SALVATION

SALVATION

CONTOURS OF ADVENTIST SOTERIOLOGY

EDITED BY

MARTIN F. HANNA • DARIUS W. JANKIEWICZ • JOHN W. REEVE

Andrews
University Press
Berrien Springs, Michigan

Andrews University Press
Sutherland House
8360 W. Campus Circle Dr.
Berrien Springs, MI 49104–1700
Telephone: 269–471–6134
Fax: 269–471–6224
Email: aupo@andrews.edu
Website: http://universitypress.andrews.edu

ISBN (paperback): 978–1-940980–24–9
ISBN (e-book): 978–1-940980–25–6

Printed in the United States of America
22 21 20 19 18   1 2 3 4 5

Library of Congress Cataloging-in-Publication Data

Names: Martin F. Hanna; Darius W. Jankiewicz; John W. Reeve, editors.
Title: Salvation : contours of Adventist soteriology / edited by Martin F. Hanna, Darius W. Jankiewicz, and John W. Reeve.
Description: Berrien Springs : Andrews University Press, 2018.
Identifiers: LCCN 2017049957 (print) | LCCN 2018011750 (ebook) | ISBN 9781940980256 (E-book) | ISBN 9781940980249 (pbk. : alk. paper)
Subjects: LCSH: Seventh-day Adventists—Doctrines. | Salvation—Seventh-day Adventists.
Classification: LCC BX6154 (ebook) | LCC BX6154 .S25 2018 (print) | DDC 234.088/2867—dc23
LC record available at https://lccn.loc.gov/2017049957

Project Director	Ronald Alan Knott
Project Editor	Deborah L. Everhart
Copy Editing	Rose Decaen
Editorial Assistance	Natanael Abriol, Jasmine Logan, Keldie Paroschi
Documentation	Pheonix M. Hardin, Samuel Pagán De Jesús
Cover and Text Design	Max Gordienko, Robert N. Mason
Typesetting	Max Gordienko, Shannon Huang
Indexing	Kellyann Falkenberg Wolfe, Jasmine Logan
Proofreading	Rose Decaen

Typeset: 11/14 Minion Pro

CONTENTS

INTRODUCTION

The salvation of humanity has been the singular purpose of God from eternity. From its introductory pages, the Scriptures testify to God's determination to restore the intimate relationship with His wayward children and His desire to return the universe to its pristine, sinless condition. For a Christian believer, the study of the theme of salvation, as presented in the Scriptures, represents the most rewarding and joyous pursuit. The study of salvation is not, however, devoid of difficulties.

This is because the Bible presents us with a description of salvation that is both simple and complex. On the one hand, throughout the Old Testament, God appears to take initiative by inviting humans to respond to His offer of salvation and providing them with the means to remain within the covenantal boundaries. Eventually, inaugurating the New Testament era, God sends His Son Jesus who proclaims the beginning of God's Kingdom. The message of salvation appears to be simple enough: "Whoever believes in the Son," Jesus said, "has eternal life" (John 3:36, NIV). Echoing the words of Jesus, the Apostle John wrote: "Believe in the name of the Son of God, so that you may know that you have eternal life" (1 John 5:13, NASB).

On the other hand, the story of human salvation is a part of an immensely complex cosmic drama described by Paul as "the mystery of godliness" (1 Tim. 3:16, NKJV). This mystery involves Christ's incarnation, the riddle of His nature, and His exemplary life of self-sacrifice that led to the sacrificial death on the cross. The mystery compounds when contemplating His miraculous resurrection and ascension to heaven, where He now sits at the right hand of God, ministering to humanity. As a response to God's initiative, the biblical writers call humans to recognize their own sinfulness and allow themselves to be led by the Holy Spirit to repentance, confession, justification, sanctification through faithful discipleship, and ultimately, glorification. Thus what Scripture has to say about salvation is far from simple for it involves complex interaction between God and sin-marred human beings.

Added to this difficulty is the ever-present question of human involvement in the process of salvation. How far does it extend, if at all? Does God do everything, reducing humans to mere spectators in the cosmic battle between good and evil? Or does He make salvation possible, while leaving all the initiative to humans to work out their salvation? When contemplating the extent of the damage Adam and Eve bequeathed to their descendants, further difficulties appear on the soteriological horizon. Are humans born in the same spiritual state as their first parents before they sinned? Do they carry only the physical consequences of the Fall? Or, is the spiritual nature of humanity also marred so that all humans are born as sinners?

These and many other questions related to the doctrine of salvation have been debated throughout history; at times diverse answers led to divisions, schisms, excommunications, anathemas, wars, and bloodshed. Today, Christians continue to be divided over these questions. Therefore, in order to introduce this volume and help the reader understand its intent, what follows is a brief overview of the history of Christian soteriology.

The early post-Apostolic Christians did not focus much on the doctrine of salvation. In general, however, they tended to assume that the Fall did not damage human nature too severely, thus leaving human beings with the natural ability to cooperate with God in the process of salvation. Many believed that God's image would eventually be restored in humans through a faithful following of Jesus as well as through their good works. This would eventually result in "divinization," or *theosis*, a becoming like God. The purpose of such a process was the unification of the believer with Christ's divine nature to such a degree that the effects of sin upon human nature would be erased, thus enabling the believer to reach a state of perfection.

The early discussions on salvation came to a head in the fourth century and resulted in what is known as the Pelagian Controversy. This controversy was mainly played out between the followers of Pelagius and Augustine, who took diverse views on the nature of humanity. Pelagius taught that humans are born perfect and therefore can perfectly obey the commandments of God. Augustine, on the other hand, embraced a dark understanding of human nature: there is nothing good in human nature, and humans have no ability to respond to God's initiative. God thus has to deal with sin by His sheer grace and without human involvement. Pelagianism, with its emphasis upon human goodness, and Augustinianism, with its emphasis upon human badness and thus innate inability to cooperate with God, form two bookends of traditional Christian soteriology. Every other soteriology finds itself somewhere in between these two views.

The Catholic understanding of salvation that emerged during the Middle Ages rejected both extremes and morphed into a soteriology that embraced both grace and works. While God initiates the process of salvation by grace, humans were expected to respond by their good works, which were then credited to them as merit. This system of human merit eventually contributed to many abuses and resulted in the rise of the sixteenth-century Reformation, which rejected the Catholic grace-works synthesis and attempted to return to the Gospel as taught by the apostles. However, instead of returning to the apostolic understanding of salvation, and in their overreaction to Catholicism, Reformers such as Luther, Zwingli, and Calvin returned to the teaching of Augustine and embraced the concept of unconditional predestination. They proclaimed that, after the Fall, humans lost the ability to freely respond to God's initiative of salvation. This situation could only be rectified by God's arbitrary election of some humans for salvation. In this way the Reformers were able to maintain that salvation was a "pure gift" from God, without any hint of human involvement—not even a possibility of making a choice. Salvation, they asserted, could not possibly depend on human choice.

While the Lutheran branch of the Reformation eventually rejected these ideas and embraced the understanding of human salvation based on God's grace and free human response to God's initiative, the Reformed branch of the Reformation continued to be increasingly entrenched in unconditional predestinarianism. A correction of this course occurred just over four hundred years ago, in 1610, when a group of Dutch preachers and theologians published a document in which they responded to the accusations of heresy leveled against the teachings of noted Reformed theologian Jacob Arminius. This document encapsulated Arminian soteriological teachings in five points and subsequently became known as *The Remonstrance*. In the years that followed, the teachings of *The Remonstrance* became a rallying point for those who were dissatisfied with traditional Calvinism. In 1618, during the Synod of Dort, Calvinist theologians fought against Arminian soteriology presented in *The Remonstrance* and formulated their own response to the five points of Arminianism. This eventually became known as the five points of Calvinism, otherwise referred to as TULIP (Total Depravity, Unconditional Election, Limited Atonement, Irresistible Grace, and Perseverance of the Saints).

Subsequent decades and centuries witnessed a wave of conflicts among many Christian Protestant religious groups that traced their theological roots to Calvinism, Lutheranism, or Arminianism, resulting in a smorgasbord of soteriologies. Eighteenth-century Methodism, which championed Arminian thought, formed the immediate theological context for the rise of Seventh-day Adventist soteriology in the nineteenth century. The Seventh-day Adventist understanding of salvation is rooted in Scripture and finds itself clearly within the strand of the sixteenth-century Protestant Reformation, which was further refined by classical Arminianism and the Wesleyan movement.

A NOTE FROM THE EDITORS

Being conscious of various soteriological strands existing within Protestant theology, we, as Adventist theologians, take a keen interest in issues relating to a biblical understanding of human nature, free will, God's grace, atonement, and predestination. In recognition of the 400th anniversary of the Remonstrance on October 14–17, 2010, the Seventh-day Adventist Theological Seminary hosted an international symposium dedicated to the study of these important issues. The idea for this book was born during that symposium. What you now hold in your hands is a result of a close collaboration of many Adventist scholars who are keen to present a biblical understanding of salvation.

Honoring our Arminian soteriological roots, we have generally organized this book according to the five points of Arminianism: Conditional Election, Unlimited Atonement, Total Depravity, Resistible Grace, and Christian Assurance/Sanctification. We have adjusted the order of the five points by presenting the sin problem before presenting the atonement solution. In this way, the cross of Christ constitutes the "chiastic" centerpiece of our presentation of Adventist Protestant soteriology. The first part introduces the book and deals with the issue of the great controversy, God's foreknowledge, and predestination. The second part deals with the problem of sin and human nature. In the third part, the authors present the biblical understanding of the work of Christ. The fourth part explores the theme of God's grace. The fifth and final part is devoted to the assurance of salvation.

As with any collaborative work, it is to be expected that the reader will encounter significant differences in presentation style and, at times, approaches. It is impossible to have a volume such as this be as unified and well integrated as a work by a single author. Rather than a liability, however, this is, in our opinion, a strength of this book, as each author brings his or her individual gifting, perspective, and personality to this project while remaining under the greater umbrella of Arminianism. This also suggests that there will be a degree of overlap between various contributions. We have chosen to permit the overlap for two reasons: first, each author approaches the material from a different angle; second, while some readers may choose to read this book from cover to cover, the most likely scenario is that readers will read first the chapters of interest to them. Therefore, occasional overlapping does not represent a significant problem.

We hope and pray that this book, the result of many years of thought and of thorough biblical and historical research, will prove to be an invaluable resource for all, specialist and non-specialist alike, who are interested in the Adventist understanding of the biblical teaching on the doctrine of salvation.

SECTION 1

God's Plan in Christ:
Is Salvation for Everyone?

The Christian doctrine of salvation includes the truth regarding what God has planned for our salvation. Since God is omniscient, knowing all things, He anticipated the sin problem and His plan for solving it *before* He created free beings who could fall into sin. The Bible refers to this plan in terms of the revealed mystery of God's eternal purpose (Eph. 1:9; 3:11).

Nevertheless, Christians have come to different conclusions about the nature of the mystery of God's plan. These various conclusions involve different answers to the following questions: How could the imperfection of sin come to exist in the universe created by a perfect and sinless God? How can created beings be free to sin or to receive salvation if God foreknew and planned, or predestined, all that they would do before He created them? These and other related questions are addressed in this section of this book.

Four authors will present historical and biblical studies of God's plan of salvation. The first chapter, authored by Nicholas Miller, provides a historical overview of Christian views on the nature of God's plan. The second chapter, written by Norman R. Gulley, presents the plan for salvation in the broad context of the cosmic controversy between Christ and Satan. In the third chapter, Martin Hanna presents a study of the role of God's foreknowledge in His pre-creation plan for restoring and preserving freedom through salvation. Finally, the fourth chapter, by Hans LaRondelle and John McVay, is a study of the role of God's predestination and election in His pre-creation plan of salvation.

CHAPTER 1

HISTORY OF THE RELATIONSHIP AMONG HUMAN FREE WILL, GOD'S CHARACTER OF LOVE, AND THE GREAT CONTROVERSY

Nicholas P. Miller

Adventists like to think that one of the unique contributions the church has made to Christian thought is the Great Controversy theme. This refers to the conflict between God and Satan that revolves around the wisdom and character of God and Satan's charges that God is arbitrary, unjust, and ultimately selfish.

It is true that Adventists have made the Great Controversy a theme and focus of their thought that is unmatched in other denominations. But the larger framework of the motif predates the birth of the Adventist church by a number of centuries. Indeed, the theological insights forming its basic outlines in the modern era go back to at least the early seventeenth century. This was when the Dutch Remonstrants—followers and supporters of famed theologian Jacob Arminius—took conceptions of human free will and God's foreknowledge and related them to the nature and government of God.

The chapters in this section explore the theological strands of the free-will/foreknowledge/God's-character tapestry to make a compelling case that there is a strong biblical foundation for the Adventist understanding of the basic freedom of all humans, enlightened by prevenient grace, to choose a God of love. God's foreknowledge of people's eternal destiny neither compels nor determines their destiny and is thus consistent with freedom given by true love, as shown in an unfolding controversy between good and evil.

This historical chapter will show how closely related the individual threads of freedom, divine knowledge, and the revelation of God's loving character were in their historical development. Seeing the early development and inter-relationship between human free will and the Great Controversy theme will reveal how that theme can play a greater role in shaping and even correcting other Adventist beliefs. The demonstration of the theme's common roots with other denominations allows the Great Controversy to be used as an effective bridge to reach other Christians with the Adventist message.

JACOB ARMINIUS, GOD'S NATURE, AND THE ROOTS OF FREE WILL THEOLOGY

To build this bridge, it is necessary to return to near the dawn of the Protestant Reformation. It was in the late sixteenth century that Jacob Arminius, the great Dutch theologian, launched a modification of Calvinist theology that set the stage for the Great Controversy theme. Arminius provided a fresh reading of the Calvinist tradition to allow for genuine human free will and the possibility of salvation for all who might believe. Since then, Arminian theology has become synonymous with a rejection of human pre-destination, limited atonement, and God's arbitrary sovereignty.

This identification of Arminius with free will theology is in one respect somewhat unfortunate, since it makes it seem as though conceptions of human freedom are a third or fourth generation addition to Protestant thought. Some claim that a free will view is thus a corruption of true, original Protestantism. But this position overlooks the earlier Protestants who embraced the idea of human freedom playing a role in salvation, including Lutheran theologian Philip Melanchthon and the entire evangelical Anabaptist movement.

The leading early magisterial Reformers, Luther and especially Calvin, reacted against a tendency in medieval scholasticism to underplay the severity humanity's fall into sin and to overplay human ability to both know and do good. Both men were struggling to move the church from a Pelagian position, which held that humans could choose to make themselves better, to one that understood the absolute necessity of God's grace to bring about any real improvement. In avoiding the theological ditch of overemphasizing human righteousness, though, they ran into the opposite ditch of overemphasizing human helplessness and God's arbitrariness.[1]

Neither Luther nor Calvin, however, made predestination the central concern of their theologies. Luther was quick to say that predestination only had to do with the hidden God, the *deus absconditus,* and that Christians should focus on the choices and grace that the revealed God has promised to all. Neither Luther nor Calvin used the term *double predestination.* It was coined by later theologians to convey the idea that God creates some people whom He will save and creates others whom He intends to damn. This stern doctrine was not expressed in these terms by Luther or Calvin but was a later addition by Calvin's successors in Geneva, Theodore Beza and others, who viewed it as a logical extension of their beliefs.

Lutheranism is not known for its strict doctrines of election and sovereignty, largely because of the influence of Melanchthon. Also a first generation reformer, Melanchthon was willing to allow the puzzle of divine foreknowledge and human freedom to go unsolved, rather than insist that there was no free will. Due to Melanchthon's influence, Lutheranism took a more moderate path in relation to predestination, with a general rejection of notions of double predestination and some openness to human choice.[2]

But there were other first generation Reformers who were even more determined than Melanchthon to defend human choice in the matter of salvation, most notably, the Anabaptists. In 1526, Anabaptist Hans Denck, no doubt provoked by the Luther/Erasmus debate over the will that occurred the previous year, set out his own views on human freedom. The title of Denck's work reveals his true concern—*Whether God is the Cause of Evil.* In this book, Denck dealt with the problem of evil and free will. He avoids Luther's wholly captive will and Erasmus's humanist/Pelagian will. He argued that "salvation is *in* man but not *of* him," and that while man naturally could not choose to oppose evil, he did have the capacity to submit to God. Thus, evil was a result of man's chosen failure to submit to God and could not be attributed to God.[3]

---

1. Gerhard O. Forde, *The Captivation of the Will: Luther v. Erasmus on Freedom and Bondage,* ed. Steven Paulson (Grand Rapids, MI: Eerdmans, 2005), 37.

2. Timothy Wengert, "'We Will Feast Together in Heaven Forever': The Epistolary Friendship of John Calvin and Philip Melanchthon," in *Melanchthon in Europe: His Work and Influence Beyond Wittenberg,* ed. Karin Maag (Grand Rapids, MI: Baker, 1999), 26–29.

3. George Huntston Williams, *The Radical Reformation,* 3rd ed. (Kirksville, MO: Truman

Influenced by Denck, Anabaptist leader Balthasar Hubmaier wrote his own works on human nature and salvation.[4] Hubmaier believed in the Fall and in sinful human nature and soul.[5] But he asserted that "whoever denies the freedom of the human will, denies and rejects more than half of the Holy Scriptures."[6] Not only did all people have the capacity to choose God, once this choice was made, they gained the ability through Christ's power to choose good. "Enlightened through the Holy Spirit, [the soul] . . . now again comes to know what is good and what is evil. It has recovered its lost freedom. It can now freely and willingly be obedient to the spirit against the body and can will and choose the good. . . ."[7]

The views of Hubmaier and Denck on human free will came to generally characterize the views of the evangelical Anabaptists, including those in Austria and the Netherlands, where Menno Simons articulated similar views. These evangelical Anabaptists represent an early Protestant free-will heritage that are as early as Luther's teachings and predate Calvin's writings by more than a decade.[8]

After the mid-sixteenth century, Beza and others began to intensify the reformed churches' emphasis on predestination and God's sovereignty. The heightened emphasis of the doctrine of election sparked concerns about human free will and God's relation to evil in theological circles outside the Anabaptist community. One such concerned onlooker was Jacob Arminius, reformed pastor and teacher, who began his ministry in Amsterdam in the late 1580s.

Arminius had contact with Mennonite Anabaptists in Holland, and his own church commissioned him to publicly debate and refute some

---

State University Press, 2000), 257–258.

4. Ibid., 257n28.

5. Hubmaier had an unusual view of the human's spirit-will not participating in the Fall, but this meant nothing and could not operate until the fallen soul received regeneration through Christ. Ibid., 335.

6. Henry Clay Vedder, *Balthasar Hübmaier: The Leader of the Anabaptists* (New York: G. Putnam's Sons, Knickerbocker, 1905), 197.

7. Balthasar Hubmaier, "On Free Will," in *Spiritual and Anabaptist Writers*, George H. Williams, ed. (Philadelphia, PA: The Westminster Press, 1962), 124.

8. Cornelius J. Dyck, ed., *An Introduction to Mennonite History: A Popular History of the Anabaptists and the Mennonites*, 3rd ed. (Scottdale, PA: Herald, 1993), 142; C. Arnold Snyder, *Anabaptist History and Theology: An Introduction* (Kitchener, ON: Pandora, 1995), 89–90.

Mennonite "heretics." While Arminius never explicitly refused to refute the Mennonites, he continually delayed the project. Eventually the consistory realized that he would never do it. Arminius differed with the Mennonites on baptism and the nature of the church. But it seems that his views on the other Anabaptist "heresy," that of the relation of grace, predestination, and free will, were similar to theirs.

Arminius also was exposed to Melanchthon's views on "conditional predestination."[9] It was in this context that Arminius developed a careful re-reading of Calvinism. He affirmed the existing reformed creeds on sin and salvation, but he did so in a way that allowed for genuine human free choice in accepting salvation. His reason for doing so was not primarily because of a concern for human dignity, importance, or freedom. Rather, his primary concern was the same as that of the early Anabaptists—the glory of God as seen in His character. He aimed to preserve God's character from the infamy and slander that He had created, ordained, or authored sin and evil.

As church historian Roger Olson puts it, "Arminius's strongest objection was that" unconditional predestination is "'injurious to the glory of God' because 'from these premises we deduce, as a further conclusion, that God really sins . . . that God is the only sinner . . . that sin is not sin.' Arminius never tired of arguing that the strong Calvinist doctrine of predestination cannot help making God the author of sin, and if God is the author of sin, then sin is not truly sin because whatever God authors is good."[10]

Both Luther and Calvin were voluntarists—they embraced the view that right and good are, by definition, whatever God does or decrees. It is ultimately a position that God's might makes right.[11] Arminius was an anti-voluntarist. He believed that God chose to do good and right *because it was good and right*—not that He was measured by some external standard, but that good and right existed as part of His very nature. In creating the world and humanity, He imbedded these truths within creation itself. While fallen, God's creation still contains traces of this divine nature.

---

9. Carl Bangs, *Arminius: A Study in the Dutch Reformation* (Eugene, OR: Wipf and Stock, 1985), 169–171, 193–194.

10. Roger E. Olson, *The Story of Christian Theology: Twenty Centuries of Tradition & Reform* (Downers Grove, IL: InterVarsity, 1999), 467.

11. Olson, *The Story of Christian Theology,* 387–388 (Luther), 410–411 (Calvin).

Arminius posited a clear connection between God's being and the beings that He created. He wrote that God "is the greatest Being and the only great One; for he is able to subdue to his sway even nothing itself, that it may become capable of divine good by the communication of himself."[12] This communication would allow lesser beings to understand and have actual knowledge of the essence of the divine Being. "In the first place he is called 'Being itself,'" he wrote, "because he offers himself to the understanding as an object of knowledge."[13]

Arminius recognized that the gap between the divine Being and the created being is huge, even "infinite," and the fact that mere beings can never be raised to "divine equality with God." But despite this gap and distance, and recognizing that "the human mind is finite in nature," Arminius believed that it is "a partaker of infinity—because it apprehends Infinite Being and the Chief Truth, although it is incapable of comprehending them."[14]

In other words, Arminius believed that humans were capable of knowing, at least in part, God as He truly is. This must be true for humans to make meaningful choices about accepting and following God. If true knowledge about God is not possible, then real choice about God is not possible either. Thus, when Christ revealed God, He showed us true things about the actual nature of God. There are no contrary, hidden natures concealed behind this revealed nature.

Concerning God's nature, Arminius was very clear: "It is worthy to receive adoration, on account of its justice; that it is qualified to form a right judgment of that worship, on account of its wisdom."[15] It is the revelation of this nature that makes human choice meaningful and thus possible.

HUGO GROTIUS AND THE MORAL GOVERNMENT OF GOD

It was in pursuit of this vindication of God's "worthy" nature that the story of the Dutch Remonstrants, supporters of Arminius, unfolded in Holland.

---

12. Jacob Arminius, *Works of Jacob Arminius*, vol. 1 (Montoursville, PA: Lamppost Books, 2009), 12.

13. Ibid., 13.

14. Ibid.

15. Arminius, *Works of Jacob Arminius*, vol. 1, 15.

Since the keepers of Calvinist orthodoxy were anxious to squash these "progressive" ideas about God, after Arminius died in 1609, his followers drafted a remonstrance, a petition, against the official orthodoxy of the state church. The five points of the Remonstrance asserted conditional election (God chose all conditioned on their exercise of faith), unlimited atonement (Christ died for all), depravity (the image of God in fallen humanity is marred, but not obliterated), prevenient grace (God's freeing grace is available to all), and continued choice (opposition to once-saved, always saved.)

These points have obvious implications for theodicy. In particular, the notions of conditional election and unlimited atonement—the view that God has made a way for all to be saved, and the choice is in their hands as to whether to respond to the grace He has given—paint a picture of God that is very different from the Calvinist view that Christ's atonement was made only for an arbitrarily chosen elect.

One of the Remonstrants, a talented thinker by the name of Hugo Grotius, wove the ideas of the nature of God, the general atonement, and human freedom into a larger conception known as the moral government of God. Grotius, a well-known name in legal circles, is considered the father of international law, the law of war and peace, and Protestant conceptions of natural law. In his day, he was equally famous for this theological writings.[16]

Grotius was convicted and imprisoned by strict Calvinists for supporting Arminius and his beliefs about freedom of the will and conditional predestination. He escaped from a life of imprisonment by hiding in a trunk that was supposedly carrying his books out of prison. But he only escaped after he had written a defense of Christianity entitled *The Truth of the Christian Religion.* It is considered the first book of modern apologetics, and it explains and justifies the Bible and Christianity in comparison to other world religions.[17]

He also wrote another book entitled *Concerning the Satisfaction of Christ,* in which he explored theories of Christ's atonement in light of the moral government of God that Arminius's free-will theology brought to light. Grotius brought his legal background to bear, constructing what came to be known as the moral government theory of the atonement.[18] (This is at times

---

16. J. B. Schneewind, *The Invention of Autonomy: A History of Modern Moral Philosophy* (New York: Cambridge University Press, 1998), 66–67.

17. Schneewind, *The Invention of Autonomy,* 68.

18. Hugo Grotius, *A Defence of the Catholic Faith Concerning the Satisfaction of Christ*

confused with the moral influence theory of the atonement, but the two are very separate ideas.)

The *moral government theory of the atonement* is best understood in relation to previous views. It did not so much displace these, as it clarified, refined, and restated them. Anselm had famously argued that Christ must die in humanity's place to satisfy the impaired honor of God. Calvin had modified this somewhat to make the necessity of Christ's substitution a response to the offended law and holiness of God. The death of Christ provides satisfaction to the offended holiness, law, and justice of God, as somehow, mysteriously, our guilt, sin, and punishment are transferred to Christ.[19]

Grotius did not deny that God's honor, holiness, justice, and law were implicated in the atonement. He accepted that these had indeed been breached and offended by sin. Rather, he answered the question as to why God could not forgive this breach by merely accepting the genuine sorrow and repentance of the sinner. Since humans can extend forgiveness without requiring sacrifice or suffering, why cannot God? This was the question that Faustus Socinus was asking, and to which Grotius responded.[20]

God could not merely freely forgive the sinner, Grotius pointed out, because it was not His role merely as an *individual* offended Deity that was involved. Rather it involved His role as *Ruler* of the universe—a universe that can only function in peace and safety according to certain principles of fairness and justice.

This shift of God as offended Being to God as offended Ruler means that in enforcing His law, He is not doing it out of some personal sense of pique, pride, or impaired glory. Rather, He is acting on behalf of the good of all the beings of the universe that depend on the stability, fairness, and morality of His government. In defending His honor, His character, He defends, as Ruler of the Universe, the very thing that allows the universe itself to have order, stability, security, peace, and, of course, love.[21]

Grotius applied these insights regarding God's government to help explain some of the mysteries surrounding the atonement. But the framework he created in doing so helped provide a foundation and basis to deal

---

Against Faustus Socinus, trans. Frank Hugh Foster (Andover: Warren F. Draper, 1889).

19. Frank H. Foster. "A Brief Introductory Sketch," ibid., xi–xiv.

20. Ibid., xv.

21. Ibid., xvi.

with many other issues as well, such as the relation of God to sin, evil, justice, and injustice. In the moral government of God, Grotius articulated the basic framework required for a larger exposition of a Great Controversy theme.

Why must God show that He is a fair, not an arbitrary, ruler? Because He cares about the opinions and good will of the onlooking universe. He is willing to have His government and His laws, which reflect His character, examined and evaluated by His created beings. This understanding of God's sovereignty and justice in relation to human free will was the key that unlocked the door to the moral government of God; the moral government of God was, in turn, the key that unlocked the door to the larger Great Controversy theme, the theological framework of Adventism. But how did these insights about God's government and human free will reach the early Adventists?

THE INFLUENCE OF GROTIUS IN ENGLAND AND EARLY AMERICA

Grotius exerted meaningful influence in the theological arena for quite some time. John Milton, when he was on a tour of Europe in 1638, stayed with Hugo Grotius in Paris for a period. Although Milton had a strong Calvinist, Puritan background, he emerged as a believer in freedom of the will, unlimited atonement, and very definitely the moral government of God. His *Paradise Lost,* of course, was written with the specific purpose to "justify the ways of God in the eyes of men." Milton's defense of God's ways and judgments is not a Calvinist ideal, which would have emphasized God's sovereignty. It is, though, a very Arminian/Grotian moral-government-of-God view of the world.

Samuel and Susanna Wesley, parents of John Wesley, the founder of Methodism, were supporters of Anglican Arminianism. Samuel's favorite biblical commentator was Hugo Grotius, and he recommended his works to John. The writings of Grotius came to be a great theological resource for Wesley and his friends at Oxford University.[22]

Through Wesley, Methodism came to inherit both Arminius's views on prevenient grace and freedom of the will, as well as Grotius's views on the

---

22. See Richard P. Heitzenrater, ed., *Diary of an Oxford Methodist: Benjamin Ingham, 1733–34* (Durham, NC: Duke Univ. Press, 1985).

moral government of God. Richard Watson, the Methodist theological sys-tematizer, wrote in 1823 that "the existence of a Divine Law, obligatory upon man, is not doubted by any who admit the *existence and government of God*. . . . It is important to keep in view the fact of the extent and severity of the punishment denounced against all transgressions of the law of God, because this is illustrative of the *character of God*; both with reference to his essential holiness and to his proceedings as *Governor of the World*."[23]

This introduction of the character of God helps answer one of the trick-ier conundrums of the Arminian, anti-voluntarist position. If God's will and power does not define God, but God only does those things that are good, then is God somehow obligated to a law or morality higher than Himself? Is there something greater than God? The riddle is solved if the laws He is bound by are the actual principles of His own character and nature.

It is of great interest to note that those who advocated freedom of human choice and the fact of God's moral government also began to seek civil free-doms and to expect higher standards of morality from human governments. Methodists were against slavery almost from its modern origins. William Wilberforce, the great British parliamentarian who ended the British slave trade, was raised a Methodist as a young man. Later in life, after his adult conversion, he associated with non-conformist ministers, including Method-ists, who opposed slavery. In the middle of his fight against the slave trade, Wilberforce received what may have been the last letter that John Wesley ever wrote, encouraging him to do all he could to end the slave trade.[24]

American Methodists voted in 1784 to expel members who bought and sold slaves. They later yielded to political and economic pressure to

---

23. Richard Watson, *Theological Institutes; or a View of the Evidences, Doctrines, Mor-als, and Institutions of Christianity,* vol. 1 (New York: J. Emory and B. Waugh, 1831), 254, emphasis added.

24. In his letter, Wesley wrote: "Unless the divine power has raised you up to be as Athanasius [against the world] in opposing that execrable villainy which is the scandal of religion, of England, and of human nature. Unless God has raised you up for this very thing, you will be worn out by the opposition of men and devils. But if God be for you, who can be against you? Are all of them together stronger than God? O be not weary of well doing! Go on, in the name of God and in the power of his might, till even American slavery (the vilest that ever saw the sun) shall vanish away before it," John Wesley to William Wilberforce, February 24, 1791, quoted in Eric Metaxas, *Amazing Grace: William Wilberforce and the Heroic Campaign to End Slavery* (Toronto, ON: HarperCollins, 2007), 144.

accept slavery in the South. But under the reviving influences of the Second Great Awakening, they once again renewed their commitments to oppose slavery. In 1844, the American Methodist Church expelled those parts of the church that continued to support slavery.

Interestingly, this anti-slavery stance came to be shared by the other branch of moral-government-of-God influence that came into America. This branch, ironically, developed within the reformed churches, becoming a renewal movement within American Congregationalism and Presbyterianism.

Grotius's theology had deep roots in American puritanism. Grotius's works were read in New England as early as the 1650s, and a copy of his *Satisfaction* was in the Harvard College Library by 1723. Grotius was also often quoted in writings of the Puritan Richard Baxter, who was widely read in New England.[25]

It would be a separate story to trace the manner in which the New England divines largely rejected Arminianism in terms of will and predestination but were influenced and eventually embraced notions of God's moral government in relation to the atonement.[26] This combination of predestination and God's moral government was an unstable coalition of thought. But while it lasted, its proponents introduced the importance of God's character in defining the laws of His universe.

New England minister Samuel Hopkins wrote that the law of God is "an eternal, unalterable rule of righteousness which cannot be abrogated or altered . . . consistent with his character, his perfect rectitude and righteousness." To do so would "put an end to all perfect moral government . . . and give full scope to the reign of rebellion, confusion, and misery forever."[27] In Hopkins's writing, the need to maintain "the law is made more evident, and grounded upon a deeper thought than Grotius reached, who neglected to state the relation existing between the government and the character of God."[28]

It is notable that the New England theologians who embraced and developed the moral government theology were, like their Arminian cousins, also involved in anti-slavery advocacy. The previous generation of

---

25. Foster, "Historical Introduction," *A Defense of the Catholic Faith,* xliv.

26. Ibid., xliii–lvi.

27. Ibid., xlviii.

28. Ibid., xlix.

Puritans had not said much about slavery. Indeed, Jonathan Edwards Sr. had owned slaves and written in defense of the practice. But the moral government of God elevated the positions of all humans, making them all participants in an examination of heavenly government. Thus, all were owed reasoned and fair treatment on this earth. And if God's government operated in a moral fashion, how could human governments be excused from doing so?[29] Both Hopkins and his moral government ally Jonathan Edwards, Jr., wrote major treatises opposing both slavery and the slave trade.[30]

But the tension between a commitment to predestination, which elevated God's arbitrary aspects, and God's moral government, which focused on His fairness, was pushing reformed theology to a point of crisis. That moment came in the rise of the New Haven theology and New School Presbyterianism in the 1820s and 1830s. These movements created much of the immediate theological context and matrix of early Adventism.

THE NEW HAVEN THEOLOGY AND THE NEW SCHOOL PRESBYTERIANISM: NATHANIEL TAYLOR, ALBERT BARNES, AND THE MATRIX OF ADVENTISM

The theologian at center of these new movements was Nathaniel Taylor, professor of theology at Yale University from 1822 to 1858. Taylor was a biblically conservative and devout Congregationalist teaching from within the reformed tradition. But he built on the insights of Edwards Jr. and Hopkins, and he followed the moral government of God theory to its logical conclusions. That is, he believed and taught that a truly moral God would provide opportunity for all to be saved.

Taylor's listeners attested to both his piety and his passion for the moral government of God. As one put it, "The Moral Government of God was the great thought of Dr. Taylor's intellect, and the favorite theme of his

---

29. A good discussion of the arguments of Edwards Jr. and Hopkins can be found in "Edwardeanism, Governmental Atonement Theology, and Slavery," by Andrew Blosser, April 2013; this is a currently unpublished paper submitted for my Seminar in History of American Religious Thought course at Andrews University.

30. Jonathan Edwards, Jr., "The Injustice and Impolicy of the Slave Trade, and of Slavery," in *The Works of Jonathan Edwards,* vol. 2, ed. Bruce Kuklick (New York: Garland, 1987); Samuel Hopkins, "A Dialogue Concerning the Slavery of the Africans," in *The Anti-Slavery Crusade in America,* ed. J. Mcpherson and W. Katz (New York: Arno Press 1969).

instructions in theology. It occupied his mind more than any and every other subject. . . . This object directed all his studies. All his investigations had their starting point from this central theme." Another former student said, "while lecturing, his voice often trembled, and at times the tears would start, especially when speaking of the moral government of God."[31]

For Taylor, it was an understanding of the absolute morality and fairness of God's government that stood against the claims of high Calvinism that only an elect few had an opportunity for salvation. He came to embrace a general view of the atonement: that Christ died for all. For Taylor, this was the good news of God's moral government. As he put it: "Let . . . the impression be made full, strong, unqualified on every guilty mind, that God in his law, and God in the invitations of his mercy, means exactly what he says. Let the full-orbed sincerity of a redeeming God, like the sun in mid-heaven, be made to pour its melting beams on the dark and guilty mind of the sinner against God."[32]

Taylor regularly taught a course called the Moral Government of God, and these lectures were collected and placed into a volume bearing the same name. He impacted a generation of Presbyterian pastors and theologians, including men like Charles Finney, the great evangelist of the Second Great Awakening, and Albert Barnes, the biblical commentator.

Albert Barnes was put on trial for heresy because of his embrace of New School principles of unlimited atonement and freedom of the will. He also wrote two major works against slavery in the period leading up to the Civil War. Finney was the evangelist of the moral government movement, but Barnes was the expositor/writer whose commentaries, which forcefully encapsulated the moral government theory, had wide and long-lasting popular impact. It is estimated that his *Notes on the New Testament* had sold nearly a million copies by the time Ellen White died in 1915. This is a remarkable number for a commentary from that age or any age and shows the breadth of his influence.[33]

---

31. Quoted in Douglas A. Sweeney, *Nathaniel Taylor, New Haven Theology, and the Legacy of Jonathan Edwards* (New York: Oxford University Press, 2003), 91.

32. Nathaniel Taylor, "The Peculiar Power of the Gospel on the Human Mind," 23–24, quoted in Sweeney, *Nathaniel Taylor,* 91.

33. T. H. Olbricht, "Barnes, Albert (1798–1870)," in *Historical Handbook of Major Biblical Interpreters*, ed. Donald K. McKim (Downers Grove, IL: Intervarsity, 1998), 281–284.

In his commentary on Romans 3:26—"that he might be just and the justifier of him which believeth in Jesus" (KJV)—Barnes sets out clearly the moral government theory. "This verse contains the substance of the gospel," Barnes argues. "It refers to the fact that God had retained the integrity of his character as moral governor; that he had shown a due regard to his law, and to the penalty of the law, by his plan of salvation. Should he forgive sinners without an atonement, justice would be sacrificed and abandoned. . . . He is, in all this great transaction, a just moral governor, as just to his law, to himself, to his Son, to the universe, when he pardons, as he is when he sends the incorrigible sinner down to hell."[34]

Ellen White was heir to a moral government of God outlook, both through her Methodist roots as well as her acquaintance with Barnes's commentaries, for which she had a deep appreciation. In January 1900, she wrote to her son Edson, asking for her library to be sent to Australia.[35] "I have sent for four or five large volumes of Barnes' notes on the Bible. I think they are in Battle Creek in my house now sold, somewhere with my books. . . . I may never visit America again, and my *best books* should come to me when it is convenient."[36]

This is not to deny the fruits of her own Bible study and visions, which expanded and grew the emphasis that the government of God was built on pure foundations of love. She developed the doctrine by enhancing its emphasis on God's love, ultimately turning it into what could accurately be called God's moral government of love and grace. "God's love is represented in our day as being of such a character as would forbid His destroying the sinner. . . . In no kingdom or government is it left to the lawbreakers to say what punishment is to be executed against those who have broken the law. . . . God is a moral governor as well as a Father."[37]

Similarly, "it is the sophistry of Satan that the death of Christ brought in grace to take the place of the law. The death of Jesus did not change or annul, or lessen in the slightest degree, the law of ten commandments.

34. Albert Barnes, *Barnes Notes on the New Testament*, ed. Ingram Cobbin (Grand Rapids, MI: Kregel, 1976), 573–574.

35. Arthur White, *Ellen G. White, Vol. 4, The Australian Years, 1891–1900* (Hagerstown, MD: Review and Herald, 1983), 448.

36. Ibid., Letter 189 (January 1, 1900), emphasis added.

37. Ellen White, *Last Day Events* (Boise, ID: Pacific Press, 1992), 241.

That precious grace offered to men through a Savior's blood, establishes the law of God. Since the fall of man, *God's moral government and His grace are inseparable. They go hand in hand through all dispensations.*"[38] Similar references to God as humanity's moral governor and ruler can be found throughout Ellen White's writings.

CONCLUSION: THE LIVING HERITAGE OF FREE WILL AND MORAL GOVERNMENT

But what difference does it make to the Adventist approach to theodicy to see this deep historical heritage in the notion of the moral government of God? Adventist theology needs a focus, a theme. At times it is suggested that that theme is the Great Controversy between Christ and Satan and the battle over His character of love. It suggests that theodicy is at the center of what Adventism is about.

The Great Controversy theodicy of God's love is a very good theme and is compatible with the theme of God's moral government of love. In this day and age, the term *love* has become ambiguous and vague. Ever since the Beatles sang "All you need is love," the cultural content of the word *love* has shifted from being a word of principle, with moral value, to a word based on feeling and emotion and largely devoid of principled elements.

Even in her day, Ellen White warned of Spiritism's corruption of love. "Love is dwelt upon," she wrote, "as the chief attribute of God, but it is degraded to a weak sentimentalism, making little distinction between good and evil. God's justice, His denunciations of sin, the requirements of His holy law, are all kept out of sight."[39] Since her time, this tendency of sentimentalizing love has worsened. The modern church's handling of this theme has been weakened by the vapid concept of love in contemporary culture. The passive, nice, kind aspects of love have virtually swamped the active, protective, accountability-seeking, heroic virtues of love.

These days, God's character of love is used to argue for acceptance of homosexual practice in the church, of avoidance of difficult doctrines like the sanctuary and 1844 (the center of the current activities of God's moral government), the rejection of the substitutionary/forensic elements of the

---

38. Ellen White, *God's Amazing Grace* (Washington, DC: Review and Herald, 1973), 144.

39. Ellen White, *The Great Controversy* (Mountain View, CA: Pacific Press, 1907), 558.

atonement (an indispensable element of the moral government under-standing of the atonement), and the avoidance of accountability in matters of lifestyle and doctrine. Many people are unable to see the core challenge that concepts such as theistic evolution or day/age creation, with their reliance on suffering and death as part of a "good" creation, make to Adventism's understanding of God's moral government of love.

But if God's moral government of love is the organizing principle of Adventist faith, then authority and righteousness become essential to an adequate conception of love, whether it be human love or God's love. It is in this context that the Adventist doctrine of divine judgment, and the importance of human accountability in spiritual matters, can be under-stood as an expression of God's character of love. It is when these active expressions of love are seen in their true light, as equally aspects of God's love, that the universe can become eternally secure.

Then, "the whole universe will have become witnesses to the nature and results of sin. And its utter extermination, which in the beginning would have brought fear to angels and dishonor to God, will now vindi-cate His love and establish His honor before a universe of beings who delight to do His will, and in whose heart is His law. . . . A tested and proved creation will never again be turned from allegiance to Him whose character has been fully manifested before them as fathomless love and infinite wisdom."[40]

Ultimately, the conundrum of human free will and eternal freedom from sin is explained by the power of the Great Controversy revelation of God's love and the justice of His government. These themes were tightly intertwined as they developed in the Protestant Reformation, and keeping them closely connected will help Adventism deal more effectively with its current doctrinal and evangelistic challenges and opportunities.

---

40. White, *The Great Controversy,* 504.

CHAPTER 2

LOVE AT WAR: THE COSMIC CONTROVERSY

Norman R. Gulley

Love is more than an attribute of God—it is His nature. John says, "God is love" (1 John 4:8, 16). The three Persons of the eternal, self-existent Trinity have always experienced an inner-history of reciprocal love. From eternity to eternity their love for each other never changes (cf. Mal. 3:6). The Father is no less loving than Christ or the Spirit. He is called the "Father of compassion" (2 Cor. 1:3). John exclaims, "See what great love the Father has lavished on us, that we should be called children of God!" (1 John 3:1). "For God so loved the world that he gave his one and only Son, that whoever believes in him shall not perish but have eternal life" (John 3:16). Christ said, "Anyone who has seen me has seen the Father" (John 14:9).[1]

THE COSMIC SCOPE OF GOD'S LOVE

It is inexplicable how such a God of love would have a controversy break out against Him when His citizens knew nothing but His love for them.

---

1. Unless otherwise indicated, all Scripture references are from THE HOLY BIBLE, NEW INTERNATIONAL VERSION®, NIV® Copyright © 1973, 1978, 1984, 2011 by Biblica, Inc.® Used by permission. Italics in Scripture quotations represent emphasis added by author. For more on God's love, see Norman R. Gulley, *Systematic Theology: God as Trinity*, vol. 2 (Berrien Springs, MI: Andrews University Press, 2011); also John C. Peckham, *The Love of God: A Canonical Model* (Downers Grove, IL: InterVarsity, 2015).

David Hume expressed the problem well: "Is he willing to prevent evil, but not able? then he is impotent. Is he able, but not willing? then he is malevolent. Is he both able and willing? whence then is evil?"[2] Nevertheless, in the midst of this rebellion, God's response is a warfare of love. God's love at war responds to Satan's war against love. The metanarrative of Scripture is the cosmic controversy. It is the ultimate framework in which all the ideas and stories in Scripture are best understood.[3]

After the cosmic war began, love motivated the Trinitarian mission to save the world. "For you know the grace of our Lord Jesus Christ, that though he was rich, yet for your sake he became poor, so that you through his poverty might become rich" (2 Cor. 8:9). "He [Christ] came to his own and his own did not receive him" (John 1:11, NKJV). No wonder he cried out, "Jerusalem, Jerusalem, you who kill the prophets and stone those sent to you, how often I have longed to gather your children together, as a hen gathers her chicks under her wings, and you were not willing" (Matt. 23:37). The same heart-love for His people is found in the Old Testament. Concerning Ephraim, He says, "'my heart yearns for him; I have great compassion for him,' declares the Lord" (Jer. 31:20).

Does Christ's mission affect the human race alone, or are there broader dimensions to consider? Is there a cosmic context that needs to be understood? Does the Bible provide a "grand unifying theory"?[4] Most theologians view Calvary as Christ dying for humans so they can go to heaven.[5] But there is more. Colossians teaches that Christ created all things in heaven and on earth (Col. 1:16), and that "in him [Christ] all things hold together" (Col. 1:17). "For God was pleased to have all his fullness dwell in him, and through him to reconcile to himself all things, whether things on earth or things in heaven, by making peace through his blood, shed on the cross" (Col. 1:19–20). In this passage, Paul clearly indicates that Christ's

---

2. See David Hume, *Dialogues Concerning Natural Religion,* Part X, *The English Philosophers From Bacon to Mill,* ed. Edwin A Burtt (London: The Modern Library, 1939), 186.

3. Richard M. Davidson, "Cosmic Metanarrative for the Coming Millennium," *Journal of the Adventist Theological Society* 11/1–2 (2000): 102–119. Norman R. Gulley, *Systematic Theology: Prolegomena,* vol. 1 (Berrien Springs, MI: Andrews University Press, 2003), 421–453.

4. Philip Yancey, *Where Is God When It Hurts?* (Grand Rapids, MI: Zondervan, 1990), 79.

5. Some of the theologians who move toward a wider metanarrative include Origen, Augustine, John Calvin, John Milton, C. S. Lewis, Gregory Boyd, and Lewis Chafer. For more on this topic, see Gulley, *Systematic Theology: Prolegomena,* 398–416.

death has cosmic implications that extend beyond the salvation of humans. In some important sense, Calvary reconciles the universe.

This wider mission of Calvary also includes the church, since Paul exclaims: "It seems to me that God has put us apostles on display at the end of the procession, like those condemned to die in the arena. We have been made a spectacle to the whole universe, to angels as well as to human beings" (1 Cor. 4:9). Similarly, Paul points out that God's "intent was that now, through the church, the manifold wisdom of God should be made known to the rulers and authorities in the heavenly realms, according to his eternal purpose that he accomplished in Christ Jesus our Lord" (Eph. 3:10–11; cf. 6:12). Why are Calvary and the church of such great interest to the entire universe? Some answers to this question are found in the biblical record of the experiences of Job.

THE TRIALS OF JOB: BEHIND THE SCENES OF THE COSMIC CONFLICT

The book of Job gives an extraordinary look behind the scenes of this world, showing the interaction between God and Satan. The author pulls aside the curtain to reveal the cosmic struggle involving humans and, at the same time, transcending human history.[6]

The book of Job begins at a special meeting convened in the presence of God, somewhere in the universe. "One day the angels came to present themselves before the Lord, and Satan also came with them" (Job 1:6). This could have been a meeting of different leaders from the inhabited planets throughout the universe. God asked Satan where he came from, and he replied: "From roaming throughout the earth, going back and forth on it" (Job 1:7).

This meeting took place long after the fall of humans in Eden, when Satan became the leader of this world and, apparently, represented the planet at this meeting. Later he tempted Christ by offering the kingdoms of this world to Him (Luke 4:5–7). So Christ calls him "the prince of this world" (John 12:31; 16:11); Paul calls him "the god of this world" (2 Cor. 4:4, ESV); and John says, "the whole world is under the control of the evil one" (1 John 5:19).[7]

---

6. Jiří Moskala, "The God of Job and Our Adversary," *Journal of the Adventist Theological Society* 15/1 (Spring 2004): 104–117.

7. Because many attended this meeting, it suggests that God has many inhabited

This is the context in which Satan came to the meeting convened by God. Satan was there as representative of earth, having wrenched that position from Adam, who capitulated to him and fell into sin (Gen. 3). At this time, the Lord spoke to Satan, calling attention to His servant Job in the following words: "There is no one on earth like him; he is blameless and upright, a man who fears God and shuns evil" (Job 1:8). Satan responded with the claim that Job served God because all his wants were supplied (1:9–11). Therefore, God allowed Satan to test Job but forbade him to touch Job's body (v. 12). Then, "On another day the angels came to present themselves before the Lord, and Satan also came with them to present himself before him" (2:1). On this occasion, the Lord repeated His former evaluation of Job, adding, "And he still maintains his integrity, though you incited me against him to ruin him without any reason'" (2:3). Satan challenged God to "'Stretch out your hand and strike his flesh and bones, and he will surely curse you to your face'" (2:5). As at the first meeting, God allowed the test proposed by Satan, this time forbidding him to take Job's life (2:6).

Here is insight into a struggle between God and Satan over Job as a test case. Both God and Satan seem to have an interest in testing Job; in fact, it was God who called attention to Job in the first place. The fact that this test case was mentioned during major meetings may suggest that the universe is involved in the same question.

Job was unlike Satan and his angels in that he remained faithful to God, "blameless," "upright," a man of "integrity," who "shunned evil." Behind the scenes the debate rages, questioning whether God is worthy of creaturely allegiance. The rebellion of Satan and his angels suggests they thought God was not worthy of their allegiance. Why else would

---

planets, which means that the cosmic controversy involves much more than just heaven and earth. The fact that only some angels and all humans sinned against God is the reason for the biblical focus on heaven and earth. These are the two levels of creaturely rebellion. However, this does not suggest that there are no other inhabited worlds interested in the cosmic controversy. Christ created worlds (*aionas*, plural, Heb. 1:2, translated "worlds" in KJV and NKJV, and "universe" in Phillips and NIV), and it is likely that He created intelligent beings in these worlds as He did on earth. (See James Strong, *A Concise Dictionary of the Words in the Greek Testament, with Their Renderings in the Authorized English Version* [McLean, VA: MacDonald, n.d.], 9.) Given that God is eternal and loves created beings, there could be innumerable populated planets in His vast interconnected universe. The depth of their interest in the cosmic controversy should not be underestimated.

they rebel? But Job remained loyal to God. This indicates that creaturely freedom to choose is gifted to created beings. It also indicates that God does not decide for created beings, but He allows them to decide. God is love, so He didn't create robots. He is a covenant God who longs for a love relationship with all created beings (Deut. 5:29).

ISAIAH 14 AND EZEKIEL 28: REBEL WARRIOR KING

Nearly all contemporary scholars confine Isaiah 14 and Ezekiel 28 to the historical king of Babylon (Isa. 14:4) and historical king of Tyre (Ezek. 28:2, 12).[8] However, there is a need to reconsider the deeper typological meaning of these chapters.[9] In examining their full hermeneutical significance (particularly Isa. 14:12–15 and Ezek. 28:13–17), it becomes clear where and why evil began, and the promise of annihilation of its leader. Here insight is gained into the two sides of the cosmic controversy where God's love is at war.

The data in the passages calls for an interpretation that transcends a local application to human kings. For example, the local king of Babylon had never been in heaven at God's throne (Isa. 14:12–13), nor had the local king of Tyre resided in Eden or appeared as a guardian cherub at heaven's throne (Ezek. 28:13–14). In both passages, the kings, because of pride (Isa. 14:13–14; Ezek. 28:17), are cast out of heaven (Isa. 14:12; Ezek. 28:16), and in the end will be annihilated (Isa. 14:15–20; Ezek. 28:18). Furthermore, the king of Tyre is said to have been perfect until sin was found in him (Ezek. 28:15), which cannot be said of any human since the Fall (Ps. 51:5; Rom. 5:16–18). Hence, this refers to a created being who had not yet sinned.

Other than God, Adam, and Eve, the only being mentioned in Scripture as being in Eden is Satan (Gen. 3:1–6; Rev. 12:9). It is his fall into rebellion that is described as follows: "You were anointed as a guardian cherub, for so I ordained you. You were on the holy mount of God; you walked among

---

8. For some exceptions and a fuller presentation of the cosmic controversy, see my *Systematic Theology: Prolegomena*, 398–416. Also, see José M. Bertoluci, *The Son of the Morning and the Guardian Cherub in the Context of the Controversy between Good and Evil* (ThD diss., Andrews University, 1985), 6–10. This is an in-depth study of Isaiah 14 and Ezekiel 28 and their contribution to the cosmic controversy. Bertoluci has made a major contribution in determining the divine intent of these two passages.

9. See Richard M. Davidson, *Typology in Scripture* (Berrien Springs, MI: Andrews University Press, 1981).

the fiery stones. You were blameless in your ways from the day you were created till wickedness was found in you" (Ezek. 28:14–15). "In the pride of your heart you say, 'I am a god' . . . you think you are wise, as wise as a god" (Ezek. 28:2; 6). "Your heart became proud on account of your beauty, and you corrupted your wisdom because of your splendor" (Ezek. 28:17). "You said in your heart, 'I will ascend to the heavens; I will raise my throne above the stars of God; I will sit enthroned on the mount of assembly, on the utmost heights of Mount Zaphon. I will ascend above the tops of the clouds; I will make myself like the Most High'" (Isa. 14:13–14).

Sin is the transgression of God's law (1 John 3:4) which is fulfilled by love (Rom. 13:10). Therefore, Satan's fall into sin was a fall from love. Sin began with Satan's bad free choice, not with God. Satan wanted to become God in place of God. He was not satisfied with the high honor of being next to God's throne; he wanted to occupy it. He must have thought he could do a better job than God. To question God was to question His rule, His law, and His government.

Scripture says "God is love" (1 John 4:8–16). Therefore, He is just in all His ways. Thus "The Lord is known by his acts of justice" (Ps. 9:16). This means that all God's attributes, as well as His rule, and the law on which it is based, reflect His love. Christ, in human history, said the law (i.e., the Torah and the Ten Commandments) is summed up as love to God and to fellow beings (Matt. 22:37–40). The Triune God experience reciprocal love among them. This means that each Person in the Trinity loves God and in so doing loves fellow beings. So the law of love is the very essence of God's nature as a God of love. Therefore, foundationally, Satan questions the love of God, which includes His justice and mercy. Satan had always known God as a God of love, but for personal gain he launched a campaign to shred the truth about Him.[10]

The human kings of Tyre and Babylon are symbols for Satan and for the final destruction of his rebellion against God. Just as Matthew 24 focuses on the destruction of Jerusalem in AD 70 (vv. 1–2, 15–20) and the end of the world (vv. 4–14, 22–31), so Isaiah focuses on the destruction of a local and an eschatological or spiritual Babylon.[11] Also, in Scripture, Jerusalem

---

10. We cannot properly judge God's justice unless He reveals it to us. See E. Edward Zinke and Roland R. Hegstad, *The Certainty of the Second Coming* (Hagerstown, MD: Review and Herald, 2000).

11. Isaiah ministered in Jerusalem from about 750–700 BC. Nebuchadnezzar was king

(Heb. 12:22–23; Rev. 21:1–3) and Babylon (Dan. 1:1–2; Isa. 21:9; 48:20; cf. Rev. 14:8; 18:1–24) represent the two sides of the cosmic controversy.

Isaiah 14 is surrounded by two prophecies against Babylon (Isa. 13 and 21). In Isaiah 21:9, a lamentation cry goes out: "Babylon has fallen, has fallen! All the images of its gods lie shattered on the ground!" This is a type of the ultimate lamentation for spiritual Babylon as portrayed in the final book of Scripture. "Fallen! Fallen is Babylon the Great, which made all the nations drink the maddening wine of her adulteries" (Rev. 14:8). "'Fallen! Fallen is Babylon the Great!' She has become a dwelling for demons and a haunt for every impure spirit" (Rev. 18:2). The first verse shows the global power of spiritual Babylon, the second the demonic power of spiritual Babylon. But God has many people in Babylon who love Him, and His final invitation is to accept His Sabbath and come out of Babylon (Rev. 18:1–4). Armageddon and the plagues (Rev. 16) find love at war climaxed by the Second Advent (Rev. 19:14–21).

The pre-Second Advent end-game of the controversy is a global confrontation between spiritual Babylon and God's people (Rev. 13–19). The roots of spiritual Babylon are embedded in the tower of Babel, where God divided the human languages in order to thwart a global unity against Him (Gen. 11:1–9). In the pre-advent end time, spiritual Babylon vents its rage against God in a global attack (Rev. 13:1–4). After the millennium, all the wicked throughout human history are raised and join Satan and his angels in their last fight against God. They are destroyed by consuming fire (Rev. 20:7–10; cf. Mal. 4:1–3). It is the New Jerusalem that comes down from heaven to the new earth and becomes the home of the redeemed forever (Rev. 21:1–5). Glorious restoration![12]

---

of Babylon from 605–562 BC. The city was captured by Cyrus in 539 BC, so Isaiah prophesied nearly 200 years before that time. Ezekiel lived during the Babylonian Captivity of Judah, when literal Babylon was the enemy of God's people, just as spiritual Babylon will be the final enemy of God's people (Rev. 14:8; 18:1–24). See Kenneth Mulzac, "The 'Fall of Babylon' Motif in Jeremiah and Revelation," *Journal of the Adventist Theological Society* 8/1–2 (Spring-Autumn 1997): 137–149.

12. Richard Davidson has identified a chiastic structure of Ezekiel that focuses on the significance of the cosmic controversy in Scripture. Building on, and going beyond, William H. Shea's pioneering work on literary structure in Ezekiel, Davidson enlarges the chiastic structure study to include the whole book. He concludes that the chiastic apex of Ezekiel is the cosmic judgment on the Fallen Cherub (Ezek. 28:17–18). So the apex of the book, where the

Isaiah presents a powerful contrast between the pride of the rebel (Isa. 14:13–14) and the humility of Christ (Isa. 53). Satan attempts to become God, which is above his status as a created being, while Jesus becomes human, which is below His status as Creator God. Here in stark boldness is epitomized the different strategies of the two sides in the cosmic controversy. This controversy led to Calvary where one killed and the other died. In the crucifixion, the injustice of the rebel and the justice of the Redeemer met head on. Calvary lavishly overflowed with Christ's love for humans (Phil. 2:5–11; 1 John 3:1) and utterly exposed Satan's hatred of Christ (Luke 22:1–6; John 13:21–30).

REVELATION 12: WAR IN HEAVEN AND ON EARTH

The last book of the Bible, Revelation, describes how the cosmic conflict begins, develops, and ends (Rev. 12). The two main combatants are also identified (12:7). The angel Lucifer (later called Satan) launched the cosmic controversy against God in heaven. As a rebel, he is known as the

---

most important fact is presented, and to which the rest is germane, is the final judgment on Satan. Here is another evidence of the cosmic importance of Ezekiel 28. That same judgment is given in Isaiah 14:12, 15. See Richard M. Davidson, "The Chiastic Literary Structure of the Book of Ezekiel," *To Understand the Scriptures: Essays in Honor of William H. Shea*, ed. David Merling (Berrien Springs, MI.: Institute of Archaeology, Andrews University, 1997), 71–93; William H. Shea, "The Investigative Judgment of Judah: Ezekiel 1–10," in *The Sanctuary and the Atonement: Biblical, Historical, and Theological Studies*, ed. Arnold V. Wallenkampf and W. Richard Lesher (Washington, DC: Review and Herald, 1981), 283–291.

Ranko Stefanovic sees in the book of Revelation a chiastic structure which also centers in the cosmic controversy.

A. Prologue (1:1–8)
    B. Promise to the overcomer (1:9–3:22)
        C. God's work for humanity's salvation (4:1–8:1)
            D. God's wrath mixed with mercy (8:2–9:21)
                E. Commissioning John to prophesy (10:1–11:18)
                    F. Great controversy between Christ and Satan (11:19–13:18)
                E'. Church proclaims the end-time gospel (14:1–20)
              D'. God's final wrath unmixed with mercy (15:1–18:24)
            C'. God's work for humanity's salvation completed (19:1–21:4)
    B'. Fulfillment of the promises to the overcomer (21:5–22:5)
A'. Epilogue (22:6–21)

Ranko Stefanovic, *Revelation of Jesus Christ: Commentary on the Book of Revelation* (Berrien Springs, MI: Andrews University Press, 2002), 36–37.

devil, and the Greek διαβάλλω means to "accuse, bring charges with hostile intent"; the word *Satan* in the Greek (Σατᾷν) means "adversary, or "slanderer." The "widespread trade" of Ezekiel 28:16a is from the Hebrew word *rekyllah* which has a wide semantic range but is best translated in this context as "gossip or slander"[13] (cf. 2 Pet. 2:10). Satan slandered God to ruin His character.[14]

The other combatant, Michael, is mentioned five times in Scripture (Dan. 10:13, 21; 12:1; Jude 9; Rev. 12:7).[15] Comparison of these references indicates that Michael is the fully divine Christ in His roles as Ruler of angels and the One who resurrects the dead. Scripture says, "The archangel Michael . . . was disputing with the devil about the body of Moses" (Jude 9; cf. Deut. 34:1–8). This seems to be at the time when Moses was resurrected since he appeared at Christ's transfiguration (Matt. 17:1–3). Christ's role in resurrection is also evident when Paul writes: "For the Lord himself will come down from heaven, with a loud command, with *the voice of the archangel* and with the trumpet call of God, and the dead in Christ will rise first" (1 Thess. 4:16). John makes the same point: "Very truly I tell you, a time is coming and has now come when the dead will hear the voice of the Son of God and those who hear will live" (John 5:25). As such, Michael is Christ who is "'very God of very God, of the same substance as the Father,'—coequal, coexistent, and coeternal with God the Father. We believe that there never was a

---

13. See Robert H. O'Connell, *"rākil"* in *New International Dictionary of Theology & Exegesis,* gen. ed. Willem A. VanGemeren (Grand Rapids, MI: Zondervan, 1997), 3:1115. My analysis is as follows: Satan's slander of God is his widespread dissemination of disinformation about God, which is altogether different from the secular trade of the king of Tyre on the local level.

14. For an examination of distorted views about God promoted by Satan in the cosmic controversy and answered by Scripture, see Norman R. Gulley, *Systematic Theology: God as Trinity.*

15. The angel said to Daniel, "Michael, one of the chief princes, came to help me" as the Persian prince had resisted him twenty-one days (Dan. 10:13). In other words Michael was able to succeed where the angel had not. The angel called Michael "your prince" (Dan. 10:21) and "the great prince who protects your people" (Dan. 12:1). In the Hebrew language, *Mikha'el* is *Micha,* "one who is like"; and *el,* "God." This title "does not in any way conflict with our belief in His full deity and eternal pre-existence." *Seventh-day Adventists Answer Questions on Doctrines: An Explanation of Certain Major Aspects of Seventh-day Adventist Belief* (Washington, DC: Review and Herald, 1957), 71.

time when Christ was not. He is God forever more, His life being 'original, unborrowed, underived.'"[16]

In Revelation 12, the first eight verses are an introduction explaining how Christ's war is motivated by His love for His church, which is represented as a woman (Rev. 12:1; cf. Jer. 6:2). She wears a crown of victory (taken from the Greek: *stephanos*, a laurel wreath worn by a victor in the Olympic Games). In the various battles in the war of love, God will take care of His church (Rev. 12:6).

The first battle of the war was before humans were created. "War broke out in heaven" between Michael and his angels and the dragon and his angels (Rev. 12:7). Satan and his angels were defeated and forced to leave heaven (Rev. 12:4). The book of Revelation describes how in the end, "The great dragon was hurled down—that ancient serpent [serpent in Eden, tempting Eve, Gen. 3:1–6] called the devil, or Satan, who leads the whole world astray" (Rev. 12:9).[17]

The second battle takes place on earth. Satan became the "prince" (John 12:31), or "god of this age" (2 Cor. 4:4), when he usurped the dominion from Adam and Eve in their fall (Gen. 1–3). That's why Satan in Old Testament times evidently represented this world when different leaders met together with Christ somewhere in the universe outside of heaven. Satan showed his colors by being critical of Job and God (Job 1–2). Again after the return of Judah from captivity, Satan accuses Joshua the high priest, whereas the pre-incarnate Christ rebuked Satan (Zech. 3:1–2).

The champion for humanity in this battle is Christ/Michael. Satan was ready to "devour" Him as soon as He was born (Rev. 12:4; cf. Matt. 2:13–17) and tried to defeat Him throughout His life. Satan worked through Judas to betray Christ so He would be crucified (John 13:21–27). Yet, Calvary was the decisive victory by Christ over Satan! At Calvary Christ won

---

16. *Questions on Doctrines*, 83.

17. From its inception, the controversy has been primarily Satan's warring against Christ. Scripture does not tell us why Satan opposed Christ, nor is the fact that sin could arise in such a perfect environment explained. The hatred of Satan toward Christ can be documented from his schemes to kill Him from His very incarnation (Rev. 12:4–5, 9) to crucifixion (John 13:21–27). It is a window through which believers can look beyond the mere emphasis on human salvation to the cosmic battle that lies behind it. See Steven Grabiner, "The Cosmic Conflict: Revelation's Undercurrent," *Journal of the Adventist Theological Society* 26/1 (Spring 2015): 38–56.

back the right, as the second or last Adam (1 Cor. 15:45–47), to be the leader of this world. In this way "the great dragon was hurled down—that ancient serpent called the devil, or Satan, who leads the whole world astray. He was hurled to the earth" (Rev. 12:9). In contrast, the resurrected Christ ascended to the heavenly sanctuary as the only qualified Person to intercede for sinners on the basis of His life (Heb. 2:18; 4:15–16) and His death (Heb. 9:12; 10:11–14). Christ "became the source of eternal salvation" (Heb. 5:9) and the only mediator between God and humans (1 Tim. 2:5).

The third battle described in Revelation 12 involves the defeated Satan venting his wrath against Christ's church. But Christ takes care of His church during the 1,260 days (representing years) of persecution (Rev. 12:14). One of the ways Christ cares for the church is through the religious freedoms promoted in the United States (12:15–16). This brought a lessening of the trials described in the book of Daniel as follows: "This horn [counterfeit system] had eyes like the eyes of a human being and a mouth that spoke boastfully" (Dan. 7:8). Daniel says, "As I watched, this horn was waging war against the holy people and defeating them, until the Ancient of days came and pronounced judgment in favor of the holy people of the Most High, and the time came when they possessed the kingdom" (Dan. 7:21–22; cf. vv. 25–27).[18] This time will fully be realized at the Second Advent of Christ.[19]

A fourth and final battle is described in Revelation 12. In response to Christ's protection of His people, the devil becomes angry and wages war

---

18. Norman R. Gulley, "Daniel's Pre-Advent Judgment in Its Biblical Context," *Journal of the Adventist Theological Society,* 2/2 (Autumn 1991): 35–66.

19. Sin brings death (Rom. 6:23). Christ upheld His law of love by paying the death penalty for humans. God really loves us. If God's law could be changed, then Christ's death was meaningless. The cosmic controversy is law-breaking, based on a broken relationship with the Lawgiver (Isa. 59:2). Redemption includes restoration of the broken relationship between God and humans, which includes law-keeping as love for redemption (see John 14:15; Phil. 1:6).

Satan's controversy is against God whose rule is based on His law of love. During the cosmic controversy God prophesied that a power would try to change the time in the law (Dan. 7:25). The Aramaic word for "time" is *zeman,* or "set point of time." The Aramaic text uses the plural *zimmin,* meaning "a recurring set time in the law," or the weekly seventh-day Sabbath (Exod. 20:8–11). By contrast the saints are persecuted for a span of time, and the Aramaic word for "time" is now *iddan* (Dan. 7:25). See William H. Shea, *The Abundant Life Bible Amplifier: A Practical Guide to Abundant Christian Living in the Book of Daniel 7–12,* gen. ed. George R. Knight (Boise, ID: Pacific Press, 1996), 139.

against God's people in the end time, against those "who keep the commandments of God and hold to the testimony of Jesus" (Rev. 12:17, ESV). The fourth battle continues throughout Revelation 13–20.[20]

After the millennium the wicked are raised so they can see that their destiny is just. Christ promised, "I, when I am lifted up from the earth, will draw all people to myself" (John 12:32, ESV). This began to be fulfilled at Calvary and will continue to be the case for eternity. On the last judgment day, even those who are lost will see that Calvary included them (cf. 1 John 2:2), and all will bow to God admitting He was right in the controversy (Isa. 45:23; Rom. 14:11; Phil. 2:10–11; Rev. 5:13; 15:3; 19:1–6). But at that point, the wicked demonstrate that they have not been changed by God's love. They join Satan and his angels in their last fight against God and those in the New Jerusalem (Rev. 20:7–9). Then in defense of the saints, and as an act of love, God brings an end to the rebellion as fire consumes the wicked (20:10; cf. Mal. 4:1–3). The New Jerusalem on the new earth becomes the home of God and the redeemed forever (Rev. 21:1–5). God really loves humanity!

CALVARY: THE DECISIVE BATTLE

Sin is breaking the law (1 John 3:4). In dying for sin, Christ demonstrated the immutability of His law, as unchangeable as God. If God's law could be changed, then Christ's death was an utter waste. The essence of the cosmic controversy is law-breaking, based on a broken relationship with the Lawgiver (Isa. 59:2). Redemption includes restoration of the broken relationship between God and humans. Resolution of the cosmic controversy includes a return to the pre-Fall state in Eden. In the cosmic controversy, Christ's work is the restoration of God's creation. Satan's work is its destruction.[21]

---

20. Attack against God is a theme in Daniel and in Revelation. Pagan nations like Egypt, Assyria, Babylon, Medo-Persia, Greece, and Rome were infused with and used by Satan in his war against God. The last four are mentioned in Daniel 2 and 7. Pagan Rome divided into ten, and the little horn "came up among them" (Dan. 7:8), replacing pagan Rome when the civil capital moved to Constantinople in 330 AD. See Jacques B. Doukhan, *Secrets of Daniel: Wisdom and Dreams of a Jewish Prince in Exile* (Hagerstown, MD: Review and Herald, 2000).

21. See Martinus C. de Boer, *The Defeat of Death: Apocalyptic Eschatology in 1 Corinthians 15 and Romans 5* (Sheffield: JSOT, 1988).

Even though millions starve at the same time, one person can only experience his or her own starvation, never the starvation of others. Not so with Calvary. "The Lord has laid on him the iniquity of us all" (Isa. 53:6). "He himself bore our sins in his body on the tree" (1 Pet. 2:24). "He was pierced for our transgressions, he was crushed for our iniquities" (Isa. 53:5). "He is the atoning sacrifice for our sins, and not only for ours but also for the sins of the whole world" (1 John 2:2). With explosive force, stunned, the universe is mightily moved by Christ's death for every sinner, including the most horrendous.

On the cross, with arms open wide, Christ hugged the world, while the devil, like a roaring lion, seeks "whom he may devour" (1 Pet. 5:8, NKJV). Calvary is the hermeneutical context to understand predestination. Not the other way round, as traditionally proposed. Calvary reveals that God predestined all humans to be saved. In that death, Christ elected all and rejected none. "God does not show favoritism" (Rom. 2:11). This is unconditional election. Christ provided the gift of eternal life for everyone. It is up to humans to either elect or reject their salvation (John 3:16). This turns the traditional priority of predestination on its head. Calvary is the ultimate or determining battle in the cosmic controversy. No need for an eternal decree hidden in mystery that is off limits to humans, so they must accept God's sovereign decision whether they like it or not, whether understood or not, whether fair or not. This is shattered by the greatest revelation of God's awesome love on the cross, which fully demonstrates His justice and mercy.

The cosmic controversy is about God's justice and mercy. Is He a God of love or not? Satan claims that He is not a God of love. Misunderstandings of predestination unwittingly aid Satan's claim. How can God choose or elect a few, dump the rest as worthless rejects, mere throw-aways? How can God give the elect irresistible grace so they cannot fail but refuse to help the rest? Then, as if this is not enough, God casts the rejects into eternal hell to suffer unspeakable anguish forever. Such behavior fully demonstrates Satan's charge that God is not love. Eternal hell would provide unending evidence that Satan's charge is legitimate. Then Satan's chances of winning the universe to his side would be guaranteed. In time, the anguish of eternal hell would define God rather than Calvary. In fact, the memory of Calvary would be smothered by the horrible and wretched suffering in an endless fiery furnace. Eternal hell overlooks the fact that there is no redemption without resolution to the cosmic controversy. If hell is forever, the cosmic controversy is never resolved.[22]

Calvary resolved the cosmic controversy. Calvary demolished Satan's charges. The mask was wrenched from that wicked wretch. His deceptive charges against God stood utterly exposed at the cross. Like roaring thunder comes from Calvary the shout "God is love!" Human destiny depends upon accepting or rejecting Calvary during human history, not upon a Sovereign God's eternal decree that is incompatible with Calvary. It is the God of Calvary who does not change (Mal. 3:6). "Jesus Christ is the same yesterday and today and forever" (Heb. 13:8).

Throughout eternity it will be seen that Calvary is the greatest revelation of God's love. Created beings will never fathom the depths of God's awesome love revealed at the cross. In utter amazement they contemplate the anguish Christ endured, allowing created beings to vent satanic rage upon their Creator. Overwhelmed by Calvary-love, in ever deepening gratitude, they will love, adore, and worship God. They realize that Christ's death was the outpouring of the Godhead for undeserving humans, and they will forever be impacted by this wondrous gift. In this context, God's love can never be questioned again (cf. Nah. 1:9).[23]

22. See Christopher M. Date and Ron Highfield, eds., *A Consuming Passion: Essays on Hell and Immortality in Honor of Edward Fudge* (Eugene, OR: Pickwick, 2015).

23. See Gustaf Aulen, *Christus Victor: An Historical Study of the Three Main Types of the Idea of Atonement* (London: SPCK, 1961).

CHAPTER 3

FOREKNOWLEDGE AND
THE FREEDOM OF SALVATION

Martin F. Hanna

This chapter presents a biblical study on God's foreknowledge of His free choices (to give and withhold salvation) and our free choices (to receive or refuse salvation). As such, this is an inquiry concerning God's foreknowledge of divine-human interactions and interactive options involved with the freedom of salvation. Foreknowledge is exhaustively definite because God has always known all the options; it is also exhaustively dynamic since, by facilitating these foreknown interactions and options, God focuses His foreknowledge of the future without adding to the content of His foreknowledge. In addition, God's foreknowledge of divine-human interactions and options complements a libertarian definition of freedom involving choices that are not decisively caused or constrained by God. This is significant because "If . . . people do not have libertarian free will, [then] God is the Creator or author of sin and evil."[1]

---

1. Roger Olson, "The Classical Free Will Theist Model of God," in *Perspectives on the Doctrine of God,* ed. Bruce Ware (Nashville, TN: B & H, 2008), 160. See also David Palmer, ed., *Libertarian Free Will: Contemporary Debates* (New York: Oxford University Press, 2014). Some persons affirm libertarian freedom while rejecting the principle of alternate options. See William Craig, "Response to Boyd," in Stanley N. Gundry and Dennis W. Jowers, eds., *Four Views on Divine Providence* (Grand Rapids, MI: Zondervan, 2011), 226; cf. John C. Peckham, "Does God Always Get What He Wants? A Theocentric Approach to Divine Providence and Human Freedom," *Andrews University Seminary Studies* 52:2 (2014): 196n2.

The libertarian definition stands in contrast with a compatibilist definition of freedom whereby interactions are decisively caused without being constrained. Proponents of this

A careful investigation of this subject is needed in response to the following problematic question: Why does God's foreknowledge seem to contradict the freedom of salvation?

> If God knows what I will do on a given occasion, it appears that it is not within my power to do otherwise. God's knowledge does not cause my action, but if he really knows it, it will occur. But if it is certain to happen, then how am I free to do other than what God knows.
>
> This is a problem not only for human freedom, but also for divine freedom . . . If God knows all future acts and events, he must know everything that he will do. But if he knows what he will do before he does it, it appears that he is not free to change his mind and do other than what he *knows* he will do.[2]

The traditional view of foreknowledge and the freedom of salvation seeks to solve the problem by proposing that God exercises His freedom and focuses His foreknowledge "by decreeing everything that occurs and then creating the world in which those things happen."[3] As such, God chooses among options when He creates the world, but He does not continue to choose among options after He creates the world. "Once God decides to create, . . . he forever after knows everything that will happen, including what he will do . . . Deliberation and decision are thereafter ruled out."[4] This means "that one is not permitted to make a separation between what God knows at a point in time, and what He does with or about that knowledge in the future."[5]

---

definition conclude: "Acting without constraint means acting in accord with one's wishes or desires. So, an act is free, though causally determined, if it is what the [free] agent wanted to do." The "causal factors" are "strong enough . . . so that there is a sense in which the [free] agent could not have done otherwise." John S. Feinberg, *No One Like Him: The Doctrine of God* (Wheaton, IL: Crossway, 2001), 637–638.

2. Feinberg, *No One Like Him*, 305. Of course, God's foreknowledge in itself need not be viewed as contradicting freedom since knowing a free choice does not cause that free choice. However, the way in which one understands the nature of foreknowledge may produce an apparent conflict with freedom. See T. R. Byerly, "Infallible Divine Foreknowledge Cannot Uniquely Threaten Human Freedom, But Its Mechanics Might," *European Journal for Philosophy of Religion*, 4:4 (2012): 73–94.

3. Ibid., 308.

4. Ibid., 314.

5. According to Kwabena Donkor, "If what God knows is as good as done, as they say, then any [libertarian] notion of free will and responsibility is negated." Donkor, "Predestination, Foreknowledge, and Human Freedom," 1, https://www.adventistbiblicalresearch.

Therefore, from this perspective, foreknowledge does not inform God's plan of salvation; rather, He foreknows only after He has made His plan.

Important aspects of the freedom of salvation remain unexplained by the traditional view of foreknowledge. As a result, Bible students propose four conflicting interpretations, or models, of the relations between God's foreknowledge and divine-human free choice interactive options and/or interactions.[6] Model 1, Simple Foreknowledge, affirms that God foreknows all interactions, but it does not define whether interactive options exist so that they could be foreknown.[7] Model 2, Augustinian-Calvinist, denies that God foreknows interactive options—they do not exist since He chooses to cause and therefore to foreknow all interactions.[8] Model 3, Middle Knowledge, affirms that God facilitates and foreknows all interactions and interactive options.[9] Model 4, Open Theism, affirms that God foreknows interactive options when He facilitates them without foreknowing the interactions involved, except when He chooses to cause them.[10]

---

org/sites/default/files/pdf/Predestination.pdf.

6. These models are described in terms that highlight the issues I address in this chapter. Specific Bible students may or may not fit completely into any of the models as I describe them. See also Feinberg's description of five models that have been used to harmonize foreknowledge with libertarian freedom: "the Boethian solution, simple foreknowledge, middle knowledge or the Molinist solution, the Ockhamist solution, and present knowledge," Feinberg, *No One Like Him,* 742.

7. David Hunt, "The Simple Foreknowledge View," in James J. Beilby and Paul R. Eddy, eds., *Divine Foreknowledge: Four Views* (Downers Grove, IL: InterVarsity, 2001), 65–103.

8. Paul Helm, "The Augustinian-Calvinist View," *Divine Foreknowledge,* 161–189.

9. William Lane Craig, "The Middle-Knowledge View," *Divine Foreknowledge,* 119–143. Model 2 fits best with the traditional model of foreknowledge. Ironically, models 3 and 4 presuppose the accuracy of the traditional view, which may be the source of the problem they are trying to solve. Models 2 and 4 deny that model 3 is able to effectively defend the harmony it proposes between the traditional view and libertarian freedom. See comments by Hunt, Helm, and Boyd in *Divine Foreknowledge,* 144–160. Significantly, Craig affirms libertarian freedom but rejects the principle of alternate options. See "Response to Boyd," in *Four Views on Divine Providence,* 226; cf. John C. Peckham, "Does God Always Get What He Wants?" 196n2.

10. Gregory Boyd, "The Open Theism View," *Divine Foreknowledge,* 13–47. Clark Pinnock points out that, according to this model, "Free actions [involving alternative options] are not actions that can be known ahead of time. They literally do not exist to be known,"

One possible way to overcome this standoff among the four models is to undertake a biblical evaluation of the traditional view of the nature of God's foreknowledge of the freedom of salvation. Biblical evaluation is a viable way forward since proponents of these competing models have a shared respect for a normative role for the Bible in matters of theology. To the extent that each of these models has insights derived from the Bible, these insights can be combined to produce a more fully biblical model. It is beyond the scope of this chapter to examine every one of the numerous biblical references to the concept of foreknowledge. Therefore, this study will examine the five biblical texts that use the words *foreknowledge* (Greek, *prognōsis*) and foreknew/foreknown (Greek, *proginōskō*) in connection with God's foreknowledge of the freedom of salvation: Acts 2:23; 1 Peter 1:2, 20; Romans 8:29; 11:2.[11] Other passages that reference the concept of foreknowledge will be mentioned as part of the explanation of the meaning of these five texts.

The examination of these biblical texts will also be informed by the fact that Peter and Paul explicitly link God's foreknowledge with His predestination of the Savior and of those who are saved. Peter refers to Christ "being delivered [to death] by the determined purpose and foreknowledge of God," "taken by lawless hands," "crucified, and put to death; whom God raised up" (Acts 2:23–24). Similarly, Paul refers to "those who love God" (Rom. 8:28), whom He "foreknew" and "predestined" (8:29). Therefore, the five texts mentioned previously (Acts 2:23; Rom. 8:29; 11:2; 1 Pet. 1:2, 20) will be examined to identify answers to the following questions: Does God's exhaustive foreknowledge of the freedom of salvation facilitate His predestination, or does His predestination facilitate His foreknowledge? Is God's definite foreknowledge static, or is it dynamically focused by divine-human interactions? Is God's foreknowledge limited to anticipating the certainty of interactions, or is it exhaustive in the sense of also anticipating the certainty of interactive options?[12]

David and Randall Bassinger, eds., *Predestination and Free Will* (Downers Grove, IL: InterVarsity, 1986), 157; cf. Donkor, "Predestination, Foreknowledge, and Human Freedom," 3.

11. The second word is also used to refer to human foreknowledge. Paul referred to the Jews who "knew me from the first [*proginōskō*]" (Acts 26:5); and Peter appeals to his readers: "Since you know this beforehand [*proginōskō*], beware" (2 Pet. 3:17). Unless otherwise indicated, all Scripture quotations are taken from the New King James Version®. Copyright © 1982 by Thomas Nelson. Used by permission. All rights reserved.

12. Foreknowledge of options and actions is greater than foreknowledge of actions

A case can be made, based on these five explicit Bible texts, that God's foreknowledge of divine-human interactive options and interactions facilitates His predestination of divine options and actions (Acts 2:23; 1 Pet. 1:2, 20; Rom. 8:29; 11:2) so as to facilitate human options and actions (Acts 2:23; 1 Pet. 1:2) which also facilitate divine options and actions (Acts 2:24; 1 Pet. 1:21).[13] For example, God "foreknew" (Rom. 11:2) His interactive options with regard to His action in the "irrevocable" (11:28–29) "election [free choice][14] of grace" (11:5) whereby He has mercy on all (11:32). God also foreknew (11:2) His continuing divine-human interactive options and interactions with those who are "elect" "by faith" and non-elect by "unbelief" (11:7, 20). Through such foreknown interactive options and interactions, the elect can become non-elect and the non-elect can become elect (11:22–23; cf. 2 Pet. 1:10; 3:9).[15] (These

---

alone. Also, since options are possible actions, foreknowledge of options anticipates actions that may not happen. In this way, the logical structures of foreknowledge and predestination are similar. God predestines actions that happen (His permissive will) and actions that may not happen (His prescriptive will). See John C. Peckham, "Does God Always Get What He Wants?", 195–212; "Providence and God's Unfulfilled Desires," *Philosophia Christi* 15:2 (2013): 453–462.

13. Traditionally, distinctions are made among God's natural knowledge of necessities, middle knowledge of contingencies, and free knowledge of future free choices. In the history of Christian reflection on these matters, two important writers are Luis de Molina (1535–1600) and Jacob Arminius (1560–1609). Molina proposes a single divine deliberation following middle knowledge; and Arminius proposes two divine deliberations, one preceding and the other following middle knowledge. God's deliberation is understood to lead to free knowledge of future free choices. Kirk M. MacGreggor, *A Molinist-Anabaptist Systematic Theology* (Lanham, MD: University Press of America, 2007), 63–81. My model highlights God's continuing use of foreknowledge (natural, middle, and free) in continuing divine deliberations. Craig writes, "We [may] take the biblical word 'foreknowledge' to encompass middle knowledge," "God Directs All Things," in *Four Views on Divine Providence,* 86. See also *The Works of James Arminius,* trans. James and William Nichols (Grand Rapids, MI: Baker, 1996), 1:653–4; cf. Timothy Arena, "Divine Foreknowledge, Predestination, and Plan" (Unpublished paper, Andrews University, December 2016).

14. Ben Witherington, III, and Darlene Hyatt, *Paul's Letter to the Romans: A Socio-Rhetorical Commentary* (Grand Rapids, MI: Eerdmans, 2004), 265.

15. "New Testament election language focuses not [primarily] on the concept of *selection* but rather [primarily] on the idea of *gracious initiative.*" Glen Shellrude, "All Are Elect, Few Are Elect," *Scottish Bulletin of the Evangelical Theology* 30:2 (Autumn 2012): 145. "Between election in the Hebrew Scriptures of Jesus and election in the formulation of theological systems there sometimes seems to be a great gulf fixed. Few and narrow are the

interpretations will be further explained and supported later in this chapter.)

The biblical model proposed here suggests that God's exhaustive definite foreknowledge operates in a dynamic way as is illustrated in the following conversation between God and David concerning King Saul and the leaders of the town of Keilah. Foreknowing Saul's impending expedition to attack David in Keilah, God said to David: "He will come down" (1 Sam. 23:11); and "they [the leaders] will deliver you [to Saul]" (23:12). In response to God's foreknowledge, David left the town (23:13). "Then it was told Saul that David had escaped from Keilah; so he halted the expedition" (23:13). Here God's interaction with David prevents an event that God foreknew: Saul will kill David in Keilah. Simultaneously, God's interaction with David facilitates another event that God also foreknew: David will become king in place of Saul (2 Sam. 2:11; 5:3).[16]

This biblical narrative illustrates that God foreknew all interactive options and interactions, some of which He excludes from actualization when He makes free choices. Also, God foreknew the interactive options that His choices make available for human beings. In addition, God foreknew the interactive options that are excluded by human choices. Therefore, God's foreknowledge focuses on different interactive options and interactions as divine-human interactions happen. In this way, God foreknew before the creation of the universe (1 Pet. 1:20) and foreknows from the perspective of His "eternal presence" within created time.[17] Being

---

bridges from one to the other," Christopher J. H. Wright, *The Mission of God: Unlocking the Bible's Grand Narrative* (Nottingham: InterVarsity, 2006), 262; cf. Stephen N. Williams, *The Election of Grace: A Riddle Without a Resolution?* (Grand Rapids, MI: Eerdmans, 2015), 5. See also Joel Kaminsky's distinctions among elect, non-elect, and anti-elect. "The Concept of Election and Second Isaiah: Recent Literature," *Biblical Theology Bulletin* 31 (Winter 2001): 135–144; "Did Election Imply the Mistreatment of Non-Israelites?" *Harvard Theological Review* 96:4 (2003): 397–425; cf. Joel N. Lohr, *Chosen and Unchosen: Conceptions of Election in the Pentateuch and Jewish-Christian Interpretation*" (Winina Lake, IN: Eisenbrauns, 2009), 35–40.

16. For more information on the incident at Keilah, see Nadav Na'aman, "David's Sojourn in Keilah in Light of the Amarna Letters," *Vetus Testamentum*, 60 (2010): 87–97.

17. Ellen White writes: "I AM means an eternal presence; the past, present, and future are alike with God" in that "He sees the most remote events of past history, and the far distant future with as clear a vision as we do those things which are transpiring daily," Letter 119, February 19, 1895. Concerning the conditionality of prophetic foreknowledge: "The angels of God in their messages to men represent time as very short. Thus it has always been

omniscient, He knows the difference among the past, the present, and the future, and focuses His foreknowledge accordingly.[18] It is important to note that this focusing does not add to God's foreknowledge since He always foreknew all things. (Additional biblical insights—concerning God's exhaustive, definite, and dynamic foreknowledge of the freedom of salvation—are presented in subsequent sections of this chapter.)

PETER'S SERMON AT PENTECOST

In Peter's sermon on the day of Pentecost, he preached about Christ "being delivered by the . . . foreknowledge of God" (Acts 2:23). The rest of the sermon shows that what God foreknew is not only revealed in this single phrase. For Peter, divine foreknowledge is also revealed in the Old Testament

---

presented to me. It is true that time has continued longer than we expected in the early days of this message. Our Saviour did not appear as soon as we hoped. But has the word of the Lord failed? Never! It should be remembered that the promises and threatenings of God are alike conditional," Ellen G. White, *Selected Messages* (Washington, DC: Review and Herald, 1980), 1:67. Herbert Douglass comments: "Conditional prophecy, or controlled uncertainty, is a Biblical principle applied to statements of a predictive nature that concern or involve the responses of human beings. Whenever an unfolding of events depends upon human choice, certain aspects of prophetic fulfillment are necessarily conditional," *Messenger of the Lord* (Napa, ID: Pacific Press, 1998), 30.

18. Patrick Todd identifies the following implications concerning the future based on his reading of the writings of Peter Geach: "the future is *mutable* in a particular way. On open future views, we often so act that we give the future a more determinate shape; we sometimes make it so that . . . what only *might* or *will probably* happen becomes such that now it simply *will* happen. Geach's view is different. We change the future in a more radical way. . . . What will happen changes. No other view—'open' or otherwise—maintains this distinctive thesis," Patrick Todd, "Geachianism," in *Oxford Studies in Philosophy of Religion,* ed. Jonathan Kvanvig (Oxford: Oxford University Press, 2011), 3:226. "Perhaps you think this is a strange, counterintuitive result. If it really is true that something is going to happen, how could it fail to? If this has been your reaction to Geach's view, then I must warn you that you may be in danger of becoming an open futurist. For it is clearly the central thesis of open future views—and logical fatalism—that if something will happen in the future, it *cannot* later fail to happen. If it will happen, then it is inevitable," ibid., 238–239. "The traditional motivation for open theism has been the thought that divine foreknowledge and human freedom are incompatible, with the consequence that we must deny that God has foreknowledge of future free actions. . . . Geach's view . . . has the consequence that mere divine foreknowledge is consistent with human freedom," ibid., 244. See Peter Geach, *Providence and Evil* (Cambridge: Cambridge University Press, 1977); Patrick Todd, "Against Limited Foreknowledge," *Philosophia* 42:2 (2014): 523–538.

prophetic Scriptures that anticipate the divine-human interactions that follow God's "determined purpose" that Christ be "delivered"—who "you have taken by lawless hands, have crucified, and put to death; whom God raised up" (2:23–24). The revelation of foreknowledge in Scripture is evident when "David said about Him, 'I foresaw the LORD'" (2:25); and "being a prophet" (2:30), he "foreseeing this spoke concerning the resurrection of the Christ" (2:31). David also spoke about Christ "being exalted to the right hand of God, and [how] having received from the Father the promise of the Holy Spirit, He poured out this" (2:33; cf. 2:34–35).[19]

In addition, Peter points out that the foreknowledge revealed in Scripture includes divine-human interactions such as God's call and believers calling on God. The prophet Joel presents God's promise that "I will pour out of My Spirit on all flesh" (2:17); and that "whoever calls upon the name of the LORD shall be saved" (2:21). Therefore, God foreknew that His initiative through the Spirit makes it possible for everyone to call on God and be saved. This motivates Peter's appeal to "every one" (2:38; cf. 3:26) to "be saved" (2:40) because God's foreknown "promise is to you and to your children, and to all who are afar off, as many[20] as the Lord our God will call" (2:39; cf. 13:48; 1 Pet. 2:8).[21]

---

19. For Ellen White, foreknowledge is revealed in prophecy and is harmonious with human freedom: "Christ quoted a prophecy which more than a thousand years before had predicted what God's foreknowledge had seen would be. The prophecies do not shape the characters of the men who fulfill them. Men act out their own free will," *Review and Herald*, November 13, 1900. She disagrees with the view of the Sadducees that God's "foreknowledge of events would deprive man of free moral agency," *The Spirit of Prophecy* (Battle Creek, MI: SDA Publishing Association, 1884), 3:44. See Joseph Corabi, Rebecca Germino, "Prophecy, Foreknowledge, and Middle Knowledge," *Faith and Philosophy* 30:1 (2013): 72–92; Eleonore Stump, Norman Kretzmann, "Prophecy, Past Truth, and Eternity," *Philosophical Perspectives* 5 (1991): 395–424.

20. A similar phrase in another text deserves consideration here: "As many as had been appointed to eternal life believed" (Acts 13:48). The word *appointed* "has been parsed in the middle voice to yield the meaning that as many as had set or disposed themselves to or for eternal life became believers," *The Election of Grace*, 64. Others propose that God's appointment "is based on his foreknowledge of what an individual would freely and voluntarily choose," ibid., 68. Still others interpret *appointed* "as a corporate and not an individual matter," ibid., 70. However this text is interpreted, the appointment of some to eternal life need not imply that the others are irrevocably appointed to eternal death, ibid., 72–81.

21. God's call may be interpreted as an invitation extended to all and/or as a designation

The implications of Peter's sermon are further clarified in the wider context of the book of Acts when, at the Jerusalem council, the Apostle James interprets Peter's ministry in terms of God's foreknowledge of all humanity as revealed in Scripture. James says, "Simon [Peter] has declared how God . . . visited the Gentiles to take out of them a people for His name. And with this the words of the prophets agree" (Acts 15:14–15). This is "'so that the rest of mankind may seek the LORD, even all the Gentiles who are called by My name, says the LORD who does all these things.' Known to God from eternity are all His works" (15:17–18; cf. 1 Pet. 1:20). If God foreknows all His choices in relation to the freedom of salvation, then He must also foreknow all divine-human interactive options and interactions, since He works in human beings so that it is possible for humans to seek salvation in Him.[22] Similarly, the book of Acts records how Paul preached in Athens that: God "has made from one blood every nation of men [humanity] . . . and has determined [predestined] their preappointed times and the boundaries of their dwellings, so that they should seek the Lord, in the hope that they might . . . find Him . . . for in Him we live and move and have our being" (Acts 17:26–28; cf. Rom. 8:20).[23] God's foreknown predestination facilitates the interactive

---

applied to some. For example: "Many are called [invited], but few are chosen" (Matt. 22:14); and "those who love God" are designated as "the called" (Rom. 8:28). What is important for the purposes of this chapter is that in Peter's sermon, God's foreknowledge (Acts 2:23) is linked with His call (2:39), and in Peter's letters he links the concepts of "foreknowledge" and "elect" (1 Pet. 1:2) and the concepts of "call and election" (2 Pet. 1:10). Also, both Peter and Paul link foreknowledge with predestination (Acts 2:23; Rom. 8:29). See William H. Willimon, "'Everyone Whom the Lord Our God Calls': Acts 2 and the Miracle of Pentecost Preaching in a Multicultural Context," *Journal for Preachers* 25:4 (Pentecost 2002): 3–10; William W. Klein, "Paul's Use of *Kalein*: A Proposal," *Journal of the Evangelical Theological Society* 27:1 (March 1984): 53–64.

22. Jesus says: "Without me you can do nothing" (John 15:5; cf. 1:3). Paul writes: "Work out your own salvation with fear and trembling; for it is God who works in you both to will and to do for His good pleasure" (Phil. 2:12–13). The fact that God foreknows all His works in concurrence with all our works does not mean that God causes us to choose one thing rather than another. "Particular creatures have distinctive contributions to make to the way God's will or intention is realized" with "the divine concurrence," Charles M. Wood, "How Does God Act?" *International Journal of Systematic Theology* 1:2 (July 1999): 148.

23. This text is similar to what Paul writes in his letter to the Romans concerning God subjecting the creation in hope for its deliverance (Rom. 8:20–21). Paul's sermon in Athens is mentioned here because it is part of the context of the book of Acts where Peter's sermon

options that make it possible for humanity to respond to His "commands [to] all men [and women] everywhere to repent" (Acts 17:30).[24]

The perspective of Peter, as presented in the context of the book of Acts, supports the concept of God's foreknowledge of interactive options and interactions. First, God possesses libertarian freedom because He foreknew His options before He determined His purpose to deliver Christ into the hands of human beings (Acts 2:23).[25] "The determined purpose and foreknowledge" of God are linked together in this statement by one article, *the,* in order to affirm the close relationship between them. Nevertheless, there is a distinction between God's purpose and His foreknowledge. God's purpose and action are informed by His foreknowledge of His options. "God's foreknowledge cannot be contingent upon His will."[26] God cannot foreknow all things unless His foreknowledge precedes all things.

Second, the wider biblical context indicates that God's foreknowledge and predestination do not exclude, but rather make possible, alternate options for interactions between the incarnate Christ and His Father in heaven. This is dramatically demonstrated when Christ affirmed in His prayer that God could reverse His will: "Father, all things are possible for you. Take this cup away from me" (Mark 14:36). After this, Christ also prayed in surrender to God's purpose: "Nevertheless, not what I will, but what you will" (14:36). Further evidence of the freedom of Christ is His statement that "I lay down my life that I may take it [up] again. No one

---

is recorded. Paul's writings on God's foreknowledge will be presented later in this chapter.

24. "Is He the God of the Jews only? Is He not also the God of the Gentiles? Yes, of the Gentiles also" (Rom. 3:29). "Christ…is over all, the eternally blessed God" (9:5).

25. The concept of foreknown free choice options helps us conceptualize how God could foreknow His free choices without compromising His freedom to choose. Defining mechanisms for the various dimensions of God's foreknowledge is beyond the scope of this chapter. At the same time, I propose that God makes free choices based on His foreknowledge of His options, not based on His foreknowledge of what His choice will be. David P. Hunt illustrates this point as follows: "The fact that you *want* to get into Harvard and that submitting an application is a *necessary means* to this end is a *reason* for submitting an application; the fact that you *will* get into Harvard . . . is not a reason for applying," "The Simple Foreknowledge View," in *Divine Foreknowledge,* 100; see also "Prophecy, Foreknowledge, and Explanatory Loops: A Reply to Robinson," *Religious Studies* 40:4 (Dec. 2004): 485–491.

26. C. Gordon Olson, *Getting the Gospel Right: A Balanced View of Salvation Truth* (Cedar Knolls, NJ: Global Gospel Publishers, 2005), 263.

takes it from me, but I lay it down of Myself" (John 10:17–18).[27] These statements make it clear that God's foreknowledge and predestination allow for both Christ and His Father to have alternate interactive options available to them within the history of creation.

In summary, Peter's sermon—interpreted in its biblical context— indicates that God foreknew in a dynamic way the following divine-human interactive options and interactions: to deliver Christ to death, to crucify Christ, to surrender to crucifixion, to resurrect and exalt Christ, to pour out the Spirit, to call human beings, and to call on God. As such, God foreknew His provision of salvation for all humanity, and He foreknew those who are saved, those who are lost, and that those who are lost may be saved. God foreknew that if He did not choose to call us through Christ and the Spirit, then we would not be free to call on God for salvation; and that if we choose to reject God's call, we will not receive the salvation He has provided. As such, God's exhaustive and definite foreknowledge is dynamically focused by His actions to accomplish His determined purpose for divine-human interactions. Peter's teaching on God's foreknowledge is further developed in his letters.

PETER'S LETTERS TO THE FOREKNOWN ELECT

In Peter's letters, he presents a second use of the noun *foreknowledge* with regard to God (1 Pet. 1:2) and two uses of the verb *foreknew/foreknown*—one refers to divine foreknowledge (1:20) and the other in refers to human foreknowledge (2 Pet. 3:17). The first two texts are more directly relevant to the biblical perspective on the focus of God's foreknowledge of the freedom of salvation. The third text is discussed briefly at the end of this section.

The dynamism of the focus of foreknowledge is evident in the way Peter links his two explicit references to foreknowledge (1 Pet 1:2, 20) with the revelation of foreknowledge in Scripture (1:10–12). Peter addresses his letter to those who are "elect according to the foreknowledge of God" (1:2). This election is an act of God that facilitates divine-human interactions since Christ "indeed was foreordained [*proginōskō,* foreknown][28] before the foundation of

---

27. See Timothy Pawl, "The Freedom of Christ and Explanatory Priority," *Religious Studies* 50:2 (2014): 157–173.

28. The literal meaning of the word is "foreknown" (not foreordained). See New

the world, but was manifest [revealed] in these last times for you who through Him believe in God, who God raised Him from the dead and gave Him glory, so that your faith and hope are in God" (1:20–21; [cf. 1:2]). Significantly, God acts in Christ to accomplish what He foreknows concerning those who are elect in Christ. God's foreknowledge of His interactions with those who believe represents His foreknowledge that all can believe and that believers can fall from faith. This may be demonstrated in the following points.

First, in between the two statements on foreknowledge (1 Pet. 1:2, 20), Peter writes about how God's foreknowledge is revealed in the prophetic Scriptures. Here the emphasis is on what God foreknew of His actions in Christ: "Of this salvation the prophets have inquired and searched carefully, who prophesied of the grace that would to come to you, searching what, or what manner of time, the Spirit of Christ who was in them was indicating when He testified beforehand the sufferings of Christ and the glories that would follow" (1:10–11).[29] These words of the prophets indicate that the revelation of God's foreknowledge in Scripture is partial and progressive; and that it continues to be revealed by God's manifestation and resurrection of Christ and by human responses to Him in faith and hope (1:20–21). However, God's foreknowledge is not only revealed through its focus on those who believe.

Second, the prophetic Scripture reveals God's foreknowledge of God's interactions with those who respond to Christ by faith or by unbelief. On the one hand, "it is also contained in Scripture" that Christ is "a chief cornerstone, elect, [and] precious" (1 Pet. 2:6; cf. Isa. 28:16); that to those "who believe, He is precious" (1 Pet. 2:7); and that in Him they are a "chosen" and "special people" (2:9).[30] On the other hand, "it is also contained in Scripture" (2:6) that that, by "those who are disobedient [by unbelief]," Christ is "rejected" as "a stone of stumbling and a rock of offense" (2:7–8; cf. Isa. 8:14).[31]

English Translation, American Standard Bible, and English Standard Version. Peter uses the same word to indicate prior knowledge (2 Pet. 3:17; cf. Acts 26:5) and makes a distinction between foreknowledge and election (1 Pet. 1:2). See William W. Klein, *The New Chosen People: A Corporate View of Election* (Eugene, OR: Wipf and Stock, 2015), 215.

29. See Klein, *The New Chosen People*, 216.

30. Klein, *The New Chosen People*, 218.

31. Peter also quotes from Psalm 118:22. As contrasted with the reference to belief

Third, God also foreknows that believers may become unbelievers and unbelievers may become believers. Peter instructs the "elect" (1 Pet. 1:2) that they are to "be even more diligent to make your call and election sure, for if you do these things you will never stumble; for so an entrance will be supplied to you abundantly into the everlasting kingdom of our Lord and Savior Jesus Christ" (2 Pet. 1:10–11; cf. 2:20–22; 3:17).[32] God foreknew that the elect might fall from faith into unbelief.[33] In addition, Peter indicates that all

---

in the same text, the reference to disobedience indicates unbelief (1 Pet. 2:7; cf. Rom. 14:23; 11:32; Gal. 3:22). The stumbling is described as that "to which they . . . were appointed" (1 Pet. 2:8). This is not a reference to their being appointed to be unbelievers. Rather, it is a reference to the stumbling that is appointed to happen to those who choose unbelief (2 Pet. 1:10–11). Peter is here interpreting Isaiah who "underlines what is in any case clear in the OT: it is the hardened heart of disobedient Israelites which brings on the judgment of God," Williams, *The Election of Grace*, 75.

32. In 2 Peter 1:10, "The language is hardly consistent with an understanding of election as the unconditional and irrevocable selection of specific individuals for salvation. However the imperative makes sense if the author assumes that election is conditional in the sense that the believer can either forfeit or retain their elected status. This understanding of the statement is consistent with the interpretation of election language as a way of speaking of God's gracious initiative and the loved status of those who respond. The point would be that believers owe their status entirely to God's drawing (calling, election). But this is a status which can be lost, so believers are encouraged to persevere in God's grace and thereby ensure that they will experience the eschatological realization of their 'calling and election,'" Shellrude, "All Are Elect, Few Are Elect," *Scottish Evangelical Bulletin*, 156. "It is abundantly clear that salvation is by faith now . . . If salvation is conditional now, it necessarily leads to the conclusion that election in eternity past was conditional," F. Leroy Forlines, *The Quest for Truth: Answering Life's Inescapable Questions* (Nashville, TN: Randall House, 2001), 403. "When believers are referred to as 'called,' it is not necessary to conclude that others have not been called," ibid., 404. Ellen White writes: "Let us make sure that we are among the number who are 'elect according to the foreknowledge of God,'" *Review and Herald*, Oct 29, 1901; *The Upward Look* (Washington, DC: Review and Herald, 1982), 366. "These words [1 Pet. 1:1–5] are all-sufficient evidence that God desires us to receive great blessings," Manuscript 71, November 12, 1912.

33. The possibility of the elect becoming non-elect is evident in the following statements by Peter. "Beware lest you also fall" (2 Pet. 3:17). "For if, after they have escaped the pollutions of the world through the knowledge of the Lord and Savior Jesus Christ, they are again entangled in them and overcome, the latter end is worse for them than the beginning. For it would have been better for them not to have known the way of righteousness, than having known *it*, to turn from the holy commandment delivered to them. But it has happened to them according to the true proverb: 'A dog returns to his own vomit,' and, 'a sow, having washed, to her wallowing

the non-elect (by unbelief) may become elect (by faith) since: "The Lord is . . . longsuffering toward us, not willing that any should perish but that all should come to repentance" (3:9). Repentance is available to everyone since Peter appealed to everyone to repent (Acts 2:38).

This indicates that God possesses a definite and dynamic foreknowledge of all things, including the elect as a corporate group, and the individuals who enter and exit that group.[34] The biblical perspective stands in contrast with the traditional concept of a divine decree that focuses a static foreknowledge of individuals who are eternally elect or eternally non-elect. Instead, God chooses to actualize His option of manifesting and resurrecting Christ so that humans could interact with Him in faith and hope. Peter instructs his readers to "rest your hope fully upon the grace that is to be brought to you at the revelation of Jesus Christ [at His Second Advent]" (1 Pet. 1:13). Therefore, God's foreknowledge of divine-human interactions is focused through the manifestation of His grace through Christ, through humanity's response to grace through hope, and through the future manifestation of grace through Christ.

Finally, Peter motivates His readers to interact with God in harmony with how their human foreknowledge is focused by Scripture concerning both their hope and the danger of falling from hope. Therefore, Peter pleads: "Looking forward to these things be diligent...and consider that the long-suffering of our Lord is salvation—as also our beloved brother Paul . . . has written to you[35] . . . in which are some things hard to understand,

---

in the mire'" (2:20–22). See also Kirk R. MacGregor and Kevaughn Mattis, eds., *Perspectives on Eternal Security: Biblical, Historical, and Philosophical* (Eugene, OR: Wipf and Stock, 2009).

34. Concerning 1 Peter 1:2, William W. Klein comments: "I insist that the reference here is corporate. The Christian *church* is elect on the basis of God's foreknowledge," *The New Chosen People,* 221. John Hall Elliott agrees: "They who believe in Jesus as the Elect and Precious One of God are gathered together as the Elect and Precious People," *The Elect and Holy* (Eugene, OR: Wipf and Stock, 1966, 2005), 222; see also Klein, *The New Chosen People,* 225.

35. Paul refers explicitly to God's "longsuffering" only in the letter to the Romans (2:4; 9:22) where God's foreknowledge is also mentioned (8:29; 11:2). Peter links God's longsuffering with His will for everyone to repent (2 Pet. 3:9; cf. 3:15–17). Paul links God's goodness and longsuffering with repentance (Rom. 2:4) and then refers to God's foreknowledge (11:2) of those who continue in His goodness by faith (11:22). Also, Paul links God's longsuffering (9:22) with God's call and "purpose . . . according to election" (9:11) which is linked with God's foreknowledge (8:29; 11:2) of the "elect" (8:33; 11:2, 7, 28), "according to the election of grace" (11:5).

which untaught and unstable people twist to their own destruction, as they do also the rest of the Scriptures. You therefore, beloved, since you know this beforehand [*proginōskō*], beware lest you also fall" (2 Pet. 3:15–17; cf. 1:10–11; 2:20–22).

PAUL'S LETTER TO THE ROMANS

As is the case with Peter, Paul's statements on foreknowledge in his letter to the Romans (8:29; 11:2) reflect his conviction that the focus of God's foreknowledge is revealed in the prophetic Scriptures. As such, wherever he mentions Scripture, Paul implies the concept of God's foreknowledge of options for interactions involved in the freedom of salvation. For example, in the prologue and epilogue of his letter to the Romans, Paul refers to "my gospel" (16:25) which is "the gospel of God" (1:1) which is "the preaching of Jesus Christ, according to the revelation of the mystery kept secret since the world began but now made manifest [by God], and by the prophetic Scriptures [through human prophets] made known to all nations . . . for obedience to the faith [the human response]" (16:25–26; cf. 1:1–5).[36]

The connection of God's foreknowledge of the freedom of salvation with the "mystery" revealed in Scripture (Rom. 16:25) is made explicit by Paul. His only other use of the word "mystery" in the book of Romans (11:25) is part of his discussion of what God "foreknew" (11:2) of the elect remnant (11:5, 7, 28) and the fullness of Israel and the nations (11:12, 25).[37] In addition, Paul's reference to the mystery kept secret since the world began and now manifest by the prophetic Scriptures (16:25–26) is conceptually parallel with Peter's reference to the truth that Christ "was foreordained [*proginōskō*, foreknown] before the foundation of the world and manifest in these last times for you who believe" (1 Pet. 1:20)[38] as announced by the prophets (1:10–11).

In other letters, Paul explicitly identifies the foreknown mystery as being Christ and those who are saved in Christ by the divine act of grace and the divine-human interaction of faith (Eph. 3:4; 5:32; 6:19;

---

36. See James C. Miller, *The Obedience of Faith, the Eschatological People of God, and the Purpose of Romans* (Atlanta, GA: Society of Biblical Literature, 2014).

37. Mark D. Nanos, *The Mystery of Romans: The Jewish Context of Paul's Letter* (Minneapolis, MN: Fortress, 1996).

38. See discussion of this text in footnote 28.

Col. 1:26–27).[39] Also, in the letter to the Galatians, Scripture is personified as possessing God's foreknowledge of divine-human interactions related to salvation: "Scripture, foreseeing that God would justify the Gentiles by faith, preached the gospel to Abraham beforehand saying 'In you all the nations shall be blessed'" (3:8). More specifically, God's foreknowledge of divine action in Christ is revealed in the following prophetic promise of Scripture: "Now to Abraham and his Seed were the promises made," and the "Seed . . . is Christ" (3:16). The focused foreknowledge implied in Paul's prologue and epilogue (Rom. 1:1–5; 16:25–26) is more explicitly presented in two other places in his letter (8:29; 11:2).

Foreknowledge in Romans 8:29

In his first explicit reference to God's foreknowledge of the freedom of salvation, Paul refers to divine-human interactions as follows. "All things work together for good [divine initiative of love] to those who love God [human response]," whom He "foreknew [divine knowledge]," "predestined [divine will]," "called," "justified," and "glorified [divine actions]" (Rom. 8:28–30). The literary structure of this text is called *sorites* and indicates an order that proceeds in steps from foreknowledge to glorification.[40] This indicates that God foreknew divine-human interactive options before He chose to predestine His interactions with human beings.[41] "God's determination that the foreknown be conformed to the

---

39. See Daniel Santos, "The Meaning of Mystery in Romans 11:25," *Fides Reformata* 17:1 (2012): 45–59. In his letter to the Ephesians, Paul refers to "the mystery of Christ" (Eph. 3:4), the "mystery" of "Christ and the church" (5:32), and "the mystery of the gospel" (6:19). To the Colossians, Paul writes about "the mystery which has been hidden from ages and from generations, but has now been revealed to His saints" (Col. 1:26), "which is Christ in you, the hope of glory" (1:27; cf. 4:3).

40. In the particular kind of *sorites* used by Paul, the predicate in each sentence is the subject of the following sentence, and each sentence logically leads to the next. Other examples include Romans 5:3–5; 10:14–15. See J. V. Fesco, "Romans 8:29–30 and the Question of the *Ordo Salutis*," *Journal of Reformed Theology* 8:1 (Jan. 2014): 35–60; Roy A. Sorenson, "Sorites Arguments," in *A Companion to Metaphysics,* ed. Jaegwon Kim and Ernest Sosa (Oxford: Blackwell, 1995).

41. See the section of this chapter on Peter's Sermon at Pentecost, where I discuss the harmony between God's foreknowledge of the future and His making free choices about predestining the future. "Romans 8:29 shows clearly that predestination presupposes

image of his Son, called, declared righteous and glorified all come after his foreknowledge of them."[42]

For Paul, there is no conflict between foreknowledge and the freedom of salvation because God foreknew the interactive options and the interactions by which He facilitates the freedom of those who are saved. The "good" toward which "all things work" (Rom. 8:28) is freedom since "the creation was subjected . . . in hope" to "be delivered from the bondage of corruption into the glorious liberty of the children of God" (8:20–21; cf. Acts 17:26–27). This freedom begins in the present time since God "predestined" human beings "to be conformed to the image of His Son" (Rom. 8:29). This image involves freedom since "there is liberty" as humans "are being transformed into the same image from glory to glory" (2 Cor. 3:17–18). God "foreknew" and "predestined" (Rom. 8:29) "the called" (8:28)—who are "called to liberty" (Gal. 5:13).

This foreknown freedom, to which believers are predestined,[43] includes alternate options since Paul appeals: "Do not use liberty as an opportunity for the flesh, but through love serve one another" (5:13). Love for God implies divine-human interaction—"We love Him because He first loved us" (1 John 4:19). In addition, the wider context of Paul's writing indicates that God's foreknown acts of calling, justification, and glorification also involve the freedom of divine-human interactive options and interactions: "The called" "who love God" (Rom. 8:28–29) are those who are "justified

---

foreknowledge but the two are different. The latter is an epistemological phenomenon; the former an activity of God. Foreknowledge is a certain attribute or capacity in God; and it is this attribute that provides the ground for, or enables the act of predestination," Donkor, "Predestination, Foreknowledge, and Human Freedom," 2.

42. A. Chadwick Thornhill, *The Chosen People: Election, Paul, and Second Temple Judaism* (Downers Grove, IL: InterVarsity, 2015), 230. "Simply put, this people who love God, whom God has foreknown, will receive future resurrection through their union with Christ. . . . [This is] a corporate and conditional notion of election," ibid., 232. "The text presupposes a loving response of the individual to God's offer of salvation," Donkor, "Predestination, Foreknowledge, and Human Freedom," 3. It "is a guarantee that those who have responded to God's call with love (and faith) can be fully assured of His purpose of final glorification for them," I. Howard Marshall, "The Problem of Apostasy in New Testament Theology," *Perspectives in Religious Studies* 14 (1987): 77; cf. Thornhill, *The Chosen People,* 232.

43. See Kyle A. Pasewark, "Predestination as a Condition of Freedom," *Lutheran Quarterly* 12:1 (1998): 57–78.

by faith" (5:1) and who "rejoice in hope of the glory [glorification]" (5:2). Similarly, in another letter Paul writes that we "wait for the hope [glorification] of righteousness [justification] by faith ... working by love [our calling in sanctification]" (Gal. 5:5–6; cf. Rom. 8:28).

Even though we are free to choose otherwise, God's perfect fore-knowledge anticipates divine-human interactions with the elect persons who will never be separated from God's love (Rom. 8:31–39). This is evident in how Paul answers the following questions. "Who shall bring a charge against God's elect? It is God that justifies. Who is he who condemns? It is Christ who died, and furthermore is also risen, who is even at the right hand of God, who also makes intercession for us" (8:33–34). These answers apply to those who are incorporated into Christ by faith since Paul writes earlier that: "There is therefore now no condemnation to those who are in Christ Jesus" (8:1); that "intercession" is made "for the saints" (8:27); and that we are "justified by faith" (5:1). This is in harmony with God's foreknowledge revealed in the prophetic Scripture since Paul writes to the Galatians about "Scripture, foreseeing that God would justify the Gentiles by faith" (3:8). Similarly, Paul describes the foreknown security of God's love relationship with His people as a group by linking it with revelation in the prophetic Scriptures: "Who shall separate us from the love of Christ? ... As it is written [in Scripture]: 'For your sake we are killed all day long; we are accounted as sheep for the slaughter.' Yet ... [no]thing shall be able to separate us from the love of God which is in Christ Jesus our Lord" (Rom. 8:35–37, 39; cf. Ps. 44:22).[44]

At the same time, it is important to note that the foreknown assurance of "God's elect" (Rom. 8:33) is grounded in God's foreknown loving initiative toward all people. This is evident in Paul's rhetorical question: "He who did not spare His own Son, but delivered Him up for us all, how shall He not with Him also freely give us all things?" (Rom. 8:32). When Paul refers to "us all," the entire human race is included in the circle of God's love. As Paul wrote earlier in his letter: "God demonstrates His own love toward us, in that while we were yet sinners, Christ died for us" (5:8). Therefore, there is a sense in which even humanity's foreknown free choice

---

44. The Apostle John points out that there is a sense in which God always loves everyone (John 3:16), for "God is love" (1 John 4:8). Also, some persons may experience a decline or fall in their love for God. To them He says: "You have left your first love" (Rev. 2:4).

to refuse salvation does not separate humanity from God's foreknown love. Human beings may separate themselves from the interactive love relationship that God intends. But they can never separate themselves from the loving initiative that God extends toward everyone.[45]

In summary, Paul's use of *sorites* (Rom. 8:29–30) indicates that God's foreknowledge precedes His predestined will and His actions which facilitate interactions with those who are called in love, justified by faith, and are rejoicing in hope of glorification. There is no conflict between foreknowledge and freedom since God foreknows His predestined purpose to focus His foreknowledge by facilitating our freedom. God foreknows His love for all His creation and for His elect who will never be separated from their interactive love relationship with Him. God's foreknowledge of His interactive options and interactions with all people and with those who receive salvation is presented in more detail in Romans 11.

Foreknowledge in Romans 11:2

The concept of the freedom of salvation is closely connected with Paul's final explicit reference to the focus of God's foreknowledge on divine actions and divine-human interactions (Rom. 11:2). Once more Paul articulates his teaching in terms of what is revealed in the prophetic Scriptures concerning divine-human interaction: "God has not cast away [but reserved] His people whom He foreknew.[46] Or do you not know what the

---

45. God's love is "foreconditional"—"freely bestowed prior to any conditions but not exclusive of conditions," John C. Peckham, *The Love of God: A Canonical Model* (Downers Grove, IL: InterVarsity, 2015), 191.

46. Paul also answers, "Certainly not! For I also am an Israelite. "Paul uses the denial formula in nine other places in Romans [3:4, 6, 31; 6:2, 15; 7:7, 13; 9:14; 11:11]. In each instance, immediately after the denial, he gives a justification for the denial in a compact summary form which contains the potential for the entire answer; then he expands the answer in the subsequent argument," Lionel J. Windsor, *Paul and the Vocation of Israel: How Paul's Jewish Identity Informs His Apostolic Ministry, with Special Reference to Romans* (Berlin: De Gruyter, 2014), 233. "Thus, when Paul is speaking positively of his status as 'Israelite,' he is speaking of his status as God's instrument to bring God's revelation to the world. For Paul, God's concern for Israel is bound up with God's choice of Israel to achieve His wider purposes," ibid., 235–236. Commenting on this text, Ellen White writes: "Even though Israel rejected His Son, God did not reject them," *Acts of the Apostles* (Nampa, ID: Pacific Press, 2005), 375.

Scripture says . . . ?" "I have reserved for Myself" those "who have not bowed the knee to Baal" (11:2, 4). In addition, Paul highlights the nature of God's foreknowledge of divine-human interactions by pointing out that while "God has not [completely/permanently] cast away [*apotheo*] His people" (11:2), they are partially and temporarily "cast away" [*apobolē*] (11:15) because of unbelief (11:20, 22). In the remainder of Romans 11, Paul explains this "mystery" (11:25; cf. 16:25) of God's foreknown people who are "not cast away" though they are "cast away."[47] The explanation involves an exposition on the focus of God's foreknowledge of interactive options and interactions involved with God's "irrevocable" (11:28–29) "election [free choice][48] of grace" (11:5) for everyone (11:32) including "the elect" "remnant" (11:5–7), "the fullness" of the elect remnant (11:12, 25), and "the rest" who are non-elect (11:7).

First, God foreknew the distinction between the divine initiative of "the election of grace" (Rom. 11:5) and divine-human interaction with those who are elect by faith and non-elect by unbelief. "There is a remnant [elect] according to the election of grace [given to Israel]" (11:5; [cf. 11:7]) since "Israel [in its completeness] has not obtained what it seeks [righteousness]; but the elect have obtained it [by faith], and the rest were blinded [hardened, *porosis*] [by unbelief]" (11:7; [cf. 9:30–32; 11:26]).[49] The remnant is elect by faith in God's grace since righteousness (4:15) "is of faith that it might be according to grace" (4:16). The remnant elect are "called, not of the Jews only, but also of the Gentiles" (9:24); as the prophetic Scripture says (9:25–29), "the remnant will be saved" (9:27; cf. Isa. 10:22–23). In this way, "the [believing] Gentiles" "have attained to" "the righteousness of faith" (Rom. 9:30), "but [unbelieving] Israel"

---

47. The casting away of some of God's people may be interpreted as a partial casting away (some are cast away because of unbelief) and/or as a temporary casting away (some who now are unbelievers will in the future become believers). See Romans 11:25–26; and F. Leroy Forlines, *Romans*, The Randall House Bible Commentary, gen. ed. Robert E. Picirilli (Nashville, TN: Randall House, 1987), 297–304.

48. Witherington and Hyatt, *Paul's Letter to the Romans*, 265.

49. It is important to note the similar language used to describe the hardening of Pharaoh (Rom. 9:17–18). Both the hardening of Pharaoh and Israel involve divine-human interactions. Therefore, there would be different results (mercy or hardening, honor or dishonor, wrath or glory) if we responded to God's initiative in different ways (9:21–24). See Nanos, *The Mystery of Romans*, 261–264.

"has not attained" (9:31), "because they did not seek it [righteousness] by faith" (9:32).

Second, God foreknew the divine initiative of "the election of grace" (Rom. 11:5) so that "the purpose of God according to election might stand, not of [human] works but of Him [God] who calls" (9:11). The nature of this call is illustrated in "the word of promise" (9:9) to Sarah and Rebecca concerning their children (9:6–12). This indicates the certainty of God's promise to: "have mercy [and compassion] on whomever I will" (9:15) indicating His will to "have mercy on all" (11:32) so that vessels of wrath are transformed into vessels of mercy. Paul illustrates the same point in terms of God as a maker of vessels: "What if God . . . endured with much longsuffering the vessels of wrath prepared [*katertismena*: ripe/fit] for destruction, and that He might make known the riches of His glory on the vessels of mercy which He had prepared beforehand [*proetoimasen*] for glory" (9:22–23).[50] Here Paul alludes to the message that Jeremiah received from God in the potter's house concerning foreknown divine-human interactive options whereby flawed pots may be remade rather than destroyed (Jer. 18:1–6). This illustration is a key to correctly understanding the foreknowledge of God as revealed in prophetic promises which may or may not be fulfilled depending on how human beings respond to God's initiative (18:6–11).[51]

Third, God foreknew that the divine initiative of "the election of grace" (Rom. 11:5) continues to be available to Israel (elect and

---

50. "Paul uses two different verbs when talking about the vessels of mercy and the vessels of wrath"—"a perfect passive participle" and "an aorist active indicative. This change cannot be accidental, and it suggests that Paul means that the vessels of wrath are ripe or fit for destruction," Witherington and Hyatt, *Paul's Letter to the Romans,* 258; cf. C. Cranfield, *Romans 9–11. International Critical Commentary* (Edinburgh: T & T Clark, 1979), 496–497; cf. Thornhill, *The Chosen People,* 241.

51. "Look, as the clay *is* in the potter's hand, so *are* you in My hand, O house of Israel! The instant I speak concerning a nation and concerning a kingdom, to pluck up, to pull down, and to destroy *it,* if that nation...turns from its evil, I will relent. . . . And the instant I speak concerning a nation and concerning a kingdom, to build and to plant *it,* if it does evil . . . then I will relent. . . . Behold, I am fashioning a disaster and devising a plan against you. Return now every one from his evil way, and make your ways and your doings good" (Jer. 18:6–11). See discussion in my introduction where I present the illustration of God's foreknowledge as indicated in the Keilah narrative (1 Sam. 23:7–13).

non-elect)[52]—as an object lesson of its continuing availability to all humanity.[53] "Concerning the gospel they [the non-elect] are enemies" but "concerning the election [of grace] they are beloved. For the gifts and calling of God are irrevocable" (11:28–29; [11:5, 7]).[54] Human rejection of the divine initiative does not cancel that initiative because "God has committed [*sugkleiō*] them all to disobedience [unbelief/non-election], that He might have mercy on all" through the election of grace (11:32; [11:5]). Paul uses similar language to make the same point in his letter to the Galatians: "Scripture has confined [*sugkleiō*] all under sin [unbelief], that the promise by faith in Jesus Christ might be given to those who believe" and are, therefore, elect by faith (3:22; cf. Rom. 14:23; 11:32; 1 Pet. 2:7).[55]

---

52. Election "should not be taken as if it [always] emphasized the selection of a smaller group out of a larger; it does not have this sense in Lk 9:35; 23:35." It is "not related primarily to individual salvation but to God's purpose," Ernest Best, *Ephesians: International Critical Commentary* (London: T & T Clark, 1998), 119; cf. Donkor, "Predestination, Foreknowledge, and Human Freedom," 2.

53. "God our Savior . . . desires all men to be saved" (1 Tim. 2:3–4). "Jesus . . . gave Himself a ransom for all" (2:5–6). "We trust in . . . God, who is the Savior of all men, especially of those who believe" (4:10). Bible scholars disagree about whether the words elect/election and Israel to refer to those in Israel who believe in Christ, to the Church, or to the fullness of Israel who will be saved in the future. However, "The blessings . . . assured to Israel are, on the same conditions and in the same degree, assured to every nation and to every individual under the broad heavens," Ellen G. White, *Prophets and Kings* (Washington, DC: Review and Herald, 1958), 500–501. See also Suzanne McDonald, *Re-Imaging Election: Divine Election as Representing God to Others and Others to God* (Grand Rapids, MI: Eerdmans, 2010); Jacques Doukhan, *The Mystery of Israel* (Hagerstown, MD: Review and Herald, 2004); *Israel and the Church: Two Voices from the Same God* (Grand Rapids, MI: Baker 2000); Charles H. Cosgrove, *Elusive Israel: The Puzzle of Election in Romans* (Grand Rapids, MI: Eerdmans, 1997).

54. "Israel's disobedience did not cancel her out, but opened the way for everyone to enter in. This, to Paul, was perhaps the ultimate mystery: One man's fall (Adam) meant the redemption of many and one nation's sin (Israel) meant the inclusion of all. The grace of God was so vast and overwhelming that it broke apart every conventional limiting structure through that very limiting structure itself (election)," Walter A. Elwell, *Baker Evangelical Dictionary of Biblical Theology* (Grand Rapids, MI: Baker, 2001).

55. On Paul's concept of commitment/confinement by God under the disobedience/sin of unbelief, see Martin F. Hanna, "The Servant-Master Roles of the Laws of Christ, of Scripture, and of Nature," *Journal of the Adventist Theological Society (JATS)*

Fourth, God foreknew that the divine initiative of "the election of grace" (Rom. 11:5) is embodied in Christ and, therefore, is available to everyone. Paul illustrates this with his parable of the olive tree from which branches are broken off and into which branches are grafted.[56] "If the root is holy, so are the branches," and "some of the branches were broken off, and you, being a wild olive tree, were grafted in among them, and with them became a partaker of the root and fatness of the olive tree, . . . you do not support the root but the root supports you" (11:16–18). Christ is this root according to God's foreknowledge revealed in the prophetic Scripture as follows. Through "Jesus Christ" (15:8), Israel and "the Gentiles might glorify God for His mercy, as it is written [in Scripture]" (15:8–9)—"there shall be a root of Jesse; . . . in Him the Gentiles shall hope" (15:12; cf. Isa. 11:10).[57]

Fifth, God foreknew that "the election of grace" (Rom. 11:5) toward Israel represents[58] the divine initiative aimed at divine-human interactions with all nations. "If their [partial and temporary] fall" and "failure" and "being cast away" is "riches for the world . . . [and] the Gentiles, how much more their fullness" benefits the Gentiles (11:12, 15). The "gospel" is "the mystery" of "Christ" "by the prophetic Scriptures" "for obedience to the faith among all nations" (1:1–5; 16:25–26). This "mystery" involves "the fullness of the Gentiles" and "all Israel" (11:25–26) since "Christ . . . is over all . . . God" (9:5)—that is, "God of the Jews" and "Gentiles" (3:29). God "made"

9/1–2 (1998): 278–309.

56. "Paul's olive tree metaphor in Rom 11:17–24 evidences the view of the corporate election perfectly. Individuals get grafted into the elect people (the olive tree) and participate in election and its blessings by faith or get cut off from God's chosen people and their blessings because of unbelief, while the focus of election clearly remains the corporate people of God, which spans salvation history," Brian Abasciano, *Paul's Use of the Old Testament in Romans 9.10–18: An Intertextual and Theological Exegesis* (New York: T & T Clark, 2011), 60–61; cf. Thornhill, *The Chosen People,* 250; Benjamin D. Gordon, "On the Sanctity of Mixtures and Branches: Two Halakic Sayings in Romans 11:16–24," *Journal of Biblical Literature* 135:2 (2016): 355–368.

57. See Jacob Stromberg, "The 'Root of Jesse' in Isaiah 11:10: Postexilic Judah, or Postexilic Davidic King?" *Journal of Biblical Literature* 127:4 (2008): 655–669.

58. See Martin F. Hanna, "Men and Women in Church Order: A Study of Paul's Use of Representative Statements," in *Women and Ordination: Biblical and Historical Studies,* ed. John W. Reeve (Nampa, ID: Pacific Press, 2015), 297–308.

Abraham the "father of many nations" (4:17–18). Therefore, God's call of Jews and Gentiles (9:24) is a fulfilment of God's foreknowledge as revealed in His prophecy that "I will call them my people, who were not my people" (9:25; cf. 9:26, 30; Hos. 1:10; 2:23).[59] Therefore, "there is no distinction between Jew and Greek, for the same Lord over all is rich to all who call upon Him" (10:12; cf. 15:9–12, 16, 18, 27).

Sixth, God foreknew that, through the divine initiative of "the election of grace" (Rom. 11:5), the elect and the non-elect are open categories—the elect can become non-elect and the non-elect can become elect. This principle is clearly stated in Paul's message to the Gentiles concerning the people of Israel as follows. "I speak to you Gentiles" (11:13). "Because of unbelief they [unbelieving Israelites] were broken off and you [Gentiles] stand by faith" (11:20).[60] "Therefore, consider the goodness and the severity of God: on those who fell [by unbelief], severity; but toward you goodness, if you continue in His goodness [by faith]. Otherwise you will also be cut off. And they also, if they do not continue in unbelief, will be grafted in [by faith], for God is able to graft them in again" (11:22–23; [cf. 11:20]). "For as you were once disobedient to God [non-elect by unbelief], yet have now obtained mercy through their disobedience, even so these also have now been disobedient, that through the mercy shown you [as elect by faith] they also may obtain mercy" (11:30–31; cf. 9:17–24; 11:20).[61] "God grants no mercy to Israel without

---

59. Here Paul quotes from Hosea 1:10 and 2:23 where God refers to His people Israel as no longer being His people and then as becoming His people again. Paul applies this principle to the Gentiles as well as to Israel.

60. See Don B. Garlington, *Faith, Obedience, and Perseverance: Aspects of Paul's Letter to the Romans* (Tubingen: Mohr, 1994).

61. "The significance of Romans 11:7, 23 for the present discussion has generally not been noticed by theologians and exegetes. . . . The 'elect' in verse 7 . . . have responded to the apostolic kerygma and recognized Jesus as the Messiah. Paul's attribution of election to these individuals is subsequent to their faith and conversion. The 'others' who have not believed are presumably among the 'nonelect,' but the crucial point to be noticed here is that while history continues, and while the gospel is still being preached, *the category of election is fluid and dynamic rather than fixed and determinate*. According to verse 23, the 'others,' presumably nonelect in light of their present unbelief, can still become 'elect,'" John Jefferson Davis, *The Frontiers of Science and Faith: Examining Questions from the Big Bang to the End of the Universe* (Downers Grove, IL: InterVarsity, 2002), 66–67. See also his discussion of bilateral *a posteriori* determination and dynamic election, ibid., 52, 54, 62, 64–70.

the Gentiles, but neither does he do so to the Gentiles without Israel."[62]

Seventh, God foreknew that "the election of grace" (Rom. 11:5) produces the fullness of the elect Israelites and the elect Gentiles since "blindness [hardening] in part has happened to Israel until the fullness of the Gentiles has come in. And so all [the fullness of] Israel will be saved" (11:25–26). Here, the fullness of the Gentiles refers to the Gentiles who will be saved; and "all Israel" refers to the "fullness" (11:12) of Israel that will be accomplished in "save[ing] some of them" (11:14). As Paul writes earlier in his letter: "They are not all [the fullness of] Israel who are of Israel" (9:6). The fullness of the Gentiles and the fullness of Israel are those who, like Paul "come in the fullness of the blessing of the gospel of Christ" (15:29; cf. Eph. 1:23).[63]

In summary, in Romans 11, Paul teaches that God focuses His foreknowledge through His loving election of grace which perseveres toward those who are non-elect by unbelief. In fact, it is this foreknown divine initiative that makes it possible for them to become elect (Rom. 11:2, 5, 7, 20–23, 28). The focus of God's foreknowledge is dynamic since "the story of election is a story of switchbacks; reversal and paradox inform its temporal shape."[64] The remnant (11:5) are elect (11:7) by faith (11:20) "according to the election of grace" (11:5). At the same time, those who are enemies of the Gospel through unbelief are beloved according to the election (11:28) of grace (11:5) which is irrevocable (11:29).

CONCLUSION

God's foreknowledge and the freedom of salvation are presented in the Bible in terms of the focus of God's foreknowledge on divine-human interactive options and interactions. God is free to give or withhold salvation, and human beings are free to receive or refuse salvation. This biblical perspective overcomes the problem of an apparent contradiction between

---

62. H. N. Ridderbos, *Paul: An Outline of His Theology* (Grand Rapids, MI: Eerdmans, 1975), 360; cf. Hans K. LaRondelle, *The Israel of God in Prophecy: Principles of Prophetic Interpretation* (Berrien Springs, MI: Andrews University Press, 1983), 127.

63. See John K. Goodrich, "Until the Fullness of the Gentiles Comes In: A Critical Review of Recent Scholarship on the Salvation of 'All Israel' (Romans 11:26)," *Journal for the Study of Paul and his Letters* 6:1 (Spring 2016): 5–32. See also LaRondelle, *The Israel of God in Prophecy*, 126.

64. Williams, *The Election of Grace*, 63.

foreknowledge and freedom. Scripture corrects the traditional view that God's foreknowledge is focused only by His free choice to cause or facilitate the free choices of human beings. God's foreknowledge actually precedes His free choices and is continually focused through His facilitation of divine-human interactive options and interactions. This model of fore-knowledge provides a way beyond the conflicting models that attempt to reconcile the traditional view of foreknowledge with human freedom. The focus of God's foreknowledge is exhaustive, definite, and dynamic.

This conclusion is supported by a contextual study of the five biblical texts that explicitly use the words *foreknowledge* and *foreknew/foreknown* (Acts 2:23; 1 Pet. 1:2, 20; Rom. 8:29; 11:2). These texts show that God reveals His foreknowledge progressively in the prophetic Scriptures (Acts 2; 1 Pet. 1), in Christ and in those who are in Christ by faith (1 Pet. 1:20–21), and in all things (Rom. 8:21, 28–29). God's foreknowledge operates from before the creation of the world—even before He predestined His actions in creation or salvation (1 Pet. 1:20; Acts 2:23; Rom. 8:29). As such, God foreknew all the divine-human interactive options and interactions before He chose to relate to humanity through "the election of grace" (11:5). The exhaustive definiteness of foreknowledge is complemented by its exhaustive dynamism so that those who are foreknown as elect by faith are instructed to make their election sure because they could become non-elect (2 Pet. 1:10). Also, the foreknown non-elect can become elect since God is not willing that any should perish but that all would repent (3:9). God's foreknowledge of the elect indicates their security in God's love (Rom. 8:31–39) and in His prom-ise of glorious liberty (8:21). God foreknows that they will not be cast away from the irrevocable election of grace (11:2, 5, 28–29). He also foreknows that some of the elect will be cast away—becoming non-elect by unbelief; and that some of the non-elect will become elect by faith (11:15, 20–23). Through this definitely foreknown yet dynamic process, the fullness of the elect will be accomplished (11:12, 25–26).

In other words, God's foreknowledge has an exhaustive, definite, and dynamic focus. What God foreknows informs all His deliberations about all interactive options and interactions that He could and would facilitate. Therefore, if human beings were to choose differently from what they do choose, God would foreknow that different choice as well.[65] As illustrated

---

65. Note the apparently small but significant difference from William Craig's statement

in the story of David at Keilah (1 Sam. 23:7–13), what God foreknew is revealed in all divine-human free choice interactive options and interactions so that He and human beings are able make free choices that transform available foreknown interactive options into foreknown interactions. God continually focuses His foreknowledge through His choices to make some interactive options available to humanity; and through His cooperation with humanity's choices which make some interactive options available for God. Therefore, God foreknows that some possible interactive options will not become actual interactive options. He also foreknows that some actual interactive options (possible interactions) will not become actual interactions. Here again, it is important to note that the choices of human beings do not add to God's foreknowledge—for He foreknew all things before He chose to create humanity.

Finally, God's exhaustive, definite, and dynamic foreknowledge remains a mystery that is revealed, but not completely explained. This is because the mechanism of how God foreknows is not explained to the writers of Scripture or to its interpreters. "God's ability to know events that have not yet occurred in a way that does not condition outcomes is perhaps the key unresolved problem. . . . But isn't this capacity that which distinguishes Him as God?"[66] As the Psalmist says: "Such knowledge is too wonderful for me; it is high, I cannot attain it" (139:6). Therefore, this study ends, as does Paul's discussion of foreknowledge, with humble, yet enthusiastic praise: "Oh, the depth of the riches both of the wisdom and knowledge of God![67] How unsearchable *are* His judgments and His ways past finding out! 'For who has known the mind of the Lord? Or who has become His counselor?' 'Or who has first given to Him and it shall be repaid to him?' For of Him and through Him and to Him *are* all things, to whom *be* glory forever. Amen" (Rom. 11:33–36).

---

that: "were they to choose differently . . . God would have foreknown this." *God, Time, and Eternity: The Coherence of Theism II—Eternity* (Dordrecht: Springer, 2001), 25.

66. Donkor, "Predestination, Foreknowledge, and Human Freedom," 3.

67. "God's foreknowledge is simply his wisdom under another name," John Milton, *Complete Prose Works* (New Haven: Yale University Press, 1973), 6:154; cf. William Pallister, *Between Worlds: The Rhetorical Universe of* Paradise Lost (Toronto: University of Toronto Press, 2008), 25.

CHAPTER 4

DIVINE ELECTION
AND PREDESTINATION:
A BIBLICAL PERSPECTIVE

Hans K. LaRondelle and John K. McVay

Since Augustine the doctrine of divine election has been an important topic in Christian theology. Even when this doctrine is avoided in teaching and preaching, the issue remains a practical need in the church. Pastors are aware of important, personal questions asked by many believers, focused not so much on the existence of God but on whether one belongs to the chosen ones, the elect. "What will be God's decision about me in the final judgment?" So the topic informs pastoral care and Gospel proclamation.

First the exegetical foundations of the themes of divine election and predestination in both testaments will be examined. This is based on the thought that the New Testament testimony on divine election is best understood against the backdrop of the theme of the election of Israel in the Hebrew Scriptures. Within the scope of this essay, fundamental turning points in the biblical revelation will be highlighted as a way of sketching the Gospel perspective. Second, and more briefly, the exegetical review of Old Testament and New Testament passages will be used to identify components in a biblical-theological framework for understanding election and predestination.

THE DIVINE ELECTION OF ISRAEL IN THE OLD TESTAMENT

The Old Testament data describe divine election as the ground for the existence of the people of Israel. This election is itself grounded in God's love for Israel and her patriarchs. In His love God chose Israel to have covenant fellowship with Himself, and to receive the call to witness to His glory and to be a blessing to all peoples on earth (Hos. 11:1, 8–9; Jer. 31:3). God's act of electing expresses the freedom of His love to choose a people and to determine their mission, together with His expectation of their response of a loving commitment to Him as Israel's Redeemer (Deut. 6). Karl Barth stressed that God created Israel "as partner in this covenant" and thereby "responsible" to Him as the meaning of her existence. He concluded: "There is no grace without the lordship and claim of grace. There is no dogmatics which is not also and necessarily ethics."[1]

The classical passage on the election of Israel is found in Moses's declaration:

> For you are a people holy to the LORD your God. The LORD your God has chosen you (*bakhar*) to be a people for his treasured possession, out of all the peoples who are on the face of the earth. . . . the LORD set his love on you and chose you (*bakhar*), . . . it is because the LORD loves you ["for love of you"; *'ahabah,* love] and is keeping the oath that he swore to your fathers, that the LORD has brought you out with a mighty hand and redeemed you from the house of slavery, from the hand of Pharaoh king of Egypt. (Deut. 7:6–8; cf. 4:37; 10:14–15; 14:2; 26:16–19).[2]

Moses reveals that Yahweh's choice to redeem Israel from slavery was rooted in His love for Israel and in His faithfulness to His promises to their patriarchs. This choice or election became a historical event, however, in Israel's miraculous deliverance from slavery in Egypt. The redemptive

---

1. Karl Barth, *Church Dogmatics,* trans. Geoffrey W. Bromiley, vol. 2 (Edinburgh: T&T Clark, 1957), 12.

2. Unless otherwise noted, all quotations from the Bible are from the English Standard Version. All italics in Scripture quotes reflect emphasis added by the authors. The ESV® Bible (The Holy Bible, English Standard Version®). Copyright © 2001 by Crossway, a publishing ministry of Good News Publishers. Unauthorized reproduction of this publication is prohibited. All rights reserved.

history of Israel begins with the Exodus (cf. Hos. 13:4). Israel's liberation was at the same time an act of divine claim on Israel: Yahweh identified them as "My firstborn son," who will be set free to "serve" (*'abad*, i.e., "worship") the Redeemer God (Exod. 4:22–23). It is significant to note Moses's repeated warning to Israel not to misunderstand her election, as if it were based on some merit or virtue in her (Deut. 7:7–8; 9:4–5; cf. Ezek. 16:4–15). Yahweh's guidance and grace are given "for his name's sake" (Pss. 23:3; 25:11; Jer.14:7; Isa. 43:25; 48:9, 11). The origin of Israel's election remains the inexplicable wonder of God's unconditioned, election love (*'ahabah*), which is expressed through God's abiding loyalty (*khesed*) to His covenant with Israel. In N. H. Snaith's succinct statement: "*Ahabah* [love] is the cause of the covenant; [*k*]*hesed* [loyalty] is the means of its continuance."[3]

The prophet Amos used a particular synonym for God's election love, when he announced to an apostate Israel: "You only have I known [*yada'*] of all the families of the earth; therefore I will punish you for all your iniquities" (3:2). For the present inquiry it is essential to define the theological meaning of this divine "knowing." Old Testament scholars seem to agree that *yada'* refers to a personal knowledge that expresses a loving care for others (for divine knowing, see Ps. 1:6; Nah. 1:7; cf. John 10:14; 2 Tim. 2:19). Amos warned Israel, however, against false conclusions from her election and against pretensions of superiority among the nations (9:7). G. C. Berkouwer clarifies: "Israel interpreted election apart from faith and thus drew illicit conclusions from it."[4]

A similar conclusion may be drawn from the prophetic ministry of Hosea. God ordered the prophet to marry an unfaithful woman, whose daughter he had to call *Lo'-rukhamah* ("not loved," 1:6), and her next child *Lo'-'ammi* ("not my people," 1:9). So it is that God emphasized that His covenant with Israel allowed no claim on the Lord apart from the obedience of faith. Likewise, Hosea looks beyond the current crisis in which Israel is destroyed through a lack of knowledge of God and a failure to practice his ways (4:6; 6:6) to the hope of a renewed relationship in which God will "betroth" Israel to Himself "in faithfulness" (2:19–20).

---

3. Norman H. Snaith, *Distinctive Ideas of the Old Testament* (New York: Schocken Books, 1964), 95.

4. G. C. Berkouwer, *Divine Election,* Studies in Dogmatics Series, trans. Hugo Bekker (Grand Rapids, MI: Eerdmans, 1960), 314.

In this context it is important to note that election and covenant are distinctive ideas yet closely connected in redemptive history. Abram was chosen and called for a universal purpose: "and in you all the families of the earth shall be blessed" (Gen. 12:3). God then placed Abram's election in the framework of his covenant with God (Gen. 15), so that the purpose of Abram's election became validated in the Abrahamic covenant. God's covenant purpose with Israel extended the Abrahamic covenant.

This redemptive objective of Israel's election received a new focal center in the Davidic covenant. David's election extends Israel's covenant blessing to all nations, as the Royal Psalms testify (Ps. 2; 72). Psalm 132 emphasizes a conditional aspect: The Davidic king must remain faithful to the Torah of Moses (vv. 11–12; cf. Deut. 18:14–20), underlining that this extension of Israel's covenant retains the need for the obedience of faith. David's kingship serves the purpose of proclaiming God's redemptive acts: "Posterity will serve him; future generations will be told about the LORD. They will proclaim his righteousness, declaring to a people yet unborn: He has done it!" (Ps. 22:30–31, NIV).

Israel's Response to Choose the LORD

What response did God expect from His chosen people? In his farewell speech, Moses appealed to the new generation that was about to enter the promised land: "Therefore choose (*bakhar*) life, that you and your offspring may live, loving the LORD your God, obeying his voice and holding fast to him" (Deut. 30:19–20). In his appeal, Moses led a renewal of the Sinai covenant, evoking Israel's fresh choice and commitment to the Lord. A similar renewal occurs later under Joshua at Shechem (Josh. 24:22).

These renewals of the covenant indicate the freedom of choice placed before Israel by Moses and Joshua. However, such choices of each generation of Israel did not happen in a vacuum but in the context of redemptive history. Israel was already redeemed and set free from slavery by Yahweh. A positive choice by Israel would be a response to God's prior, electing love. Such renewed commitments required nonetheless "the careful activity of choosing itself."[5]

---

5. H. Seebass, "בָּחַר" (*bakhar*) in *Theological Dictionary of the Old Testament*, vol. 2, ed. G. Johannes Botterweck and Helmer Ringgren (Grand Rapids, MI: Eerdmans, 1977), 86.

The act of "choosing" Israel's God by believing Gentiles and foreigners would also be recognized, since the divine message of Isaiah 56 assures for the post-exilic temple cultus:

> And the foreigners who join themselves to the LORD, to minister to him, to love the name of the LORD, and to be his servants, everyone who keeps the Sabbath and does not profane it, and holds fast my covenant—these I will bring to my holy mountain and make them joyful in my house of prayer; their burnt offerings and their sacrifices will be accepted on my altar; for my house shall be called a house of prayer for all peoples. (vv. 6–7)

This revelation of Isaiah includes believing Gentiles in Israel's election and marks a turning point in the history of divine election. The Mosaic regulation of Exodus 12:43, 45 (banning foreigners from participating in the Passover and presumably the entire Israelite cultus) is canceled by a new, divine oracle. Now Gentiles are also solemnly granted a place in Israel as a worshiping community. Yet two conditions are mentioned: (1) keeping the Sabbath and (2) holding fast to God's covenant (Isa. 56:3, 6). The purpose is universal worship: "for my house will be called a house of prayer for all nations" (56:7, NIV).

The Prophetic Remnant Theology

If God's elective purpose broadens to include believing Gentiles, there is also a sense in which it narrows to focus on a "remnant" of Israel. While earlier Old Testament documents introduced the idea of remnant (especially 1 Kings 19:13–18), the theme is most clearly developed in the prophetic literature. According to Amos, the covenant God whose election of Israel has produced only a false sense of security will punish her for her iniquities: "All the sinners of my people shall die by the sword, who say, 'Disaster shall not overtake or meet us'" (9:10; cf. 3:2). Amos holds out one tentative ray of hope: "It may be that the LORD, the God of hosts, will be gracious to the remnant of Joseph" (5:15). With stronger conviction, Amos argues that God will accomplish His purpose for the world through this faithful remnant. God Himself will "raise up the booth of David that is fallen" so that "'they may possess the remnant of Edom and all the nations who are called by my name,' declares the LORD who does this" (9:11–12). This prophetic perspective includes: (1) the restoration of the Davidic dynasty as Yahweh's work and (2) embracing the "remnant" of

Israel's arch-enemy Edom and of all the other nations.[6]

If Amos is the first of the writing prophets to develop the idea of remnant, the concept is most central in Isaiah's theology. For him, a faithful remnant assures the fulfillment of Israel's divine election. That remnant of Israel "will inherit the election promises and form the nucleus of a new faith community (Isa. 10:20f.; 28:5f.; 30:15–17)."[7] Isaiah portrays this remnant displaying a quiet, confident trust in Yahweh during times of threat to the nation (8:16–18; cf. 7:1–9).

To highlight one additional example of prophetic remnant theology, Zechariah offers a similar hope in his vision concerning Satan's accusation of the high priest Joshua, who represented post-exilic Israel: "The LORD rebuke you, O Satan! The LORD who has chosen [*bakhar*] Jerusalem rebuke you! Is not this a brand plucked from the fire?" (3:2). The assurance of God's continued election is revealed in a graphic picture of God's justifying grace of His guilty people (3:3–5). Those whom God chose, He also justified. The immediate context commissions Joshua to "walk in my ways and keep my charge" (3:7) before being entrusted with a future rulership in the kingdom of God (8:1–19). Zechariah thus connects election, justification, sanctification, and glorification, in a mounting chain of God's eternal purpose, a sequence of divine election similar to that which Paul validates for Christian believers in Romans 8:28–30.

It was a real and constant danger for Israel to assume that her election gave her a claim on God. Jeremiah's temple speech presents God's rejection of Judah's unconditional claim as "deceptive words": "This is the temple of the LORD" (Jer. 7:4). Otto Weber states: "Yahweh's claim on his people could easily be transformed into Israel's claim on Yahweh. Wherever that happened, the gracious freedom of election was placed in question."[8] To counteract this trend to trust in a false security seems to be the purpose of covenant renewals (Deut. 30:19–20; Josh. 24:19–24; 2 Kings 23:1–3). Every

---

6. Christians may look to an apostolic application of Amos 9:11–12. During the apostolic council in Jerusalem, James interpreted the purpose of God in the passage (via the Septuagint rendering) as "to take from them [the Gentiles] a people for his name" (Acts 15:14).

7. Gerhard Hasel, "Remnant," in *International Standard Bible Encyclopedia,* ed. Geoffrey W. Bromiley (Grand Rapids, MI: Eerdmans, 1988), 4:133.

8. Otto Weber, *Foundations of Dogmatics,* vol. 2 (Grand Rapids, MI: Eerdmans, 1983), 439.

seven years the Law of Moses had to be read publicly during the Feast of Tabernacles so that Israel may "learn to fear the LORD your God" (Deut. 31:10–12; cf. Lev. 19:2). This spiritual qualification of Israel brought the prophets to their remnant theology (Amos 5:15; Isa. 6:13; 11:11–16; Jer. 23:3; 31:7; Joel 2:32; Zeph. 3:12–13) and their understanding of the messianic promise (Isa. 11:1, 10; 53). Most revealing in the Old Testament revelations is the persistent love of God to provide a faithful remnant of Israel in spite of wholesale apostasy and covenant breaking (see Ezek. 16; 23). God has demonstrated His faithfulness notwithstanding Israel's faithlessness.

The Messiah as the Chosen One

Promises concerning Israel as a chosen or elect people are not self-contained, isolated ones only for the sake of Israel; rather, they are integral parts of God's progressive plan of salvation for the world and the human race. God's elective purpose does not end in the cul-de-sac of Israel's rebellion. In His covenant loyalty (*khesed*), the Lord finds a way to further salvation history. This divine, progressive plan is revealed in both narrowing and widening patterns of election.

As has been seen, the rebelliousness of Israel led to a "narrowing" of God's elective purpose in a righteous remnant. The language of election is applied in a still narrower and more focused way in Old Testament messianic prophecies regarding the Servant of the Lord who is described by the Lord as "my chosen" (Isa. 42:1). Isaiah used the image of a tested foundation stone in Zion to describe the mission of the Davidic Messiah: "Behold, I am the one who has laid as a foundation in Zion, a stone, a tested stone, a precious cornerstone, of a sure foundation: 'Whoever believes will not be in haste'" (28:16).[9]

This narrowing from people to remnant to Messiah is in service, though, of a fresh broadening of the purposes of God since the Messiah is linked to the gathering of an eschatological remnant of Israel (Isa. 11:1–16). And God's plans are wider still as the eschatological, believing, and worshiping remnant is to include representatives of "the nations" (Isa. 45:20–23; 66:18–21; Zech. 14:16).[10]

---

9. The LXX translates "tested" with *eklektos*, "chosen." The passage is quoted as being fulfilled in Jesus Christ in 1 Peter 2:5–6; cf. Romans 9:33; 10:11.

10. Portions of this section are adapted from Hans K. LaRondelle, *The Israel of God in*

ELECTION AND PREDESTINATION
IN THE NEW TESTAMENT

Terms communicating the idea of election, used in the Old Testament to highlight the identity of Israel as the elect people of God, are taken up frequently in the New Testament, with writers employing the following words: *eklektos*, "chosen"; *eklogē*, "selection," "choice," or "election"; *eklegomai*, "choose"; *suneklektos*, "also chosen" (only in 1 Pet. 5:13); *hairetizō*, "to choose" (Matt. 12:18 only); *haireomai*, "to choose" (2 Thess. 2:13 only); *tassō*, "to appoint" (Acts 13:48 only). Broadly speaking, these terms are used to identify Jesus as the elect one *par excellence* and to describe believers.[11]

The authors of the New Testament employ several terms to communicate ideas of foreknowledge and pre-determination on the part of God, often in the context of the idea of election: *proorizō*, "decreed before" or "determined beforehand" or "predestined" or "predetermined" (Acts 4:28; Rom. 8:29–30; 1 Cor. 2:7; Eph. 1:5, 11); *proginōskō*, "know beforehand" (Rom. 8:29; 11:2; 1 Pet. 1:20); *prognōsis*, "foreknowledge" (Acts 2:23; 1 Pet. 1:2); *prothesis*, "plan" or "purpose" (Rom. 8:28; 9:11; Eph. 1:11; 3:11; 2 Tim. 1:9); *proetoimazō*, "prepare beforehand" (Rom. 9:23; Eph. 1:20).

It is important to note that the themes of election and predestination are sometimes present in the New Testament apart from this specific terminology.[12] The New Testament everywhere exhibits the conviction that God's actions in Christ to redeem humankind are not haphazard ones

---

Prophecy: Principles of Prophetic Interpretation, vol. 13, Andrews University Monographs, Studies in Religion (Berrien Springs, MI: Andrews University Press, 1983), 17–18. See also Gerhard Hasel, *The Remnant*, 3rd ed., Andrews University Monographs, 5 (Berrien Springs, MI: Andrews University Press, 1980); Kenneth D. Mulsac, "Remnant," in *Eerdmans Dictionary of the Bible*, ed. David Noel Freedman (Grand Rapids, MI: Eerdmans, 2000); Angel Manuel Rodriguez, ed., *Toward a Theology of the Remnant: An Adventist Ecclesiological Perspective* (Silver Spring, MD: Biblical Research Institute, 2009).

11. In one instance, 1 Timothy 5:21, *eklektos* is used of angels.

12. With regard to the idea of predestination, I. Howard Marshall, having reviewed specific vocabulary employed in the New Testament, notes that "the *idea* is much more widespread and a larger word-field demands investigation" including verbs employing the prefix *pro-* that are related to God's decision-making as well as "all texts in which God is described as willing, planning and purposing," "Predestination in the New Testament," in *Grace Unlimited*, ed. Clark H. Pinnock (Minneapolis, MN: Bethany Fellowship, 1975), 127–128.

crafted in a moment of crisis but carefully pre-determined by God (Col. 1:24–27 and Eph. 3:1–13 offer examples of explicit treatment of this theme).

Jesus's Testimony

While the Old Testament theme of the "chosenness" of the messianic Servant of the Lord may be regarded as "a minor Old Testament theme," from another point of view it may be argued that the messianic promise is the central focus of all God's covenants with humankind from the beginning.[13] The servant of Yahweh as chosen messiah is a theme that does indeed have "far-reaching consequences."[14] Isaiah's designation of the Servant of Yahweh as "chosen" (42:1) is taken up by the Gospel authors of the New Testament to describe Jesus (Matt. 12:15–21; Luke 9:35; 23:35). Jesus's own convictions about His status as the "chosen One" and who constitute chosen people of God are evident in parables He told and in direct assertions He made.

After His triumphal entry in Jerusalem, Jesus experienced the rejection of His messiahship by the religious leaders. He then delivered His most comprehensive indictment in the form of an updated Song of Isaiah about the "vineyard" of Israel (Matt. 21:33–46; Mark 12:1–12; Luke 20:9–19; cf. Isa. 5:1–7). Jesus added a new feature in that the owner of the vineyard now has a son who is therefore the legitimate heir: "But when the tenants saw him, they said to themselves, 'This is the heir. Let us kill him, so that the inheritance may be ours'" (Luke 20:14). Jesus concludes, "What then is this that is written: 'The stone the builders rejected has become the cornerstone'? Everyone who falls on that stone will be broken to pieces, and when it falls on anyone, it will crush him" (Luke 20:17–18). Jesus quoted Psalm 118:22 as a prefiguration of His messianic mission. He would first meet rejection by Israel but would be recognized by God in the resurrection and ascension and would be chosen as the cornerstone of a "holy temple in the Lord" (Eph. 2:21–22; see Peter's post-Easter proclamation in Acts 4:11–12; 1 Pet. 2:4–8).

---

13. Robert A. Peterson, "The Bible's Story of Election," *Presbyterion* 33, no. 1 (2007): 32. See also Walter C. Kaiser Jr., *Toward an Old Testament Theology* (Grand Rapids, MI: Zondervan, 1978), 12, 32–35.

14. Peterson, "The Bible's Story of Election," *Presbyterion*, 32.

In the Parable of the Wedding Feast (Matt. 22:1–14; Luke 14:15–24) Jesus offered a surprising differentiation between the "called" and the "chosen." The repeated invitations of the king to attend the feast were all met with an unwillingness to come, even when banquet was fully prepared (Matt. 22:3–5; Luke 14:17). Finally the king invited all that could be found, "both bad and good" so that the wedding hall was filled with guests (Matt. 22:10; cf. Luke 14:23). The parable is commonly understood to refer to the mixture of true and false disciples in the church. The king's coming to "look over" the dinner guests "implies divine inspection of professing disciples at the last judgment."[15] One invited guest appeared to have refused the appropriate wedding garment and was "cast into the outer darkness" (Matt. 22:11–13). Jesus's concluding statement was: "For many are called, but few are chosen" (Matt. 22:14). Jesus's surprising contrast between the invited (or called) ones and the chosen ones becomes meaningful in this narrative. It reveals the personal responsibility of choosing to accept the call to the kingdom of God from the God-sent Messiah (cf. John 6:44–45).

As reflected in the Gospel of John, Jesus viewed boasting of descent from Abraham as a misappropriation of Israel's status as the elect people of God. To be truly God's people required the response of faith, rather than the rejection of Him and His mission that they offered. The authentic "chosen ones" would respond to Him in faith like Abraham did to God's promises (John 8:31–59, esp. vv. 37, 39–42; cf. Matt. 24:22, 24, 31; Eph. 4:1; Phil. 2:12–13). This idea, that God's elect are those who exercise faith in Jesus, carries through the New Testament. In the Apocalypse, "those with him [the Lamb] are called [*klētos*] and chosen [*eklektos*] and faithful [*pistos*]" (Rev. 17:14). Matthew and Mark designate the "chosen" ones as "his elect" when the Son of Man appears in His glory (Matt. 24:31; Mark 13:27).

Jesus claimed to be sent by God as His unique Son, endowed with divine power and authority, something especially evident in the Gospel of John (especially 6:22–59). Jesus exercised that authority in choosing His apostles. As He announced to them: "You did not choose me, but I chose you and appointed you that you should go and bear fruit and that your fruit should abide, so that whatever you ask the Father in my name, he may give it to you" (John 15:16). Yet Jesus emphasized the necessity of individual choice to do the

---

15. Robert H. Gundry, *Matthew: A Commentary on His Literary and Theological Art* (Grand Rapids, MI: Eerdmans, 1982), 439.

will of God and to judge His messianic teachings: "Anyone who resolves to do the will of God will know whether the teaching is from God or whether I am speaking on my own" (John 7:17, NRSV). In this way, Jesus elicited a decision of the worshipers at the Feast of Tabernacles to recognize His teaching as God's own teaching (cf. John 7:15–16; 6:45). Jesus asked them to "not judge by appearances" but to "judge with right judgment" (7:24) regarding His identity as the God-sent Messiah (7:12, 25–31). John records Jesus's pathos-filled invitation extended on the last day of the feast: "If anyone thirsts, let him come to me and drink" (7:37–39). Note that Jesus evoked a decision of faith from the chosen people even as He appealed to "all people" (12:32; cf. 3:16, 36).

The New Testament emphasis on God's foreordained will or plan focuses on the messianic fulfillment of "God's own purpose" in the life, death, and resurrection of Jesus Christ (2 Tim. 1:9–10; cf. Rom. 16:25–26; Eph. 3:1–13). Peter announced on the day of Pentecost that the men of Israel had handed over Jesus for crucifixion "according to the definite plan and foreknowledge of God" (Acts 2:23, *tē hōrismenē boulē kai prognōsei tou theou*). Peter referred to messianic prophecies that were misunderstood by Israel, as appears from his explanation: "But what God foretold [*prokatēngeilen*] by the mouth of all the prophets, that his Christ would suffer, he thus fulfilled" (Acts 3:18). Similarly, the grateful prayer of the church in Jerusalem regarded the hostile acts against Jesus and His disciples as "predestined" by God's "hand" and "plan" (Acts 4:28), as predicted in Psalm 2:1–3. This understanding accords with Paul's announcement that he had taught the Ephesians "the whole counsel [*pasan tēn boulēn*] of God" (Acts 20:27; "the whole will of God," NIV).

Peter's Testimony

On the day of Pentecost Peter proclaimed the surprising news to the crowd that their act of handing over Jesus to death was *both* their personal responsibility, incurring guilt before God, *and* an act according to "the definite plan and foreknowledge of God" (Acts 2:23). Luke's narrative repeats this assessment. In prayer to God, the early Christian believers acknowledged that the political leaders and the people simply did "whatever your hand and your plan had predestined to take place" (Acts 4:28, *hosa hē cheir sou kai hē boulē [sou] proōrisen genesthai*). In the face of this divine "predestination" or "deciding beforehand," Peter nonetheless appealed to faith and repentance in view of God's new act in Christ (Acts 2:38; 3:18–19; 5:31).

This same shared emphasis on God's plan, or election, on the one hand and personal responsibility, or choice, on the other is evident as well in Peter's epistles. Peter addresses his first pastoral letter to "God's elect [*eklektois*] . . . who have been chosen according to the foreknowledge of God the Father, through the sanctifying work of the Spirit, to be obedient to Jesus Christ and sprinkled with his blood" (1 Pet. 1:1–2, NIV). He assures the suffering Gentile Christians in Asia Minor that they are "a chosen race [*genos eklekton*], a royal priesthood, a holy nation, a people for his own possession" (2:9), applying to them the same calling that ancient Israel had received (cf. Exod. 19:5–6; Deut. 7:6; Isa. 43:20–21). Peter explains that the purpose of their election is to "proclaim the excellencies" of their Redeemer and, to "offer spiritual sacrifices acceptable to God through Jesus Christ" as a "holy priesthood" (1 Pet. 2:5, 9).

In his second letter, Peter stresses the responsibility of Christian believers to "confirm" (NRSV) their "calling and election" (1:10) by practicing godliness (1:3–9) and by growing "in the grace and knowledge of our Lord and Savior Jesus Christ" (3:18; cf. 1:8). Notice carefully that Peter unites God's "calling" and "election" for believers that they might glorify Him as the Redeemer and Sanctifier of His chosen ones. The implication for Peter seems to be that a failure to "confirm" their election in a pattern of committed living amounts to their repudiation of the election. Peter's purpose, though, is not so much to warn as to encourage. Every Christian believer who sanctifies Christ in heart and life shall enter "into the eternal kingdom of our Lord and Savior Jesus Christ" (1:10–11). This assurance echoes Peter's declaration to insecure believers in his first letter that God has "chosen" and "foreknown" them and that Jesus Christ came to earth "for the sake of you" (1 Pet. 1:1, 2, 20).

Paul's Testimony

During their first missionary journey, Paul and Barnabas visited the synagogue in Pisidian Antioch. Paul reminded the Jews and God-fearing Gentiles there that God "chose" (*eklegomai*) Israel to bring forth the Davidic Messiah and announced Jesus of Nazareth to be this Messiah (Acts 13:17–23). While the residents of Jerusalem did not recognize Jesus as Messiah and had rejected Him (v. 27), the invitation was open to them: "through this man [Jesus] forgiveness of sins is proclaimed to you" (v. 38). Those who believed among the Jews and God-fearing Gentiles were counted as "appointed [*tassō*] to eternal life" (v. 48). Here Luke qualifies the appointment, or assignment, to "eternal life" in relationship to the divine purpose of faith in the hearers of the gospel (cf. v. 46).

Early in his First Letter to the Corinthians, Paul stresses that God "chose" the church in Christ in her low and weak appearance "to shame the wise" and "the strong," "so that no human being might boast in the presence of God" (1:27–29; the term *eklegomai*, "choose," is used three times). He describes Christ as the secret "wisdom" that God had "decreed [*proorizō*] before the ages for our glory" (2:7). Paul claims that the prophecy of Isaiah (64:4) about the inconceivable glory of "what God has prepared [*etoimazō*] for those who love him" has been revealed now by God's Spirit to the Christian believers who love God (2:9–10), even while the full, consummated glory is still future (15:20–28).

Paul addressed his most comprehensive theology of divine election to the Ephesians. In his opening blessing (1:3–14), Paul paints on a canvas of cosmic dimensions and in doing so provides one of the most significant and sweeping vistas of the plan of salvation in the entire Bible. It covers the full span of salvation history, from eternity past, through God's grace-filled actions in Christ, to eternity future. God's redemption of believers is rooted in divine initiatives taken "before the foundation of the world" (v. 4) and worked out in the lives of believers (esp. vv. 7–8, 13–14). These pre-creation strategies will be finally and fully accomplished at the end of time when God's pre-ordained plan will come to fruition (vv. 9–10). Then, "all things," both "in heaven" and "on earth" will be "headed up" or "united" in Christ and God's plan for "the fullness of time" will be fulfilled (v. 10). Then, believers will fully experience God's mysterious plan (v. 9), which through God's revelation they can already know, that the marvelous, Christ-centered salvation in which they stand is part of God's wide-reaching plan for the redemption of "all things."

In the passage Paul employs a variety of terms to describe God's planning and activity for the salvation of humankind. Two such terms are often taken to describe predestination in the Calvinist sense. One is the verb *eklegomai*: God "chose" us in Christ "before the foundation of the world" (1:4). Here the verb means "to select someone or something for oneself."[16]

---

16. Walter Bauer and Frederick William Danker, *A Greek-English Lexicon of the New Testament and Other Early Christian Literature* [*BDAG*], 3rd ed. (Chicago, IL: University of Chicago Press, 2001), 305.

It should be noted that this divine choice is made "in him" (Christ), "before the foundation of the world" and for a specified purpose, "that we should be holy and blameless before him."

The other term is the verb *proorizō* (vv. 5, 11). God "predestined" for "adoption as sons" (v. 5) and, in turn, believers have been "predestined" (v. 11). In each context this "predestination" occurs through God's "will" and "purpose" ("according to the purpose of his will," v. 5; "according to the purpose of him who works all things according to the counsel of his will," v. 11). The verb means to decide upon beforehand, to "predetermine."[17] As with the use of *eklegomai* in verse 4, in each of the two uses of *proorizō*, Christ's role is determinative, since the choice occurs "through Jesus Christ" (v. 5) or "in him" (v. 11).

It is important to understand the full context of Ephesians 1:3–14 and the many terms used to describe God's work for the salvation of humankind. The passage exhibits not only language about the choice, predestination, purpose, and will of God, it also contains most vivid and relational language about God's work of salvation. God is "Father" (v. 3) and human beings are destined through Jesus Christ for "adoption" as His children (v. 4). And God is no stinting parent carefully parsing out family privileges to His newly adopted children. Instead, He offers them "every spiritual blessing" (v. 3), including His grace (vv. 6–7), redemption (v. 7), forgiveness of sins (v. 7), an eternal inheritance (vv. 11, 14), salvation (v. 13), and the sealing gift of the Holy Spirit (vv. 13–14). These blessings are "lavished" upon believers (v. 8) bountifully from the limitless supply of "the riches of his grace" (v. 7). The language Paul employs in the passage to describe the choice, predestination, purpose, and will of God, then, should not be misunderstood as though in contradiction to this rich, relational language, but in company with it. Both God's sovereignty and His love are highlighted in the passage.

Imposing a Calvinist understanding on the passage violates the overall tone of the passage in another way as well. It has been noted that, at the heart of the passage, is God's plan, being worked out through Jesus Christ, "to unite all things" in Christ, "things in heaven and things on earth" (v. 10). It would be difficult to imagine a more inclusive portrayal of the Gospel. In the context of the letter, Paul deals in broad categories, imagining

---

17. Ibid., 873.

disparate segments of human society being joined together in Christ. In this way he offers a most vivid example of what he means by God's plan "to unite all things" (2:11–22; 3:4–6). To argue that Paul, in 1:3–14, is highlighting a small group of elect who have been destined for salvation over against a wider group destined for damnation is to disrupt the bracing, inclusive, redemptive tone of the passage set within this wider literary context. To take a restrictive view of a passage that expansively proclaims God's purpose to "sum up all things" in Christ (v. 10) in a letter that swings the door wide for the two great divisions of humankind, Jews and Gentiles, risks truncating the purposes of God and the intentions of the author.

Moreover, phrases such as "in Christ," "in the beloved," and "in him" are used eleven times in the passage. This suggests that God's election and predetermination are exercised corporately—in and through Christ—rather than individually.[18] Paul's focus is not on individual salvation but on the redemptive call for all believers and on the Christocentric structure of the entire universe. The passage, near its end, does become more personal in tone. And it is just here that the Spirit-inspired human actions of "hearing" and "believing" the Gospel, exercised by Paul's addressees, are seen as important (v. 13), in line with the divine, pre-creation choice that believers "should be holy and blameless before him" (v. 4).

In his earlier letter to the Romans, Paul also presents God's electing love for the pastoral purpose of uniting Jewish and Gentile believers in one new covenant people. It is enlightening to compare Paul's theological exposition of divine election and predestination in Ephesians and Romans and to watch a similar pattern emerge in Ephesians 1:3–14 and Romans 8:28–30. The following outline highlights this pattern, with an emphasis on broad themes and the order in which they are developed:

---

18. "Because the Father loves the Son he loves those who are in the Son. . . . What the New Testament affirms, and on which Ephesians 1 rests, is that Jesus Christ is now the elect of God and that the Christian's election can be spoken of only as being election *in him.* . . . Here God does not choose to elect individuals, but has chosen to elect Christ and those who are found in him. For this reason this passage presents a theology of election in the context of *corporate* worship, and with a clear pastoral note that affirms Christians as loved and chosen by God," John Lewis, "Doing Theology Through the Gates: A Bible Study on Ephesians 1:3–14," *Evangelical Review of Theology* 28, no. 4 (2004): 364–365.

	EPHESIANS 1		ROMANS 8
v. 3	. . . God . . . has blessed us in Christ with every spiritual blessing in the heavenly places	v. 28	. . . for those who love God all things work together for good . . .
v. 4a	. . . even as he chose [*ekle-gomai*] us in him before the foundation of the world, . . .	v. 29a	For those whom he fore-knew [*proginōskō*] he also predestined [*proorizō*]
v. 4b	. . . that we should be holy and blameless before him.	v. 29b	to be conformed to the image of his Son . . .
v. 5	. . . he predestined [*proorizō*] us for adop-tion as sons through Jesus Christ, according to the purpose of his will,	v. 30a	And those whom he pre-destined [*proorizō*] he also called, and those whom he called . . .
v. 7	In him we have redemption through his blood, the for-giveness of our trespasses . . .	v. 30b	. . . he also justified, . . .
vv. 10–11	. . . to unite all things in him. . . . In him we have obtained an inheritance, having been predestined [*proorizō*] according to the purpose of him . . .	v. 30c	and those whom he justi-fied he also glorified.
vv. 13–14	In him you also, when you . . . believed in him, were sealed with the prom-ised Holy Spirit, who is the guarantee of our inheri-tance . . . to the praise of his glory.	vv. 33, 38–39	Who shall bring any charge against God's elect [*eklek-tos*]? It is God who justifies. For I am sure that neither death nor life . . . will be able to separate us from the love of God in Christ Jesus our Lord.

This comparison suggests that Paul offers, in both Ephesians and Romans, a broad pattern of salvation history that includes the ideas of pre-temporal, divine initiative, a Christ-centered election of believers, their faith response to the salvation offered in Christ, and the eschatological fulfillment of the Christian hope.

In the context of the history of interpretation, Paul's discussion in Romans 8:28–30 requires close attention. With few exceptions, modern

New Testament exegetes and systematic theologians find no ground in this passage for a predecision of God (*Deus nudus,* "pure God in isolation") about a "decree" of double predestination. This medieval scholastic assumption created the problem that "the electing God is not understood seriously anymore as the One who elects and discloses himself in Christ."[19] Barth concluded: "There is no such thing as a *decretum absolutum.* There is no such thing as a will of God apart from the will of Jesus Christ."[20] Ridderbos points out that the term "election" of itself does not contain the thought of "decree," and it is used originally to describe the manner in which Israel became the people of God and had its cause only in God's "good pleasure."[21]

In this majestic outlook on redemptive history, Paul develops first God's purpose in Christ (in 8:29); and then God's way to realize this purpose (in 8:30):

1. "For whom he foreknew, he also predestined to become conformed to the image of his Son, that he might be the first-born among many brethren" (8:29, NASB);
2. "and whom he predestined, these he also called; and whom he called, these he also justified; and whom he justified, these he also glorified" (8:30).

Paul stresses how God's plan of salvation is realized in human history: by God's acts of calling, justifying, and glorifying (8:30). This exclusive focus on God's redemptive acts does not refer to any human response— neither to an act of faith, nor to a decision to obey God's will, nor to perseverance in a sanctified life—not because such responses are irrelevant or superfluous but rather because these are not meritorious works that contribute to an individual's salvation. John Wesley's explanation of Romans 8:30 is pertinent:

He [St. Paul] does not deny, that a believer may fall away and be cut off, between his special calling and his glorification, chap. xi. 22. He only affirms, that this is the method whereby God leads us step by step toward heaven.[22]

---

19. Weber, *Foundations of Dogmatics,* 420.

20. Barth, *Church Dogmatics,* 115.

21. Herman Ridderbos, *Paul: An Outline of His Theology* (Grand Rapids, MI: Eerdmans, 1975), 344.

22. John Wesley, *Explanatory Notes Upon the New Testament,* vol. 2 (London: Thomas Cordeux, 1813), 34.

As noted earlier, Paul's teaching in Romans 8:28–30 should not be iso-lated from that in his Ephesians letter, where he stresses the Christ-centered character of God's eternal purpose and counsel (Eph. 1:4–11; 2:4–10; 3:8–12). The structure of the divine plan is explicitly Christocen-tric. In Romans, Paul's intention is to assure all believers of both their present and future salvation by rehearsing the calling of God through the Gospel proclamation (1:6; 5:1; 8:1; 11:32; 16:25–26). As in Ephesians 1:10, Paul's scope of God's redeeming grace widens to embrace all of cre-ation that "waits with eager longing for revealing of the sons of God" (8:19). For that future glory of "the sons of God" Christ Jesus was sent to earth, "in order that he might be the firstborn among many brothers" (8:29). To assure the believers of the absolute certainty of the fulfillment of God's plan of salvation, Paul introduces the concept that "for those who love God all things work together for good, for those who are called according to his purpose" (8:28).

Themes of election and predestination come to the fore again in a major section of Romans, chapters 9–11, in which Paul ponders God's faithfulness in the face of rejection of Christ by many Jews. Following a heartfelt expression of concern for these, his own people (9:1–5), Paul begins his defense of the faithfulness of God by arguing from examples drawn from the history of Israel, that physical descent—genetics—is not determinative for belonging to God's people since God declares, "Jacob I loved, but Esau I hated" (9:6–13). And God is free to do whatever He wishes, including calling Gentiles "my people" and saving only a "remnant" of the "sons of Israel." This point is affirmed by reciting the story of God hardening Pharaoh's heart and an appeal to the potter's power over the clay (9:14–29). Read in isolation, these early segments of the wider passage could lead to the conclusion that God is arbitrary and human choice of no consequence in the plan of salvation. However, when read in the context of the wider passage, a rather different picture emerges.[23]

---

23. Hultgren offers a sustained defense of the general conclusion, widely held among exegetes today, that "Romans 9–11 makes up a section that can hardly be treated as a series of units lifted out of their contexts. It reads as one large unit, and it must be read in its entirety. Too often in the history of interpretation it has been the practice of interpreters to stop along the way between the beginning and the end and then draw out a theological position attributable to Paul on a particular topic (e.g., predestination, election, or the rise of faith from hearing) or to describe his views on some matter (such as an alleged spiritual

Paul next turns to an explanation of the curious irony at which he has just hinted—that Gentiles, who did not seek out righteousness, have obtained it, while Jews, who have energetically, if misguidedly, sought for righteousness have not (9:30–10:21). Embedded here amid passages often employed to defend concepts of "double predestination" comes one of the most profound biblical statements of salvation being based on faith and one's confession of Jesus Christ as resurrected Lord (10:5–10). This is joined to one of the great affirmations that God has made salvation available to all (10:11–13; cf. 1:16–17). Paul's answer to the irony he has elaborated is provided in these inspiring statements about faith and salvation: While the Gospel is accessible to all who trust in Christ, the majority of Israelites did not accept this good news but instead clung to "the old search for righteousness on the basis of the exclusive privilege of ancestry."[24]

Paul has a definite conclusion in mind in these chapters, which are now widely acknowledged as central to the whole theology and purpose of the letter. Answering the question, "Did God reject His people?" in the negative—and citing his own situation and the case study of Elijah in defense of that response—Paul turns to his understanding of what God is about in the face of the rejection of Jesus by most Jews: Jewish rejection has led to the Gospel going to the Gentiles (11:1–11).

The culmination of Paul's argument comes in 11:12–36 where Paul discloses his firmly held eschatological hope that, having seen the Gentiles accept Christ, the Jews will, in a jealous reaction, also accept Him. The hardening of his co-religionists is only a temporary phenomenon, one that will give way to "all Israel" being saved (11:26) and, broader still, God having mercy on all (11:32).[25] For Paul, the wonder of this eschatological vision cues a doxology,

---

obduracy of the Jewish people). But to isolate smaller units as providing Paul's last word on any matter is to do violence to the argument being made in the section as a whole," Arland J. Hultgren, *Paul's Letter to the Romans: A Commentary* (Grand Rapids, MI: Eerdmans, 2011), 347. Hulgren's cogent discussion of Romans 9–11 and his excellent, thorough bibliographies of secondary literature are to be commended.

24. John C. Brunt, *Romans: Mercy for All*, Abundant Life Bible Amplifier Series, ed. George R. Knight (Boise, ID: Pacific Press, 1996), 192.

25. For a critique of dispensationalist understandings of Romans 11:26 and Romans 9–11 as a whole, see Hans K. LaRondelle, "The Church and Israel in Romans 9–11," in *The Israel of God in Prophecy: Principles of Prophetic Interpretation*, Andrews University Monographs, Studies in Religion 13 (Berrien Springs, MI: Andrews University Press, 1983), 123–134.

one that appropriates divine inscrutability as a cause for praise (11:33–36).

A central question regarding Romans 9:1–29 is this: Does Paul address himself in the passage to the salvation of individuals *qua* individuals? Or is he discussing broader patterns of salvation? For example, what does he mean to communicate on this topic by citing the Old Testament story of Jacob and Esau? One way of approaching this question is to examine the ways in which Paul thinks about his "kinsmen" in Romans 9–11. Frequently, he thinks of them *en masse,* as a group. This is true in the introduction, where they are described as "my brothers, my kinsmen according to the flesh" and "Israelites" who share an important and sacred heritage and elsewhere (9:1–5; cf. 10:1–2, "Brothers, my heart's desire and prayer to God for them is that they may be saved . . . they have a zeal . . . they did not submit"). This type of thinking is reflected in 11:11–12 ("did they stumble," "through their trespass"; "to make Israel jealous"; "their trespass"; "their failure"; "their full inclusion"). In a context where Paul has just referred to stories and citations from the Old Testament, the group seems timeless. That is, it would seem to the reader that the same individuals are performing these actions across time when, of course, in the historical events themselves, different individuals would necessarily be involved.[26]

At other times Paul seems to differentiate among "my fellow Jews" (11:14), elsewhere viewed as a single group. This perspective, too, emerges early on with Paul's contrast of "children of the flesh" and "the children of the promise" among the descendants of Abraham (9:8). Later, he sees himself and others as part of "a remnant chosen by grace" (11:5), a select group within the larger one. Paul contrasts these two groups as "the elect" and "the rest" (11:7; note that he identifies "the rest" who failed to obtain God's favor with "Israel," though it is clear that some within Israel did succeed in obtaining God's blessing).

In the illustration of the olive tree (11:17–24), Paul again differentiates. Here his tone becomes more personal, with individuals more in view. There are "branches" that "were broken off" and the "others" who remained part of the tree (11:17; cf. v. 20). And, interestingly, it is just here that he is

---

26. I find helpful Frank J. Matera's description of Paul's three "movements: Israel's past (9:1–29), Israel's present (9:30–10:21), and Israel's future (11:1–36)," Frank J. Matera, *Romans,* Paideia Commentaries on the New Testament, ed. Mikeal C. Parsons and Charles H. Talbert (Grand Rapids, MI: BakerAcademic, 2010), 253.

clearest about the element of personal choice in speaking of some Jews, under the figure of branches, as being "broken off because of their unbelief" (11:20), while holding out the possibility that they may choose to abandon that unbelief (11:23).

So, while Paul's major lens is to understand his countrymen as a (sometimes timeless) group, he can differentiate groups within them and in the context of reflecting on the exercise of faith can become more personal still. The conclusion seems appropriate if somewhat imprecise that it is God's plan for salvation of the Jews as a people that is under discussion:

> Paul is addressing the problem of Israel as chosen people and its relation to Christ, present and future. Paul is *not* addressing the fate of some individual—a modern Christian, for example—who may, from time to time, distrust God's redemptive word in Jesus Christ.[27]

Another key to the passage is to work out what Paul means by the dichotomy between, on the one hand, "children of the promise" (9:8), salvation through God's mercy and compassion (9:14–18), and "the righteousness based on faith" (10:6), and, on the other hand, "the children of the flesh" (9:8), salvation through "human will or exertion" (9:16), and "the righteousness that is based on law" (10:5) since these latter categories relate to the exercise of human choice.

In this regard it is crucial to note that Paul is illustrating the same fundamental point in his discussion of God's sovereign election of "Jacob" (9:6–18) and his lengthy consideration of the need for human beings to exercise faith and confess that Jesus is Lord (10:1–21). Salvation does not come through human will, exertion, work, or law-keeping. It comes through something else—the work of God in Christ—and is accessed through faith and confession (esp. 10:5–13). This means of salvation and the way to access it, Paul argues, is in contrast to futile attempts to gain salvation through law-keeping. Note carefully that, for Paul, the exercise of faith and confession are viewed in contrast to human works. This does not mean that faith and confession are imposed upon humans and are inauthentic, not really their own. Rather,

---

27. Paul Achtemeier, *Romans*, ed. James Luther Mays (Louisville, KY: John Knox, 1985), 154–55. Achtemeier continues, "The context of this discussion, namely the fate of Israel as chosen people, must be honored, especially in verses 6–13 and 24–29, or what we hear from these chapters will be quite different from what Paul wants to say."

it means that they are so influenced by and attached to the work of God in Christ that Paul views them as part and parcel of God's salvation. They are not, from this point of view, human works at all. So it is that those who acknowledge God's predestined plan for the salvation of humankind, with its ample provision for salvation *and* its call to exercise faith in Christ who is at the heart of that provision, are "chosen by grace" (11:5).

Salvation is under discussion in both Romans 9:14–29 and the wider frame of Romans 9–11, but in a special sense. The particular topic is the salvation of the Jews as the people of God and, still more broadly, the offer of salvation to all people.[28] By using the Old Testament citation, "Jacob I loved but Esau I hated," Paul takes a considerable rhetorical risk, especially that some auditors/readers might take "Esau" as a type of the Gentiles and conclude that Gentiles are not chosen for salvation. Paul limits that risk, though, in the wider framework of Romans 9–11 by carefully detailing the importance of the decision of faith (esp. in 10:5–13) and the fact that salvation is conditional based on the response of faith (11:17–24). It becomes clear that his point has been to argue more narrowly for the freedom of God to elect or choose who belongs to His people. To build a theology of double predestination on Romans 9:1–29 is to ignore the important ways in which Paul directs the meaning of this segment through the context of the wider passage, Romans 9–11.

It remains to mention in brief two more of those ways. First, notice the multiple times that Paul underlines the accessibility of salvation to all "by faith" (9:32): "whoever believes in him will not be put to shame" (9:33); "For Christ is the end of the law for righteousness to everyone who believes" (10:4); "The word is near you, in your mouth and in your heart" (10:8); "Everyone who believes in him will not be put to shame" (10:11); "For there is no distinction between Jew and Greek; for the same Lord is Lord of all, bestowing his riches on all who call on him. For 'everyone who calls on the name of the Lord will be saved'" (10:13). Given the many times Paul

---

28. In holding that salvation is under discussion in the passage, I am in agreement with Thomas R. Schreiner in his critique of Arminian views of Romans 9. However, he unnecessarily pits the idea that Paul is discussing salvation in the passage against the idea that Paul is "making a general statement about God's strategy in history." I believe that Paul is doing both. See "Does Romans 9 Teach Individual Election Unto Salvation? Some Exegetical and Theological Reflections," *Journal of the Evangelical Theological Society* 36 (1993): 27.

reiterates this idea, the passion with which it seems to be communicated, and how close it is to the heart of Paul's understanding of the Gospel (Rom. 1:16–17), this is a clear, defining revelation: Salvation is authentically and genuinely accessible to anyone who believes in Christ. And when one identifies "God's accusers" in Romans 9:14 as Paul's Jewish opponents, it becomes clear that this point is linked tightly to the theological infrastructure of Romans 9: "When Paul asserts God's freedom to have mercy on whomever he wishes, Paul is not forging a doctrine of unconditional individual election but establishing God's freedom to pour out his mercy beyond the boundaries of Jewish ethnic identity."[29]

A second, important way that Paul controls the meanings of the discussion of 9:1–29 is through a very clear, if parenthetical, reminder that he does not hold the position that the "elected" saints will, invariably, persevere to the end: "Note then the kindness and the severity of God: severity toward those who have fallen, but God's kindness to you, provided you continue in his kindness. Otherwise you too will be cut off" (10:22).

Romans 9:1–29 should not be viewed as a unique passage that teaches double predestination but understood within the wider framework of Romans 9–11 and the New Testament as whole as affirming God's careful, advance preparation of a plan to redeem humankind, a plan that included inviting all human beings to choose the salvation offered through it.

A BIBLICAL-THEOLOGICAL FRAMEWORK FOR UNDERSTANDING ELECTION AND PREDESTINATION

Drawing on this survey of biblical materials, this study will conclude by identifying elements that provide a biblical-theological framework for understanding election and predestination.

Election and Predestination in the Great Controversy

The language of election and predestination in the New Testament assures believers that sin did not catch God off guard. When sin entered the world, God had already acted in "deep time" to make provision for

---

29. Jerry L. Walls and Joseph R. Dongell, *Why I Am Not a Calvinist* (Downers Grove, IL: InterVarsity, 2004), 91.

the salvation of humankind. "In contrast to ancient mythology, which speculated on the cosmic struggles of various divine and suprahuman powers as the background to all that happens on earth, the Bible concentrates on the history-shaping, personal decisions of the one God."[30]

The provision God planned "before the foundation of the world" (Eph. 1:4) and the actions that have unfolded that provision in salvation history (most centrally the Incarnation of Jesus, e.g. 2 Tim. 1:9–10) disclose God's nature and character. They illustrate His love (Eph. 1:4–5; 1 Thess. 1:4), mercy (Rom. 9:16), grace (Rom. 11:5), wisdom and knowledge (Rom. 11:33).[31]

Patterns of Election, Predestination, and Salvation in Old and New Testaments

God's character of love is expressed down through the ages of salvation history. It is God's character that brings both continuity and sequence between the Old and New Testaments. God pledges Himself to His people, Israel. They forget Him or, more blatantly, rebel. God expresses His covenant loyalty and mercy by calling them back to Himself through discipline and revelation. When, after durable and extreme efforts, God's people refuse to repent, His covenant loyalty motivates fresh efforts and new strategies. A remnant and the messianic Servant of Yahweh become the bridges to a renewed and widened mission encompassing both Jews and Gentiles. What seem to be surprising twists and turns in the journey come to be understood as fulfillments of earlier prophecy and are always rooted in the election and predestination of God.

---

30. John E. Alsup, "Predestination," in *Harpercollins Bible Dictionary,* ed. Paul J. Achtemeier (San Francisco: HarperSanFrancisco, 1996), 878. Ivan T. Blazen's statement of the theme is an excellent one: "The salvation of humankind does not result from a divine afterthought or improvisation made necessary because of an unexpected turn of events after sin arose. Rather, it issues from a divine plan for man's redemption formulated before the founding of this world (1 Cor. 2:7; Eph. 1:3, 14; 2 Thess. 2:13, 14) and rooted in God's everlasting love for humanity (Jer. 31:3)," "Salvation," in *Handbook of Seventh-day Adventist Theology,* Commentary Reference Series, ed. Raoul Dederen (Hagerstown, MD: Review and Herald, 2000), 275.

31. I borrow this list of qualities and passages from W. A. Elwell, "Election and Predestination," in *Dictionary of Paul and His Letters,* ed. Gerald F. Hawthorne, Ralph P. Martin, and Daniel G. Reid (Downers Grove, IL: InterVarsity, 1993), 225.

God Offers Salvation to All

A theme that is oft-stated and seemingly everywhere assumed in the Bible is the idea that God actively seeks the salvation of all people: "God our Savior . . . desires all people to be saved and to come to the knowledge of the truth" (1 Tim. 2:3–4). In the New Testament this idea figures so strongly as to become thematic in some documents (esp. Luke, Acts, John, Romans, and Galatians).[32] God's pre-determined, Christocentric plan cannot be any threat to human freedom, because it is a call and summons to all people to believe the Gospel (e.g., Acts 17:22–31). In fact, "Wherever the NT speaks of predestination, it does so with the intent of underscoring God's will to embrace all his creation in the saving help predestined for it."[33] Possessing intimate knowledge of people as individuals (Matt. 10:39–40; Luke 12:6–7; Acts 9:10–19; 1 Cor. 13:12), God seeks to draw them to Himself and save them.[34] This is as sure and clear a biblical truth as exists. No candidate for truth dare make a charade of this deep, central understanding of the character and work of God.[35]

The Importance of Human Choice

In the divine plan of salvation, human choice is exceptionally important. Throughout Scripture, God and His agents are portrayed as pleading with human beings to exercise their ability to choose right and truth. In the Old

---

32. Explicit statements of the theme include: Ezekiel 18:23, 32; John 1:9–13; 3:16–17; Romans 1:16–17; 3:27–31; 11:32; 1 Timothy 2:3–4; 4:10; Titus 2:11; 2 Peter 3:9; Revelation 22:17. See our focused treatment of this theme in dealing with Romans 9–11, p. 28.

33. Alsup, "Predestination," in *Harpercollins Bible Dictionary*, 879.

34. Marshall extends this thought: "A solution to the problem of predestination must do justice to the way the Bible speaks of God as one who places his will over against ours and acts like another person, rather than as a being who does not enter into real relationships with his creatures but simply treats them as the unconscious objects of his secret will," *Grace Unlimited*, 139.

35. "God wants the wicked man to turn from his wickedness and live; he has no delight in the death of the sinner, and that is his last word on the matter. We have no right to go beyond Scripture and assert that he determines otherwise in the secret counsel of his heart. He is not willing that any should perish but that all should come to a knowledge of the truth and be saved (1 Tim. 2:4). 'Whoever wishes, let him take the free gift of the water of life' (Rev. 22:17). That is God's final word on the matter," ibid., 141–142.

Testament, the pattern of exhortation established in Deuteronomy and carried through the prophets assumes the importance of human choice. In the New Testament, the appeal to human choice is evident in narratives (e.g., John 20:30–31). And in the letters of the New Testament, exhortation, or paraenesis, is prominent, with constant appeals to human choice. The New Testament presents the topics of election and predestination without communicating any contradiction to the ubiquitous assumption: Human beings possess the God-given ability to exercise choice and faith and those commitments matter.

The Purpose of Divine Revelation Concerning Election and Predestination

God's purpose in communicating the truths of election and predestination aligns with His character—He intends to encourage and uplift. To use Ephesians 1:3–14 as an example, contemporary readers must put themselves in the place of Paul's listeners as they consider ideas of election and predestination. It will not do to approach the passage from the standpoint of individualism and self-determination, which are so valued in modern democratic societies. Paul's readers, imbedded as they are in the first century, would have heard these words from a very different mind-set than that of contemporary individuals. They had no sense that they could decide their own destiny or fate. Rather, they believed that through the power of the stars and planets their destinies had already been fixed.[36]

So when those first-century people hear the Gospel—that God has chosen their destiny in offering them salvation through Jesus Christ—it comes as very good news indeed. Their lives are not in the hands of chance and fate; their destinies are not determined by the astral powers. Instead,

---

36. Ralph P. Martin summarizes the first-century mind-set this way: "Oriental astrology and occultism . . . with [their] . . . accompanying astral religion and dominant fatalism, haunted like a nightmare the soul of first-century people. The vacuum (caused by disillusion over the collapse of the Homeric gods who were like magnified men and women on Mount Olympus) was quickly filled with an all-embracing capitulation to 'chance.' People who came under the spell of star worship were made to feel that all things were ruled by 'fate.' The particular conjunction of the stars or planets under which people were born was of decisive importance and settled irretrievably their destiny," *Ephesians, Colossians, and Philemon*, Interpretation (Atlanta: John Knox, 1991), 91.

God offers them eternal life through Jesus Christ who, above any competing power, is now the Lord of their lives. Instead, God has "chosen" or "predetermined" another destiny, that they might be "holy and blameless before him" (v. 4) and might forever be His sons and daughters "through Jesus Christ" (vv. 5–6). This announcement of God's "predestination" was surely good news to those who had been under the thrall of astral religion. They would have known with certainty that their lives had been destined by the astral powers. That their lives were destined was not the innovation offered by Paul in Ephesians, but by whom and for what purpose.

To put oneself in place of the first readers of the Epistle to the Ephesians is to hear the passage as the good news that it was and is. To read the passage as teaching that the individual destinies of human beings are, before the creation of the world and apart from any element of human choice, forever fixed is to mutate its message into bad news. And to do so communicates to believers the type of sad, fatalistic, and deterministic message conveyed to first-century people through the worldview of astral religion.

The Limitations of Human Knowledge

In pondering the themes of election and predestination, believers often find themselves at the outer limits of human knowledge, even when aided by divine revelation (1 Cor. 2:10–16): "The affirmations of predestination belong to those ultimate dimensions of life on the extreme outer limits of what humans can perceive and talk about. Humans enter these outer limits by permission, as it were, where faith is mingled with mystery."[37] So it is no surprise if some move beyond what is truly accessible to humanity, creating scholastic distinctions and constructions of God's "foreknowing" and "preordaining" that are problematic.[38] Many have interpreted such terms as referring to God's foreseeing the faith of believers (*praevisa fides*), as the ground of their predestination to salvation. But who can claim to understand the order of divine decisions in God's eternal counsel? In view of the truths of election and predestination, Paul exclaimed, "How unsearchable are his judgments and how inscrutable his ways! 'For who has known the

37. Alsup, "Predestination," in *Harpercollins Bible Dictionary,* 878.

38. For example, M. J. Erickson's *priority* of predestination, *Christian Theology* (Grand Rapids, MI: Baker, 1985), 926.

mind of the Lord, or who has been his counselor?'" (Rom. 11:33–34). Elsewhere, Paul was overwhelmed in realizing that God's electing love existed already before anyone loved Him (Eph. 1:4; 2:4–5; cf. 1 John 4:19). Why God loved humanity beforehand cannot be explained by a simple decree of God's sovereign will. God chose us beforehand in His unfathomable and merciful love. From the perspective of divine election and predestination, believers do not stand as believers, but rather as sinners and enemies of God (see Rom. 5:6, 8, 10). Wishing to be more specific about any ground for God's redemptive love seems to "go beyond what is written" (1 Cor. 4:6). In affirming both the foreknowledge of God and the Spirit-aided freedom of human choice, there is room for mystery, wonder, and a humble admission of the limits of human knowledge.[39]

These elements—the thematic setting of the great controversy; the trajectory of God's grace evidenced in both the Old and the New Testaments; that God offers salvation to all; the importance of human choice; the positive purpose of divine revelation concerning election and predestination; and an acknowledgment of the limits of human language—provide the framework within which believers grapple with God's revelation on the themes of election and predestination.

---

39. Thomas R. Schreiner also acknowledges the limits of human knowledge ("There are times when Scripture strongly affirms two realities that cannot finally be resolved logically by us"), and he argues that the mystery is to be located between the idea that God "does elect individual and groups unto salvation, and he determines who will exercise faith" and the thought that "those who do not exercise faith are responsible and should have done so," "Does Romans 9 Teach Individual Election Unto Salvation?" *Journal of the Evangelical Theological Society,* 39. We agree with the principle that human knowledge has limits and reaches its boundaries in contemplating some aspects of election and predestination. However, we would locate the mystery between the thought that God allows for freedom of choice and the idea that God knows who will exercise faith without interfering with the authenticity of that choice.

SECTION 2

The Sin Problem:
Are Humans Born
in Need of a Savior?

All Bible-believing Christians tend to agree that the Fall of the first humans, as described in the early chapters of the book of Genesis, has left lasting effects upon humanity. While the reality of the impact of original sin upon humanity has rarely been denied, its extent has been hotly debated throughout the history of the church. The questions remain today: Did the Fall of the first couple leave their posterity with only the physical effects of their sin, or did the damage extend to their spiritual nature? Was human nature affected to the point that individuals became unable to respond to God's offer of salvation, or do they have unaltered free will, much like Adam and Eve themselves before the Fall? What is the extent to which Adam and Eve's children are able to cooperate with God in the process of salvation? Has their human nature become so damaged by sin that humanity is no longer able to cooperate at all, forcing God to act alone in the process of salvation? At the basis of all these questions lies the inquiry of the ages: What is sin?

Problems regarding sin occupied the minds of Christian thinkers throughout the centuries and continue to do so in the twenty-first century. Clear biblical answers to sin-related questions are crucial as they have powerful implications for the biblical doctrine of salvation. An error in understanding sin and its impact upon human nature may result in a faulty understanding of God's nature and the way He saves humanity.

In this section the authors attempt to grapple with the problem of sin and its nature. The first chapter, authored by Darius Jankiewicz, provides a brief history of Christian views on sin and its impact upon humanity.

The second chapter, written by Jiří Moskala, presents an anatomy of sin as found in Genesis 3. In the third chapter, Roy Adams provides an in-depth discussion of the nature and complexity of sin as presented in the Bible. Finally, in the last chapter of this section, George Knight deals with human nature in the context of sin.

CHAPTER 5

SIN AND HUMAN NATURE: HISTORICAL BACKGROUND

Darius W. Jankiewicz

The book of Genesis begins with the account of Creation and a short statement that sums up God's work: "God saw all that he had made, and it was very good" (Gen. 1:31).[1] Included in this was the creation of Adam and Eve as perfect, free, moral beings who were to rule over Creation. Subsequently, through the actions of the first couple, sin entered the human world and changed the dynamics of God's relationship with humanity. In a mysterious and inexplicable way, the entry of sin also affected the inner workings of human nature. While the Creation account found in Genesis presents human beings as the crown and climax of Creation, clothed in glory and possessing freedom of choice, the subsequent narratives of both the Old and New Testaments depict humanity as apparently unable to change their sin-affected nature and in desperate need of salvation. Although acknowledging human freedom, the Old Testament writers view humans as mired in sin in its various forms and unable to break away.[2] Thus David writes: "Surely I was sinful at birth" (Ps. 51:5) and "Even from birth the wicked go astray;

---

1. Unless otherwise indicated, all Scripture quotations are taken from THE HOLY BIBLE, NEW INTERNATIONAL VERSION®, NIV® Copyright © 1973, 1978, 1984, 2011 by Biblica, Inc.® Used by permission. All rights reserved worldwide.

2. For an excellent treatise on sin and the variety of ways in which it touches humanity, see John M. Fowler, "Sin," in *Handbook of Seventh-day Adventist Theology*, ed. Raoul Dederen (Hagerstown: Review and Herald, 2000), 244–255.

from the womb they are wayward, spreading lies" (Ps. 58:3); Isaiah laments: "your whole heart [is] afflicted" (1:5); and Jeremiah chimes in: "Can the Ethiopian change his skin or a leopard its spots?. . . . The heart is deceitful above all things and beyond cure" (13:23; 17:9). In the midst of the ocean of human sin, God is presented as the only Savior of humanity (Isa. 43:11; 45:21).

The New Testament also presents a rather dim view of human nature, while at the same time acknowledging the possibility of genuine freedom of choice. In the book of Romans, for example, the Apostle Paul is emphatic when he describes the sinful state of all human beings (3–8); because of the sin of one man, *all* sinned, are subject to death, and are in need of repentance (5:12—6:4). In Ephesians 2:3 he refers to humanity as being "by nature deserving of wrath." Likewise, the apostles John and James despair of the state of humanity. In 1 John 1:8, 10, John states this to his readers: "If we claim to be without sin, we deceive ourselves and the truth is not in us" and again "If we claim we have not sinned, we make him out to be a liar and his word has no place in our lives." James agrees that: "We all stumble in many ways" (3:2). Speaking of corrupted human nature, he lays the symbolic blame on the human tongue: "No human being can tame the tongue. It is a restless evil, full of deadly poison" (3:8). At the same time, like the Old Testament prophets, the New Testament writers proclaim God, Jesus Christ, as the only Savior of humanity (Acts 4:12; 1 Tim. 2:5; 4:10). Despite such a dismal assessment of human nature, much of the New Testament appears to affirm the existence of a grace-endowed human freedom of choice (e.g., Acts 17:30; Rom. 6:16).[3]

While the Scriptures clearly present the wretched state of humanity and its desperate need of the Savior's grace, they do not include a systematic explanation of sin and its nature. Moreover, the inspired authors do not provide theological explanations for questions such as: What was the impact of Adam's sin (the original human sin) on human nature? What are the inner workings of its apparent transmission from parent to child, for countless generations of humanity? Are sinful actions a result of a free moral choice of an unspoiled human will, or they are a result of

---

3. There are some passages that seem to deny this assertion. See, for example, Romans 9:11 or 2 Timothy 1:9. Passages such as these are dealt with in other parts of this book.

a deep-seated perversion of human nature? When born, are humans innocent and good, or are they, by nature, evil and depraved?

Faced with various heretical teachings, post-Apostolic Christianity took upon itself the task of clarifying these issues, resulting in many, often contradictory, perspectives. Over the centuries, Christian understandings of the impact of original sin upon human nature and the level of God's grace needed to rescue sinners tended to oscillate between two extremes of a high (optimistic) and a low (pessimistic) anthropology; the former signified a minimal impact of Adamic sin upon the human nature and the existence of a relatively unspoiled human free will, and the latter represented a significant impact upon human nature, rendering it unable to choose good.

The purpose of this chapter is to briefly introduce Christian interpretations with regard to original sin and its influence upon human nature. The anthropological questions that have troubled Christian thinkers throughout the centuries also lie at the center of the Seventh-day Adventist understanding of sin, atonement, and salvation. A historical review of these developments might thus be helpful in providing a context for the current Adventist discussions on salvation.

PRE-FIFTH CENTURY VIEWS ON ORIGINAL SIN AND HUMAN NATURE

The discussion of the nature of original sin and its impact on human nature did not begin in earnest until the early fifth century and is known today as the Pelagian controversy.[4] This debate was significantly influenced by a slow re-discovery of Christ's full divinity during the pre- and post-Nicaean period and a growing understanding of His role in the process of salvation. All this does not mean, however, that the pre-Nicaean Christian writers had nothing to say about sin and its impact on human nature.

References to Adam's sin and its relationship to human nature do not feature prominently in the writings of the earliest post-Apostolic Christian writers, known as the Apostolic Fathers, although most recognize the

---

4. Parts of what follow have already appeared in print. See Darius and Edyta Jankiewicz, "Let the Little Children Come: Toward a Seventh-day Adventist Theology of Childhood," *Andrews University Seminary Studies* 49 (2011): 213–242.

universality of sin.[5] This group of writers appeared to be more concerned with the moral living of believers than with developing coherent theological systems.[6] In the writings of such authors as Clement of Rome and Ignatius of Antioch and in the first Christian Catechism, *Didache*, therefore, one finds scant allusions to sin, and none to its origin and influence upon human nature.[7] In general, however, it may be stated that because of their moralistic emphases directed at Christian believers, the Apostolic Fathers appeared to hold an optimistic view of human nature and its natural abilities. Bernhard Lohse thus commented that "the generally prevailing conviction among the early fathers is that man is equipped with a free will, and that no sin can effectively keep him from deciding for the good and from avoiding the bad."[8] This understanding of sin, notes J. N. D. Kelly, decidedly weakened the atonement idea so prevalent in the New Testament.[9]

A more sophisticated group of theologians, known as the Apologists, emerged during the second part of the second century and preoccupied themselves with the defense of Christianity and a struggle against a number of heretical teachings of the day.[10] It is in their writings that one begins to witness the gradual emergence of various theories regarding sin and its impact upon humanity. In general, however, it may be stated that the Apologists appear to follow in the footsteps of the Apostolic Fathers in their optimism with regard to sin's influence upon human nature and the ability of humanity to contribute to the process of

---

5. The Apostolic Fathers is the name given to those authors writing immediately after the New Testament period and include Clement of Rome, Ignatius, Hermas, Polycarp, Papias, and the authors of the *Epistle of Barnabas, 2 Clement,* and *Didache.* For more on this topic, see *The Oxford Dictionary of the Christian Church* (1997), s.v. "Apostolic Fathers."

6. Bernhard Lohse, *A Short History of Christian Doctrine* (Philadelphia: Fortress Press, 1966), 102.

7. *The Oxford Dictionary of the Christian Church* (1997), s.v. "Original Sin"; Thomas A. Smith, "Original Sin," *The HarperCollins Encyclopedia of Catholicism* (1995), 943.

8. Lohse, *A Short History of Christian Doctrine,* 104.

9. "Although satisfied that Christ died for us . . . they assign a relatively minor place to the atoning value of [Christ's] death," J. N. D. Kelly, *Early Christian Doctrines* (New York: Harper and Brothers, 1960), 165.

10. These theologians flourished throughout the Roman Empire between c. 140 and c. 250 AD.

salvation. Justin Martyr (d. ca. 165) is probably the first Christian thinker to speak of the universal problem of sin. He thus taught that while the human race found itself under the curse of sin, this curse was nothing else but a physical death. "The human race . . . from Adam had fallen under the power of death."[11] Although humans struggle with evil tendencies,[12] these were apparently the result of demonic action and the bad example of other people.[13] Having affirmed the existence of human free will, Justin believed that obedience to the law of God provided the universal remedy for sin.[14] Justin's contemporary, Theophilus of Antioch (d. ca. 181), believed that human beings were originally created neutral, although in an unfinished state, with the capacity for both mortality and immortality. Becoming immortal depended on an individual's ability to remain obedient to the commandments of God. From the time of the first sin, human beings are subjected to the weakening power of the evil spirit, which they must conquer through the exercise of their will.[15]

The writings Irenaeus of Lyons (d. ca. 202), which eventually became normative for early Christian theology, represent the first theological discussion on sin and its nature. Irenaeus appears to be the first of the early theologians to develop the incipient doctrine of original sin.[16] As did his predecessors, however, he continued to adhere to a strongly optimistic anthropology. Like Theophilus, Irenaeus believed that God created human beings with a capacity to reach perfection through obedience. They were created in God's image, he believed, but not in His likeness. Adam and Eve had a chance to attain to the rich fullness of perfection in the Garden of Eden. However, through their disobedience they lost the original opportunity[17] and death came into the world "as an act of mercy

11. Justin Martyr, *Dialogue with Trypho* 95, 88, *ANF* 1:247, 243; cf. Linwood Urban, *A Short History of Christian Thought* (New York: Oxford University Press, 1995), 137–138.

12. Justin Martyr, *First Apology* 10, *ANF* 1:165–166.

13. Justin Martyr, *Second Apology* 5; *First Apology* 61, *ANF* 1:190, 183.

14. Justin Martyr, *Dialogue with Trypho* 88, 95, 116, 124, 134, *ANF* 1:243, 247, 257, 262, 267.

15. Rick Rogers, *Theophilus of Antioch: The Life and Thought of a Second-Century Bishop* (Lanham: Lexington Books, 2000), 44.

16. Irenaeus, *Against Heresies* 3.23; 4.37, *ANF* 1:455–458, 518–521.

17. Irenaeus, *Against Heresies* 3.38, *ANF* 1:521.

towards Adam and Eve, especially in view of their immaturity and inexperience, and to prevent their remaining forever disobedient adolescents."[18] All was not lost, however, as through their obedience and despite the presence of sin in the world, God could continue working with human beings and bring them to the state of perfection originally designed for humanity.[19] All they needed to do was to be obedient to God for one day and they could become incorruptible again.[20] Sin, in the writings of Irenaeus, is thus understood as disobedience. Sinful nature is the state of immaturity, compounded by the sin of the first couple, and which is passed on to their posterity. It was up to those who followed Irenaeus to explain the mechanics of this transmission, since he does not address the issue. The ultimate goal of the plan of salvation is the restoration of human beings, who, while continuing as creatures, may eventually share in the glory of God through their obedience.[21] The incarnated Christ serves as a model of the final perfection that can be achieved by the human race.[22] "Through His transcendent love," Irenaeus writes, "[Christ became] what we are, that He might bring us to be even what He is Himself."[23]

While Irenaeus was the first to speculate on sin and its nature, it was his younger contemporary, Tertullian (ca. 160–ca. 225), who was the first Christian thinker to develop the notion of what later became designated as original sin.[24] Believing that the soul is transferred from human to human by the act of physical procreation,[25] he taught that when Adam fell, all

---

18. Denis Minns, *Irenaeus* (Washington, DC: Georgetown University Press, 1994), 65.

19. Irenaeus, *Against Heresies* 4.39, ANF 1:522–523; cf., Minns, *Irenaeus*, 63–64.

20. Ibid., 3.20, ANF 1:450.

21. Minns, *Irenaeus*, 62–66.

22. Matthew Craig Steenberg, *Irenaeus on Creation: The Cosmic Christ and the Saga of Redemption* (Leiden: Brill, 2008), 9.

23. Irenaeus, *Against Heresies* 5, ANF 1:526; Irenaeus, *Against Heresies* 4.38, ANF 1:521–522; cf. R. A. Norris, *God and World in Early Christian Theology* (New York: The Seabury Press, 1965), 94; Kelly, *Early Christian Doctrines,*172–174; Otto W. Heick, *A History of Christian Thought,* vol. 1 (Philadelphia: Fortress Press, 1965), 109.

24. J. L. Neve, *A History of Christian Thought* (Philadelphia: Fortress Press, 1946), 139.

25. This view is also known as Traducianism (from Latin *tradux*, which means "shoot" or "sprout"), a theory that goes back directly to Tertullian. For more on this topic, see *The*

humans fell with him. The soul was sinful, therefore, simply because it was related to its first "sprout," Adam. Through his sin, the human race, thus, became infected not only with its result, death, but his fallen nature became part of his posterity.[26] Such an understanding of the human situation, however, did not prevent Tertullian from also strongly emphasizing complete freedom of will[27] and the ability of humans to free themselves from sin by obedience, works of self-humiliation, asceticism, and even martyrdom. Once God was satisfied with human self-humiliation, He would then infuse the soul of the offender with His re-creative grace.[28]

The Eastern Christian thinkers of the early third century, Clement of Alexandria and Origen, did not share Tertullian's views that the entire human race was present in Adam when he sinned.[29] They agreed, however, with the universal sinfulness of humanity, which they attributed to the bad influence of parents upon their children rather than to any inherited weaknesses. Adam, they believed, was created in God's image but not in His likeness (i.e., in a state of perfectibility). God created Adam with the ability to sin and Adam chose that path. As a result, he came under Satan's influence and became subjected to death and corruption.[30] This did not extend, however, to Adam's free will but only affected his intellect. Through the exercise of their unaided free will, humans could choose to embark on a way of salvation known as *theosis*, or divinization.[31] Within this context, it

---

Oxford Dictionary of the Christian Church (1997), s.v., "Traducianism."

26. Neve, *History of Christian Thought,* 139.

27. In fact, as James Morgan notes, Tertullian was responsible for coining the Latin term for "free will," *The Importance of Tertullian on the Development of Christian Dogma* (London: K. Paul, Trench, Trubner, 1928), 52.

28. Neve, *History of Christian Thought,* 140.

29. It must be noted that while Clement and Origen differed in the details of their anthropological views, they were, in substance, in agreement. Their views may thus be presented together.

30. Louis Berkhof, *The History of Christian Doctrines* (Edinburgh: The Banner of Truth Trust, 1937), 128–129.

31. Clement, *The Stromata* 6.9, 14, *ANF* 2:497, 506. Clement was one of the earliest Christian theologians to use the term *theopoieo*, "being made like God." This term is closely associated with the concept of *theosis* (usually translated as "divinization," "deification," "being made divine"), which became the hallmark of pre-Nicaean Eastern Christian theology. G. W. Butterworth notes that while there are slight differences among early Christian

must be noted that, like their predecessors, Clement and Origen were sub-ordinationists[32] and believed that Jesus Christ provided the clearest way for humans to achieve a state of perfect unification with the divine.[33]

It was not until the third century, within the context of the debate over infant baptism, that Christian thinkers began to pay more careful attention to human anthropology and the way sin is passed from human to human. While the practice of infant baptism was still divisive and subject to debate in the second century, third-century thinkers appear to accept the practice as more or less universal.[34] The first unambiguous reference to infant baptism appeared in the third century in writings attributed to Hippolytus (d. ca. 235).[35] The thinkers of later decades begin to prescribe the practice universally. Cyprian (d. ca. 258), for example, was supportive of infant baptism, arguing that although children were not guilty of their own sin, they were "born after the flesh according to Adam," and thus in need of remission for

---

theologians who wrote in Greek, all (and this includes Origen) are essentially in agreement with Clement's views on deification, "The Deification of Man in Clement of Alexandria," *JTS* 17 (1916): 162; cf. Eric Osborn, *Clement of Alexandria* (Cambridge: Cambridge University Press, 2005), 234–235; cf. Origen, *Against Celsus* 3.28.41, ANF 4:475, 480.

32. Although early Christian subordinationism manifested itself in various forms, the common underlying theme was that the Son and the Holy Spirit are subordinate to the Father. According to various thinkers, the Son and the Holy Spirit were either created or generated at some point in eternity past, or eternally generated, as in the teaching of Clement and Origen. As I have documented elsewhere, any form of subordinationism in history has often led to aberrant soteriological views where salvation is viewed in legalistic, and even perfectionistic, terms. Subordinationism and especially the doctrine of eternal generation have strong roots in pagan Greek philosophy. See Darius Jankiewicz, "Lessons from Alexandria: The Trinity, The Soteriological Problem, and the Rise of Modern Adventist Anti-Trinitarianism," *Andrews University Seminary Studies* 50 (2012): 5–24.

33. Origen, *Against Celsus* 3.28, ANF 4:475.

34. In the second century, for example, Tertullian argued for a "delay of baptism." "Why does the innocent period of life hasten to the 'remission of sins'?" he asked. Children, he believed, should know what they are asking for as far as salvation is concerned. "Let them know how to 'ask' for salvation, that you may seem (at least) to have given 'to him that asketh,'" Tertullian, *On Baptism* 18, ANF 3:678.

35. "And they shall baptize the little children first. And if they can answer for themselves, let them answer. But if they cannot, let their parents answer or someone from their family," Hippolytus, *The Apostolic Tradition* 21.4, ed. Gregory Dix (London: SPCK, 1968), 33.

"the sins of another."[36] Cyprian's views constitute the foundation upon which Augustine, one of the most important early church fathers, developed his views on infants and original sin, which became a watershed for the Christian understanding of the nature of human beings.[37]

In summary, it appears that, for the most part, the earliest post-Apostolic thinkers adhered to a rather optimistic anthropology.[38] They all strongly affirmed human freedom which, while weakened by sin, was strong enough, with the assistance of God's grace, to lift the human being from the degradation of sin. According to many, "freedom and grace [stood] side by side in producing the acts of goodness; or more correctly, man's free will begins and grace follows in a supplementary manner. . . . Faith is man's own work."[39] It is not surprising, therefore, that, in Berhnard Lohse's words, their writings were characterized by "a confirmed moralism which really amounted to nothing more than a pure righteousness by works."[40]

THE PELAGIAN CONTROVERSY

The fifth-century controversy between Pelagius (ca. 390–418 AD)[41] and Augustine (354–430 AD) is the most important early discussion on

---

36. Cyprian, *Epistle* 58.5, *ANF* 5:353–354.

37. Brinley Roderick Rees, *Pelagius: Life and Letters* (Rochester: The Boydell Press, 1991), 58; cf. Alister E. McGrath, *Christian Theology* (Oxford: Blackwell, 2007), 18–19.

38. Scholars generally agree that the presence of such optimistic anthropology in these early Christian writings can be ascribed to their authors' opposition to Gnostic fatalism. Heick, *History of Christian Thought*, vol. 1, 191; Neve, *History of Christian Thought*, 137. On the basis of my study, I would add two more reasons. First, the influence of various Greek philosophies, most of which (with the notable exception of Stoicism) espoused an optimistic view of the human nature; second, the inability of these early Christian thinkers to come to terms with the full divinity of Christ. As noted previously, all were subordinationists and unable to reconcile the relationships within the Trinity if Jesus was to be considered as fully divine and co-equal to God the Father. Only during the fourth century did the church begin to come to terms with the full, co-equal divinity of Christ and the implications of such view on human salvation. See my "Lessons from Alexandria."

39. Heick, *History of Christian Thought*, vol. 1, 193–194.

40. Lohse, *Short History of Christian Doctrine*, 102.

41. It is assumed that Pelagius was a British monk who came to Rome around 405 AD and then moved to Carthage about 411 AD, where he met Augustine.

Christian anthropology and the first systematic effort to settle the issues relating to the original sin, its impact upon human nature, and the way it is passed on. The views of these two thinkers[42] constitute two opposite extremes that created the framework within which all future theological controversies relating to sin and its influence were fought.

Pelagius was a Christian ascetic who, like many of the second- and third-century Christian thinkers, held a highly optimistic view of human nature. Pelagius goes beyond the earlier Christians by asserting that the human person was essentially good and endowed with an undetermined free will. Nothing that could be classified as a sinful nature or a bent toward sinning was passed on from Adam to his children. As such, a person was endowed with the ability to choose between sinning and not sinning equally. Sin is the personal choice of a person rather than something passed on from generation to generation. People become sinners by following the bad example given by their parents and friends and by wrong educational methods. Pelagius appears to have believed that since people are born sinless, they can eventually return to the state of sinlessness if they choose to. God, in His mercy and grace, provided humanity with a set of guidelines, the Ten Commandments, which every human being is capable of obeying perfectly. They also have the example of Christ's perfect obedience, as witnessed by the New Testament. And the very fact that God expects obedience is a positive proof that humans are capable of obeying God's commandments perfectly. God, thus, did everything possible to show humans the correct path of living. The possibility of human perfection was, according to Pelagius, hinted at in Jesus's words: "Be perfect, therefore, as your heavenly Father is perfect" (Matt. 5:48). In this system of thought, the salvation of a person was, in its entirety,

---

42. It must be noted at this point that very little is known about Pelagius and his life and none of his writings survive. His views, however, may be gleaned from the writings of others, most importantly, Augustine and Julian of Aeclanum (c. 386–c. 455), the latter eventually becoming known as the "architect of Pelagian dogma." For this reason, it is impossible to reconstruct the actual beliefs of Pelagius himself. When using the name "Pelagius," therefore, I actually refer to a theological position rather than to what the man Pelagius actually believed. For a detailed discussion, see Jairzinho Lopes Pereira, *Augustine of Hippo and Martin Luther on Original Sin and Justification of the Sinner* (Bristol: Vandenhoeck & Ruprecht, 2013), 129–140.

dependent upon his or her obedience to the commandments of God.[43] It is for this reason that, for subsequent generations of Christians, Pelagianism became synonymous with salvation by works. This fundamental assumption that human beings are essentially good and unhindered in their choice for good eventually drew the ire of Augustine, who pushed Christian anthropology into the opposite extreme.

While, prior to his involvement with Pelagius, Augustine appeared to affirm the innocence of infants,[44] later in his life, after reflecting on his own infancy and in response to Pelagius, he firmly rejected any form of innate innocence of newborn human beings. Against Pelagius's argument that infants were born in the same state as Adam before the fall, thus possessing perfect free will, and that sin was the result of forming a habit of sinning as a result of "evil examples" of sinning individuals such as parents,[45] Augustine argued that "the sin of Adam was the sin of the whole human race."[46] The entire human race is, thus, *massa damnata* (a condemned crowd), with their natures completely depraved and unable to do any good or respond to God's offer of salvation; the free will is thus denied by Augustine. From this sin-cursed race God chooses some individuals for salvation. This is an act of pure grace by God, uninfluenced by any form of human behavior, and that includes choice. While it is God's desire to save all, only those who are chosen will experience salvation.[47] Because of his insistence on the absolute nature of God's grace, Augustine was the first early thinker to systematically develop the doctrine of divine predestination. Human beings could not choose God, he believed; therefore, God had to choose them.[48]

---

43. Berkhof, *History of Christian Doctrines,* 132–133; Justo L. González, *A History of Christian Thought,* vol. 2 (Nashville: Abingdon Press, 1987), 29–32. See also Pelagius, quoted in Augustine's *De gratia Christi,* in Henry Bettenson, *Documents of the Christian Church* (Oxford: Oxford University Press, 2011), 56.

44. In his treatise *On the Freedom of the Will,* for example, and with reference to the children "slain by Herod," he suggested that, even though they had died unbaptized, these children were to be considered "martyrs" for whom God had some "good compensation," Augustine, *Free Will* 3.23.67–69, in S. Aurelii Augustine, *De libero arbitrio,* trans. Carroll Mason Sparrow (Richmond: Dietz, 1947), 141–142.

45. Neve, *History of Christian Thought,* 142.

46. Ibid., 144.

47. Richard P. McBrien, *Catholicism* (New York: HarperCollins Publishers, 1994), 187.

48. Augustine, "On Predestination of the Saints," in *Four Anti-Pelagian Writings,* trans.

The Augustinian version of *original sin* (a term coined by Augustine himself), thus, teaches that infants are born carrying Adam's personal moral guilt and cannot be considered "innocent."[49] Although they lacked the physical ability to do harm, infants were sinful from birth. Baptism was then needed to remove the guilt of sin and to cement the infant's status as belonging to the family of God (i.e., the church).[50] In addition to inheriting Adam's guilt, their natures are totally depraved, bent toward evil, and unable to respond to God's mercy. Augustine believed that original sin is transmitted from human to human via sexual desire and intercourse, which arouses disordered (sinful) passions in humans.[51] In simplified terms, it could be said that the traditional Augustinian doctrine of original sin embraces three basic consequences for Adam and his posterity: guilt, complete depravation (or total corruption), and a bent or tendency to evil.[52]

As stated previously, the theological interaction between Pelagianism and Augustine constitutes the two opposite ends of the theological spectrum of human anthropology.[53] Throughout the rest of Christian history, all thinkers found themselves somewhere in between Pelagius and Augustine, more often closer to Pelagius than they would be willing to admit.

John A. Mourant and William J. Collinge, in *Fathers of the Church* (Washington, DC: Catholic University of America Press, 1992), 86:259–60.

49. *Augustine Conf. 1.7,* trans. Vernon J. Bourke (New York: Fathers of the Church, 1953), 12. Augustine thus states: "The injustice of the first man is imputed to little ones when they are born so that they are subject to punishment, just as the righteousness of the second man," *Answer to Pelagians III: Unfinished Work in Answer to Julian* (New York: New City Press, 1999), 85.

50. Augustine, *On Marriage and Concupiscence* 1.22, 1.28, *NPNF* 5:273, 275; Augustine, *Reply to Faustus the Manichean* 12.17, *NPNF* 4:189; cf., Roger Olson, *The Story of Christian Theology* (Downers Grove, IL: IVP Academic, 1999), 270–274.

51. McBrien, *Catholicism*, 187; cf., Justo L. González, *Heretics for Armchair Theologians* (Louisville, KY: Westminster John Knox Press, 2008), 116–118.

52. Louis Berkhof, *Systematic Theology* (Grand Rapids, MI: Wm. B. Eerdmans Publishing Co., 1939), 245; Greg R. Allison, *Historical Theology* (Grand Rapids, MI: Zondervan, 2011), 342; cf., McGrath, *Christian Theology,* 364–365.

53. For a deeper study of Augustine's response to Pelagianism, see Augustine, *Four Anti-Pelagian Writings: On Nature and Grace, On the Proceedings of Pelagius, On the Predestination of the Saints, On the Gift of Perseverance.*

THE MEDIEVAL CHURCH

The Pelagian controversy left Christian anthropology in flux. For the most part, however, medieval theologians were not willing to commit themselves to either Augustinianism or Pelagianism. The first attempt to reconcile these opposing views on sin, free will, and salvation resulted in a system that became known as Semi-Pelagianism.[54] On the one hand, Semi-Pelagianism denied Augustinian *monergism* (from Greek *monos*—one, *ergos*—work); this is the doctrine that God alone is responsible for all the work of salvation since humans are so damaged by sin that they cannot possibly respond to God's offer. On the other hand, they also denied Pelagian anthropology, which taught that humans are born morally perfect, just as Adam before the Fall. In contrast, Semi-Pelagian theologians postulated that while infants are born morally weak and sinful, they somehow retained a natural capacity to take the first step toward God in the process of salvation. By His grace, God joins in the process and helps the willing humans along their journey toward heaven. Salvation was thus conceived as a result of synergistic (Greek *syn*—with, *ergos*—work) co-operation between God and humans.[55] To simplify things, William Shedd compares the three systems in this way: "Augustinianism asserts that man is morally *dead*; Semi-Pelagianism maintains that he is morally *sick*; Pelagianism holds that he is morally *well*."[56] Ultimately, Semi-Pelagianism proved unviable to many Catholic theologians because too much was claimed for human beings.[57] Two of these theologians, Pope Gregory the Great (ca. 540–604 AD) and Thomas Aquinas (1225–1274 AD), became instrumental in creating what later became the official Catholic doctrine of salvation.

Gregory the Great, one of the most important pope-theologians of the Middle Ages, proposed an alternative that was closer to Augustine than

---

54. The leading proponents of Semi-Pelagianism, which had many shades during the post-Augustinian era, were fifth-century theologians John Cassian (ca. 360–435 AD) and Faustus of Riez (ca. 410–495 AD). For a detailed description of Semi-Pelagianism and its shades, see Olson, *Story of Christian Theology,* 278–285.

55. Marcia L. Colish, *The Stoic Tradition from Antiquity to the Early Middle Ages* (Leiden: Brill, 1990), 116.

56. William G. T. Shedd, *A History of Christian Doctrine,* vol. 2 (New York: Charles Scribner and Co., 1871), 110.

57. Semi-Pelagianism was eventually condemned by the Council of Orange in 529 AD.

that offered by Semi-Pelagianism. Like Augustine, he believed that, upon their birth, infants are in the chains of original sin and cannot rescue themselves. God, thus, must initiate the process of salvation. This chain is broken by God's grace, given through the work of Christ, with baptism being an essential part of this process because it removes the guilt of condemnation. The baptized infant or adult receives an infusion of God's grace, which enables him or her to cooperate with God's grace in the process of salvation. Since it is expected that most people will continue to sin after their baptism, some form of repayment is necessary. This repayment may be completed through the works of merit which believers are expected to complete with the assistance of God.[58] Participating in church-prescribed rituals, such as the Lord's Supper, praying to the saints, as well as various good works of charity, were considered by Gregory as the means to atone for any post-baptismal sin, and ultimately, the reception of eternal life.[59] It thus appears that the only way in which Gregory's system differed from that of Semi-Pelagians was that the beginning of Christian life was ascribed to God's grace alone. With Semi-Pelagians and against Augustine, however, he affirmed the existence of the natural, albeit weakened, free will and the ability of humans to cooperate with God in the process of salvation through accumulation of merits prescribed by the church.[60] If this sounds somewhat confusing, it is. While Gregory's writings form the foundation upon which the Catholic doctrine of sin and salvation was built, he did not develop his views systematically and consistently, and many questions were left unanswered. The final refinement of the medieval doctrines of sin, free will, and salvation was left to the greatest of all Catholic systematicians, Thomas Aquinas (ca. 1214–1274).

Thomas endeavored to reconcile the Augustinian doctrine of original sin with a more optimistic, Aristotelian vision of humanity, which tended

---

58. Gregory, *The Books of the Morals* 33.40, http://www.lectionarycentral.com/GregoryMoralia/Book33.html (accessed on February 1, 2018); cf., Williston Walker, *A History of the Christian Church* (New York: Charles Scribner's Sons, 1970), 174.

59. Walker, *History of the Christian Church*, 174; cf. Berkhof, *The History of Christian Doctrines*, 140–141.

60. Carole Straw, *Gregory the Great: Perfection in Imperfection* (Berkeley: University of California Press, 1988), 140–141.

to view human infants as essentially innocent but immature.[61] Thus, although Aquinas accepted the official Augustinian position of the fundamental sinfulness of human beings, he viewed them as having "potential for spiritual growth, with the aid of grace."[62] The greatest challenge to Aquinas's thinking was the apparent contradiction between his acceptance of an Augustinian understanding of original sin as an impediment to salvation[63] and his Aristotelian belief in the actual innocence of unbaptized children.[64] As his solution to this theological quandary, Aquinas embraced the doctrine of *limbus infantium*, or limbo,[65] a state between heaven and hell where unbaptized infants were consigned.[66] As bearers of original sin, Aquinas asserted, the souls of unbaptized infants know that they do not deserve heaven; thus they do not "grieve though being deprived of what is beyond [their] power to obtain,"[67] but rather "enjoy full natural happiness."[68] Infant baptism, according to Aquinas, cancels out the guilt but leaves the tendencies to sinful behavior. God has to reach to humans with His grace first to awaken the natural tendencies toward goodness and to provide

61. Christina L. H. Traina, "A Person in the Making: Thomas Aquinas on Children and Childhood," in *The Child in Christian Thought*, ed. Marcia J. Bunge (Grand Rapids, MI: William B. Eerdmans, 2001), 106; cf. Joseph James Chambliss, *Educational Theory as a Theory of Conduct: From Aristotle to Dewey* (Albany, NY: State University of New York Press, 1987), 34–35, and A. Scott Loveless and Thomas Holman, *The Family in the New Millennium: Strengthening the Family* (Santa Barbara: Praeger Publications, 2006), 6–9.

62. Traina, "A Person in the Making," *The Child in Christian Thought*, 106.

63. Thomas Aquinas, *Summa Theologica* III, Q68. Art.2 in St. Thomas Aquinas, *Summa Theologica*, trans. Fathers of the English Dominican Province (Allen, TX: Christian Classics, 1981), 4:2393–2394; cf. Aquinas, Appendix 1, Q1, Art.2 in *Summa Theologica* 5:3002.

64. Eileen Sweeney, "Vice and Sin," in *The Ethics of Aquinas*, ed. Stephen J. Pope (Washington, DC: Georgetown University Press, 2002), 158–159.

65. Christopher Beiting, "Limbo in Thomas Aquinas," *Thomist* 62 (1998): 238–239.

66. Aquinas, *Summa Theologica* Suppl. Q69, Art.6, in St. Thomas Aquinas, *Summa Theologica*, 5:2822–2823; cf. Shulamith Shahar, *Childhood in the Middle Ages* (London: Routledge, 1990), 45.

67. Aquinas, *Summa Theologica* Appendix 1, Q1, Art. 2, in *Summa Theologica*, 5:3004.

68. *The Oxford Dictionary of Christian Faith* (1997), s.v. "Limbo." Cf. Beiting, "Limbo," *Thomist*, 238. In recent centuries, Aquinas's doctrine of limbo has created much theological difficulty for Roman Catholic theologians. See George J. Dyer, "Limbo: A Theological Evaluation," *Theological Studies* 19 (1958): 32–49.

continual healing for the effects of original sin. As a result, Richard McBrien perceptively notes in his description of Aquinas's teaching, "the theological counterpart to grace is not sin, but human nature. Original Sin is presented as an 'illness' which, though it weakens and injures human nature, does not render human nature ugly or radically perverse," as is found in Augustinian theology.[69] With Thomas Aquinas placing the capstone on medieval anthropology, therefore, Catholicism departed from Augustinian anthropological pessimism and turned to a softer view that rendered a human being sick or wounded (in contrast to being dead) and with an innate ability to respond to God's offer of salvation.[70]

In the end, Catholic soteriology offered a view of salvation as a type of transaction between God and humans involving the church as the intermediary. Ecclesiology thus became enmeshed with soteriology.[71] Through His grace, God does His part by providing the initial grace, which awakens natural goodness in humans and assists them in the process of sanctification, accomplished mainly by participating in the rituals and works approved by the church. In return, believers are required to fulfill their part of the transaction by doing what God and the church requires of them. If, through their diligent obedience, they are able to prove to God that they are worthy of heaven, they will be saved. In this system, justification becomes enmeshed with sanctification, thus resulting in what is sometimes referred to as "ontological righteousness"[72] and encouragement of human merit in the process of salvation.[73]

---

69. McBrien, *Catholicism*, 188.

70. Tatha Wiley, *Original Sin* (New York: Paulist Press, 2002), 94–100.

71. The early signs of amalgamation between soteriology and ecclesiology were already evident in the writings of second-century thinkers, such as Ignatius, Irenaeus, and Tertullian, and it found its classic expression in Cyprian's famous dictum *Quiasalus extra ecclesiam non est!* ("Outside of the Church there is no salvation"), Cyprian, *Epistle* 72.21, *ANF* 5:384.

72. Carter Lindberg, *The European Reformations* (Oxford: Blackwell Publishers, 1996), 353.

73. *The Canons and Decrees of the Council of Trent*, chaps. VII, X, XI in *Creeds of the Churches: A Reader in Christian Doctrine from the Bible to the Present*, ed. John H. Leith (Louisville, KY: John Knox Press, 1982), 411–416; cf., Olson, *Story of Christian Theology*, 446; John W. O'Malley, *Trent: What Happened at the Council* (Cambridge: Belknap Press, 2013), 115.

Catholic Christianity that emerged from the Middle Ages thus possessed a fine-tuned soteriologico-ecclesiological system, which attempted to balance God's grace with human merit. This system, unfortunately, resulted in many soteriological abuses that plagued the medieval church and was eventually challenged by the Protestant Reformation of the sixteenth century. The Reformation, however, did not significantly affect the Catholic understanding of human nature. During the Council of Trent (1545–1563), a more optimistic view of human nature prevailed and was codified in its canons. The Council thus stated that while, as a result of the Fall, human beings "immediately lost the holiness and justice in which [they] had been constituted," "the free will was [not] lost and destroyed."[74] "Trent," therefore, writes Roger Olson, "clearly denied salvation by grace through faith alone and made justification a process involving human cooperation of the will and meritorious good works. . . . The righteousness of justification is not a sheer gift. The ability to merit and possess it may be a gift, but it is itself partly earned."[75] It could thus be once again stated that too much is claimed for human beings. This understanding of humanity, sin, and salvation eventually found its way into modern official Catholic documents, such as *Catechism of the Catholic Church* issued in 1994.[76]

THE MAGISTERIAL REFORMATION

In many ways, the Protestant Reformers' views on sin and human nature constitute a reversal of Catholic medieval anthropology and a return to Augustinian anthropology. What in 1517 began as a small-scale reaction against various sacramental abuses eventually evolved into a massive rebellion against any form of synergistic understanding of salvation. It seemed natural for Martin Luther (1483–1546), an Augustinian monk, to reach deeply into the writings of his ancient mentor to fight against various sacramental abuses of the medieval Catholic Church. In the process,

---

74. Leith, *Creeds of the Churches,* 406, 420. The actual statement is as follows: "If anyone says that after the sin of Adam man's free will was lost and destroyed . . . let him be anathema." cf. O'Malley, *Trent,* 115.

75. Olson, *Story of Christian Theology,* 447.

76. *Catechism of the Catholic Church* (Liguori: Liguori Publications, 1994), 102, 483.

Luther embraced the deeply pessimistic anthropological views of Augustine and his understanding of original sin. Like Augustine, he believed that humans enter the world not merely inclined to evil, but as fallen sinners, evil from birth and infected with "irreversible egoism," which he saw as the "all-pervading symptom of human perversion."[77] While, following an experience of conversion, a believer may exhibit external signs of improvement, the internal corruption lingers in him or her even after the sin is forgiven. This is the basis for Luther's famous dictum *simul peccator et iustus,* or "at the same time both a sinner and a righteous man."[78] In tandem with his views on human nature, and in a proper Augustinian manner, Luther proclaimed the utter inability of human beings to contribute to their salvation. His views are best explained in *On the Bondage of the Will*, where in strong language he rejected Erasmus's tepid approach to human depravation.[79] As a result of his anthropological views, and in agreement with Augustine, Luther embraced election and predestination as the only mode of human salvation. God's righteousness is thus a pure gift that cannot be refused by the believer.[80]

---

77. Gerald Strauss, *Luther's House of Learning: Indoctrination of the Young in the German Reformation* (Baltimore, MD: John Hopkins University Press, 1978), 33–34. Luther wrote of the human will that it is "innately and inevitably evil and corrupt," *Disputation Against Scholastic Theology*, in *Luther's Works* 31, ed. Harold J. Grimm (Philadelphia, PA: Muhlenberg Press, 1957), 10.

78. Martin Luther, *Romans*, in *Luther's Works* 25 (Saint Louis, MO: Concordia Publishing House, 1972), 260.

79. Luther thus writes: "So you see that free choice is completely abolished by this passage [Romans 3], and nothing good or virtuous is left in man, since he is flatly stated to be unrighteous, ignorant of God, a despiser of God, turned aside from him, and worthless in the sight of God," *On the Bondage of the Will*, in *Luther and Erasmus: Free Will and Salvation*, ed. E. Gordon Rupp and Philip S. Watson (Philadelphia, PA: The Westminster Press, 1969), 300.

80. While it is not widely known, Luther was just as staunchly predestinarian as John Calvin and Huldrych Zwingli. For Luther on predestination, see Martin Luther, *On the Bondage of the Will* (Westwood, NJ: Fleming H. Revell Company, 1957); cf., Harry Buis, *Historic Protestantism and Predestination* (Philadelphia, PA: Presbyterian and Reformed Publishing Company, 1958), 2, 48; Millard J. Erickson, *Christian Theology* (Grand Rapids, MI: Baker Academic, 2013), 846; Roger E. Olson, *The Story of Christian Theology*, 388; Jairzinho Lopes Pereira, *Augustine of Hippo and Martin Luther on Original Sin and Justification of the Sinner*, 362, 453. Influenced by Philip Melanchthon, Luther's successor, later

In the same vein as Luther, John Calvin (1509–1564) also espoused a deeply pessimistic anthropology, spawned by the Augustinian concept of original sin. In fact, his position on the nature of humanity is often seen as even "more pessimistic than that of any of his predecessors or contemporaries."[81] Adam's sin, Calvin taught, "enkindled God's fearful vengeance against the whole of mankind."[82] Because the "heavenly image was obliterated" in Adam, all who come after him also suffer his punishment by inheriting complete corruption of their natures.[83] He thus wrote, "Even infants bear their condemnation with them from their mother's womb; for, though they have not yet brought forth the fruits of their own iniquity, they have the seed enclosed within themselves. Indeed, their whole nature is a seed of sin; thus it cannot be but hateful and abominable to God."[84] Calvin's affirmation of Augustinian original sin resulted in his becoming the most visible proponent of God's election and predestination. Since humans are totally depraved and have a proclivity only toward evil, salvation is left up to God alone, who can only save them through the decree of election that was accomplished in eternity past. God's grace, thus, is absolute, with no human input into the event of salvation. In the mind of Calvin, thus, even a simple human "yes" in response to God's offer of salvation would constitute "human work," thus chipping away from the glory of God and negating the Reformation's slogan: *Soli Deo Gloria!*[85] This is the very reason why the Reformers, in their desire to preserve God's sovereignty over human beings and their salvation, chose the predestinarian solution.

Lutheranism rejected the predestinarian doctrines as incompatible with the Gospel.

81. Barbara Pitkin, "The Heritage of the Lord: Children the Theology of Calvin," in *The Child in Christian Thought*, ed. Marcia J. Bunge (Grand Rapids, MI: William in B. Eerdmans, 2001), 167.

82. John Calvin, *Institutes of the Christian Religion* 2.1.4 in *The Library of Christian Classics (LCC)*, vol. 20, ed. John T. McNeill (Philadelphia, PA: The Westminster Press, 1960), 1:244, 245.

83. Calvin, *Institutes* 2.1.5 and 9, *LCC* 20, 1:246, 252–253.

84. Calvin, *Institutes* 4.15.9, *LCC* 21, 2:1311. Like Augustine, Calvin taught that baptism is necessary to remove the guilt and condemnation inherited by humans. See *Institutes* 4.15.10, *LCC* 21, 2:1311.

85. See, for example, Calvin's commentary on Luke 18:9–14. John Calvin, *Commentary on a Harmony of the Evangelists, Matthew, Mark and Luke* (Edinburgh: The Calvin Translation Society, 1845), 2:201–207.

The monergism of the Magisterial Reformation was clearly the strongest possible response to the Catholic synergism of the Middle Ages and a powerful reminder that salvation is only from God (*Soli Deo Gloria*). The doctrine of total depravity, thus, became a hallmark of the Protestant Magisterial Reformation, and it was left up to future theological traditions to provide a correction of the predestinarian soteriology of the Magisterial Reformers.

THE POST REFORMATION ERA

The first serious challenge to the Augustinian/Magisterial Reformation doctrine of original sin did not occur, primarily, within a discussion of the nature of humanity, but rather transpired within the debate over baptism. The Anabaptists, the "step-children" of the Protestant Reformation,[86] agreed with much of the teachings of other Reformers; however, they also departed in some ways from the Magisterial Reformation's anthropology. One issue that became of central importance to the Anabaptists was baptism, which, they believed, should be voluntary and based on an understanding of the Gospel of Jesus Christ.[87] Menno Simons[88] (1492–1559), a former Catholic priest and a prominent Anabaptist leader, asserted that since infants "have no faith by which they can realize what God is and that he is a rewarder of both good and evil, as they plainly show by their fruits—therefore they have not the fear of God, and consequently they have nothing upon which they should be

---

86. For a detailed study of Anabaptism, see Leonard Verduin, *The Reformers and Their Stepchildren* (Grand Rapids, William B. Eerdmans, 1964).

87. Williston Walker notes that the Anabaptists' opposition to infant baptism stemmed from the larger issue of "their opposition to the use of force in matters of faith and their abandonment of the age-old requirement of religious uniformity," *A History of the Christian Church* (New York: Charles Scribner's Sons, 1970), 327; cf. Menno Simons, "Christian Baptism," in *The Complete Writings of Menno Simons,* trans. Leonard Verduin, ed. J. C. Wenger (Scottdale, PA: Herald Press, 1956), 257; Keith Graber Miller, "Complex Innocence, Obligatory Nurturance, and Parental Vigilance: 'The Child' in the Work of Menno Simons," in *The Child in Christian Thought*, 195.

88. While a variety of perspectives existed among the Anabaptists, Menno Simons is considered the quintessential theologian of the Anabaptist tradition. The nature of this paper prevents a thorough and comprehensive treatment of the Anabaptist perspective on the issues of sin and its impact upon human nature.

baptized."[89] Instead of baptizing infants, "who cannot be taught, admonished, or instructed," Simons exhorted Christian parents to nurture their children's faith until they had reached the "years of discretion,"[90] when they could make the decision to be baptized. [91] Implicit in Simons's rejection of infant baptism was his understanding of human nature. Although he acknowledged that humans are born with an innate tendency to sin, "inherited at birth by all descendants and children of corrupt, sinful Adam," a tendency that "is not inaptly called original sin,"[92] he appears to differentiate "between a *nature* predisposed toward sin and actual *sinning*, disallowing the former to obliterate childhood innocence."[93] Thus, according to Simons, although children inherit corruption from Adam, their natures are damaged by sin, they are innocent, "as long as they live in their innocence," and "through the merits, death, and blood of Christ, in grace," they are "partakers of the promise."[94] Children who die "before coming to the years of discretion," declares Simons, "die under the promise of God."[95] The Anabaptist perspective, which affirmed the depraved and sinful nature of children and the need for God's grace for salvation, while at the same time rejecting the deterministic understanding of salvation, impacted some Christian traditions that continue to this day.[96]

---

89. Simons, "Christian Baptism," in *The Complete Writings of Menno Simons,* 240. Baptizing infants, Simons asserted, gave parents a false sense of security about their children's salvation, resulting in the possibility of children being "raised without the fear of God," and thus living "without faith and new birth, without Spirit, Word and Christ," "Reply to False Accusations," in *The Complete Writings of Menno Simons,* 570.

90. Simons, "Christian Baptism," in *The Complete Writings of Menno Simons,* 241.

91. Ibid.

92. Simons, "Reply to False Accusations," *The Complete Writings of Menno Simons,* 563.

93. Miller, "Complex Innocence, Obligatory Nurturance, and Parental Vigilance," in *The Child in Christian Thought,* 201, emphasis in original.

94. Simons, "Reply to Gellius," in *The Complete Writings of Menno Simons,* 708; Menno Simmons, *A Foundation and Plain Instruction of the Saving Doctrine of Our Lord Jesus Christ* (Lancaster: Boswell and M'Cleery, 1835), 415.

95. Simons, "Christian Baptism," in *The Complete Writings of Menno Simons,* 241; Furthermore, Simons suggests that children of both believing and unbelieving parents remain innocent through the grace of Christ. See, for example, "Christian Baptism," in *The Complete Writings of Menno Simons,* 280 and "Reply to Gellius," in *The Complete Writings of Menno Simons,* 707.

96. Today, the Amish, some Baptists, the Brethren, Hutterites, Mennonites, Bruderhof

Another theological challenge to the Calvinistic doctrine of salvation came from within the Reformed tradition itself. A Dutch Reformed theologian, Jacobus Arminius (1560–1609), took exception to Calvinistic determinism and its overemphasis on the sovereignty of God. Fiercely accused of departing from traditional Protestantism, Arminius considered himself a thoroughbred Protestant who strongly affirmed the traditional Protestant teachings of *Sola Scriptura* and *Sola Gratia et Fides*[97] but who chose not to affirm the Calvinistic teaching on election and predestination. In classical Protestant fashion, however, he did affirm the total depravity doctrine. How could he do that without also affirming the doctrine of predestination? Consider this statement from Arminius:

> In his lapsed and sinful state, man is not capable, of and by himself, either to think, to will or to do that which is really good; but it is necessary for him to be regenerated and renewed in his intellect, affections or will and in all his powers, by God in Christ, through the Holy Spirit, that he may be qualified rightly to understand, esteem, consider, will and perform whatever is truly good. I ascribe to Divine grace—the commencement, the continuance, and the consummation of *all good*—and to such an extent do I carry its influence, that a man, though already regenerated, can neither conceive, will, nor do any good at all, nor resist any evil temptation, without this preventing and exciting, this following and co-operating grace.[98]

It is evident, from this statement, that Arminius embraced the Protestant doctrine of the total depravity of human nature, while at the same time steering clear of the trap of predestinarianism. For him *total depravity* meant that all aspects of human nature have become corrupted by the Fall of the first couple. As a result their descendants are incapable of

---

Communities, and Quakers are considered successors of the Continental Anabaptists. See Holly Catterton Allen, "Theological Perspectives on Children in the Church: Anabaptist/Believer Churches," in *Nurturing Children's Spirituality: Christian Perspectives and Best Practices*, ed. Holly Catterton Allen (Eugene, OR: Cascade Books, 2008), 115. Seventh-day Adventists also consider themselves within the Anabaptist theological tradition. George Knight, *Search for Identity* (Hagerstown, MD: Review and Herald Publishing Association, 2000) 30, 177.

97. Olson, *Story of Christian Theology*, 464–465.

98. James Arminius, in *The Works of James Arminius, D.D*, vol. 1, trans. James Nichols (London: Longman, Hurst, Rees, Orme, Brown and Green, 1825), xxxi, emphasis in original.

initiating the process of salvation without the assistance of God's super-natural, enabling grace. It is indisputable, thus, that for Arminius the entire work of salvation, including sanctification, is ascribed to God's grace. It is that grace, known in history as "preventing," "prevenient," or the grace that "comes before," that awakens the "lifeless faculties of the soul" and attracts humanity to God.[99] Restored humanity now has a choice to reject the salvific grace—or accept it and lead a sanctified life. This grace, however, and in contrast to Calvinism, is resistible. Arminius was thus, in Roger Olson's words, "optimistic about grace but not about human nature!"[100] With the Magisterial Reformers, thus, Arminius could cry out *Soli Deo Gloria* as far as human salvation was concerned. At the same time, Arminius further adjusted the Protestant idea of original sin by rejecting the notion that the guilt of Adam's sin was imputed to humans upon their conception. Because of the atoning work of Christ, Arminius asserted, newly born humans were innocent, and if they died in infancy, their salvation was secure.[101] Arminius's contemporaries, par-ticularly those influenced by Calvinism, vehemently opposed his views. This situation continues to this day. His thinking, however, ultimately influenced the beliefs of John Wesley (1703–1791) and the Methodist movement.[102] According to Wesley scholar Herbert B. McGonigle, it is indisputable that Wesley was a careful student of Arminius.[103]

---

99. It is striking that Ellen G. White in her *Steps to Christ* would follow the same lines of reasoning (Mountain View, CA: Pacific Press Publishing Association, 1956), 18. It is to be noted that Arminius was not the first theologian to use the term *prevenient grace*. It is he, however, who appears to be the first to frame this concept within a uniquely Protestant context.

100. Roger Olson, *Arminian Theology: Myths and Realities* (Downers Grove, IL: IVP Academic, 2006), 150.

101. Jacobus Arminius, *Apology or Defence* 13 and 14, in *The Works of James Arminius*, trans. and ed. James Nichols (Grand Rapids, MI: Baker Book House, 1996), 10–14; cf. *Works of James Arminius* (Buffalo, NY: Derby, Miller and Orton, 1853), 1:479–531.

102. Late in his life, Wesley began publishing a periodical entitled *The Arminian Magazine* as a protest against the predestinarian tendencies of his Calvinistic contemporaries. In 1822 it was renamed *Wesleyan Methodist Magazine*.

103. Herbert B. McGonigle, *Sufficient Saving Grace: John Wesley's Evangelical Arminianism* (Waynesboro, GA: Paternoster Press, 2001), 12, 71–105.

Scholars often consider Wesley's anthropology as eclectic,[104] neither "fully consistent" nor "complete."[105] Most of Wesley's interpreters agree, however, that Wesley accepted the notion of original sin,[106] which he seemed to have understood as an inherited "corruption of nature" that affects "all mankind," and requires "even infants [to be] born again."[107] Wesley saw this corruption as so pervasive that even the "holiest parents beg[a]t unholy children, and [could] not communicate their grace to them as they [did] their nature."[108] Thus he wrote: "Is man by nature filled with all manner of evil? Is he void of all good? Is he wholly fallen? Is his soul totally corrupted? Or, to come back to the text, is 'every imagination of the thoughts of his heart evil continually?' Allow this, and you are so far a Christian. Deny it, and you are but a Heathen still."[109] In his views on human nature, Wesley thus emphatically declared, he was not a "hair's-breadth" away from Calvin.[110] Even though Wesley appeared to be in agreement with the Reformed Tradition on the natural evil state (total depravity) of every human being, he nevertheless asserted that God's grace was also at work from the beginning of life. God extended this grace, which, like Arminius, Wesley termed "preventing grace" (or "prevenient grace"), to every human being, without waiting "for the call of man."[111] It was because of God's love and His

---

104. See Susan Etheridge Willhauck, "John Wesley's View of Children: Foundations for Contemporary Christian Education" (PhD diss., Catholic University of America, 1992), 123.

105. See Richard P. Heitzenrater, "John Wesley and Children," in *The Child in Christian Thought*, 298, 286.

106. Willhauck, "John Wesley's View of Children," 123.

107. John Wesley, *The Doctrine of Original Sin According to Scripture, Reason and Experience In Answer to Dr. Taylor* (New York: The Methodist Episcopal Church in the United States, 1817), 340–341.

108. Ibid., 340.

109. John Wesley, *Original Sin*, Sermon 38.3.2, in *Wesley's Standard Sermons*, vol. 2, ed. Edward H. Sugden (London: The Epworth Press, 1951), 223.

110. John Wesley, "To John Newton," in *John Wesley*, ed. Albert C. Outler (New York: Oxford University Press, 1964), 78.

111. John Wesley, "On Working Out Our Own Salvation" in *The Works of John Wesley*, ed. Albert C. Outler (Nashville: Abingdon Press, 1986), 3:207. Roger Olson defines *prevenient grace* as follows: "it is simply the convicting, calling, enlightening and enabling grace of God that goes before conversion and makes repentance and faith possible," *Arminian Theology*, 35.

prevenient grace that all human beings had the ability to respond to God.[112] Although Wesley's understanding of the nature of humanity has been interpreted in many ways,[113] it appears that he held a belief in original sin "in dynamic tension" with a conviction that God's grace was at work in the life of every human.[114]

Thus while agreeing with the Protestant belief that salvation is *sola gratia et fide,* Arminian theology and, by extension Wesleyan theology, provided a necessary correction to the Calvinistic anthropological pessimism that led the Magisterial Reformers to embrace predestinarianism. While on the one hand both Arminius and Wesley strongly aligned themselves with the Protestant principle of total depravity, they also emphasized God's love and believed in the power of God they labeled as "prevenient grace." This Holy Spirit-driven power first enables genuine human freedom; second, it leads to Christ those who would not resist its appeal to experience His justifying grace; and third, it prompts the justified believers to lead a sanctified life.[115] Thanks to the concept of

---

112. Michael J. Scanlon, "The Christian Anthropology of John Wesley" (PhD diss., Catholic University of America, 1969), 100–101; cf. Wesley, "On Working Out Our Own Salvation," in *The Works of John Wesley,* 207–209.

113. For a detailed examination of Wesley's Christian anthropology, as well as an overview of the many ways it has been interpreted by commentators, see Willhauck, "John Wesley's View of Children," 102–173.

114. Catherine Stonehouse, "Children in Wesleyan Thought," in *Children's Spirituality: Christian Perspectives, Research and Application,* ed. Donald Ratcliffe (Eugene, OR: Cascade, 2004), 140. This same tension is inherent in Wesley's views on baptism and conversion. Although scholars disagree on Wesley's understanding of infant baptism, Wesley himself affirmed and practiced the baptizing of infants. He did not, however, view baptism as necessary for salvation. Rather, Wesley's position was that baptism was the "initiatory sacrament which [sic] enters us into covenant with God;" but being part of the covenant did not automatically secure salvation. Each individual still needed to experience conversion or new birth through justifying faith, Willhauck, "John Wesley's View of Children," 164 and John Wesley, "On Baptism," in *John Wesley,* 319. For Wesley, infant baptism was clearly equivalent to the Jewish rite of circumcision; both required a converted heart, or "inward circumcision," for salvation, Wesley, "On Baptism," *John Wesley,* 322–323. For a detailed discussion of Wesley's views on infant baptism and conversion, see Willhauck, "John Wesley's View of Children," 125–173.

115. While the term *prevenient grace* itself is not found in the New Testament, it is present there conceptually. See, for example, Romans 2:4; 1 Corinthians 15:10; Ephesians 2:4–5; John 1:9; and Titus 2:11.

prevenient grace, therefore, two otherwise seemingly mutually exclusive concepts (according to the Reformed Tradition) could be harmonized: that salvation is *Soli Deo Gloria*, with all of its aspects depending on God's grace (Heb. 12:2), and that humans have genuine freedom of choice and responsibility with regard to their salvation. The Protestant principle of total depravity can therefore be embraced without accepting predestinarianism or denying a possibility of genuine, freewill-driven sanctification.

It is an incontestable fact that, while coming from a variety of Christian denominations, early Sabbatarian Adventists were strongly influenced by Wesleyanism.[116] The most prominent founder of the Seventh-day Adventist Church, Ellen G. White, grew up as a Methodist, and to a significant extent her writings reflect the Arminian/Methodist understanding of sin's impact upon human nature and salvation. While the phrase *prevenient grace* is not found in her writings, the idea clearly permeated her thinking. She thus wrote of total depravity and God's prevenient grace:

> It is impossible for us, of ourselves, to escape from the pit of sin in which we are sunken. Our hearts are evil, and we cannot change them. . . . Education, culture, the exercise of the will, human effort, all have their proper sphere, but here they are powerless. They may produce an outward correctness of behavior, but they cannot change the heart; they cannot purify the springs of life. There must be a power working from within, a new life from above before men can be changed from sin to holiness. That power is Christ. *His grace alone* can quicken the *lifeless faculties of the soul*, and attract it to God, to holiness.[117]

---

116. George Knight, *A Search for Identity: The Development of Seventh-day Adventist Beliefs* (Hagerstown: Review and Herald Publishing Association, 2000), 33–34.

117. Ellen White, *Steps to Christ* (Mountain View, CA: Pacific Press Publishing Association, 1956), 18, emphasis added. In another place White writes of total depravity and prevenient grace: "There is in [every man's] nature a bent to evil, a force which, *unaided*, he cannot resist"; "As through Christ every human being has life, so also through Him every soul receives *some ray of divine light*. Not only intellectual but spiritual power, a perception of right a desire or goodness, exists in every heart," *Education* (Mountain View, CA: Pacific Press Association, 1952), 29, emphasis added. The following excerpt is very specific: the exercise of free will is a gift of God: "Because of their transgression they [Adam and Eve] were sentenced to suffer death, the penalty of sin. But Christ, the propitiation for our sins, declared: 'I will stand in Adam's place. I will take upon myself the penalty of his sin, He shall have another trial. I will secure for him a probation. He shall have the privileges and opportunities of a free man, and be allowed to exercise his God-given power

Note the word "lifeless," which clearly implies "total depravity." On another occasion she wrote of prevenient grace: "The very first step to Christ is taken through the drawing of the Spirit of God; as man responds to this drawing, he advances toward Christ in order that he may repent."[118]

Thus, Ellen White's writings, while firmly grounded in the classical Protestant soteriology with its understanding of sin and its effect on human nature, exhibit an unmistakable affinity with the evangelical Arminianism that she appears to have assimilated through the teachings of her own Wesleyan theological tradition. In agreement with classical Protestant soteriological tradition, she could thus emphatically exclaim *Soli Deo Gloria!* for our salvation in Christ.

---

of choice. I will postpone the day of his arraignment for trial. He shall be bound over to appear at the bar of God in the judgment," White, "Christ the Propitiation for Our Sins," *Atlantic Union Gleaner,* August 19, 1903.

118. Ellen G. White, "Justified by Faith," in *Selected Messages,* vol. 1 (Washington, DC: Review and Herald Publishing Association, 1958), 390.

CHAPTER 6

ORIGIN OF SIN AND SALVATION ACCORDING TO GENESIS 3: A THEOLOGY OF SIN

Jiří Moskala

Humanistic perceptions of evil and of human nature have deeply influenced Christian thinking regarding sin and its effects. Believers can at times be naïve about the nature of sin and may deceive themselves by not seriously considering the power and deceitfulness of sin. Accordingly, sin tends to be understood as a mere mistake, fault, problem, foolishness, error, disease, illness, forgetfulness, or ignorance. In order to perceive the nature of sin clearly, it is necessary to investigate the origin of sin, its nature, and consequences according to God's revelation.[1]

---

1. Insightful studies about sin include: G. C. Berkouwer, *Sin* (Grand Rapids, MI: Eerdmans, 1971); Mark E. Biddle, *Missing the Mark: Sin and Its Consequences in Biblical Theology* (Nashville, TN: Abingdon, 2005); Mark J. Boda, *A Severe Mercy: Sin and Its Remedy in the Old Testament* (Winona Lake, IN: Eisenbrauns, 2009); Iain D. Campbell, *The Doctrine of Sin* (Fearn, Great Britain: Mentor, 1999); Paul Chamberlain, *Can We Be Good Without God?: A Conversation About Truth, Morality, Culture and a Few Other Things That Matter* (Downers Grove, IL: InterVarsity Press, 1996); John M. Fowler, "Sin," in *Handbook of Seventh-day Adventist Theology* (Hagerstown, MD: Review and Herald Publishing Association, 2000), 233–270; Norman R. Gulley, "Preliminary Consideration of the Effects and Implications of Adam's Sin," *Adventist Perspectives* 2, no. 2 (Summer 1988): 28–44; Gulley, *Systematic Theology: Prolegomena* (Berrien Springs, MI: Andrews University Press, 2003), 191–192, 436–441; Chad Meister, *Evil: A Guide for the Perplexed* (New York: Continuum, 2012); Christopher W. Morgan and Robert A. Peterson, *Fallen: A Theology of Sin* (Wheaton, IL: Crossway, 2013).

This biblical-theological study focuses principally on God's Word as revealed in Genesis chapter 3.

ANATOMY OF ORIGINAL SIN AND THE DYNAMICS OF TEMPTATION (GEN. 3:1–6): EXEGETICAL OBSERVATIONS

The biblical explanation of the origin of sin on earth is conveyed in the form of a story. In the Fall account of Genesis 3, the term *sin* does not appear, yet it is the best interpretation of what sin is. This model story is historical, telling what actually happened, but at the same time has a deep symbolic meaning that explains the nature of sin as a paradigm and archetype with its vast consequences.

The biblical narrative regarding original sin[2] presupposes the knowledge of the creation accounts found in Genesis 1–2. According to these accounts, God created the first humans in His image in a pristine state, not marred by evil, and placed them in the Garden of Eden. The first creation story demonstrates that the world was made without a trace of sin by stating six times that everything was "good" (Gen. 1:4, 10, 12, 18, 21, 25). Moreover, after the completion of the physical creation, the creation account culminates with a seventh expression: "God saw all that he had made . . . was very good" (Gen. 1:31).[3] This means that Adam and Eve did not have a corrupted nature and that God had endowed them with the power of free will and choice (Gen. 2:16–17). In addition, the first couple was "naked" (*'arom*), yet without "shame" (Gen. 2:25). This innocence indicates the wholeness of their being, not broken or affected by the presence of sin. Allen Ross summarizes: "They were at ease with one another, without fear of exploitation for evil. . . . *God has prepared human beings, male and female, with the spiritual capacity and communal assistance to serve him and keep his commands so they might live and enjoy the bounty of his*

---

2. In this study, the term *original sin* refers to the first sin of Adam and Eve in the Garden of Eden and does not imply the bearing of the original guilt of the first couple by their posterity. Their offspring are not responsible for their committed sin, even though humans now have a sinful nature resulting from Adam's and Eve's disobedience.

3. Unless otherwise indicated, all Scripture quotations are taken from THE HOLY BIBLE, NEW INTERNATIONAL VERSION®, NIV® Copyright © 1973, 1978, 1984, 2011 by Biblica, Inc.® Used by permission. All rights reserved worldwide.

creation."[4] However, this verse is a springboard text that anticipates the coming change in Genesis 3 that describes how the pre-Fall atmosphere of harmony, peace, love, and joy was abruptly interrupted and marred by sin.

Humans were not only created in a perfect world without guilt, shame, fear, corruption, or death,[5] but the Genesis creation account teaches that they were primarily made for (1) close fellowship with God, (2) a total dependence on Him, and (3) cultivating His presence in their lives.[6] All of this abruptly ended with the first couple's disobedience.

The Fall account also presupposes the existence of Satan, who used the disguise of the serpent's form. Thus chapter 3 begins with the serpent as a known entity to the reader; this is alluded to in the Hebrew by the definite article. The insight into Satan's rebellion against God before humanity's fall into sin is provided in only a few biblical passages (e.g., Job 1:6–13; Isa. 14:12–15; Ezek. 28:11–19).[7]

The account of the Genesis fall begins with three surprises. First, a serpent speaks, a very unusual phenomenon that should have immediately indicated to Eve that this creature was endowed with abnormal and unusual power. Second, the serpent addresses the woman. The text does not explicitly give Adam's location, but the imagery alludes that Eve was curious about the forbidden tree and walked there alone.[8]

---

4. Allen P. Ross, *Creation and Blessings: A Guide to the Study and Exposition of Genesis* (Grand Rapids, MI: Baker Book House, 1988), 127.

5. Jacques B. Doukhan, "When Death Was Not Yet: The Testimony of Biblical Creation," in *The Genesis Creation Account and Its Reverberations in the Old Testament*, ed. Gerald A. Klingbeil (Berrien Springs, MI: Andrews University Press, 2015), 329–342.

6. See my article, "The Sabbath in the First Creation Account" in *Journal of the Adventist Theological Society* 13, no. 1 (Spring 2002): 55–66.

7. We will not engage in a discussion about the identification of the serpent in the Garden of Eden but presuppose that he was used as a medium by Satan, our adversary of salvation, as it is biblically documented (Job 1:7–9; 2:2; Matt. 4:1–11; Luke 4:5–8; 10:18; John 8:44; 2 Cor. 11:3; 1 Tim. 2:14; 1 John 3:8; Rev. 12:7–12; 20:2). For an outstanding exegetical and theological discussion on the identification of the serpent in the Fall account of Genesis 3 and the Fall and role of Satan before humanity's disobedience, see José M. Bertoluci, *The Son of the Morning and the Guardian Cherub in the Context of the Controversy between Good and Evil* (ThD diss., Andrews University, 1985).

8. This is not contradicted by the fact that "she also gave some to her husband, who was with her" (Gen. 3:6). The preposition "with" (*'im* in Hebrew) here means "whom she belonged to." There are two prepositions in Hebrew with the meaning "with": one is *'et* and

Third, the serpent knows exactly what God said previously in the Garden of Eden (Gen. 2:16–17) and directly contradicts His command. He engages in deceptive activity even though he never forces Adam or Eve to eat the forbidden fruit. The fall narrative records the targeted statement of the serpent (i.e., Satan) when he probes the woman: "Did God really say, 'You must not eat from any tree in the garden'" (Gen. 3:1)?[9] Satan thus opens his discourse with Eve by establishing doubt regarding God's word and authority. If one takes this sentence as declarative, it has the sense of questioning God's command and authority with an even greater force. Accordingly, Speiser states: "The serpent is not asking a question; he is deliberately distorting a fact."[10] Thus one needs to ask, What was the purpose of this first emphatic question recorded in the Bible and expressed as a powerful attack against God?

The best way to discover the actual aim of Satan's utterance is to compare it with God's previous command. In the beginning, the Creator gave two commandments: the first was positive and the second negative (Gen. 2:16–17). He first created free space for humans, because the Lord is the author of ultimate freedom: "You are free to eat from any tree in the garden." He thus created Adam and Eve as free moral beings. In order to enjoy their freedom, humans needed to accept the boundaries and limits of freedom. This is why He gave the restriction, the second command: "You must not eat from the tree of the knowledge of good and evil." The gift of freedom presupposes choice and free will. To retain their freedom, they also needed to respect the boundaries imposed by God. By accepting the limits of freedom, they were free; they had a safe space in which they could grow and develop all their potential, true humanity, and the image of God in which they were created.

Satan's goal was more than simply an invitation to dialogue. He wanted to accomplish more than to create doubt. Doubt would certainly come as a

---

the second is *'im*. The first preposition stresses space (standing by, being in close proximity to someone); however, the second is a more relational preposition in addition to meaning accompaniment, thus underlying closeness and relationship.

9. Umberto Cassuto, *A Commentary on the Book of Genesis [Part One]: From Adam to Noah* (Jerusalem: The Magnes Press, 1989), 144.

10. E. A. Speiser, *Genesis: Introduction, Translation, and Notes*, The Anchor Bible Series (Garden City, New York: Doubleday, 1981), 23.

result of his tactics when suspicions were born. Satan could succeed in his intrigue only when he was able to create a skewed picture of God! Thus, his primary goal was to paint a false image of God, suggest a wrong impression of His character and intentions, and thus impregnate Eve's mind with erroneous thinking about God. Satan was well aware that if he succeeded here and gained victory over Eve's thoughts, he would win the entire war, because spiritual life directly depends on a correct mental picture of God. Thus, Satan knew where to strike first: against God's character of love. The anatomy of the first sin begins with this attempt to create a false picture of God.[11]

Instead of abandoning the conversation (the only proper reaction; cf. Gen. 39:12), Eve tried to defend God. However, in defending God, Eve did not quote Him correctly. She altered His words slightly, and her interpretation of the divine statements created a trap for her. Her small modifications provide some hints to the reader of what may have been going on in the mind of Eve.

The dialogue between the serpent and Eve was "the first conversation about God."[12] Walter Brueggemann excellently explains: "God is treated as a third person. God is not a party to the discussion but is the involved object of the discussion. This is not speech *to* God or *with* God, but *about* God. God has been objectified."[13] Phyllis Trible underlines: "The serpent and the woman discuss theology. They talk about God," but "only using the appellative God, they establish that distance which characterizes objectivity and invites disobedience."[14]

It is noteworthy that by referring to the divine Person only as God (Elohim) instead of speaking about Him in a personal way with His proper covenant name, the Lord (Yahweh), Eve is distancing herself from her

---

11. Satan repeats the same strategy in the Garden of Eden that he used against God in heaven. He leads humans to sin by "the same misrepresentation of the character of God as he had practiced in heaven, causing Him to be regarded as severe and tyrannical," Ellen G. White, *The Great Controversy* (Mountain View, CA: Pacific Press, 1950), 500.

12. Dietrich Bonhoeffer, *Creation and Fall: A Theological Interpretation of Genesis 1–3* (London: Collins, 1959), 70.

13. Walter Brueggemann, *Genesis Interpretation: A Bible Commentary for Teaching and Preaching* (Atlanta, GA: John Knox Press, 1982), 48.

14. Phyllis Trible, *God and the Rhetoric of Sexuality* (Philadelphia, PA: Fortress, 1985), 109.

Creator.[15] Eve also makes four changes to the Lord's explicit command. First, instead of stressing their freedom to eat and enjoy every fruit of "any" tree in the Garden of Eden, she mentions that they "may eat fruit from the trees in the garden." Second, instead of speaking about the nature of the forbidden tree ("the tree of the knowledge of good and evil"), she points to its geographical location ("which is in the middle of the garden"). For her, this forbidden tree has become the most important tree, the center and focus of her attention.[16] Third, she adds to God's words about the forbidden fruit: "We cannot even touch it." Undoubtedly, this is a correct interpretation of what the Lord said, because if one cannot eat the forbidden fruit, then such a person certainly should not come close to admire, smell, or touch it. But when she exaggerates and adds these words, she may suddenly realize that her empirical experience (what she sees with her own eyes) contradicts God's word ("when you eat of it you will surely die"), because the serpent is on the tree, touching the fruit, and is not dying.[17] By contrast, the serpent is alive and has the extraordinary ability to speak. The fourth, minute but significant alteration relates to God's statement: "You will surely die." She downplays this command by stating simply: "You will die," omitting the crucial emphatic word "surely." This is a textual signal that Eve began to question the certainty of death after disobedience.[18]

---

15. It is significant that the serpent, as well as Eve, does not speak about God in a personal, relational term as the Lord (Yahweh), but simply as the transcendent God (Elohim), indicated in the conversation of Genesis 3:1–5. This type of description is understandable for Satan because there is no close or covenantal relationship between him and God (as the usage of the proper name the Lord would presuppose). However, the lack of employment of the name Yahweh in Eve's reaction to the serpent's question is surprisingly missing, because chapters 2–3 consistently use the term *Lord* for God (except in the dialogue between the serpent and Eve), which may indicate that Eve lightens the personal aspect of her relationship with the Lord.

16. Umberto Cassuto aptly comments: "Her interest is focused at the moment on the *forbidden tree*, and for her it is *the tree*—with the definite article—in the center of the garden," *Commentary on the Book of Genesis*, 145.

17. The biblical story creates the imagery that the serpent is on the tree and touching or eating fruit, even though it is not stated explicitly. The text makes this assumption by the flow of the event and does not provide a detailed description of everything. Cf., with Ellen G. White, *Patriarch and Prophets* (Nampa, ID: Pacific Press, 2005), 54–56.

18. The Hebrew language contains a special grammatical syntactical structure when the infinitive absolute stands before its cognate verb. In this case, it serves to intensify or

Thus, the next step in the anatomy of the first sin was the apparent contradiction between empirical experience and the Word of God. This deepened her doubts and built distrust. Only after this situation transpired was the serpent able to come with a full frontal attack that would completely oppose what the Creator stated. The Lord said: "In the day you will eat, *you will surely die*," and Satan boldly contradicts: "If you will eat *you will not surely die*!" Satan uses the same syntactical structure as God Himself in order to give certainty to his categorical statement, but reversing it with a forceful "not," and putting this negation in front of the entire construction, thus literally saying, "not—you will surely die." The conversation began with a subtle quasi-question regarding God's prohibition, transforming to a complete "denial of the consequences of disobedience."[19] Thus, Satan categorically denied the penalty for sin and promised a false immortality. Eve now faced a critical decision—whom would she trust, God or the serpent? Should she follow the word of the Lord or the other word?

This was an opportunity for the serpent to act on his own interpretation. With his cardinal attack, he brought two offers: (1) your eyes will be opened, and (2) you will be like God, knowing good and evil. If only they would eat the forbidden fruit, the serpent insisted, they would not die but would be like God, knowing good and evil. This specific gain would elevate them to a higher level of existence. Satan subtly suggested that the forbidden fruit possessed a unique power similar to the fruit from the tree of life, which would give them access to the unknown and mysterious.

Satan also claimed that he knew of God's motivation for the prohibition not to eat from the tree of the knowledge of good and evil: "For God knows that when you eat from it your eyes will be opened, and you will be like God, knowing good and evil" (Gen. 3:5). He pictured God as a jealous, selfish, self-centered, and self-contained Deity, who retained ultimate good only for Himself. Ross eloquently explains: "Adam and Eve lived in a setting that God himself had pronounced 'good.' Yet they were now led to believe that there was greater good held back from them, that somehow they could elevate life

---

reinforce the verbal idea. This strengthening is expressed in English translations with words like *surely, verily,* or *indeed.* See *Gesenius' Hebrew Grammar,* 2nd ed., ed. and enl. E. Kautzsch and A. E. Cowley (Oxford: Clarendon Press, 1910), 342–343. Eve does not use this syntactical construction, and thus the statement does not look so strict and severe.

19. Ross, *Creation and Blessings,* 135.

for better. . . . In raising doubt about God's integrity, the serpent motivated them to sin with the promise of divinity. The idea of becoming like God had an appeal that was almost irresistible."[20] In their rationalization they fell into the temptation of divinization. They desired what did not belong to them, to get what they never could obtain or should ever be.

Verse 6 reveals that Eve engaged in incorrect meditation, perception of reality, and thinking about the forbidden fruit (the Hebrew text uses the term *ra'ah*, "see"). Eve was not previously blind; this verb suggests an intense inner struggle and intellectual activity. In her thinking she "saw" that eating from the forbidden tree was profitable on three levels: "good for food," "delight of the eyes," and "desirable to gain wisdom."[21] Eve observed the forbidden fruit, thought about it, and then made her decision. Satan seemingly promised a so-far unexperienced pleasure, a great future, and superior knowledge. He appealed to the physical, emotional, and spiritual dimensions of life, and a forbidden fruit was now associated with beauty and wisdom. "Eve's reflection concentrates on the potential good of the fruit and ignores the evil that there is in disobedience."[22]

When Eve lost the true picture of a loving and caring God, doubts about His word were cultivated, apparent contradictions were met without an answer, and offers were mentally accepted; then "she took it and ate." Mistrust brought fruit—a visible act of disobedience. When a loving relationship is broken, the word/law of God is broken. Note that Eve, and later Adam, were not forced by Satan to eat the forbidden fruit or to disobey. The choice to do so was their deliberate action. Adam and Eve faced a dilemma—who is right, who is to be trusted? God and His word—or the serpent (self, their own eyes, feelings, experience)? Behind the struggle and agony of this decision lies a foundational issue, namely, whether God can be trusted. Thus, at the core of every temptation lies the basic question: Whom will I trust? Misunderstanding God's character produces wrong thinking that leads to poor choices and false decisions, followed by the tangible act of disobedience.

---

20. Ibid., 136.

21. A similar statement is in 1 John 2:16, which speaks of the trilogy of sin in the following terms: the desire of the flesh, the desire of the eyes, and the pride of life (cf. Ezek. 16:49–58; Sir. 23:4–5).

22. Ross, *Creation and Blessings,* 136.

DEFINITIONS OF SIN

Sin is described in Genesis 3 primarily in theological and relational terms as it is aimed against God the Creator and what He represents. A colorful wide-ranging terminology for sin in the Bible reveals its devastating nature. The rich biblical vocabulary demonstrates the complexity of sin. In Hebrew there is a trilogy of the main terms for sin—the strongest biblical language consists of the following terms: *hattah* (the most common term for sin in the sense of missing the target, deviating from the right way, or going astray from a straight path; the Greek word *hamartia* expresses the same idea); *avon* (transgression, something that is bent, twisted, or crooked); and *peshah* (rebellion, revolt). God forgives all of these variants of sin and trespasses mentioned in crucial passages of the Hebrew Scriptures (Exod. 34:6; Lev. 16:21; Ps. 32:1–2; Isa. 53:5–6, 8–12; Dan. 9:24). Besides these three main Hebrew words for sin, the Bible contains additional terms that describe the complexity of sin and of our sinful nature. Additional vocabulary includes evil, guilt, wickedness, trespass, impurity, deceit, dishonesty, falsehood, offense, abomination, desecration, perversion, unrighteousness, error, injustice, arrogance, failure, and so on.[23]

One may summarize this explicit biblical terminology that describes the vast array of the sin problem in five main definitions of sin that are all built and expanded upon in the theology of sin presented in Genesis 3:

Sin, according to Genesis 3, is a broken relationship with God; it is an attempt to live an independent and autonomous life apart from God (from Greek *autos* "self," and *nomos* "law," i.e., to be a law for oneself), a life without God, His authority, His law, and separated from Him. Sin is thus de-creation, the undoing of God's creation. Sin reverses all three foundational functions and purposes of life for which humanity was created according to the Genesis

---

23. "One may count over fifty words for 'sin' in biblical Hebrew, if specific as well as generic terms are isolated," David Noel Freedman, et al., eds., *The Anchor Bible Dictionary* (New York: Doubleday, 1992), 6:31. There are seven main Greek words that describe the plethora of sin in the New Testament: *hamartia, paraptoma, parakoe, adikia, asebeia, kakia,* and *opheiletes.* For details on the biblical Hebrew and Greek terminology on sin and the concept and understanding of sin, see *The Anchor Bible Dictionary,* 6:31–47; Geoffrey W. Bromiley, et al., eds., *The International Standard Bible Encyclopedia* (Grand Rapids, MI: William B. Eerdmans Publishing Company, 1979), 4:518–525; George Arthur Buttrick, et al., eds., *The Interpreter's Dictionary of the* Bible (Nashville, TN: Abingdon Press, 1962), 4:361–376.

account. Sin severs humanity's closeness to God, destroys a trusting fellowship, and alienates humanity from the Lord's presence. Thus, evil destroys the basic qualities of life, separates the individual from God, and isolates humanity from Him. A person living in sin does not trust God, decides by his or her own authority what is right or wrong, and is a law to himself or herself. Sin comes as a result of refusing God's authority and an unwillingness to acknowledge Him as the Creator to whom one must be accountable. God's law is first broken in the mind and then in behavior. Thus, sin is mistrust or disbelief in God; it is a state of mind that directly rejects God's law.[24] This quest for autonomy leads to separation from God and His presence. Ted Peters excellently expresses this reality: "At the heart or essence of all sin is the failure to trust God. Sin is our unwillingness to acknowledge our creatureliness and dependence upon the God of grace."[25]

This crucial definition of sin leads theologians to differentiate between sin and sins by stating that sins derive from the basic understanding of sin as a broken relationship with God. Sin is thus something more than an action; it is an attitude and rebellion against God, His command, and His values. It is present where people love themselves more than God and His creation. Such an attitude leads to visible, concrete, sinful actions (Ezek. 18:5–9, 11–13, 15–17; 22:1–12; 33:25–26; Matt. 15:18–19; Gal. 5:19–21; Col. 3:5–9; Rev. 22:15).[26] The difference between the sin and sins is similar to the difference between the root and the fruit. All other biblical explanations of sin spring from this foundational understanding of sin provided in the Fall narrative.

Another well-known biblical definition of sin, firmly rooted in Genesis 3, is found in the writings of the Apostle John: sin is a breaking of the law (1 John 3:4; Greek word *anomia* literally means "lawlessness"), a concrete act of disobedience. It is a visible result of a broken relationship, an outcome of wrong

---

24. Ellen G. White keenly defines the first sin of Adam and Eve in the Garden of Eden as "distrust of God's goodness, disbelief of His word, and rejection of His authority, that made our first parents transgressors, and that brought into the world a knowledge of evil," *Education*, 25. The nature of sin is thus explained by the concept of a broken relationship and a hostile state of mind toward God.

25. Ted Peters, *Sin: Radical Evil in Soul and Society* (Grand Rapids, MI: Eerdmans, 1998), 8.

26. George Knight, *I Used to be Perfect: A Study of Sin and Salvation*, 2nd ed. (Berrien Springs, MI: Andrews University Press, 2001), 18–24; Peters, *Sin: Radical Evil in Soul and Society*, 23–24.

thinking, an effect of broken faith, and a product of mistrust. God's question, "Have you eaten from the tree that I commanded you not to eat from?" (Gen. 3:11), revealed that disobedience is the result of disrespecting God's commandment. In this way, sin is defiant, arrogant rebellion against God and a proud rejection of His word, will, and authority. Living in sin means living without focusing on God and fulfilling His will. Thus, sin is understood as an external deed or action.

Third, sin is a state in which humans are born. This is already reflected in Genesis 5:1–3, which states that Adam was created in God's image, but Seth was born in the image of Adam, his father. The difference between Adam created in God's image (Gen. 1:26–27) and Seth made in Adam's image (Gen. 5:3) can be explained by the event that brought this change: the Fall that Genesis 3 describes. After Adam and Eve sinned, human nature became corrupted, and their posterity was born with a sinful nature. David states plainly: "Surely I was sinful at birth, sinful from the time my mother conceived me" (Ps. 51:5). Also in Psalm 58:3, David speaks about the wrong attitude of wicked people toward God: "Even from birth the wicked go astray; from the womb they are wayward, spreading lies." The sinner does not consider God when making life decisions. "All humanity's righteous acts are like filthy rags" (Isa. 64:6); human hearts are perverted and deceptive (Jer. 17:9). Humans are not able to change their nature, just as a leopard cannot change its skin (Jer. 13:23). Without exception, all are born sinners (Eccl. 7:20; Rom. 3:23; 1 John 1:8), naturally afraid and alienated from God (Gen. 3:10; Eph. 2:1, 12, 19).[27]

The Apostle Paul clearly explains: "I do not understand what I do. For what I want to do I do not do, but what I hate I do. And if I do what I do not want to do . . . it is sin living in me. I know that nothing good lives in me, that is in my sinful nature [literally "in my flesh"]. For I have the desire to do what is good, but I cannot carry it out. For what I do is not the good I wanted to do; no, the evil I do not want to do—this I keep on doing. Now if I do what I do not want to do, it is no longer I who do it, but it is sin living in me that does it" (Rom. 7:15–20). This passage clarifies that sin lies at the core of human nature. While being a human in itself is not sinful, human beings are born with a sinful nature, and consequently born as sinners separated from God and in need of salvation. As sinners, they love and produce sin, and their sinful nature is

---

27. Only Jesus was born as "the holy One" (Luke 1:35); all humans are born hostile to God (Rom. 8:7), alienated from Him, and dead in their sin (Ps. 51:5; Eph. 2:1–3).

characterized by selfishness, tendencies to evil, propensities to sin, and inclinations to do wrong. The power of sin enslaves humans (Rom. 5:6; 6:6–7, 14; 7:25). As an apple tree bears apples and the fig tree figs, so sinners produce sin because the whole person is affected and corrupted by sin.

In his epistle, James underlines the same truth when he explains that sin begins with the inner cravings, the "evil desire" that lies within. When the desire is cultivated, a person reaches for the forbidden fruit, which produces sin. Unless cherished, this wrong desire is not yet sin, but when it is yielded to, it leads to wrong actions and death. Wrong thinking and imagination urge the individual to have what he or she seemingly lacks; by yielding to the urge, sin is thus accomplished (James 1:14–15). Humans are not culpable for this sinful tendency and propensity to sin rooted in their nature, but this fact places them under condemnation and alienation toward God (John 3:36; Eph. 2:1–3). Humans sin because they are sinners, marked by wrong thinking and orientation. They are guilty when they play and associate with these evil desires.

Fourth, sin is a neglect to do good, an omission to do what is right (James 4:17), an attitude of indifference. This attitude can also be called apathy or lukewarmness (Rev. 3:15–18). It is not enough not to do wrong. Sin of omission leads to sin of commitment, to incorrect actions or non-action. Christianity is not only about avoiding wrong, although this is included (James 1:27), but true religion is about doing what is good, right, and profitable (Mic. 6:8; John 5:29; Tit. 3:8; James 1:27; cf. Phil. 4:5–6). It is not enough to simply confess faith; good deeds are important (Gal. 5:4; James 1:27; 1 Pet. 2:9; Eph. 2:10). However, good deeds are not the cause, but the result and fruit of salvation. Obedience and good works are not important for building the highway to heaven (all are saved by God's grace through faith in Christ Jesus), but for the salvation of other people (Matt. 5:16). They are also crucial to show believers whether they are consistent in their faith, if they are living lives of integrity, and if their faith is a living faith (James 2:14, 17, 20, 26). To know the truth and practice it should always go hand in hand.

And fifth, sin constitutes not believing in Jesus Christ, because He is the only solution to human sinfulness (John 16:8–9). Humans cannot help themselves, cure the problem of sin, and heal their own brokenness. Christ is the only and unique Savior of the world (Acts 4:12; 16:31; Rom. 8:1; 1 John 5:12–13). Sin is disbelief in Jesus, a refusal of His saving activity on our behalf because He is the only One who can rescue us from bondage to sin. In other words, no one will be condemned to eternal death at the last judgment because he or she is a sinner (the reality is that all are sinners, all have all sinned—Eccl. 7:20; Rom. 3:23; 1 John 1:8), but because the person does not repent and refuses to accept Jesus as the solution to his or her sinfulness. To fail to accept Jesus as one's personal Savior, to choose to remain in sin, is fatal (Prov. 24:16; John 3:36).

CONSEQUENCES OF SIN ACCORDING TO GENESIS 3

The modern world is dominated by evil and sinful behavior. The world is incurably sick. The presence of evil brings terrible results to the human race. Genesis 3 not only explains how paradise was lost, but also presents the consequences of disobedience and how God reacts to transgression of His command.

After the sin of Adam and Eve, the imagery in Genesis 3 changes. Shame, guilt, fear, degradation, and humiliation suddenly appear. The brightness of life changes to darkness. Brueggemann comments: "What had been a story of trust and obedience (chapter 2) now becomes an account of *crime and punishment* (3:1–7)."[28] Sin is a curse that brings terrible consequences. Like an avalanche, it begins seemingly as nothingness, but then breaks and tears down everything that is beautiful, valuable, and meaningful, completely destroying life. Sin disrupts meaningful relationships, causing misery, suffering, separation, and complications. What was originally very good is now corrupted and marred by sin. Genesis 3 mentions the multiple consequences of sin:

Sin/disobedience opened the eyes of the first couple, showing them their nakedness. Upon eating the forbidden fruit, Satan suggested that their "eyes will be opened" (Gen. 3:5), and following their disobedience, the narrator states that "the eyes of both of them were opened" (Gen. 3:7). Yet, their eyes were opened differently than they had contemplated. In this deception, Adam and Eve actually lost what they had and realized that they were naked. They began to perceive the reality of life differently after losing their innocence (Gen. 3:7). Not only did they lose their garment of light,[29] but after the break in

---

28. Brueggemann, *Genesis: A Bible Commentary*, 48.

29. Genesis 2:25 does not explicitly indicate in what manner Adam and Eve were without clothes, but the semantic range of *'arom* in connection with Psalm 104:1–2 suggests that the original "garments" of Adam and Eve were "garments of light and glory," Richard M. Davidson, *Flame of Yahweh: Sexuality in the Old Testament* (Peabody, MA: Hendrickson Publishers, 2007), 56; cf., Jacques B. Doukhan, *The Literary Structure of the Genesis Creation*

their relationship with God, their very nature became corrupted. The broken relationship with God led to a broken relationship with "self."

When Adam and Eve saw their nakedness, they realized and felt for the first time their sense of shame and guilt. They felt miserable and experienced remorse of conscience (2:25; 3:7). Adam's and Eve's nakedness refers to more than a physical bodily exposure. Genesis 3:7 and 10 reveal that when God appeared in the Garden of Eden, Adam and Eve were no longer physically naked because they were covered with fig leaves (v. 7), yet Adam stated, "I was afraid, because I was naked" (v. 10). They were "clothed" but still naked. Thus, this nakedness was greater than a physical phenomenon. As a result of their broken relationship with God, their nature was broken and their posterity would inherit the same sinful nature, a nature corrupted by sin, with its propensities, inclinations to evil, and tendency to sin (Gen. 3:7, 10; 5:1–3; 6:5). This means that every part of each human being is corrupted by sin; the whole person is lost and cannot be saved without God's redemptive activity.

For the first time, Adam and Eve felt intense shame, and their covering made from fig leaves could not help them. The term *'erom* used in Genesis 3 denotes elsewhere in the Old Testament a shameful exposure of nakedness (Deut. 28:48; Ezek. 16:7, 22, 39; 18:7, 16; 23:29), which they tried to cover with fig leaves (3:7). Victor Hamilton correctly clarifies their attempt as a self-justifying act: "Rather than driving them back to God, their guilt leads them into a self-atoning, self-protecting procedure: they must cover themselves."[30] Their covering activity can be theologically characterized as "righteousness by works."

The nakedness after sin signifies inner nakedness, being unmasked, a consciousness of guilt, total shame, loss of integrity, feelings of degradation, defeat, ruined innocence, and the disappearance of light. Gordon Wenham rightly asserts: "A more complete transformation could not be imagined. The trust of innocence is replaced by the fear of guilt."[31] The first sin deeply affected human

---

Story, Andrews University Doctoral Dissertation Series 5 (Berrien Springs, MI: Andrews University Press, 1978), 83–90.

30. Victor P. Hamilton, *The Book of Genesis: Chapters 1–17,* The New International Commentary on the Old Testament Series (Grand Rapids, MI: Eerdmans, 1990), 191.

31. Gordon J. Wenham, *Genesis 1–15,* vol. 1, Word Biblical Commentary Series (Waco, TX: Word Books, 1987), 76.

nature. While the traces of God's image in humans remained, they became lost, broken, alienated, and condemned to death. Love for sin and inclinations to evil became superposed on them and an integral part of their human nature.

Sin/disobedience caused Adam and Eve to fear God. Instead of enjoying God's presence and rejoicing in His company, they hid from Him. Their disobedience, resulting from a broken vertical relationship with God, caused their separation from Him (Gen. 3:10). They hid in shame, guilt, and fear. Consequently, all human beings are now born with an alienated and antagonistic attitude toward God and are naturally afraid of Him (Eph. 2:1–3).

Sin/disobedience led Adam and Eve to blame each other for their failure (the horizontal dimension of life was broken). They now experienced a broken relationship with each other (Gen. 3:12; 4:5–8). Sin thus alienates people from one another: "But something in them and between them *does* die. Their sense of themselves and their relationship with each other is shattered."[32] "Sin has undermined both the sense of self and the sense of belonging to another."[33] Sinners refuse to accept accountability for their wrong behavior. Eve blamed the serpent for the seduction. Adam not only blamed Eve for giving him the forbidden fruit, but actually blamed God Himself because it was God who gave her to him. Self-vindication causes one to find fault beyond, and not within, oneself.

Sin/disobedience brought death because the relationship with real life was broken (Gen. 2:17; 3:3, 19; cf. Rom. 6:23). Adam and Eve would return to dust, the symbol of fragility and death: "until you return to the ground, since from it you were taken; for dust you are and to dust you will return" (Gen. 3:19). Death was not a primary theme in Genesis 2, even though it was mentioned by God (Gen. 2:17), because the God of creation is about life and abundance. Death "was not a threat but a candid acknowledgment of a *boundary* of life. But the boundary is now altered to become a *threat*. It is transformed into a terror which puts everything in question. It is not God, but the serpent who has made death a primary human agenda."[34]

Sin/disobedience would make giving birth and raising children a painful experience (Gen. 3:16).

---

32. Craig G. Bartholomew and Michael W. Goheen, *The Drama of Scripture: Finding Our Place in the Biblical Story* (Grand Rapids, MI: Baker Academic, 2014), 41.

33. Bartholomew and Goheen, *The Drama of Scripture*, 43.

34. Brueggemann, *Genesis: A Bible Commentary*, 48.

Sin/disobedience would make marriage a place of fighting for dominance and supremacy instead of a loving, caring, emotional, and intimate relationship between equal heterosexual partners (Gen. 3:16).

Sin/disobedience would make work a painful experience (Gen. 3:18). Sweat and tiredness would become part of that endeavor.[35]

Sin/disobedience broke the relationship with nature. The ground would produce thorns and thistles, and it would be exploited and corrupted (Gen. 3:18; 6:11).

Sin/disobedience would bring violence, pain, hatred, polygamy, and so on. Everything good, meaningful, and beautiful became corrupted by sin (Gen. 6:11–13) as evidenced by the subsequent Genesis narratives.

Sin/disobedience blinded people. One of the terrible characteristics of sin is that sinners tend to deny their real condition, and signs of lostness are not often discerned and accepted. Sin leads to the denial of truth about one's own sinfulness.

In his outstanding study of sin, Ted Peters describes the progressive nature of sin in its logical pattern (not so much in its chronological order). He points out the path toward the radical nature of evil, which he defines as "evil pursued in the name of evil"[36] and explains the evolution of evil in the following seven steps: (1) anxiety, (2) unfaith, (3) pride, (4) concupiscence, (5) self-justification, (6) cruelty, and finally (7) blasphemy.[37] He describes the last step of blasphemy or radical evil not so much as "the defilement of God's name," but rather as "the misuse of divine symbols . . . to prevent the communication of God's grace."[38]

GOD'S SOLUTION

Hope appears in Genesis 3 against all hopelessness. In the midst of darkness, disobedience, despair, judgment, and condemnation, God secures

---

35. However, troublesome work was a blessing in disguise, a means for stopping the avalanche of evil and a learning process in how to do what was right and to help develop character. We need to realize that certain punishments described in Genesis 3 "were also promises of future relief," Ross, *Creation and Blessings,*142.

36. Peters, *Sin: Radical Evil in Soul and Society,* 9.

37. Ibid., 10–17.

38. Ibid., 16.

humanity's future despite the fact that Adam and Eve do not deserve to live. Sin cannot be undone, the clock cannot be turned back, and reality cannot be reversed. However, the solution to the problem of sin comes from God Himself: "Salvation comes from the LORD" (Jon. 2:9; Ps. 27:1; Isa. 12:2). Covenant theology is the key to the theology of sin and salvation. "The Eden Narrative speaks of a radical choice, a choice between obedience and disobedience to the divine commandment."[39] Ross states: "Sinful rebellion against God brings pain, conflict, and death; but confession to God ensures God's gracious provisions."[40] However, God's grace precedes human repentance and change. The Lord always takes the first step and is the Initiator of our salvation. God confronts evil and responds to it as the loving Creator and gracious Judge. "The scene becomes a trial."[41] He did not abandon or destroy Adam and Eve in their sin. On the contrary, He is in search of humanity. God is on His way to find them.

There are at least seven indicators of God's saving activities in regard to humanity according to Genesis 3.

1. God comes to Adam and Eve with grace. He cries for His lost and missing children: "Where are you?" (Gen. 3:9). Because of divine and undeserved grace streaming from Calvary, they could live (Rev. 13:8). Sinners are lost; however, God graciously calls all sinners back to Himself as He called Adam and Eve (e.g., Isa. 45:22; Ezek. 18:31–32; Joel 2:12–14). This principle is revealed in the Bible from the very beginning—humans sin, but God takes the initiative and invites them back to Himself. Humans thus respond to God's amazing, prevailing grace, and His goodness leads people to repentance (Rom. 2:4). God's first question is an invitation of grace, an expression of His deep love in search of humanity that simultaneously reveals God's judgment (see Exod. 34:6–7; John 3:16; Rom. 5:8; 2 Cor. 5:21).[42]

---

39. Tryggve N. D. Mettinger, *The Eden Narrative: A Literary and Religio-historical Study of Genesis 2–3* (Warsaw, IN: Eisenbrauns, 2007), 52.

40. Ross, *Creation and Blessings,* 150.

41. Brueggemann, *Genesis: A Bible Commentary,* 49; Claus Westermann, *Genesis 1–11, A Continental Commentary* (Minneapolis, MN: Fortress Press, 1994), 252–255.

42. God's question: "Where are you?" had a multiple purpose: (1) an invitation to dialogue; (2) an offer of grace (God did not appear to kill them, but to provide a very costly solution to their new situation as sinners; Gen. 3:15; Rev. 13:8; Eph. 1:4; 1 Pet. 1:20); (3) help for them to realize their position/attitude toward God (instead of enjoying His presence, they

2. God provides a real garment (Gen. 3:21). Because the nakedness of the first couple was more than a physical phenomenon, so it follows analogically that the garment represents more than a physical dress. There is a contrast in the biblical text between "they made" and "He made." What Adam and Eve could not do for themselves in covering their guilt and shame, God did for them. He gave them a garment of skin and thus covers sinners with the garment of His righteousness (1 Cor. 1:30; 2 Cor. 5:21; Rev. 7:14; 22:14). He sacrificed the first animal in order to provide the solution for their sin problem in view of the Messiah (Rev. 13:8; Eph. 1:4; 1 Pet. 1:20).[43] Forgiveness and their redemption was secured through God's gracious sacrifice represented by the death of the animal whose skin they were wearing.[44]

3. God creates enmity between the powers of good and evil (Gen. 3:15a) in the context of spiritual warfare. This theme of the great controversy introduces the imagery of war and tension. Because as sinners we love sin, God helps humans by introducing enmity toward evil and enables them to hate evil.

4. God promises to send the Seed (Gen. 3:15b) who will do for humans what they cannot do for themselves: He will defeat their enemy, Satan. God's statement to the serpent lies at the center of chiastic literary structure of chapter 3.[45] The Messiah will become humanity's Redeemer and Savior; His victorious deliberate death will ultimately destroy Satan and consequently everyone and everything associated with him. The Messiah is the Victor

---

were now hiding from Him); and (4) a trial/investigative judgment, because they were accountable for their past actions to God as their Creator. God is presented here as their Judge.

43. The word *tunic* and the specific Hiphil form of the verb *wayyalbishem*, translated as "clothed," belongs to sanctuary language, specifically referring to the dress of the priests (Exod. 28:41; 29:8; 40:14; Lev. 8:13). In our text, the reference to "skin" implies that an animal had been sacrificed. The ritual of sacrifice was instituted then, with all "the awareness of substitutionary atonement," Richard M. Davidson, "The Theology of Sexuality in the Beginning: Genesis 3," *Andrews University Seminary Studies* 26, no. 2 (1988): 127.

44. The garments of skin God gave to the first couple symbolize the righteousness of God that is given to sinners as a free gift of God's grace accepted through faith. Adam and Eve did not ask for the garment, God provided it for them (Gen. 3:21). This reference to skin alludes to the first sacrifice in view of the fact that it was the skin of an animal.

45. Afolarin O. Ojewole, *The Seed in Genesis 3:15: An Exegetical and Intertextual Study,* Adventist Theological Dissertation Series (Berrien Springs, MI: Adventist Theological Society, 2002), 98.

and gives victory to all who connect with Him (Rom. 8:1–4). The final victory is assured by Him (Rev. 12:7–12; 19:6–7, 15–21; Jude 24–25). Thus, God has the solution to the problem of sin, but this solution is very costly, demanding, painful, and full of suffering despite the fact that it is a decisive and victorious action. God did not leave humans to the power of evil. He would step down, and as a promised Seed, defeat the enemy even though He knew it would cost Him His life. He deliberately died for humankind. "God does not give up his purposes for his creation and his kingdom. Though Adam and Eve flee from him, God graciously takes the initiative to seek them out. . . . The woman's offspring will crush the serpent's head—in other words, God promises to extinguish the evil forces Adam and Eve have unleashed. This is the first biblical promise of the gospel: Christ is to be woman's offspring and will defeat Satan, though at great cost to himself, as the serpent 'will strike his heel.'"[46] Norman Geisler underlines in a summary statement: "God *desires* to restore man to a vital personal relationship with Himself through man's faith in God through the death of Jesus Christ for man's sin."[47] Jesus Christ came to earth to reveal the true character of His Father because the image of God was radically distorted among people, as well as to unmask and destroy Satan (John 17:6; 1 John 3:8). Christ is the second Adam (1 Cor. 15:45) as well as the Seed of the woman (Gal. 3:16–19; 4:4; cf. Dan. 9:24–27). Victory over evil comes only through the Seed's ultimate sacrifice, humility, and unselfish service; humans add nothing to this offering. He takes upon Himself the entirety of the curse of disobedience (Gal. 3:13). The main motifs of Genesis 3 such as "toil, sweat, thorns, the conflict, the tree, death, dust, and the seed—all will be reflected in the experience of the Christ."[48] Steps to victory for humans are made by God. The promised Seed will die, not humans, and His death will be a substitutionary death on their behalf. Jesus brings victory, liberation from the domination of sin, and freedom from the power of evil.

5. Paradoxically, God expels Adam and Eve from the Garden to prevent and protect them from becoming "eternal" sinners and to live under the curse of sin permanently. Ross aptly explains: "The story closes with

---

46. Bartholomew and Goheen, *The Drama of Scripture,* 42.

47. Norman L. Geisler, *The Roots of Evil* (Eugene, OR: Wipf and Stock Publishers, 2002), 81.

48. Ross, *Creation and Blessings,* 141.

the Lord's reasoned decision to prevent humankind from extending life in such a painful state. . . . God acted to prevent them from continuing on perpetually in that condition."[49] He will lead and teach them to trust Him and walk humbly with Him, and be transformed in their characters by knowing Him personally and factually. "The way to life is available, but only in the way God would provide it."[50] Their future seemed uncertain, but they were in God's caring hand. He would bring victory over their enemy and secure their salvation. If they turned to Him in faith, His victory would be theirs.

6. He teaches humans how to worship (Gen. 4:3–9). Giving to Adam and Eve garments made of skin (Gen. 3:21) alluded to the death of an animal, a sacrifice for their sin. On that occasion, God gave insights into true worship, which is the cultivation of a genuine relationship with God.[51]

7. God provides the gift of faith, the ability to cling to God's Word as an affirmative response to His kindness. Even though the word "faith" is not explicitly mentioned in chapter 3 (for the first time, the verb to "believe" appears in Genesis 15:4 in relation to Abraham's faith in God's promises), it is implied in the actions of Adam and Eve: (1) they both accept the garments God provided for them (faith is trust in God's grace and word); (2) Adam gave a special name to his wife—"Eve" (meaning "a mother of the living" according to Gen. 3:20), a designation full of hope, a sign of trust, an indicator of life that will continue in spite of the existence of evil, and an expectation by which he expresses faith in God's merciful guidance and that He will provide, care, and hold the future in the midst of crisis; (3) Eve expresses her hope in the coming Redeemer, the promised Seed (3:15), by naming her firstborn son Cain—"I have received a man, the Lord."[52] She hoped that through him salvation would be secured and thus they would return to the lost paradise. What a disappointment when he instead became

---

49. Ross, *Creation and Blessings*, 149.

50. Ibid., 141.

51. Jiří Moskala, "The Mission of God's People in the Old Testament," *Journal of the Adventist Theological Society* 19, nos. 1–2 (2008): 40–60.

52. Translation is mine. The Hebrew particle *'et* is to be taken as an indicator of a direct object (not as a preposition "with"). It means "the Lord" and is in apposition to the previous word, "man." Thus, Eve's explanation should be translated as follows: "I have received a man, namely (that is) the Lord."

the first murderer! Humanity would need to painfully learn how to trust the Lord and to patiently and consistently follow Him and His will.

Faith brings victory. "This is the victory that has overcome the world, even our faith" (1 John 5:4; cf. Jude 24). However, faith itself is not humankind's savior, but only a means by which we receive God's victory for ourselves.[53] Faith is a relationship of trust, a reliance upon God's Word. Saving faith is not an innate quality of believers and not their achievement, but a gift of God (Eph. 2:8; Phil. 1:29; Jude 3). Humans are responsible if they do not believe, because faith is communicated through hearing the Gospel (Rom. 10:17) and through God's general revelation (Rom. 10:18–20). This is a biblical paradox. Human beings cannot on their own overcome sin; only God can solve the problem of sin and give them victory over it by His divine power. Victory comes from an external source outside of humanity as a gift from God through faith. Human beings can fight against different symptoms of sin and try to overcome wrong habits, but what they really need is a transformation of heart, the experience of a new birth, a pure heart (John 3:3, 5; Ps. 51:10), because their real problem is their unchanged hearts.[54]

Where the first Adam failed, the Second Adam won (Rom. 5:14–21; 1 Cor. 15:22, 45–49). What humans lost in the Garden of Eden, Christ came to restore at the cross. Humanity's new, true identity can and must be shaped and built according to the victory accomplished by Jesus Christ. God did not leave humanity to the power of Satan and sin—the Spirit of God brings victory when individuals cling by faith to God and His Word because the Holy Spirit and the Word of God alone can produce true life (Ezek. 36:25–27; Rom. 8:4, 14).[55] The solution to sin involves not only

---

53. In Greek, it is expressed by the preposition *dia* plus genitive of *pistis,* meaning "faith"; *dia pisteos* means literally "through faith" (and not by *dia* plus accusative of *pistis* which would then mean "on account of faith" or "because of faith").

54. Victory comes from above as a gift from God. We need to be born again, which means to be born from above (the Greek word "*anothen*" means "again," but also "above"). Only when we decide for God, surrender to Him, allow the Holy Spirit to work in us, and accept continually the Word of God are we sons and daughters of God (John 1:12–13; Rom. 8:14), a new creation (2 Cor. 5:17).

55. The first verses of the Bible provide the first definition of true life. Life can happen only when the Spirit of God (Gen. 1:2b) and the Word of God (Gen. 1:3) come together and reign (in the first creation account the phrase "and God said" occurs ten

forgiveness, but renewal and restoration to the image of God and freedom from slavery to sin. A new life is word- and Spirit-oriented (Rom. 8:2–6; Col. 3:1–4, 10). Those who do not live according to the flesh but according to the Spirit, and those who are led by the Holy Spirit are sons and daughters of God (Rom. 8:14). Only when individuals surrender to God, decide for Him, and allow Him to be God in their lives do they experience the difference and a new life. Believers need to strive each day for a close relationship with God so that nothing and no one can take it from them (Rom. 8:31–39). Only Jesus can impart true joy of a new victorious life (Rom. 7:25). To Him alone be glory (Jer. 9:23–24; Rom. 11:33–36).

The good news is that Jesus Christ regenerates and changes the hearts of individuals (John 3:3–5); forgives all their sins (Isa. 1:16–19; 1 John 1:8–9); liberates them from the bondage of sin (John 12:31–32); and transforms their lives (Rom. 12:1–2; 2 Cor. 5:17; 1 John 3:1–3). If the Son gives freedom, every person is indeed free. There is hope for all because sin was overcome by the humble person of Jesus Christ who is the guarantor of freedom, peace, and joy. The sinful nature of humanity does not change or disappear through an individual's conversion or repentance; however, the sinful nature, tendencies, or inclinations (inherited or cultivated) can be controlled by the power of the Holy Spirit, His Word, and God's grace (Rom. 7:25; 8:1–11). Not until the second coming will believers be completely transformed and receive an incorruptible body (1 Cor. 15:50–57; Phil. 3:20–21; 1 John 3:2–5). Believers are not able on their own to perform good deeds, which are a result of the transforming power of God's grace and the work of the Holy Spirit (John 1:12; 15:1–5; Rom. 1:16–17; 8:1–4; 1 Cor. 1:18–25, 30–31; 2:12–15; Gal. 5:22–23; Eph. 1:10; Phil. 4:13; 1 Pet. 2:9–10).

CONCLUSION

God created a perfect world that was distorted by sin, a fatal wound that ushered in terrible consequences. Eugene Peterson describes humanity's lost

---

times). Spirit + Word = Life. This is correct not only for the creation of physical life, but also for the birth of spiritual life. A person can be born again only when he or she is born from above—when this person opens himself or herself to the influence of the Holy Spirit (John 3:5–8; Rom. 8:14; Tit. 3:5) and believes in the Word of God (John 1:12–13; 1 Pet. 1:23; James 1:18). Regeneration is possible and can be experienced because God is our Creator. He creates in us new life (Ps. 51:10).

situation: "A catastrophe has occurred. We are no longer in continuity with our good beginning. We have been separated from it by a disaster. We are also, of course, separated from our good end. We are, in other words, in the middle of a mess."[56] Because of the sin problem, human beings live in a "deeply wounded"[57] world destined for death. At creation, God endowed humans with a free will, and being human means possessing freedom of choice. However, that freedom has been compromised because humans have tasted the forbidden fruit that misleads and perverts their judgment of what is good and evil. The problem is the sinful nature that inclines them toward evil, love for sin, and a desire for selfish self-realization and self-centeredness. Humans no longer respect God's Word and will. This disrespect for divine guidance tragically complicates life.

God's Word reveals the origin of sin and evil in the world. In Genesis 3, sin is described as a broken relationship, a mistrust of God, a refusal to follow His Word, and unbelief. It is an egocentric life, selfish, and a rejection of God's authority, His Word, His command, and His law, which is not a mere code of norms but an expression of His loving and holy character. Sinners do not recognize and appreciate His goodness, love, justice, order, and care. Sin underestimates, blurs, and blinds the real values of life and the severe consequences of sin. Sin is a wrong attitude, an enslaving power that changes human nature and leads to violence, problems, and death.

Some tend to view sin in a shallow, mechanical, and one-sided way, as a deed or simply as an external act. However, sin has a deeper basis and larger connotations. It cannot be defined only as the transgression of the law. Sin is first a theological term aimed against God (Gen. 3:1; Ps. 51:4) that ruins relationships and personal integrity. Transgression dishonors humanity but primarily dishonors God, and disobedience robs God of His honor as humanity's Creator. When God's creatures rebel against Him, His glory, reputation, and name are belittled, and the splendor and majesty of His Person and character are degraded. When the vertical relationship with God is broken, it causes the breakdown of all other relationships (the self, each other, life, and nature). The consequence of sin is death (Rom. 6:23). Its negativity is plainly seen in the Flood account where everything

---

56. Eugene H. Peterson, *Working the Angles: The Shape of Pastoral Integrity* (Grand Rapids, MI: Eerdmans, 1987), 82–83.

57. Bartholomew and Goheen, *The Drama of Scripture*, 40.

was corrupted (i.e., destroyed by sin),[58] and the antediluvian people are portrayed as possessing continuous evil thoughts (Gen. 6:5). Sin is complex, even though its nature is clear. Sin is not only an inner brokenness, but disobedience, depravity of the heart with selfish tendencies and propensities to sin, as well as a dominating power—sin is all inclusive (Rom. 1:18–3:20; Gen. 6:5; Isa. 1:5–6; Jer. 11:8; Matt. 7:18–23; Rom. 5–8). Sin is a state of thinking and being, as well as a concrete act of active rebellion.

The Fall account teaches people not to be ignorant of the power of sin and Satan's devices (Rom. 6:5–7; 2 Cor. 2:11). John Toews asserts: "The serpent asked the woman and Adam to make a judgment about God. They did. They . . . decided to mistrust God, to mistrust the Word of God, in quest for autonomy that would make them wise. Their mistrust of God led them to disobedience, to disobey the Word of God."[59] Sin is a separation from God, and salvation is a restoration of that broken relationship with God. In the Bible, sin is associated with alienation from God, self-love, straying from the right path, missing the target, injustice, guilt, slavery, death, darkness, hopelessness, selfishness, and twisting truth. Various Hebrew and Greek terms testify regarding the vast array of sin's influence and decay.

The anatomy of the first sin and the dynamics of temptation is as follows: First, a wrong picture of God is created that casts Him into a false light and distorts who He is. Second, this skewed view generates doubts regarding His love and purposes, followed by misunderstandings and

58. Moses plays with one Hebrew word *shachat*, which has two meanings in English: (1) corrupt and (2) destroy. This play is best described in Genesis 6:11–13 which shows that God is not coming to destroy what is good, meaningful, beautiful, and has the potential to grow, but He intervenes to destroy what has already been destroyed (corrupted), and those who are agents of destruction: "Now the earth was corrupt in God's sight and was full of violence. God saw how corrupt the earth had become, for all the people on earth had corrupted their ways. So God said to Noah, 'I am going to put an end to all people, for the earth is filled with violence because of them. I am surely going to destroy both them and the earth.'" Compare this with the statement of John in the book of Revelation, which alludes to Genesis 6, where the purpose of the second coming of Jesus is explained as follows: "The time has come for judging the dead, and for rewarding your servants the prophets and your people who revere your name, both great and small—and for destroying those who destroy the earth" (Rev. 11:18).

59. John E. Toews, *The Story of Original Sin* (Eugene, OR: Pickwick Publications, 2013), 6.

distrust. Third, the discrepancy between God's Word and observations in life are pointed out or found out. Fourth comes the direct attack against the validity of God's Word, His law, and will. Fifth, the offer of something apparently better culminates the deception (Gen. 3:13). Finally, an act of disobedience follows. Satan first wants to obtain a hold on a person's mind, impregnate his or her thinking, and finally control his or her behavior. The most decisive battle is fought over the mind, over thinking. If he succeeds here, he will win the entire war. In other words, a breaking of the law first occurs in the mind of a person, followed by a breaking of the law in actual behavior. Sin affects the whole life of an individual.

The narrative on the Fall teaches that God is not the author of evil, but that He is the only One who can provide a lasting and thorough solution to the sin problem, even though this resolution is extremely costly, painful, and surprising. Despite humanity's sinfulness, brokenness, and lostness, God loves people and wants to save them. Because the human will is self-centered, humans do not desire to seek God on their own. There is no capacity in humans by which they can connect with God. It is God who condescends, pursues, and connects with humans. He initiates this encounter; He takes the first step. God's cry "Where are you?" (Gen. 3:9) is a model of how God is in search of humanity all the time.

CHAPTER 7

THE NATURE OF SIN: UNDERSTANDING ITS CHARACTER AND COMPLEXITY

Roy Adams

From start to finish, the Bible considers sin, in all its manifestations, a matter of grave concern. S. J. De Vries is correct: "The Bible takes sin in dead seriousness. Unlike many modern religionists, who seek to find excuses for sin and to explain away its seriousness, most of the writers of the Bible had a keen awareness of its heinousness, culpability, and tragedy."[1]

It seems clear, though, that the Bible, taken as a whole, provides its own calibration of this human disorder, weighing the relative gravity of its many expressions. This chapter seeks to identify and describe the most prominent attributes of this complex universal malady, with a view to better understanding its nature and character.

Because the biblical materials cover thousands of years of human life and experience, they understandably contain a wide variety of words and expressions to describe the human estrangement from God and the aberrant behavior that results from it. This makes it impossible to be comprehensive, so the aim here will be to focus on the most theologically significant allusions to this syndrome.

---

1. S. J. De Vries, "Sin, Sinners," *The Interpreter's Dictionary of the Bible* (IDB), 4:361.

SIN—GENERAL AND UNIVERSAL

The most fundamental patterns of human language have not changed over the centuries. Every society has felt the need for words expressing general ideas and for appropriate modifiers to provide specific meaning within particular contexts. This is the case with the Bible, as its writers grapple with the universal phenomenon known as sin.

As he tried to get a handle on the multitude of terms for sin employed by the Old Testament writers, Gottfried Quell identified "four different roots" associated with the idea: *khet'*, *pesha`*, *`awon,* and *shegh.*[2] Quell argued that though often used synonymously, these (and other) terms for sin in the Old Testament are not identical. Rather, they exhibit "strong qualitative differences among themselves."[3] But because these words must be translated using the single English term *sin,* it's often impossible to "bring out the etymologically derived nuances of the Hebrew."[4]

Quell also notes the significance of *context* in determining the specific meaning of these and other terms for sin.[5] But at this point, slightly to the contrary, it is necessary to call attention to *the general nature* of many of the Old Testament references to sin, instances where no "etymologically derived nuances of the Hebrew" come into play.

The term *`asham,* for example—a common word for "sin" or "guilt"—primarily refers to sin, without any inherent "color" of its own. For example, consider Proverbs 14:9, which says that "fools mock at making amends for sin [*`asham*]."[6] Here the author simply assumes he is talking about a reality whose currency all his readers already know—hence no need to characterize it further. The sense is the same in

---

2. Gottfried Quell, ἁμαρτάνω, *Theological Dictionary of the New Testament* (*TDNT*) ed. Gerhard Kittel (Grand Rapids, MI: Eerdmans, 1964), 1:270, 271. The last word in Quell's list, which we shall not return to, means "to err." It refers to sin as "creaturely conditioned error," ibid., 1:271. Quell sees the term and its derivatives as "the mildest expression of the reality of sin" in the Old Testament, ibid., 1:274.

3. *TDNT,* 1:271.

4. Ibid., 270.

5. Ibid., 279.

6. Unless otherwise indicated, all Scripture quotations are taken from THE HOLY BIBLE, NEW INTERNATIONAL VERSION®, NIV® Copyright © 1973, 1978, 1984, 2011 by Biblica, Inc.® Used by permission. All rights reserved worldwide.

Jeremiah 51:5, which describes the land of Israel and Judah as full of
'asham ("full of guilt").

The word khet' ("sin," "error," "failure"), one of the four terms on which
Quell focused, provides another example. It occurs in Leviticus, Numbers,
and Deuteronomy, where it appears to have no specific connotation of its
own, other than suggesting the violation of a norm. An Israelite is admonished to rebuke a neighbor, so as not to share in that neighbor's khet' (guilt)
(Lev. 19:17); Israelites are forbidden to approach certain sacred spaces, lest
they incur khet' (sin) (Num. 18:22). In such passages the word appears as a
general term for sin, with no distinguishing specificity.

Three other Hebrew terms, derivatives of khet and virtually identical to
each other in both form and meaning, provide additional examples of this
general usage. To avoid confusion, just one term, khatta'ah will be used
and applied in all cases, without distinction. The basic meaning is "sin"
(sometimes "sin offering").

The use of khatta'ah as a general term for sin occurs in Leviticus 4:3,
13, and 14, the passages outline what needs to happen "if the anointed
priest sins [khatta'ah], bringing guilt on the people," or "if the whole Israelite community sins [khatta'ah] unintentionally and does what is forbidden." It is clear that in this context "if" ('im) carries the sense of "when,"
the passages taking for granted that such infractions *will* occur. As sins,
they would not be unimportant, of course; but they would not rise to the
seriousness that disqualifies the anointed priests from continuing as God's
special agents, or the Israelites from being God's chosen people. Atonement must be made; but clearly such trespasses do not rise to the level seen
at Sinai with the golden calf (Exod. 32:9–10) or in the crisis at Kadesh following the return of the spies (Num. 14:10–12). In both of these instances
Israel came under serious threat of divine disinheritance.

Khatta'ah is probably the most common Old Testament word for sin,
in all its forms occurring some 500 times and signifying general human
failings and shortcomings.

In the New Testament, *hamartia* ("error," "offense," "sin") corresponds
to those Old Testament terms that describe sin in a general sense, being
especially close, however, to khatta'ah and its cognates.[7] Messiah was to be

---

7. According to *TDNT* 1:268, hamartia is used in the LXX to translate khatta'ah and its
cognates some 274 times.

called Jesus, "because he will save his people from their sins [*hamartia*]" (Matt. 1:21; cf. 1 Pet. 2:24).

In Romans, Paul not only uses *hamartia* as a general term for sin, but by personalizing it, he also dramatizes its pervasive grasp on humanity: Sin came into the world (Rom. 5:12). Humans are slaves to it, sold into its service (Rom. 6:6; 7:14); they can be set free from it (6:22); it has its law (7:23; 8:2); and it pays its wages (6:23).[8] Sin (*hamartia*) has taken the whole world prisoner (Gal. 3:22); humans are all "dead in trespasses and sins [*hamartia*]" (Eph. 2:1, NKJV). And "if we claim to be without sin [*hamartia*], we deceive ourselves and the truth is not in us" (1 John 1:8).

SIN—SPECIFIC AND PARTICULAR

With appropriate modifiers, a word used for sin in general can take on new meaning, becoming defined, particularized—even personal. That is the case in 2 Kings 10:29, which speaks of "the sins [*khet'*] of Jeroboam son of Nebat, which he had caused Israel to commit—the worship of the golden calves at Bethel and Dan." Here *khet'* refers to the serious offense of idolatry, the modifiers signaling the gravity of the particular violation.

Another good example of this phenomenon is Exodus 32:30, where Moses described Israel's action in the matter of the golden calf as "a great *khatta'ah*"—"a great sin." So serious, in fact, that God was ready to "destroy" His chosen people and raise up a new nation through Moses (32:9–10). In 1 Samuel 2, after describing the despicable practices of Eli's "wicked" sons (vv. 12–16), the writer then says: "This sin [*khatta'ah*] of the young men was very great in the LORD's sight, for they were treating the LORD's offering with contempt" (v. 17).

In that last passage, *khatta'ah* by itself does not describe the sin in question. Only the modifier alerts the reader to the seriousness of the case. The same is true in 1 Samuel 15:23, which describes rebellion (*meri*) as equivalent to "the sin [*khatta'ah*] of witchcraft" (KJV). Here *khatta'ah* functions simply as a general term for sin, with the modifier ("witchcraft") indicating the level of its gravity in the specific instance.

---

8. W. Arndt, F. W. Gingrich, and W. Bauer, *A Greek-English Lexicon of the New Testament and Other Early Christian Literature* (*GELNT*; Chicago, IL: The University of Chicago Press, 1979), 43, s.v. ἁμαρτια.

One of Elihu's accusations of Job shows how sin as *khatta`ah* might be exceeded by offenses of a more serious nature. Elihu charged that Job, "to his sin [*khatta`ah*]" had added "rebellion" (Job 34:37). Had Elihu's insinuation been correct, Job's infraction would have become exponentially more egregious.

As already indicated, the terms for sin in the Bible are numerous—more than twenty distinct words in the Old Testament alone—making it impossible to do them justice in a single chapter.[9] In addition, Scripture contains a multitude of references to human decrepitude, where no specific term for sin is mentioned. In Galatians 5:19–21, for example, Paul speaks about "sexual immorality, impurity and debauchery; idolatry and witchcraft; hatred, discord, jealousy, fits of rage, selfish ambition, dissensions, factions and envy; drunkenness, orgies" (cf. Col. 3:5–9).

In the wake of this plethora of specific and non-specific terms for sin, there is a biblical passage that helps to focus the fundamental issue. It centers around four terms for sin, three of which are featured among the four mentioned by Quell.

INSIGHTS FROM DAVID'S GREAT TESTIMONY[10]

David's testimony in Psalm 32 stands out as one of the most instructive passages in the Bible on the nature of sin. Overwhelmed by the painful knowledge of his own wickedness, David passionately bared his soul before his great Redeemer, in the process sharing with all succeeding generations the joy of God's forgiving grace. The vocabulary he employed, under the Spirit, has vastly helped to enrich our understanding of the complex ramifications of this universal human condition.

Beyond Hebrew Parallelism

David says: "Blessed is he whose *transgression* [*pesha`*] is forgiven, whose *sin* [*khatta`ah*] is covered. Blessed is the man to whom the LORD does not

---

9. For a helpful listing and discussion of several of these terms, see *IDB*, 4:361–362, 370–372.

10. For this and the following segment, I have borrowed here and there (without attribution) from chapter 6 of my book, *The Nature of Christ: Help for a Church Divided over Perfection* (Hagerstown, MD: Review and Herald, 1994).

impute *iniquity* [`awon], and in whose spirit there is no *deceit* [*remiyyah*]"
(Ps. 32:1–2, NKJV).

The terms used in this passage go far beyond Hebrew literary parallelism. Carefully considered, they spell out the broad and multifaceted parameters of this universal malady. Given the enormity of the spiritual crisis that elicited David's confession, it seems far from accidental that he would utilize just those four terms from the many at his disposal. Rather, it would seem that he was reaching into covenant language going clear back to Moses.

In Exodus 34:5–10, in the context of a solemn iteration of the covenant, God proclaimed Himself the God who abounds "in love and faithfulness ... forgiving wickedness [`awon], rebellion [*pesha*`], and sin [*khatta`ah*]" (vv. 6–7). Toward the end of the solemn ceremonies on the great Day of Atonement, the high priest was to lay his hands on the goat for Azazel and "confess over it all the iniquities [`awon] of the children of Israel, and all their transgressions [*pesha*`], concerning all their sins [*khatta`ah*], putting them on the head of the goat," and sending the animal away (Lev. 16:21, NKJV). Isaiah, spelling out the covenant violations of his people, confessed that "our offenses [*pesha*`] are many in your sight, and our sins [*khatta`ah*] testify against us. Our offenses are ever with us, and we acknowledge our iniquities [`awon]" (Isa. 59:12–13).

And in Daniel's great intercessory prayer (Dan. 9), the prophet, his mind filled with concerns about God's covenant with His people, fell back on the same kind of terminology employed by the Lord in Exodus 34 and repeated in David's testimony. "We have *sinned* and committed *iniquity*," he began, using derivatives of *khatta`ah* and `awon. And though he used the word *marad* (to rebel), rather than a derivative of *pesha*` to describe the seriousness of Israel's offense (v. 9), the angel Gabriel, in a summary of Messiah's work, returned to the same key words as in earlier covenant passages: "Seventy weeks are determined for your people ... to finish the transgression [*pesha*`], to make an end of sins [*khatta`ah*], to make reconciliation for iniquity [`awon]" (v. 24, NKJV).

Thus David's vocabulary in Psalm 32:1–2 has its foundation deep in God's ancient covenant and gets to the very heart of the human problem, heightened by the addition of *remiyyah* (deceit), a word used only here in the Old Testament.

For convenience and clarity, the four terms, clause by clause, will be examined—but in the following order: *transgression; deceit; sin;* and *iniquity*.

The first two will be featured in the present section, the other two in the section that follows.

1. "Blessed is he whose *transgression* is forgiven." The Hebrew word is *pesha`* ("rebellion," "defection," "revolt"). It implies "willful sin."[11] "By all counts," says De Vries, *pesha`* "is the Old Testament's most profound word for 'sin,' indicating its theological meaning as 'revolt against God.'"[12] It is not "a mere failure or mistake, like [*khatta'ah*] . . . , since it consists of willful disobedience."[13] Isaiah had *pesha`* in mind when he charged Israel with "rebellion and treachery against the LORD, turning our backs on our God, inciting revolt and oppression" (Isa. 59:13).

With *pesha`* one comes to an offense of the most serious gravity: open hostility toward God, insubordination, sacrilege. It implies premeditation, as in David's case. He violates Uriah's wife, summons the poor man from the battlefield to use as cover for his adultery, then, as the scheme collapses, sends him back to the battlefront with a sealed death sentence in his own hand. It was calculating, methodical, intentional, cold-blooded. That is *pesha`*.

Quoting David's words from Psalm 32, Paul used the term *anomia* to translate *pesha`*. Thus, one may consider *anomia* (lawlessness) as the New Testament equivalent of *pesha`*. Jesus employed it in the judgment scene He painted during the Sermon on the Mount. "Depart from me," He will say to all counterfeits on the last day, "you who practice lawlessness [*anomia*]" (Matt. 7:23, NKJV). At the end of time, the angels "will gather out of His kingdom all things that offend, and those who practice lawlessness [*anomia*]" (Matt. 13:41, NKJV; cf. 23:28; 24:12). In 2 Thessalonians 2:7, Paul refers to "the secret power of lawlessness [*anomia*]" as being already in operation. This is the ultimate *pesha`*, the ultimate *anomia*, involving the usurpation of God's power and prerogatives.

Pesha` involves a deliberate "decision of the human will."[14] Along these lines, says Quell, "Amos (4:4) need only say [*pesha`*] . . . without any further explanation to denote this challenging and almost impetuous attitude towards

11. F. D. Nichol, ed., *Seventh-day Adventist Bible Commentary* (Washington, DC: Review and Herald, 1954), 3:706.

12. *IDB*, 4:361.

13. Ibid.

14. *TDNT*, 1:273–274.

God."[15] It is what the book of Numbers describes as sinning "defiantly"; it is blasphemy—or, to use the literal Hebrew, it is sinning "with a high hand" (Num. 15:30). To borrow an expression, it is "an outraging of God."[16]

According to David, this offensive attitude must be surrendered, so it can be forgiven. "Blessed is he whose transgression [*pesha`*] is forgiven" (Ps. 32:1, NKJV). With *pesha`*, the stakes reach as high as they can get! And in Psalm 51:1, David pleads with God to "blot out" this revolting malady completely from his heart.

2. "And in whose spirit there is no *deceit*." The Hebrew word here is *remiyyah* ("deceit," "guile," "falsehood," "duplicity," "fraud"). Its New Testament equivalent is *dolos* ("deceit," "cunning," "treachery").

It represents an extremely undesirable trait for the Christian. Peter called on believers to rid themselves "of all malice and all deceit [*dolos*]" (1 Pet. 2:1); and John's glowing description of the 144,000 is that "in their mouth was found no deceit" (Rev. 14:5, NKJV). (Textual evidence favors here the word *pseudos* ["lie," "falsehood," "deception"], but the basic meaning remains the same.)

Every indication suggests that the posture represented by *remiyyah, dolos,* or *pseudos* is exceedingly offensive in the eyes of God. None of these terms is present in Matthew 23, yet the seven woes of verses 13–32 paint an accurate picture of the same mind-set. Here, on the eve of His passion, Jesus directed the most scathing denunciation of His entire ministry against the duplicity and deceitful treachery of the Scribes and Pharisees who "do not practice what they preach" (Matt. 23:3). "Everything they do," He said, "is done for people to see" (v. 5). "You snakes, you brood of vipers!" (v. 33, NRSV). He thundered, as he brought His withering litany to an end, "How can you escape being sentenced to hell?" (v. 33, NRSV).

All sins are serious and harmful, and any discussion of their relative gravity can very easily be misunderstood. But the reality of the situation is that, however subtle, Scripture itself does make those very distinctions, indicating that God regards some sins as particularly repugnant. How else to explain Jesus's outrage in Matthew 23 over the lying hypocrisy (read *dolos/pseudos*) of His professed people?

Given its seriousness, "transgression" (*pesha`*) must be abandoned by the believer; and given its lethalness, "deceit" (*remiyyah*) must vanish

---

15. Ibid., 274.

16. *TDNT,* 1:289.

completely from the Christian's spirit. When that happens, believers are *right with God.*

Unfortunately, however, this does not mean that believers have achieved sinlessness. And that is because they still must contend with two intractable and annoyingly unpredictable aspects of sin, which David mentions in the middle of the passage.

The Complexity of Sin

In the middle of the Psalm 32:1–2, David mentions *khatta`ah* and *`awon*.

**3. "Blessed is he . . . whose *sin* [*khatta`ah*] is covered."** Throughout the Old Testament, as indicated above, *khatta`ah* stands as one of the most common terms for sin, "used of all kinds of misdemeanors."[17] But to the extent that the word carries any inherent meaning of its own, there is general consensus that, like *hamartia* in the New Testament, it refers to the specter of "missing the mark" (like a dart thrower missing the target), "falling short," "failing in one's duty."[18] As T. O. Hall, Jr. puts it, "The OT distinguishes between deliberate sins and those committed through ignorance, weakness, or where the sinner was not totally responsible."[19] Leviticus 4, 5, and 6 are full of examples of *khatta`ah* in reference to the common, unpremeditated offenses of the people.

To put things in contemporary terms, *khatta`ah* arises from everyday interpersonal interactions in community—the way we relate to our children in the multitude of dealings we have with them; the way we relate to our spouses; to our colleagues on the job; to other drivers on the roadway; to the poor and disadvantaged in our own communities; and in the world at large; it includes our response (or non-response) to human exploitation and injustice.

Khatta`ah arises from animosity cherished in the heart; from hatred, resentment, jealousy, envy, greed, harshness, discourtesy, unkindness, compromise, stinginess, carelessness, neglect, resentment, pride. The list is endless. And added to the mix are a believer's repeated failures in respect to the social requirements of the gospel, as spelled out by the ancient

17. *TDNT,* 1:272.

18. See *SDA Bible Commentary,* 3:706; *IDB,* 4:361; cf. *TDNT,* 1:271.

19. T. O. Hall, Jr. "Sin, Christian and Jewish Concept," *Perennial Dictionary of World Religions,* gen. ed. Keith Crim (San Francisco, CA: Harper Collins, 1981), 694.

prophets: Amos 5:11–15; Isaiah 1:1–17; 58:1–10; Jeremiah 22:13–17; or as distilled by Jesus in His Matthew 25 judgment parable (vv. 41–45).

These are difficult and complex areas of human experience—precarious and unpredictable. The situation becomes even more perilous, in that *khatta`ah* also involves "sins of omission." In the words of the Apostle James: "Anyone . . . who knows the right thing to do and fails to do it, commits sin [*hamartia*]" (Jas. 4:17, NRSV). If one thinks, for example, of the responsibility of taking the Gospel to one's neighbors, then who can say that he or she is doing everything possible in this important area of Christian responsibility? And what about the kind word left unspoken? Or the downward trend in someone's life that could have been prevented by some timely action left undone? "Many are deceived as to their true condition before God," wrote Ellen G. White. "They congratulate themselves upon the wrong acts which they do not commit, and forget to enumerate the good and noble deeds which God requires of them, but which they have neglected to perform."[20]

The point here is that *khatta`ah* involves a whole range of reactions, interactions, activities, relationships, and emotions that often are completely unpredictable and constantly changing. The ancient prophet said it right: "Who can say, 'I have kept my heart pure; I am clean and without sin [*khatta`ah*]?" (Prov. 20:9). It would have been unthinkable for him to make that statement about *pesha`* or *remiyyah*. But in regard to *khatta`ah*, it is an instructive observation, a pivotal admission—correct for all times.

**4. "to whom the Lord does not impute *iniquity* [`*awon*]."** Apart from its reference to sin in general, `*awon* stands for "iniquity," "vanity," "perversity." It signifies moral distortion, crookedness, a congenital malfunction in the human soul[21]—what Charles Wesley in one of his hymns called "our bent to sinning." Perhaps it was in this respect that David spoke of being "brought forth in iniquity [`*awon*]" and "conceived" "in sin" (Ps. 51:5, NASB).

A common conception of sin among many Christians centers (almost exclusively) on sexual and other sensual indulgences. Such preoccupation with one class of sin, however, can obscure the fact that sin is much deeper than behavior—that it is a malady that pervades as well as precedes behavior and is buried deep in the human psyche. William Hordern was correct

20. Ellen G. White, *Great Controversy* (Mountain View, CA: Pacific Press, 1888), 601.

21. *TDNT*, 1:270–271.

in distinguishing between "sin as a state and sins as individual actions." "Sin," he says, "is the prideful state in which man revolts against God and makes himself the measure of all things. From this state of sin the various sins flow in the form of unethical and immoral actions."[22]

Long after believers are converted and cease their willful rebellion against the Lord, the influence of this congenital deformity (`awon`) plagues them. There are shades of crookedness buried deep within the soul, just waiting for a certain combination of circumstances to trigger them. This is seen in the life of Simon the sorcerer. Observing the operation of the Holy Spirit in the ministry of Peter and John, this new convert succumbed to the perversity that had formed the basis of his previous life of witchcraft. Offering to purchase the Spirit with money, he found himself facing the righteous anger of Peter for his sinful treachery: "Repent of this wickedness," Peter said to him, "for I see that you are full of bitterness and captive to sin [*adikia*]" (Acts 8:18–25).

If *adikia* (unrighteousness, wickedness) is the New Testament equivalent of `awon,` then the Simon story gives believers a reason to resist this particular sin with every ounce of power God provides. Harbored in the soul, it can become chronic, leading to what Jesus called the sin against the Holy Spirit, for which there is no forgiveness (Matt. 12:32; Mark 3:29; Luke 12:10); and from which, says the author of Hebrews (in a slightly different context), one cannot "be brought back to repentance" (6:4–6).

Against this backdrop, it should be clear that John's definition of sin as "the transgression of the law" (1 John 3:4, KJV) was never meant to be all-inclusive. Indeed, there are other biblical definitions, such as that in Romans 14:23: "everything that does not come from faith is sin." But relying exclusively on that single Johannine definition, some Christians (Adventists among them) have come to understand sin primarily in terms of acts that we commit. From this restricted outlook have come spirited admonitions to *stop sinning*.[23]

---

22. William Hordern, "Man, Doctrine of," *Dictionary of Christian Theology,* ed. Alan Richardson (Philadelphia, PA: Westminster Press, 1969), 204.

23. For example, leading one-time Adventist theology professor, M. L. Andreasen (1876–1962) regarded baptism as the sixth "step" to Christ, a step in which the sinner is made dead to sin. From that point, the new convert is to "abstain from sin," Andreasen, *A Faith to Live By* (Washington, DC: Review and Herald, 1943), 96–97. He admonished new believers to "get rid of every sin"; to "gain the victory over every besetment"; to "break every

When John says that the person who is "born of God . . . cannot go on sinning" (1 John 3:9), he is using *hamartia* in a heightened sense.[24] His reference in the passage to the sin of the devil (v. 9) suggests he is really talking about weighty violations—sins that "lead to death," so to speak (cf. 1 John 5:16–17)—offenses like *pesha`* and *remiyyah* (or *anomia* and *pseudos*). In other words, sins of rebellion, revolt, sacrilege, guile, and deceit. Sin as "missing the mark" (*khatta'ah*), for example, is not something the Bible ever associates with the devil. He is into the heavy stuff.

If one is talking about sin as *pesha`*, then it is obvious that true Christians would have put such attitudes behind them. While this does not mean that they will never know times of relapse, it does mean that they have set a course that consistently runs in tandem with the will of God. The spirit of revolt, insubordination, and stubborn resistance has surrendered. And sin as *remiyyah* (deceit, duplicity) has ceased.

But the other categories of sin will continue to torment the soul, as Paul acknowledged in that much-misunderstood passage of Romans 7:14–24. Such shortcomings and mistakes are common to the entire human family from cradle to grave, egged on by that congenital imbalance (*`awon*), with which we struggle daily. "If you, O LORD, kept a record of sins [*`awon*], LORD, who could stand? But with you there is forgiveness" (Ps. 130:3–4). Evidently God does not miraculously remove this problem from us, but rather, in His providence, uses it to help us grow.

So what happens if a person dies (or if Jesus comes) before he or she can "gain the victory" over every besetment?

Only God can definitively answer that, of course; but the words of David may shed some light on the sensitive issue: God, David says, "does not treat us as our sins [*khatta'ah*] deserve or repay us according to our iniquities [*`awon*]. For as high as the heavens are above the earth, so great is his love for those who fear him; as far as the east is from the west, so far has he removed our transgressions [*pesha`*] from us. As a father has compassion on his children, so the LORD has compassion on those who fear him; for he knows how we are formed, he remembers that we are dust" (Ps. 103:10–14).

---

chain that binds"; and to "do it now, to-day," *Isaiah, the Gospel Prophet* (Washington, DC: Review and Herald, 1928), 2:78.

24. I base this observation on the fact that the LXX, with which John would have been familiar, uses *hamartia* 19 times to translate *pesha`* (see *TDNT*, 1:268).

The God who reads the inmost souls of His children understands when a believer is fully surrendered and committed to Him and is no longer in revolt. And He knows when the shortcomings he or she experiences do not constitute defiance of His will and purpose.

CONCLUSION

Surrendered Christians will experience continual growth; yet they will never come to the place in this life where they move beyond the reach of certain infirmities; they will never outgrow the need for God's forgiving grace. Thus the only hope of salvation—from beginning to end—is the sheer mercy and grace of God. He covers His children's *khatta'ah*, says David, and "does not count" their *'awon* against them (Ps. 32:1–2). What a God! What a Savior! To understand this is to know the true joy of assurance in Christ.

CHAPTER 8

THE SINFUL NATURE AND SPIRITUAL INABILITY

George R. Knight

Previous chapters have dealt with the origin of sin, the biblical vocabulary of sin, and the nature of sin as both a state, or condition, of human nature and a series of actions that flow out of that sinful orientation. The present chapter will discuss the practical implications of sin on human nature and how the fallen nature affects views of salvation.

POLLUTION, DEPRAVITY, AND INABILITY

One of the undeniable facts of human existence is not only that human nature is polluted or corrupted but that that pollution is universal. That truth is captured by Paul's conclusion to his extensive treatment on sin, when he declares that "all have sinned and fall short of the glory of God" (Rom. 3:23).[1] John enunciates the same point when he writes that "if we say we have no sin, we deceive ourselves" and "if we say we have not sinned, we make [God] a liar" (1 John 1:8, 10). Henri Blocher captures the truth of universal pollution when he notes that being sinners is "an

---

1. Unless otherwise indicated, all Scripture quotations are taken from the Revised Standard Version of the Bible, copyright © 1946, 1952, and 1971 the Division of Christian Education of the National Council of the Churches of Christ in the United States of America. Used by permission. All rights reserved.

existential, spiritual, *fact* for human beings since Adam."[2] And William Horndern points out that "even theologians who have denied that Adam's fall corrupted later generations and who have denied the doctrine of original sin have been forced none the less to admit the strange fact that the line of least resistance for man never leads into the paths of righteousness."[3] The downward bent of human nature is captured by the concept of concupiscence, which "affirms the basic truth that each human being is born with a prejudice to sin."[4] Ellen White captures the idea when she writes that human nature has a "bent to evil."[5]

Both biblical testaments highlight the fact of human pollutedness. Thus Jeremiah points out that "the heart is deceitful above all things, and desperately corrupt" (17:9). And Paul highlights the fact that those without God are "darkened in their understanding, alienated from the life of God," ignorant of spiritual realities, hard of heart, "have become callous and have given themselves up to licentiousness," and are "greedy to practice every kind of uncleanness" (Eph. 4:17–19).

The Bible is clear on the fact that pollution is not an end in itself but leads to what theologians call total depravity and spiritual inability. Many are tempted to avoid the phrase *total depravity* because they mistakenly think it means that people are as wicked as they could be and have no good in them. But the real implication is that sin has affected their entire being. That is the picture being described in Romans 3, in which Paul notes that sinners' *throats* are as open graves, their *tongues* practice deceit, their *lips* spread snakelike poison, their *mouths* utter bitter curses, and their *feet* don't merely pursue violence, but are swift to do so (vv. 13–16). The passage goes on to deal with the shortcoming of people's *eyes* (v. 18). Thus the depravity is total in the sense that it affects every part of a person. James Denney captures Paul's meaning when he writes that "the depravity which sin has produced in human nature extends to the whole

---

2. Henri Blocher, *Original Sin: Illuminating the Riddle* (Downers Grove, IL: InterVarsity, 1997), 129.

3. William Horndern, "Depravity," in *A Dictionary of Christian Theology*, ed. Alan Richardson (Philadelphia, PA: Westminster, 1969), 92.

4. Bernard Ramm, *Offense to Reason: A Theology of Sin* (San Francisco, CA: Harper & Row, 1985), 88.

5. Ellen G. White, *Education* (Mountain View, CA: Pacific Press, 1952), 29.

of it. There is no part of man's nature which is unaffected by it." As a result, "when the conscience is violated by disobedience to the will of God, the moral understanding is darkened, and the will is enfeebled. We are not constructed in water-tight compartments, one of which might be ruined while the others remain intact."[6]

In line with Denney's insight, the Bible moves beyond Paul's discussion of depravity being related to the totality of body parts by teaching that the *mind* is affected and darkened by sin (Rom. 1:28; Eph. 4:18; Tit. 1:15); the *conscience* is defiled (Tit. 1:15; Heb. 10:22; 1 Tim. 4:2); and the *heart* is deceitful (Jer. 17:9). Thus it is that Jesus roots depravity in the inner nature when He declares that "from within, out of the heart of man, come evil thoughts, fornication, theft, murder, adultery, coveting, wickedness, deceit, licentiousness, envy, slander, pride, foolishness" (Mark 7:21–22).

The defilement of the heart, or *kardia,* is a particularly rich concept in Scripture. The heart is not only the center of physical life as in modern thinking, but is variously described as "the seat of thought and will,"[7] "the centre and seat of spiritual life,"[8] and the "source of the whole inner life," including "its thinking, feeling, and volition."[9] A. Sand sums up the implications of heart nicely, writing that *kardia* "refers thus to the *inner person,* the seat of understanding, knowledge, and will, and takes on the meaning of *conscience.*"[10]

Given that richness of meaning, the Bible teaching that humans have corrupted and sinful hearts has wide implications. With evil thoughts coming from the heart (Matt. 15:19), shameful desires dwelling in the heart (Rom. 1:24), and the heart being disobedient and impenitent (Rom. 2:5) and dull, darkened, and hardened (Eph. 4:18), it is little wonder that the Bible not only emphasizes the need of a new birth (John 3:3, 5), but

---

6. James Denney, *Studies in Theology* (Grand Rapids: Baker, 1976), 83; cf. Ramm, *Offense to Reason,* 86.

7. R. T. France, *The Gospel of Mark,* The New International Greek Testament Commentary Series (Grand Rapids: Eerdmans, 2002), 292.

8. Joseph H. Thayer, *Thayer's Greek-English Lexicon of the New Testament* (Peabody, MA: Hendrickson, n.d.), 325.

9. Walter Bauer, *A Greek-English Lexicon of the New Testament and Other Early Christian Literature,* 3rd ed., ed. and rev. Frederick William Danker (Chicago: University of Chicago Press, 2000), 508.

10. Horst Balz and Gerhard Schneider, eds., *Exegetical Dictionary of the New Testament* (Grand Rapids: Eerdmans, 1991), 2:250.

also the need of a "new heart" (Ezek. 18:31) with God's principles infusing it (Heb. 8:10).

Previously it was mentioned that total depravity is a concept that is often misunderstood. As a result, before moving forward, depravity needs to be examined in order to see what it is and what it is not. Negatively, depravity does not mean (1) that unrenewed individuals cannot do actions that are socially good. It is outwardly obvious that Christians have no monopoly on such things as civic morality. Every community, for example, contains secular individuals of moral character who unselfishly give of their time and finances to those in need. (2) Total depravity does not mean people are devoid of conscience or some knowledge of God. Paul argues just the opposite in such passages as Romans 1:20 and 2:14–15. (3) Nor does it imply that every unregenerate person will indulge in every form of sin or sin to the greatest extent possible. (4) Finally, total depravity does not mean that sinful beings are incapable of recognizing virtuous character and actions in others.

Thus it is that the biblical understanding of total depravity represents the potential for complete evil but not the reality of total evil. In order to account for the evidence of residual goodness in all people, theologians have developed the concept of common grace. Thomas Oden writes that "that grace is called *common* which is shared by all humanity even amid all conceivable forms of fallenness." As a result, "we may be thankful that by common grace God 'upholds the universe by his word of power' (Heb. 1:3, RSV), 'causes his sun to rise on the evil and the good' (Matt. 5:45), restrains social sin from becoming ungovernable (Rom. 13:1–4), enables society to live together in a proximately just and orderly manner, and enables it to cultivate scientific, rational, and economic pursuits of civilization."[11] Without common grace, life would be impossible due to the effects of sin. Common grace came into effect at the very time that God chose not to let the results of sin take Adam's life on the very day he rebelled (Gen. 2:17). God upheld Adam in life in spite of his fallen condition. Thus it is that by common grace God curbs the ravages of sin in both individuals and societies and thereby provides all individuals with some knowledge of Himself and goodness. Closely linked with common grace is the fact that at the Fall the image of God in people was not

---

11. Balz and Schneider, *Exegetical Dictionary of the New Testament*, 2:250.

destroyed even though it has been fractured and grossly distorted (Gen. 9:6; 1 Cor. 11:7; Jas. 3:9). As John Calvin put it, a "residue" of the image continued to exist in humanity after the Fall, "some sparks still gleam" in the "degenerate nature."[12] Therefore, although people are twisted and lost as a result of the Fall, they are still human with humans potentials, albeit potentials limited by the effects of sin.

At this point it is important to discuss the positive meaning of total depravity. First, as noted previously, it means that inherent corruption extends to every part of an individual's nature. Second, total depravity reflects the fact that "corrupt motives also lie behind the good things we do."[13] That dynamic is reflected in the Pharisee's temple prayer, in which his self-righteous attitude, rather than genuine piety, motivated what outwardly appeared to be pious acts (Luke 18:9–14). Third, because depravity affects the entire being and all of its faculties, there is nothing a person can do to merit saving favor with God.

That third point moves our discussion beyond sin's pollution of the human being and total depravity to the topic of spiritual inability. Or as Bernard Ramm puts it, "Total Depravity translated into the area of salvation means total inability."[14] The point Paul makes so effectively in Romans 1:17–3:20 is that universal human inability makes it impossible for people of their own accord and by any means to appear justified before God. That fact also undergirds Paul's presentation in Ephesians 2 and 4:17–24, in which he presents Christ and saving grace as absolutely necessary because human beings are sinners who live in darkness.

Spiritual inability or total spiritual inability is directly tied to the effect of sin upon the human will. The will, as Ellen White so nicely phrases it, "is the governing power in the nature of man."[15] Disorient the will and the entire life is out of kilter. That disorientation took place in Genesis 3 when the still free Eve chose "to dethrone love to God from its place of supremacy in the soul," and to place her own will there.[16] With

---

12. John Calvin, *Institutes of the Christian Religion,* book 2, chap. 2:12.

13. Stanley J. Grenz, *Theology for the Community of God* (Nashville, TN: Broadman & Holman, 1994), 240.

14. Ramm, *Offense to Reason,* 87.

15. Ellen G. White, *Steps to Christ* (Mountain View, CA: Pacific Press, n.d.), 47.

16. James Orr, *God's Image in Man and Its Defacement in the Light of Modern*

that disorientation of the center of life, Ramm argues, "the whole psyche" became "like a ship whose rudder is fixed at a wrong angle or like an airplane whose wing adjustments are permanently set askew."[17] Stanley Grenz makes the same point when he writes that "sin affects a person's entire heart. It infects our personal 'control center.'"[18]

Thus at the very center of the human predicament is the perversion of the will leading to a perverted inclination of the will that is hostile to God. It is for that reason that the unaided human will loves darkness rather than light (John 3:19) and that people become "slaves to various passions and pleasures" (Tit. 3:3), even those that lead to their destruction.

The key word in the last sentence is "slaves." One of Paul's favorite metaphors for the effects of sin on humanity is enslavement. Thus he writes of those outside of Christ as being "slaves of sin" (Rom. 6:17). And Jesus teaches that even a person who proclaims that he or she is not in bondage may still be "a slave to sin" (John 8:33–34). Such is the deceptiveness of the sinful heart (Jer. 17:9).

From the biblical perspective sin "is a cosmic power that enslaves its prey. . . . Just as conquering armies enslaved subjected peoples, so also we find ourselves slaves of a hostile, foreign force called sin. No longer able to exercise choice, we discover that we must obey sin, for it exercises power over us."[19] It was that understanding of the power of sin that led to the Reformation idea of "the bondage of the will."

Here it is important to stop for a moment to explore the amount of freedom inherent in the unrenewed human will. On one level there is freedom of the will in what Luther and Calvin identified as the "things below." That is, individuals have freedom in social and moral matters. As a result, people are free to choose their path in terms of daily activities, such as selecting a spouse, job, or college. Likewise, an individual is free to either care for or abuse his or her children, to refuse or accept certain temptations, or to seek religion or God from motives of self-interest. Even those with a strong predestinarian

---

Denials (London: Hodder and Stoughton, 1905), 223, 216; cf. George R. Knight, *Sin and Salvation: God's Work for and in Us* (Hagerstown, MD: Review and Herald, 2008), 38–43.

17. Ramm, *Offense to Reason*, 149.

18. Grenz, *Theology for the Community of God*, 239.

19. Ibid., 272.

belief system recognize that sinful humans still have "reason, conscience, and the freedom of choice in their daily affairs."[20]

On the other hand, given the disorientation of the human will in its relation to God, humans do not have free will in spiritual matters. Rather, as Ellen White points out, "there is in" every person's "nature a bent to evil, a force which, unaided, he cannot resist."[21] Grenz makes the same point when he writes that "the choosing individual faces moral choice already predisposed." Thus "freedom" of the will "means the release from the predisposition toward evil in order to be able [to] choose the good."[22] As a result, sinful humanity is never neutral. Its free actions are limited by the propensity or tendency to sin residing in the heart and will—a propensity lodged there when humans put themselves and their wills at the center of their lives rather than God and His will. In that event what looked like the path to freedom ended up as the road to enslavement and spiritual death and inability (Prov. 14:12).

The New Testament teaching is that sinners are slaves to sin and are unable of themselves to turn to God and true righteousness. Spiritual freedom is the great lack among those under bondage to sin. Their essential need is to be enlightened by the Holy Spirit so that they will not remain in darkness (1 Cor. 2:14), to be born from above by the Spirit (John 3:3, 5), and to become new creatures in Christ (2 Cor. 5:17). Human beings cannot regenerate themselves, but must be born of God (John 1:12–13). Even their choices toward morality find their righteousness as nothing but "filthy rags" (Isa. 64:6, KJV).

James Denney sums up the problem of spiritual inability nicely when he writes that "there is *one* thing which man cannot do *alone*. . . . He cannot fulfil the destiny for which he was created." Denney then offers the ultimate challenge to those who deny spiritual inability: "When a man has been discovered, who has been able, *without Christ*, to reconcile himself to God, and to obtain dominion over the world and over sin, *then* the doctrine of inability, or of the bondage due to sin, may be denied; *then*, but *not till then*."[23]

Thus far this chapter has discussed the effects of sin on human nature in terms of pollution, total depravity, and the resulting spiritual inability. In that discussion the role of the will proved to be a central feature. The next

---

20. L. Berkhof, *Systematic Theology*, 4th ed. (Grand Rapids, MI: Eerdmans, 1941), 248.

21. White, *Education*, 29.

22. Grenz, *Theology for the Community of God*, 273.

23. Denney, *Studies in Theology*, 85.

section of the chapter will focus on the four major ways of relating to human inability and the bondage of the will in church history. That will be followed by a Seventh-day Adventist approach to the topic.

THEOLOGICAL PERSPECTIVES RELATED TO TOTAL DEPRAVITY AND SPIRITUAL INABILITY

The topics of depravity, inability, and the freedom of the will have played a central role across the history of the church in its discussion of salvation. Four quite distinct orientations developed across time. The first perspective on these topics is Pelagianism. Pelagianism arose about the year 400 when Pelagius, a British monk based in Rome, became alarmed at the moral laxity of the Roman Church. He argued forcefully for the need for human moral responsibility and insisted on the need for constant self-improvement in the light of Christ's example and Old Testament law. He affirmed freedom of the will and that all humans have the power not to sin. The choice is theirs to follow Adam's evil example or Christ's good one. Pelagius not only denied original sin and its results (inherited depravity and inability), but also assertively taught that humans have a natural ability to live sinless lives apart from empowering grace. Sin was viewed as an act willfully committed against God. Grace for Pelagius was external enlightenment provided for humanity by God through such things as the Ten Commandments and the example of Christ. Thus grace informs people regarding their moral duties but does not assist them in performing them. People are able to avoid sin through following the example of Jesus. In short, humans are morally neutral rather than depraved and they have the free will to choose good and evil. Thus sin is a problem of the human will rather than being rooted in human nature.[24] Following that line of thought, Hans LaRondelle points out that according to the Pelagian soteriology, "sinless perfection after baptism was not merely possible but a duty to

24. For helpful overviews of the Pelagian/Augustinian controversy, see Alister E. McGrath, *Historical Theology* (Oxford, UK: Blackwell, 1998), 35–37, 79–85; Geoffrey W. Bromiley, *Historical Theology* (Grand Rapids, MI: Eerdmans, 1978), 117–123; Edwin Harry Zackrison, "Seventh-day Adventists and Original Sin: A Study of the Early Development of the Seventh-day Adventist Understanding of the Effect of Adam's Sin on His Posterity" (PhD diss., Andrews University, 1984), 108–113.

achieve."[25] Success is a matter of choice and will power. While Pelagianism had its birth in the fifth century, it has had a vigorous existence ever since.

The second perspective on depravity, inability, and the freedom of the will was set forth by Pelagius's adversary, Augustine of Hippo (354–430), and passed on to the modern world largely through Luther and Calvin. Augustine's understanding can be viewed as the polar opposite to that of Pelagius. Pelagius held that after the Fall the human will was neutral and thus individuals were able to make in their own power a decision for God once the evidence was in, while Augustine held that the Fall had biased the will toward evil to the extent that it was enslaved to sin and could not unaided make a decision for God. While Pelagius viewed sin as an act performed by each individual on the basis of free choice which in itself frees people from a life of sin, Augustine argued that sin was a hereditary disease and that the effects of sin on the human will had enslaved it to the extent that unaided humans could not break free from its power. While Pelagius viewed grace as God's mercy in revealing the true way of life to people so that they could then choose to walk a sinless life, Augustine viewed grace as the saving act of God rather than mere moral guidance. Thus for Augustine humanity is justified by God as an act of grace, while for Pelagius people are justified on the basis of their merits in imitating the example of Christ.

Augustinian tradition held a firm belief in the pollution of humanity, total deprivation, and spiritual inability, while those in the Pelagian tradition rejected those beliefs—but how do those teachings relate to salvation in the real world? For Pelagius it was quite simple. A person had only to choose God and then choose to follow the example of Christ in daily life. But for those believing in total depravity, the bondage of the will, and spiritual inability, the problem was more complex. One possible solution was highlighted by the followers of John Calvin. Their response to total depravity was total grace to the extent that human choice did not even enter the picture. How could it, since the will was fallen and under the power of sin? Instead, God in His sovereignty made the choice by predetermining some individuals to be saved eternally while others were

---

25. H. K. LaRondelle, *Perfection and Perfectionism: A Dogmatic-Ethical Study of Biblical Perfection and Phenomenal Perfectionism* (Berrien Springs, MI: Andrews University Press, 1971), 290–291.

predetermined to eternal damnation. In the process the extreme Calvinists "simply annihilated human freedom."[26]

A third theological perspective on salvation in relation to depravity and inability is semi-Pelagianism, which is basically a compromise between Pelagianism and Augustinianism. On the one hand, the name semi-Pelagianism is misleading in the sense that its proponents do not accept the extreme position of Pelagius on human ability and grace as being merely informative toward the moral life. But, on the other hand, it has a major Pelagian element. Roger Olson highlights the essence of the semi-Pelagian contribution to the debate over salvation when he writes that the movement "embraces a modified version of original sin but believes that humans have the ability, even in their natural or fallen state, to initiate salvation by exercising a good will toward God."[27] However, after that free will decision has been made, saving grace in the Augustinian sense takes over.[28] Olson suggests that a large number of modern religions are semi-Pelagian by "default" due to the fact that many pastors and lay people have not fully thought through their understanding of free will in relationship to their understanding of the effects of sin on human nature.[29]

A fourth theological perspective on depravity, the fallen will, and human inability is Arminianism. Arminianism developed from within Dutch Calvinism, but it spread widely in the English world through the Wesleyan/Methodist movement. Both Arminians and Calvinists agreed that post-Fall humans in their natural state do not have free wills in the sense that they can choose to follow God. Yet the two theological traditions differ on their solution to that inability. Calvinists have God overriding the will through the unconditional predestination of individuals to salvation, while Arminians, who hold that "the human will ultimately determines whether the divine grace proffered to man is accepted or

---

26. Denney, *Studies in Theology,* 84. For an overview of the main positions of Calvinism, see Edwin H. Palmer, *The Five Points of Calvinism* (Grand Rapids, MI: Baker, 1972).

27. Roger E. Olson, *Arminian Theology: Myths and Realities* (Downers Grove, IL: IVP Academic, 2006), 17–18.

28. "Semipelagianism," in *The Oxford Dictionary of the Christian Church,* 3rd ed., ed. F. L. Cross and E. A. Livingstone (New York: Oxford University Press, 1997), 1481.

29. Roger E. Olson, *The Mosaic of Christian Belief: Twenty Centuries of Unity and Diversity* (Downers Grove, IL: InterVarsity, 2002), 274.

rejected," believe that God predestined Christ to become the potential Savior for every human being who would believe and repent.[30]

But that is where the problem comes in. Given the facts of the effects of original sin on human nature, including depravity and bondage of the will, there is no way that individuals can choose for God. Something has to wake them up to spiritual realities and enable them to choose. That something the Arminians called prevenient grace, the grace that works in a person's life before he or she accepts saving grace. The result of prevenient grace's enabling power through the Holy Spirit is a "freed will"—"one which, though initially bound by sin, has been brought by the prevenient grace of the Spirit of Christ to a point where it can respond freely to the divine call."[31] Thomas Oden refers to this concept as "grace-enabled freedom."[32] The end result is that Arminianism stands firmly in the grace-oriented Augustinian tradition and objects to Pelagianism with its denial of depravity, bondage of the will, and spiritual inability, while at the same time rejecting semi-Pelagianism.

SEVENTH-DAY ADVENTIST PERSPECTIVES ON DEPRAVITY AND SPIRITUAL ABILITY

Various Adventists have been tempted to embrace all the positions discussed up until now, except the Calvinistic option. The Adventist belief in free will is strong, even though the concept is largely misunderstood. With the denomination's traditional emphasis on the Ten Commandments, obedience, and sanctification, some of its adherents have been drawn to the Pelagian perspective, especially those with a theological orientation focused on sinless perfectionism.[33]

But more central to Adventism, with its clearer understanding of the centrality of grace since its 1888 General Conference session, is the divide

---

30. H. Orton Wiley and Paul T. Culbertson, *Introduction to Christian Theology* (Kansas City, MO: Beacon Hill Press of Kansas City, 1946), 263.

31. Olson, *Arminian Theology,* 164.

32. Ibid., 95.

33. For a fuller discussion, see George R. Knight, "Seventh-day Adventism, Semi-Pelagianism, and Overlooked Topics in Adventist Soteriology: Moving Beyond Missing Links and Toward a More Explicit Understanding," *Andrews University Seminary Studies,* vol. 51, no. 1 (2013): 3–24.

between semi-Pelagian and Arminian understandings. Having said that, it is important to realize that Adventists have by and large neglected a discussion of those aspects of the plan of salvation that have divided the Arminians and semi-Pelagians. The reason for that neglect is not difficult to discover. Namely, while much of the discussion among Arminians, semi-Pelagians, and Calvinists has been focused primarily on the beginning of salvation for individuals, Adventists, with their concern with the law and end-time events, largely neglected beginnings while focusing on how people ought to live and what they had to do to be ready for the coming of Christ.

While that is true, many twentieth century Adventist authors explicitly stated their belief in total depravity and spiritual inability, but then inconsistently went on to provide a semi-Pelagian solution to the sin problem by stating that by free will one could choose to accept the grace of Christ and become a Christian.[34]

There were exceptions to that rule, including Hans LaRondelle and Edward Vick.[35] But perhaps the most important exception was Ellen White. In the 1890s she made several points to clarify the issue. She not only explicitly stated her perspective on human depravity and spiritual inability, but she explicitly denied that free will could initiate the plan of salvation for an individual.[36] Even more to the point is her statement that "many are confused as to what constitutes the first steps in the work of salvation. Repentance is thought to be a work the sinner must do for himself in order that he may come to Christt. . . . Yet the sinner cannot bring himself to repentance, or prepare himself to come to Christ. . . . The very first step to Christ is taken through the drawing of the Spirit of God; as man responds to this drawing, he advances toward Christ in

34. William Henry Branson, *How Men Are Saved: The Certainty, Plan, and Time for Man's Salvation* (Nashville, TN: Southern Publishing Assn., 1941), 8, 10, 18, 19, 23, 27, 29; Edward Heppenstall, *Salvation Unlimited: Perspectives in Righteousness by Faith* (Washington, DC: Review and Herald, 1974), 14–15, 17–18, 23–25; see also the discussion of these authors in Knight, "Seventh-day Adventism."

35. Hans K. LaRondelle, *Christ Our Salvation: What God Does for Us and in Us* (Mountain View, CA: Pacific Press, 1980), 12–20; Edward W. H. Vick, *Let Me Assure You: Of Grace, of Faith, of Forgiveness, of Freedom, of Fellowship, of Hope* (Mountain View, CA: Pacific Press, 1968), 1, 12. See also, Knight, *Sin and Salvation*, 73–74, 87.

36. White, *Steps*, 18. We will return to this passage in my other chapter—"The Grace That Comes Before Saving Grace"—in its discussion of prevenient grace.

order that he may repent. . . . Repentance is no less the gift of God than are pardon and justification, and it cannot be experienced except as it is given to the soul by Christ."[37]

With such statements Ellen White placed herself firmly in the Arminian camp, while rejecting the semi-Pelagianism of many of her fellow believers. In the process she took into full account the biblical teachings on total depravity, the bondage of the will, spiritual inability, and the absolute need of grace in every step of the Christian journey. Above all, she highlighted what those in the Arminian/Wesleyan sector of Protestantism called prevenient grace—the grace that comes before saving grace and frees the will so that an individual can make the grace-inspired choice to accept the saving grace of God in Christ.

---

37. Ellen G. White, *Selected Messages* (Washington, DC: Review and Herald, 1958), 1:390–391.

SECTION 3

Jesus Saves: A Perfect Solution?

The willingness of God to restore His relationship with fallen humanity has rarely been questioned by Christian believers. After all, Scripture testifies that already in the Garden of Eden God initiated the plan of salvation that would ultimately reconcile humanity to Himself (Gen. 3:15). Most Christians also agree that Jesus Christ plays a crucial role in the plan of salvation and that His role has been defined in the plan of God "from the foundation of the world" (Rev. 13:8).[1] While this much has been agreed on, Christians often have different views on exactly how the atonement is accomplished. Was the incarnation necessary for reconciliation between God and humanity to occur? What exactly happened on the cross? Did Christ have to die? Was Christ's atoning mission completed at the cross, or is it continued in His priestly ministry? Has humanity's fate been sealed on the cross, or is the final reconciliation still awaiting us in the future? These and other questions have troubled Christian believers throughout the centuries and continue to do so today. The clear biblical answers to these questions are necessary in order to understand what God accomplished through Christ for humanity.

The authors of the chapters in this section will attempt to address these questions. The first chapter, authored by Denis Fortin, provides the historical background to the biblical concept of atonement. It also traces the historical development of various models of atonement. In the second chapter, Jon Paulien specifically focuses on the completeness and unlimited nature of the atoning sacrifice of Christ on the cross. The third chapter, written by Jiří Moskala, focuses on the continuing ministry of

---

1. Unless otherwise indicated, all Scripture quotations are taken from the New King James Version®. Copyright © 1982 by Thomas Nelson. Used by permission. All rights reserved.

Christ on behalf of humanity in the heavenly sanctuary. Finally, in the fourth chapter, Roy Gane writes about the eternal reconciliation that will be realized in the kingdom of God.

CHAPTER 9

HISTORICAL AND THEOLOGICAL BACKGROUND OF THE DOCTRINE OF ATONEMENT

Denis Fortin

The book of Revelation gives a glimpse of a scene in the heavenly courtroom in which the entire host of heaven sing praises to Christ.

> Now when He [the Lamb] had taken the scroll, the four living creatures and the twenty-four elders fell down before the Lamb, each having a harp, and golden bowls full of incense, which are the prayers of the saints. And they sang a new song, saying: "You are worthy to take the scroll, and to open its seals; for You were slain, and have redeemed us to God by Your blood out of every tribe and tongue and people and nation, and have made us kings and priests to our God; and we shall reign on the earth." (Rev. 5:8–10, NKJV)

The reason given for this magnificent worship of the Lamb is because He was slain and thus has redeemed God's people. At the core of the message of salvation is this belief that Christ died on the cross to redeem humanity, that His death is the catalyst that makes salvation possible. Without His death there would be no salvation.

The doctrine of atonement seeks to explain the reasons why the divine pre-existent Son of God became a human being and why Christ's death redeems humanity. This doctrine is closely dependent on what is explained in the doctrines of Christ (Christology) and salvation (soteriology). This chapter will explain some of the theories theologians have proposed to explain Christ's death on the cross.

NO SIMPLE EXPLANATION

In the eleventh century, Anselm (1033–1109), archbishop of Canterbury, asked: "Why did God become man? For what purpose did Christ come down from heaven?"[1] Before Anselm's time and since then, numerous theologians have pondered the same questions and have come up with multiple reasons to explain both the incarnation and the death of Christ. Hence books on this topic are legion and there seem to be almost as many theories on atonement as there are authors. Anglican theologian Leon Morris notes,

> It is an interesting fact that through the centuries the Church has agreed that the cross is at the very heart of the faith, but it has never come to an agreed conclusion as to how the cross saves men. Some Christians have thought of it as the means of God's winning a great victory. Some have seen in it a revelation of divine love. Some have regarded it as the payment of the debt that sinners owed. And we could go on. The theories are many, and the Church has never officially declared her mind on the matter.[2]

One reason for this, Morris observes, is the complexity of the subject and limited human understanding of sin is part of the complexity. Sin can be understood from many angles: all at once it is a transgression of God's law, a debt, an incurring of guilt, a coming under the power of some evil, and much more. "Obviously anything that is able to deal effectively with all the aspects of all the sins of all men will itself be exceedingly complex. . . . And when a thing is necessarily complex there is bound to be a certain amount of disagreement as to what it means essentially."[3] Thus for Morris, and for many theologians,

> a recognition that the atonement is many-sided is a first essential if we are to make progress in the subject. A good deal of harm has been caused by well-meaning people who have had such a firm grasp of one aspect of the subject that they have proceeded to maintain that all else is immaterial. There is a well-known saying that "Theories of the atonement are right in what they affirm and wrong in what they deny." . . . Since the atonement is

---

1. The Latin title of the book is *Cur Deus Homo? Ad quid Christus descendebat?*

2. Leon Morris, *Glory in the Cross: A Study in Atonement* (Grand Rapids, MI: Baker Book House, 1966), 58.

3. Ibid., 58–59.

God's perfect provision for man's need it is necessarily many-sided. And since man's perception is at best partial each of us can perceive part of the truth only. . . . We must always bear in mind that this subject is a large one, and that there are many ways of looking at it.[4]

THEORIES OF ATONEMENT

Over the centuries various explanations of the doctrine of atonement have been proposed. All of them sought to answer the question of why Jesus died on the cross. When Jesus said, "It is finished" (John 19:30)—what was finished? Of the various theories offered, the five most prominent ones will be reviewed in the order they were developed.[5]

The Ransom Theory: Atonement as Victory over the Forces of Sin and Evil

In the first two centuries, redemption was a fact rather than a doctrine and few attempts were made to clarify the reasons for Jesus's death on the cross. In fact, the Apostles' Creed, one of the earliest confessions of faith, simply stated about Christ that He "suffered under Pontius Pilate, was crucified, died, and was buried; he descended into hell, the third day he rose again from the dead; he ascended into heaven, and sits on the right hand of God, the Father almighty; from thence he shall come to judge the quick and the dead." Nothing is said about the reasons for Jesus's death.

But the Apostle Paul in the New Testament offered two initial perspectives. One identified Christ's death on the cross as the dramatic moment of a cosmic victory over the forces of evil and the means of a reconciliation between God and His estranged world (Col. 1:20; 2:15). Additionally, Christ's death also provided the price for the redemption of all humanity (1 Cor. 6:20; Col. 1:13, 14; see also Matt. 20:28; Mark 10:45). These two aspects of atonement—victory and ransom—provided the biblical framework to understand the death of Christ.

---

4. Ibid., 59–60.

5. Millard J. Erickson provides a good summary of the various theories of atonement presented in this chapter. See *Christian Theology*, 2nd ed. (Grand Rapids, MI: Baker Books, 1998), 798–817.

It is only after the second century that tangible attempts at formulating a theory of atonement began to be constructed. When the subject of atonement was discussed, it was simply believed that a transaction between God and the devil had occurred, and on the cross Jesus had paid the price for the redemption of humanity.

This ransom (or bargain) theory was the dominant view for about nine centuries until the time of Anselm of Canterbury. The first suggestion of this theory among early church fathers appears in Irenaeus (d. 202) in his treatise *Against Heresies*. Origen (184–253) left no doubt about his belief in the ransom theory.

> If then we were "bought with a price," as also Paul asserts, we were doubtless bought from one whose servants we were, who also named what price he would for releasing those whom he held from his power. Now it was the devil that held us, to whose side we had been drawn away by our sins. He asked, therefore, as our price the blood of Christ.[6]

In the twentieth century, this view of atonement was revived by Gustaf Aulén (1879–1977), a Swedish Lutheran theologian.[7]

This view builds on the biblical imagery of ransom and redemption (Matt. 20:28; Mark 10:45). Origen, for example, makes much of Paul words in 1 Corinthians 6:20, "You were bought at a price." If Christ bought humanity, it must certainly have been from the one whose servants humans were, namely, the devil. Logically, the ransom could not have been paid to God, but it was determined by, paid to, and accepted by Satan.

Taking this metaphor too far has led to all kinds of speculations. If the price for the ransom demanded by the devil was Christ's soul, did the devil know that Jesus was divine and that His soul could not remain in the devil's possession even after Christ died? There has been also a lot of discussion as to whether God used some kind of deception to trick the devil into accepting the soul of Jesus as the price for redeeming humanity, while knowing that Jesus's soul could not remain in hell since He was sinless.

---

6. *Commentary on Romans* 2.13, quoted in L. W. Grensted, *A Short History of the Doctrine of the Atonement* (Manchester: Manchester University Press, 1920), 37.

7. See *Christus Victor: An Historical Study of the Three Main Types of the Idea of Atonement* (New York: Macmillan, 1951), 26–27.

In many ways, Ellen White also affirmed the classical theory of atonement that Calvary was the sign of Christ's ultimate victory over the powers of evil and Satan. In her small brochure on the "The Sufferings of Christ," first published in 1869,[8] she wrote, "He [Christ] was about to ransom His people with His own blood. . . . This was the means through which an end was to be finally made of sin and Satan, and his host to be vanquished."[9] At the cross, "Satan was then defeated. He knew that his kingdom was lost."[10] White devoted an entire chapter to this theme in the *Desire of Ages*. In this chapter, she affirmed unequivocally that Christ's death on the cross was God's appointed means to gain the victory over the forces of evil and Satan. "Christ did not yield up His life till He had accomplished the work which He came to do, and with His parting breath He exclaimed, 'It is finished.' . . . The battle had been won. . . . All heaven triumphed in the Saviour's victory. Satan was defeated."[11]

The Satisfaction Theory: Atonement as Compensation to the Father

The most objective of all the theories of atonement is the satisfaction theory. While some Latin Fathers had anticipated this theory of the atonement (for example, Augustine and Gregory the Great),[12] it was Anselm of Canterbury who articulated it in the Middle Ages. His book *Cur Deus Homo* has become a classic on the subject.

In this theory, Christ died to satisfy a principle in the very nature of God the Father. Inspired by the medieval feudal system, Anselm argued that God is like a feudal lord who needs to maintain his honor and that there must be adequate satisfaction for any encroachment upon it. In this setting, sin is understood to be a failure to render God His due. Thus sinners dishonor God.

In response, God must act to preserve His own honor. He cannot merely forgive or remit sin without punishing it. Sin left unpunished would leave God's

---

8. "The Sufferings of Christ" has been published in Ellen G. White, *Testimonies for the Church* (Mountain View, CA: Pacific Press, 1948), 2:200–215.

9. White, *Testimonies for the Church*, 2:209.

10. Ibid., 211.

11. Ellen G. White, *The Desire of Ages* (Mountain View, CA: Pacific Press, 1898, 1940), 758.

12. See Grensted, *A Short History of the Doctrine of the Atonement*, 120–121.

economy out of order. God's violated honor can be put right again either by His punishing sinners or by accepting satisfaction made in their behalf. This satisfaction, however, could not possibly be rendered by a human being because humanity is sinful. To set things right in the economy of God's kingdom, something had to be done for human beings by someone qualified to represent them.

To be effective the satisfaction rendered had to be greater than what all created human beings are capable of doing. Thus only God could make satisfaction. However, if it was to restore humanity's relationship with God, it had to be made by a human being. Therefore, the satisfaction had to be rendered by someone who is both God and human and, consequently, the incarnation of the Son of God became a necessity. Christ, being both God and sinless human, did not deserve death. Thus, the sacrifice of His life to God on behalf of the human race went beyond what was required of Him. And thus His substitutionary death satisfied God's honor and justice.

The logic of this view is remarkable, and many texts of Scripture support its key elements. In Romans, Paul is clear in his description of God's wrath toward sinners; God is offended by sin (1:18–32). Jesus's death is described as a propitiatory sacrifice for humanity (Isa. 53:4–6; Rom. 3:23–26; 1 John 2:2) and as a substitutionary ransom (1 Tim. 2:6).

Notwithstanding the biblical support, this view is not without its challenges. Of all the views on atonement, this one is the most readily rejected because of the portrayal of God as a vengeful god, as having a gripe with humanity and intent on its destruction. God needs the atonement to appease His wrath. Many theologians object to the violence this view requires. Why would God require the violent death of His Son in order to forgive sinners?[13]

However, as a partial response to these objections, John 3:16 teaches that atonement is also an act of love from the Father. Jesus's death did not cause the Father to love humanity. God's wrath and His love need to be kept in balance. He hates sin, but He loves humanity.

For Ellen White, Christ's death was a substitutionary sacrifice; Christ suffered our penalty for sins, died our death, and bore our sins. "Christ consented to die in the sinner's stead, that man, by a life of obedience, might escape the penalty of the law of God."[14] At Calvary, "The glorious

---

13. An example of a recent publication addressing this issue is John Sanders, ed., *Atonement and Violence: A Theological Conversation* (Nashville: Abingdon, 2006).

14. White, *Testimonies for the Church*, 2:200–201.

Redeemer of a lost world was suffering the penalty of man's transgression of the Father's law."[15]

White argued as well that Christ's substitutionary sacrificial death is the means by which sinners can be justified by faith. Without this substitutionary atonement, there can be no justification of sinners. Her classic statement in *The Desire of Ages* is clear: "Christ was treated as we deserve, that we might be treated as He deserves. He was condemned for our sins, in which He had no share, that we might be justified by His righteousness, in which we had no share. He suffered the death which was ours, that we might receive the life which was His. 'With His stripes we are healed.'"[16]

White also clarified her understanding of how Jesus bore the wrath of God on the cross. "Through Jesus, God's mercy was manifested to men; but mercy does not set aside justice. The law reveals the attributes of God's character, and not a jot or tittle of it could be changed to meet man in his fallen condition. God did not change His law, but He sacrificed Himself, in Christ, for man's redemption. 'God was in Christ, reconciling the world unto Himself.'"[17] In White's understanding of this concept of propitiation, there is no dichotomy or irreconcilable chasm between God's love and God's justice. She does not believe that on the cross Jesus attempted to make God love humanity; in fact, in this context she never uses the verb *to appease*. God does not need to be appeased. Rather, it is a self-renouncing God who is sacrificing Himself to redeem a lost humanity. Jesus Himself bears the wrath of God.

The Moral-Influence Theory: Atonement as a Demonstration of God's Love

In contrast to the satisfaction theory that is strictly focused on God benefiting from the atonement, the moral influence theory speaks only of the benefits that Christ's death achieved for humanity. This theory emphasizes the divine dimension of Christ's death as a demonstration of God's love. This view was first developed by Peter Abelard (1079–1142) in response to Anselm's satisfaction theory.

---

15. Ibid., 209.

16. White, *Desire of Ages*, 25.

17. Ibid., 762.

The moral-influence theory emphasizes the primacy of God's love and insists that Christ did not make some sort of sacrificial payment to the Father to satisfy His offended dignity. Rather, Jesus demonstrated to human beings the full extent of the love of God for them. It was humanity's fear and ignorance of God that needed to be rectified. This was accomplished by Christ's death. So the major effect of Christ's death was for the benefit of humanity rather than for God.

Among other aspects of the atonement, Abelard emphasized the moral influence aspect of the atonement. In his *Commentary on the Epistle to the Romans*, he presented "the Cross as the manifestation of the love of God, and to the thought of this love he continually returns."[18] The justification of humanity is in the kindling of this divine love in their hearts in the presence of the Cross. To love is to be free from the slavery of sin, to attain to the true liberty of the children of God. The justification and the reconciliation of human beings to God consist in the grace shown to humanity in the incarnation of Christ and in the endurance of Christ in teaching by word and by example, even unto death.

This view of atonement understands that God is essentially love. Other aspects of God's character are minimized (e.g., justice, holiness, and righteousness). Therefore, human beings need not fear God's justice and punishment. Humanity's problem is not that they have violated God's law and God will punish them. Rather, their problem is that their own attitudes keep them apart from God.

Sin is perceived as a type of sickness from which humanity must be healed. It is to correct this defect in humanity that Christ came. Sin manifests itself by fear of God, separation and alienation from Him. Human nature is essentially free from the effects of sin. In a Pelagian fashion an individual can accept salvation and turn from sin after receiving a revelation of the love of God.

Jesus's death is a demonstration of divine love. His death was only one of the modes in which His love was expressed. It was not the purpose of His coming; rather, it was a consequence of His coming. The healing of sin-sick souls is the real work of Jesus. As Horace Bushnell states,

> Only to have seen one perfect life, to have heard the words and received the pure conceptions of one sinless spirit, to have felt the working of his charities,

---

18. Grensted, *A Short History of the Doctrine of the Atonement,* 104.

and witnessed the offering of his sinless obedience, would have been to receive the seeds of a moral revolution that must ultimately affect the whole race. This was true even of a Socrates. Our world is not the same world that it was before he lived in it. Much less the same, since the sinless Jesus lived and suffered in it. Such a character has, of necessity, an organific power.[19]

By His death on the cross, Jesus fulfilled three most basic human needs. The first is humanity's need for openness to God, an inclination to respond to Him. Human beings are naturally fearful of God. Christ understands humanity's situation, and He came to open the way, to show the love of God by dying the most cruel death, obliterating humanity's fear of God.

A second human need satisfied by the cross is a genuine and deep conviction of personal sin and a resultant repentance. By His death Jesus accomplishes this need in humanity. When individuals seek Him whom they have pierced by their sin, then they are softened. And they repent and turn to Jesus in love.

Thirdly, humanity's need for inspiration to live a holy life is fulfilled in the cross. In Jesus human beings see the practical and personal exposition of real holiness in a person's life. Thus Jesus's death on the cross exerts a moral influence on the lives of people in every generation. When people see Jesus God's love, God's suffering, and God's holiness in the man Jesus, they are morally influenced to abide by God's Word.

One can argue that the most basic aspect of Ellen White's theology of atonement centers on the death of Christ as a demonstration of the love of God for lost humanity. "Who can comprehend the love here displayed! . . . All this in consequence of sin! Nothing could have induced Christ to leave His honor and majesty in heaven, and come to a sinful world, to be neglected, despised, and rejected by those He came to save, and finally to suffer upon the cross, but eternal, redeeming love, which will ever remain a mystery."[20] Moreover, she also affirms that such a demonstration of the love of God exerts a powerful moral influence on humanity. She writes that reflecting on the events of Calvary will "awaken tender, sacred, and lively emotions in the Christian's heart" and remove "pride and self-esteem."[21]

---

19. Horace Bushnell, *God in Christ: Three Discourses* (New York: Scribner, Armstrong, and Company, 1877), 205–206.

20. White, *Testimonies for the Church,* 2:207.

21. Ibid., 212. Years later, Ellen White offered this same theme as the starting point of her book *The Desire of Ages*: "It was to manifest this glory [of God] that He came to our world. To

Eternal interests are here involved. Upon this theme it is sin to be calm and unimpassioned. The scenes of Calvary call for the deepest emotion. Upon this subject you will be excusable if you manifest enthusiasm. . . . The contemplation of the matchless depths of a Saviour's love should fill the mind, touch and melt the soul, refine and elevate the affections, and completely transform the whole character.[22]

The Socinian Theory: Atonement as Example

This theory was first articulated by a sixteenth-century Polish theologian, Faustus Socinus (1539–1604), and today this view is held by Unitarians. Basically, this view rejects any idea of Christ's death having any vicarious satisfaction and maintains that Christ's ministry on earth was prophetic rather than priestly. Embracing Arianism, Socinianism emphasized only Christ's humanity.

The covenant of which Jesus spoke involves an absolute forgiveness rather than some form of substitutionary sacrifice. The real value of the death of Jesus lies in the beautiful and perfect example that it gives us. It is the type of dedication that all Christians are to practice. Socinianism points to 1 Peter 2:21 as the explicit connection between Christ's example and His death: "To this you were called, because Christ suffered for you, leaving you an example, that you should follow in his steps" (NIV).

Several doctrinal concepts feed into the Socinian understanding of atonement. A Pelagian view of the human condition is foundational: humanity is spiritually and morally capable of doing God's will, of fulfilling God's expectations. Furthermore, God is not perceived as a God of retributive justice, and therefore He does not demand some form of satisfaction from or on behalf of those who sin against Him.[23] And what about Jesus?

---

this sin-darkened earth He came to reveal the light of God's love,—to be 'God with us.' . . . In the light from Calvary it will be seen that the law of self-renouncing love is the law of life for earth and heaven; that the love which 'seeketh not her own' has its source in the heart of God" (19–20). The same sentiments are echoed at the beginning of *Patriarchs and Prophets*, "The history of the great conflict between good and evil, from the time it first began in heaven to the final overthrow of rebellion and the total eradication of sin, is also a demonstration of God's unchanging love," *Patriarchs and Prophets* (Mountain View, CA: Pacific Press, 1890, 1958), 33.

22. Ibid., 213.

23. The *Racovian Catechism* states, "For although we confess, and hence exceedingly

He is merely a human. The death He experienced was simply that of an ordinary human being in a fallen and sinful world. His death is an example for all humans of what it means to fulfill God's requirements.

This view of atonement also explains that humanity has in Jesus a perfect example of that total love for God humans must display if they are to experience salvation. The death of Jesus gives humanity inspiration. It is possible for humans to love God wholeheartedly since Jesus did it.

This theory, however, exhibits some evident weaknesses. It fails to come to grips with other texts of Scripture that speak of Jesus's death quite differently. Scripture speaks also of ransom, sacrifice, and sin-bearing in reference to Jesus's death. Three verses after Socinianism's major text, Peter says that Jesus "himself bore our sins in his body on the cross, so that we might die to sins and live for righteousness; by his wounds you have been healed" (1 Pet. 2:24, NIV).

For Socinianism the atonement is only a metaphorical concept. All that is necessary for God and human beings to have fellowship with one another is for humanity to have faith in and love for God. For God to have required something more would have been contrary to His nature, and to have punished the innocent (Jesus) in place of the guilty (humanity) would have been contrary to justice. "Rather, God and humans are restored to their intended relationship by our personal adoption of both the teachings of Jesus and the example he set in life and especially in death."[24] Clearly Socinianism is a subjective view of atonement: only humanity benefits from the death of Jesus.

The Governmental Theory: Atonement as a Demonstration of Divine Justice

Another major view of the doctrine of atonement was developed by Hugo Grotius (1583–1645), a seventeenth-century Dutch theologian. He developed his theory in response to the Socinians, whose view of atonement he regarded as too human-centered.

---

rejoice, that our God is wonderfully merciful and just, nevertheless we deny that there are in him the mercy and justice which our adversaries imagine, since the one would wholly annihilate the other." Quoted in Millard J. Erickson, ed., *Man's Need and God's Gift: Readings in Christian Theology* (Grand Rapids, MI: Baker Book House, 1976), 364.

24. Erickson, *Christian Theology,* 802.

For Grotius, God is holy and righteous. As the ruler of the universe, He has established certain laws and transgressions of His laws are assaults upon His government. But God's love is also the basis of His actions and He loves the human race. He has the right to punish sin (since He is the ruler of the universe), but it is not mandatory that He do so. He can forgive sin and absolve the guilty. The way He does this manifests both His clemency and severity. God can forgive sin, but He also takes into consideration the interests of His moral government. To forgive guilty people too often would undermine the authority of His administration.

Hence, Christ's death accomplished the means of atonement. It provides grounds for forgiveness and simultaneously retains the structure of the moral government. His death was not a penalty inflicted on Jesus as a substitute for the penalty that is attached to the sins of humanity (like Anselm advocated). Christ's death was a substitute for a penalty, an example of what will happen to humanity if they persist in sin. In Christ's death God demonstrated that His justice will require humanity to suffer if they continue in sin. Looking at the sufferings of Christ is enough to deter people from sin. And if human beings turn from sin, they can be forgiven and God's moral government can be preserved.

Grotius believed that the death of Christ was not a punishment because Christ was sinless. No penalty could be attached or transferred to Christ. Punishment is personal to the individual. If it could be transferred, the connection between sin and guilt would be severed. Christ's suffering was not a vicarious bearing of humanity's punishment, but a demonstration of God's hatred of sin, a demonstration intended to induce in human beings a horror of sin. Grotius's theory is a form of the "penal substitution" view, because he believed only Christ's sufferings, not His death, are the substitution to the rightful punishment that should be inflicted upon sinners.

To some extent, Ellen White's understanding of atonement falls also within the governmental theory and, in ways, is reminiscent of Hugo Grotius's thought. She affirmed that Calvary is a vindication of God's character, law, and just government. (But in contrast to Grotius, Ellen White believed that Jesus died a substitutionary, vicarious death.) Her concept of the great controversy argues that the universal government of God has been threatened by the rebellion of Lucifer and his angels and the sin of humanity. Satan has claimed that God's law and character are unfair and harmful to the harmony of the universe. To prove these accusations wrong, God sent His Son to live and die for humanity, and in a broader sense to save the universe from chaos. In Jesus, God's character is demonstrated as love and justice, and His law as fair and equitable.

> His death did not make the law of non effect; it did not slay the law, lessen its holy claims, nor detract from its sacred dignity. The death of Christ proclaimed the justice of His Father's law in punishing the transgressor, in that He consented to suffer the penalty of the law Himself in order to save fallen man from its curse. The death of God's beloved Son on the cross shows the immutability of the law of God. . . . The death of Christ justified the claims of the law.[25]

As is now clear, there exists inter-connectedness among various theological concepts or doctrines, and the view one holds in one area affects the interpretation of Scripture dealing with other doctrines. In other words, one's conclusions on one doctrine constitute the presuppositions for another. "In the doctrine of the atonement we see perhaps the clearest indication of the organic character of theology, that is, we see that the various doctrines fit together in a cohesive fashion. The position taken on any one of them affects or contributes to the construction of the others."[26]

As Leon Morris has rightly pointed out, all theories have something good to say about atonement and all these views possess a dimension of the truth. "Since the atonement is God's perfect provision for man's need it is necessarily many-sided. And since man's perception is at best partial each of us can perceive part of the truth only."[27] Together they present the entire picture of the meaning of Christ's death on Calvary. For Adventists, Morris's approach makes sense since it takes into account all that Scripture has to say on the subject.

---

25. White, *Testimonies for the Church*, 2:201. In *The Desire of Ages*, White affirmed the same concept: Christ's death vindicated the character, law, and government of God against all Satan's accusations. "In the opening of the great controversy," she wrote, "Satan had declared that the law of God could not be obeyed." But, "by His life and His death, Christ proved that God's justice did not destroy His mercy, but that sin could be forgiven, and that the law is righteous, and can be perfectly obeyed. Satan's charges were refuted. God had given man unmistakable evidence of His love," 761–762.

26. Erickson, *Christian Theology*, 799–800.

27. Morris, *Glory in the Cross*, 59.

CONCLUSION

In His death Christ (1) triumphed over the forces of sin and death, liberating humanity from their power, (2) rendered satisfaction to the Father for humanity's sins by sacrificing His life on their behalf, as their substitute, (3) demonstrated the great extent of God's love for humanity, (4) gave humanity a perfect example of the type of dedication God desires of them, and (5) underscored the seriousness of sin and the severity of God's righteousness and the impact sin has upon God's government in the universe.

In many ways, Ellen White affirmed all the major aspects of the theories of atonement that we have surveyed. Her writings support the view espoused by many theologians that all the theories together bring out the full meaning of the death of Christ.

CHAPTER 10

ATONEMENT: ACCOMPLISHED AT THE CROSS

Jon Paulien

One of the most debated topics of Christian theology is expressed in these questions: Why the cross? What really happened at the cross? The answers to these questions have been widely debated under the general heading of the atonement. But when Seventh-day Adventists (SDA) approach the matter of atonement, an immediate dilemma is perceived. When Adventists talk about the atonement, they refer specifically to what Jesus is doing now in the heavenly sanctuary. On the other hand, when scholars outside the Seventh-day Adventist Church discuss the atonement, they refer specifically to the cross of Jesus Christ and what God was doing there.[1] The purpose of

---

1. Siegfried H. Horn, "Atonement," *Seventh-day Adventist Bible Dictionary (SDABD)*, ed. Don F. Neufeld (Washington, DC: Review and Herald, 1960), 92; Interestingly, English dictionaries do feature both meanings of the word; it is not an either/or situation among the major linguists. For example, *Webster's New International Dictionary of the English Language* (2nd ed., ed. William Allan Nelson [Springfield, MA: Merriam, 1960], 176) notes under theological meanings both "the saving or redeeming work of Christ wrought through his incarnation, sufferings and death," and "reconciliation between God and men, esp. as effected by Christ." The *American Heritage Dictionary of the English Language* (ed. William Morris [New York: American Heritage Publishing, 1973], 84) also gives two theological meanings: 1) "redemptive life and death of Christ," and 2) "reconciliation of God and man as brought about by Christ." Joel Green agrees with this assessment of the biblical materials when he says, "In doctrinal statements in the Christian tradition, it [atonement] typically denotes Jesus' sacrifice on the cross.... In the biblical materials, however, the concept of 'atonement' refers more broadly to various means by which particular persons

this chapter is to focus on what the Bible has to say about atonement at the cross without denying the traditional view of atonement inherited from the Adventist pioneers. To get a fuller picture of the issues involved in this discussion, the English word *atonement* needs to be defined.

THE ENGLISH WORD *ATONEMENT*

The English word *atonement* does not originate in ancient or biblical languages as many other theological words do. It is a compound word constructed from English components.[2] It seems to have originated early in the sixteenth century with the word *onement,* then came *at onement,* and by the end of the century it appeared as "atonement."[3]

The closest root meaning is "reconciliation"[4] with an extended meaning in English of "propitiation, expiation."[5] Elaborations of the root meaning include "restoration of friendly relations," "the state or act of bringing into concord,"[6] "the action of setting at one, or condition of being set at one, after discord or strife,"[7] and/or "amends or reparation made for an injury or wrong."[8] To "atone for a wrong is to take some

---

(or humanity) are restored to right relationship with God." "Atonement," in *The New Interpreter's Dictionary of the Bible (NIDB),* vol. 1, ed. Katharine Doob Sakenfeld (Nashville: Abingdon Press, 2006), 344–345.

2. Raoul Dederen, "Christ: His Person and Work," in *Handbook of Seventh-day Adventist Theology,* Commentary Reference Series, vol. 12, ed. Raoul Dederen (Hagerstown, MD: Review and Herald Publishing Association, 2000), 173; C. L. Mitton, "Atonement," in *The Interpreter's Dictionary of the Bible: An Illustrated Encyclopedia (IDB),* ed. George Arthur Buttrick (New York: Abingdon Press, 1962), 1:309.

3. *The Oxford English Dictionary,* ed. James A. H. Murray et al. (1933; repr., London: Oxford University Press, 1961), 1:539; Green, "Atonement," *NIDB,* 1:344.

4. Dederen, "Christ: His Person and Work," in *Handbook of Seventh-day Adventist Theology,* 173; Mitton, "Atonement," *IDB,* 1:309; W. S. Reid, "Atone, Atonement," in *The International Standard Bible Encyclopedia (ISBE),* rev. ed., ed. Geoffrey W. Bromiley (Grand Rapids, MI: Eerdmans, 1979), 1:352; *SDABD,* 74; Clark M. Williamson, "Atonement Theologies and the Cross," *Encounter* 71:1 (Winter 2010): 2.

5. *Webster's New International Dictionary,* 176; *The Oxford English Dictionary,* 1:539.

6. Green, "Atonement," *NIDB,* 1:344–345; *Webster's New International Dictionary,* 176.

7. *The Oxford English Dictionary,* 1:539.

8. *The American Heritage Dictionary,* 84.

action that cancels out the ill effects of alienation and brings harmonious relationship."[9]

Use of the word in English can reflect both a process and a state. *Atonement* can be the process of righting wrongs, making amends and bringing people into friendly relations with each other. On the other hand *atonement* can mean to state of being in harmony, or at-one with others.[10] As noted above, the basic root meaning of the word *atonement* in English has tended to expand in the direction of propitiation and expiation. One must be very careful in doing theology to not distort the biblical text on account of changes in the meaning of the English words that are used or have been used to translate the biblical text.

It is also clear from the major English dictionaries that linguists see a twofold application of the word *atonement* in the arena of theology. Atonement occurs both at the cross and in the application of what the cross achieved. So it is not an either/or situation in terms of the English word.

ATONEMENT IN THE BIBLE

Greek and Hebrew Words Translated *Atonement*

In the King James Version of the English Bible,[11] the word *atonement* occurs 81 times in the Old Testament[12] and only one time in the New (Rom. 5:11). Of the 81 occurrences in the Old Testament, 77 are clustered in the section of the Pentateuch that focuses primarily on the regulations for the Hebrew tabernacle.[13] All of them belong to the *kpr* Hebrew word group.[14] Fifteen of

---

9. Dederen, "Christ: His Person and Work," *Handbook of Seventh-day Adventist Theology*, 173.

10. Mitton, "Atonement," *IDB*, 1:309, notes that while the English word *atonement* originally meant primarily the state of being at one, modern usage focuses almost entirely on the derived meaning of "the process by which the hindrances to reconciliation are removed."

11. Usage of *atonement* in the King James Version is mentioned because it was the primary source text for early Seventh-day Adventist reflection on the meaning of the atonement.

12. 11 times in Exodus; 49 times in Leviticus; 17 times in Numbers; and once each in 2 Samuel 21:3; 1 Chronicles 6:49; 2 Chronicles 29:24; and Nehemiah 10:33.

13. From the second half of Exodus through the book of Numbers.

14. The noun form is *kippur* and the verb form *kaphar*. The noun form *kippur* occurs nine times and the verb form *kaphar* occurs seventy-two times.

the occurrences are in Leviticus 16, which describes the services on the Day of Atonement. So it is not surprising that the Adventist pioneers, utilizing the King James Version, would be drawn to a view of atonement that focuses on the rituals of the Hebrew sanctuary and particularly the Day of Atonement. And the general lack of references in the New Testament would also drive SDA pioneers to treat the subject in terms of the Old Testament evidence more than the New.

The root meaning of *kpr* in the Hebrew is to cover (i.e., cover one's face) or cover up (e.g., trouble or sin).[15] It has the extended meaning of making amends and providing reconciliation, expiation, cleansing, and atonement.[16] An expanded noun form of *kpr* is *kapporeth*, which is used 23 times for the "mercy seat" on the Ark of the Covenant.[17] The Ark, of course, played a central role in the services on the Day of Atonement.

Looking at the contexts in which these words for atonement are found reveals some interesting things.[18] The passage that seems to most clearly define *atonement* is Leviticus 17:11.[19] This passage could easily leave the

15. William L. Holladay, *A Concise Hebrew and Aramaic Lexicon of the Old Testament: Based upon the Lexical Work of Ludwig Koehler and Walter Baumgartner* (Grand Rapids, MI: William B. Eerdmans Publishing Company, 1971), 163. Some scholars suggest a related meaning, to "wipe or rub." See Green, "Atonement," *NIDB*, 1:345; Mitton, "Atonement," *IDB*, 1:310; *SDABD*, 74; Christopher J. H. Wright, "Atonement in the Old Testament," in *The Atonement Debate: Papers from the London Symposium on the Theology of the Atonement*, ed. Derek Tidball, David Hilborn, and Justin Thacker (Grand Rapids, MI: Zondervan, 2008), 75–76.

16. Holladay, *A Concise Hebrew and Aramaic Lexicon*, 163. See also G. K. Beale, *A New Testament Biblical Theology: The Unfolding of the Old Testament in the New* (Grand Rapids, MI: Baker Academic Press, 2011), 487–488.

17. Another related word, *kôpher*, implies ransom or redemption. See Henri Blocher, "Biblical Metaphors and the Doctrine of the Atonement," *Journal of the Evangelical Theological Society (JETS)* 47:4 (December 2004): 644.

18. In order to be able to weigh all the evidence carefully, I felt it would be important to examine every instance in which the Hebrew words underlying the English word *atonement* occurred. The categorizations of this evidence are my own and can certainly be disputed, but I think the larger picture is reasonably clear and not affected by the fine points of these categorizations.

19. Terry Briley, "The Old Testament 'Sin Offering' and Christ's Atonement," *Stone-Campbell Journal* 3 (Spring 2000): 97–100; Samuel J. Mikolaski, "The Cross of Christ: The Atonement and Men Today," *Christianity Today* (March 13, 1961): 3–4; Leon Morris,

impression that the every word for "atonement," in every case, is focused solely on blood and its manipulation. And this is certainly true of the Day of Atonement (Lev. 16:14–19).[20] But the larger picture of the word group's usage in the Old Testament requires that this impression be qualified. Atonement in the Old Testament is not always made by sacrifice and application of blood but can be granted on the basis of a number of other actions as well.[21]

A number of Greek words are used to translate *kpr* in the Greek Old Testament (LXX). The most common translation is by the verb *exilaskomai* and the noun *exilasmos*. The Hebrew word *kapporeth* (mercy seat) is normally translated *hilasterion*. On occasion, the LXX translates *kpr* with the Greek word *lutron*, which means "ransom or redemption."[22] Since variations of these words are found in the New Testament, they will help make it clear how atonement was understood to have occurred at the cross of Jesus Christ.

Reading *atonement* through the lens of the Sanctuary ceremonies and particularly the Day of Atonement led the Adventist pioneers to see the atonement as having a particular focus on the investigative judgment and the final cleansing of the universe from sin. This larger view of God and the cosmic conflict led them often to deny that atonement was completed at the cross.

The Atonement: Its Meaning and Significance (Leicester, England: InterVarsity Press, 1983), 53. The serious importance of blood in atonement is underlined further in Leviticus 10:16–20, where Moses chides the sons of Aaron for burning the sin offering rather than bringing its blood into the sanctuary.

20. See the discussion in Beale, *New Testament Biblical Theology*, 487.

21. Green, "Atonement," *NIDB*, 1:345; Mitton, "Atonement," *IDB*, 1:310. There are multiple passages in which there is an absence of blood and sacrifice and the atonement is granted on other grounds. Atonement can be granted after application of oil (Lev. 14:29), burning flour (Lev. 5:11–13), burning incense (Num. 16:41–50), payment of money (Exod. 30:11–16), execution (Num. 25:1–13; 2 Sam. 21:1–6), gifts of jewelry (Num. 31:48–54), the release of a live animal (Lev. 16:10), and simple appeals to God with words (Exod. 32:30). In the Psalms, sin is put right largely in the absence of sacrificial or atonement language. See Christopher J. H. Wright, "Atonement in the Old Testament," 81–82. In the non-ritual texts of the Old Testament, the proper atonement for moral wrong doing is repentance. See J. Milgrom, "Atonement in the OT," in *The Interpreter's Dictionary of the Bible: An Illustrated Encyclopedia*, suppl. vol., ed. Keith Crim (Nashville: Abingdon Press, 1976), 80–81. Sacrifice can also be used for purposes other than atonement. See Blocher, "Biblical Metaphors and the Doctrine of the Atonement," *JETS*, 642.

22. Based on the "ransom/redemption" meaning of the related Hebrew word *kôpher*. See Milgrom, "Atonement in the OT," *IDB Supplement*, 80.

While SDA pioneers were truly on to something important, the one reference to atonement in the New Testament portion of the King James Bible should have given them pause. That reference is found in Romans 5:11.

Atonement Language in the New Testament

In Romans 5:11, according to the King James Version, atonement is clearly in the context of the cross: "We also joy in God through our Lord Jesus Christ, by whom we have now received the atonement."[23] It is true that the King James wording ("we have now received") can be read in terms of the ongoing process of intercession in the heavenly sanctuary. But the aorist indicative form in the Greek (*elabomen*) points to a singular conclusive action in the past, at the cross of Christ.[24] The benefits of that action are now (*nun*) made available to those who are rejoicing (present continuous tense—*kauchômenoi*) in Him. So a full picture of the atonement language in Scripture indicates an either/or approach is incorrect.[25]

It is interesting that the King James Version translates only the noun form of the word for atonement (*katallagên*) as "atonement." Verbal forms of the same word occur in verse 10 (*katêllagêmen*—"were reconciled," *katallagentes*—"having been reconciled") and are translated as "reconciled."[26] So the King James translation actually masks the fact that "reconciled" in

---

23. Romans 5:1–10 is about the benefits that flow from justification and Romans 5:12–21 contains the famous Adam/Christ typology in which death and sin enter the human race through Adam and these are undone through the obedient life and sacrificial death of Jesus Christ.

24. Beale, *New Testament Theology*, 541.

25. Romans 5:11 is at the heart and pivot of the whole chapter. See the analysis in Beale, *New Testament Theology*, 540–542. Romans 5:11 defines *atonement* as follows: Through the death of Christ people have been restored from a state of hostility into a peaceful relationship with God. This builds on verse one of the same chapter (NIV), where believers, "hav[ing] been justified through faith ... have peace with God through our Lord Jesus Christ." The hostile state of alienation from God introduced by the first Adam is overcome by the death and resurrection of the last Adam (Rom. 5:12–21).

26. There are no differences in Romans 5:10–11 between the Byzantine text (upon which the King James Bible was based) and the scholarly text generally accepted today. So text critical issues do not impact the interpretation of these verses.

verse 10 translates a root form of the same word as *atonement* in verse 11. The more modern translations, therefore, are correct in using "reconciliation" instead of "atonement" in Romans 5:11. Furthermore, since the translators of the King James used "atonement" for the noun form but translated "reconciled" for the verb form, it is clear that they understood "atonement" as a synonym of "reconciliation."

Extended Meaning of the Greek Word *katallassô*

The root meaning of the verb form *katallassô* is difficult to determine, but it has a basic idea of "change" or "exchange."[27] From there it isn't far to the idea of "reconcile," as in "the exchange of hostility for a friendly relationship."[28] When applied to God, the verb is always active; when applied to human beings it is always passive.[29] So reconciliation is something that flows from God to us, not the other way around. The noun form *katallagê* corresponds to the meaning of the verb, with the sense of "exchange" or "reconciliation."[30] Surprisingly, both terms are extremely rare in the LXX (Greek Old Testament). Within the canonical books, *katallagê* is found only in Isaiah 9:5 and there its meaning is obscure.[31]

Reconciliation in the New Testament

The Bible begins with the assumption that humans from the beginning were designed to be in harmonious relationship with God (Gen. 1:26–28). But a radical breach has broken this unity (Gen. 3:22–24; 6:5; Isa. 59:1–2;

---

27. Friedrich Büchsel, "*Katallassô*, etc." in *Theological Dictionary of the New Testament (TDNT)*, ed. Gerhard Kittel, trans. and ed. Geoffrey W. Bromiley (Grand Rapids, MI: William B. Eerdmans Publishing Company, 1964), 1:254.

28. *A Greek-English Lexicon of the New Testament and other Early Christian Literature*, 3rd ed., rev. and ed. Frederick Danker, based on Walter Bauer, *Griechisch-deutsches Woerterbuch zu den Schriften des Neuen Testaments und der fruehchristlichen Literatur*, 6th ed. (Chicago: University of Chicago Press, 2000), 521.

29. Büchsel, "*Katallassô*, etc." in *TDNT*, 1:255.

30. Ibid., 1:258. In the Bauer/Danker lexicon (521), *katallagê* is defined as "reestablishment of an interrupted or broken relationship."

31. Ibid., 1:258.

Rom. 5:12; Eph. 2:1).[32] So human beings became alienated from (Eph. 4:18) and hostile to God and each other (Col. 1:21; Rom. 5:10; 8:7).[33] This is not only true of Gentiles (Rom. 1:23ff.), but also of Jews (Rom. 3:9–20, 23). The cause of this estrangement is human disobedience toward God and His law (1 John 3:4) arising out of a lack of trust (faith) in who He is (Rom. 14:23).[34] This is where the concept of reconciliation comes in.

The concept of reconciliation is grounded in the realm of personal relationships, severed and restored.[35] In contexts where there is enmity, distrust, or broken relationships of all types, reconciliation is about the healing and restoration of those relationships.[36] So atonement in the New Testament has to do with how the cross of Jesus Christ heals the breach between God and the human race. To gain a clearer understanding of this concept, the main texts where this word group is used, beginning with Romans 5:8–11, will be examined.[37]

Paul declares in Romans 5:8 that the death of Christ, which occurred at a time when humans were still sinners (before they turned to God), demonstrates God's own love toward humanity.[38] When the cross took place, all

---

32. Mark L. Y. Chan, "The Gospel and the Achievement of the Cross," *Evangelical Review of Theology* 33 (1, 2009): 20; Reid, "Atone, Atonement," *ISBE*, 1:353.

33. Mitton, "Atonement," *IDB*, 1:311.

34. Dederen, "Christ: His Person and Work," *Handbook of Seventh-day Adventist Theology*, 174.

35. I. Howard Marshall, "The Theology of the Atonement," in *The Atonement Debate: Papers from the London Symposium on the Theology of the Atonement*, ed. Derek Tidball, David Hilborn, and Justin Thacker (Grand Rapids, MI: Zondervan, 2008), 60; Morris, *The Atonement*, 132–150; C. M. Tuckett, "Atonement in the NT," in *The Anchor Bible Dictionary* (Garden City, NY: Doubleday, 1992), 1:521.

36. Dederen, "Christ: His Person and Work," *Handbook of Seventh-day Adventist Theology*, 181.

37. Although Paul is the only writer of the New Testament who uses the terminology of reconciliation (Rom. 5:8–11; 2 Cor. 5:14–21; Eph. 2:11–16; Col. 1:20–23), it is central to his understanding of the cross and is implied in many other parts of the New Testament, such as Luke 15:11–31 and Matthew 5:23–24. A related concept is the word *peace* which describes the outcome of the reconciliation process. Those in Christ have peace with God and also with others (Acts 10:36; Rom. 5:1; 8:6; Gal. 5:22; Eph. 2:14–17; Col. 1:20). See Green, "Atonement," *NIDB*, 1:346–347.

38 Green, "Atonement," *NIDB*, 1:347; P. Jewett, "Atonement," *Zondervan Pictorial Encyclopedia of the Bible (ZPEB)*, ed. Merrill C. Tenney (Grand Rapids, MI: Zondervan, 1975), 1: 410.

humans were not only sinners, but enemies of God (v. 10) and the death of God's Son reconciled humanity to God. Sin was the root cause of the enmity, and since humans were unable to remove it, God put it out of the way at the cross.[39] Paul's use of "were reconciled" (Rom. 5:10, NIV)[40] clearly places the reconciliation in the past rather than the present from the point of our experience. As a passive, the word also makes it clear that the reconciliation that took place on the cross was entirely God's work, humanity had no part in it.[41] It is objective, outside of humans.

Paul reiterates his point in verse 11, but from the standpoint of the converted person rather than preconversion. Through our Lord Jesus Christ "we have now received the reconciliation (or atonement)" (NASB). The "now" in verse 11 is in contrast with the time of the believer's enmity and sinfulness. Paul moves from the time of the cross (in vv. 8 and 9) to the moment when that past act of atonement is applied to the new believer (v. 11). Reconciliation is something to be "received" (*elabōmen*), it exists objectively before an individual experiences it, and it is outside of and prior to an individual's response.[42] Arising out of God's love, the cross was God's act of reconciliation and atonement which is applied to human beings as they respond to the preaching of the gospel.[43] While Jesus Christ is the active agent of reconciliation, the Father is its author.[44] "The grief of the

---

This reconciling love was demonstrated at the cross but goes all the way to eternity past (John 17:6ff.; Eph. 1:4; 2 Tim. 1:9–10). See Reid, "Atone, Atonement," in *ISBE*, 1:353.

39. Dederen, "Christ: His Person and Work," *Handbook of Seventh-day Adventist Theology*, 181; I. Howard Marshall, "The Death of Jesus in Recent New Testament Study," *Word and World* 3:1 (Winter 1983): 18.

40. This translation of the aorist passive participle (*katallagentes*) is standard, being found, for example, in the King James Version, the New International Version, and the English Standard Version.

41. Dederen, "Christ: His Person and Work," *Handbook of Seventh-day Adventist Theology*, 181.

42. Ibid., 181; Morris, *The Atonement*, 139.

43. Rohintan K. Mody, "Penal Substitutionary Atonement in Paul," in *The Atonement Debate*, 116.

44. Dederen, "Christ: His Person and Work," *Handbook of Seventh-day Adventist Theology*, 181; Arland J. Hultgren, "Salvation: Its Forms and Dynamics in the New Testament," *Dialogue: A Journal of Theology* 45:3 (Fall 2006): 216, 221.

Father is as important as the death of the Son."[45] The death of Christ, then, "made it possible for a holy God to do for sinners what otherwise He could not have done."[46]

In 2 Corinthians 5:14–21, Paul grounds reconciliation completely in the death of Christ. The crucial act is that "one died for all" and so there is a sense that all have somehow died in that action (2 Cor. 5:14). Then Paul gives his classic statement about reconciliation in verses 18–20. Reconciliation comes from God and God here (v. 18) is clearly distinguished from Christ, so God the Father is in view. Through the actions of Jesus Christ at the cross, God the Father is reconciled to humanity and gives humanity the ministry of reconciliation.

He elaborates on this in verse 19: "God was in Christ, reconciling the world unto himself" (KJV). J. I. Packer expressed this beautifully: "The two loves, love of Father and Son, are one."[47] That reconciliation is grounded in "not reckoning to them their sins" (my translation). The message regarding that reconciliation is then committed or entrusted to "us." This last point is elaborated in verse 20. Paul and the apostles have become God's ambassadors to invite others to participate in that reconciliation.

The passage in 2 Corinthians 5 makes several critical points. First, it clearly distinguishes the work of Christ on the cross from the prior purpose of the Father to provide the reconciliation. Christ does not change the heart of the Father by the action He does at the cross; rather, the Father Himself was acting in our behalf through the work of Christ.[48]

---

45. Gabriel Fackre, "A Theology of the Cross," *Andover Newton Quarterly* 16:2 (November 1975): 155, quoting Jürgen Moltmann, *The Crucified God*, trans. R. A. Wilson and John Bowden (London: SCM Press, 1974), 243.

46. Dederen, "Christ: His Person and Work," *Handbook of Seventh-day Adventist Theology*, 182.

47. J. I. Packer, "What Did the Cross Achieve? The Logic of Penal Substitution," *Tyndale Bulletin* 25 (1974): 40. Packer does not see any contradiction between the full, loving engagement of the Father in the atonement and the concept of penal substitution. To him, penal substitution heightens the love of God rather than diminishes it. The highest measure of divine love is seen in Jesus experiencing the full measure of the divine reaction against sin.

48. This point is also made by Jesus in John 3:16 and 14:10. See Grace Adophsen Brame, "The Cross: Payment or Gift?" *Perspectives in Religious Studies* 33:2 (Summer 2005): 170–172. In the New Testament, God and Jesus are always portrayed as the subject of the atonement, never as its object. If God were the object, Jesus would be giving up His life to

Second, there is a "now and not yet" aspect to reconciliation.[49] It is a completed action at the cross, outside of humanity, once for all.[50] On the other hand, reconciliation is also a task humans are to do (vv. 18–19); it has not yet happened in the fullest sense.[51] Reconciliation is only complete when human beings respond to what God has already done.[52] Third, there is a strong sense of exchange or substitution in the passage. Through one death "all died" (5:14, NIV, NKJV), and the One who knew no sin was made sin so "that we might be made the righteousness of God in him" (5:21, KJV).

In Colossians 1:19–22, the concept of reconciliation is expanded beyond the human race to the entire universe.[53] Christ "is the image of the invisible God" (Col. 1:15, KJV), pre-eminent (1:18), and one in whom all the fullness of God dwells (v. 19). Through Him everything in heaven and earth is reconciled,[54] making peace through the blood of the cross (v. 20). What happened on the cross, therefore, provides atonement not just for the human race, but for the entire universe. In verse 21, however, Paul steps back and addresses the condition humanity was in before the cross. Human beings were alienated (estranged), hostile (enemies) in mind, and doing evil deeds. These very same people were reconciled (*apokatêllaxen*) "in the body of His flesh through death" (v. 22, KJV). The end result is human beings who are holy, blameless, and unreproachable in God's sight.

The passage in Colossians 1 brings out a number of important things. The focus in this passage is not on the Father (as was the case in 2 Cor. 5), but on Jesus Christ, who carries the fullness of God in Himself and thus is qualified to be the agent on God's side of the reconciliation process.

---

appease God. If Jesus were the object, God would be punishing Jesus in His death. But the atonement is never expressed in the latter two ways. Green, "Atonement," *NIDB*, 1:346.

49. Dederen, "Christ: His Person and Work," *Handbook of Seventh-day Adventist Theology*, 181.

50. The Greek expresses this in the indicative mood combined with past tenses. Reconciliation is an established fact that cannot be altered.

51. In verse 20 this is expressed with an aorist imperative (*katallagête*), which means it does not fully happen until humans respond to what God has done.

52. Morris, *The Atonement*, 145.

53. Tuckett, "Atonement in the NT," *ABD*, 1:521.

54. Aorist infinitive (*apokatallaxai*), implying a point in time rather than a process.

The one-time death of Jesus Christ on the cross has reconciled (i.e., made atonement) to God not only the human race, but in some sense the entire universe. While not denying the biblical teaching about continuing atonement in the heavenly sanctuary, Paul is clear in this passage that the decisive act of atonement occurred on the cross. And atonement does not end at the cross, but results in transformed lives.

The final text that centers on the language of reconciliation is Ephesians 2:11–16. The focus there is not on God's side in the atonement, but on the need for human response.[55] The condition of the Gentiles before conversion is described in verse 12 (ESV) as "separated from Christ, alienated from the commonwealth of Israel and strangers to the covenants of promise, having no hope and without God in the world." But "now" (2:13) in Christ, those who were afar "have been brought near"[56] through the blood of Christ, a reference to the cross.[57] In the flesh of Christ on the cross (2:14), He brought an end to the hostility (enmity) between God and humanity and also the "dividing wall" (2:14, ESV) between humans. Through Christ, Gentile and Jew have become one. Christ acted as He did on the cross in order that He "might reconcile"[58] both Jew and Gentile to God and to each other. The impact of the cross included "killing" (2:16, ESV) the enmity.

This passage in Ephesians reiterates the one-time act on the cross as the decisive event in the atonement, but it focuses more than the previous passages on the outcome of the cross—the ongoing nature of the atonement in its effects on the Ephesian church. While there is no talk here of a heavenly sanctuary, or Christ's ongoing intercession in heavenly places, the atonement on the cross and the ongoing atonement in the sanctuary are not in conflict with each other. They are two parts of a larger concept. Reconciliation and atonement involve both an indicative (i.e., past, completed action) and an imperative (i.e., something that still needs to happen).[59]

---

55. Dederen, "Christ: His Person and Work," in *Handbook of Seventh-day Adventist Theology,* 182; Tuckett, "Atonement in the NT," *ABD,* 1:521.

56. Aorist passive indicative (*egenêthête*), implying a one-time act in the past that the Ephesians had nothing to do with, but that had a powerful effect on their lives.

57. Hultgren, "Salvation," in *Dialogue: A Journal of Theology,* 220.

58. Aorist active subjunctive (*apokatallaxê*). The subjunctive express probability, in this context, the purpose of God, so there is an implication of future reconciliation here.

59. This is beautifully expressed by N. T. Wright, *Evil and the Justice of God* (Downers

Conclusion

The examination of the biblical use of the word *atonement,* along with its equivalent, *reconciliation,* has led to some significant conclusions. First, while atonement is not limited to the cross, it is clearly grounded there in the biblical sense.[60] It is a one-time objective act that removes all barriers to reconciliation except the human response. Second, there is a now and a not-yet sense to atonement. The cross is an established fact, a one-time event in the past. But atonement and reconciliation don't end there—they continue in the work of Christ in heaven and in the ministry of reconciliation on earth.[61] These continuing actions work to effect that human response that was not completed at the cross. So in one sense, atonement is complete at the cross, and in another sense it is not.

THE PROBLEM OF METAPHOR

A small aside will be helpful before tackling the why and the how of the cross. When it comes to spiritual matters, it is very difficult to use direct speech.

Grove, IL: InterVarsity Press, 2006), 98: "The cross is not just an example to be followed, it is an achievement to be worked out, put into practice."

60. While Ellen G. White can say "The intercession of Christ in man's behalf in the sanctuary above is as essential to the plan of salvation as was His death upon the cross" (*The Great Controversy Between Christ and Satan* [Mountain View, CA: Pacific Press Publishing Association, 1911], 489), she is also very firm that "The sacrifice of Christ as an atonement for sin is the great truth around which all other truths cluster" (Francis D. Nichol, ed., *The Seventh-day Adventist Bible Commentary* [SDABC], seven volumes [Washington, DC: Review and Herald Publishing Association, 1956], 5:1137) and "the cross . . . is the means of man's atonement" (6T 236). In speaking about the cross she could say, "The conditions of the atonement had been fulfilled" (Manuscript 138, 1897). On Ellen White's view, see Denis Fortin, "The Cross of Christ: Theological Differences Between Joseph H. Waggoner and Ellen G. White, *Journal of the Adventist Theological Society* 14:2 (Autumn 2003): 134–139.

An excellent summary of what the New Testament has to say about the centrality of the cross can be found in John R. W. Stott, *The Cross of Christ* (Downers Grove, IL: Inter-Varsity Press, 1986), 17–46. An argument for a much more marginal role for the cross in the New Testament can be found in Robert M. Price, "The Marginality of the Cross," *Journal of Unification Studies* 6 (2004–2005): 23–38.

61. Joel B. Green and Mark K. Baker, *Recovering the Scandal of the Cross: Atonement in New Testament and Contemporary Contexts* (Downers Grove, IL: IVP Academic, 2000), 133–134.

Knowing God is like gazing into the sun.[62] God is real, yet in everyday human experience people do not see, hear, or touch God (in the Bible, Moses and Jesus were notable exceptions).[63] All talk of God, therefore, involves the stretching of human language. When it comes to spiritual matters, God is generally spoken about using metaphors, analogies, or other figures of speech.[64]

When it comes to getting right with God, for example, the Bible frequently makes use of law court metaphors. The human condition is described in terms of guilt and condemnation.[65] Human beings are legally out of synch with God. Salvation is then described in legal terms such as *justification, acquittal,* and *vindication.* On the other hand, if the human condition is described in terms of debt (a banking or financial metaphor), the appropriate salvation word would be *forgiveness* or possibly *redemption.*

People often treat such language as if it were scientifically precise with reference to their salvation (which itself is a metaphor based either in the realm of rescue operations or healing), but it is actually metaphorical, speaking about something beyond the five senses in the language of concrete, everyday existence (*concrete* itself is here a figure of speech!). Other well-known biblical metaphors are *the body of Christ, the fruit of the spirit,* and *the bread of life.*

When it comes to explaining how the cross of Jesus Christ reconciles humanity to God, language moves immediately into the realm of metaphor. Metaphor is based on a similarity between something that cannot be described directly and something that known from everyday experience. The analogy between the two conceptual worlds expresses something that

---

62. Packer, "What Did the Cross Achieve?" in *Tyndale Bulletin,* 6–8, also notes scriptural support for this theme in Ephesians 3:19 (ESV: "the love of Christ that surpasses knowledge"); Romans 11:33–36 (KJV: "How unsearchable are His judgments, His ways past finding out"); and 1 Corinthians 13:9, 12 (KJV: "For we know in part and we prophesy in part").

63. "It is a unique kind of knowledge which, though real, is not full; it is knowledge of what is discernible within a circle of light against the background of a larger darkness; it is, in short, knowledge of a *mystery,* the mystery of the living God at work," Packer, "What Did the Cross Achieve?", *Tyndale Bulletin,* 6.

64. Green and Baker, *Recovering the Scandal of the Cross,* 38–43, 124; I. Howard Marshall, "The Theology of the Atonement," in *The Atonement Debate,* 50.

65. Tuckett, "Atonement in the NT," *ABD,* 1:518.

is real and true, but it rarely does so in a complete way.[66] There is both commonality and difference. To press any single metaphor into doing the job of explaining everything is to distort the understanding of the whole.

This does not imply some sort of post-modern "anything goes" approach to Scripture. Even God speaks in analogies and models, but they are "revealed models" or "controlling models."[67] God's models are revelation, not specula-tion. They are ways of thought that God Himself has taught His children. The biblical metaphors operate as controls for unrestrained theological modeling.[68] While humans know only in part, what the Bible teaches them is adequate for both salvation and a living relationship with God.

Throughout history, Christian theology has often focused on one or another New Testament model of the atonement and tried to absolutize that metaphor, as if it explained everything. But that is never the perspective of the New Testament writers, as will be demonstrated.[69] The greatest justice is done to the atonement at the cross if believers are open to the great variety of metaphors and figures of speech that were used in the New Testament to express how God reconciled the world to Himself at the cross.[70]

Coming back to Romans 5:8–11, one notes the wide variety of meta-phors for the atonement that occur in that single passage. The language of sin and blood (vv. 8–9) is drawn from the cultic context of the ancient tab-ernacle. The language of enmity and reconciliation comes from the realm of relationships. And the language of justification comes from the law court. Paul does not limit himself to a single metaphor to describe what

---

66. A good discussion of metaphor can be found in Blocher, "Biblical Metaphors and the Doctrine of the Atonement," *JETS*, 634–640.

67. Packer, "What Did the Cross Achieve?", *Tyndale Bulletin*, 14–16.

68. Ibid., 12.

69. Tuckett, "Atonement in the NT," *ABD*, 1:518; Ben Wiebe, "Cross Currents: Rethink-ing Atonement (with Reflection on Campbell, Stone, and Scott)," *Stone-Campbell Journal* 13 (Fall 2010): 202.

70. Packer, "What Did the Cross Achieve? *Tyndale Bulletin*, 10, recalls Calvin, who noted that God's love for us and hostility to sin (at one and the same time) are compatible "in a way that cannot be put into words." See John Calvin, *Institutes of the Christian Religion*, II, xvii. 2. See also Mark D. Baker, "How the Cross Saves," *Direction* 36:1 (2007): 45; Steve Chalke, "The Redemption of the Cross," in *The Atonement Debate*, 37; Chan, "The Gospel and the Achievement of the Cross," *ERT*, 23–24; Green and Baker, *Recovering the Scandal of the Cross*, 124–126, 134.

happened at the cross, and he can mix several metaphors into a single paragraph![71] When it comes to describing what God did for humanity in Christ, human language is exposed in all its weakness. The Word of God is expressed in the language of humanity![72]

WHY AND HOW THE CROSS?

Though conservative Christians agree on the facts of Jesus's death and resurrection, they differ widely on the "why" of the cross.[73] Throughout Christian history churchmen and scholars have debated the meaning of the cross as atonement without coming to a settled conclusion.[74] Most of these debates were grounded at one point or another on specific metaphors or models found in the New Testament. There was often the attempt to put forward a particular metaphor as if it were the only possible one. But, as has been seen, the full richness of the biblical testimony pushes the readers toward a multiplex approach. So this chapter will close with a survey of the main metaphors[75] by which the New Testament writers expressed their understanding of what the atonement was all about.[76] These are usually

---

71. Tuckett, "Atonement in the NT," *ABD*, 1:521.

72. Ellen G. White, *Selected Messages, Book One* (Washington, DC: Review and Herald Publishing Association, 1958), 21.

73. S. Mark Heim, "Cross Purposes: Rethinking the Death of Jesus," *Christian Century* (March 22, 2005): 20.

74. A good summary of the classic views on the meaning of the atonement can be found in John Sanders, "Introduction," in *Atonement and Violence: A Theological Conversation* (Nashville: Abingdon Press, 2006), xiii–xv. A good summary of the most recent issues in the debate over the meaning of the atonement can be found in Sanders, *Atonement and Violence*, ix–xi.

75. Green and Baker, *Recovering the Scandal of the Cross*, 41, 123, list five major metaphors in the New Testament, as does Blocher, "Biblical Metaphors and the Doctrine of the Atonement," *JETS*, 629–630. Wayne Northey, "The Cross: God's Peace Work Towards a Restorative Peacemaking Understanding of the Atonement," in *Stricken by God? Nonviolent Identification and the Victory of Christ*, ed. Brad Jersak and Michael Hardin (Grand Rapids, MI: Eerdmans, 2007), 356–357, lists ten, as does Mark D. Baker, "How the Cross Saves," *Direction* 36:1 (2007): 46–55.

76. One could argue that *reconciliation* is one metaphor among many in the New Testament. And that is certainly true. But since the goal of this paper is an understanding of the *atonement* (an English word) and *atonement* is a translation of *katallásso* in Romans 5:11,

grounded both in the Old Testament Scriptures and in the New Testament writers' perception of who Jesus was and is.[77]

The Cross as a Sacrifice

As noted previously, the Hebrew words for atonement (*kpr, kapporeth*) are heavily associated with the Old Testament sacrificial system (Exod. 29:36; Lev. 4:20; Num. 15:25).[78] Given the nature of Christ's death, therefore, it is not surprising that the New Testament uses sacrificial language to describe the cross.[79] It is a major theme in Hebrews, where Jesus is described as the fulfillment and extension of that sacrificial system.[80] Other explicit

---

it seemed appropriate to begin with *reconciliation* as expressing the fundamental meaning of what the translators of the King James Bible and the Adventist pioneers understood by *atonement*. Further aspects of the atonement at the cross will be discerned by looking at other metaphors of what God did on the cross.

77. N. T. Wright, "The Reasons for Jesus' Crucifixion," in *Stricken by God? Nonviolent Identification and the Victory of Christ*, ed. Brad Jersak and Michael Hardin (Grand Rapids, MI: Eerdmans, 2007), 135–142.

78. Brame, "The Cross: Payment or Gift?" *Perspectives in Religious Studies*, 167; Briley, "The Old Testament 'Sin Offering' and Christ's Atonement," *Stone-Campbell Journal*, 94–97; Dederen, "Christ: His Person and Work," in *Handbook of Seventh-day Adventist Theology*, 175; Green, "Atonement," *NIDB*, 1:345–346. Briley points out that while sacrifice was widespread in the ancient world, there were significant differences between pagan and Hebrew sacrificial understandings. In the Hebrew understanding there was no magical power in the sacrifice; its value was solely in the blessing of God. Also blood played no role in ancient pagan sacrifices, and holiness was required of the offerer. Among the Church Fathers, the sacrificial metaphor appears relatively late in Cyprian, Eusebius, and John of Damascus. See G. W. Bromiley, "Atone; Atonement: History of the Doctrine," in *ISBE*, 1:356.

79. Dederen, "Christ: His Person and Work," *Handbook of Seventh-day Adventist Theology*, 175–180; Paul Jewett, "Atonement," *ZPEB*, 1:408; Marshall, "The Theology of the Atonement," in *The Atonement Debate*, 59–60; Mikolaski, "The Cross of Christ," *Christianity Today* 3; Mitton, "Atonement," *IDB*, 1:312; Kathryn Tanner, "Incarnation, Cross and Sacrifice: A Feminist-Inspired Reappraisal," *Anglican Theological Review* 86:1 (Winter 2004): 48–56; Tuckett, *ABD*, 1:518–520.

80. Dederen, "Christ: His Person and Work," in *Handbook of Seventh-day Adventist Theology*, 176; Green and Baker, *Recovering the Scandal of the Cross*, 131; Geoffrey Grogan, "The Atonement in the New Testament," in *The Atonement Debate*, 92; Steve Motyer, "The Atonement in Hebrews," in *The Atonement Debate*, 136–149. Explicit texts in Hebrews include 9:13–15, 22–28; 10:10, 12, 26 and 13:11–12.

references to the death of Jesus Christ as a sacrifice include 1 Corinthians 5:7 (KJV: "Christ our passover is sacrificed for us") and Ephesians 5:2 (ESV: "a fragrant offering and sacrifice to God").

The cross as a sacrifice is also implied in frequent references to the blood of Christ (Matt. 26:28; Mark 14:24; Rom. 3:25; 5:9; Eph. 1:7; 2:13; Col. 1:20; 1 Pet. 1:18–19).[81] It is also implied in John 1:29, NIV, where Jesus is described as "the Lamb of God, who takes away the sin of the world!"[82] For the writers of the New Testament, the great Old Testament text that led them to apply sacrificial language to the death of Christ was Isaiah 53,[83] where the Suffering Servant was led as "a Lamb to the slaughter" (Isa. 53:7), died as "an offering for sin" (Isa. 53:10, KJV), and "bare the sin of many" (53:12).

Why the cross? The metaphor of sacrifice implies that death is the penalty for sin (Gen. 2:16–17; Ezek. 18:4, 20) and that the death of a sacrificial victim would substitute or be exchanged for the death of the sinner.[84] Since the book of Hebrews denies that the sacrifices in the Old Testament sanctuary were the ultimate basis for remission of sin, the sacrifice of Christ is not one sacrifice among many, but the single sacrifice that was truly

81. James D. G. Dunn, "Paul's Understanding of the Death of Jesus," in *Reconciliation and Hope: New Testament Essays on Atonement and Eschatology Presented to L. L. Morris on His 60th Birthday*, ed. Robert Banks (Carlisle: The Paternoster Press, 1974), 125–141; Morris, *The Atonement*, 52–53, 63; Tuckett, "Atonement in the NT," *ABD*, 1: 518. Dederen, "Christ: His Person and Work," *Handbook of Seventh-day Adventist Theology*, 175–177, points to Leviticus 17:11 as a key text in the association of sacrificial blood with the atonement.

82. George L. Carey, "The Lamb of God and Atonement Theories," *Tyndale Bulletin* 32 (1981): 97–122. On the relation of Passover to sacrifice, see Bruce H. Grigsby, "The Cross as an Expiatory Sacrifice in the Fourth Gospel," *Journal for the Study of the New Testament* 15 (July 1982); Morris, *The Atonement*, 88–105. See also Green and Baker, *Recovering the Scandal of the Cross*, 130–131; Tuckett, "Atonement in the NT," *ABD*, 1:518.

83. Mikolaski, "The Cross of Christ," *Christianity Today*, 3; Tuckett, "Atonement in the NT," *ABD*, 1:518–519. Excellent interpretations of Isaiah 53 in light of atonement at the cross can be found in Chan, "The Gospel and the Achievement of the Cross," *ERT*, 21–22; E. Robert Ekblad, "God Is Not to Blame: The Servant's Atoning Suffering According to the LXX of Isaiah 53," in *Stricken by God? Nonviolent Identification and the Victory of Christ*, ed. Brad Jersak and Michael Hardin (Grand Rapids, MI: Eerdmans, 2007), 180–204; Sue Groom, "Why Did Christ Die? An Exegesis of Isaiah 52:13—53:12," in *The Atonement Debate*, 96–114.

84. Dederen, "Christ: His Person and Work," in *Handbook of Seventh-day Adventist Theology*, 176, 178. According to 2 Corinthians 5:14, in this one death "all died" (NIV, NKJV). The concept of substitution or exchange is also clear in verse 21 of the same chapter.

meaningful and put an end to all others (Heb. 9:25–26; 10:1–14). Through the sacrifice of Christ, the sins of the world could be forgiven.[85] Unfortunately, the biblical texts concerning sacrifice never fully reveal the inner logic behind such ritual acts. It is clear that sacrifice is effective in restoring right relations with God, how this is so is less clear.[86] Jesus's death was "for us" (1 Thess. 5:10), "for our sins" (1 Cor. 15:3),[87] and "for the forgiveness of sins" (Matt. 26:28, NIV, ESV).

The Cross as a Ransom or Redemption

It has also been noted that in the LXX the Hebrew words for "atonement" (*kpr, kapporeth*) were sometimes translated by the Greek word for "ransom/ redemption" (*lutron*). So it should not be surprising if *lutron* and its derivatives (*apolutrosis* and *antilutron*) are used to explain the atonement in the New Testament.[88] In any case, the language of ransom or redemption had a rich background in the first century. In the Gentile world, slaves and prisoners of war could be "redeemed" by paying a suitable ransom price.[89] Among the Jews this language was grounded in the Israelite deliverance from Egyptian slavery at the time of the Exodus (Exod. 6:6; 15:13; Deut. 7:8).[90]

In the New Testament, the cross of Christ is described in ransom/ redemption language (Mark 10:45 and parallels; Rom. 3:24; Heb. 9:12, 15;

---

85. Tuckett, "Atonement in the NT," *ABD*, 1:519.

86. Briley, "The Old Testament 'Sin Offering' and Christ's Atonement," *Stone-Campbell Journal*, 93; Green, "Atonement," *NIDB*, 345. Perhaps the meaning of sacrifice in biblical times was so self-evident to the ancients that it needed no explanation.

87. For an in-depth look at the implications of 1 Corinthians 15:3 for the death of Christ, see Chan, "The Gospel and the Achievement of the Cross," *ERT*, 29–30; Grogan, "The Atonement in the New Testament," in *The Atonement Debate*, 88; Martin Hengel, *The Atonement: The Origins of the Doctrine in the New Testament* (Philadelphia: Fortress Press, 1981), 36–39; Mitton, "Atonement," *IDB*, 1:312.

88. The ransom idea was very popular among the early church fathers. It was mentioned by Athanasius, Gregory of Nyssa, Gregory of Nazianzus, Ambrose, Ambrosiaster, and in the Epistle to Diognetus. See Bromiley, "Atone; Atonement: History of the Doctrine," *ISBE*, 1:355–356.

89. Morris, *The Atonement*, 107–110; Tuckett, "Atonement in the NT," *ABD*, 1:520.

90. Green, "Atonement," *NIDB*, 346; Green and Baker, *Recovering the Scandal of the Cross*, 126; Morris, 113; Tuckett, "Atonement in the NT," *ABD*, 1:520.

Eph. 1:7; 1 Pet. 1:18–19).[91] Paul can also use the language of having been "bought with a price" (1 Cor. 6:20; 7:23, KJV). Scholars have debated whether God's redeeming of Israel in the Exodus and of the human race at the cross did indeed require the payment of a price or not.[92] But there is a strong sense of substitution or equivalence in the Greek form *antilutron* ("ransom in place of," see 1 Tim. 2:6) and the way *ransom* is expressed in Mark 10:45 ("ransom [*lutron*] in place of [*anti*] many"—my translation).[93] Ransom in the New Testament, however, may be less about a transaction than about the value that God places upon the human race.[94]

If one understands that the New Testament points to the payment of a price, there is no indication to whom the price was paid, whether to God, Satan, or some other entity.[95] What is clear from this language is that the atonement at the cross was costly to the godhead. The forgiveness that humans receive is free through the cross, but it was not cheap to God. What Jesus endured on the cross was in behalf of, in place of, all of humanity.[96]

The Cross as a *Hilasterion*

A third Greek word associated with Old Testament atonement language is *hilasterion*, which was consistently applied in the LXX for the "mercy seat" on the ark of the covenant (e.g., Lev. 16:2ff.). It is transliterated here because

91. Marshall, "The Theology of the Atonement," in *The Atonement Debate*, 60.

92. The classic debate over whether the language of redemption in the Bible requires payment of a price was between Leon Morris, *The Apostolic Preaching of the Cross*, 3rd ed. (1965; repr., London: The Tyndale Press, 2000), 11–64 and David Hill, *Greek Words and Hebrew Meanings: Studies in the Semantics of Soteriological Terms*, Society for New Testament Studies Monograph Series, 5 (Cambridge: Cambridge University Press, 1967), 49–81. See also Green, "Atonement," *NIDB*, 346; Morris, *The Atonement*, 116–119.

93. Dederen, "Christ: His Person and Work," in *Handbook of Seventh-day Adventist Theology*, 177–178; Green and Baker, *Recovering the Scandal of the Cross*, 127; Tuckett, "Atonement in the NT," *ABD*, 1:521.

94. Brame, "The Cross: Payment or Gift?" *Perspectives in Religious Studies*, 172–173.

95. Green and Baker, *Recovering the Scandal of the Cross*, 128; Jewett, "Atonement," *ZPEB*, 1:410. This issue was a major point of contention in the course of church history. See Bromiley, "Atone; Atonement: History of the Doctrine," *ISBE*, 1:355–360.

96. Dederen, "Christ: His Person and Work," in *Handbook of Seventh-day Adventist Theology*, 178.

there is no settled English equivalent. In Hebrews 9:5 *hilasterion* is used in common Old Testament fashion to describe or name the mercy seat in the Most Holy place of the Hebrew sanctuary.[97] There is no direct theological meaning stated there.[98]

The other usage of *hilasterion* is in Romans 3:25.[99] *Hilasterion* in Romans 3:25 is usually translated as "propitiation" (KJV, ESV) or as "expiation" (RSV, NAB). The New International Version clarifies without clarifying by translating *hilasterion* as "sacrifice of atonement." In pagan Greek sources *hilasterion* carries the idea of propitiation, to turn away someone's anger or to conciliate, usually by the offer of a gift.[100] In Jewish and Christian sources the word usually means expiation, to cancel guilt or pay the penalty for a crime, to nullify sin and its effects.[101] The first meaning considers *hilasterion* in personal terms, while the second considers it in impersonal terms.[102] Pagan views of wrath and propitiation are absent from the

---

97. G. K. Beale applies this meaning also to Romans 3:25; see G. K. Beale, *A New Testament Biblical Theology: The Unfolding of the Old Testament in the New* (Grand Rapids, MI: Baker Academic, 2011), 486–489, while Morris argues strongly against applying this usage to Romans 3:25. See Morris, *The Atonement*, 168.

98. Related nouns and verbs are found in Hebrews 2:17 and 1 John 2:1–2 and 4:10. See Morris, *The Atonement*, 170–172, for a discussion of these. They have similar meaning to the likely usage in Romans 3:25.

99. Romans 3:25 stands at the culmination of a process of reasoning that goes all the way back to the first chapter of the epistle. After an introductory summary of the gospel (Rom. 1:16–17), Paul speaks of the wrath of God being revealed against sin (1:18), but since sin has left the entire human race in a hopeless condition (1:18—3:20), a mighty intervention from God is needed. That intervention is described by means of multiple metaphors. It is the manifestation of the righteousness of God through the faith of Jesus Christ (3:21–22). It is justification by His grace through the redemption (*apolutroseôs*) which is in Christ Jesus (3:24). That redemption is further explained as a *hilasterion* through His blood (3:25). So the word *hilasterion* is a crucial part of the solution God offers on account of human sin.

100. Dederen, "Christ: His Person and Work," in *Handbook of Seventh-day Adventist Theology*, 178; Rohintan K. Mody, "Penal Substitutionary Atonement in Paul," in *The Atonement Debate*, 124–127; Tuckett, "Atonement in the NT," *ABD*, 1:519.

101. Dederen, "Christ: His Person and Work," in *Handbook of Seventh-day Adventist Theology*, 178; C. H. Dodd, *The Bible and the Greeks* (London: Hodder, 1935), 82–95; Green, "Atonement," *NIDB*, 345; Milgrom, "Atonement in the OT," *IDB Supplement*, 80–81; Mitton, "Atonement," *IDB*, 1:313; Tuckett, "Atonement in the NT," *ABD*, 1:519.

102. Morris, *The Atonement*, 151–152, says you can propitiate a person, but you

scriptural view of God: He is not a capricious and vindictive deity whose mind must be changed by an overwhelming sacrifice.[103] But in the context of Romans 3:25, wrath and negative judgment are too central to ignore in relation to the solution that God provides, so there is an element of propitiation in Paul's use of *hilasterion*.[104] How does one reconcile the love of God with His wrath against sin?[105]

From this point of view, God's holiness made the penalty for sin inescapable. But God's love endured the penalty of sin in humanity's place. God took upon Himself the penalty of sin. "What the holiness of God required, His love provided."[106] At the cross both God's wrath against sin and His love for the sinner are revealed. There justice and mercy kiss each other (Ps. 85:10). "Love does not gloss over sin, but effectively grapples with it."[107] Whatever is understood by the phrase "the wrath of God," it is important to note that the wrath of God is not removed by human activity, its removal is due solely to God Himself.[108]

---

expiate a sin or a crime. So this translational dilemma has major significance for the role of God in the atonement. Is there someone who needs to be addressed or only an object that needs to be removed?

103. Dederen, "Christ: His Person and Work," in *Handbook of Seventh-day Adventist Theology,* 178; Dodd, *The Bible and the Greeks,* 82–95.

104. Dederen, "Christ: His Person and Work," in *Handbook of Seventh-day Adventist Theology,* 179; Mitton, "Atonement," *IDB,* 1:310. For a strong defense of propitiation as an important aspect of *hilasterion* in the New Testament, see Morris, *The Atonement,* 151–176. Some recent scholars are concerned that views such as this encourage violence in the name of God. See, for example, Jürgen Moltmann, "The Crucified God: Yesterday and Today: 1972–2002," trans. Margaret Kohl, in Marit Trelstad, *Cross Examinations: Readings on the Meaning of the Cross Today* (Minneapolis: Augsburg Fortress, 2006), 127–138; Marit Trelstad, *Cross Examinations: Readings on the Meaning of the Cross Today*; J. Denny Weaver, "The Nonviolent Atonement: Human Violence, Discipleship, and God," in *Stricken by God? Nonviolent Identification and the Victory of Christ,* ed. Brad Jersak and Michael Hardin (Grand Rapids, MI: Eerdmans, 2007), 316–355.

105. For an extensive discussion of the wrath of God in both testaments and its implications for today, see Morris, *The Atonement,* 153–157, 163–166.

106. Dederen, "Christ: His Person and Work," in *Handbook of Seventh-day Adventist Theology,* 179.

107. Dederen, "Christ: His Person and Work," in *Handbook of Seventh-day Adventist Theology,* 179–180.

108. Morris, *The Atonement,* 157.

He dealt with this while humans were still sinners, so the way to reconciliation is completely open to everyone.

This element of wrath and propitiation does not necessarily diminish the love of God, it can even raise it to unimaginable heights.[109] The greater the challenge that sin presents, the greater the action of love that was needed to overcome it. The challenge of sin highlights the love of God all the more. While *hilasterion* as a metaphor is challenging in today's world and easily misunderstood, it too provides a biblical dimension for understanding atonement at the cross.

The Cross as Acquittal in Court (Justification)

Why the cross? If the problem of sin is described in terms of a broken law that results in a state of guilt, the solution is acquittal (justification) in God's court of judgment.[110] This acquittal is made possible by two realities; the cross exhausting the penalty for breaking the law and the perfect law-keeping of Jesus providing the "righteousness" that is needed in the final judgment (Rom. 3:21–26; 5:12–21; 8:3–4).[111] To put it in other terms, Christ redeemed the human race from the curse of the law, having become that curse for them (Gal. 3:13). The concept is used in a similar fashion outside of Paul in Luke 18:9–14.

Today, *legalism* is often a dirty word, lending a negative connotation to the Bible's concern for covenant, law, righteousness, and judgment. But

---

109. Packer, "What Did the Cross Achieve?" *Tyndale Bulletin*, 41, notes that the divine withdrawal from Jesus on the cross was all the more intense because Jesus had experienced the full depth of the Father's love. For him, penal substitution demonstrated the depth of the Father's love, what He was willing to take on Himself to save humanity. Timothy Keller, in *King's Cross: The Story of the World in the Life of Jesus* (New York: Dutton, 2011), 141–142, points out that when you love wounded or needy people, there is always a cost to yourself. Philip Yancey points out that only someone who has been hurt can forgive. At Calvary, God chose to be hurt, "Surveying the Wondrous Cross: Understanding the Atonement Is About More Than Grasping a Theory," *Christianity Today* 53:5 (May 2009): 72.

110. The Greek word for justification (*dikaiosunê*) means essentially the same thing as righteousness and/or acquittal. See Mikolaski, "The Cross of Christ," *Christianity Today*, 4; I. Howard Marshall, "The Death of Jesus in Recent New Testament Study," *Word and World* 3:1 (Winter 1983): 17–18; Morris, *The Atonement*, 183–185.

111. The only Church Father who comes close to expressing this viewpoint is Cyril of Jerusalem. See Bromiley, "Atone; Atonement: History of the Doctrine," *ISBE*, 1:356.

legal systems do not need to be seen as impersonal, harsh, cold, and unfeeling. Rightly handled, constitutional law enables people with differing goals and interests to live together in peace. And the application of even-handed justice comes very close to mercy in the experience of those whose wrongs have been set right.[112]

Paul argues that God is completely just in both condemning and punishing sin and in pardoning and accepting sinners (Rom. 3:23–26).[113] Jesus Christ, acting on the sinner's behalf has both put away human sin by His death (3:25; 5:9) and fulfilled the just requirement of the law by His perfect thirty-three and a half years on this earth (8:4). So, according to this model, Christ's sacrifice is not a compromise of justice, but actually demonstrates it (3:26). Because of justification, relationship can be restored.[114]

It is important to note at this point that all of these first four metaphors of atonement have an element of substitution in them. God in Christ does for the sinner what the sinner is incapable of doing.[115] Many writings on atonement, therefore, highlight substitution as a metaphor of atonement in the New Testament.[116] This study does not, simply because there is no Greek word for "substitution" in the New Testament. Substitution is a natural by-product of most other metaphors rather than a central metaphor in its own right. It is assumed in the Scriptures rather than proved and explained.[117]

---

112. Morris, *The Atonement*, 178–179.

113. Dederen, "Christ: His Person and Work," in *Handbook of Seventh-day Adventist Theology*, 180.

114. Ibid., 180.

115. According to the Scriptures, at the cross Jesus substituted for both Adam and Israel. Hans Boersma, "Eschatological Justice and the Cross: Violence and Penal Substitution," *Theology Today* 60 (2003): 186–199. See also Richard L. Mayhue, "The Scriptural Necessity of Christ's Penal Substitution," *Master's Seminary Journal* 20:2 (Fall 2009): 139–148; Thomas R. Schreiner, "Penal Substitution View," in *The Nature of the Atonement: Four Views*, ed. James Beilby and Paul R. Eddy (Downer's Grove, IL: IVP Academic, 2006), 67–98.

116. The language of substitution, representation, and/or vicarious suffering was extremely popular among the early church fathers, being expressed by Irenaeus, the Epistle to Diognetus, Tertullian, Athanasius, Eusebius, Cyril of Alexandria, Gregory of Nyssa, Chrysostom, Nestorius of Constantinople, and Augustine. See Bromiley, "Atone; Atonement: History of the Doctrine," *ISBE*, 1:355–356.

117. While some prefer words like *representation* and *vicarious* to *substitution*, Packer, Packer, "What Did the Cross Achieve?" *Tyndale Bulletin* 17, notes that the three words are

The Cross as a Victory over Satan/Sin/Evil

The idea of ransom/redemption recalls the Exodus, where God's redemption of Israel proved also to be a victory over the evil powers under Pharaoh.[118] In fact, Israel's freedom could not have been obtained without such a prior victory. The language of victory is widespread in the New Testament.[119] It presupposes a somewhat dualistic view of the universe in which spiritual powers and sin hold sway over the human race.[120]

Perhaps the clearest text asserting victory over the evil powers is Colossians 2:14–15. While parts of this passage are difficult, the main message of these two verses is clear: The cross of Jesus Christ has "disarmed the powers and authorities" (Col. 2:15, NIV) through the cross, resulting in forgiveness of sins for the human race (2:13). The language of powers (*archas*) and authorities (*exousias*) translates Greek words that have consistent reference to the demonic realm (see Rom. 8:38; 1 Cor. 15:24; Eph. 3:10; Col. 2:10). A further clear reference is Revelation 12:9–11, where Satan is cast down from heaven as the accuser of the "brothers" and is overcome on earth by "the blood of the Lamb."[121] The ultimate

---

essentially synonyms, meaning putting a person or thing in place of others. They mean to do something so that others don't have to do it (Rom. 5:8; Gal. 3:13). See also Marshall, "The Death of Jesus," *Word and World,* 20; Samuel J. Mikolaski, "The Nature of Atonement; The Cross and the Theologians," *Christianity Today,* 5.

118. The classic exposition of this view of the atonement is by Gustav Aulén, *Christus Victor: An Historical Study of the Three Main Types of the Idea of the Atonement,* trans. A. G. Herbert (1931; repr., London: SPCK, 1965). More recent summaries of the "Christus Victor" view are in Gregory A. Boyd, "Christus Victor View," in *The Nature of the Atonement: Four Views,* ed. James Beilby and Paul R. Eddy (Downers Grove, IL: IVP Academic, 2006), 23–49; Paul R. Eddy and James Beilby, "The Atonement, an Introduction," in *The Nature of the Atonement: Four Views,* 12–14; Weaver, "The Nonviolent Atonement: Human Violence, Discipleship, and God," in *Stricken by God?,* 321–337. See also Tuckett, "Atonement in the NT," *ABD,* 1: 521.

119. It was also popular among the early church fathers, including Justin, Origen, Eusebius, and Augustine. See Bromiley, "Atone; Atonement: History of the Doctrine," *ISBE,* 1:355–356.

120. Tuckett, "Atonement in the NT," *ABD,* 1:521. Sin itself is seen as a malignant power in Romans 7:7–11.

121. See further references such as John 12:31; 16:11; Romans 8:35–38; 1 Corinthians 15:24–25; Philippians 2:9–11; Hebrews 2:14; 1 John 3:8; Revelation 5:5–10. This perspective

victory, of course, is the victory over death (1 Cor. 15:57). This was won by Christ at His resurrection and culminates in the resurrection of those who believe in Christ (1 Cor. 15:20–22).

Why the cross? Because it was needed to defeat the powers of sin and Satan, freeing human beings to return to God.[122] Jesus is the Champion (substitute) who defeats Satan for humanity (cf. 1 Sam. 17:8–11).[123] At the cross, Satan and his henchmen directed all the evil they could upon Jesus Christ, but He did not respond in kind. He thereby exhausted the power of evil and defeated it.[124] An additional way the cross defeated Satan may be hinted at in the next idea of how the cross effects the atonement.

The Cross as the Revelation of God's Character

While the New Testament models of atonement addressed so far all focus on what God has done by way of sacrifice, redemption, propitiation/expiation, justification, and victory to pave the way for human beings to be reconciled to Him, this model of the atonement focuses on the human side of the equation, the effect the cross has on human beings.[125] One way the New Testament portrays the human condition is in terms of ignorance or blindness.[126] Jesus is the One "who brings light and knowledge and who reveals the true nature of God."[127] This perspective is, therefore, particularly prevalent in the Gospel of John.[128]

---

often puts more emphasis on the cosmic significance of Christ's death than on its role in human salvation. See Boyd, "Christus Victor View," in *The Nature of the Atonement*, 33.

122. Theung-Huat Leow, "'The Cruciality of the Cross:' P. T. Forsyth's Understanding of the Atonement," *International Journal of Systematic Theology* 2:2 (April 2009): 197–198.

123. Chan, "The Gospel and the Achievement of the Cross," *ERT*, 26–27; Packer, "What Did the Cross Achieve?" *Tyndale Bulletin*, 20.

124. N. T. Wright, *Evil and the Justice of God* (Downers Grove, IL: InterVarsity Press, 2006), 88–90.

125. Packer, "What Did the Cross Achieve?" *Tyndale Bulletin*, 19.

126. Green and Baker, *Recovering the Scandal of the Cross*, 132.

127. Tuckett, "Atonement in the NT," *ABD*, 1:521; Chan, "The Gospel and the Achievement of the Cross," *ERT*, 24–26.

128. Chan, "The Gospel and the Achievement of the Cross," *ERT*, 24–26; Terence Forestell, *The Word of the Cross* (Rome: Biblical Institute Press, 1974), 113, 120: Green and Baker, 132–133. Church Fathers who speak of the atonement in these terms include

In the Prologue to the Gospel of John, the coming of Jesus reveals the glory and character of God (John 1:14). Jesus's intimate relationship with God enables Him to rightly "exegete" (*exêgêsato*) God (1:18). Jesus is the "light of the world" (8:12; 9:5) who not only reveals God but exposes the true character of human beings as well (3:18–21; 13:1–17). Helping His disciples to know God is at the core of Jesus's mission (17:3). And at the center of that "making known" (17:26) is the cross, which in John is described as a "lifting up" (3:14) which enables all to see the glory of God (17:1). The cross of Christ is, therefore, the supreme moment of revelation.[129]

In the Gospel of Mark, everyone, including the disciples of Jesus, struggles with who Jesus is (Mark 1:27; 2:6–7; 3:21; 4:10–13; 8:13–21). It is only at the moment Jesus dies that the centurion recognizes what the narrator and God have been saying all along, Jesus is the Son of God (Mark 1:1, 9–11; 9:2–8; 15:39).[130] It is the cross that reveals who Jesus is.

This focus on knowledge is not gnostic in character, but echoes the Hebrew concept of knowledge as involving close personal relationships (Gen. 4:1,17,25; Deut. 34:10; 2 Chron. 33:13; Isa. 55:5; Hos. 6:3; 13:5).[131] Why the cross? To provide human beings with the kind of knowledge that will draw them back to God.[132]

The Cross as a Pattern/Model

While "What would Jesus do?" is a common enough phrase, the focus here is not Jesus's life as a model for human beings to imitate, but specifically

---

Justin, Clement of Alexandria, and Origen. See Bromiley, "Atone; Atonement: History of the Doctrine," *ISBE*, 1:355–356.

129. Tuckett, "Atonement in the NT," *ABD*, 1:521.

130. Green and Baker, *Recovering the Scandal of the Cross*, 132.

131. Tuckett, "Atonement in the NT," *ABD*, 1:522.

132. This model seems most effective when combined with one or more of the objective models of atonement like sacrifice, ransom, or victory. The cross best reveals the love of God if it was necessary in some way, if it had a purpose other than revelation as well. See Chan, "The Gospel and the Achievement of the Cross," *ERT*, 25–26. A parent racing into a house to save a child demonstrates love. Racing into an empty burning house to "demonstrate love" is not nearly as effective. See Blocher, "Biblical Metaphors and the Doctrine of the Atonement," *JETS*, 645; Marshall, "The Theology of the Atonement," in *The Atonement Debate*, 62–63.

His death on the cross.[133] The New Testament frequently encourages believers to imitate the crucified Christ.[134] The cross as a pattern or model for Christian behavior is explored under two terms, "missional suffering" and "cruciformity."[135] There are multiple passages in the New Testament that call on believers to self-sacrificial suffering in behalf of the kingdom and after the pattern of Jesus's own suffering on the cross.[136]

Perhaps the best-known call to "cruciformity" is found in the Gospels. In Mark 8:34 (NAB) Jesus said, "Whoever wishes to come after me must deny himself, take up his cross, and follow me" (8:35–38; cf. Matt. 16:24–27; Luke 9:23–26). It is in the context of the cross that Jesus invites the first to be last and to become the servant of all (Mark 9:30–35; cf. Matt. 17:22–23; 18:1–5). The cross sets a new standard for leadership, servant leadership (Mark 10:42–45; Matt. 20:25–28). Jesus invites His followers to follow Him in the context of the cross (John 12:26; cf. 20–25), then sets the example by washing the disciples' feet (John 13:12–17; cf. 34–35; 15:12–13). Hebrews 12:1–2 describes the Christian life as a race looking to the crucified Christ as a model. John exhorts the believers that if they know Jesus laid down His life for them, they should do the same for each other (1 John 3:16). And nowhere in the New Testament is this message clearer than in 1 Peter 2:21 (ESV): "For to this you have been called, because Christ also suffered for you, leaving you an example, so that you might follow in his steps."

Paul delights in becoming one of Christ's "fools" and urges the Corinthians to follow his steady and constant example of living the cross (1 Cor. 4:8–17; 11:1). For Paul, this is not so much a doctrine as a "cruciform way of life."[137] This cruciform teaching becomes explicit in 2 Corinthians 5:14–15 where he urges that One died for all so that we may be constrained to live no longer for ourselves, but for the One who died for us

---

133. Church Fathers who spoke of the cross as an example or model include Justin and Origen.

134. Jason B. Hood, "The Cross in the New Testament: Two Theses in Conversation with Recent Literature (2000–2007)," *Westminster Theological Journal* 71 (2009): 286.

135. Michael J. Gorman, *Cruciformity: Paul's Narrative Spirituality of the Cross* (Grand Rapids, MI: Eerdmans, 2001), 35, 48; Hood, "The Cross in the New Testament," 287–291.

136. Hood, "The Cross in the New Testament," 287.

137. Ibid., 288.

(cf. Gal. 5:24; 6:14,17; Eph. 5:1–2). This teaching reaches an exalted height when Paul counsels in Ephesians 5:25–28 (KJV): "Husbands, love your wives, even as Christ also loved the church, and gave himself for it." So for Paul it is clear that the self-sacrificing love of the cross provides the model for every aspect of life.[138]

The Cross as a New Covenant

The final model of the atonement[139] in the New Testament explains the cross in terms of a new covenant. According to the Synoptic Gospels, Jesus offers His own interpretation of the cross in His comments at the last supper (Mark 14:24; Matt. 26:28; Luke 22:20).[140] In all three versions, the cup represents the blood of the covenant and Luke clearly adds the qualifier "new": "the *new* covenant in my blood."[141] Jesus's (new) covenant blood is "poured out for many" (Mark 14:24, ESV), "for the forgiveness of sins" (Matt. 26:28), or simply "for you" (Luke 22:20).

When Jesus said "*the* covenant," He was talking about the one and only covenant of the Old Testament, grounded in the fundamental event of

---

138. In the title of a book, Richard Hays identifies the cross as one of the main sources of New Testament ethics. Richard B. Hays, *The Moral Vision of the New Testament: Community, Cross, New Creation, a Contemporary Introduction to New Testament Ethics* (San Francisco, CA: Harper, 1999).

139. This model comes last for two reasons only. First, it has only received attention in the last few years as a model of the atonement. See Michael J. Gorman, "Effecting the New Covenant: A (Not So) New, New Testament Model for the Atonement," *Ex Auditu* 26 (2010): 26–59. Gorman builds on the work of R. Larry Shelton, *Cross and Covenant: Interpreting the Atonement for 21st Century Mission* (Milton Keynes, UK: Paternoster Press, 2009) and Thomas F. Torrance, *Atonement: The Person and Work of Christ*, ed. Robert T. Walker (Milton Keynes, UK: Paternoster Press, 2009). Second, I realized as this chapter was almost complete that I had written on this model in the past without connecting the idea to "the atonement." See Jon Paulien, *Meet God Again for the First Time* (Hagerstown, MD: Review and Herald, 2003), 77–112, 126–136. It was the reading of Gorman's article (previous note) that made me realize that he and I were saying the same things, but he was talking about atonement on the cross. This is probably my favorite model of the atonement because it is so solidly biblical and clearly goes back to Jesus Himself.

140. Gorman, "Effecting the New Covenant," *Ex Auditu*, 29.

141. Some manuscripts leave out Luke 22:20 entirely and some manuscripts of Matthew and Mark add the word "new," but I am working with the standard scholarly Greek text.

Israel's history, the Exodus.[142] After all, Jesus was presiding at a Passover meal as He spoke these words and a review of the events of the Exodus was part of the Passover ritual.[143] *The* covenant of the Exodus was the covenant with Abraham, which was grounded in the language of Eden.[144] Clearly, Jesus saw His upcoming death as the decisive event in all of Israel's history, and by extension, the history of the whole human race.[145]

In the only New Testament account of the last supper outside the Gospels (1 Cor. 11:23–25), Paul passes on a similar tradition, "this cup is the new covenant in my blood" (v. 25). In the book of Hebrews, the word *covenant* appears 16 times, nearly half the 33 occurrences in the New Testament as a whole. Jesus is there described as the Mediator of a new (Heb. 9:15; 12:24), eternal (13:20), or better (8:6) covenant that is made effective by His blood or by His death (10:19; 12:24; 13:20). Not only that, the new covenant promise of Jeremiah is quoted twice in the book (Heb. 8:8–13; 10:16–18).[146]

What makes this line of interpretation exciting is that covenant is not only a major category throughout the New Testament,[147] even where the word *covenant* is not used, but this model has the potential of drawing a common thread through nearly all of the previous models.[148] In summary, the new covenant promised in the Old Testament (Jer. 31:31–34; Ezek. 11:17–20; 36:23–28) was to be a transforming, creative act of God that would generate a renewed covenant people of God. They would be liberated, restored, forgiven, empowered, and permanent.[149] The New Testament writers understood that transforming act of God to have occurred at the cross.[150]

---

142. Gorman, "Effecting the New Covenant," *Ex Auditu*, 29.

143. Paulien, *Meet God Again*, 102–103; Gorman, "Effecting the New Covenant," *Ex Auditu*, 29.

144. Ibid., 29–34.

145. Ibid., 55–75.

146. Ibid., 30–31.

147. Jon Paulien, *Meet God Again*, 77–112, 126–136.

148. Gorman's working attempt to do this is on pages 55–58 of his seminal article, "Effecting the New Covenant," *Ex Auditu*.

149. Ibid., 33–36.

150. Spelled out from Matthew to Revelation in ibid., 36–55.

CONCLUSION

There are a wide variety of metaphors for the atonement in the New Testament. Not only are these metaphors diverse, but they tend to be intertwined with each other, making it difficult to separate them and to favor one over the others. The more these various metaphors are understood and respected, the richer will be the understanding of the message of the cross. And as the Gospel is embodied in a variety of cultures, it may yet be discovered that there are new biblical metaphors that have been overlooked up until now. Believers may also be led by the Spirit to express the cross in a way the New Testament writers had not thought of. But in all thinking regarding the atonement, believers need to be guided by the inspired models placed for them in the Scriptures.

What conclusions can believers draw from this brief survey of the relationship between the atonement and the cross?[151] The English word for *atonement* is most closely related to the concept of reconciliation. Atonement provides both the means and the incentive for human beings to become reconciled to God. In the New Testament atonement is clearly focused on the cross, but in the book of Hebrews the principle of the atonement continues in the heavenly work of Jesus Christ.

The human race is in great need of atonement, being unable to save itself. There are barriers between the human race and God on both sides of the equation. Because of sin reconciliation is, first of all, very costly to God. He cannot set its implications aside lightly. Also because of sin, human beings need to be drawn away from rebellion and back to relationship with God.

Although sin is a barrier between God and the human race, God does not require sacrifice in order to desire reconciliation with the human race; instead, He Himself lovingly provides the sacrifice/ransom/atonement needed to reconcile all to Himself. Human beings are called to respond to God's reconciling action with an action of their own.

Although God has given humans over to the consequences of their own sinful actions, He continually desires fellowship with sinful humans. His love provides all that they cannot perform in order for atonement to

---

151. This conclusion is modeled on the style of the conclusion to the article by W. S. Reid, "Atone, Atonement," *ISBE,* 1:354–355.

take place. The atonement made at the cross is not limited to some humans or even all humans, but in some sense affects the entire universe.

The New Testament offers a variety of models to explain the atonement. There was no attempt to set one view as normative over against the others, and various models could be mingled in a single sentence or paragraph.

In many ways, the atonement is as inscrutable to humans as God is. What humanity knows for sure is that God is portrayed in Scripture as infinitely loving and infinitely gracious to erring humanity. However one expresses the atonement at the cross, it is clear that God has provided all that human beings need in order to be reconciled to Him. So the word from Paul continues to ring out, "We implore you on Christ's behalf: Be reconciled to God" (2 Cor. 5:20, NIV).

CHAPTER 11

THE MEANING OF THE INTERCESSORY MINISTRY OF JESUS CHRIST ON HUMANITY'S BEHALF IN THE HEAVENLY SANCTUARY

Jiří Moskala

The intercessory ministry of Jesus Christ in the heavenly sanctuary is a core teaching of Seventh-day Adventism. Jesus's mediatory work is made possible only because of His exceptional, unselfish, and once-for-all death for humanity (Heb. 9:28). The view of Christ's mediatorial work in heaven does not in any way diminish what happened on the cross as a unique, unparalleled, non-repeatable, and unprecedented divine act of salvation (Heb. 10:12, 14) from which all benefits flow to humans.[1] Nothing can improve or supplement it, and no one can add anything to Christ's extraordinary sacrifice. Salvation on the cross is indeed complete (Rom. 3:21–6; 1 Cor. 1:18, 23–24; 2:2; Gal. 2:16, 21; Eph. 2:4–10). Adventist theology differentiates

---

1. Everett Ferguson underlines that Jesus's "atoning death was [a] unique and unrepeatable work for human salvation (Heb 10:12, 14). Jesus' sacrificial death, therefore, was a ministry that the church cannot continue. . . . Jesus' redemptive sufferings were complete and cannot be added to," Everett Ferguson, *The Church of Christ: A Biblical Ecclesiology for Today* (Grand Rapids, MI: Eerdmans, 1996), 282.

Ellen G. White explains: "The intercession of Christ in man's behalf in the sanctuary above is as essential to the plan of salvation as was His death upon the cross. By His death He began that work which after His resurrection He ascended to complete in heaven. . . . There the light from the cross of Calvary is reflected," *The Great Controversy* (Boise, ID: Pacific Press, 1950), 489.

between the "complete" atonement accomplished by Jesus Christ on the cross, and the "completed" atonement in relationship to His intercessory ministry in heaven on humanity's behalf.[2] Atonement-salvation is therefore not completed, because we still live in a sinful world. Christ's ministry involves the security of the entire universe as He applies His work of redemption to individual believers (Dan. 7:9–10, 13–14; 9:24–27; Eph. 1:7–10; Rev. 12:7–12).[3] A lasting solution to the problem of evil, however, is complex, involving Christ's mediatory work in heaven over a long period of time.

A DIFFICULT PUZZLE

Theologians encounter seemingly unsurmountable problems regarding the meaning of Jesus's work on earth today. Philip Yancey eloquently declares:

> I have concluded, in fact, that the Ascension represents my greatest struggle of faith—not whether it happened, but why. It challenges me more than the problem of pain, more than the difficulty of harmonizing science and the Bible, more than belief in the Resurrection and other miracles. . . . For me what has happened since Jesus' departure strikes at the core of my faith. Would it not have been better if the Ascension had never happened? If Jesus had stayed on earth, he could answer our questions, solve our doubts, mediate our disputes of doctrine and policy.[4]

---

2. See, for example, the statement of the former dean of the Seventh-day Adventist Theological Seminary, Dr. W. G. C. Murdock, at the 1980 General Conference session in Dallas, Texas: "Seventh-day Adventists have always believed in a complete atonement that is not completed," quoted in Morris L. Venden, *Never Without an Intercessor: The Good News About the Judgment* (Boise, ID: Pacific Press, 1996), 140.

The full at-one-ment (i.e., the complete harmony between God and His creation) will be reached when sin is eradicated and evil is no longer present (1 Cor. 15:24–28; Eph. 1:10). This full harmony will be restored at the end of the Millennium (Rev. 21–22).

3. "Christ is mediating in behalf of man, and the order of unseen worlds is preserved by His mediatorial work," Ellen G. White, *Messages to Young People* (Nashville, TN: Southern Publishing, 1930), 254. "Not only men, but angels, will ascribe honor and glory to the Redeemer, for even they are secure only through the sufferings of the Son of God. It is through the efficacy of the cross that the inhabitants of unfallen worlds have been guarded from apostasy. Not only those who are washed by the blood of Christ, but also the holy angels, are drawn to him by his crowning act of giving his life for the sins of the world," Ellen G. White, "The Home Missionary," May 1, 1897.

4. Philip Yancey, *The Jesus I Never Knew* (Grand Rapids, MI: Zondervan, 1995), 229.

He adds: "By ascending, Jesus took the risk of being forgotten."[5] God's distance and invisibility disturbs humanity. His obvious physical absence frustrates humans, especially in view of atrocities such as war, rape, exploitation, natural disasters, death, suffering, and pain. People often ask, Where is God now, and what is He doing?

BIBLICAL AFFIRMATION

The Bible powerfully declares that Jesus Christ is in heaven (Mark 16:19; Luke 24:50–51; Acts 1:9–11) and is interceding for humans (hinted at in Rom. 5:10–21, but explicitly taught in Rom. 8:34; 1 John 2:1). This fundamental teaching attests that Christ's intermediatory role is needed to accomplish the plan of salvation. Jesus Christ is humanity's Intercessor, Mediator, and High Priest, in the heavenly sanctuary (Heb. 4:15–16; 8:1–2). The author of Hebrews presents an elaborate picture of Jesus Christ as our High Priest and Mediator-Intercessor who is alive and makes intercession for sinners (Heb. 7:25). The Old Testament points to God Himself as a heavenly Witness or Advocate (Job 16:19–20; cf. 33:23), and explains that the Servant of the Lord makes "intercession for the transgressors" (Isa. 53:12).[6] This Suffering Servant, whom the early church identified as Jesus Christ (Acts 8:27–35), died for humans on their behalf, forgives their sins, and gives them His righteousness. Thus, His work bestows the benefits of His substitutionary death to sinners (Isa. 53:3–12).[7]

According to the book of Daniel, at the time of the end, Michael will stand for His people in order to deliver them from oppression (Dan. 12:1–2). Likewise, Jesus was standing for Stephen when he was stoned to death (Acts 7:55–56). Standing at the right hand of God is biblical imagery for the intercessory ministry of Jesus Christ.[8] Numerous biblical scholars and

---

5. Ibid., 230.

6. Unless otherwise indicated, all Scripture quotations are taken from THE HOLY BIBLE, NEW INTERNATIONAL VERSION®, NIV® Copyright © 1973, 1978, 1984, 2011 by Biblica, Inc.® Used by permission. All rights reserved worldwide. Italics in Scripture quotes reflect emphasis added by author.

7. There are five songs of the Servant of the Lord in the book of Isaiah (42:1–9; 49:1–7; 50:4–9; 52:12–53:12; 61:1–3).

8. A difference exists between standing and sitting at the right hand of God. "Standing" points to intercession, whereas "sitting" refers to the rulership, victory, authority,

theologians confirm the biblical teaching that Jesus Christ is humanity's Intercessor,[9] but what does it mean? What does the Bible want to convey by this terminology? What difference does it make for everyday problems that He "always lives to intercede" (Heb. 7:25) for humanity?

WHAT CHRIST'S INTERCESSION DOES NOT MEAN

Before describing the current role of Jesus in heaven, it is first necessary to underline what the intercessory ministry of Jesus Christ in the heavenly sanctuary does not mean. It does not imply that Jesus must (1) plead with the heavenly Father or beg Him to forgive our sins; (2) appease an angry God; (3) change the Father's attitude toward us; (4) nor reconcile God to humanity. Jesus and the Heavenly Father are not involved in a celestial arm-wrestling match to ascertain who is stronger in order to show either favor or anger toward humans.

The Scriptures clearly explain the reasons for these conclusions. First, Jesus does not need to implore our Heavenly Father to love us. He Himself declared it: "In that day you will ask in my name. I am not saying that I will ask the Father on your behalf. No, the Father himself loves you because you have loved me and have believed that I came from God" (John 16:26–27). Second, Jesus does not need to change the Father's attitude toward us— "For God so loved the world that He gave His one and only Son, that whoever believes in him shall not perish but have eternal life" (John 3:16). Christ died for us, because the Father loved humans. Finally, humans must be reconciled to God, not vice versa. This is our message of reconciliation

---

and kingship of Christ's ministry (Matt. 26:64; Mark 16:19; Rom. 8:34; Eph. 1:20; Col. 3:1; Heb. 12:2; cf. Ps. 110:1). *Standing* also refers to the action of the judge who is ready to pronounce the legal verdict regarding the indicted person. Thus, the verdict brings deliverance and victory or condemnation.

9. See, for example, Louis Berkhof, *Systematic Theology*, 4th rev. and enl. ed. (repr.; Grand Rapids, MI: Eerdmans, 1979); G. C. Berkouwer, *The Work of Christ* (Grand Rapids, MI: Eerdmans, 1965); Emil Brunner, *The Mediator: A Study of the Central Doctrine of the Christian Faith*, trans. Olive Wyon (Philadelphia, PA: Westminister Press, 1947); Millard J. Erikson, *Christian Theology*, 3rd ed. (Grand Rapids, MI: Baker Academics, 2013); Wayne A. Grudem, *Systematic Theology: An Introduction to Biblical Doctrine* (Grand Rapids, MI: Zondervan, 1994); Edward Heppenstall, *Our High Priest: Jesus Christ in the Heavenly Sanctuary* (Washington, DC: Review and Herald, 1972).

as God's ambassadors: "Be [you people] reconciled to God" (2 Cor. 5:20). Sinners need to be brought back to Him; God is constantly searching for the lost (Gen. 3:9).[10]

If Jesus Christ needed to appease an angry heavenly Father, then He would not differ from pagan gods that require pacification and the expiation of their anger through sacrifices and gifts. One cannot buy God's favor; thus Jesus does not need to plead with the Father on our behalf, but satisfies God's righteousness-justice in dealing with sin. Thus, He is both "just and the justifier of the one who has faith in Jesus" (Rom. 3:26, NKJV). Our Heavenly Father loves people (Deut. 33:3); He and Christ are fully united in their efforts to save humanity (Eph. 1:3–10).[11]

NECESSARY PREREQUISITE

The essential precondition for Christ's mediation is the oneness of His being God and man (i.e., the divinity and humanity of the person of Jesus Christ). He came to save fallen humanity. The incarnation of Christ and His atoning death on Calvary are foundational qualifications that opened the way for His intercessory ministry. The cross was a necessary prerequisite for His salvific mediatory work for humanity (Rom. 3:23–26). His victory over sin (Matt. 4:1–11; Rom. 8:3) and His voluntary and substitutionary death for humanity qualified Him to be their Intercessor.

The intercessory ministry of Jesus puts into practice the results of the cross by expanding the efficacy of Calvary. Jesus became sin and a curse for humanity (Isa. 53:3–6; 2 Cor. 5:21; Gal. 3:13). What was accomplished on the

---

10. Romans 5:10 states: "For if when we were enemies we were reconciled to God through the death of His Son, much more, having been reconciled, we shall be saved by His life" (NKJV). Regarding a sense in which God was reconciled to humanity in order that His justice could be satisfied through the substitutionary death of Jesus Christ, and His wrath propitiated (Rom. 3:25; 2 Cor. 5:18), see point no. 4 in the section "Linguistic Connotations."

11. Ellen G. White notes: "The atonement of Christ was not made in order to induce God to love those whom He otherwise hated. . . . We are not to entertain the idea that God loves us because Christ has died for us, but that He so loved us that He gave His only-begotten Son to die for us," *The Signs of the Times*, May 30, 1895. "The atonement of Christ was not the cause of God's love, but the result of that love. Jesus died because God loved the world," *The Review and Herald*, September 2, 1890. "The Father loves us, not because of the great propitiation, but He provided the propitiation because He loves us," *Bible Echo and Signs of the Times*, August 1, 1892.

cross nearly two thousand years ago must now be applied, actualized, and incorporated into the lives of men and women for them to be restored to His image and have abundant life (John 10:10). He is the God-Man, the Mediator of humanity, because He "gave himself as a ransom for all people" (1 Tim. 2:6; cf. Mark 10:45). He is humanity's Mediator because He is their Savior. His intercession is a continuation of His saving activity on humanity's behalf, the realization and integration of His work for all people on the cross. Every person needs His death and life in order to be spiritually alive (Rom. 3:24–25; 5:10; 1 Cor. 1:24, 30; 2 Cor. 5:14–17; Eph. 2:1, 4–6; Col. 3:3–4).

Raoul Dederen emphasizes the role of Christ's death on the cross: "While His sacrifice for sin was made once for all on the cross (Heb. 7:27; 9:28; 10:11–14), the ascended Christ is making available to all the benefits of His atoning sacrifice."[12] At the moment sin entered the world, Jesus reached down from heaven and stepped in as humanity's Intercessor in anticipation of His victory at the cross. This proleptic reality is best described in the book of Revelation: "The Lamb who was slain from the creation [or better 'foundation'; Greek: *katabolē*] of the world" (13:8).

CHRIST'S TWOFOLD MINISTRY

Christ's role as Intercessor is twofold: (1) revealing and ministering the mysteries of God's goodness and richness to humankind; and (2) presenting humanity's existential needs to God and securing their salvation. In other words, His intercessory ministry is both a revelatory and redemptive process for humanity, forming one unit that cannot be separated. Alister McGrath correctly explains that "the presence of God in Christ is intended to mediate between a transcendent God and fallen humanity. This idea of 'presence as mediation' takes two quite distinct, yet ultimately complementary, forms: the mediation of revelation on the one hand, and of salvation, on the other."[13]

First of all, Jesus being divine (John 1:1–3; Rom. 9:5; Col. 1:15–18) represents the Godhead. As the Mediator, meaning communicator, of the

---

12. Raoul Dederen, "Christ: His Person and Work," in *Handbook of Seventh-day Adventist Theology* (Hagerstown, MD: Review and Herald, 2000), 187.

13. Alister E. McGrath, *Christian Theology: An Introduction*, 2nd ed. (Cambridge, MA: Blackwell Publishers, 1997), 346–347.

divine, He reveals the Father, His character, and all the values of the God-head (Matt. 11:27; Luke 10:22; John 1:14–18; 17:6). Because He and the Father are one (John 10:30), Christ also discloses the Holy Spirit by explaining the Spirit's ministry (John 14:16–17; 15:26–27; 16:7–15) and interceding (*entynchanein*) for the saints (Rom. 8:27).[14] With the entrance of sin (Gen. 3:1–10) and the ensuing distortion of God's character, Christ's birth and sacrifice on the cross for humanity demonstrates, credibly and convincingly, that God is the God of love, truth, and justice (2 Chron. 15:3; Ps. 31:5; 89:14; Jer. 10:10; John 1:14; 3:16; 14:6; Rom. 1:17; 3:21; 5:5–8; 1 John 4:16).

Proverbs 8:22–31 hints at the special role Jesus took upon Himself as Mediator and Communicator between the triune God and created beings. From the moment God began to create beings in the universe,[15] Christ was presenting the principles of love, government, and the will of the Godhead to the created worlds.

When the New Testament uses the term *mesites* (Gal. 3:19–20; 1 Tim. 2:5; Heb. 8:6; 9:15; 12:24) or *mesiteuein* (Heb. 6:17), it denotes what God is doing for humans through Jesus Christ. He came from above to be with us, Emmanuel (Isa. 7:14; Matt. 1:20–23), a movement from God toward humanity, not the reverse. He came to live among humankind as a fragile human being to reveal God's values, truth, teachings, and how God hates sin and evil. He never stands on the side of the oppressor, but on the side of the oppressed. In humanity's suffering and distress, He suffers with human-ity (Isa. 63:9). Jesus is the optimal self-revelation of God, the revealer of truth, because He is the Way, the Truth, and the Life (John 14:6; cf. Exod. 34:6–7). He not only reveals God and proclaims the Word of God, but is Himself the revelation and personified Word of God in the flesh (John 1:1–3; Col. 2:9). In His humanity, He served as an exegete (*exegeomai*) by imparting a right interpretation of the true character of His Heavenly Father (John 1:18). Upon this existential knowledge depends eternal life (John 17:3). He desires to unveil the lies regarding the Godhead and rebuild a loving and trusting relationship between Himself and humanity.

---

14. In the case of the Spirit, the Greek word *mesites* (mediator) is not used.

15. See on this point a seminal article by Richard M. Davidson, "Proverbs 8 and the Place of Christ in the Trinity," *Journal of the Adventist Theological Society* 17, no. 1 (Spring 2006): 33–54.

Second, by experiencing true humanity, Jesus Christ (Matt. 4:1–11; Luke 2:52; John 1:14; Rom. 8:3; Phil. 2:5–11; Col. 2:9; 1 John 1:1–2; 4:2–3) understands humanity's struggles (Heb. 4:15–16) and thus, as their Representative (1 Tim. 2:5), can efficiently mediate on their behalf between the Holy Father and sinful humanity. The remainder of this chapter focuses on this aspect of Jesus's role as humanity's Intercessor in the heavenly sanctuary and pursues a clearer understanding of His ministry.

LINGUISTIC CONNOTATIONS

The Scriptures attest that Jesus Christ intercedes (*entynchanein*) on humanity's behalf before the heavenly Father (Rom. 8:34; Heb. 7:25; 9:24) and that He is humanity's Advocate (*parakletos*, 1 John 2:1). A careful study of the biblical vocabulary related to Christ's intercessory ministry can assist a serious student of Scripture in discovering the meaning of Jesus's function as our Intercessor.

The Hebrew word for "intercede" is *paga'* which means basically "to meet" or "encounter" (Gen. 23:8). Another verb is *palal*, translated as "to pray" or "intercede" (1 Sam. 2:25; 7:5). Also, the term *khalah* (II; only in pi'el) means to "pacify," "appease," or "intercede" (1 Kings 13:6).

The Greek verb *entynchano* means also "to meet" or "encounter," and as its Hebrew counterpart it conveys according to the context whether this meeting is positive or negative (Acts 25:24; Rom. 11:2).

The notion of *parakletos* literally means "someone who is called (to help or to stand by)," thus "Helper," "Advocate," "Intercessor." Jesus Christ, as well as the Holy Spirit, is called *parakletos* (John 14:16 [the Holy Spirit]; 1 John 2:1 [Jesus Christ]), which means, "He is Someone called to help" or "Someone to stand by." He can effectively help in every person with his or her daily struggles.

Jesus Christ is a *hilasterion* (atonement, expiation, propitiation) according to Romans 3:25. The Hebrew equivalent of this expression is *kapporet* (a mercy seat; see Lev. 25:17; 16:15–17).[16] Christ is a reconciling or atoning

---

16. A significant debate exists among New Testament scholars regarding whether the correct translation of the word *hilasterion* means "to expiate" or "to propitiate." See James E. Allman, "*hilaskesthai*: To Propitiate or to Expiate?" *Bibliotheca Sacra* 172 (July–September 2015): 335–355; C. H. Dodd, "*hilaskesthai*, Its Cognates, Derivatives, and Synonyms, in the Septuagint," *Journal of Theological Studies* 32 (1930–31): 352–360; Leon Morris, *The*

sacrifice (Greek: *hilasmos*; 1 John 2:2; 4:10). He experienced God's wrath because He became sin for humanity (2 Cor. 5:21) and took upon Himself the curse for humanity's transgressions (Gal. 3:13–14) that humans may live and have eternal life (John 5:24–25; 11:25). The biblical understanding of the Lord's anger or wrath (Rom. 1:18) is God's antagonistic, irreconcilable, and burning reaction toward sin. It is His passionate attitude toward every-thing that is irreversibly associated with evil because sin destroys what is good, valuable, and beautiful. God cannot tolerate evil because it opposes His good nature (Ps. 107:1). God is love by definition (Deut. 7:9; 1 John 4:16) and is only perceived as wrathful in revealing His uncompromising attitude toward sin and anything that destroys life. The Triune God devised a very costly solution to the problem of sin: Christ Himself. His sacrifice of love bestows reconciliation and peace with the Godhead (Rom. 5:9–11; 2 Cor. 5:18–19; Col. 1:19–20). He is the mercy seat, the atoning sacrifice who cov-ers all repentant sinners with His righteousness, thus removing the cause of God's wrath (2 Cor. 5:18). All sinners who admit they have transgressed His Word, the law of God, openly, honestly, and sincerely confess their sins, and accept Christ as their Savior are forgiven; God is their righteousness (Ps. 32:1–2; 51:1–12; Jer. 23:5–6; 33:16; Rom. 3:26; 1 John 1:7–9). Michael Bird states: "We might say that when sin is expiated, then God's wrath is propitiated. When sin is removed, God's wrath is appeased."[17] However, unrepentant sinners remain under God's wrath (John 3:36).

God's wrath is revealed against all iniquity, but Jesus Christ is a *hilaste-rion*, a mercy seat, a *kapporet*.[18] The cross was a revelation of God's love and

---

Apostolic Preaching of the Cross (Grand Rapids, MI: Eerdmans, 1955): 144–213; Roger Nichol, "C. H. Dodd and the Doctrine of Propitiation," *Westminster Theological Journal* 17 (May 1955): 117–157; Valentin Zywietz, "Representing the Government of God: Christ as the *Hilasterion* in Romans 3:25" (MA thesis, Andrews University, 2016).

17. Michael F. Bird, *Evangelical Theology: A Biblical and Systematic Introduction* (Grand Rapids, MI: Zondervan, 2013), 406–407.

18. In the sanctuary, the *kapporet* covered the ark of the covenant under which was the law of God, the Decalogue (see Exod. 25:17–22). In the Septuagint, the *kapporet* is trans-lated as *hilasterion* (see, for example, Exod. 25:17, 20–21; 31:7; Lev. 16:13–15; cf. Heb. 9:5). This mercy seat or covering lid represented Jesus Christ, His atoning sacrifice on the cross. He was the sacrifice of atonement that God provided in order to cover sinners and give them transforming grace. Paul identifies Jesus as a mercy seat—"*hilasterion*" or "*kapporet*" (Rom. 3:25; 1 John 4:15). Jesus makes propitiation or atonement (*hilaskomai*—Heb. 2:17), and is the

justice (Pss. 85:10; 101:1). By the cross, God demonstrated that He is just, while justifying "those who have faith in Jesus" (Rom. 3:26) and accept Christ as the Mercy Seat (Rom. 3:25). His righteousness is manifested through His ultimate sacrifice of life.

Jesus Christ is humanity's only Intercessor (1 Tim. 2:2–6). This assertion by Paul was intended to counter the Gnostic teaching of his time, a world teeming with diverse intercessors.[19] But Paul assures his listeners that no other power can come between God and this world, and that Christ is fully God and fully human. He is humanity's Intercessor because He gave Himself for humanity in order to redeem humanity. No one and nothing on earth or in the entire universe can separate humanity from God's love (Rom. 8:35–39).

WHAT IS THE MEANING OF THE INTERCESSORY MINISTRY OF JESUS CHRIST ON OUR BEHALF?

Christ Meets the Father in Order to Help

Jesus Christ and the heavenly Father meet (*paga'* and *entynchano*) together in order to help (*parakletos*) humans with their everyday problems and enable them to be victorious Christians. All heaven—the Father, Jesus Christ, and the Holy Spirit—is united in helping humans in their struggle with sin, Satan, and temptation. Without His assistance, people are powerless and cannot resist evil, change, or grow spiritually (John 15:5; cf. Phil. 4:13).

The first tangible result of the meeting after Christ's ascension was the sending of the Holy Spirit to believers (Acts 2). Everett Ferguson rightly states:

> God gives help in living out one's salvation (Phil. 2:12) in the Christian way of life. The Holy Spirit provides the link between baptism and the Christian life. The Holy Spirit not only sanctifies (1 Cor. 6:11; 1 Pet. 1:2) but also gives new life in baptism (John 3:5) and takes up residence in the one converted (Acts 2:38; 5:30; Rom 8:9; 1 Cor. 6:19). The Holy Spirit provides the

---

propitiation or the atoning sacrifice for sins (1 John 2:2; cf. "an offering for sin"—Isa. 53:10).

19. Thus, for example, Ivan T. Blazen in his article "Jesus: Priest and Coming King," in *The Essential Jesus: The Man, His Message, His Mission*, ed. Bryan W. Ball and William G. Johnsson (Boise, ID: Pacific Press Publishing Association, 2002), 251.

continuing present benefits of God's one-time action in the cross and the one-time commitment in baptism (there is "one baptism"—Eph. 4:5). He is the power of the Christian life.[20]

Because humanity now has free access to God, people can approach Him directly through Christ without the need of any human mediation (Heb. 4:16; 10:19). "Christ has made direct access to God in the heavenly sanctuary possible. That access is also related to the Holy Spirit. 'For through [Christ Jesus] both [Jew and Gentile] have access in one Spirit to the Father' (Eph 2:18). The Holy Spirit provides a life that in some measure already participates in the future life (Eph 1:13–14; Heb 6:4)."[21]

John's comment: "Up to that time the Spirit had not been given, since Jesus had not yet been glorified" (John 7:39) needs to be correctly understood.[22] This proclamation does not mean that the Holy Spirit was not present, active, and engaged during the Old Testament period (ample evidence testifies against this popular standpoint),[23] but signifies that the Spirit of the Lord could only work proleptically during Old Testament times and was acting in anticipation of Christ's glorification, (i.e., Jesus's

---

20. Everett Ferguson, *The Church of Christ: A Biblical Ecclesiology for Today* (Grand Rapids, MI: Eerdmans, 1996), 204. Consider also the following statements of Ellen G. White: "By a union with Christ, by living faith, we are privileged to enjoy the efficacy of His mediation. We are crucified with Christ, buried with Christ, risen with Christ, to walk in newness of life," *Signs of the Times*, October 11, 1899. "Everyone who will break from the slavery and service of Satan, and will stand under the blood-stained banner of Prince Immanuel will be kept by Christ's intercessions. Christ, as our Mediator, at the right hand of the Father, ever keeps us in view, for it is as necessary that He should keep us by His intercessions as that He should redeem us with His blood. If He lets go His hold of us for one moment, Satan stands ready to destroy. Those purchased by His blood, He now keeps by His intercession," MS 73, 1893, in Francis D. Nichol, ed., *The Seventh-day Adventist Bible Commentary* (Washington, DC: Review and Herald, 1980), 6:1078.

21. Ferguson, *The Church of Christ*, 217.

22. See Luke 24:49; John 14:16–17, 26; 15:26; 16:7; Acts 1:8. See also seven New Testament statements about the "baptism of/with/in/by the Holy Spirit" (Matt. 3:11–12; Mark 1:8; Luke 3:16–17; John 1:33; Acts 1:5; 11:16; 1 Cor. 12:13). Compare with Luke 1:15 (John the Baptist); 1:41 (Elizabeth); 1:67 (Zechariah)—all these Old Testament saints were filled with the Holy Spirit before Pentecost or Jesus's glorification.

23. John Goldingay, "Was the Holy Spirit Active in Old Testament Times? What Was New About the Christian Experience of God?" *Ex Auditu* 12 (1996): 14–28; Wilf Hildebrandt, *An Old Testament Theology of the Spirit of God* (Peabody, MA: Hendrickson Publishers, 1995).

victory on the cross, His resurrection and ascension). James Hamilton states: "The sense in which the Spirit is yet to be given is that *believers* are about to receive Him at the glorification of Jesus."[24]

The cross historically validated the Spirit's activities. Jesus's glorification (see John 13:31–32; 17:1–5)[25] was the seal authenticating the involvement of the Holy Spirit's work during Old Testament times and onward. Thus, the triumphant death of Jesus was the prerequisite for giving the Spirit of God to the world. And, at the same time His activity was real, in the justification and affirmation of the work of the Holy Spirit in the Old Testament dispensation.[26]

Jesus's intercession is also compared to His praying for us. By praying for His followers, He helps them become strong in faith and united in love and truth (see John 17). Jesus's intercessory prayer for His disciples and successive generations of His followers is that they be a model of unity and faithfulness. A good example of this is Jesus praying for Peter: "I have prayed for you, that your faith should not fail" (Luke 22:32, NKJV). He wants believers to know Him (John 17:3; 2 Pet. 3:18); be victorious in Him (Rev. 3:5, 21); love each other (John 13:34–35); and be His

---

24. James M. Hamilton, Jr., *God's Indwelling Presence: The Holy Spirit in the Old and New Testaments,* New American Commentary Studies in Bible and Theology, ed. E. Ray Clendenen (Nashville, TN: B&H Publishing Group, 2006), 62, emphasis in original. See also, Geoffrey W. Grogan, "The Experience of Salvation in the Old and New Testaments," *Vox Evangelica* 5 (1967): 12–17; Sidney H. Hooke, "The Spirit Was Not Yet (John 7:39)," *New Testament Studies* 9 (1963): 372–380.

25. By the sacrificial life and victorious death for sinners, Jesus Christ glorified His Father and saved humanity. Each believer in Him has eternal life, the glorious result of His ultimate sacrifice for humanity. The Father glorified Jesus, that is, resurrected Him to life and restored Him to His previous position of glory (John 17:5; Acts 2:32, 36; 5:30–31; Phil. 2:8–9).

Christ's death started not only a new dimension of His ministry, but also approved and authenticated all that was previously accomplished in Old Testament times.

26. Walter C. Kaiser, Jr., "The Indwelling Presence of the Holy Spirit in the Old Testament," *Evangelical Quarterly* 82, no. 4 (2010): 315, "The coming of the Holy Spirit at Pentecost was a most significant work wherein the Spirit arrived in state, visibly and dramatically, thereby showing in time and space what had been experienced all along in the Old Testament was not unreal, but was fully part of the whole plan of God." He also asks a pertinent question: "How could all of these old covenant persons have believed and been enabled to live sanctified lives if the Spirit of God did not dwell in them?" To prove the point, he provides examples of Old Testament believers such as Enoch, Noah, Joseph, Job, Bezalel, and David, ibid., 309.

bold and courageous disciples (Matt. 14:27; Acts 4:13, 29; 23:11; 27:22, 25; 28:31; Phil. 1:20).[27]

Through Christ's mediatory work, the Intercessor purifies the actions, prayers, worship, obedience, and praises of believers who seek to express their gratitude to God. All need His purification. Ellen White powerfully comments on this aspect:

> Christ, our Mediator, and the Holy Spirit are constantly interceding in man's behalf, but the Spirit pleads not for us as does Christ who presents His blood, shed from the foundation of the world; the Spirit works upon our hearts, drawing out prayers and penitence, praise and thanksgiving. The gratitude which flows from our lips is the result of the Spirit striking the cords of the soul in holy memories, awakening the music of the heart.
>
> The religious services, the prayers, the praise, the penitent confession of sin, ascend from true believers as incense to the heavenly sanctuary; but passing through the corrupt channels of humanity, they are so defiled that unless purified by blood, they can never be of value with God. They ascend not in spotless purity, and unless the intercessor who is at God's right hand presents and purifies all by His righteousness, it is not acceptable to God. All incense from earthly tabernacles must be moist with the cleansing drops of the blood of Christ. He holds before the Father the censor of His own merits, in which there is no taint of earthly corruption. He gathers into this censor the prayers, the praise, and the confessions of His people, and with these He puts His own spotless righteousness. Then, perfumed with the merits of Christ's propitiation, the incense comes up before God wholly and entirely acceptable. Then gracious answers are returned.
>
> O, that all may see that everything in obedience, in penitence, in praise and thanksgiving must be placed upon the glowing fire of the righteousness of Christ. The fragrance of this righteousness ascends like a cloud around the mercy seat.[28]

Finally, as Intercessor, Jesus Christ helps His followers to be connected to Him and be active in His Church. "To be in Christ is to be in the church, and

---

27. Exodus 32:31–32 provides an excellent example of such a praying ministry where Moses intercedes for the people of God who have sinned against Him by making a golden calf. Moses asks for God's forgiveness and even offers his own life for them.

28. Ellen G. White, MS 50, 1900, in *Seventh-day Adventist Bible Commentary*, 6:1077–1078. See also Ellen G. White, *Patriarchs and Prophets* (Boise, ID: Pacific Press, 1958), 353.

to be in the church is to be in Christ."[29] Ferguson fittingly comments: "One is not 'in Christ' because of being 'in the church,' but one is 'in the church' because of being 'in Christ.' . . . To be saved is to be in Christ, and to be a Christian is to be a member of the church."[30] Jesus gives His followers the Holy Spirit in order to be His faithful witnesses: "But you will receive power when the Holy Spirit comes on you; and you will be my witnesses in Jerusalem, and in all Judea and Samaria, and to the ends of the earth" (Acts 1:8).

Christ Saves

Jesus Christ justifies and saves (Zech. 3:1–7; Rom. 8:1). Consequently, believers identify with Him (Rom. 6:1–4; Eph. 2:4–10). He is their Substitute and Representative because He died for their sins (1 Cor. 1:30; 15:3; 2 Cor. 5:21). His substitutionary death brought victory over the evil forces and Satan. He defeated death (Rom. 6:24; 1 Cor. 15:21–22, 26, 54–55), which is why He can now give His followers eternal life (John 5:24–25; 11:25).

According to Hebrews 7:25, Jesus "is able to save completely." Humanity's Intercessor saves all who come to Him as they are, confessing their sins. Christ the Intercessor reflects the Old Testament function of the priest and high priest who made atonement for the people (Lev. 16:19, 30) and reconnected the sinner with the holy and gracious God. However, Jesus gave Himself as an ultimate sacrifice for humanity (Heb. 9:25–26, 28), and His blood purifies all from their sins (Heb. 5:9; 9:12; 1 Pet. 1:18–19). Believers are perfect in Him, "*en Christo,*" and Paul strongly emphasizes their dwelling in Christ (Rom. 6:23; 8:1; 9:1; 12:5; 1 Cor. 1:30; 4:15).

Jesus Christ identifies with His people individually, and this identification is so close that it is compared to the most sensitive part of the body: the pupil of the eye. "For this is what the LORD Almighty says . . . 'whoever touches you touches the apple of his [Lord's] eye'" (Zech. 2:8). "The King will reply, 'Truly I tell you, whatever you did for one of the least of these brothers and sisters of mine, you did for me'" (Matt. 25:40). Additional biblical examples demonstrate how Jesus closely unites Himself with His followers: "He will reply, 'Truly, I tell you, whatever you did not do for one of the least of these, you did not do for me'" (Matt. 25:45). "He fell to the ground and heard

---

29. Claude Welch, *The Reality of the Church* (New York: Scribner's, 1958), 165.

30. Ferguson, *The Church of Christ,* 205.

a voice say to him, 'Saul, Saul, why do you persecute me?' 'Who are you, Lord?' Saul asked. 'I am Jesus, whom you are persecuting,' he replied" (Acts 9:4–5). "Whoever listens to you listens to me; whoever rejects you rejects me; but whoever rejects me rejects him who sent me" (Luke 10:16).

Jennings rightly comments:

> Jesus interceded in the course of sinfulness itself. . . . He took on himself our terminal condition in order to conquer, overcome and cure. 'Surely he took up our infirmities and carried our sorrows' (Is 53:5 NIV 1984). Yes, Jesus became one of us in order to reverse all the damage sin has done to his creation and to restore us, his children, back to unity with God. Jesus came to crush the serpent's head (Gen 3:15)—to destroy Satan and eradicate the sin infection from this world (Heb 2:14).[31]

Jesus takes each person into the very presence of God the Father and applies the results of the cross (Eph. 2:5; Heb. 9:24). Ellen White powerfully summarizes the biblical teaching:

> If you give yourself to Him [Jesus Christ], and accept Him as your personal Saviour, then, sinful as your life may have been, for His sake you are accounted righteous. Christ's character stands in place of your character, and you are accepted before God just as if you had not sinned.[32]
>
> Make friendship with Christ today. Put your case in the hands of the great Advocate. He will plead your cause before the Father. Though you have transgressed the law, and must plead guilty before God, Christ will present his precious blood in your behalf, and through faith and obedience, and vital union with Christ, you may stand acquitted before the Judge of all the earth, and he will be your friend when the final trump shall sound, and the scenes of earth shall be no more.[33]

Because Jesus Christ is humanity's Intercessor, all people can come to Him with full confidence, assurance, and boldness (Heb. 3:6; 4:16; 10:19, 35; 1 John 2:28; 4:17). People can come to Him without fear, doubt, or wavering, for in Him they have hope (Heb. 6:19; 7:19; 10:23; 1 Pet. 1:3). He is highly and uniquely qualified to be humanity's Intercessor since He is one of

---

31. Timothy R. Jennings, *The God-Shaped Brain: How Changing Your View of God Transforms Your Life* (Downers Grove, IL: IVP Books, 2013), 82–83.

32. Ellen G. White, *Steps to Christ* (Nampa, ID: Pacific Press, 1956), 62.

33. Ellen G. White, *Signs of the Times*, July 27, 1888.

them, their older Brother, and He was "tempted in every way, just as we are—yet he did not sin" (Heb. 4:15; cf. 2:17–18). He is the Source of salvation for everyone who comes to Him (Heb. 4:16; 5:7–9), and "there is now no condemnation for those who are in Jesus Christ" (Rom. 8:1).

Christ Changes and Transforms

Salvation means healing (Pss. 6:2; 41:4; Jer. 17:14; Hos. 14:4) and transformation (Rom. 12:1–2; 2 Cor. 6:14; 1 Thess. 5:23–24). Jesus Christ did not come to save humanity "in" sin but "from" sin (Matt. 1:21). He desires the sanctification of each person (1 Thess. 4:3–4; Heb. 12:14; 13:12) as he or she walks humbly with the Lord (Mic. 6:8), persevering (Rev. 12:14), and living with eyes fixed on Him (Heb. 12:1–2). In this way, each believer will ever more fully reflect the character of God (2 Cor. 3:18).

Hebrews 4:16 eloquently spells out why humans need the intercessory ministry of our High Priest:[34] "Let us then approach God's throne of grace with confidence, so that we may receive mercy and find grace to help us in our time of need." As broken and fragile human beings, people are constantly in need of Jesus and totally dependent upon Him. Each believer is crucified with Christ (Rom. 6:5–6) in order to live a new life (Rom. 6:4; 8:11; Eph. 1:15–21; 2:1–10). Being a new creation in Christ (2 Cor. 5:17) does not mean that believers no longer have a sinful nature (Ps. 51:5; Rom. 7:14–20), but that their sinful desires are under the control of His Spirit (Rom. 6:11–14; 8:1–4). Christ lives in each person (Gal. 2:20; Phil. 1:21). The sinful nature will be changed only at the second coming of the Lord Jesus Christ (1 Cor. 15:50–54; Phil. 1:6; 3:20–21; 1 John 3:1–3).

Jesus proclaimed: "Without me you can do nothing" (John 15:5, NKJV). Paul confesses: "I can do all this through him who gives me strength" (Phil. 4:13). To fight against temptation, overcome sin, fight a successful fight of faith (1 Tim. 6:12; 2 Tim. 4:7), and bear lasting good fruit are impossibilities without Christ or His Spirit. Christ alone is able to keep believers from falling (Jude 24), because His intercession breaks the power of sin, gives freedom, and liberates from addictions and slavery to

---

34. The book of Hebrews explicitly states nine times that Jesus Christ is the High Priest (Heb. 2:17; 3:1; 4:14–15; 5:5, 10; 6:20; 7:26; 8:1; 9:11), and implies such twice (Heb. 7:28; 8:13). In the same book, Jesus is called the Priest six times (5:6; 7:16–17, 21).

evil. He saves believers from the consequence of sin—eternal death, but He also enables them to live new lives according to His will (Ezek. 36:26–29; Rom. 8:13–14). Only He can transform believers by His grace so that they may replicate His loving, compassionate, and serving character. He wants to change each person by the power of His Word, Spirit, and grace in order to rid each person of selfishness, self-centeredness, self-justification, and striving to be the strongest. "Godly love is at war with the survival-of-the-fittest principle."[35] He desires believers to be governed by the Spirit, experience His fruit, against which there is no condemnation (Gal. 5:22–23).

Christ Vindicates/Defends His People

Jesus Christ vindicates His children against the accusations of Satan. The book of Job offers insight into Satan's charges against God's followers (Job being a typological figure for them), and how God stands against Satan and for His people (Job 1:8–9; 2:4; 42).[36] The book of Revelation presents God as humanity's defender, describing His victory on the cross:

> Then I heard a loud voice in heaven say: "Now have come the salvation and the power and the kingdom of our God, and the authority of his Messiah. For the accuser of our brothers and sisters, who accuses them before our God day and night, has been hurled down. They triumphed over him by the blood of the Lamb and by the word of their testimony; they did not love their lives so much as to shrink from death. Therefore rejoice, you heavens and you who dwell in them! But woe to the earth and the sea, because the devil has gone down to you! He is filled with fury, because he knows that his time is short." (Rev. 12:10–12)

Jesus Christ personally withstood Satan's accusations when He defeated Him on the cross (John 8:31; 16:11; Rev. 12:7–10). He was the victor, and His followers can be victorious only because of Him. His victory is His gift to His children. Jesus Christ not only opposes Satan, the powers of darkness, and the principalities of evil (Eph. 6:10–13), but He also defends His children against Satan's accusations (Rev. 7:1; 12:10–12). Jesus places a hedge of protection around His people (2 Kings 6:17; Job 1:10; Ps. 34:7; 91:1–3; 103:1–5).

---

35. Jennings, *The God-Shaped Brain*, 83.

36. For details, see my article "The God of Job and Our Adversary," *Journal of the Adventist Theological Society* 15, no. 1 (Spring 2004): 104–117.

Thus, the intercessory ministry of Jesus Christ means that He personally stands against Satan to defend His children and to silence their accuser.

Jesus Christ as Intercessor vindicates His people before the whole universe (Dan. 7:9–10, 13–14, 22; Eph. 3:10–11). He is simultaneously both Advocate and Judge, so His children can look forward with bold assurance and without fear to the day of judgment (1 John 2:28; 4:17). For who He is, for what He accomplished, and for what He does, He deserves to be eternally praised (Rom. 9:5; Rev. 5:9–10, 12–13).

Jesus Christ is His children's Intercessor until the close of probation (Rev. 15:7–8; 22:11). However, this does not mean that after this time, believers live without the help of the Holy Spirit or without Christ (though He ends His specific role and ministry as their Intercessor). Believers will never live on their own, independent of Him. This dependence will be maintained throughout eternity (Rev. 22:1–4). The Holy Spirit will be with His people and carry them through the last short period of time, when they will live without the intercessory ministry of Christ. His intercessory ministry will no longer be necessary because He has saved them completely, begun in them the process of powerful transformation, and vindicated them before the universe (for details, see Matt. 25:1–10; 28:20; John 15:5; Rom. 8:14; 2 Cor. 3:5; Phil. 1:6; 3:12–15; 4:13; 1 Thess. 5:23, 24; 2 Thess. 3:3; Jude 24, 25; Heb. 12:1, 2; Rev. 3:10).[37] During this short period before the second coming of Christ, between the close of probation and His children's glorification, true believers will need to be covered by the results of the cross, the atoning merits of Christ, because of their sinful natures. Believers will still need a "constant dependence upon the atoning blood of Christ."[38]

An incredible pattern is observed throughout the Bible regarding Christ's intercessory ministry for His people. He is for them, never against them, and wants to save them. This crucial ministry is indispensable, as the following statement indicates:

What does intercession comprehend? It is the golden chain which binds finite man to the throne of the infinite God. The human agent whom Christ has died to save importunes the throne of God, and his petition is taken up by

37. Ellen G. White, *Testimonies to Ministers and Gospel Workers* (Nampa, ID: Pacific Press, 1962), 431; White, *Early Writings* (Washington, DC: Review and Herald, 1945), 86; idem, *Great Controversy*, 615, 623.

38. White, *Patriarchs and Prophets*, 352.

Jesus who has purchased him with His own blood. Our great High Priest places His righteousness on the side of the sincere suppliant, and the prayer of Christ blends with that of the human petitioner.[39]

Ellen White properly explains the vast efficacy of Christ's intercessory ministry:

All blessings must come through a Mediator. Now every member of the human family is given wholly into the hands of Christ, and whatever we possess—whether it is the gift of money, of houses, of lands, of reasoning powers, of physical strength, of intellectual talents—in this present life, and the blessings of the future life, are placed in our possession as God's treasures to be faithfully expended for the benefit of man. Every gift is stamped with the cross and bears the image and superscription of Jesus Christ. All things come of God. From the smallest benefits up to the largest blessing, all flow through the one Channel—a superhuman mediation sprinkled with the blood that is of value beyond estimate because it was the life of God in His Son.[40]

His children can go to Jesus with full confidence because whatever He does, He does for their salvation. His actions are transparent to them, as well as to the entire universe. He is a great communicator with His created beings because He wants all to understand who God is, as well as His character, purposes, and will. He does not hide His purposes from His created beings; on the contrary, He opens Himself and His thoughts, feelings, actions, and the future to all who want to know and understand. Christ's intercessory ministry is twofold: He reveals God's character and His values to humanity, and presents their needs, struggles, and issues to God. The Triune God closely collaborates in this double mission.

CONCLUSION

A decision for Jesus Christ means complete salvation—eternal life (John 5:24), and He is always ready to help (Heb. 4:15–16; 7:25; 1 John 2:1; 1:8–9). The following summarizes the four main functions of Jesus Christ as

---

39. Ellen G. White, *That I May Know Him* (Hagerstown, MD: Review and Herald, 1964), 78, emphasis added.

40. Ellen G. White, *Faith and Works* (Nashville, TN: Southern Publishing, 1979), 22, emphasis added.

our Intercessor. First, on Jesus Christ's return to heaven, He and the heavenly Father met together in order to help humans in their everyday struggles with evil. The first tangible result of that meeting on humanity's behalf is that the Holy Spirit is given to believers—see Acts 2. All heaven is united in helping believers in their struggles with sin, Satan, and temptation (John 15:5; Phil. 4:13). Jesus prays for His children (John 17; Luke 22:32). They are covered by Christ's perfect life and atoning sacrifice and are enabled through His power to witness to others. Second, Jesus Christ saves completely and identifies with His children when they give their lives to Him (Zech. 2:8; Matt. 25:40, 45; Acts 9:4–6). Jesus Christ saves, justifies, sanctifies, and changes believers into His image (Zech. 3:1–7). Because of His goodness (Rom. 2:4; Eph. 1:7) His children identify with Him (Rom. 6:1–4; Eph. 2:4–10). Third, Christ's intercessory ministry transforms His followers into His likeness; they grow in Him and His grace, and become increasingly more like Him (2 Cor. 3:18; Col. 1:25–28; 2 Pet. 1:3–4; 3:18). Finally, Jesus Christ vindicates His children against the accusations of Satan (Rev. 12:10–12; Job 1:8–9; 2:4; 42). He personally stands up against them; and because He is the victor, His children's victory is secure in Him when they accept Him as the Lord of their lives.

Knowing this magnificent work of Jesus Christ "for" and "in" each individual, one cannot do otherwise but give Him glory. Doxology is the only proper response to His kindness: "Now to him who is able to do immeasurably more than all we ask or imagine, according to his power that is at work within us, to him be glory in the church and in Christ Jesus throughout all generations, for ever and ever! Amen" (Eph. 3:20–21).

AT-ONE-MENT FOREVER IN GOD'S NEW HEAVEN AND NEW EARTH

Roy E. Gane

The canonical record of the Bible began with God's flawless Creation on planted Earth (Gen. 1–2). Then came the disloyalty of the first humans in failing to observe a boundary set by their Creator, which precipitated a cluster of devastating consequences, culminating in death, which would afflict them and subsequent generations. These consequences include estrangement from the divine presence, lack of harmony between people, pain, exhausting labor for survival, as well as suffering and death throughout the natural world that God created as the dominion of the human race (Gen. 3; cf. Rom. 5:12, 14, 17–19; 8:19–23). Nevertheless, God promised the eventual destruction of the source of evil, namely, the one who had deceived Adam and Eve and led them into sin (Gen. 3:15). This implied that God would undo the effects of evil and restore the perfection of His Creation so that the end would be like the beginning.[1]

The last chapters of the Bible prophesy the final fulfillment of the divine promise of deliverance: Satan, his followers, death, and all evil will be destroyed (Rev. 20), and then God will re-create our world (Rev. 21–22). This destruction and re-creation mirror the initial Creation and Fall in chiastic order:

---

1. T. Desmond Alexander, *From Eden to the New Jerusalem: An Introduction to Biblical Theology* (Grand Rapids: Kregel, 2008), 14.

| A. *Creation (Gen. 1–2)* | B. Fall into Evil (Gen. 3) |
| B´. Destruction of Evil (Rev. 20) | A´. *New Creation (Rev. 21–22)* |

The chiasm is not merely a literary construct. Evil, including the evil beings that marred the original Creation, must be removed before God makes the New Creation. When Peter referred to the "period of restoration [*apokatástasis*] of all things about which God spoke by the mouth of His holy prophets from ancient time" (Acts 3:21),[2] he did not mean that all human or angelic beings would be restored. This is clear from the fact that the "holy prophets," whom Peter cited, did not teach universal salvation, even in their eschatological writings (cf. Isa. 66:24). Furthermore, Peter subsequently referred to the utter destruction of those who would not heed Jesus (Acts 3:22–23; cf. Deut. 18:15, 18–19). Peter preached that people needed to repent (Acts 3:19; cf. v. 26) in order to be saved (cf. 2:21, 38–40). Thus, he understood the biblical teaching of dual fates: life for those who accept salvation through Christ, and death for those who persist in rebellion (cf., e.g., John 3:16–18; Rom. 6:23).[3] The restored cosmos, with everything and everyone in it, will be perfect according to the Creator's original plan—after the removal of all evil.

Between the slim bookends of Genesis 1–3 and Revelation 20–22, the rest of the Bible deals with God's epic struggle to liberate earth from evil in order to fulfill his plan for it. Just as the reign of evil began with a fracture of the relationship between humans and their Creator, the New Creation must commence with the difficult process of divine-human relational reconciliation to reintegrate planet Earth into the community of God's universe on the corporate and individual levels (2 Cor. 5:17–21). Other aspects of reconciliation (human-human) and physical healing follow.

A common English word for the divinely provided basis of reconciliation is *atonement,* etymologically derived from "at-one-ment" (i.e., reintegration). Vast amounts of scholarly research have been devoted to the

---

2. Unless otherwise indicated, all Scripture quotations are taken from the NEW AMERICAN STANDARD BIBLE®, Copyright © 1960, 1962, 1963, 1968, 1971, 1972, 1973, 1975, 1977, 1995 by The Lockman Foundation. Used by permission. Italics in Scripture quotes reflect emphasis added by author.

3. The term *apokatástasis* (often transliterated *apocatastasis*), which appears in Acts 3:21 in the sense of "restoration," is associated with the teaching of universal salvation in patristic theology, especially of Origen (c. 185–251 AD). See John R. Sachs, "Apocatastasis in Patristic Theology," *Theological Studies* 54 (1993): 617–40.

process of atonement through the death of Christ, which is equivalent to the death of all humans as the penalty for sin (Rom. 6:23; 2 Cor. 5:14), because He is the Creator/Father of all (Isa. 9:6 [Heb. v. 5]; Luke 3:38; John 1:1–3, 14; Heb. 1:2), and therefore all are in Him (cf. Heb. 7:9–10). However, relatively little attention has been paid to the ultimate goal of atonement: an eternally reintegrated, restored state of harmony with God and all of His Creation.[4] This is the topic of the present chapter.

To discuss the goal of atonement, the scope of this word must be delineated in order to determine what is to be reintegrated and restored. Christians tend to think of atonement primarily in terms of what Christ accomplished through His death on the cross to make it possible for God to forgive humanity's sins (1 John 2:2; 4:10), and secondarily as the symbolic efficacy of Israelite animal sacrifices that typologically foreshadowed and taught about the sacrifice of Christ, "the Lamb of God who takes away the sin of the world" (John 1:29). In Old Testament texts regarding animal sacrifices, "make atonement" is a common translation of the Hebrew verb *kipper*. However, this rendering is imprecise. In contexts of divine-human interaction, *kipper* denotes removal of an impediment to the relationship (NJPS Lev. 4:20, 26, 31: "make expiation") that is required before completion of reconciliation. So that which *kipper* accomplishes is more limited than what "make atonement" would indicate, given that *atonement* refers to reconciliation as a whole, which would also include forgiveness.[5]

Because *kipper* represents a crucial step in the reconciliation process, its usage is instructive regarding the scope of atonement. The basic sense of *kipper* does not include substitution. Rather, someone accomplishes *kipper* for the community by destroying those who disrupt the relationship between God and His people (Num. 25:13). In this sense, the final destruction of those who persist in rebellion against God (Rev. 20) can be regarded as *kipper* that cleanses the cosmic community.[6]

---

4. See, e.g., Daegeuk Nam, "The New Earth and the Eternal Kingdom," in *Handbook of Seventh-day Adventist Theology,* ed. Raoul Dederen (Hagerstown, MD: Review and Herald, 2000), 947–968 and the brief but helpful treatment by Roy Adams, *The Sanctuary: Understanding the Heart of Adventist Theology* (Hagerstown, MD: Review and Herald, 1993), 146–148.

5. Roy Gane, *Cult and Character: Purification Offerings, Day of Atonement, and Theodicy* (Winona Lake, IN: Eisenbrauns, 2005), 194.

6. Cf. *kipper* on the goat of Azazel (Lev. 16:10), which represents Satan, who bears his own responsibility with regard to the sins of God's people; see Roy Gane, *Leviticus, Numbers,*

Substitution adds a special dynamic: An innocent party dies in place of sinners. The Israelite sacrificial system illustrates this: The blood of an animal victim applied to God's altar ransomed the life of the one bringing the sacrifice (Lev. 17:11).[7] The life of an animal owned by a human was not really an adequate substitute for human life (Heb. 10:1–4, 11; cf. Ps. 49:7–8 [Heb. vv. 8–9]), but offering it signified acceptance by faith of Christ's ultimately efficacious sacrifice (Heb. 10:5–18). Those who accept (now without animal sacrifice) the sacrifice of the divine Lamb of God are ransomed to enjoy eternal life in the new heaven and new earth (Rev. 5:6–14; 21:22–27; cf. John 1:29; 3:16).

Substitutionary *kipper* through animal sacrifices pointing to Christ's sacrifice remedied two basic kinds of problems:[8]

First, it was relational. Such *kipper* could serve as a token payment of "debt" to compensate for moral faults (i.e., sinful actions) that damaged the divine-human relationship, prerequisite to divine forgiveness (Lev. 4:20, 26, 31).

Second, it was physical. Sacrificial *kipper* could provide purification from severe physical ritual impurity (Lev. 12:7–8; 14:19), which had to be kept away from the sphere of holiness connected to the God of life (7:20–21; 15:31), because impurity represented the birth to death cycle of physical decay and mortality (i.e., the state of sinfulness) that results from sinful action (Rom. 6:23).[9] *Kipper* could also symbolize removal of an agent of deterioration, analogous to human physical impurity, that had affected a house (i.e., in the human environment; Lev. 14:53).

In light of the scope of effects of Christ's sacrifice reflected by these functions of sacrificial *kipper,* this chapter analyzes the outcome of atonement in the new heaven and new earth for (1) divine-human and human-human relationships, and (2) physical conditions of humans and their environment. Each section explores evidence for the goal of atonement from Revelation 21–22 and other eschatological passages, along with indirect evidence of comparison with the initial Creation order and what changed at the Fall (esp. Gen. 1–3).

NIV Application Commentary (Grand Rapids, MI: Zondervan, 2004), 290–291, 295–297.

    7. Cf. ibid., 302–304.

    8. Gane, *Cult and Character,* 49–50, 198–202.

    9. Hyam Maccoby, *Ritual and Morality: The Ritual Purity System and Its Place in Judaism* (Cambridge: Cambridge University Press, 1999), 49; cf. esp. 31–32, 48, 50, 207–208; Gane, *Cult and Character,* 201.

RELATIONAL RESTORATION AND RECONCILIATION WITH GOD

In Eschatology

Revelation 21:3 announces the restored state of divine-human relations: "Behold, the tabernacle of God is among men, and He will dwell among them, and they shall be His people, and God Himself will be among them." Verse 7 emphasizes this idea with language of adoption for individuals who have overcome in the battle with evil: "I will be his God and he will be My son."[10] Paul describes how this victory is achieved by God's children allowing the Spirit to control them (Rom. 8:6, 9). The Spirit living in them brings life and makes them God's children, heirs of God (Rom. 8:11, 15–17). The unity expressed in Revelation 21 culminates realization of the "Immanuel" ("God is with us") principle that binds together the successive phases of the divine covenant throughout salvation history (e.g., Gen. 17:7–8; Exod. 25:8; Isa. 7:14; Jer. 31:33).[11]

Restoration of divine-human unity, which Adam and Eve initially enjoyed but then lost, was foreshadowed by the residence of God's presence among His chosen people in the Israelite sanctuary/temple (Exod. 25:8).[12] The difference is that the New Jerusalem needs "no temple in it, for the Lord God the Almighty and the Lamb are its temple" (Rev. 21:22). The point is not that God will be homeless; in fact, Revelation 7:15 says that those who are saved will serve God "in His temple." But in the New Jerusalem there will be no need for a temple in the sense of a place of restricted, incomplete, and mediated access to God that would allow interaction with Him by faulty, mortal people in such a way that they would not be consumed by His unveiled glory (Exod. 33:20; Lev. 16:2; Heb. 12:29). Freed from sin and consequent mortality, God's people will enjoy full access to Him: "they will see His face, and His name will be on their foreheads (Rev. 22:4). Just as the incarnate Christ, the "Lamb of God" (John 1:29), dwelt among humans (1:14) as a temple (John 2:19–21), with

---

10. Rev 21:7. Cf. Hosea 1:10; 2:23; contrast with the language of rejection in 1:9.

11. Cf. O. Palmer Robertson, *The Christ of the Covenants* (Phillipsburg, NJ: Presbyterian and Reformed, 1980), 45–46.

12. Cf. Alexander, *From Eden to the New Jerusalem*, 20–25, 190–91.

no barriers between Him and them, so the glorified Lamb and "the Lord God the Almighty" (Rev. 21:22) will serve as the unrestricted focus of worship for His glorified people.

The fact that the people of God will dwell with God inside the New Jerusalem, which is a holy city (Rev. 21:2, 10), indicates that they will be holy as He is holy. Long ago, God commanded His covenant people to emulate Him in holiness (which requires purity) by living according to his principles (Lev. 11:44–45; 19:2; 20:26) because they were to be "a kingdom of priests and a holy nation" (Exod. 19:6; cf. 1 Pet. 2:9). But the God-initiated holiness of the inhabitants of the New Jerusalem and their access to God will be greater. The fact that their white robes are purified by the blood of the Lamb (Rev. 7:13–14) qualifies them for priestly service in God's temple "day and night" (v. 15). There are several indications that their entire city will constitute an especially holy space, and in this sense it will serve as a temple—a temple city.

First, the entire New Jerusalem will be a temple city, corresponding to the holy of holies in the Israelite temple, in that "its length and width and height are equal" (Rev. 21:16; cf. 1 Kings 6:20). This implies that its people will dwell in the eschatological equivalent of the holy of holies, as confirmed by the fact that "the throne of God and of the Lamb will be in" the city (Rev. 22:3). Whereas only the Israelite high priest was permitted to enter the most holy apartment of the sanctuary, where the divine Presence was enthroned, and then only once per year on the Day of Atonement and with special rituals (Lev. 16), all of God's people will be able to maintain a level of proximity to Him that would have been lethal to them before their glorification.[13]

Second, the main material of the New Jerusalem is gold (Rev. 21:18, 21), the metal that covered the interior of the tabernacle and its furniture (Exod. 25; 26:29; cf. 1 Kings 6:20–22, 28, 30).

Third, twelve kinds of gemstones adorning the foundation stones of the city wall, on which are the names of the twelve apostles (Rev. 21:14, 19–20), are reminiscent of twelve kinds of jewels mounted on the high priest's breastpiece, which were engraved with the names of the tribes of Israel, so that he carried their names over his heart (Exod. 28:17–21, 29). It is as

---

13. Fiorenza, Beale, and Mounce, quoted in Ranko Stefanovic, *Revelation of Jesus Christ: Commentary on the Book of Revelation* (Berrien Springs, MI: Andrews University Press, 2002), 588, 600; cf. Alexander, *From Eden to the New Jerusalem*, 20, 139.

though the entire city constitutes a massive breastpiece on the heart of God to signify His love for His people, represented by the apostles.

Fourth, the names of the twelve tribes are written on the twelve gates of the city, three gates at each of the four directions (Rev. 21:12–13; cf. Ezek. 48:30–34), just as three tribes at each of the four directions were camped around God's sanctuary in the wilderness (Num. 2).

Fifth, an angel stationed at each gate of the city (Rev. 21:12) recalls the cherubim that God appointed to bar Adam and Eve from the entrance to the Garden of Eden, which was like the holy New Jerusalem in that it contained the tree of life (Gen. 3:24). By contrast, however, the angels at the New Jerusalem represent the ongoing security of humans inside its sacred space, even after all threats from evil forces will have been eliminated (Rev. 21:8; cf. Rev. 20) so that its gates can always remain open (Rev. 21:25; contrast Ezek. 44:2). There is much more to the new earth than the capital city of the divine King, but the names of the tribes (representing God's people) on its gates indicate that the city is theirs (cf. Num. 17:2–3 [Heb. vv. 17–18]) and they are entitled to enter there any time they wish and enjoy access to the tree of life (Rev. 22:2, 14). The curse that for so long estranged them from God and kept them from the source of eternal life (Gen. 3) will be gone (Rev. 22:3), removed by Christ's forgiveness (Rom. 5:1–2), and by the Spirit of Christ living in them (Rom. 8:9), and by the redemption of their bodies (Rom. 8:22–23).

Sixth, "nothing unclean, and no one who practices abomination and lying, shall ever come into" the city (Rev. 21:27).[14] Impurity is excluded from the sacred space, because holiness, connected to the Creator of life, and impurity, associated with the domain of death, are antithetical.[15] Impurity must not be allowed to defile things that belong to the holy sphere centered at the sanctuary (cf. Lev. 15:31) in order to protect God's reputation from association with the state of mortality, which results from sinful action (Rom. 6:23). Thus, Israelites were forbidden to contact holy things while in a state of physical ritual impurity (e.g., Lev. 7:20–21) and seriously impure individuals were sent outside the wilderness camp, where God dwelt in their midst in His sanctuary

---

14. Cf. the purity of the entire eschatological Temple City in the *Temple Scroll* from Qumran, 11Q19. However, the concern in this text is with exclusion of physical ritual impurity; see Hannah K. Harrington, *The Impurity Systems of Qumran and the Rabbis: Biblical Foundations*, SBL Dissertation Series 143 (Atlanta: Scholars Press, 1993), 55–58.

15. Jacob Milgrom, *Leviticus 1–16*, Anchor Bible 3 (New York: Doubleday, 1991), 731–3.

(Num. 5:1–4). The fact that Revelation 21:27 refers to those who practice abomination and lying, as opposed to those "whose names are written in the Lamb's book of life," implies that the impurity in view here is moral rather than physical ritual in nature. In Pentateuchal law, moral impurities that result from serious sinful actions (e.g., sexual immorality, idolatry, murder), rather than from physical states, are irremediable and ultimately lead to exile from the Promised Land (Lev. 18, 20, 26; Num. 35:31–34).[16] In Christ, even these sins are forgiven for those who want His forgiveness (Jer. 31:34; 1 Cor. 6:11; Rom. 5:1, 6). In Revelation, those who ultimately refuse to give up the moral impurities that separate them from God, who knowingly cling to cherished sin and absolutely refuse Christ's forgiveness, will be irrevocably barred from the ultimate Promised Land, the new heaven, new earth, and New Jerusalem.

Seventh, Revelation 22:1–2 prophesies regarding the New Jerusalem habitat for humanity:

> Then he showed me a river of the water of life, clear as crystal, coming from the throne of God and of the Lamb, in the middle of its street. On either side of the river was the tree of life, bearing twelve kinds of fruit, yielding its fruit every month; and the leaves of the tree were for the healing of the nations.

These verses allude to Ezekiel 47:1–12, which predict that water would flow toward the east from under the threshold of a future ideal temple. The volume of water would grow to become a life-giving river. "By the river on its bank, on one side and on the other, will grow all kinds of trees for food. Their leaves will not wither and their fruit will not fail. They will bear every month because their water flows from the sanctuary, and their fruit will be for food and their leaves for healing" (v. 12). The source of the water in Ezekiel is the temple residence of God; in Revelation it is the place of divine enthronement in the holy city where God dwells with His people.[17]

The eternal reign (Rev. 22:5) of God's dependent people over the lost dominion (Gen. 1:26–28) that Christ reclaims for them (Dan. 7:13, 14, 18, 22, 27; Rev. 3:21), which they inherit as children of God (Rev. 21:7), will always be

---

16. Jacob Milgrom, *Leviticus 17–22*, Anchor Bible 3A (New York: Doubleday, 2000), 1326; Jonathan Klawans, *Impurity and Sin in Ancient Judaism* (Oxford: Oxford University Press, 2000), especially 21–31; Jay Sklar, *Sin, Impurity, Sacrifice, Atonement: The Priestly Conceptions* (Sheffield: Sheffield Phoenix Press, 2005), 139–53.

17. Cf. water flowing from Jerusalem in verse 8 of the eschatological oracle of Zechariah 14.

under His supreme sovereignty and they will serve Him (Rev. 7:15; 22:3). "His name will be on their foreheads" (22:4; cf. 14:1), signifying that they belong to Him. But the fact that "they will see His face" (Rev. 22:4; i.e., have access to his presence) means that they will be high-ranking servants in His kingdom (cf. 2 Kings 25:19; Esther 1:14—literally, "those who see the king's face").

Human service for God will always be voluntary. He saves human beings by first empowering their freedom of choice. Without this freedom, they could not love Him.[18] Those who "follow the Lamb wherever He goes" (Rev. 14:4; cf. 7:17) will do so in the new earth because they formed the habit of depending upon Him before the eradication of sin. Empowered by grace (Rom. 5:20–21) and filled with the Spirit (1 Cor. 3:16), they will have kept themselves "chaste" (Rev. 14:4), totally honest, and blameless (v. 5).[19] In spite of extreme challenges ("great tribulation"), the saved "have washed their robes and made them white in the blood of the Lamb" (7:14). It is evident that God's law of love (Matt. 22:37–40) is in their hearts, put there by God himself (Jer. 31:33), because they love Him with all their heart, soul, and strength (Deut. 6:5). The fact that they no longer sin does not mean that there is no room for further moral growth; their love for Him and for other created beings will expand throughout eternity as they learn and experience more of His grace.

By Comparison with the Initial Creation Order and the Fall

The fact that the New Creation restores what was lost at the Fall (Gen. 3) implies that humanity can learn about the eschatological scenario from the protological one. In the earlier perfect world, God created the first humans in His image to exercise benevolent dominion as His representatives (1:26–28). They would work to maintain order in their garden (2:15), but not to laboriously provide food for survival (contrast 3:17–19). They were permitted to freely eat from the "tree of life" (2:9, 16), could be in God's immediate presence (vv. 19–22), and needed no clothes to prevent shame (v. 25).

---

18. Cf. Gregory A. Boyd, *Satan and the Problem of Evil: Constructing a Trinitarian Warfare Theodicy* (Downers Grove, IL: IVP Academic, 2001), 50–57. However, Boyd also points out that God has established limits to the ability of His angelic and human creatures to continue exercising freedom to rebel against him, Boyd, *God at War: The Bible & Spiritual Conflict* (Downers Grove, IL: InterVarsity, 1997), 287.

19. Cf. the Suffering Servant (Christ) of Isaiah 53, who was slaughtered like a lamb and there was no deceit in his mouth (vv. 7–9).

The fact that God met with them in their Eden home and it contained the tree of life (like the holy New Jerusalem in Revelation) indicates that Eden was holy space. Like Ezekiel's temple and the New Jerusalem, it had a river flowing from it (v. 10).

The only restriction on the first couple was the prohibition to eat the fruit of a certain tree (Gen. 2:17; 3:3). When they were deceived into disobedience, they experienced shame of their nakedness and fear of God (3:7–10). When God confronted Adam, the man indirectly blamed God, who had given his wife to him (vv. 11–12). The divine-human relationship was fractured. No longer could morally impure Adam and Eve benefit from the tree of life or enjoy God's presence in holy Eden (vv. 23–24). Moreover, planet Earth came under the destructive control of Satan, the mighty fallen being who usurped human dominion by deceiving our first parents into following him (Rev. 12:7–9), thereby establishing himself as the ruler of this world (John 12:31). Humans were now controlled by chaos and alienation in relation to themselves, others, and God, and this affected them physically, socially, and spiritually.[20]

In light of Genesis 1–3, restoration to full harmony and happiness by the end of the process of atonement would first require healing of the estrangement between humans and their Creator. This process is initiated by God because of His great love and mercy (Gal. 3:15–16; Eph. 2:4–5). It requires humble admission of guilt and a divinely provided remedy for sin, guilt, shame, and fear (cf. Rom. 5; 1 John 1:9). Those who would accept the remedy could return to God's presence and the tree of life in holy space, and they would recover the lost dominion of earth. The process of atonement accomplishes all these things, climaxing in Revelation 21–22. However, the new paradise is a city rather than a garden, there is no forbidden tree, and its occupants are countless descendants of Adam and Eve, rather than just the original pair. As Desmond Alexander points out, "while *Endzeit* [the end] resembles *Urzeit* [the beginning], there is progression. Whereas Genesis presents the earth as a potential building site, Revelation describes a finished city."[21]

---

20. Graham McFarlane, "Atonement, Creation and Trinity," in *The Atonement Debate: Papers from the London Symposium on the Theology of Atonement*, eds. Derek Tidball, David Hilborn, and Justin Thacker (Grand Rapids, MI: Zondervan, 2008), 196–197.

21. Alexander, *From Eden to the New Jerusalem*, 14. It also appears that whereas Adam

RECONCILIATION WITH HUMANS

In Eschatology

There are several indications that relations between humans in the new earth will be harmonious. In the New Jerusalem there will be no troublemakers—"the cowardly and unbelieving and abominable and murderers and immoral persons and sorcerers and idolaters and all liars"—because they will have been destroyed (Rev. 21:8; cf. Rev. 20; 21:27; 22:15). There will be a vast diversity of nations and ethnic groups (5:9; 21:24, 26), but there will be no conflicts or racism; all will dwell together in peace under the rule of the "Prince of Peace" (Isa. 9:6–7 [Heb. vv. 5–6]). The fact that the gates of the New Jerusalem will never be closed shows that there will be no danger of attack (Rev. 21:25). The massive walls and gates, with an angel stationed at each gate, signify the grandeur and absolute security of the royal capital of the omnipotent divine King, whose presence provides ultimate protection (cf. Zech. 2:5), but all threats will have been vanquished (Rev. 20).

There will be no bad neighbors there. Everyone in the city will have deep love for Christ in appreciation for what He has done for them. Forgiven and empowered by God, they have allowed God to transform their characters. They are "those whose names are written in the Lamb's book of life" (Rev. 21:27), who voluntarily belong to God (22:4), because they have felt their need of His free grace (21:6; 22:17). They are not "cowardly and unbelieving" (21:8), but have overcome by faith (v. 7).[22] Righteousness and holiness involve keeping God's law of love in all relationships and interactions, both toward Him and toward those whom He has created (cf. 1 Thess. 3:12–13).

By Comparison with the Initial Creation Order and the Fall

Human society began with the creation of Eve and her marriage to Adam. The first couple was united as "one flesh" (Gen. 2:24) in God's image to

---

and Eve were naked before the Fall (Gen. 2:25), saved humans in the new earth will wear clothes (Rev. 7:9).

22. Cf. 2 Peter 3:13—"But according to His promise we are looking for new heavens and a new earth, in which righteousness dwells."

equally co-rule the earth (1:26–28).[23] But when Adam admitted eating the forbidden fruit, he directly blamed his wife: "The woman whom You gave to be with me, she gave me from the tree, and I ate" (3:12). Happy harmony in the home was gone; rapture had given way to rupture of relationship. As part of the negative result of leading her husband into sin (cf. v. 6), God informed her: "Yet your desire will be for your husband, and he will rule over you" (v. 16). Marriage remained, but the full equality intended by God was destroyed. This was not a command, per se, but a description of a new situation that the woman would face in a fallen world.

The Big Bang of the Fall blew human relationships apart. To blaming was added murder (Gen. 4:8, 23) and many other kinds of moral evils. Already by Genesis 6:5, God's assessment of humanity is hopelessly negative: "every intent of the thoughts of his heart was only evil continually."

Divine healing of human relationships, which is absolutely necessary for God's people (cf. Mal. 4:5–6; Eph. 4:32), requires restoration of unselfish love in harmony with His character of love (1 John 4:8), as demonstrated by Christ (John 13:34; 15:12). Christians who receive divine love into their hearts through the Holy Spirit (Rom. 5:5), so that God's law of love for Him and for other people (Matt. 22:37–40) is written on their hearts (Jer. 31:33), can go a long way toward realizing the Creation ideal for human relationships. This includes enjoyment of tightly bonded, egalitarian marriage that represents the image of the triune God (cf. John 17:21–23; Col. 1:19; 2:9). But complete renewal of human society awaits the *eschaton*, when sin and its curse and temptation will be removed by God (Rev. 20; 21:8, 27; 22:3, 15) and sorrow will be no more (21:4).

PHYSICAL RESTORATION

In Eschatology

Revelation 21 begins with the stunning observation: "Then I saw a new heaven and a new earth; for the first heaven and the first earth passed away, and there is no longer any sea" (v. 1). This is nothing less than a total New Creation of planet Earth and its atmosphere after the destruction of all evil,

---

23. On the full equality of the sexes at Creation, see Richard M. Davidson, *Flame of Yahweh: Sexuality in the Old Testament* (Peabody, MA: Hendrickson, 2007), 22–35.

decay, and pollution (Rev. 20). Unlike Genesis 1–2, Revelation 21 does not describe the process; it simply announces the result. In Genesis 1, seas remained after dry land appeared (v. 10), but the eschatological new earth will have no sea to separate and reduce the habitable areas of its terrestrial inhabitants. The multitude of saved people (Rev. 7:9) will be able to spread out, and God has plenty of dwelling places for everyone (John 14:2).

In the New Jerusalem divine glory will provide constant daylight (no urban nightlife or danger after dark!), with no need for light from the sun or moon (Rev. 21:23, 25; 22:5). This does not mean that the sun or moon will have ceased to exist or that their day-night cycles of light will not occur elsewhere on earth (cf. 7:15—"day and night"). Rather, the point is to emphasize the brilliance and permanence of God's Presence. Days, weeks, and months will continue, as indicated by the fact that new moons and Sabbaths will be special times of worship (Isa. 66:23; cf. Rev. 22:2 on the monthly cycle of the tree of life).[24]

God will transform the life experience of His creatures, which was devastated by the Fall. After evil and death are finally eradicated (Rev. 20:9–10, 14–15), all of the former physical and emotional suffering (hunger, thirst, scorching from sun, excessive heat, tears, mourning, crying, pain) will be gone in the new earth (7:16–17; 21:4). This will be the ultimate fulfillment of Isaiah's prophecy of "new heavens and a new earth," where "the former things" will not even be remembered, but will be replaced by joy, long life, satisfaction, safety, blessing, and peace (Isa. 65:17–25).[25] In Revelation 7,

---

24. Cf. Emmanuel Uchenna Dim, *The Eschatological Implications of Isa 65 and 66 as the Conclusion of the Book of Isaiah*, Bible in History (Bern: Peter Lang, 2005), 196, on Isaiah 66:23—"Thus, as the first creation culminated in the institution of the Sabbath (Gen 2,2–3), so will this new creation culminate in the reinforced observance of the same Sabbath."

25. The apocalyptic prophecy of Revelation, in which there is a more definitive break between the present era and the next, goes beyond Isaiah, where long life does not exclude death (Isa. 65:20; on this verse, see Dim, *The Eschatological Implications,* 107–110). In the historical foreground, Isaiah 65–66 appears to be hyperbolically providing hope for a grand renewal of Judah after the Babylonian exile. For example, see Daniel K. Bediako, "Isaiah's 'New Heavens and New Earth' (Isa 65:17; 66:22)," *Journal of Asia Adventist Seminary* 11.1 (2008): 1–20. However, the universal creation language in Isaiah 65:17–25 (with affinities to Gen. 1) evokes a more radical picture of eschatological transformation, including re-creation of the cosmos. For example, see Wann M. Fanwar, "Creation in Isaiah" (PhD diss., Andrews University, 2001), 134–7. On the telescoping of chronologically distinct but spiritually related aspects in Isaiah 65:17–25, see John N. Oswalt, *The Book of Isaiah: Chapters 40–66,* New International

the fact that people can serve God "day and night" (v. 15) also implies that fatigue will be no more.

The absence of death does not mean that human life will be independent of God, who alone possesses unborrowed, inherent immortality (1 Tim. 6:16). Glorified humans will continue to depend on the Creator for their life-support.[26] The "river of the water of life ... coming from the throne of God and of the Lamb" (Rev. 22:1) is for their benefit (cf. Rev. 7:17; 21:6; 22:17), as is the "tree of life" that receives the divinely provided water, which regularly bears fruit for food and its leaves are "for the healing of the nations" (Rev. 22:2; cf. Ezek. 47:12).[27] God's people will also receive their light from Him (Rev. 22:5).

The fact that glorified humans will need water and food indicates that they will have been resurrected from the temporary "sleep" of the first death (Dan. 12:2; 1 Cor. 15:51; 1 Thess. 4:13–15) to live forever in bodily form, not with the present natural/unspiritual (Greek *psuchikos*) body (*soma*) that decays and dies, but with the body (*soma*) that is immortal because it is spiritual (*pneumatikos*; 1 Cor. 15:44; cf. the context in vv. 42–43, 45–54). The body is changed (v. 52), but the person does not become a disembodied spirit. Paul's contrast here is between mortality versus immortality, not between material versus nonmaterial. So there is no contradiction with Luke 24:39, where the post-resurrection state of Jesus includes "flesh and bones."[28] Interpreting aspects of life in the new earth—water, tree, fruit—to be metaphorical expressions rather than material entities would create more problems than it would solve. If there is no real "river of the water of life" (Rev. 22:1), should the reality of the throne of God, from which the river flows, or the city street down which it flows (vv. 1–2) also be discounted? What about the whole city itself, or the new earth? These elements are interlinked and interdependent, and

---

Commentary on the Old Testament (Grand Rapids, MI: Eerdmans, 1998), 656–662.

26. Cf. Daniel 5:23—"the God in whose hand are your life-breath and all your ways."

27. On possible explanations for this "healing" function of the leaves in Revelation 22 (in the new earth, where suffering is gone: 21:4) and its background in Ezekiel 47, see, Alexander, *From Eden to the New Jerusalem*, 156; Jacob Milgrom and Daniel I. Block, *Ezekiel's Hope: A Commentary on Ezekiel 38–48* (Eugene, OR: Cascade, 2012), 233; Stefanovic, *Revelation of Jesus Christ*, 585–593.

28. John C. Brunt, "Resurrection and Glorification," in *Handbook of Seventh-day Adventist Theology*, 361–362.

there is no textual indication that they are metaphors. "Western Christendom has inherited an allegorical view of heaven from the Platonism of some of its early interpreters, but the New Testament emphasizes resurrection for bodily existence, ultimately on the new earth."[29] "The earth may be purged or recreated, but it remains 'the earth, not a transcendent realm beyond it.'"[30]

The "tree of life" in the New Jerusalem appears to have the same function as the tree with the same name in the Garden of Eden: to continually sustain life (Gen. 3:22; Rev. 2:7; 22:2, 14). In Eden, the perfect lives that were to be sustained were those of Adam and Eve, whose descendants (us) are carbon-based. So it appears that glorified humans will also have carbon-based bodies. It is true that God, the Sovereign of the New Jerusalem, is intrinsically immortal spirit (John 4:24; 1 Tim. 6:15–16) and therefore does not depend on food (e.g., Ps. 50:13). However, He can appear to and interact with those of His creatures who are limited to bodily form (e.g., Gen. 18).

The fact that perpetuation of human life will depend on the tree of life in the New Jerusalem (Rev. 22:14) indicates that anyone denied access to it there would die. Therefore, the fact that "Outside are the dogs[31] and the sorcerers and the immoral persons and the murderers and the idolaters, and everyone who loves and practices lying" (v. 15) means that such individuals, who reject God, will perish. There is no indication that their lives will be sustained in an eternally burning hell so that the redeemed must witness their writhing and endure their shrieking throughout the ceaseless ages of eternity. There are several major problems with the notion of an ever-burning hell:

1. Would God feed fruit from the tree of life to the wicked to keep them alive in hell? If so, this would contradict the biblical teaching that only those who are saved enjoy the right to this fruit (Rev. 22:14). Consider Genesis 3, where God barred sinful Adam and Eve from the tree of life

---

29. Craig S. Keener, *Revelation,* NIV Application Commentary (Grand Rapids, MI: Zondervan, 2000), 502.

30. Ibid., 502n80, quoting Norman Perrin, *The Kingdom of God in the Teaching of Jesus* (Philadelphia, PA: Westminster, 1963), 69; cf. Nam, "The New Earth and the Eternal Kingdom," in *Handbook of Seventh-Day Adventist Theology,* 957.

31. Cf. Deuteronomy 23:18.

precisely to prevent them from living forever (vv. 22–24), and as a result, they died (Gen. 5:5 regarding Adam's death).

2. In Revelation 20, the "lake of fire" that destroys the wicked covers a vast area on the surface of the earth around the New Jerusalem (vv. 8–10). There is no indication in Revelation 21–22 that the molten "lake" remains as a feature of the new earth.

3. Those who are thrown into the "lake of fire" suffer the "second death," which is the last death (Rev. 20:14–15; 21:8). Therefore, they die; they do not go on living eternally in infernal misery. Language of eternal torment (20:10; cf. 14:10–11) means that they are tormented without relief until they are completely burned up. This fire is "forever" in the sense that its results are eternal (cf. Jude 7 re: Sodom); it is the death from which there is no return.[32]

By Comparison with the Initial Creation Order and the Fall

Genesis 1–2 records the Creation of heaven/sky and of earth, on which there were rivers, trees, and other kinds of vegetation, precious metal and stones, as well as many kinds of living creatures. Initially there was no rain, but mist watered the earth's surface. The first humans were to tend the Garden of Eden (2:15), but they did not need to till the ground. For food, it appears that they simply picked from seed-bearing plants and fruit-trees (1:29; 2:9, 16). Animals and birds were to eat green plants (1:30). There is no evidence of predation here.

The Fall did not disrupt the overall cosmology of planet Earth. However, the curse on the ground because of Adam appears to have reduced its fertility and brought about undesirable plants, so that considerable effort would be required to till the ground in order to grow food outside

---

32. Cf. Edward W. Fudge, *The Fire That Consumes: A Biblical and Historical Study of the Doctrine of Final Punishment*, 3rd ed. (Eugene, OR: Cascade, 2011), 239–52; Boyd, *God at War*, 288–90. Isaiah 66:24 is commonly adduced as support for eternal torment. For example, see Dim, *The Eschatological Implications*, 197—"Thus, though dead, the rebels will continue to suffer forever, all on account of their obstinate rebellion," but here the rebels are "corpses" who suffer permanent shame, not unending pain. For more on this topic, see Edward W. Fudge and Robert A. Peterson, *Two Views of Hell: A Biblical & Theological Dialogue* (Downers Grove, IL: IVP Academic, 2000), 32–33 versus 130–133.

the Garden of Eden (Gen. 3:17–19, 23).[33] Genesis 3:21 implies the first death(s) in recorded history: "The LORD God made garments of skin for Adam and his wife, and clothed them." These garments of animal hides would cover their nakedness and keep them warm, needs they did not have before they sinned. Humans created in the image of God to have dominion over the earth (1:26–28) were now dependent on the lives of lower creatures.

The great Flood, which was due to radical expansion of human sin, had a much greater impact on the surface of the earth (Gen. 7–8) than did the immediate aftermath of the Fall. The Flood deepened the effects of the Fall upon the surface of the earth and may have changed the distribution of land versus sea. Since then, human population growth, exploitation of natural resources, and pollution have damaged our environment, including the earth's atmosphere, at an accelerating rate.

Therefore, God's remedy needs to be comprehensive: re-creation not only of a new earth, but also of a new heaven (Rev. 21:1). Undoing the natural effects of the Fall involves removal of death (1 Cor. 15:54–55; Rev. 20:14), sickness, hunger, thirst, excessive heat (Rev. 7:16), need for artificial means of warmth or laborious agriculture, and physical harm and predation by humans or by animals, which will again be vegetarian (Isa. 11:6–9; 65:25). There will be restoration of access to the fruit of the "tree of life" (Rev. 2:7), renewal of earth's fertility, and pure rivers (22:1). Then the lives of humans will be dependent on the life of another, but this time the life will be that of the divine Lamb (21:22–23, 27; 22:1, 3).

CONCLUSION

The goal of at-one-ment through Christ's sacrifice is ultimate fulfillment of God's original plan for relational harmony and physical well-being on planet earth after the deadly detour caused by sin. Having defeated the evil deceiver and his hosts in the Great War, God will bring His salvific, covenant purposes to fruition by restoring the lost dominion of Adam and Eve and a multitude of their descendants in a perfect new world and a resplendent city where God Himself dwells.

---

33. Cf. covenant curses on rebellious Israelites through negative effects on the natural world in Leviticus 26 and Deuteronomy 28.

The eschatological visions of John in Revelation and of other prophets in earlier biblical books reveal God's character and give humanity hope by unveiling the contours of His goodwill toward humans, which are greater than anything humans could imagine (1 Cor. 2:9). This God-given hope motivates humanity to accept God's gift of salvation and to work with Him in extending the Gospel invitation to all others so that they too can enjoy Paradise with the loving Creator. Even now, in a broken, groaning world that anticipates unprecedented alienation, upheaval, and suffering (e.g., Dan. 12:1), the followers of Christ form a new temple by their access to God through the Holy Spirit (Eph. 2). Therefore, His children are to live together in unity "as citizens of the New Jerusalem."[34]

---

34. Alexander, *From Eden to the New Jerusalem*, 191.

SECTION 4

Amazing Grace: Can Believers Earn Their Salvation?

One of the issues concerning salvation that Christians seek to understand is the relationship between God's grace and human works. The Bible teaches that salvation is accomplished by God's grace through faith and therefore not by human works. At the same time, it also teaches that God provides the gift of faith which works by love to fulfill God's law (Eph. 2:8–9; see also Rom. 11:6; 13:8, 10; Gal. 5:6, 14). This biblical teaching indicates that there are various dimensions of the reality of salvation that need to be understood in proper relation to each other.

Salvation is all grace because the sin problem disqualifies humanity for an eternal relationship with God and because a perfect atonement has been accomplished in Christ so that humanity may be reconciled with God. Therefore, because humans have been corrupted by sin, they are totally unable even to receive God's salvation without His assistance. Also, because God has provided a complete atonement in Christ, there is nothing humans can do to earn salvation.

In addition, however, God has enabled human beings to exercise faith and receive salvation so that the righteousness of God's law is fulfilled in them (Rom. 8:4). Does this mean that God in some sense enabled humans to earn their salvation? Is salvation begun by grace and then continued and perfected by works? How are justification, sanctification, and glorification related to each other in salvation by grace? These and other related questions are answered in this fourth section.

The authors of the chapters in section four present historical and biblical studies on salvation by God's grace. The first chapter, authored by John Reeve, provides a historical overview of Christian views of salvation by grace. The second chapter, written by George Knight, presents a study of

God's prevenient grace that enables humans to receive or refuse God's gift of salvation. In the third chapter, Ivan Blazen provides a study of how God's grace accomplishes the justification and sanctification of sinners. Finally, in the fourth chapter, Woodrow Whidden and Hans LaRondelle present how God's grace perfects and glorifies those who are eternally saved.

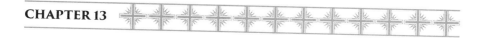

CHAPTER 13

GRACE: A BRIEF HISTORY

John W. Reeve

Grace is unmerited favor.[1] Paul begins and ends his letters with pronouncements of grace. The book of Acts is full of God's grace working in and through the disciples. According to John, all have received grace and it comes through Jesus Christ (John 1:16–17). Paul tells believers that they are justified by grace (Rom. 3:24) and that they stand by grace (Rom. 5:2). Ephesians 2:8 declares that believers are saved by grace. Hebrews 4:16 both describes God's throne in terms of grace as well as saying that all are invited to receive grace there. Grace as a free gift is a major theme in the New Testament. It seems a bit jarring then, when one reads in Origen's (ca. 185–254)[2] *On First Principles* (written ca. 230)[3] the suggestion that some may deserve,

---

1. "Grace," *Oxford Encyclopedia of the Reformation*, ed. Hans J. Hillerbrand (New York: Oxford University Press, 1996), 2:184; "Grace," *Webster's New World College Dictionary*, 5th edition, ed. Andrew N. Sparks, et al. (Boston: Houghton Mifflin Harcourt, 2016), 628. Whereas the dictionary definition of the word *grace* based on its usage within the English language is varied and complex, I have chosen to focus on the theological definition which dominated the sixteenth-century reformation.

2. Ronald E. Heine, "The Alexandrians," in *The Cambridge History of Early Christian Literature* (*CHECL*), ed. Frances Young, Lewis Ayres and Andrew Louth (Cambridge: Cambridge University Press, 2004), 117.

3. Originally written in Greek under the title Περὶ Ἀρχῶν (*Peri Archōn, Concerning the Archons*) see the *Ante-Nicene Fathers* (*ANF*), 4:235. Origen's *On First Principles* was written during his Alexandrian years, which Eusebius places before 232, when he left for Caesarea in Palestine. It is only available to us in small pieces and fragments in Greek, but is complete in Latin, as translated in 397 by Rufinus, in Heine, "The Alexandrians," in *CHECL,* 121–122.

or merit, the gifts of the Spirit and how some may deserve to be sanctified by His grace.[4] How one views grace depends on how one views salvation. Is salvation brought about by human action, church action, or God's action? The history of Christian teachings on grace suggests that all three of these sources of actions have been credited with human salvation, and often with an intermingling of two or more of them.

Paul's teaching on grace and salvation, as famously summarized in Romans 3–8, highlights justification as a free gift of grace (3:24) and that all humans are sinners who do not do good (3:10–12, 23), meaning that law-keeping cannot be the way to righteousness (3:20–21). Yet Paul's teaching also emphasizes the ethical claims of the new life in Christ (Rom. 6:1–2), which life is made possible through the reconciliation by His blood (Rom. 5:9–11), and in which believers are to offer themselves to God as instruments of righteousness (Rom. 6:13) through the indwelling of the Spirit (Rom. 8:11). Thus Paul says that believers have an obligation (*opheiletai*) to live according to the Spirit (Rom. 8:12) and can expect to share in the sufferings of Christ as well as in His glory (Rom. 8:17). It is this last detail, the ethical obligation to live a righteous life in the power of the Spirit, that became the focus of the discussion of grace by the second- and third-century Christians.[5]

GRACE PLUS MERIT

Throughout the early Christian centuries, before the best-known controversy on grace between Augustine and Pelagius in the fifth century, there was a stress on the ethical demands of living out one's faith that included an aspect of human merit. Initially this conceptualization of living saintly lives was perceived to be the responsibility of all Christians, but it was especially

---

4. Origen, *On First Principles*, Preface 3; Book 1.3, *ANF*, 4:239, 255. In both places Rufinus, the Latin translator of this work by Origen, uses the Latin word *merēre*, meaning "to merit," to denote the deserving character of the person receiving the grace and the gifts of the Spirit. Origen's original Greek, of which we only now have fragments, was probably some form of the word ἀξιόω (*axioō*), which has the basic meaning of to "consider worthy." See *A Greek-English Lexicon of the New Testament and Other Early Christian Literature*, 3rd ed., ed. Frederick William Danker (Chicago, IL: University of Chicago Press, 2001).

5. B. Studer, "Grace," in *Encyclopedia of Ancient Christianity* (*EAC*), ed. Angelo Di Berardino, trans. Eric E. Hewett, et al. (Downers Grove, IL: IVP Academic, 2014), 2:168.

perceived in Christian martyrs.[6] Later, it became associated primarily with monasticism.[7] J. William Harmless suggests that, "Early Christian monks were in the business of doing ordinary Christianity extraordinarily well."[8] This section will follow the passage from an understanding that all Christians have a responsibility to live ethical lives in response to the salvation provided by God, as Paul taught, to an understanding that human effort adds to, or even prepares the way for, God's grace. As the focus on human merit towards salvation intensified, it was perceived that only a small group of saintly Christians could achieve this merit, the martyrs and ascetics.

Ignatius of Antioch (ca. 110)[9] appealed to the Christians in Rome not to save him from martyrdom but to allow him through death to achieve life through copying Christ: "permit me to be an imitator of the passion of my God."[10] In this context Ignatius stressed the obligation of copying Jesus Christ, but he went beyond to stress a reward for such an achievement. However, in another letter, Ignatius also suggested that "if He were to reward us according to our works, we would cease to be."[11] As such, Ignatius illustrates the tension felt throughout Christian history between meriting a reward for moral actions in following the example of Christ, and unmerited favor in receiving better than believers deserve.

Later, Justin Martyr (ca. 110–ca. 165)[12] spoke in terms that emphasized human ability to choose good or evil actions: "We hold it to be true, that

---

6. Susan Ashbrook Harvey, "Martyr Passions and Hagiography," in *The Oxford Handbook of Early Christian Studies*, ed. Susan Ashbrook Harvey and David G. Hunter (Oxford: Oxford University Press, 2008), 603.

7. Eva-Maria Faber, "Grace," in *Encyclopedia of Christian Theology (ECTh)*, ed. Jean-Yves Lacoste (New York: Routledge, 2005), 2:647.

8. J. William Harmless, SJ, "Monasticism," in *The Oxford Handbook of Early Christian Studies*, 510.

9. It is impossible to accurately date Ignatius (see *ANF*, 1:45, 48), and the discussion is ongoing; see Graydon F. Snyder, "Ignatius of Antioch," in *Encyclopedia of Early Christianity* (*EEC*), 2nd ed., ed. Everett Ferguson (New York: Garland, 1999), 559.

10. Ignatius of Antioch, *Epistle to the Romans* 6, 8, in *ANF*, 1:76–77. See the thread of references throughout his letters to his own achievement of martyrdom in imitation of Christ in Snyder, "Ignatius of Antioch," *EEC*, 559–560.

11. Ignatius of Antioch, *Epistle to the Magnesians* 10, in *ANF*, 1:63.

12. *ANF*, 1:159; Theodore Stylianopoulos, "Justin Martyr," in *EEC*, 647.

punishments, and chastisements, and good rewards, are rendered according to the merit of each man's actions."[13] In this context, he found himself arguing against those who falsely accused Christians of fatalism on account of their belief in prophecy, so, Justin argued strongly in favor of human responsibility. He went on to insist that "unless the human race have the power of avoiding evil and choosing good by free choice, they are not accountable for their actions."[14] In another context, arguing that Christians teach a punishment of wrongdoing in afterlife similar to, but more rigorous than, the teachings of Plato,[15] Justin uses the argument that those who choose well, and "by their works show themselves worthy of His (God's) design, they are deemed worthy . . . of reigning in company with Him, being delivered from corruption and suffering."[16] Note that Justin is speaking of humans as they came from the hand of God, with free will. In keeping his argument simple, Justin makes no distinction in human ability to choose before or after the Fall. Though the context of his argument in his apologetic purpose makes him speak more forcefully, and simply, of Christian ethical behavior, nevertheless, Justin's actual words speak in favor of salvific rewards for human works. Note his words to Trypho: "The Holy Ghost reproaches men because they were made like God, free from suffering and death, provided they kept His commandments, and were deemed deserving of the name of His Sons, and yet they, becoming like Adam and Eve, work out death for themselves."[17]

Theophilus of Antioch,[18] in his only extant work, *To Autolycus* (*Ad Autolycum*, ca. 180),[19] also emphasizes the choice set before pre-Fall humans,

---

13. Justin Martyr, *1 Apol.* 43, in *ANF,* 1:177.

14. Ibid.

15. Ibid., 8.

16. Ibid., 10, in *ANF,* 1:165.

17. Justin Martyr, *Dial.* 124, in *ANF,* 1:262.

18. I choose not to attempt a life dating of Theophilus of Antioch. The date of birth given by Marcus Dods (*ANF,* 2:87–88), he admits, is one of pure conjecture. Dods goes on to suggest that the only solid date in Theophilus's life from any source is Eusebius's date of his succession as bishop in Antioch as the eighth year of Marcus Aurelius, or 168.

19. The date for *Ad Autolycum* is quoted in Frederick W. Norris, "Theophilus of Antioch," in *EEC,* 1122. Significantly, Norris dates only Theophilus's work, not his life. This date is based on the terminus of the chronology Theophilus gave in book three. The final

and then he argues a similar choice for post-Fall humans. In reference to Adam, the first created human, Theophilus wrote: "If he were to turn to the life of immortality by keeping the commandment of God, he would win immortality as a reward from him and would become a god; but if he turned to deeds of death, disobeying God, he would be responsible for his own death." Theophilus went on, now in reference to all humans: "For as by disobedience man gained death for himself, so by obedience to the will of God whoever will can obtain eternal life for himself." Continuing, the next statement contains Theophilus's idea of grace and salvation: "God gave us a law and holy commandments; whoever performs them can be saved."[20] This emphasis of Theophilus suggests a shared dependence between humans and God for salvation.

The Christian writers of the second century were primarily interested in ethics and lifestyle rather than in clear theological distinctions,[21] including distinctions about grace. Irenaeus of Lyon (writing ca. 190)[22] can be included in that statement, but his articulation that there is "one God who is the creator of the world and the Father of Jesus Christ, [and] that there is one divine economy of salvation and one revelation"[23] shows Irenaeus to be a more systematic thinker than his predecessors. To understand Irenaeus on salvation is to see his stress on Christ's recapitulation of Adam. Jesus Christ, as human, succeeds where Adam, the first human, failed,[24] and also died as the redemptive sacrifice, in order to give the gift of eternal life to humans: "through the flesh of our Lord, and through His blood, we have been saved."[25] As such,

---

entry (*Auto.* 3.27–28) is the death of "Emperor Aurelius Verus," in 169, which leads us to believe that the book was written before the death of Marcus Aurelius, who died in 180.

20. Theophilus of Antioch, *Auto.* 2.27. Quotations from Theophilus of Antioch are from the translation by Robert M. Grant, *Theophilus of Antioch: Ad Autolycum* (Oxford: Clarendon Press, 1970).

21. Frances Young, "Christian Teaching," in *CHECL*, 103.

22. Mary Ann Donovan, *One Right Reading? A Guide to Irenaeus* (Collegeville, MN: Liturgical Press, 1997), 8–10. Whereas the only solid date we have in the life of Irenaeus is his trip to Rome as Christian leader from Gaul in regards to the martyrdoms of 177, Irenaeus does denote Eleutherius as twelveth and current bishop of Rome (ca. 174–ca. 189) as he wrote his lists of bishops now found in *Against Heresies* 3.3.3.

23. Mary T. Clark, RSCJ, "Irenaeus," in *EEC*, 587.

24. Irenaeus, *Against Heresies* 5.21.1–2, in *ANF,* 1:548–550.

25. Ibid., 4.14.2, 3, *ANF,* 1:541–542; see also 3.19.1–3, in *ANF,* 1:448–449.

Irenaeus anticipates, but does not clearly differentiate, several of the ingredients of salvation which are later articulated: freedom to choose, substitution, saved by grace, and growing in grace.

Clement of Alexandria (ca. 160–215)[26] and Origen both talk in terms of becoming "worthy to receive the power of grace from God,"[27] but Origen develops the idea more thoroughly. In his preface to his work now known as *On First Principles*, Origen suggests that the gifts of the Spirit are given only to those who deserve them, and that the correct meaning of the scriptures "is not known to all, but to those only on whom the grace of the Holy Spirit is bestowed in the word of wisdom and knowledge."[28] He calls such people "lovers of wisdom" who "prepare themselves to be fit and worthy receivers of wisdom" and who have obtained from the Holy Spirit "the gift of language, of wisdom, and of knowledge." These few, as Origen further describes, are ones who "turn to the Lord" and are able to view scriptures "with unveiled faces" having "deserved to be sanctified by His grace."[29] So, according to Origen, salvation and the understanding of scripture are only available to those in whom the Holy Spirit works: "The operation of the Holy Spirit does not take place at all in those . . . who are endued indeed with reason, but are engaged in evil courses." Origen makes it even more clear when he continues: "In those persons alone do I think that the operation of the Holy Spirit takes place, who are already turning to a better life, . . . who are engaged in the performance of good actions, and who abide in God."[30] In Origen's view, sanctifying grace, salvation, and the Holy Spirit are only available to those who have already changed their lives and actions, people Origen calls "saints."

One could argue that Origen and Clement are speaking in these places only of sanctifying grace, and that they would understand that there is also grace which precedes. It must be granted that Origen also argues that the Father and the Son are always working in both saints and sinners, but that this work is largely to be understood as having provided them with existence

---

26. Walter H. Wagner, "Clement of Alexandria," in *EEC*, 262–263.

27. Clement of Alexandria, *Strom.* 4.22, in *ANF*, 2:435; see also 5.1, in *ANF*, 2:445: "'For by grace we are saved:' not, indeed, without good works."

28. Origen, Preface to *Princ.* 3, 8, in *ANF*, 4:240–241.

29. Origen, *Princ.* 1.1.2, 3, in *ANF*, 4:242.

30. Origen, *Princ.* 1.3.5, in *ANF*, 4:253.

and rational thought.[31] He actually speaks of a "special ministry of the Lord Jesus Christ to those upon whom he confers by nature the gift of reason, by means of which they are enabled to be rightly what they are." This is clearly a manifestation of grace, but Origen immediately turns his attention to "another grace of the Holy Spirit, which is bestowed upon the deserving." This grace Origen equates with the new wine which cannot be poured into old wineskins. "Men should walk in newness of life, that they may receive the new wine, i.e., the newness of grace of the Holy Spirit." He concludes, "The Holy Spirit is conferred on the saints alone."[32] Origen overtly argues that people are to turn to a life of good works on their own, before they can merit the gifts of the Holy Spirit. His stress on the human ability to behave is built on his view of Christ, as our brother, offering a salvation by example.[33] Origen goes on to teach a perfectionism empowered by the Holy Spirit, but the initial change is made by the saints for themselves. For Origen, saints begin their own salvation and then depend on the Holy Spirit to finish it.

Many other early Christian teachers and bishops from many locales follow a similar pattern as that of these Alexandrians, Clement and Origen. Gregory of Nyssa (ca. 340–ca. 395) "preserved the primacy of God as the source of all good, while maintaining human responsibility in freely responding to God's call by a continuous process of conversion."[34] Nyssa taught that human ascetic exertions were met by God's responsive grace. "Gregory articulated this as *synergia*, a working together of human effort and God's grace."[35]

---

31. Ibid., 1.3.8, in *ANF,* 4:255.

32. Ibid., 1.3.7, in *ANF,* 4:254.

33. Origen views the Son as "being God through participation in the Father's divinity," not by nature. John W. Reeve, "The Trinity in the Third and Fourth Centuries," in Woodrow Whidden, Jerry Moon, and John W. Reeve, *The Trinity: Understanding God's Love, His Plan of Salvation, and Christian Relationships* (Hagerstown, MD: Review and Herald, 2002), 138. For a discussion of the ramifications on salvation from Origen's low Christology, see Darius Jankiewicz, "Lessons from Alexandria: The Trinity, the Soteriological Problem, and the Rise of Modern Adventist Anti-Trinitarianism," *Andrews University Seminary Studies* 50.1 (2012): 5–24.

34. David L. Balás, O. Cist., "Gregory of Nyssa," in *EEC,* 495–497.

35. Karen Jo Torjesen, "Grace," in *EEC,* 482. For an in-depth discussion of Gregory's position in contrast to both Augustine and Pelagius, see Ekkehard Mühlenberg, "Synergism

One of the dominant views that come out of the first five centuries of Christian writers concerning salvation is that humans are born in a sinful condition, walking away from God, but are capable on their own of turning toward God, and on their own begin to walk toward God. Grace enters the picture to forgive past sins and empower the walk toward God into a walk with God. In the fifth century two very different ideas come to light.

AUGUSTINE AND THE PELAGIAN CONTROVERSY

Pelagius (ca. 350–ca. 425),[36] a monk from the British Isles, came to Rome around 405 and endeavored to reform the Christians in Rome until the invasion of Aleric forced many to flee Rome in 409.[37] Pelagius then made a circuit through Christian Europe, ending up in Palestine, espousing an idea that humans were not that bad off at birth but learned sinful behavior patterns by being raised in a sinful environment. What came to be known as Pelagianism was the idea that all humans are born without sin, but that each person falls victim to sin by choosing it, much like Adam and Eve did. The obvious implication of this view is that if sin is merely a choice and not an integral part of a sinful nature, then it only takes a choice to overcome it. In Pelagianism, Jesus Christ is not so much Savior as example. Grace is for forgiveness of past sins, but the choice to no longer sin is a human capability, not a special grace of Christ.

Augustine of Hippo (354–430)[38] could not have disagreed more, though his actual understanding of Pelagianism may well have come more from the teachings of Celestius, his fellow fifth-century North African,[39] than from Pelagius himself.[40] Augustine strongly held that all humans since Adam, except Jesus, the second Adam, are born with a sinful nature. Augustine does correct this major wrong from Pelagianism by teaching

---

in Gregory of Nyssa," *Zeitschrift für die Neutestamentliche Wissenschaft* 68 (1977): 93–122, especially 109.

36. Joanne McWilliam, "Pelagius, Pelagianism," in *EEC,* 887.

37. Brinley Roderick Rees, *Pelagius: A Reluctant Heretic* (Rochester, NY: Boydell, 1988), 1.

38. Margaret R. Miles, "Augustine," in *EEC,* 148.

39. Michael P. McHugh, "Celestius (Fifth Century)," in *EEC,* 228–229.

40. Rees, *Pelagius,* 2–3, 10–11.

that humans are born sinful and are unable to change under their own power.[41] Augustine argued that only through grace can humans recognize their sinful condition, perceive the forgiveness offered by the sacrifice of Christ, experience the invitation of God drawing them to Himself, and respond by choosing to allow Him to save them and change them.[42] In other words, Augustine identified that grace was not just the forgiving of those who have chosen God and turned toward him. Rather, God initiates the process by giving His grace before any action, knowledge, or choice from the human. This concept is called prevenient grace, the grace that comes before salvation. It is this prevenient grace that ensures that God initiates salvation by wooing sinners and empowering them to change. This prevenient grace is not needed by Pelagians or those earlier teachers who held that humans were able to turn toward God on the own, like Origen, John Chrysostom, and many others.

The problem with Augustine's solution to the error of Pelagianism was that he went too far. He rightly taught that humans were born sinners, unable to initiate a saving relationship with God, and that God's prevenient grace initiated the salvific relationship, but he turned the whole process of salvation into a monergism from God's side. The term is built on *monos* (one, singular, or only) and *ergos* (work), and in the context of salvation means that all activity of salvation is from God, humans can do nothing, not even have an empowered choice. In Augustine's understanding, even prevenient grace could not be resisted. Monergism contrasts the term *synergism* (working together), where both God and the human have a role in salvation. Most Christian theologians before Augustine and also after him until the Protestant Reformation were synergists of some kind. Augustine's monergism was based on the concept that saved humans were predestined to be saved and had no choice in the matter at all. Though Augustine's view of predestination was centered much

---

41. This is not to say that all aspects of Augustine's teaching on original sin are biblically correct. For example, his explanation that sin is transmitted through sexual impregnation clearly lacks biblical support.

42. J. Patout Burns, "Grace: The Augustinian Foundation," in *Christian Spirituality: Origins to the Twelfth Century*, ed. Bernard McGinn, John Meyendorff, and Jean Leclercq, World Spirituality 16 (New York: Crossroad, 1997), 336–337.

more on church[43] and nations[44] than the more individualistic predestination embraced later by Luther and John Calvin, it shared some of the same problems. Namely, it left no room for any human choice concerning salvation. "It was Paul's teaching on grace that provided Augustine with the foundation of his own much more comprehensive and sophisticated doctrine; but he carried his interpretation of that teaching to limits which left him with a theory of predestination unacceptable to the majority of later theologians—though not to Calvin."[45]

So in the Pelagian controversy Pelagius got it right that humans do have a choice in their own salvation, but he got it wrong that humans were born without sin, chose sin based on the sinful environment, and then chose to not sin based on their own abilities. Pelagianism had far too large a role for the human in his understanding of synergism.

Augustine got it right in that humans are sinful from birth and are unable to even consider salvation or a relationship with God without God's prevenient grace wooing, inviting, and empowering their choices and faith. What Augustine got wrong is that salvation is only for the predestined, born in Christian churches and nations, and for a few that are called out of paganism. Augustine taught that those predestined to salvation have no choice in the matter: they cannot refuse salvation. Though he did not coin the Calvinistic term *irresistible grace*, Augustine taught something very similar to that in his monergistic understanding of salvation.

---

43. "Now if the binding and shutting up of the devil means that he cannot deceive the Church, must his loosing therefore mean that he will be able to do so again? God forbid! For he will never deceive the Church which was predestined and chosen before the foundation of the world, of which it is said that 'the Lord knoweth them that are His,'" Augustine, *Civ.* 20.8, in *Augustine: The City of God Against the Pagans,* trans. R. W. Dyson, Cambridge Texts in the History of Political Thought Series, ed. Raymond Guess and Quentin Skinner (Cambridge: Cambridge University Press, 1998), 982–983.

44. "Because he is thus bound and shut up, then, the devil is prohibited and prevented from seducing those nations which belonged to Christ: the nations whom he formerly seduced or held in bondage. For God chose those nations before the foundation of the world, to deliver them from the power of darkness and to translate them into the kingdom of His dear Son, as the apostle says. (Cf. Eph 1:4)," ibid., 20.7, in *Augustine: The City of God,* 981.

45. Rees, *Pelagius,* 53.

TWO KINDS OF SEMI-PELAGIANISM

As the name suggests, semi-Pelagianism is like Pelagianism in that it places too much responsibility for salvation on the human rather than on God, just not to the extent of Pelagianism. There is no single, simple definition of semi-Pelagianism because it comes in many forms, as well as being viewed from many different perspectives. For instance, a stark Calvinist would view any human input in salvation as semi-Pelagianism, even a God-empowered response to God's gracious call.

The two kinds of semi-Pelagianism addressed in this section represent (1) those who believe humans can individually cooperate with God in the works of salvation and (2) those who believe the works of the corporate church ensure their salvation.

Most of the Christian teachers before Augustine taught that humans have the innate ability to turn toward God and initiate the process of their own salvation. In the immediate aftermath of Augustine's monergism, including a selective predestination and a grace that could not be refused, there was a reaction in favor of human choice. Unfortunately, this return to free will also included a return to the first kind of semi-Pelagianism: humans can cooperate in the works of salvation.

John Cassian (ca. 365–ca. 433)[46] opposed Augustine's monergism as too simplistic in regard to divine grace and human will. The synergistic models he developed within his work *Conferences,* written as a record of conversations between ascetic monks, were later named "semi-Pelagianism" and condemned at the Council of Orange in 529.[47] Cassian's two models of grace and will, developed in *Conf.* 13, have recently been labeled the "cooperative model" and the "alternative model."[48] Both of these models include the human cooperating with God in the works of salvation and correspond to the first kind of semi-Pelagianism previously discussed. In spite of their condemnation at Orange, they reflect two ongoing threads in monastic thought. Also, Cassian's appeal to the rule of faith in the church in *Conf.* 13.11.4, 5 suggests the second kind of semi-Pelagianism.

---

46. Paul C. Burns, CSB., "John Cassian," in *EEC,* 219.

47. Faber, "Grace," in *ECTh,* 2:648; Karen Jo Torjesen, "Grace," in *EEC,* 483.

48. Alexander Y. Hwang, "Manifold Grace in John Cassian and Prosper of Aquitaine," *Scottish Journal of Theology* 63.1 (2010): 97–101.

In the cooperative model, Cassian suggests that some people, and he specifically means the strong-willed ascetics of the type that are participating in his recorded conversations, desire to practice holiness and live righteous lives and they engage their wills in this practice. Cassian argues that all humans have the seeds of virtue in their soul on account of being created by God, and though he recognizes that God provides the germination of the seeds unto perfection, he also reacts against accounting all good works to God: "Therefore, we must be on the watch lest we attribute all the good works of the holy persons to the Lord in such a way that we ascribe nothing but what is bad and perverse to human nature."[49] In this cooperative model, "the grace of God initiates and inspires the free will towards the good, but the free will can choose to follow or resist the actions of grace at each stage in the process of perfection."[50] Cassian seems to be asserting a shared power of the will between God and humans in the good actions of salvation. The analogy of a diligent farmer attempting to grow crops is used to illustrate the cooperation between the human and God: "Consequently, just as the divine goodness does not bestow an abundant yield on sluggish farmers who do not plow their fields frequently, so neither will night-long anxiety be profitable to those who labor if it has not been smiled upon by the Lord's mercy."[51]

The cooperative model of John Cassian contains a high view of human ability in cooperating with God in salvation. It is similar to the earlier models which suggested that humans prepare for their own salvation. It compares well with what Augustine complained was the position of Tyconius (fl. 370–390),[52] the Donatist writer of the seven *Rules* of scripture interpretation. Concerning rule five, "about the promises and the law," which Augustine says should rather be called "about grace and the commandments," Augustine repined, "Tychonius did some good work in his treatment of it, but still left something to be desired. While discussing faith and works, he said that our works are given to us by God on the strength of our faith, but that faith itself comes from us in such a way that we do not have it from God."[53] This

---

49. John Cassian, *Conlatio*, 13.12.5–7; quoted in Boniface Ramsey, OP, trans., *John Cassian: The Conferences*, ACW 57 (New York: Paulist, 1997), 479–480.

50. Hwang, "Manifold Grace," *SJT*, 98.

51. Cassian, *Conlatio* 13.3.3; Ramsey, *John Cassian: The Conferences*, 468.

52. Pamela Bright, "Tyconius," in *EEC*, 1148.

53. Augustine, *Doctr. chr.*, 3.46; quoted in Edmund Hill, O.P., trans., *Teaching*

understanding of Tyconius represents many who have said that humans initiate their own faith, a position shared by John Cassian's cooperative model, though sometimes Cassian speaks in terms of humans having perfecting faith. Ironically, in the second model identified within the thirteenth of the *Conferences*, the "alternate model," John Cassian appears to be saying the exact opposite.

After quoting a series of passages from Paul, Cassian asserts that for some people, God "draws the unwilling to salvation, removes from those who want to sin the means of fulfilling their desire, and graciously hinders those who are hastening on to what is evil."[54] This sounds more like Augustine's irresistible predestination than Cassian's synergism. However, Cassian goes on to quote "seven sets of scriptural passages, each containing at least one passage that supports divine initiative (grace) and at least one passage that supports human initiative (free will)."[55] Cassian then concludes that this all means "that in each of these cases both the grace of God and our freedom of will are affirmed, since even by his own activity a person can occasionally be brought to a desire for virtue, but he always needs to be helped by the Lord."[56]

So both the cooperative model and the alternative model described by John Cassian include cooperation between God's grace and natural abilities, including free will and internal virtues. As such, both of Cassian's models represent the first kind of semi-Pelagianism, that of individual cooperation in salvation. Cassian's cooperative model works for the strong, ascetic monks whereas the alternative model is aimed at the weak, but both retain the internal seeds of virtue as well as at least some free will. In his summary of the thirteenth of the *Conferences*, Cassian records concerning God's handling of salvation that "sometimes he inspires the beginning of salvation and places in each person a fervent good will, while sometimes he grants the performance of the work and the perfection of virtuousness. . . . Some he supports as they hasten and run, while others he draws unwilling and resisting and compels them to a good will."[57]

Christianity: De Doctrina Christiana, The Works of Saint Augustine: A Translation for the 21st Century, vol. 1, ed. John E. Rotelle, OSA (Hyde Park, NY: New City Press, 1996), 190.

54. John Cassian, *Conlatio* 13.9.1; Ramsey, *John Cassian: The Conferences,* 474.

55. Hwang, "Manifold Grace," *SJT,* 99.

56. John Cassian, *Conlatio* 13.9.4; Ramsey, *John Cassian: The Conferences,* 475.

57. John Cassian, *Conlatio* 13.18.2; Ramsey, *John Cassian: The Conferences,* 490.

John Cassian also represents the second kind of semi-Pelagianism, depending on the corporate church, though to a much lesser degree than many others. Near the end of *Conferences* 13.11, Cassian refers to the "rule of the Church's faith"[58] as something he purposefully retains in regard to salvation. Later, he asserts that he is in line with all the fathers of the universal church. To teach within the rule of faith has been an important goal by most Christian teachers clear back to Irenaeus and Origen.[59] It was Cyprian of Carthage (ca. 200–258)[60] who most dramatically initialized the teaching that the church is in charge of salvation.

Cyprian of Carthage and his experiences surrounding the Decian persecution in 249–251 clarified for Catholics, and even for the later Donatists, the relationship between salvation and the Church. In the aftermath of the persecution, the Christians of Carthage and the surrounding areas who had looked to the martyrs and those in prison as confessors for spiritual direction and even forgiveness now had to deal with their returned bishop who had fled the city during the persecution, against the distinct writing of his North African predecessor and theological mentor, Tertullian (fl. 200).[61] Cyprian had to reestablish order in the church with his own moral authority called into question. He summoned a synod of North African bishops, who would recognize him as their leader as the metropolitan bishop of the province of North Africa. There he asserted his official authority to reestablish the unity of the Church. In his letters and in his treatise entitled *On the Unity of the Church*, he summarized three principles which became standards of Catholic Church order:

1. "He can longer have God for his Father, who has not the Church for his Mother."[62] This attested to Cyprian's belief, that was gaining universal appeal, that salvation is only available through the Church. Through baptism and the Eucharist the Church offered salvation to its members.

---

58. Quoted in Ramsey, *John Cassian: The Conferences,* 477–478.

59. John W. Reeve, "Understanding Apostasy in the Christian Church," in *Message, Mission and Unity of the Church* (Hagerstown, MD: Review and Herald, 2013), 156–160.

60. Robert D. Sider, "Cyprian," in *EEC,* 306.

61. "More glorious the soldier pierced with a javelin in battle, than he who has a safe skin as a fugitive," Tertullian, *De fuga,* 10 in *ANF,* 4:122. Tertullian's flourish date is from Robert D. Sider, "Tertullian," in *EEC,* 1107.

62. Cyprian, *Unit. eccl.,* 6; in *ANF,* 5:423.

2. "The Church is founded upon the bishops, and every act of the Church is controlled by these same rulers."[63] "For Cyprian the unity of the church, and thus the very possibility of salvation, resides in the office of the bishop."[64]

3. "It is manifest where and by whom remission of sins can be given; to wit, that which is given in baptism. For first of all he gave that power to Peter, upon whom he built the Church, and whence he appointed and showed the source of unity—the power, namely, that whatever he loosed on earth should be loosed in heaven. . . . Whence we perceive that only they who are set over the Church and established in the Gospel law, and in the ordinance of the Lord, are allowed to baptize and to give remission of sins."[65]

This placed the spiritual authority of salvation firmly into the hands of the bishops alone; it denied that either the confessors or the presbyters on their own authority could offer God's grace. Through this Cyprian also asserted that no heretic or schismatic could offer salvation. This concept is built on Tertullian's understanding of the *ordinatio*,[66] which set the bishop up as the high priest, at the apex of the hierarchy of spiritual authority, which was built up, throughout the Middle Ages, into the church as the conduit of grace. This second semi-Pelagian position is on the institutional level: the human institution of the church cooperating with God to bestow grace. So both the individual semi-Pelagianism and the corporate semi-Pelagianism put too much emphasis on the human side of synergism. Both individual and corporate semi-Pelagianism portray humans as cooperating with God in the works of salvation instead of depending on God for the works of salvation and cooperating in a God-empowered response to salvation.

---

63. Cyprian, *Ep.* 26.1, in *ANF,* 5:305.

64. Roger E. Olson, *The Story of Christian Theology: Twenty Centuries of Tradition and Reform* (Downers Grove, IL: IVP Academic, 1999), 121.

65. Cyprian, *Ep.* 72.7, in *ANF,* 5:381.

66. "It is the authority of the Church, and the honour which has acquired sanctity through the joint session of the Order, which has established the difference between the Order and the laity," Tertullian *Exh. cast.,* 7; in *ANF* 4:54; "Of giving [baptism], the chief priest (who is the bishop) has the right: in the next place, the presbyters and deacons, yet not without the bishop's authority, on account of the honour of the Church, which being preserved, peace is preserved," Tertullian, *Bapt.,* 17, in *ANF,* 3:677.

GRACE IN THE MIDDLE AGES

Though Cyprian never intended this exact outcome, in the Middle Ages the church asserted exclusive control over salvation, highlighting the difference and distance from the church as portrayed in the New Testament. Cyprian himself felt that all of salvation was from God. Roger Olson defends Cyprian personally, while still showing the damage of his theological trajectory in Olson's ably nuanced chapter on Cyprian:

> In spite of later Protestant polemics against the penitential system that grew out of Cyprian's theology, Cyprian himself was not guilty of works righteousness or self-salvation. Nowhere did he suggest that a person can earn salvation as a reward for good works. . . . On the other hand, the suspicion that Cyprian unintentionally contributed to a growing tendency toward moralism and works righteousness within the church is not entirely unjustified.[67]

There was a shift in understanding from being saved through right practice (orthopraxy) during the second century, into being saved through right belief (orthodoxy) from the third century and on. Both of these are semi-Pelagian in their focus because they put human actions and beliefs into a cooperative balance with God's grace as the means of salvation. Cyprian's assertion that there was no salvation outside the church came to be applied to the sacramental system of orthodox bishops using the storehouse of merits from martyrs and ascetic saints to apply to weak and needy common Christians.

Augustine supplies the protection of church orthodoxy in his argument from Revelation 20:1–3 that Satan cannot cause the church to err because he is bound:

> Now if the binding and shutting up of the devil means that he cannot deceive the Church, must his loosing therefore mean that he will be able to do so again? God forbid! For he will never deceive the Church which was predestined and chosen before the foundation of the world, of which it is said that "the Lord knoweth them that are His."[68]

---

67. Olson, *Story of Christian Theology,* 120.

68. Augustine, *Civ.,* 20.8, in Dyson, trans., *City of God,* 982–983.

Peter Lombard (c. 1100–1160)[69] secures the seven sacraments for the church in book 4 of *The Sentences* both in number and in meaning, not by being original, but by systematizing.[70] As a theologian, he makes careful distinctions as to who is the author of grace and who is the servant of grace. As in his description of the efficacy of baptism, Lombard argues that the Lord is the author of the invisible grace that remits sins in baptism, but that the servant who does the baptizing remits sins "by the visible sacrament."[71] He gets it right that the Lord is the only source of grace, but he gets it wrong that the human action remits sins. But that is not the worst of it by far. Others who follow him without his fine theological distinctions simply use the sacraments as if the power were their own on the basis of their ordination.

Bernard of Clairvaux (1090–1153) heightens the level of church hierarchy, especially the papacy, as *amicus sponsa,* friend of the bride. The pope was charged with protecting the church as the bride of Christ, leading believers to salvation. "Bernard developed in this work a theory of the plentitude of papal power which was to be of immense importance for the later Middle Ages. His idea was that the Pope stood in the hierarchy of heaven and earth, not only above every secular power, but also above all others in the Church."[72]

By the end of the Middle Ages, the church in Europe had taken on the task of exclusively tending salvation on behalf of God through the seven sacraments provided through the hierarchical structure from the pope through the ordained to the laity and was believed to be without error in the understandings of God, humans, and the saving grace it dispensed. On top of that, the system empowered unscrupulous people to take advantage of the authoritarian system, bringing to themselves power, money, and license to act as they wanted. The free gift of God's grace had been largely overshadowed. It is indeed amazing grace that God reached people in the midst of all that, but He did.

---

69. Tony Lane, *A Concise History of Christian Thought,* rev. and exp. ed. (Grand Rapids, MI: Baker Academic, 2006), 113.

70. Justo L. González, *A History of Christian Thought in One Volume* (Nashville, TN: Abingdon, 2014), 202.

71. Peter Lombard, *Sent.,* 4.5.3.4, in Giulio Silano, trans., *Peter Lombard: the Sentences, Book 4 On the Doctrine of Signs,* Mediaeval Sources in Translation, vol. 48, ed. Joseph Goering and Guilio Silano (Toronto: Pontifical Institute of Mediaeval Studies, 2010), 31.

72. G. R. Evans, *Fifty Key Medieval Thinkers* (New York: Routledge, 2002), 96.

THE PROTEST TO REASSERT GOD'S GRACE

The protests against both the system and the abuses of the system came about as a rediscovery of grace. Many different concepts of understanding grace were tried. Some felt that the removal of the abuses and the unscrupulous people would solve the problem of belittling God's grace. Others thought that reducing the number of sacraments to just the two from the New Testament, baptism and the Lord's Supper, would suffice. However:

> those who claim that the sacraments have the power to justify and to bestow grace are also mistaken. Their mistake consists in confusing the "figure" of the sacrament with the "truth" in it. . . . Such confusion leads to superstition, which consists in placing one's faith in what is not God. This perverts the very nature of the sacrament, whose purpose is precisely to exclude any other claim to justification, and to focus faith in Jesus Christ. In fact, Christ himself is the true substance of all sacraments, for he is the source of their strength, and they promise and grant nothing but him.[73]

Luther and Calvin: Monergism Again; Common Grace

Though William of Ockham (1285–1347),[74] John Wyclif (ca. 1329–1384),[75] and Jan Hus (died 1415)[76] all contributed to the idea of a reform to Christianity that went back not to laws of Justinian (Emperor 527–565),[77] but back to the message of the Bible itself, Martin Luther (1483–1546)[78] is usually

---

73. González, *Christian Thought in One Volume*, 259.

74. Evans, *Fifty Key Medieval Thinkers*, 150–151. Ockham taught that secular rulers and church councils had more authority than popes.

75. Ibid., 158–164. Wyclif not only urged and labored for translation of the Bible into the vernacular, but he taught that the Scriptures had more authority than all the popes, clerics, and orders of monks. He encouraged biblical preaching as more important for salvation than the Eucharist.

76. Olson, *The Story of Christian Theology*, 370: "So similar was Martin Luther's theology to Hus's that many labeled him 'the Saxon Hus.'"

77. F. Donald Logan, *A History of the Church in the Middle Ages* (New York: Routledge, 2002), 30; "Canon law, with its enormous impact on the medieval church, took its shape and, indeed, much of its substance from the law reforms of Emperor Justinian," ibid., 33.

78. Olson, *Story of Christian Theology*, 375.

credited with starting the Protestant Reformation in 1517 with his 95 Theses against the sale of indulgences. Thesis 82 struck at the very essence of the problem of the papal church being the conduit of grace as it challenged: "Why does not the pope liberate everyone from purgatory for the sake of love (a most holy thing) and because of the supreme necessity of their souls? This would be morally the best of all reasons. Meanwhile he redeems innumerable souls for money."[79] This protest would flower into a renewed understanding of grace, over and against the church-oriented semi-Pelagianism that was so prevalent in medieval scholasticism.

The spiritual struggles of Martin Luther as a young man were largely caused by Gabriel Biel's [ca. 1425–1495] teaching on grace.[80] Biel taught that God infuses grace into the souls of those who themselves remove the obstacles of grace "by ceasing from the act of sin, by ceasing to consent to it, and by eliciting a good movement toward God."[81] This sounds a lot like the grace earned by Origen's saints and taught in John Cassian's cooperative model. Luther was troubled because he "could not meet the precondition for salvation."[82] Luther discovered, first in the Psalms, and later in the book of Romans, that grace is not earned, but received as a free gift from God. "True repentance is to be seen as the result, rather than the precondition, of grace."[83] To put it simply, Luther learned to depend on God to do what Luther could not: initiate salvation with gifts of grace.

This breakthrough brought Luther to want to study and teach only the Bible and Augustine, not the medieval scholastics.[84] Unfortunately, Luther failed where Augustine failed, and where John Calvin (1509–1564)[85] failed, in turning from an incorrect synergism that gave too much responsibility to

---

79. Ibid., 378.

80. Lane, *Concise History of Christian Thought,* 143–144.

81. Gabriel Biel, *Commentary on the Sentences* 2.27.1, quoted in Lane, *Concise History of Christian Theology,* 145.

82. Alister McGrath, *Reformation Thought: An Introduction,* 2nd ed. (Oxford: Blackwell, 1993), 94. Note the excellent discussion of Luther's coming to term with God's righteousness as a gift rather than as His wrath in ibid., 93–101.

83. Ibid., 96–97.

84. McGrath, *Reformation Thought,* 102.

85. Olson, *Story of Christian Theology,* 408.

the human for salvation to a monergism where the human will is always bound[86] and the response to God's work of salvation is purely passive.

Before addressing Jacob Arminius and the theological answer to total passivity in predestination, there is another understanding of grace that is adopted by John Calvin: common grace. The basic idea of common grace is not bad, since it teaches that God gives gifts to all persons, not just those who respond positively to Him. That is true. God gives the blessings of life and rain to all kinds of people, not just to those who have accepted His salvation. So, this gift of grace is common to all. Where Calvin gets it wrong is when he argues that this common grace *is not* an invitation to salvation. For Calvin, God's will is absolute. So, if He wants to save you, you'll be saved. If not, you'll be lost. Period.[87] Calvin himself downplayed predestination as a consequence of God's sovereignty and His initiative in salvation. His successors reimaged predestination as a central tenet of reformed thought on the sovereignty of God.[88] With regard to grace, however, a complete lack of human choice in the matter of salvation, as in monergism, leaves saving grace as only for some and not for others (limited atonement) and as irresistible. But here is the flaw in Calvin's concept of common grace: since it is for all, it cannot be useful toward salvation. It looks like a false gift. An individual can be thankful to God for the blessings, but he or she cannot respond to God in a relationship. That is awkward. Rather, what seems to be true is that all God's gifts are invitations toward a saving relationship, so common grace is a subset of prevenient grace.

Jacob Arminius: Prevenient Grace, Empowered Choice

Jacob Arminius (1560–1609)[89] taught that all grace is of one kind, and it all leads to salvation, and it is offered to everybody. This is not to say that he did not recognize different forms of grace, or that there are many different gifts freely given by God; it's just that God is attempting to save everyone (John 12:32), so all His gifts are meant as invitations to salvation. Similar to

---

86. Lane, *Concise History of Christian Thought,* 158. Lane points out that Luther goes even farther than Augustine in regard to the predestined human will having no choices, not just the inability to choose the good.

87. McGrath, *Reformation Thought,* 125–126.

88. Ibid., 123.

89. Olson, *Story of Christian Theology,* 454.

Augustine's use of prevenient grace, Arminius describes it as the initial steps in God's calling out to each person to allow Him to save that person. God, as Arminius sees Him, wants to be in a close relationship with humanity. That is starkly different from the scholastic view of God as timeless, and therefore, all knowing.[90] In this way Theodore Beza (1519–1605)[91] and other post-Calvin Calvinists explain how it is that God both predestines, elects, and knows the outcome at the same time. In their estimation, for God, all time is one. Arminius, also a post-Calvin Calvinist, trained by Beza, is trying to understand how predestination can be understood so as to not leave God responsible for both the sin of Adam and the sins of those predestined to eternal loss. In establishing "the final cause in predestination," Arminius argues that it is fine if God foreknows and from that knowledge predestines:

> But if you think that God, from eternity, without any pre-existence of sin, in His prescience, determined to illustrate His own glory by mercy and punitive justice, and, that He might be able to secure this object, decreed to create man good but mutable, and ordained farther that he should Fall, that in this way there might be a place for that decree, I say that such an opinion cannot, in my judgment, be established by any passage of the Word of God.[92]

Arminius is clearly more concerned with biblical truth and a correct view of God than only in the sovereignty of God. A few pages later he asserts: "For in that case, the fault could be justly and deservedly charged upon God, who would be the cause of sin."[93]

John Wesley, Sanctification Without Perfectionism

John Wesley (1703–1791)[94] took to heart this message of Arminius on prevenient grace allowing personal choice in salvation. John Wesley, along with

---

90. Olson, *Story of Christian Theology*, 457.

91. Ibid., 456.

92. Jacob Arminius, "An Examination of Predestination and Grace in Perkins' Pamphlet," Part 1, quoted in John D. Wagner, ed., *Arminius Speaks: Essential Writings on Predestination, Free Will, and the Nature of God* (Eugene, OR: Wipf and Stock, 2011), 97.

93. Ibid., 104.

94. Ibid., 510–511.

his brother Charles (1707–1788),[95] the great hymn writer, George Whitfield (1714–1770),[96] and others shared the pietism[97] of their time and first started a "Holy Club" at Oxford University. They later experienced an awareness of personal salvation and sparked the Great Awakening in England and the American colonies. Wesley expressed his experience of personal assurance of God's grace and salvation in his journal:

> In the evening I went very unwillingly to a society in Aldersgate Street, where one was reading Luther's preface to the Epistle to the Romans. About a quarter before nine, while he was describing the change which God works in the heart through faith in Christ, I felt my heart strangely warmed. I felt I did trust in Christ, Christ alone, for salvation; and an assurance was given me that he had taken away my sins, even mine, and saved me from the law of sin and death.[98]

John Wesley's stress on the converted life of holiness made him susceptible toward perfectionism; he even experimented for a while with the concept of instant perfection. What saved Wesley from a perfectionistic understanding of salvation was his twofold emphasis on prevenient grace and the love of God. For Wesley, Christian perfection is not "spiritual infallibility. Wesley made it plain that the Christian is still liable to sin, and does not possess absolute knowledge, absolute judgment, or absolute performance."[99] As quoted previously, Wesley trusted "Christ, Christ alone," for his salvation. This includes his stress on "the power to begin," or prevenient grace, that Christ initiates salvation.[100] It also includes that Christ provides justification, "the turning point."[101] It also includes the new birth experience, or

---

95. Lane, *Concise History of Christian Thought*, 214.

96. González, *Christian Thought in One Volume*, 307.

97. Lane, *Concise History of Christian Thought*, 166–167. Pietism is a Christian religious attitude that stressed a personal, heartfelt faith in Jesus Christ and the need to be born again. Within this attitude it is not enough to be a baptized member or to believe a set of doctrines; one must "experience the Holy Spirit in conversion and new life."

98 John Wesley, *Journal of John Wesley,* 24 May 1738, quoted in Lane, *Concise History of Christian Thought*, 213.

99. Wesley, "Christian Perfection," in Steve Harper, *John Wesley's Message for Today* (Grand Rapids, MI: Zondervan, 1983), 92.

100. Ibid., 39–46.

101. Ibid., 49–59.

transformation: "Wesley called it God's activity of 'renewing our fallen natures.'"[102] Wesley was a strong proponent of God-empowered sanctification. However, he did not move to a semi-Pelagian understanding that somehow humans can do without grace and forgiveness after renewal. In fact, Wesley charged those who felt they had experienced Christian perfection to "go on to perfection," referring to growth in Christian love. "Christian perfection is like that. There is a sanctifying grace that may operate in one's life 'in a moment.' The experience can be noted and described. But the experience loses its full significance when it is divorced from the larger activity of grace before and after. God's grace leads us to the place of Christian perfection (narrowly viewed), and it leads us on after the experience itself."[103]

John Wesley placed God's love at the center of his preaching and teaching,[104] which enabled him to place trust in God at the center of his understanding of salvation. This emphasis on God's trustworthiness, along with prevenient grace, allowed Wesley to evade Pelagian tendencies and to depend on God for his salvation, from start to finish, every step depending on God.

Ellen White, *Steps to Christ*: God-Empowered Synergism

Along with Joseph Bates (1792–1872)[105] and James White (1821–1871),[106] Ellen White (1827–1915)[107] was a founder of the Seventh-day Adventist Church.[108] She played a prophetic role in the shaping of Adventism as well as a theological role as she confirmed the biblical theological choices of the denomination, guided the application of policies, and led in nuancing how to

---

102. Wesley, "The New Birth," in Harper, *John Wesley's Message for Today*, 65.

103. Ibid., 94.

104. Olson, *Story of Christian Thought*, 512.

105. George R. Knight, ed., *Autobiography of Joseph Bates*, Adventist Classic Library (Berrien Springs, MI: Andrews University Press, 2004), viii, xiv.

106. Ellen G. White, *Life Sketches: Ancestry, Early Life, Christian Experience, and Extensive Labors, of Elder James White, and His Wife, Mrs. Ellen G. White* (Battle Creek, MI: Steam Press, 1880), 9.

107. Arthur L. White, *Ellen G. White: The Early Years, 1827–1862* (Hagerstown, MD: Review and Herald, 1985), 9.

108. George R. Knight, *Joseph Bates: The Real Founder of Seventh-day Adventism* (Hagerstown, MD: Review and Herald, 2004), ix.

live the Christian life as an Adventist. She wrote prolifically both on the personal level as well as articles and books for the corporate church. Her most read and bestselling book is her 1892 book titled *Steps to Christ*.[109] It contains thirteen chapters that are mostly easy to see as following a path of steps to a deepening relationship with Jesus Christ as savior. At each step she shows how God initiates the interaction and empowers the step. Starting with God's love for humanity and the sinner's absolute inability to even recognize his or her lack and need of God, White shows that the very desire to have something better is an empowered gift from God to each sinner who allows the thoughts to continue. The same can be said of repentance: "We can no more repent without the Spirit of Christ to awaken the conscience than we can be pardoned without Christ."[110] Confession also is an empowered gift from God: "Unless he yields to the convicting power of the Holy Spirit he remains in partial blindness to his sin. His confessions are not sincere and in earnest."[111] Faith does not come from the sinner, but it is empowered within the sinner who is willing to let God work.

In the work of salvation, the sinner isn't cooperating with God so much as allowing God to work in him or her. God does the work of calling, wooing, enabling repenting and confessing, forgiving, and changing. The sinner's role in White's description of the saving relationship is a willingness to let God work in each step as God moves the sinner through prevenient grace to forgiving grace and saving grace and on to changing grace, repeating steps and moving on as needed.[112] This is no semi-Pelagian cooperation between God and sinner to share the work of salvation. This is salvation from God's side and willingness to be saved on the sinner's side. It is synergistic, but all the work is initiated and empowered by God:

> The heart of God yearns over His earthly children with a love stronger than death. In giving up His Son, He has poured out to us all heaven in one gift. The Saviour's life and death and intercession, the ministry of

---

109. Ellen G. White, *Steps to Christ* (Chicago, IL: F. H. Revell, 1892).

110. Ellen G. White, *Steps to Christ* (Washington, DC: Review and Herald, 1908), 26.

111. Ibid., 40.

112. "God's work of grace upon all human beings prepares them to receive His offer of salvation" (*The Ellen G. White Encyclopedia*, ed. Denis Fortin and Jerry Moon [Hagerstown, MD: Review and Herald, 2013], 250. For a fuller conversation of Ellen White's understanding of prevenient grace, see the section titled "Wesleyan Methodism," pp. 248–255).

angels, the pleading of the Spirit, the Father working above and through all, the unceasing interest of heavenly beings,—all are enlisted in behalf of man's redemption.[113]

Ellen White talks boldly of human effort in working for God and for the salvation of others. She speaks of Christ's life on earth being one of effort, not ease, and is an example for all believers: "He toiled with persistent, earnest, untiring effort for the salvation of lost mankind. . . . So those who are partakers of the grace of Christ will be ready to make any sacrifice, that others for whom He died may share the heavenly gift."[114] For Ellen White, the efforts and works of humans, then, are not to gain salvation, but are in loving response to the free gifts of salvation bestowed in love by God.

CONCLUSION

In the history of the interpretation of grace, from the Apostle Paul to the Seventh-day Adventist Church, there has been a constant struggle between depending on the church and depending on the self for salvation, rather than depending on God. For those who do depend on God for their salvation, there has been a struggle between seeing God's choice to save as either selective and irresistible, or universal and resistible. Within the history of the Seventh-day Adventist Church, there have been these same kinds of struggles. Fortunately, *Steps to Christ* was written and is widely read. Unfortunately, it was sorely needed by an Adventist denomination that was so intent on restoring a correct understanding of God's law that it was tending toward a view of salvation that depended far too much on the sinner's abilities and not enough on God. Bluntly, there were many semi-Pelagians in the ranks that needed the message that salvation is from God alone, not from cooperation with God. Cooperation with God in salvation has been far too prevalent throughout the history of the Christian church, both in terms of humans having a part of the works, or operations, in salvation (as was apparent in John Cassian), and in the operations of the church being the guarantor of salvation (as became the norm in the medieval church as summarized by Peter Lombard).

---

113. Ellen G. White, *Steps to Christ* (Mountain View, CA: Pacific Press Publishing Association, 1956), 21.

114. Ibid., 78.

The problem with the concept of human cooperation in salvation is that only God has the power to operate in the context of sin. The sinner has no abilities to operate his or her way out of sin; the sinner is dependent on God's operations on his or her behalf. Yet if salvation were a complete monergism, as Augustine, Luther, and Calvin asserted, there would be no freedom to choose. Worse yet, freedom to choose is precisely what the sinner lacks, without prevenient grace. The strand of the history of grace that runs through Jacob Arminius, John Wesley, and Ellen White restores human choice in the context of God's empowering invitations through prevenient grace. Prevenient grace also logically allows for God to invite all to accept salvation without making these invitations irresistible. With the God-empowered choice restored through prevenient grace, the sinner's role in salvation is to allow or reject the gracious gifts of God's saving operations on behalf of each and every sinner, empowering the saved sinner to will and act in accordance with God's law in response to God's love.

CHAPTER 14

THE GRACE THAT COMES BEFORE SAVING GRACE

George R. Knight

Grace has many flavors. There is *justifying grace* by which God counts individuals righteous, *transforming grace* through which He makes them into new creatures, *empowering grace* by which He energizes them to walk the new life, and *forgiving grace* when they fail in the Christlike walk. And those are just a few of the flavors.

Grace is absolutely central to the whole plan of salvation in the Bible, and in the context of a sinful humanity, living on a sinful planet, all grace is intended by God to lead to salvation. However, the nature of grace doesn't get much air time apart from its definition as unmerited favor or God giving sinners what they don't deserve. A more accurate and helpful definition is "grace is an overarching term for all of God's gifts to humanity, all the blessings of salvation, all events through which are manifested God's own self-giving. Grace is a divine attribute revealing the heart of the one God, the premise of all spiritual blessing."[1] Again, "grace is the favor shown by God to sinners. It is the divine goodwill offered to those who neither inherently deserve nor can ever hope to earn it. It is the divine disposition to work in our hearts, wills, and actions, so as actively to communicate God's self-giving love for humanity (Rom. 3:24; 6:1; Eph. 1:7; 2:5–8)."[2]

---

1. Thomas C. Oden, *The Transforming Power of Grace* (Nashville: Abingdon, 1993), 33.
2. Ibid.

From those definitions it is clear that the topic of grace is much more inclusive than most people imagine it to be. The topic for this chapter is "the grace that goes before." But the question that needs to be asked is, Before what? And the answer is *before saving grace*. Here is an absolutely essential form of grace that has been all but ignored in Adventist discussions of salvation and even in most of the denomination's teachings on salvation. Yet it is central to the biblical understanding of God's saving work.

THE PROBLEM AND THE NEED

The problem is that most people have confused free will with free grace. But do sinners in their unrenewed state really have free will? The Bible's answer is an unequivocal no. As was noted in chapter 8, individuals are born with a sinful nature, or what Ellen White calls "a bent" to sin.[3] The scriptural teaching on sin and total depravity means that every part of human life has been infected by sin, including the heart, mind, and will, so much so that Paul refers to unrenewed individuals as being enslaved to sin, living in darkness, hard of heart, and alienated from God (Rom. 6:12–17; Eph. 4:18).

How is it that people in such a condition can choose God? The short answer is that they can't. Only divine aid makes such a choice possible.

At this juncture there needs to be an examination of the three arguments against free will in unrenewed individuals and in favor of their need of the grace that goes before saving grace. The first argument, foundational to the discussion, is that Jesus flatly denied the idea that unrenewed people could choose to follow Him. "No one," He asserted, "can come to me unless the Father who sent me draws him" (John 6:44).[4] Again, "I, when I am lifted up from the earth, will draw all men to myself" (John 12:32). According to Jesus, it is not free will but His grace-filled power that draws individuals to Him. Free-will turning to God is not even a possibility. But why?

---

3. Ellen G. White, *Education* (Mountain View, CA: Pacific Press, 1952), 29.

4. Unless otherwise indicated, all Scripture quotations are taken from the Revised Standard Version of the Bible, copyright © 1946, 1952, and 1971 the Division of Christian Education of the National Council of the Churches of Christ in the United States of America. Used by permission. All rights reserved. Italics in Scripture quotations represent emphasis added by the author.

That question leads to two other biblical reasons against the initiation of salvation through free will. One is, as noted previously, the Bible's teaching on depravity and the enslavement of the human will. Paul puts the matter bluntly when he writes that people are "dead in trespasses and sins" (Eph. 2:1, NKJV). With that passage in mind, one thinker on the topic has suggested that a sinner can no more turn to God than corpses can turn themselves in their graves.[5] Romans 3:9–20 repeatedly drives that thought home when it demonstrates that "no one seeks for God" (v. 11). And Jesus affirms it when He claims that "apart from me you can do nothing" (John 15:5). And those dead in sin cannot understand spiritual things (Rom. 8:7–8; 1 Cor. 2:14), so how could they turn to God? They will remain in that dead condition until God's grace makes them alive (Eph. 2:1–5).

While before the Fall Adam had free will, since that time humans in their unrenewed state have twisted wills that are unable to choose God. John Wesley summarizes the Bible position on the topic succinctly when he writes that "the condition of man after the fall of Adam is such that he cannot turn and prepare himself, by his own natural strength and good works, to faith and calling upon God."[6]

That conclusion leads to another important scriptural reason as to why humans cannot initiate the salvation process by choosing to follow God: salvation is one hundred percent by grace alone from beginning to end. "For by grace you have been saved through faith; and this is not your own doing, it is the gift of God—not because of works, lest any man should boast" (Eph. 2:8–9).

The problem with the idea that sinners can initiate the process of salvation in their lives through free will is that this very teaching not only contradicts Jesus and Paul, but it also makes that free-will choice a work of human merit and gives credit to some humans who have made better choices than others. Thus by a misunderstanding of free will, many have trucked in works righteousness and will indeed have something to boast of throughout all eternity. Yet the Bible gives all the credit for all of salvation to God alone. Salvation is by grace alone. Period. The Bible has no conditional statements that

5. John W. Fletcher, *The Works of the Rev. John Fletcher*, vol. 1, ed. Abraham Scott (London: Thomas Allman, 1836), 229.

6. John Wesley, *The Works of John Wesley*, vol. 5, ed. John Emory (New York: J. Emory and B. Waugh, 1831), 39.

might allow for human free will to initiate the process. "*No one,*" Jesus claims, "can come to me unless the Father who sent me *draws* him" (John 6:44). Ellen White is fully in harmony with that position:

> Many, are confused as to what constitutes the first steps in the work of salvation. Repentance is thought to be a work the sinner must do for himself in order that he may come to Christ. . . . While it is true that repentance must precede forgiveness, . . . yet the sinner cannot bring himself to repentance, or prepare himself to come to Christ. . . . *The very first step to Christ is taken through the drawing of the Spirit of God*; as man responds to this drawing, he advances toward Christ in order that he may repent. Repentance is no less the gift of God than are pardon and justification, and it cannot be experienced except as it is *given* to the soul by Christ.[7]

This genuine theological problem has been solved in two basic ways. The first is absolute predestination, in which the will is basically annihilated as God decrees that some individuals will be saved. The second is that God's grace goes into operation before saving grace, thus restoring free will and giving individuals the possibility of choosing to follow the drawing of Christ. Theologians have given the name of *prevenient grace* to that grace which precedes and prepares the way for saving grace.

THE CHARACTERISTICS OF PREVENIENT GRACE

Before exploring the characteristics of prevenient grace, the term needs to be defined and its relationship to common grace must be examined. The term *prevenient* comes from Latin and means "to come before." In terms of salvation, it comes before everything else in the process of redemption. In relation to Jesus's statement in John 6:44, it can be viewed as the beginning of the process by which Jesus "draws" a person to Himself. As such, it prepares the heart of the non-believer to respond to the good news of salvation in Christ.

H. Orton Wiley offers a helpful definition when he describes prevenient grace in this way:

> . . . that grace which "goes before" or prepares the soul for entrance into the initial state of salvation. It is the preparatory grace of the Holy Spirit

7. Ellen G. White, *Selected Messages* (Washington, DC: Review and Herald, 1958), 1:390–391, emphasis added.

exercised toward man helpless in sin. As it respects the guilty, it may be considered mercy; as it respects the impotent, it is enabling power. It may be defined, therefore, as that manifestation of the divine influence which precedes the full regenerate life.[8]

Thomas Oden's definition is also insightful and helps fill out the picture. Prevenient grace, he writes, "antecedes human responsiveness so as to prepare the soul for the effective hearing of the redeeming Word. This preceding grace draws persons closer to God, lessens their blindness to divine remedies, strengthens their will to accept revealed truth, and enables repentance. Only when sinners are assisted by prevenient grace can they begin to yield their hearts to cooperation with subsequent forms of grace."[9]

It should be noted that *prevenient grace* is not a biblical term. On the other hand, it is a scriptural concept that is consistently evident in the biblical presentation of salvation. Examples are found in John 6:44 and 12:32, in which Jesus makes clear the limitations of human ability and speaks of His drawing power; John 1:9, which speaks of Jesus enlightening every person coming into the world; and Romans 2:12–14, which presents God's work in the hearts of pagans.

Another preliminary topic in the discussion is the relationship of prevenient grace to common grace. Common grace is defined by Millard Erickson as "grace extended to all persons through God's general providence" in such things as "his provision of sunshine and rain for everyone."[10] Common grace provides for not only God's sustaining of a sinful world but also furnishes the theological foundation for an awareness of God and consciousness of right and wrong, even for secular people (Rom. 1:19—2:15), and for civil justice in secular societies in spite of human depravity.

Still, those in the Arminian/Wesleyan theological tradition "did not believe common grace alone was sufficient for willing the good." Rather, Roger Olson points out, "a special infusion of supernatural grace is

---

8. H. Orton Wiley, *Christian Theology* (Kansas City, MO: Beacon Hill Press of Kansas City, 1952), 2:345–346.

9. Oden, *Transforming Power of Grace*, 47.

10. Millard J. Erickson, *The Concise Dictionary of Christian Theology* (Grand Rapids: Baker, 1986), 69.

required for even the first exercise of a good will toward God."[11] That special infusion is prevenient grace.

But what is prevenient grace? What are its general characteristics?. A first is that it is universal. Just as the results of Adam's sin are universal, so in the justice of God is the gift of prevenient grace through the Holy Spirit a universal gift to every person. Thus just as Christ died "as a ransom for *all*" (1 Tim. 2:6), so also "the grace of God has appeared for the salvation of *all* men" (Titus 2:11). It was with that universal perspective in mind that Christ claimed that "when I am lifted up from the earth," I "will draw *all* men to myself" (John 12:32). And John 3:16 proclaims that "God so loved the world that he gave his only Son," so "that *whoever* believes in him should not perish but have eternal life." "All" and "whoever" include everyone who has ever been born and not merely those who were fortunate to be born in a Christian nation or near a mission station. Christ is the "true light" who "enlightens *every* man" (John 1:9, NASB).

Adventist author Ellen White recognized the universal nature of the grace that comes before saving grace when she wrote that "wherever there is an impulse of love" that "reaches out to bless and uplift others, there is revealed the working of God's Holy Spirit. In the depths of heathenism, men who have had no knowledge of the written law of God, who have never even heard the name of Christ," have performed actions demonstrating "the working of a divine power. The Holy Spirit has implanted the grace of Christ in the heart of the savage." She goes on to point out that the "'Light which lighteth every man that comes into the world' (John 1:9), is shining in his soul; and this light, if heeded, will guide his feet to the kingdom of God."[12] The universal gift of prevenient grace is a fact of God's justice in His desire that not "any should perish, but that all should reach repentance" (2 Pet. 3:9).

One of the unfortunate aspects of Christian history is that some have confused universal prevenient grace with universal justification. The first is a scriptural teaching but the second is not.

A second major characteristic of prevenient grace is that it is irresistible grace even though its work in the human heart can be resisted. It is

11. Roger E. Olson, *Arminian Theology: Myths and Realities* (Downers Grove, IL: InterVarsity Press, 2006), 42.

12. Ellen G. White, *Christ's Object Lessons* (Washington, DC: Review and Herald, 1941), 385; cf. Ellen G. White, *The Desire of Ages* (Mountain View, CA: Pacific Press, 1940), 638.

irresistible because the Holy Spirit works with every person who comes into the world whether that person wants His ministration or not. Still, simply because God provides prevenient grace to each person born into the world does not mean that he or she must respond positively to it. Since one aspect of prevenient grace is the restoration of freedom to choose for or against God, the work of that grace may be resisted (Matt. 23:37; John 5:40; Acts 7:51; Heb. 10:29). Thus while prevenient grace is irresistible, its work in a person's life may be resisted. Wiley notes that a person "may resist it, but he cannot escape it."[13] As a result, prevenient grace provides universal possibility but not universal salvation. It opens the way to saving grace, but that further provision must be accepted or rejected.

That thought brings the discussion full circle—back to the topic of free will. In chapter 8 it was noted that since the Fall the human will has been damaged and has a bent toward evil. In short, unrenewed humans do not have a free will but a will biased toward evil and away from God. On the other hand, the Bible portrays individuals as being free to choose for God or against Him and His ways (Josh. 24:15; Matt. 23:37; John 5:40; 7:17; Rev. 22:17).

It is not difficult to see how people can choose to resist God if their wills are corrupted and bent toward evil. But how is it that they can choose for God? The answer is a "freed will, one which, though initially bound by sin, has been brought by the prevenient grace of the Spirit of Christ to a point where it can respond freely to the divine call."[14] Oden refers to that freed will as "grace-enabled freedom."[15] Adam Clarke, in commenting on Philippians 2:12, highlights the process when he notes that "God gives *power* to will, man wills through that power."[16] With these facts in mind, and with the teaching of the New Testament on the will in view, it should not be said that people who have responded to God have free will, but rather that they have *freed will*, which is the third major characteristic of the work of prevenient grace.

The fourth characteristic is that conversion is the hinge that ties the work of prevenient grace to that of saving grace. When reacted to positively, prevenient grace results in saving grace. Grace clearly has a progressive nature:

---

13. Wiley, *Christian Theology*, 2:355.

14. Olson, *Arminian Theology*, 164.

15. Oden, *Transforming Power*, 95.

16. Adam Clarke, *The New Testament of Our Lord and Saviour Jesus Christ* (New York: Abingdon, n.d.), 2:497.

Prevenient grace is the stage of grace that enables a positive response to God, but it does not forgive sin or save. Rather, it leads to the conviction of sin and enables faith to develop, but it does not compel a faith response. However, it does position a person to make a positive faith choice for God through the freed will. It is at that point that grace progresses to saving faith in terms of justification, sanctification, and eventual glorification. In the process freed will comes to act as free will in making spiritual decisions and choosing to cooperate with God, who is active in the life "both to will and to work for his good pleasure" (Phil. 2:13). Or as Oden phrases it, "prevenient grace is the grace that begins to enable one to choose further to cooperate with saving grace," it is "that grace that helps us to receive more grace."[17]

Finally, prevenient grace is responsible grace, because it positions a person to make a faith choice for God, which leads to ongoing responsibility throughout a person's post-conversion life. The alternative, of course, is the predestination understanding of the fallen will which places all of the responsibility and choice upon God and theoretically could lead to a passive Christianity that sees no compulsion to choose to continue to live according to God's will. From the perspective of prevenient grace, the power for responsible choices and living exists from the dawn of moral life. Those choices move right into the post-conversion life as individuals live in line with saving grace.

THE FUNCTION OF PREVENIENT GRACE AS THE HOLY SPIRIT OPENS UP THE POSSIBILITY OF CONVERSION

Roger Olson highlights the various functions—or what might be thought of as sub-graces—when he writes that "prevenient grace is simply the convicting, calling, enlightening and enabling grace of God that goes before conversion and makes repentance and faith possible."[18] The Bible presents the Holy Spirit as the active agent in each of those processes, drawing human beings toward God and conversion.

---

17. Thomas C. Oden, *John Wesley's Scriptural Christianity: A Plain Exposition of His Teaching on Christian Doctrine* (Grand Rapids, MI: Zondervan, 1994), 243–244.

18. Olson, *Arminian Theology,* 35.

In regard to conviction, Jesus told His disciples shortly before His crucifixion that He would send the Spirit who "will convict the world concerning sin and righteousness and judgment" (John 16:8). A part of that convicting process is to bring individuals to an awareness of their personal sinful status. That function is absolutely crucial in the process of conversion, since without an awareness of personal sinfulness, people will feel no need for something better. Conviction of sin, and the accompanying hope for a fuller life, leads to confession and desire for that life.

A second function of prevenient grace is the calling of people by the Spirit, a process identified by some as "summoning grace."[19] At its most nebulous and universal level, this calling is what Jesus refers to as His drawing of all people to Himself (John 6:44; 12:32). At a more concrete and specific level, this calling function of the Spirit is directly related to the Word of God and the preaching of the good news of salvation in Christ. In that vein Paul can write to the Thessalonians that God "called you through our gospel" (2 Thess. 2:14). That same relationship between the Spirit and the human agent in calling is also illustrated in 2 Corinthians 5:20, in which Paul writes: "We are ambassadors for Christ, God making his appeal through us." Because of the calling effect of prevenient grace, Christians are defined as those who God "called out of darkness into his marvelous light" (1 Pet. 2:9).

A third function of the Holy Spirit in prevenient grace is enlightenment, or illumination, of the minds of individuals so that they can better see the truth of God. The importance of enlightenment in the calling/convicting process that leads to conversion becomes evident in light of the fact that unspiritual persons cannot grasp spiritual truth (1 Cor. 2:14). Part of the difficulty is that "the god of this world has blinded the minds of the unbelievers, to keep them from seeing the light of the gospel of the glory of Christ" (2 Cor. 4:4). Thus if clear understanding is to be developed, it must be at God's initiative.

Illumination, it should be noted, comes on two levels. At its broadest level it is through that general revelation that God has given to all people in the natural world (Rom. 1:19–20). On a narrower front it refers to the added advantage of special revelation provided by God in scripture (2 Tim. 3:15–17). The Spirit works through both of these agencies in His work of illumination. Thus every individual has some witness to God when it comes to the drawing work of prevenient grace.

---

19. Oden, *Transforming Power*, 49.

A fourth function of prevenient grace is to enable sinners to respond to God's call. It is one thing to hear the truth, to be convicted, and to feel the call of God, but without the power to respond, it is all for naught. It is the energizing power of the Holy Spirit that makes repentance and faith possible. Because of the bondage of the will and human enslavement to sin (Rom. 6:12–16), people lack the necessary power to respond to God's call. Sinners must be enabled if they are to respond to God's drawing and conviction.

Stanley Grenz illustrates the dynamics in the enabling process when he writes that "whereas the primary focus of the Spirit's illuminating work is the mind, he directs enablement toward the human will. The task of the Spirit is to woo and strengthen the will, in order that the individual both desires and is able to respond to God's call."[20] Other descriptions of the enabling process state that "grace works to enable the will to will the good"[21] and "it breaks the bondage of the will to sin and frees the human will to decide against sin and submit to God."[22]

While prevenient grace is not the stage of grace which forgives sin or saves, it is the stage that enables the will to respond to God's call so that people can be saved. The end result is that the good news is at every stage of the salvation process. It is "the power of God for salvation" (Rom. 1:16) that leads men and women who have responded to the Spirit's work of convicting, calling, illumination, and enabling the will to choose the way of faith. Thus faith is the proper response of the sinner to prevenient grace, but even that faith must be viewed as a gift of the Spirit. That faith choice leads to the new birth (John 3:3, 5) which is of itself a divine experience, rather than natural, as God provides "power" for individuals "to become children of God" (John 1:12–13).

RESULTING BENEFITS OF PREVENIENT GRACE

Beyond exploring the major work accomplished in humans through prevenient grace, it is important to appreciate some of its theological "side benefits." A first is that it helps people make sense of Bible teachings that are

---

20. Stanley J. Grenz, *Theology for the Community of God* (Nashville, TN: Broadman & Holman, 1994), 541.

21. Oden, *Transforming Power*, 95.

22. Olson, *Arminian Theology*, 172.

problematic or seem contradictory. Thus it is that prevenient grace helps people make sense of both divine sovereignty and human freedom.[23] Without an understanding of prevenient grace, a person is forced to choose between those two concepts, predestination (i.e., human will has no part) on one hand, or Pelagianism (i.e., works) on the other. Kenneth Collins highlights the fact that the doctrine of prevenient grace helps people "to hold together, without any contradiction, the four motifs of total depravity, salvation by grace, human responsibility, and the offer of salvation to all."[24] That is quite an accomplishment—one quite beyond alternative theological approaches to those biblical teachings.

A second theological benefit of prevenient grace is that it provides a logical understanding for the justice of God. Its teaching that God is drawing all to Him through His grace presents a God who loves all of His created beings, not just some of them. Those opting for the predestinarian alternative are stuck with an inescapable dilemma—namely, "if salvation is in no way conditioned by human response, then why does God not save all?"[25] How just is a God who condemns eternally a portion of the population who had no ability to respond to divine truth or, alternately, lived too far away from Christianity to hear the gospel message preached?

A third theological benefit of prevenient grace, one closely related to the justice of God, is that it uplifts the kinds of human responsibility taught in the Bible. In contrast to the temptation to passivity and antinomianism (i.e., lawlessness) encouraged by predestination or other theologies that imply that it doesn't make any difference how people live because God makes all the important decisions unilaterally, the doctrine of prevenient grace reflects the biblical position that every human being is responsible to God at some level for the choices he or she makes. It is only in line with such an understanding of human responsibility that God could possibly be viewed as a just judge.

---

23. See Thomas A. Langford, *Practical Divinity: Theology in the Wesleyan Tradition*, rev. ed. (Nashville, TN: Abingdon, 1998), 1:28.

24. Kenneth J. Collins, *The Scripture Way of Salvation: The Heart of John Wesley's Theology* (Nashville, TN: Abingdon, 1997), 45.

25. John B. Cobb, Jr., *Grace and Responsibility: A Wesleyan Theology for Today* (Nashville, TN: Abingdon, 1995), 36.

ADVENTISM AND PREVENIENT GRACE

Prevenient grace stands at the heart of Seventh-day Adventist theology, even though most church members probably have never heard the term before reading this book and even though the majority of them have an inadequate view of free will. Adventist concerns with the justice of God, human responsibility, and the tension between the sovereignty of God and the importance of human response make insights related to prevenient grace important to the denomination.

Adventism's current statement of fundamental beliefs reflects both depravity and prevenient grace even though neither term is used. Article 7 notes that Adam's "descendants share" his "fallen nature and its consequences. They are born with weaknesses and tendencies to evil."[26] That statement implicitly sets forth the effects of sin as pollution, depravity, and spiritual inability (see chapter 8) even though they are not defined explicitly using that terminology.

In a similar manner, the core ideas of prevenient grace are set forth in article 5, on the Holy Spirit, even though the terminology is missing. The key sentence is "He draws and convicts human beings; and those who respond He renews and transforms into the image of God." Article 10, on the experience of salvation, also reflects a definite understanding of prevenient grace: "Led by the Holy Spirit we sense our need, acknowledge our sinfulness, repent of our transgressions, and exercise faith in Jesus. . . . This faith which receives salvation comes through the divine power of the Word and is the gift of God's grace."

Some twentieth-century Adventist theologians presented clear understandings of prevenient grace and a few even used the phrase itself,[27] but by and large they were clearer on depravity and inability than they were on the

---

26. All editions of the *Seventh-day Adventist Church Manual* and the denomination's *Yearbook* since 1980 contain a complete copy of the current statement of the church's "fundamental beliefs."

27. Irwin Henry Evans, *This Is the Way: Meditations Concerning Justification by Faith and Growth in Christian Graces* (Washington, DC: Review and Herald, 1939); Edward W. H. Vick, *Let Me Assure You of Grace, of Faith, of Forgiveness, of Freedom, of Fellowship, of Hope* (Mountain View, CA: Pacific Press, 1968); Hans K. LaRondelle, *Christ Our Salvation: What God Does for Us and in Us* (Mountain View, CA: Pacific Press, 1980); George R. Knight, *Sin and Salvation: God's Work for Us and in Us* (Hagerstown, MD: Review and Herald, 2008).

initial starting point of salvation. For many there was confusion regarding free will being the point of origin, since they had demonstrated the fallenness of that very will.[28]

The clearest writer on the topic for most of the denomination's history has been Ellen White. She was quite explicit on both depravity and spiritual inability and prevenient grace, even though she never used those specific terms. Regarding the effects of sin, she states that "through sin the whole human organism is deranged, the mind is perverted, the imagination corrupted. Sin has degraded the faculties of the soul."[29]

With her explicit understanding of the corrupting effects of sin, it is not surprising that she also held a well-defined view of prevenient grace. Consider her statement that "many are confused as to what constitutes the first steps in the work of salvation." She went on to note that "the very first step to Christ is taken through the drawing of the Spirit of God; as man responds to this drawing, he advances toward Christ in order that he may repent."[30]

Another very explicit statement on spiritual inability and prevenient grace is found in *Steps to Christ*, in which she notes:

> . . . it is impossible for us, of ourselves, to escape from the pit of sin. . . . Our hearts are evil, and we cannot change them. . . . Education, culture, the exercise of the will, human effort, all have their proper sphere, but here they are powerless. They may produce an outward correctness of behavior, but they cannot change the heart. . . . There must be a power working from within, a new life from above, before men can be changed from sin to holiness. That power is Christ. His grace alone can quicken the lifeless faculties of the soul, and attract it to God, to holiness.[31]

That is about as clear a statement as could be desired when contemplating an Adventist understanding of the grace that comes before saving grace.

---

28. George R. Knight, "Seventh-day Adventism, Semi-Pelagianism, and Overlooked Topics in Adventist Soteriology: Moving beyond Missing Links and toward a More Explicit Understanding" (paper, Arminian and Adventism Symposium, Andrews University, October 2010).

29. Ellen G. White, *The Ministry of Healing* (Mountain View, CA: Pacific Press, 1942), 451; see also Woodrow W. Whidden II, *Ellen White on Salvation: A Chronological Study* (Hagerstown, MD: Review and Herald, 1995), 41–46.

30. White, *Selected Messages*, 1:390.

31. Ellen G. White, *Steps to Christ* (Mountain View, CA: Pacific Press, n.d.), 18.

CHAPTER 15

THE GRACE THAT JUSTIFIES AND SANCTIFIES

Ivan T. Blazen

The words *justification* and *sanctification* find their fullest conceptual development in the writings of the Apostle Paul. Therefore this chapter will focus upon Paul's presentation of these two themes.[1]

THE MEANING OF JUSTIFICATION

At the outset it is important to note the relationship between the terms *justification* and *righteousness*. They seem to be two different words, but in the language of the New Testament, they are basically the same word based on the same Greek stem which in English means "right." *Justification* could better have been translated as "rightification." Consequently, it is important to understand that to *justify* means "to bestow righteousness," and to *grant righteousness* means "to justify."

Forensic Background and Relational Foreground

Justification is a forensic word, which indicates that it is to be understood in terms of the pronouncement which a judge renders in a courtroom

---

1. Unless otherwise indicated, all Scripture quotations are taken from the New Revised Standard Version Bible, copyright © 1989 the Division of Christian Education of the National Council of the Churches of Christ in the United States of America. Used by permission. All rights reserved. Italics in Scripture reflect emphasis added by author.

proceeding. If the judge finds against the accused, the verdict is one of condemnation, but if the judge finds for the accused, a verdict of acquittal (justification) is rendered. In other words, guilt or innocence is established by the findings and pronouncement of a judge. Thus, justification has a declarative sense in which the defendant is not made right but is pronounced right.

This forensic usage is the primary background for the New Testament teaching on justification. However, the forensic character of justification, while vital to the biblical understanding of the term, does not exhaust Scripture's teaching. Particularly in the New Testament, court judgments and relationships are translated into the higher key of forgiving grace and personal relationship with God, and the concept of God as Judge is exceeded, though not superseded, by the idea of God as Father. In other words, the forensic meaning of justification flows into the theology of the inexhaustible and super-abounding riches of God's gift of grace in Christ. It is this that establishes an altogether new and right relationship between God and humanity.

The Righteousness of God

To speak of a right relationship with God is to speak of God's righteousness. Paul's letter to the Romans, with important support from Galatians and Philippians, is Scripture's most salient source for understanding God's righteousness and the justification it brings. Paul's initial approach to the topic begins in Romans 1:16–17. Here he presents the thesis which he will pursue in the rest of the letter. He declares that the Gospel—the proclamation of God's Son as Messiah (Savior) and Lord (1:3)—powerfully leads to salvation. It does so because the gospel is the locus for the revelation of God's righteousness. This revelation is absolutely essential if humans are to be saved from their unrighteousness and God's just wrath upon it.

Paul paints a sordid picture of the depths of human sin in Romans 1:18—3:20. Here are the primal sin of Gentile idolatry as it flows into immorality (1:18–32) and the Jewish sin of judgmentalism upon Gentiles being accompanied by hypocrisy (2:1). Thus, whether it be the Jew who has the written law or the Gentile who has the inner law of conscience, all have sinned (2:12–15; 3:9). Consequently, no one escapes sin's clutches, and the law, though giving the knowledge of sin, cannot deliver from it and bring justification (3:19–20).

In Romans 3:21, which picks up the theme of 1:16–17, an entirely new dimension is brought to view, introduced by the revolutionary word *but*. The whole world stands guilty before the judgment seat of God and awaits execution (3:19–20) . . . *"but."* Clearly a revolution and reversal of the human situation is signaled here, for the word *but* turns things the opposite way. The human *but* often changes hope into despair, but the divine *but* transposes despair into hope. In place of human unrighteousness (3:19) comes the restorative righteousness of God which is appropriated solely by faith (3:22; cf. 1:17), and by which God saves guilty humankind from His just wrath.

What is meant by the righteousness of God, then, is not a static state of rightness in God, but God's covenant faithfulness in action for the salvation of God's people. This comports with a significant class of Old Testament texts, particularly in Isaiah and the Psalms, where God's righteousness, sometimes translated as "deliverance," or "vindication," is synonymous with His salvation. This can be seen clearly, for example, in Isaiah 46:13: "I bring near my deliverance [righteousness] . . . and my salvation will not tarry." Verses of the same import in Isaiah are 51:5; 54:8; 56:1; 59:16; 61:10. God Himself is spoken of as One "announcing vindication [righteousness], mighty to save" (Isa. 63:1). Indeed, God is "a righteous God and a Savior" (45:21; also Pss. 31:1; 40:10; 51:4; 71:15; 98:2; 143:11).

There are a number of facets in God's bestowal of His saving righteousness and justification of sinners. These may be enumerated as follows.

Justification as Acquittal

Directly related to the forensic or juridical background of justification is the concept of acquittal, the opposite of which is condemnation. This contrasting word pair is found in Deuteronomy 25:1; Proverbs 17:15; Matthew 12:37; Romans 5:16, 18; 8:33–34; and 2 Corinthians 3:9. Thus, in justification, God saves sinners from condemnation for their sins (Rom. 8:1) by acquitting them at the bar of divine justice.

Justification as the Reckoning of Righteousness

The most important passage for defining the meaning of justification is Romans 4. Here Abraham, who in the Jewish tradition of Paul's day was thought to be a paragon of virtue and a man of perfection,[2] is brought forth as an illustration of what Christianity's forefather according to the flesh found, and what the rest of humanity, the ungodly, may find as well (4:1, 22–24). In Jewish thought, as echoed in the first part of verse 2, it was believed that Abraham was justified by his works, the inference being that he had a boast. Paul demolishes this view at the end of verse 2 by making it clear that Abraham could not boast before God, which renders all boasting empty. The corollary of this is that justification cannot be by works. Thus, Romans 4:2 shows what Abraham did not find, while verse 3, quoting Genesis 15:6, describes what he did find. He found that his faith, engendered by God's promise, "was reckoned to him as righteousness." This means that justification, which from one standpoint is acquittal, may from another be understood as the reckoning of righteousness. This reckoning, counting, or imputing of righteousness occurred when Abraham believed God.

Observation of the line of argument from Genesis 15:1 to 15:6 is instructive. Three major stages emerge: the divine promise of blessing, the human response of faith, and the divine pronouncement of righteousness. In other words, when God confronts humankind with His Word of grace, and humans accept it in faith, God's verdict goes forth: "Your faith is reckoned as righteousness," that is, "Your faith is pronounced to be a right response to My grace and indicative of a right relationship with Me." A right standing with God results from the cause-effect interaction between promise and faith. The promise elicits faith, and faith receives the promise. Paul's argument in Romans 4:3 is that if there is a divine *reckoning* of righteousness, such righteousness can never be considered as humanity's achievement, but only as God's grace. This is clarified in Romans 4:4–5. Verse 4 indicates how things operate on the human level: people work and get wages, not grace, for it. Verse 5, on the other hand, indicates how things operate on the divine level: by abandoning working for righteousness in favor of trusting (having faith in) the God who justifies the ungodly, this trust or faith is reckoned as righteousness.

To speak of the ungodly as being justified or reckoned as righteous was a radical, indeed a shocking, statement. To Paul's Jewish contemporaries it seemed supportive of ungodliness—hence the charges against Paul in

---

2. C. K. Barrett, *The Epistle to the Romans*, rev. ed., Black's New Testament Commentary (London: A & C Black, 1991), 82.

Romans 3:8; 6:1; and 6:15—and directly contrary to the Hebrew Scriptures, which say that God will not acquit the wicked (Exod. 23:7) and that those who justify the wicked or condemn the righteous are an abomination to God (Prov. 17:15; cf. Isa. 5:23). In this world of thought God pronounces only the just to be just (cf. 1 Kings 8:32).

What answer can be given to the apparent ethical dilemma Paul's words pose? According to the Psalms, God Himself is justified in His condemnation of evil (Ps. 51:4). What justifies God, then, in justifying the ungodly rather than the godly? The Psalmist further pleaded: "Do not enter into judgment with your servant, for no one living is righteous before you" (143:2). Thus, for the Psalmist, God's judgment upon the unrighteous could only be "Guilty!" However, in Paul's use of the forensic terms *righteousness* and *justification,* he teaches that God *does* enter into judgment with His unrighteous people and, incredibly, the verdict is not "Guilty!" but "Righteous!" What justifies this seeming contradiction? First, it must be remembered that Paul taught that "all, both Jews and Greeks, are under the power of sin" (Rom. 3:9). Thus, if anyone were to be justified, it would have to be from among the ungodly. Second, Paul did not teach merely that God justified the ungodly, but that God justified the ungodly *who placed their faith and trust in Him* (4:5). These are people who have repentantly responded "Yes!" to God's verdict upon them as sinners and have cast themselves upon the mercy of God. This is already a new alignment with God, a saying "Amen!" to God. To have faith is, indeed, the right response to God. Third, the faith these people have is in the atoning sacrifice which God has provided as the means of justification (3:24–25).

Justification as Divine Forgiveness

In Romans 4:6–8 Paul gets to the heart of the matter. After discussing Abraham and a prominent text, Genesis 15:6, now he turns to David and another prominent text, Psalm 32:1–2. It was an Old Testament dictum that an important testimonial was to be established by at least two witnesses (Deut. 17:6), so Paul presents Abraham and David. Further, Paul had proffered his belief that the law and the prophets witness to righteousness by faith (Rom. 3:21), so he presents Abraham as the witness of the law and David as the witness of the prophets (i.e., from the rest of the Old Testament). What Paul, in effect, does is to use the testimony of David to explain more fully the meaning of the reckoning of righteousness to Abraham. The basis on which Paul did this was by applying the second of Rabbi Hillel's seven rules of biblical interpretation, *gezerah shawah,* which deals with equivalent expressions.[3] According to this principle, a word or phrase found in one text of Scripture could be explained by the meaning it bears in another biblical text. Since the word *reckon* appears not only in Genesis 15:6 but also in Psalm 32:1–2, considered as a unit of thought, Paul uses the latter text from Psalms, with its threefold parallelism, to illumine the former text from Genesis. When this is done, the inner meaning of justification or the reckoning of righteousness unfolds. *Justification* comes to mean the forgiveness of sin or, what amounts to the same thing, the covering of sin or its *non*reckoning to the believer. Guilt is gone, sin is covered so that it does not appear for judgment, and all charges are dropped. The latter member of this triad of ideas which explain the content of justification finds a meaningful echo in 2 Corinthians 5:19: "in Christ God was [at the cross] reconciling the world to himself, not counting their trespasses against them." Thus, through one nuance or another, forgiveness lies at the heart of justification. In harmony with this, Ellen White says: "Pardon and justification are one and the same thing."[4]

Justification as Eschatological Life and New Creation

There is a further ingredient in the meaning of *justification* which is also found in Romans 4. *Justification* not only refers to the reckoning of righteousness but also to the bestowal of eternal life. Paul mentions this in a pungent phrase in Romans 5:18, where he speaks of "one man's act of righteousness" (the cross) as leading to "justification and life." This translation could equally as well and, perhaps better, be rendered "lifegiving justification" or "justification which issues in life." Thus, justification brings not only pardon but life. In Romans 4:17 this is seen with utter clarity. Paul speaks here of Abraham standing "in the presence of the God . . . who gives life to the dead and calls into existence the things which do not exist." Paul here utilizes two great realities of Scripture to explain the fullness of

---

3. Herman L. Strack, *Introduction to the Talmud and Midrash* (Philadelphia, PA: The Jewish Publication Society of America, 1931), 93–94.

4. Ellen G. White, Ms 21, 1891.

justification: *Creation*—God calls into existence the things which do not exist—and *Resurrection*—God gives life to the dead. In other words, justification is a new creation in which the power of God is present to bring life to those who are spiritually dead. Second Corinthians 5:17 affirms: "If anyone is in Christ, there is a new creation: everything old has passed away; see, everything has become new!" Galatians 6:15 comports with this when, in a letter in which justification is the main theme, Paul says that circumcision and uncircumcision count for nothing, but what really counts is a new creation. This is in line with Paul's rabbinic background according to which when a Gentile was converted to Judaism, that Gentile was considered to be a "new creature" through the forgiveness of sins.[5] The concept of newness is found in Romans 6:4 which speaks of one who has been united to Christ as walking in "newness of life," a reference to the eschatological life of the age to come manifesting itself in present existence.

In terms of Romans 4, justification, while having a legal setting in the pronouncement of a judge, goes beyond it by speaking of the believer's personal relationship to God who both forgives his or her sin (judges do not forgive sin) and, as Creator, makes him or her a new creature in whom eternal life is already present.

Justification as Exchange of Lordships

Another component, without which the full implications of justification will not be seen, is found in Romans 6. Often this chapter is thought to deal primarily with the subject of sanctification as a reality following after justification. To be sure, sanctification as both a word (vv. 19, 22) and a concept (vv. 2, 4, 6, 13, 17–19, 22) is present in the chapter. However, these references must be seen in the light of the purpose for which Romans 6 was written in the context of Paul's argument. The occasion for the chapter was the misunderstanding of Paul's teaching on justification by faith alone apart from the law (Rom. 3:21—4:25). That teaching had been misconceived to mean that believers could justifiably perform

---

5. Joachim Jeremias, *Infant Baptism in the First Four Centuries*, trans. David Cairns (London: SCM Press, 1960), 33, 36; W. D. Davies, *Paul and Rabbinic Judaism: Some Rabbinic Elements in Pauline Theology*, 2nd ed. (London: SPCK, 1955), 119; Arthur Darby Nock, *Early Gentile Christianity and Its Hellenistic Background*, Harper Torchbooks (New York: Harper and Row, 1964), 64.

evil that good may come (3:8), which meant that Christians could continue in sin so that grace might abound (6:1). This was an erroneous deduction from Paul's teaching that when the law came in at Sinai, far from sin being abated, trespasses abounded, only to be met by the super-abounding of grace (5:20). Some of Jewish background thought that such a construction was tantamount not only to the justification of the ungodly, but also to the justification of ungodliness. To quash this view, Paul wrote Romans 6. His primary argument in clarification of his teaching is that in the life of believers there has occurred a transfer or exchange of lordships. Sin *used to be* lord (vv. 17, 20), but as a result of baptism *into* Christ and His death (vv. 3–4), death to sin's lordship occurs, and the lordship of Christ begins. In the forensic language of Romans 8:3, Christ judicially condemned sin in the flesh, and thus sin has lost its case in court and is thereby deprived of authority over, or custody of, the life of the Christian. In other words, *freedom* from sin as lord is the result of union with Christ. It is remarkable and illuminating that the Greek word employed in Romans 6:7 to state that freedom from sin's reign has taken place is the word ordinarily meaning "to justify." This word, when used with the preposition *from* means, in the passive voice, "being freed from," as in Acts 13:39. In a parallel construction in Romans 6:18, 22, the Greek verb "to free" is used in the passive voice with *from* to indicate freedom from sin's slavery. There can be no question that for Paul justification, in addition to forgiveness of sins, involves liberation from the old lordship of sin. This newfound liberty is the root out of which the fruit of sanctification, spoken of in Romans 6, emerges. Justification is a far more powerful reality than a mere legal adjustment in the books of heaven. It is a dethroning of that illegitimate authority which prevents a sanctified life and the establishment of that divine authority which enables it. The rest of this chapter will focus on sanctification as a result, or fruit, of justification.

THE MEANING OF SANCTIFICATION

Sanctification, or holiness, in one form or another, is one of the most significant and frequent (more than one thousand occurrences) concepts referred to in Scripture. So crucial is the matter that believers are admonished to strive for "the holiness without which no one will see the Lord" (Heb. 12:14).

Sanctification is grounded in the Christological reality of Christ as both Savior and Lord. As Christ's Saviorhood can never be severed from His lordship, so salvation as gift can never be severed from salvation as claim; grace and faith can never be separated from works or fruit; life from Christ can never be divided from living for Christ; and justification can never be disconnected from sanctification. In what follows, sanctification will be discussed in terms of its two major components: the relational and the moral.

A New Relationship and Status

Sanctification, like *justification,* is a relational word. Its basic meaning has to do with being set apart or separated. This is illustrated by the seventh day which God set apart from the rest of the week to be His special day (Gen. 2:3; Exod. 20:8–11). In this relational sense, the word *sanctification,* as applied to humankind, is not first of all a matter or morals but of belonging to God as one consecrated or separated for Him. God's call to holiness is well expressed in Leviticus 19:2: "You shall be holy, for I the LORD your God am holy." God's holiness means that He is "Wholly Other," totally unique and transcendent. God is holy in and of Himself, so that He can be called the "Holy One" (Isa. 10:17; Hos. 11:9) to whom the Seraphim cry "Holy, holy, holy is the LORD of hosts" (Isa. 6:3). God's people are holy or sanctified only in a derivative sense, holy by virtue of a relation to Him. By His own action God has consecrated them to Himself.

It is in this context that 1 Corinthians 1:2 is to be understood. Notwithstanding the many serious moral and theological problems the Corinthians had, Paul still addresses them as "those who are sanctified in Christ Jesus, called to be saints." The perfect tense in Greek which is used here in "sanctified" points to a completed action in the past which has continuing results in the present. The Corinthians already have been sanctified or set apart as His people by the consecrating power of His call. This is not sanctification in the ethical, but in the relational sense. While sanctification in the moral sense is the work of a lifetime,[6] sanctification in the relational sense, whereby believers become God's property and part of His people, is, like justification, the work of a moment. This is corroborated by 1 Corinthians 6:11, which

---

6. Ellen G. White, *Acts of the Apostles* (Mountain View, CA: Pacific Press, 1911), 560–61.

places washing, sanctification, and justification alike in the past as the product of the activity of the Lord Jesus Christ and the Spirit of God—for which reason each verb is in the passive voice, the so-called divine passive. The fact that sanctification can be coupled with justification, itself a relational term, as a past event and even listed before justification shows that both sanctification, in the relational sense, as well as justification, itself a relational term, are twin roots of moral growth.

In the sense discussed so far sanctification refers to God's setting apart of a people to belong to Himself. The note of being the people of God is also found in 1 Corinthians 1:2 where, following the statement that the Corinthians have been sanctified, it is said that they were "called to be saints." Here "to be" is not in the Greek text and, while appropriate to use in English, should not be understood as referring to a status which will take place sometime in the indefinite future. By virtue of the fact that the Corinthians were already sanctified, they were already saints. The same root is used in Greek for both *sanctification* and *saint*. It is because people belong to Jesus Christ (i.e., are sanctified in Him)—that they can be called saints. That is why Paul addresses his letters to the saints. They have become such by God's action in sanctifying or setting them apart. The term *saints,* then, which almost always occurs in the plural, means "the people of God," or "God's own people."

Moral Growth in Goodness

Out of the root of sanctification as *belonging* emerges sanctification as *becoming.* The former, as the "already" of God's consecrating activity, leads to the "not yet" of God's transforming activity (2 Cor. 3:18). The former has previously been completed; the latter continues on. Heaven itself will be a ceaseless approaching unto God.[7]

One of the most important passages of scripture for sanctification as moral change is Romans 6. In this chapter Paul affirms that the Christian, as one who has died to sin as lord, no longer lives under its domination (vv. 2, 14). With the crucifixion of the old self, sin's possessive power over the body has been broken so that the believer need no longer render slavish service to sin (v. 6). This definitive death is symbolized by the rite of baptism.

---

7. Ellen G. White, *The Desire of Ages* (Mountain View, CA: Pacific Press, 1898), 331–332.

Baptism not only represents a Christian's commitment to Christ, accepting Him as his or her new Lord. It is also a sign of the believer's unification with those main soteriological events by which complete redemption has been acquired, namely, Christ's death and resurrection (vv. 3–4). In consequence of the believer's union with the crucified and risen Lord, he or she is to (1) walk in newness of life (v. 4); (2) not let sin reign in his or her mortal body (v. 12); and (3) yield his or her members to God as instruments or weapons of righteousness rather than to sin as instruments or weapons of wickedness (v. 13).

As to the first of these, newness of life is a reference to the eschatological life of the age to come. The Christian has been grasped by this life, and his or her life-walk in this world is to be transformed thereby.

Thus, the believer's participation in the realities of the age to come is manifested and attested by the way he or she walks (i.e., conducts his or her moral life).[8] There is to be a profound contrast between the unconverted and converted person: "For just as you once presented your members to impurity . . . so now present your members as slaves to righteousness for sanctification" (Rom. 6:19). Since believers are not their own because they have been bought with a price, they are empowered to glorify God in their bodies (1 Cor. 6:19–20).

The second consequence of the believer's union with the crucified and risen Lord is that the Christian need not and therefore should not let sin reign in his or her mortal body, to obey the body's continuing desires (Rom. 6:12). Though the old self has been crucified, and sin's kingly hold over the body has been broken (v. 6), the body still belongs to the old aeon—that is why it is called a mortal body (v. 12)—and, thus has continuing desires. These are the avenues through which sin seeks to regain the throne of its former subject. Thus, while the Christian is freed from the reign of sin, he or she is not freed, this side of the resurrection to immortal life, from sin's influence. The only thing which can keep sin from reestablishing its rule is the same thing that ended it in the first place, the grace of God (v. 14). Thus, the Christian is still subject to temptation through the old bodily appetites, but by the grace of God and the Spirit of God, the believer may find victory over appetites becoming life-characterizing deeds of the flesh (Rom. 8:13; Gal. 5:16–25).

---

8. For more on this topic see Ivan T. Blazen, "Salvation" in *Handbook of Seventh-day Adventist Theology,* ed. Raoul Dederen (Hagerstown, MD: Review and Herald, 2000), 297.

In the third place, as Romans 6:13 instructs, believers are asked to yield their bodies and its members to God as instruments or weapons of righteousness instead of to sin as weapons of wickedness. This is the Christian warfare, and it helps to define the implications of death to sin mentioned in 6:2. Death to sin does not mean, even after the exchange of lordships from sin to Christ, that sin has no further relation to the lives of believers. Rather, death to sin means that having been freed from sin as lord, believers are to fight sin as enemy. Having been released from sin's sovereignty, they are to battle sin's solicitation. The Christian has peace with God, but he or she is never again to be at peace with sin, but aggressively hostile to it.

The sanctification of the Christian is one of constant movement forward. The will of God for human life cannot be reduced to any fixed level of attainment. There is no boundary on the ethical commitment to which the gospel calls believers (Phil. 1:27; cf. Eph. 4:1). The reason for this is that Christ is the norm of Christian existence, as Scripture testifies: "For to me living is Christ" (Phil. 1:21). As He loved, forgave, and welcomed sinners, they are to do the same (Rom. 15:7) as His newly adopted children. In other words, what believers have learned of Christ is to determine their behavior (Eph. 4:20). He is the One who illustrates in His own existence the principles of love, humility, and service believers are to emulate because He is Lord (Phil. 2:5–11). When it comes to Christian demeanor, the example of Christ in suffering is to be imitated by His people. They are to "follow in his steps" (1 Pet. 2:21–23).

To consider Christ in this way is to see that there is no ultimately reachable height or depth of the sanctified life, no end to the journey of sanctification. There is fulfillment, but not finality. At whatever stage Christians arrive, there is always further advance to be made. Christians may already be living to please God, but they are to do so "more and more" (1 Thess. 4:1). Even when they have exemplified love itself, the apostolic call is to love "more and more" (4:9–10)—to "increase and abound in love" (3:12). The fundamental reason for the "more" of these texts is not because original sin keeps believers from doing the good, but because of the inexhaustible nature and challenge of Christ's love.

According to Philippians 1:9–11, Christian love is to abound with knowledge and all discernment so that believers may "determine what is best, so that in the day of Christ you may be pure and blameless, having produced the harvest of righteousness that comes through Jesus Christ for the glory and praise of God." This text uncovers an important aspect of sanctification. As the Christian lives in the insight of Christ's love, he or she is to learn the excellent way which meets with God's approval. This concept coheres with that expressed in Romans 12:2: "Do not be conformed to this world, but be transformed by the renewing of your minds, so that you may discern what is the will of God, what is good and acceptable and perfect." Within the framework of the love of Christ transforming the mind, the Christian is called to *discover* or *discern* what God's will is in the varied circumstances of life. According to Ephesians 5:8–10: "For once you were darkness, but now in the Lord you are light." Thus, believers are to "live as children of light—for the fruit of the light is found in all that is good and right and true"—and to "try to find out what is pleasing to the Lord." In other words, the Christian is one who in every situation seeks for the will of God, for what pleases Him. This is not a static standard but a dynamic one which calls us to ever new and increasing sanctified insight and moral fulfillment.

CHAPTER 16

THE GRACE OF CHRISTIAN PERFECTION

Hans K. LaRondelle and Woodrow W. Whidden

Christ explained how the love of the heavenly Father, flowing out impartially to both the good and the evil, is a perfect love that must be imitated or reflected by the true children of God. This New Testament concept of Christian perfection is found in Matthew 5:43–48. Christian perfection implies a personal experience of the saving love of the God of Israel and the manifestation of its sanctifying power in wholehearted love to all who need our help.

CHRISTIAN PERFECTION AS EMBEDDED IN NEW TESTAMENT SOTERIOLOGY

The context of self-sacrificing service to others found in the story of the rich young ruler in Matthew 19:21 lays the foundation for the entire experience of perfecting grace. Perfection, then, is not the striving after ethical ideals or even the endeavor to imitate or copy Christ's life independent of Him, but it is the wholehearted, undivided belonging to Him and living with Him by His saving and sanctifying power. Thus Christian perfection is defined not by one's living according to moral law only but by belonging to and following the living Lord Jesus with a pure heart. All such follow the Lamb wherever He goes (Rev. 14:4).

The very foundation of any Christian experience of perfecting grace includes grace-empowered obedience to the will of God and is experienced in the heart of any disciple that is totally dedicated to the service of Christ and to His human children. Such dedication can only arise out of a heart that

has been led to trust in Christ Jesus as the converting, forgiving, and transforming (sanctifying) Christ. It thus becomes quite apparent that the experience of Christian perfection is woven into the very fabric of the various facets
of every true believer's personal experience of salvation.

For any person who is on the path of conversion, full surrender to
Christ as Lord is the essential, initial step in the process of conscious character change. This includes six subsequent, definitive phases. Included in
these experiences are:

1. Pardon, or forgiveness for all sins, or as it is more technically known,
   justification by faith alone in the imputed merits of Christ;
2. Sanctification by faith in the imparted merits of Christ;
3. Coming to the place in the experience of sanctification where the
   believer is finished with sins of willful premeditation and attitudes
   which are constantly excusing known sins or character defects;
4. The experience of perfection will then reach a stage where there will be
   no compromise with sin and temptation, no matter how severe the test
   may be. In other words, those who receive the "seal of the living God"
   described in Revelation 13 and 14 will be so perfect that they would
   rather die than knowingly disobey any clearly revealed command of
   God;
5. Sinless perfection, in both nature and character will only be fully realized when glorification of the body transpires at the second coming of
   Christ. For the first time in human history, since the Fall, the people of
   God will then be able to say that they are "sinless" in the more absolute
   sense of the word. And then there is the final phase of the redeemed
   experience of Christian perfection;
6. The constant character growth that all of the saved will experience as
   they dynamically grow in the likeness of Christ for all eternity!

Thus what follows will be a brief exposition of each of these varied facets
of what can be called the biblical taxonomy of perfection. The redemption of Christ in its fullness is in the New Testament distinguished by two
aspects or phases, the *present salvation* of justification and sanctification
by faith in Christ on the one hand, and the *future salvation* of glorification at the second advent of Jesus Christ, on the other. Like the concept
of the kingdom of God, so also *perfection* is a present gift and reality;
yet, in another sense, it is a promise to be realized only at the ultimate

establishment of the kingdom of glory. This dual distinction Paul also applies to the concept of believers *as God's children*. In Romans 8:14, he assures the Christians that they have become already "sons [and daughters] of God," since they are led by the Spirit of God. "For those who are led by the Spirit of God are the children of God."[1]

This present redemptive assurance Paul then underlines by stating: "And by him we cry 'Abba, Father.' The Spirit himself testifies with our spirit that we *are* God's children" (vv. 15–16; emphasis added). However, when the apostle proceeds to dwell on the future glory to be revealed to believers, he makes the remarkable statement that "[while we humans have the Spirit of God, we] groan inwardly *as we wait eagerly for adoption to sonship*, the redemption of our bodies" (v. 23; emphasis added).

The relationship of God and the believer as Father and child, therefore, is both a *present reality*, in one real sense, and a *future reality*, in another sense. The difference is determined by the meaning of the two advents of Christ. The same principle applies to the use of perfection with the Apostle Paul. On the one hand, he can say that believers in Christ are *perfect* in Him and may grow up together into one perfect body or spiritually mature manhood and womanhood (Col. 1:28; 3:14; 4:12; Eph. 4:13; 1 Cor. 14:20). On the other hand, Paul stresses that the ultimate perfection *has not yet* arrived and is still future (1 Cor. 13:10). Only at the glory of the second advent will Christ sweep away the imperfect.

Phase 1: Perfection as Justification by Faith Alone

When the believer responds to the drawing power of God's convicting grace and surrenders to the lordship of Christ, such a one is then accepted for the sake of the doing and dying of Christ, and is declared to be perfectly sinless in a legal or forensic sense. This then becomes the effectual foundation of all subsequent experience of character transformation into the likeness of Christ. The key Bible verses are 1 John 1:9 and 2:1–2: "If we confess our sins, he is faithful and just and will forgive us our sins and purify us from all unrighteousness." "But if anyone does sin, we have an

---

1. Unless otherwise indicated, all Scripture quotations are taken from THE HOLY BIBLE, NEW INTERNATIONAL VERSION®, NIV® Copyright © 1973, 1978, 1984, 2011 by Biblica, Inc.® Used by permission. All rights reserved worldwide.

advocate with the Father—Jesus Christ the righteous One. He is the aton-ing sacrifice for our sins, and not for ours only but also for the sins of the whole world." Thus the newly converted believer stands in a new legal rela-tionship to God and the "in Christ" status brings with it the blessing of absolute legal perfection (2 Cor. 5:17–21).

Phase 2: Perfection as the Fruit of Sanctification

Perfection as sanctification includes dynamic growth in the likeness of Christ's character. Paul upheld the human body as a good and holy creation of God, which was to be consecrated to the service of God. In contrast, with those whose "god is their stomach, and . . . [whose] glory is in their shame. Their mind is set on earthly things" (Phil. 3:19), Paul explicitly renounced every self-righteousness or perfection (vv. 8–12). Seeking his righteousness exclusively in Christ, Paul looked forward to his ultimate perfection in the resurrection from the dead (v. 11): "Not that I have already obtained all this, or have already arrived at my goal, but I press on to take hold of that for which Christ Jesus took hold of me" (v. 12).

Philippians 3:12–15 provides one of the clearest definitions of perfec-tion in the New Testament. For those who are pressing toward the goal for the prize of the upward call of God in Christ, the very fact of their progress in reaching out to the prize is called Christian maturity or being perfect: "All of us, then, who are mature (perfect) should take such a view of things" (v. 15). Thus genuine Christian perfection or maturity includes dynamic growth into the likeness of Christ's perfect righteousness. Per-fection as growth in grace has to with the fact that such growth involves a struggle, which strongly suggests that such perfection is not strictly sin-less. Paul had such a close fellowship of heart with the living Christ that he could testify, "For to me, to live is Christ" (Phil. 1:21), and "I have been crucified with Christ; it is no longer I who live, but Christ who lives in me; and the life I now live in the flesh I live by faith in the Son of God, who loved me and gave himself for me" (Gal. 2:20). With this profound testimony the apostle touches upon the inward Christian struggle, which he also knows himself (1 Cor. 9:27), and which he develops more fully in Galatians 5:16–24 and Romans 7:14–25.

Paul did not say that his *I*, his self, was shot to death or was hanged to death, but it had been crucified, which indicates a prolonged dying process.

Although a crucified one was legally dead and exterminated, in actual reality such a one could live on for several days and nights on the cross, but in increasing sufferings and agonies. This illustration may serve to clarify the apostle's message in Galatians 5 and Romans 7. On the one hand, baptized Christians have to consider themselves, by faith in Christ, legally dead to sin and the condemning law of God (Rom. 6:11; 7:4). On the other hand, they discover that the old self is still alive in empirical reality; that the inherited and cultivated tendencies to evil and wrongdoing still send their desires and impulses to the cleansed heart.

It is a significant fact that not one apostolic letter in the New Testament presupposes a sinless church or a Christian life without the abiding battle with self. All the New Testament writings abound with moral exhortations and admonitions to fight the good fight against the flesh, the world, and the powers of darkness. For the baptized believers, however, there is no despair or defeat necessary in this battle. Christ dwells in their hearts and gives the victory (1 Cor. 15:57). The believers are called to be "strong in the Lord and in his mighty power" (Eph. 6:10). Being led by His Spirit, the fruit of the Spirit may be developed: "love, joy, peace, forbearance, kindness, goodness, faithfulness, gentleness and self-control" (Gal. 5:22–23). Paul, therefore, summons: "So I say, walk by the Spirit, and you will not gratify the desires of the flesh. . . . But if you are led by the Spirit, you are not under the law" (Gal. 5:16–18).

James adds the important idea that the various trials of life for the Christian operate as the *testing* of his faith, which produces steadfastness and, in this way of battle, perfection of character (James 1:2–4; compare also Rom. 5:3–4). These apostolic admonitions show that the Christian life is not one of mere peace and joy. On the contrary, the way of Christian perfection or sanctification knows inexpressible depths of struggle, sorrow, and repentance, besides the heights of redemptive joy. The way of Christian perfection can never be one of feeling holy or sinless, because God will gradually reveal more and more the defects of a person's character through an ever-increasing understanding and efficacy of His holy, spiritual law.

The consciousness of both truths *simultaneously* in Paul's mature Christian experience is the most profound proof that Christian perfection is not just a life of ecstatic joy or emotional elation, but it is also a life of faithful obedience and wrestling submission to our divine Lord and Savior.

Fighting in the divine power of the whole armor of God (Eph. 6:13ff), the Christian is called to destroy every obstacle to his or her living connection with God and to "take captive every thought to make it obedient to Christ" (2 Cor. 10:5). The Christian can accept no other gods before Him. Christ wants to reproduce His own perfection of character in those who were originally created in His likeness and image.

"And we all, who with unveiled face contemplate the Lord's glory are being transformed into his image with ever-increasing glory, which comes from the Lord, who is the Spirit" (2 Cor. 3:18). This is the dynamic, increasing Christian perfection which the Apostle Paul extols and with holy passion urges upon the primitive church and thus on the church of all ages. The Old Testament covenant imperative to follow Yahweh is not annulled, but fulfilled and concretized in the true following of Christ. For believers to know Christ and to love Him with all their soul and all their heart means neither the renouncing of Yahweh nor apostasy from Moses and the prophets of Israel. On the contrary, only through the Son, "who is himself God" (John 1:18), can the Father be known, loved, obeyed, and fully honored.

Phase 3: No Acts of Sinful Premeditation and Attitudes of Excuse for Sinning

John's exposition on love in his first letter mounts a most compelling case for this important phase of Christian perfection: "No one born of God will continue to sin, because God's seed remains in them; they cannot go on sinning, because they have been born of God" (1 John 3:9). The Apostle John evidently proclaims only a Christian love, which consumes sin in the lives of the believers. When Christians are really in Christ, and Christ in them, they will "walk in the light, as he is in the light" (1 John 1:7). "Whoever says, 'I know him,' but does not do what he commands is a liar, and the truth is not in that person. But if anyone obeys his word, love for God is truly made completed (perfected) in them. This is how we know we are in him: Whoever claims to live in him must live as Jesus did" (1 John 2:4–6). Thus to John, Christian perfection is more than sinlessness; it is a moral communion and dynamic love relationship of the soul with Christ, revealing the same character of holy love as Christ. Then there will be no fear in the believer's heart for the day of judgment or shame when Christ appears in His holy glory: "This is how love is made complete (perfected) among us so that we will have confidence on the day of judgment: in this world we are like Jesus. There is no fear in love. But perfect love drives out fear, because fear has to do with punishment. The one who fears is not made perfect in love. We love because he first loved us" (1 John 4:17–19; also 2:28).

As long as the soul is united with Christ and the Spirit of Christ abides in that person, that soul cannot sin, says the apostle in 1 John 3:9. The walk of the regenerated Christian in the light does not imply, however, any consciousness or feeling of sinlessness. On the contrary, to walk in the light means a continued dependence on God's forgiving and keeping grace. In other words, the victorious life of the Christian is not the automatic result of a sinless nature. There is no inherent righteousness in the Christian before his or her final glorification in the day of God. Therefore the believer can fall into sin again, as appears from John's consolation: "My dear children, I write this to you so that you will not sin. But if any one does sin, we have an advocate with the Father—Jesus Christ the Righteous One" (1 John 2:1).

Far from being written as an excuse for sinning or for a walk in darkness, this comforting message reveals the consciousness that in the reborn children of God, the old, sinful nature is at work, always striving for the mastery. The knowledge of inherent lusts of the flesh and of the eyes (1 John 2:16), will lead the believer to a deepening repentance of heart and self-condemnation. Only implicit trust in the word of acquittal from a God who is "greater than our hearts" (1 John 3:20), while walking in loving obedience to Him, will "set our hearts at rest in his presence" (1 John 3:19). Such implicit trust in the word of acquittal from God will not lead to presumptuous acts of sin on the part of a true believer.

When John distinguishes between mortal sin and non-mortal sin (1 John 5:16–17), he is only continuing the old-covenant doctrine of sin, which differentiated sharply between deliberate, presumptuous sin and unintentional sin, which is afterward repented (Num. 15:27–31; Ps. 19:13–14). The apostle wants to clarify, finally, that the Christian is kept from mortal or presumptuous sin because he or she is being *kept* from this way of sinning by the indwelling Spirit of Christ. The child of God is no longer under the overruling power of the evil one, as is the world (1 John 5:18–19).

Phase 4: Sinless Loyalty in the Final Crisis of Christian History

Very closely related to perfection, defined as the absence of acts of sinful, willful premeditation and attitudes of excusing sin, is the fourth phase. There will be a great eschatological test of perfect obedience for those who have cultivated the habit of constant trust in the power of forgiving and transforming grace (and not thinking "about how to gratify the desires of the flesh" [Rom. 13:14]) and who live to see the coming of the Lord. This takes place in the great struggle between the seal of God versus the mark of the beast crisis that is graphically laid out in Revelation 12–14, especially in the key passages of 12:17 and 14:12. These familiar verses strongly suggest that in history's final end time on earth there will be a group of Christ's faithful followers who will loyally follow the Lamb, even in the face of the threat of death. While they do not appear to claim any sinless perfection of nature, the imagery does strongly suggest a perfect character of those "who keep the commandments of God and the faith of Jesus."

Phase 5: Sinless in Nature and Character
at the Second Coming: Glorified Sinlessness

The redemption of Christ it its fullness distinguishes between the two aspects of *present salvation,* justification and sanctification, and the *future salvation* of glorification at the second advent of Jesus Christ, which ushers in the ultimate establishment of the kingdom of glory. And it is at this glorious juncture of the salvation plan that it can be positively affirmed that the saints are sinless, not only in character, but also in nature bodily, morally, and mentally. Paul classically states this glorious future reality: "And we eagerly await a Savior from there, the Lord Jesus Christ, who, by the power that enables him to bring everything under his control, will transform our lowly bodies so that they will be like his glorious body" (Phil. 3:20–21; cf. 1 Cor. 15:51–54).

Phase 6: Dynamic Growth in Grace Through All Eternity

This final phase of perfection refers to the eternal growth in character of the people of God during the ceaseless ages of eternity. This is based on the understanding that God's love is infinite; and thus, those who are with Him "in Christ" for all eternity will have endless possibilities of growth in knowledge, joy, and love. Truly now believers only see as "in a mirror dimly" (NKJV) but then there will come a time when they will be "face to face" and with Paul will then be able to say "then I shall know fully, even as I am fully known" (1 Cor. 13:12). Maranatha!

SUMMARY

So what does it mean to be a perfect believer in Christ? First of all, it means to be fully submitted to the lordship of Christ in life—perfectly committed to do His will as one consistently draws the mighty draughts of His concerted convicting, justifying, and sanctifying grace. It means to be growing into the likeness of the loving Christ by being daily filled with the fruitful work of the Holy Spirit of God. To be pardoned, forgiven, or justified means to legally stand perfect in Christ and to be no longer under the condemnation of the holy law of God. Such a perfectly forgiven believer will never presume on the grace of God through sins of willful premeditation or indulge in attitudes of excuse for any known sin or sinful propensity, be it inherited or cultivated. This attitude of full, daily loyalty to Christ will also be open to obedience by grace no matter what the earthly cost may be. And for those who live through the last great testing crisis described in Revelation 12–14, they will aspire to experience the apex of perfection that character and nature change which will be bestowed with the finishing touch of immortality at the second coming of Jesus. And then it will be their supernal purpose to grow in the likeness of Christ's loving and righteous character for all eternity in the blessed heavenly realm. *Even so, come, Lord Jesus, and do whatever is needed to bring about such a glorious eventuality!*

SECTION 5

Blessed Assurance: Can Believers Be Sure About Their Salvation?

In previous sections of the book it has been shown that all parts of every human person have been adversely affected by sin, leaving humans unable to save themselves, or even to turn toward God on their own. Therefore, salvation is of necessity grounded in God's grace. God reinvigorates the power of choice through prevenient grace. This grace is not limited, but it is indeed offered to all (Matt. 18:14; John 3:15). At the same time, this grace is not irresistible; it can be turned down by those who refuse God's forgiveness. God woos and invites all to accept His gift of salvation.

This brings us to a number of questions concerning perseverance, security, assurance, and confidence in salvation. Can believers be sure that they are saved? Can they lose their salvation? Is it true that once believers are saved they will always be saved? How can believers be sure that they will continue to experience salvation? How can they be sure that they have salvation now and in the future and will not be rejected in the coming judgment?

This section on the blessed assurance of salvation begins with a chapter by Abner Hernandez-Fernandez and Jerry Moon that addresses the history of perseverance and assurance. Then there is a chapter on the Holy Spirit and assurance by Jo Ann Davidson. In the third chapter Woodrow Whidden discuss the issue of assurance in connection with the biblical teaching on Christian perfection. The final chapter, by Richard Davidson, addresses the all-important question of how believers can have assurance in relation to the biblical teaching on God's end-time judgment. Each of these chapters contributes to the understanding that the assurance of salvation comes from God rather than from the self.

CHAPTER 17

FROM THE APOSTLES TO ADVENTISM: A BRIEF HISTORY OF ASSURANCE

Jerry Moon and Abner Hernandez-Fernandez

The quest for certainty regarding the future eternal life is as old as humanity. The terms *assurance* of salvation, *perseverance* in salvation, and *once saved, always saved* have a history going back two millennia. The purpose of this chapter is to provide a practical introduction of these terms and what they meant in particular historical eras and contexts, beginning the story with Christ and the apostles, through the early church to Augustine, past the Middle Ages to Luther, who rediscovered the New Testament certainty of salvation—by then a completely revolutionary idea. After Luther bulldozed the medieval denial of assurance, Calvin sought to replace it with a thoroughly systematic biblical doctrine. Many thought Calvin had succeeded. But Jacobus Arminius, who regarded Calvin so highly as to credit him with "a certain spirit of prophecy,"[1] was the very man who pointed out the weakness in Calvin's system. Arminius denied that God purposely created anyone for eternal destruction, even though that was one of the contemporary arguments thought to bolster the assurance of the "elect" (i.e., those predestined for eternal life). Arminius died without seeing the fruit of his work, but John Wesley, a century later, wove Arminian presuppositions into a Methodist theology that reinforced the certainty of present assurance, while pointing toward a solution for the

---

1. Carl Bangs, *Arminius: A Study in the Dutch Reformation* (Eugene, OR: Wipf & Stock, 1998), 287.

problem of ultimate assurance. Ellen G. White, who was raised Methodist, formed a bridge from Wesley to the Seventh-day Adventists, who still retain an essentially Wesleyan view of the way of salvation.

ASSURANCE IN THE EARLY CHURCH

The gospel of Christ and the apostles included two opposing emphases: the certainty of present salvation in Jesus (John 3:16; 10:28), and a wary recognition of human weakness and potential for losing salvation (e.g., 1 Cor. 9:27; 10:12). In the New Testament, the basis of salvation and the security against future apostasy are the same: an intimate knowledge of Christ through a lifelong personal relationship with Him (John 17:3). The operative word is *lifelong* because the life consists of a faith relationship with Jesus. The Scripture says, "God has given us eternal life, and this life is in His Son. He who has the Son has life; he who does not have the Son of God does not have life" (1 John 5:12).[2] Therefore the essential protection against future apostasy is simply to make the relationship with Jesus lifelong (John 15:1–8). Thus the New Testament emphasis on the necessity of endurance to the end was never a one-sided behavioral exhortation, but a reminder to persist in a personal relationship with Jesus. The need for perseverance was always connected with a relationship of faith and assurance. But as the church's aggressive spread of the Gospel gave way to a more passive coexistence with the ancient world, the influence of the world subtly shifted the church's focus away from the all-sufficient Savior to a pessimistic emphasis on human frailty and the potential for losing salvation, until the message of the church became largely legalistic.

In this context, the New Testament emphasis on the necessity of endurance to the end (see, e.g., Matt. 24:13; John 15:5–7; Rom. 2:7; 5:3–4; 2 Thess. 1:4; 3:5; 1 Tim. 4:16; Heb. 6:11; 10:36; James 1:12; and Rev. 2:2–3) remained a popular topic in the writings of the early church. Because Christians faced the continual possibility of persecution and trials for their faith, church leaders underlined the importance of faithful perseverance and steadfastness. Writing to the Philippians, Polycarp urged them to

---

2. Unless otherwise indicated, all Scripture quotations are taken from the New King James Version®. Copyright © 1982 by Thomas Nelson. Used by permission. All rights reserved.

"continually persevere" together in "our hope, and the earnest of our righteousness, which is Jesus Christ."[3] His calling to perseverance was carefully constructed on Jesus Christ's faithfulness to the end as an exemplary model for all believers. As Jesus "endured all things for us," so the believers should become "imitators of His patience."[4]

Indeed, the goal to perfectly replicate the life of Christ led the early church fathers to place a strong emphasis on the role of individuals in Christian perseverance in faith.[5] They taught that believers should live a moral and ethical life bearing plentiful fruit of good works. For instance, Ignatius (c. 110) preached that as "the tree is made manifest by its fruit; so those who profess themselves to be Christians shall be recognised by their conduct. For there is not now a demand for mere profession, but that a man be found continuing in the power of faith to the end."[6] Daily perseverance implies, then, a daily life of ethical and moral behavior for the sake of the Gospel and Christ.

This does not mean, however, that all the emphasis was placed upon human effort. Instead, they believed that the human role in the continual faithfulness of Christians is sustained by the grace of God. It is the grace of God that empowers human ability to persevere. It is also God who protects the believers' faith from falling away from Him. Thus the Church Fathers understood the role of grace in perseverance as an assisting and protecting power. Tertullian clearly pointed out that no true believer could yield to Satan's temptations, deceptions, and persecutions, because Christ is "absolutely committed" to the protection of the believer's faith.[7] Similarly, Cyprian pointed out that God has provided "more than abundant care ... for preserving man after he is already redeemed!"[8] Thus, while humans exercise daily perseverance, God empowers and preserves their faith.

---

3. Polycarp of Smyrna, *The Epistle of Polycarp to the Philippians* 8, in *The Apostolic Fathers, Justin Martyr, Irenaeus,* vol. 1 of *The Ante-Nicene Fathers (ANF),* ed. Alexander Roberts, James Donaldson, and A. C. Coxe (Peabody, MA: Hendrickson, 2012), 1:35.

4. Ibid.

5. See Irenaeus, *Against Heresies* 4.37 (*ANF,* 1:518–521).

6. Ignatius of Antioch, *Epistle of Ignatius to the Ephesians* 14 (ANF, 1:55).

7. Tertullian, *De fuga in persecutione* 2 (*ANF,* 4:117).

8. Cyprian, *On the Works and Alms* 8.1 (*ANF,* 5:476).

The understanding that perseverance must be the result of a joint effort of God and humans is directly related to the early church's strong emphasis on human freedom of will. For Irenaeus "all men are of the same nature" and God made all of them "free agents from the beginning," in both works and faith. Therefore, on the one hand, individuals are able "to hold fast and to do what is good," or on the other hand "to disobey God, and to forfeit what is good."[9] This understanding of the liberty of human nature helped to explain why bodily temptations, heretical ideas, or brutal persecution could lead many Christians to fall away from their allegiance to Christ.

Tertullian accurately expressed the possibility of falling. God foresaw "that faith, even after baptism, would be endangered; that the most, after attaining unto salvation, would be lost again, through soiling the wedding-dress, through failing to provide oil for their torchlets."[10] Tertullian believed that due to the weakness and volatility of the human will it is impossible to have present assurance of final salvation. To lose salvation is always possible. The Church Fathers were afraid of having absolute conviction of future salvation and perseverance, because this could lead to self-confidence, spiritual pride, and complacency.[11] They felt that if believers were absolutely certain about future assurance, they could become self-satisfied with their spiritual life and lose their vigilant attitude toward sin.

Therefore, the early church generally viewed complete assurance as not only impossible, but dangerous, inclining to overconfidence or false confidence, pride of heart, and negligent conduct. As long as life endures, believers must continually fight "the battle of the faith." In the Patristic period before Augustine, present assurance and the hope of perseverance to the end were in continual tension with the possibility of future falling from faith.

AUGUSTINE ON ASSURANCE

One of the earliest systematic treatments of the doctrine of perseverance appeared from the pen of Augustine of Hippo (354–430). His treatise *On the Gift of Perseverance*, written in 428–429 in the middle of his battle

---

9. Irenaeus, *Against Heresies* 4.37 (*ANF*, 1:519).

10. Tertullian, *Antidote for the Scorpion's Sting* 6 (*ANF*, 3:639).

11. Gregg R. Allison, *Historical Theology: An Introduction to Christian Theology* (Grand Rapids, MI: Zondervan, 2011), 544.

against Pelagius, defended the unique role of God's grace in the perseverance of the saints. It is only by a divine gift, says Augustine, that believers "persevere in Christ to the end."[12] Therefore, perseverance to the end is as completely dependent on God's grace to individuals as is faith's beginning.[13] Citing Jeremiah 32:40, Augustine insisted that just as God works so "that we come to him, so He works that we do not depart."[14] Logically, he concluded: "This, therefore, is God's hand, not ours, that we depart not from God."[15]

For Augustine, unless believers receive the gift of perseverance, faithfulness to the end is impossible. He even argued that the reason Adam and Eve, who enjoyed all kinds of moral, ethical, and spiritual capacities, were unable to maintain their unblemished nature, was because God did not grant them the grace of perseverance.[16] Likewise, contemporary believers could possess various holy virtues, but if they finally desert from faith, it is assuredly and justly said that they did not have "in any degree that perseverance ... by which one perseveres in Christ even to the end."[17] So, the ever-present possibility of falling from faith is a warning. Believers should never assume "that perseverance is given to any one to the end, except when the end itself has come, and he to whom it [perseverance to the end] has been given has been found to have persevered unto the end."[18]

At this point it is important to observe two essential characteristics of Augustine's doctrine of perseverance. First, for Augustine the grace of perseverance as a divine gift will not only endure for a while, but believers will

---

12. Augustine, *On Perseverance* 1, in *Augustin: Anti-Pelagian Writings*, vol. 5 of *The Nicene and Post-Nicene Fathers (NPNF¹)*, Series 1, ed. Philip Schaff, trans. Peter Holmes and Robert Ernest Wallis, intro. by Rev. Benjamin B. Warfield (Peabody, MA: Hendrickson, 2012), 5:526, 548.

13. "I maintain that both the beginning of faith and the perseverance therein, even to the end, are, according to Scripture—of which I have already quoted many—God's gift." Augustine, *On Perseverance* 54 (*NPNF¹*, 5:547).

14. Augustine, *On Perseverance* 14 (*NPNF¹*, 5:530), translation modernized.

15. Ibid.

16. Augustine, *On Rebuke and Grace* 26 (*NPNF¹*, 5:482).

17. Augustine, *On Perseverance* 1 (*NPNF¹*, 5:526).

18. Augustine, *On Perseverance* 10 (*NPNF¹*, 5:529).

continually enjoy it to the end. "Perseverance even to the end," emphatically wrote Augustine, "is not indeed lost when it has once been given."[19] He further explained, "when that gift of God is granted . . . none of the saints fails to keep his perseverance."[20] He supported his case by quoting 1 John 2:19: "They went out from us, but they did not really belong to us. For if they had belonged to us, they would have remained with us; but their going showed that none of them belonged to us" (NIV).

For Augustine, unfaithfulness, rebellion, and falling into temptation demonstrate that such a believer, although regenerated,[21] did not have the grace of perseverance. On the other hand, evidences of victory over sin and a daily life of sanctification to the end confirm the gift of perseverance in the believer's life. Indeed, like many of his predecessors, Augustine held that to endure persecution and face death for Christ is the ultimate proof of perseverance and the reception of the grace of perseverance.[22]

Second, Augustine closely tied his concept of perseverance to his doctrine of election (i.e., predestination to salvation). Because those God elects receive the gift of perseverance, no elect person can fail to persevere in grace.[23] Curiously, Augustine did not hold that every believer is one of the elect. According to him, regeneration does not necessarily involve continual perseverance to the end.[24] Not all believers, but only the elect are granted the grace of perseverance. Thus for Augustine, true believers face the real possibility of losing salvation, while the elect have no such risk, because in his view, election guarantees the reception of the gift of perseverance.

Finally, it should be noted that, for Augustine, only God knows for certain who will persevere to the end. This raises the question: Does God's knowledge of final salvation offer any assurance for believers? The answer is that God's knowledge does not give assurance to individual believers, because

---

19. Augustine, *On Perseverance* 11 (*NPNF¹*, 5:529).

20. Augustine, *On Perseverance* 9 (*NPNF¹*, 5:529).

21. Norman Geisler rightly observes, "Augustine and his followers up to the Reformation believed that some of the regenerated are not elect and would not persevere." *Chosen But Free: A Balanced View of God's Sovereignty and Free Will* (Bloomington, MN: Bethany House, 2010), 106n60.

22. Augustine, *On Perseverance* 2 (*NPNF¹*, 5:526).

23. *Oxford Dictionary of the Christian Church*, 1997 ed., s.v. "Election."

24. Augustine, *On Perseverance* 10, 33 (*NPNF¹*, 5:529, 538).

believers cannot know for certain whether they are elected. Thus Augustine left his readers (supposedly believers) in a total state of uncertainty.[25] To be fair with Augustine, it should be noted that in order to give believers a measure of hope, he gave some advice. First, he advised believers to continually pray for the gift of perseverance, for that gift is given in response to sincere prayer.[26] Second, he advised believers to "trust in God" and not in human power for perseverance to the end, because Christians "are bidden to have their hope in Him."[27] Finally, Augustine advised preachers to present this doctrine carefully in order to not give offense, to not discourage the faith or obedience of their hearers. Even preachers, advised Augustine, should not "mention the possibility of the hearers' being rejected."[28]

In summary, according to Augustine the grace of perseverance is a gift of God sovereignly bestowed on the elect believers. No one, except by a special revelation, can be sure of perseverance resulting in final salvation. For Augustine there is neither present assurance of present salvation nor present assurance of final salvation. Christians must wait until the moment of death to discover God's will for their eternal destiny.

ROMAN CATHOLIC VIEW OF ASSURANCE

The dominant view of the Middle Ages was that salvation is God's reward for good works. "Even Augustine had succumbed to the notion that salvation is attained as a reward for doing good." He taught that "grace empowers the believer to do works that are pleasing to God, and thus to attain salvation."[29] The unavoidable consequence of making human works the ground of God's favor is that unclouded assurance becomes impossible. The consensus of medieval theology was that ordinary believers can have no certainty of salvation. Thomas Aquinas, the greatest of the Scholastic theologians, argued that, apart from a direct

25. Augustine, *On Perseverance* 62 (*NPNF¹*, 5:550).

26. Augustine, *On Perseverance* 10 11 (*NPNF¹*, 5:529).

27. Augustine, *On Perseverance* 62 (*NPNF¹*, 5:550).

28. Eugene TeSelle, *Augustine* (Nashville, TN: Abingdon, 2006), 69; cf. Augustine, *On Perseverance* 57–62 (*NPNF¹*, 5:549, 550).

29. Justo L. González, *A Concise History of Christian Doctrine* (Nashville, TN: Abingdon, 2005), 174.

revelation from God to the individual, it is impossible to know whether one has received God's grace.[30]

This theological error eventually precipitated the Reformation. The earthquake that shook the church in the sixteenth century had many contributing causes. But the chief cause of the Reformation was that "the church was unable to satisfy man's desire for genuine assurance of salvation." The church taught there could be no certainty of salvation apart from a special revelation from God to the individual, and for one to seek such a revelation "would have been regarded as presumptuous."[31] A key text was Ecclesiastes 9:1 (Vulgate), "Man knows not whether he is worthy of God's love or hate."[32] The whole scholastic tradition agreed that in this present life "man is not able to know . . . with full certitude, whether or not he has grace."[33] If one cannot know whether one even has God's grace, neither present justification nor future salvation can be known for sure. The only exception would be a direct revelation such as the promise to Paul in 2 Corinthians 12:9: "My grace is sufficient for you." But ordinary Christians could not expect direct revelation; they could only hope for a "conjectural certitude" based on indicators such as "joy in what is good" and "peace of conscience"—but since these may appear in heretics and other deceived persons, they are only a possible indicator, not a guarantee of grace.[34] Thus Joel Beeke describes Aquinas's view of assurance as "a conjectural certainty based on works."[35]

What Aquinas asserted, the Council of Trent defined as dogma—a teaching whose "acceptance is necessary for salvation."[36] The twelfth chapter

---

30. Matthew C. Hoskinson, *Assurance of Salvation: Implications of a New Testament Theology of Hope* (Greenville, SC: Bob Jones University Press, 2010), 16–18.

31. Bernhard Lohse, *A Short History of Christian Doctrine from the First Century to the Present* (Philadelphia, PA: Fortress, 1966), 159.

32. The Protestant consensus would be that no human is "worthy" of God's love, but God loves them anyway, because it is His nature to love, and because they are His children.

33. Gabriel Biel, "Luther's Most Important Scholastic instructor," quoted in Sven Grosse, "Salvation and the Certitude of Faith: Luther on Assurance," *Pro Ecclesia* 20, no. 1 (Winter 2011): 68.

34. Ibid.

35. Joel Beeke, *The Quest for Full Assurance* (Carlisle, PA: Banner of Truth, 1999), 13.

36. *Our Sunday Visitor's Catholic Encyclopedia*, 1991 ed., s.v. "Dogma."

of Trent's "Decree of Justification" declares as dogma the teaching that "assurance of grace is virtually impossible 'in this mortal life.'"[37] Canons I–XXXIII "On Justification" anathematizes all the major aspects of the Protestant understanding of assurance.[38] This remains the official Roman Catholic position on assurance.[39]

LUTHER ON ASSURANCE

The doctrine of the impossibility of certain assurance brought Martin Luther (1483–1546) to the personal crisis through which he discovered the truth about assurance. Luther's breakthrough was simply this: that since God's promises are based on His unchanging character, not on the variable performance of the believer, the promises are for everyone who chooses to believe them. Luther's doctrine of assurance was not merely a theoretical construct, but a robust confidence and security that triumphed over all fear. As early as his first lecture series on the Psalms (1513–1515), he began to move away from the medieval tradition of "uncertainty" regarding assurance. Commenting on Psalm 119:49–50, 111, Luther exclaimed,

> That which God has promised gives joy to the hearts of those who believe in it and who hope for it. Therefore, we exult in the interim, in faith, and in the hope of future things, those future things that God has promised us. Therefore, indeed, we exult because we are certain that He does not deceive, but rather, that He will do what He has promised, and that He will take all affliction of body and soul from us, and will give us all that is good, and that without end.[40]

Sven Grosse points out that in lecturing on Romans 8:16 ("The Spirit Himself bears witness with our spirit that we are children of God"), "Luther identifies this testimony, which the Holy Spirit gives to the human spirit, with the human heart's trust in God."[41] Luther affirms that Romans 8:33,

---

37. Philip Schaff, *The Creeds of Christendom*, vol. 2 (New York: Harper & Brothers, 1919), 103, quoted in Hoskinson, *Assurance of Salvation*, 19.

38. Schaff, quoted in Hoskinson, *Assurance of Salvation*, 19, n. 9–13.

39. See Hoskinson, *Assurance of Salvation*, 18–21.

40. Martin Luther quoted in Grosse, *Salvation and the Certitude of Faith*, 69.

41. *"Testimonium istud sit fiducia cordis in Deum*—'this witness is the heart's trust in

"'Who will bring any charge against God's elect?' means that 'we are certain that no sin will be charged against us.' Likewise, the apostle speaks of how 'we know that in everything God works for good with those who love him, who are called according to his purpose' (Rom 8:28). Finally, he declares in Rom 8:38f. that he is *certain* that nothing will separate him from the love of God."[42]

In contrast, Luther charged the church with deliberately producing pervasive doubts about assurance.

> [Catholic] theologians . . . have twisted [Ecclesiastes 9:1] in such a way that they . . . completely extinguished the certainty of faith in Christ . . . teaching and inculcating nothing more religious upon suffering hearts than to tell them that they must be in doubt and uncertainty about the grace and love of God toward us, regardless of how blameless our lives may be.[43]

To Luther, those fostering fundamental doubts about the merciful character of God committed nothing less than "an awful and exceedingly common blasphemy" because "they either smugly despise and hate the words and promises, or . . . they say that they have doubts and do not know whether God is compassionate to such an extent."[44] This idea "originates from a blasphemous heart which does not think that God is truthful."[45] Thus they "attribute fickleness and untrustworthiness to God."[46] Such a view of God, Luther concluded, "publicly declares God a liar."[47] Thus Luther's discovery of assurance became a major factor in his break with Rome.[48] Luther's

---

God.'" Luther, quoted in Grosse, *Salvation and Certitude,* 69.

42. Luther quoted in Grosse, *Salvation and Certitude,* 69 (emphasis in original).

43. Martin Luther, *Notes on Ecclesiastes,* in *Luther's Works,* vol. 15, ed. Jaroslav Pelikan (Saint Louis, MO: Concordia Publishing, 1972), 3–4.

44. Martin Luther, *Lectures on Genesis, Chapters 21–25,* in *Luther's Works,* vol. 4, ed. Jaroslav Pelikan (Saint Louis, MO: Concordia Publishing House, 1964), 144.

45. Ibid., 145.

46. Ibid.

47. Ibid.

48. "To a certain extent it is not incorrect when it is said that the reformatory discovery consisted formally in the discovery of the word of promise which forgives and makes certain." Martin Brecht, *Martin Luther: His Road to Reformation 1483–1521,* trans. James L. Schaaf (Philadelphia, PA: Fortress Press, 1985), 236; cf. Grosse, *Salvation and Certitude,* 67; Lohse,

doctrine of assurance is basic to his theology, because the lack of assurance makes true faith and confidence in God nearly impossible.[49]

Matthew C. Hoskinson shows that Luther based his doctrine of assurance on three grounds. The first and foremost was "the unchanging character of God" mediated to humans through Christ, our High Priest. "The second and third grounds of assurance . . . are both subjective, flowing from the objective promises of God through Christ. One of these is the life of obedience that saving faith produces." Obedience constitutes "inferential evidence that one is a recipient of God's grace." But assurance comes first, even before obedience; only after assurance produces the faith that results in obedience can obedience provide assurance.[50]

The third ground of assurance, the testimony of the Holy Spirit (Rom. 8:16; Gal. 4:6; 1 Thess. 1:5), is also based on the promises of God in Scripture. Hoskinson explains that this "connection of God's promises with both the believer's obedience and the Spirit's testimony," guards the believer "against legalism on the one hand and subjectivism on the other. There may be three bases of assurance . . . but only one right object of saving faith"—the character and promises of God in Christ.[51]

In a sermon on Galatians 4:1–7, Luther explained that the believer should have "no fear or wavering that he is devout and is God's child through grace, but there should rather only be fear and concern about how he will therefore remain constant until the end . . . for such faith does not boast of works or of itself, rather of God alone and His grace."[52] Here Luther portrays the believer, not as vacillating between fear and hope, but rather using both fear and hope as "two guardrails" to protect from "false extremes."[53] In Luther's words, "Fear bars the way to the right, but mercy bars the way to the left; one is the [false] certainty, the other is despair, one is vainglory, the other

---

A Short History of Christian Doctrine, 159, and Hoskinson, *Assurance of Salvation*, 21–24.

49. "The sum of our religion is this: that a man be certain and secure in his own conscience." See Martin Luther, "Lectures on 1 Timothy," in *Luther's Works*, vol. 28, ed. Hilton C. Oswald (St. Louis, MO: Concordia, 1973), 325; cf. Hoskinson, *Assurance of Salvation*, 24.

50. Hoskinson, *Assurance of Salvation*, 26–28.

51. Ibid., 29.

52. Martin Luther, quoted in Grosse, *Salvation and Certitude*, 77.

53. Ibid.

is loss of hope in God."⁵⁴ On Romans 4:7, "Blessed are those whose lawless deeds are forgiven," Luther commented that believers are "simultaneously unjustified and justified. . . . For so long as the saints keep their sins always in mind and beseech God for justification by virtue of His mercy, then God will accept them as justified. . . . The truth of the matter is that they are sinners, but on account of the acceptance of our merciful God, they are justified."⁵⁵ In short, those who humble themselves as sinners before God will be justified; but those who trust in their own merits will be disqualified. When believers look at themselves, they can see nothing good, but they cast themselves on the mercy of God and are accepted and justified. But if they presume to base assurance on their obedience or good works, God exposes their works as nothing but sin. Therefore, true faith always remains focused on the merciful Savior, never on any human worthiness.

Thus Luther affirmed present assurance based on present faith in the character and promises of God. The believer can know without doubt that God is merciful, keeps His promises, hears prayer, and forgives sinners. In Grosse's words, "If he believes, and so long as he believes, his future salvation is assured, and he is also certain of his election."⁵⁶ On the other hand, Luther acknowledged that *absolute* certainty of ultimate salvation is beyond human knowing. As Grosse explains, "no one attains salvation unless he is elected to it by God, so the certainty of salvation would simultaneously have to be the certainty of predestination to salvation."⁵⁷ Luther did not believe one could have infallible certainty of one's own election (i.e., predestination to salvation). The assumption that one could have absolute certainty of one's own election was a later development within Calvinist theology.

CALVIN ON ASSURANCE

John Calvin (1509–1564), twenty-six years younger than Luther, belonged to the next generation of reform. Born in France, spending his mature career in Geneva, Switzerland, he built on Luther's foundation, elaborating

---

54. Ibid., 78.

55. Ibid., 72.

56. Ibid., 77.

57. Grosse, *Salvation and Certitude,* 76.

and systematizing what Luther had begun. A standard edition of Calvin's *Institutes* gives more than three hundred pages to the exposition of faith and assurance.[58] Foremost among his objections to the Roman doctrine was the inclusion of meritorious human works as a basis for justification.

Calvin agreed with Luther that assurance rests on one objective and foundational basis—the character and promises of God—plus two subjective supporting bases, the inner witness of the Spirit and the obedient life of the believer.[59] Calvin defined faith as "[1] a firm and certain knowledge of God's benevolence toward us, [2] founded upon the truth of the freely given promise in Christ, both [3] revealed to our minds and [4] sealed upon our hearts through the Holy Spirit."[60] Unpacking this definition, (1) "firm and certain knowledge" means the kind of certainty based on personal experience. The true believer regards the goodness of God as beyond doubt. (2) This sense of certainty is founded first of all on "the truth of the freely given promise" of God's word in Christ. The promise is trustworthy because God Himself is true and unchanging, and because His Word in Christ and in Scripture is utterly trustworthy. (3) The trustworthiness of God's promise is "revealed to our minds" by general revelation, the evidences of God's power and love in His created works; by special revelation and a believer's personal verification that His written word is reliable; and by the believer's own experience of His love and power at work in his or her life. (4) God's promise is also "sealed upon our hearts through the Holy Spirit" (i.e., by a subjective revelation of His love to each person individually). By this definition, Calvin asserts that a so-called faith that does not produce assurance is not genuine faith.[61] Thus Calvin insists that one who believes Christ died for the world, but does not know whether Christ died "for me," does not yet have true faith. "He alone is truly a believer who, convinced by a firm conviction that God is a kindly and well-disposed Father to him, promises himself all things on the basis of [H]is generosity; who relying on the promises of divine benevolence toward him, lays hold

---

58. John Calvin, *Institutes of the Christian Religion*, vols. 20 and 21 of Library of Christian Classics, ed. John T. McNeill, trans. Ford Lewis Battles (Philadelphia, PA: Westminster, 1960), 3.1–19.

59. Hoskinson, *Assurance of Salvation*, 39.

60. Calvin, *Institutes* 3.2.7.

61. Hoskinson, *Assurance of Salvation*, 32; Calvin, *Institutes* 3.2.16.

on an undoubted expectation of salvation."[62] This is a bold statement, which Calvin later qualifies, conceding that "even weak faith is real faith,"[63] but his point is clear. The one who believes Christ died for the world, but does not know whether Christ died "for me," does not yet have full, strong faith. By thus making assurance intrinsic to faith, Calvin links present assurance with ultimate assurance. He believes that until one has present assurance, he or she does not have true faith, and if one has true faith, he or she has ultimate assurance. Calvin concludes that believers do not "well comprehend the goodness of God unless we gather from it the fruit of great assurance."[64] Assurance must be grounded on the goodness of God because "the lack of assurance breeds an inability to obey."[65] Assurance enables obedience. Since "whatever is not from faith is sin" (Rom. 14:23), whenever the believer takes a course of action which he or she doubts is God's will, he or she is not acting in faith, but presumptuously. "It is only when we have lost all anxiety on our own account that we can be wholehearted in sacrificing ourselves for the service of God."[66]

For all his emphasis on assurance as intrinsic to true faith, Calvin cited Peter's boasting that he would never deny Christ as a warning to all believers against the danger of pride and self-confidence. "Identifying a lack of confidence as one extreme, and self-confidence as the other, Calvin charts a 'middle course' expounded in Philippians 2:12–13": "Work out your own salvation with fear and trembling; for it is God who works in you both to will and to do."[67] Thus Calvin implicitly recognized that only as the believer continues in the relationship with Christ which gives present assurance does one maintain that assurance into the future.

Calvin's view on assurance was closely related to his belief in double predestination: the premise that before the Creation of the world, God had irrevocably predetermined who would be lost and who would be saved.

---

62. Calvin, *Institutes* 3.2.16.

63. Ibid. 3.2.17–19.

64. Ibid. 3.2.16.

65. Hoskinson, *Assurance of Salvation*, 34.

66. Ronald Wallace, *Calvin's Doctrine of the Christian Life* (Grand Rapids, MI: Eerdmans, 1989), 299, quoted in Hoskinson, 34.

67. Hoskinson, *Assurance of Salvation*, 39.

In Calvin's favor, it should be noted that he strongly *denied* that believers "ought to *begin* with predestination in seeking assurance of salvation."[68]

The Calvinist concept of double predestination appealed to many because it seemed to make it possible for one to determine with certainty whether one is among the elect, and thus to know one's ultimate destiny. The idea of an irreversible guarantee ("once saved, always saved") is based on pre-destinarian reasoning: that no one could be converted unless he or she were already predestined (elected) to salvation, therefore conversion proves election (predestination to salvation). The syllogism continues that those pre-destined to salvation can under no circumstances be lost; therefore, "perseverance" in salvation is guaranteed.

Though it is commonly thought that the doctrine of double predestination offers the believer greater security, it really doesn't. If one loses faith, the Calvinist view could easily lead the backslider to think he or she was divinely predestined to damnation and therefore hopeless. Calvin warned his readers against drawing such a conclusion,[69] but it remains a logical possibility from his presuppositions. If it were true that God had predetermined the majority of humankind to damnation, then the chances would be better than 50–50 that a person who is going away from Christ might not be merely slipping temporarily, but could be among the eternally non-elect. It is more scriptural to affirm that there is no biblical assurance apart from a continuing relationship with Christ. "This is eternal life, that they may know You, the only true God, and Jesus Christ whom You have sent" (John 17:3; cf. 15:1–7).

ARMINIUS ON ASSURANCE

Jacobus Arminius (1560–1609) approached the issue of perseverance and assurance motivated essentially by pastoral concerns rather than by

68. Calvin, "Second Defense of the Sacraments," in *Tracts and Treatises on the Doctrine and Worship of the Church,* vol. 2 of *Calvin's Tract and Series,* trans. Henry Beveridge (Grand Rapids, MI: Eerdmans, 1958), 2:343, quoted in Hoskinson, *Assurance of Salvation,* 40–41 (emphasis added). Calvin's *Institutes* included predestination, not under the doctrine of God, but as a supporting argument within the doctrine of salvation, *after* he had firmly established the doctrine of assurance on the basis of faith. See Calvin, *Institutes* 3.21.1.

69. Calvin, *Institutes* 3.24.4; see also Hoskinson, *Assurance of Salvation,* 40–41.

theological speculations. Carl Bangs reports that while Arminius performed pastoral duties during the bubonic plague in Amsterdam, he spiritually supported two individuals on their deathbeds who were completely in despair due to their lack of assurance.[70] Arminius's own account of his intervention serves as an example of his theological understanding of the certainty of salvation. According to Arminius's dialogue with these two individuals, assurance could be defined as the certainty in the believer's heart of the remission of sins, confirmed by the testimony of the Holy Spirit. Indeed, the firm belief that one's own sins have been forgiven is *necessarily* followed by assurance of salvation; assurance is the predictable result of believing that "God had reconciled the world to himself in Christ."[71]

In this manner, Arminius directly correlated personal faith in Jesus Christ with certainty of salvation. Faith, says Arminius, makes it possible "to be persuaded with certainty."[72] From Arminius's perspective, faith in what God has done for the redemption of human beings through Jesus Christ is the solid ground of assurance. He strongly pointed out the source of his confidence: "'I am a believer,' or 'I believe in Christ;—therefore I shall be saved,' or I am elect."[73] Keith Stanglin and Thomas McCall rightly assert that according to Arminius's theology, "for assurance, one need only look to Christ and the God of love and grace that he [Christ] reveals."[74] In sum, for Arminius, present faith in Christ and His reconciling work is the basic ground for present assurance. Christian assurance of salvation is simply a matter of trusting in Christ, His love, and His grace.

In addition, Arminius affirmed that the inner testimony of the Holy Spirit, a pure conscience, and the actual evidence of the fruits of faith corroborate the certainty of salvation that faith in Christ brings to the life of

70. Bangs, *Arminius,* 174.

71. Ibid. (emphasis in original).

72. W. Stephen Gunter, *Arminius and His Declaration of Sentiments: An Annotated Translation with Introduction and Theological Commentary* (Waco, TX: Baylor University Press, 2012), 142.

73. James Arminius, *The Works of James Arminius,* vol. 3, trans. James Nichols and William R. Bagnall (Grand Rapids, MI: Baker Book, 1956), 497.

74. Keith D. Stanglin and Thomas H. McCall, *Jacob Arminius: Theologian of Grace* (New York: Oxford University Press, 2012), 187.

believers.[75] Indeed, the Holy Spirit testifies to the believer's conscience about His own salvific work in the believer's heart. The Holy Spirit not only empowers the human will to believe, but He is also the operative instrument of God for perseverance in goodness.[76] With such a certitude of salvation, Christians can face death and "appear before the throne of grace without anxious fear or terrifying dread of damnation."[77] Thus, after the promises of Scripture, the actual evidence of a Christian life, the testimony of the Holy Spirit, and a pure conscience also produce assurance of salvation in the life of the believer.

Arminius went to great lengths to reevaluate the Reformed idea regarding the eternal security of the saints. On the one hand, he held that believers to whom God has given true faith have the spiritual power to obtain victory over "Satan, sin, the world, and their own flesh."[78] Divine assistance, says Arminius, continually provides the necessary means for the believers to overcome temptations and to "remain diligent, on guard."[79] Therefore, "it is not possible for Satan by his cunning, craftiness, or power to seduce or drag them out of the hands of Christ."[80] In other words, for Arminius there are no efficient or deficient causes in God's work of salvation that could lead believers to a falling away from their Christian experience. God has provided sufficient means for all believers to endure in faith and good works and obtain the final purpose of God, eternal salvation.

On the other hand, however, Arminius's more synergistic view of salvation led him to carefully consider the testimony of Scripture regarding the possibility of apostasy.[81] One strongly emphasized argument in his writings is that humans, assisted by the grace of God, are not passive but

75. See Gunter, *Arminius and His Declaration,* 142.

76. Arminius, *Works,* 3.372–373.

77. Gunter, *Arminius and His Declaration,* 142.

78. Ibid., 141.

79. Ibid.

80. Ibid.

81. Arminius found a real tension between passages that assert the possibility of falling away from Christ and those that seem to indicate the unconditional perseverance of the saints. Regarding the possibility of apostasy, Arminius wrote "there are passages of Scripture that seem to indicate such." However, "other passages of Scripture may be produced [supporting] the opposite doctrine (asserting unconditional perseverance)," Gunter, *Arminius and His Declaration,* 142. Cf. 141–142.

active agents in the dynamic of salvation.[82] Therefore, in the same manner that they can freely decide to believe and accept God's offer of salvation, they can also decide to disbelieve in God, turn away from good works, and as a consequence completely lose their salvation. Stanglin and McCall point out that "taking the entire body of his writings into account, it is clear that Arminius assumed that true believers can fall away" from grace.[83]

Yet, while true believers do actually fail in their battles against sin, they are "in most cases . . . brought back" to repentance by the work of the Holy Spirit.[84] Indeed, this seems to be the context in which his statement "I have never taught that a true believer either totally or finally falls away from the faith and perishes"[85] should be understood. The balance proposed by Arminius seems to be that while actual sins are both a possibility and a reality in the lives of believers, absolute apostasy according to his reading of Scripture remains only as a possibility in their experiences. He took very seriously the warning passages of Scripture. Such passages led Arminius to believe that the only safe attitude[86] for Christ's disciples is to "remain diligent, on guard, and implore" the continual assistance of God.[87] Consequently, as long as believers hold their faith in God's promises of salvation, as long as they continually accept God's

---

82. Arminius, *Works,* 2:192.

83. Stanglin and McCall, *Jacob Arminius: Theologian of Grace,* 173; Arminius, *Works,* 1:530: Arminius, in his article *On Regeneration and the Regenerate,* clearly points out that the regenerate persons are still "capable of committing sin" and "grieving the Holy Spirit by their sins," *Works,* 2:502. In this context he cites David as the example showing that even true believers could completely lose their salvation unless they repent. "If David had died in the very moment in which he had sinned against Uriah by adultery and murder, he would have been condemned to death eternal" (ibid.).

84. Stanglin and McCall, *Jacob Arminius: Theologian of Grace,* 173.

85. Gunter, *Arminius and His Declaration,* 142.

86. Ellen White makes a similar statement: "There is *no safety* for the child of God unless he daily receives a new and fresh experience in looking unto Jesus. By beholding him day by day, he will reflect his image, and thus represent his divine attributes. His *only safety* lies in daily placing himself under the guidance of God's word, in daily bringing his course of action to the test inquiry, 'Is this the way of the Lord?' A divine life will represent Jesus Christ, and will be antagonistic to the customs, practices, and standards of the world," "Why the Lord Waits," *The Review and Herald* (July 28, 1896).

87. Gunter, *Arminius and His Declaration,* 141.

assisting and subsequent grace, they will not fall away from the eternal blessing given to the saints.

Arminius's understanding of perseverance strongly influenced the theological ideas of his followers on this topic. Surely, if Christians sin and do not repent, the possibility that they can lose their salvation is a real one.[88] For example, the Remonstrant pastors in 1621 stated, "we believe that it is entirely possible, if not rarely done, that they [true and holy believers] fall back little by little and until they completely lack their prior faith and charity."[89]

To conclude, according to Arminius, the Christian's assurance of salvation relies on a daily faith in Christ supported by the conjoint testimony of the Holy Spirit and the human conscience. This faith looks to Christ as its "pioneer and perfecter" (Heb. 12:2, NIV). In addition, daily perseverance in such faith and good works, by the assisting grace of God, enhances assurance of salvation in the life of the believer. Nevertheless, Arminius recognized that the possibility of apostasy is always a present reality in human experience. Christians, then, should continually pray, claiming God's assistance to confront their flesh and the trickery of Satan. For this reason, one could agree with Bangs that from the perspective of human fragility and weakness, in Arminius's theology "there is not *present* assurance of *final* salvation."[90] However, from the perspective of God's love, power, and passionate desire to save His beloved children, in Arminius's theology there truly is present hope of final salvation that brings lasting joy and peace to the believing heart.[91]

WESLEY ON ASSURANCE

While Arminius dealt with assurance of salvation mainly as a pastor trying to comfort some of his members, John Wesley (1703–1791) approached the topic from his own experience as one who knew Jesus but was uncertain of his own salvation. During severe storms while crossing the Atlantic

---

88. See Mark A. Ellis, ed. and trans., *Arminian Confession of 1621* (Eugene, OR: Pickwick, 2005), 82.

89. Ibid.

90. Bangs, *Arminius*, 348 (emphasis in original).

91. See Keith Stanglin, *Arminius on the Assurance of Salvation: The Context, Roots, and Shape of the Leiden Debate, 1603–1609* (Leiden: Brill, 2007), 234–235.

to Georgia, Wesley noticed how sharp was the contrast between his own fear of death and the peaceful attitude of the Moravians.[92] In a conversation with Moravian leader August Spangenberg in Georgia in 1736, Wesley received from his interlocutor the most jarring question of his life: "Does the Spirit of God bear witness with your spirit that you are a child of God?"[93] Wesley did not know how to answer. That interview revealed that, despite his theological training, he "lacked the witness of the Holy Spirit that he was a child of God."[94] He had not yet found the assurance confidence, and certainty of salvation enjoyed by the Moravian Christians.

Two years later, May 24, 1738, Wesley finally began to enjoy the assurance of salvation for which he had been searching.

> In the evening I went very unwillingly to a society in Aldersgate Street, where one was reading Luther's preface to the Epistle to the Romans. About a quarter before nine, while he was describing the change which God works in the heart through faith in Christ, I felt my heart strangely warmed. I felt I did trust in Christ, Christ alone for salvation; and an assurance was given me that He had taken away my sins, even mine, and saved me from the law of sin and death.[95]

From that moment forward he wanted every follower of Christ to experience what he had, because he viewed assurance as the only alternative to "a constant state of fear regarding his soul's salvation."[96] In his sermons, Wesley defended threefold grounds for the Christian assurance of salvation. First, assurance is obtained by the inner testimony of the Holy Spirit to the human conscience. Second, the fruit of the Holy Spirit in the life of believers gives evidence that they are children of God. Finally, these two grounds of assurance are supported by the testimony of holy Scripture.

---

92. Kenneth J. Collins, *John Wesley: A Theological Journey* (Nashville, TN: Abingdon, 2003), 56–58.

93. John Wesley, *Journal of the Rev. John Wesley*, ed. Nehemiah Curnock (London: Epworth Press, 1938), 1:151.

94. Kenneth J. Collins, "Wesley's Life and Ministry," in *The Cambridge Companion to John Wesley*, ed. Randy L. Maddox and Jason W. Vickers (New York: Cambridge University Press, 2010), 46.

95. Wesley, *Journal*, 475–476.

96. Allan Coppedge, *John Wesley in Theological Debate* (Wilmore, KY: Wesley Heritage, 1987), 140.

Wesley defined the inner testimony of the Spirit as "an inward impression on the soul, whereby the Spirit of God immediately and directly witnesses to my spirit, that I am a child of God; that Jesus Christ hath loved me, and given himself for me; that all my sins are blotted out, and I, even I, am reconciled to God."[97] Wesley held that the witness of the Holy Spirit is necessarily the first ground of assurance:

> We must be holy of heart, and holy in life before we can be conscious that we are so; before we can have the testimony of our [human] spirit, that we are inwardly and outwardly holy. But we must love God, before we can be holy at all. . . . Now we cannot love God, till we know that He loves us. . . . And we cannot know his pardoning love to us, till his Spirit witness it to our spirit.[98]

Thus the testimony of the Holy Spirit gives Christians the certainty of God's love for them, their own love for God, their justification and regeneration, before there can be any life of holiness. This implies that the testimony of the Holy Spirit brings assurance of present justification, acceptance as a child of God, and pardon of all sin.

Yet, Wesley was well aware of the subjectivity of such inner testimony. Christians could become easy prey of the "presumption of a natural mind, and the delusion of the devil."[99] For this reason he closely tied the testimony of the Holy Spirit to a more objective ground of salvation, the observable presence of the fruit of the Holy Spirit in the believer's life. According to Wesley, Scripture evidences that validate the inner testimony of the Holy Spirit include conviction of sin, repentance, faithful obedience to God's commandments, and the fruit of the Spirit (Gal. 5:22–23).[100] Wesley reasoned, "The Word of God says everyone who has the fruit of the Spirit is a child of God; experience, or inward consciousness, tells me, that I have the fruit of the Spirit; and hence I rationally conclude, therefore I am a child of God."[101]

Arguably, in Wesley's theology, while the *inner testimony of the Holy Spirit* brings assurance of justification, the *testimony of a pure conscience* in

97. John Wesley, "The Witness of the Spirit," in *The Works of the Reverend John Wesley*, vol. 1, ed. John Emory (New York: J. Emory and B. Waugh, 1831), 94.

98. Ibid., 89.

99. Ibid.

100. Ibid., 64–68.

101. Ibid., 94.

harmony with God brings the assurance of daily sanctification or continual regeneration. Wesley observes that the evidence of the fruit of the Spirit may be "clouded for a while" and "not always indeed [visible] in the same degree." "Neither joy nor peace . . . nor love" always stays at the same level.[102] Obviously, Wesley anticipated that the conviction obtained at the moment of justification by the inner testimony of the Spirit would be reinforced by a continual growing in the likeness of Christ.

Additionally, for Wesley, it is in the joint testimony of the Holy Spirit and the human conscience that the assurance of salvation becomes complete. Although he spoke of the testimony of the Holy Spirit as prior to the testimony of the human conscience, he really rejected the idea that they could testify separately. In his Sermon 11, Wesley warned, "Let none ever presume to rest in any supposed testimony of the Spirit, which is separate from the fruit of it. If the Spirit of God does really testify that we are the children of God, the immediate consequence will be the fruit of the Spirit."[103] At the same time, he also urged his hearers:

> Let none rest in any supposed fruit of the Spirit without the witness. There may be foretastes of joy, of peace, of love . . . before the Spirit of God witnesses with our Spirit that we have "redemption in the blood of Jesus, even the forgiveness of sin." Yea, there may be a degree of long-suffering, of gentleness, of fidelity, meekness, temperance (. . . by the preventing grace of God,). . . . but it is by no means advisable to rest here; . . . If we are wise we, shall be continually crying to God, until his Spirit cry in our heart, *Abba, Father!*[104]

Therefore, according to Wesley, assurance of salvation is only a real certainty when the Spirit of God and the human spirit at once testify regarding the reality of faith, justification, and sanctification. This combined witness assures believers that they are truly children of God.

Finally, Wesley continually appealed to Scripture as the supporting pillar of his theology of assurance. The testimony of the Holy Spirit and the testimony of the human conscience are more or less based on personal experience and, therefore, in some measure subjective evidences. While he conceded that "strictly speaking," assurance "is a conclusion drawn partly from the Word of

---

102. Ibid., 100, 95.

103. Ibid., 100.

104. Ibid., 100 (emphasis in original).

God, and partly from our own experience," he several times pointed out, "this doctrine is founded on Scripture."[105] Human experience, then, though largely palpable in the life of "a great multitude" of believers, is only an indication, though a critical one, confirming the biblical teaching.[106] Allan Coppedge correctly points out that for Wesley Scripture "served as his standard, and if a man saw in his own life what the Bible described as evidence of sonship, then he could rationally be assured that he was a son of God."[107]

Thus Wesley insisted that every Christian should enjoy full assurance "beyond reasonable doubt"[108] of present justification, regeneration, sanctification, and participation as a child of God in the benefits of salvation. Assurance, he maintained, is "a common privilege of the children of God"[109] and "the very foundation of Christianity."[110]

Wesley seems to make a careful distinction between the doctrine of assurance and the doctrine of Christian perseverance in faith. While *assurance* concerns the *present reality* of the believer, *perseverance* mainly deals with what is future. Richard P. Heitzenrater thus observes that, for Wesley, "assurance is never a conviction or guarantee of final perseverance or a place in heaven."[111] In his treatise on perseverance, Wesley maintained that assurance of salvation "does not prove that every believer shall persevere, any more than that every believer is thus fully persuaded of his perseverance."[112]

How, then, does Wesley understand the doctrine of the final perseverance of the saints? In his treatise, *Serious Thoughts upon the Perseverance of*

---

105. Ibid., 94, 97.

106. Ibid., 96.

107. Coppedge, *Wesley in Theological Debate,* 141.

108. Wesley, "The Witness of the Spirit," 107.

109. Wesley, quoted in Robert Southey, *The Life of Wesley: The Rise and Progress of Methodism* (London: Paternoster-Row, 1820), 1:295.

110. Wesley, quoted in Kenneth J. Collins, *A Real Christian: The Life of John Wesley* (Nashville, TN: Abingdon, 1999), 87.

111. Richard P. Heitzenrater, "The Founding Brothers," in *The Oxford Handbook of Methodist Studies,* ed. William J. Abraham and James E. Kirby (New York: Oxford University Press, 2009), 47; cf. Coppedge, *Wesley in Theological Debate,* 142; Kenneth J. Collins, *The Theology of John Wesley: Holy Love and the Shape of Grace* (Nashville, TN: Abingdon Press, 2007), 137.

112. John Wesley, "Serious Thoughts upon the Perseverance of the Saints," *The Works of the Reverend John Wesley,* vol. 10, 3rd ed. (London: James Nichols, 1830), 291.

the Saints, Wesley complains that although large volumes have been written on the topic, they have not clarified the issue for common believers. Therefore he prepared a "short, plain treatise" on what he understood as the Scriptural teaching on perseverance.[113] He began by defining saints as those who presently enjoy the salvation that brings assurance through the testimony of the Holy Spirit and the fruits of the Spirit. His main question is: Can any of these saints with full assurance fall totally away from faith to the point of losing eternal salvation?

Wesley went to great lengths to explain that, sadly, the biblical answer to this question is yes. He affirmed, "On this authority, I believe a saint may fall away; that one who is holy or righteous in the judgment of God himself may nevertheless so fall from God as to perish everlastingly."[114] Nevertheless, Wesley encourages his followers not to despair but to trust in God. "It is the power of God only, and not our own, by which we are kept one day or one hour."[115] For him, the future of a believer remains secure in the hands of God. Indeed, it is not to the future that believers should look, but to their present joy in the assurance of forgiveness, to the reality of the fruit of the Spirit presently evident in their lives, and to the continual testimony of the Spirit that they are children of God.[116]

Summarizing, Wesley understood that Christians can enjoy a full assurance of present salvation. Like Arminius before him, he maintained that although there could be no present proof of final perseverance, there is abundant evidence of present assurance, and the grace that gives present assurance will also sustain to the end all who continue in a trusting, obedient relationship with Jesus.

AN ADVENTIST VIEW OF ASSURANCE

The Adventist movement began in the 1830s as an interdenominational rediscovery of the doctrine of the premillennial second advent of Christ.

---

113. Ibid., 284.

114. Ibid., 285. Wesley's treatise cites passage after passage of Scripture to prove that perseverance is conditioned on a day-to-day walk in sanctity of life; see, for example, Ezekiel 18:24; 33:13–18; John 8:51; 15:1–6; Romans 11:17, 20–22; and 1 Timothy 1:18–19.

115. Ibid., 293.

116. Ibid., 295–297.

The disappointment of the expectation that Christ would come in 1844 splintered the movement, but it motivated further Bible study that led to the formation of the Seventh-day Adventist denomination in 1863.

A major influence in the development of the Adventist church and its belief system was the prophetic gift exercised by Ellen G. White (1827–1915). Adventists find striking similarities between her visions and teachings and the visions and teachings of the biblical prophets. While they hold that she is not a canonical prophet, and her writings do not carry the same level of authority as Scripture, nevertheless they believe that she did receive special revelation by the inspiration of the Holy Spirit.[117] She often upheld the ideal that "we are reformers,"[118] and she regarded the Adventist movement as a continuation of the Reformation carried on by Luther, Calvin, and Wesley.

White's overall understanding of the way of salvation has much in common with classical Protestantism. Like Luther, she utterly repudiated the idea that human merit could contribute anything to the justification of a sinner, and she exalted the cross of Christ as the foundation of all assurance.

> Let the subject be made distinct and plain that it is not possible to effect anything in our standing before God or in the gift of God to us through creature merit. Should faith and works purchase the gift of salvation for anyone, then the Creator is under obligation to the creature. Here is an opportunity for falsehood to be accepted as truth. If any man can merit salvation by anything he may do, then he is in the same position as the Catholic to do penance for his sins. Salvation, then, is partly of debt, that may be earned as wages. If man cannot, by any of his good works, merit salvation, then it must be wholly of grace, received by man as a sinner because he receives and believes in Jesus. It is wholly a free gift. . . . Justification is wholly of grace and not procured by any works that fallen man can do.[119]

---

117. *Seventh-day Adventist Believe: An Exposition of the Fundamental Beliefs of the Seventh-day Adventist Church,* 2nd ed. (Silver Spring, MD: Ministerial Association of the General Conference of Seventh-day Adventists, 2005), 247–261; George E. Rice, "Spiritual Gifts," in *Handbook of Seventh-day Adventist Theology,* ed. Raoul Dederen (Hagerstown, MD: Review and Herald, 2000), 610–650.

118. See, e.g., Ellen G. White, *Testimonies for the Church,* vol. 6 (Boise, ID: Pacific Press, 1948), 179.

119. Ellen G. White, *Faith and Works* (Hagerstown, MD: Review and Herald, 2003), 19–20; cf. 23. Originally in Ellen G. White, *1888 Materials* (Washington, DC: The Ellen G. White Estate, 1987), 812–813.

Like Calvin, White cited Peter's fall as a perpetual warning to all who are tempted to equate present assurance with ultimate future perseverance. "Peter's fall was not instantaneous, but gradual. Self-confidence led him to the belief that he was saved, and step after step was taken in the downward path, until he could deny his Master. Never can we safely put confidence in self or feel, this side of heaven, that we are secure against temptation."[120]

Although she never mentioned Arminius in her writings, she certainly agreed with him that sin was not part of God's original plan.[121] It was Satan who pictured the "Creator as the author of sin and suffering and death," leading people to view God as "hard and exacting" and "watching to denounce and condemn, unwilling to receive the sinner so long as there was a legal excuse for not helping him."[122] White portrays God as passionately loving the lost, despite their depravity, and imparting grace to those who do not yet love Him. She did not use the technical terms *total depravity* or *prevenient grace,* but she expressed similar concept in different language.

[Depravity:] Man through sin has been severed from the life of God. His soul is palsied through the machinations of Satan, the author of sin. Of himself he is incapable of sensing sin, incapable of appreciating and appropriating the divine nature. Were it brought within his reach there is nothing in it that his natural heart would desire it. The bewitching power of Satan is upon him. All the ingenious subterfuges the devil can suggest are presented to his mind to prevent every good impulse. Every faculty and power given him of God has been used as a weapon against the divine

120. Ellen G. White, *Christ's Object Lessons* (Washington, DC: Review and Herald, 1941), 155. The quotation continues: "Those who accept the Saviour, however sincere their conversion, should never be taught to say or to feel that they are [finally, irrevocably] saved. This is misleading. *Every one should be taught to cherish hope and faith;* but even when we give ourselves to Christ and *know that He accepts us,* we are not beyond the reach of temptation. . . . Those who accept Christ, and in their first confidence say, I am saved, are in danger of trusting to themselves. They lose sight of their own weakness and their constant need of divine strength. They are unprepared for Satan's devices, and under temptation many, like Peter, fall into the very depths of sin. We are admonished, 'Let him that thinketh he standeth take heed lest he fall.' 1 Corinthians 10:12. Our only safety is in constant distrust of self, and dependence on Christ," emphasis added. White believed in biblical assurance; she only opposed the self-confidence or complacency that so easily precipitates a fall.

121. Ellen G. White, *Great Controversy* (Mountain View, CA: Pacific Press, 1911, 1950), 535–536.

122. Ellen G. White, *Prophets and Kings* (Mountain View, CA: Pacific Press, 1917), 311.

Benefactor. So, although He loves him, God cannot safely impart to him the gifts and blessings He desires to bestow.

[Grace:] But God will not be defeated by Satan. He sent His Son into the world, that through His taking the human form and nature, humanity and divinity combined in Him would elevate man in the scale of moral value with God.

[Grace:] There is no other way for man's salvation. "Without me," says Christ, "ye can do nothing" (John 15:5). Through Christ, and Christ alone, the springs of life can vitalize man's nature, transform his tastes, and set his affections flowing toward heaven. Through the union of the divine with the human nature Christ could enlighten the understanding and infuse His life-giving properties through the soul dead in trespasses and sins.[123]

Against the idea that God predestined any to reprobation, she set forth a metanarrative of cosmic conflict between good and evil that pictures God creating only perfect creatures—and honoring them with a gift of genuine moral freedom in spite of their Fall into utter helplessness. She held that only freely given love gives God any joy. A mechanistic affection from creatures who had no ability to do otherwise would not be a true reflection of God's love. Thus she portrayed God as voluntarily self-limiting the exercise of His sovereignty, in order to create angels and humans as free moral agents, because, unless they were free to reject God, they could not voluntarily love Him.

White was directly influenced by Wesley, because she was born (1827) into a devout Methodist family just thirty-six years after John Wesley's death (1791). At fourteen, Ellen Harmon White was baptized into the Methodist Episcopal Church in Portland, Maine. Her description of her own conversion experience was strongly colored by Methodist understandings of justification and sanctification. She recalled that "as I prayed, the burden and agony of soul that I had endured so long, left me, and the blessing of the Lord descended upon me like the gentle dew."[124] Many American Methodists in the 1830s held to a view of instantaneous sanctification. White sought this experience and apparently thought she

---

123. Ellen G. White, *Selected Messages* (Washington, DC: Review and Herald, 1958), 1:340–341.

124. James White, *Life Sketches: Ancestry, Early Life, Christian Experience, and Extensive Labors of Elder James White, and His Wife, Mrs. Ellen G. White* (Battle Creek, MI: Steam, 1880), 159, 160; White, *Testimonies,* vol. 1, 31–32.

had received it, but she later reinterpreted her experience, not as instantaneous sanctification, but as the witness of the Holy Spirit that God had forgiven her sins and accepted her as His child.[125]

Her mature writings describe sanctification as "the work of a lifetime," not in the sense that sanctification cannot be immediately experienced, but in the sense that as a product of a freely chosen personal relationship with Christ, it remains free and fluid, a relationship that must continue to be chosen as long as life lasts.[126] It is a secure relationship because Christ continues to choose the believer, and His choice of the believer does not waver. For the believer who carefully guards every impulse toward independence from Christ, in order to abide in constant trusting submission to Christ as Lord and Master, Christ's grace and power virtually guarantees the outcome of faith.[127] But the believer is not preserved by a static decree that prevents falling. Rather, the believer is held by the power of divine love, a Love so great that it will succeed in saving "all who do not interpose a perverse will and thus frustrate His grace."[128]

---

125 Ellen G. White, *Testimonies*, vol. 1, 31–32.

126. Ellen White saw the redeemed as remaining completely free moral agents throughout eternity. "The death of Christ upon the cross made sure the destruction of him who has the power of death, who was the originator of sin. When Satan is destroyed, there will be none to tempt to evil; the atonement will never need to be repeated; and there will be no danger of another rebellion in the universe of God. That which alone can effectually restrain from sin in this world of darkness, will prevent sin in heaven. The significance of the death of Christ will be seen by saints and angels. Fallen men could not have a home in the paradise of God without the Lamb slain from the foundation of the world. Shall we not then exalt the cross of Christ? The angels ascribe honor and glory to Christ, for *even they are not secure except by looking to the sufferings of the Son of God. It is through the efficacy of the cross that the angels of heaven are guarded from apostasy. Without the cross they would be no more secure against evil than were the angels before the fall of Satan. Angelic perfection failed in heaven. Human perfection failed in Eden, the paradise of bliss. All who wish for security in earth or heaven must look to the Lamb of God. The plan of salvation, making manifest the justice and love of God, provides an eternal safeguard against defection in unfallen worlds, as well as among those who shall be redeemed by the blood of the Lamb.* Our only hope is perfect trust in the blood of Him who can save to the uttermost all that come unto God by Him. The death of Christ on the cross of Calvary is our only hope in this world, and it will be our theme in the world to come," Ellen G. White, "What Was Secured by the Death of Christ," *Signs of the Times* (Dec. 30, 1889), par. 4 (emphasis added).

127. See Philippians 1:6; 2:12–13; 2 Peter 1:10–11.

128. "In every command or injunction that God gives there is a promise, the most positive, underlying the command. God has made provision that we may become like unto

Wesley's concept of "perfected in love" describes a life of loving service that springs not from selfish motives, fear or guilt, but from love to God and humankind (1 John 4:17). White's concept is very similar: "When self is merged in Christ, love springs forth spontaneously. The completeness of Christian character is attained when the impulse to help and bless others springs constantly from within—when the sunshine of heaven fills the heart and is revealed in the countenance."[129] For her, "character perfection" (i.e., moral or ethical maturity and a non-compromising attitude toward sin) signified the goal of sanctification.[130]

One aspect of White's teaching is that she makes a clear distinction between salvation and assurance of salvation. She held that it is possible to have salvation without assurance,[131] or false assurance without salvation,[132] but that genuine biblical assurance is essential to the normal Christian life. "It is essential," she wrote, "to have faith in Jesus, and to believe you are saved through Him; but there is danger in taking the position that many do take in saying, 'I am saved.'"[133] But while she cautioned against overconfidence, she urged the necessity of the faith that brings assurance.

> You are not to look to the future, thinking that at some distant day you are to be made holy; it is now that you are to be sanctified through the truth. . . . No one can make himself better, but we are to come to Jesus as we are, earnestly desiring to be cleansed from every spot and stain of sin, and receive the gift of the Holy Spirit. *We are not to doubt his mercy, and say, "I do not*

Him, and He will accomplish this for all who do not interpose a perverse will and thus frustrate His grace"; Ellen G. White, *Thoughts from the Mount of Blessing* (1896; repr., Mountain View, CA: Pacific Press, 1955), 76.

129. White, *Christ's Object Lessons,* 384.

130. Regarding Wesley and Ellen G. White on perfection, see Woodrow W. Whidden II, "Adventist Soteriology: The Wesleyan Connection," *Wesleyan Theological Journal* 30 (Spring 1995): 173–186; Whidden, "The Soteriology of Ellen G. White: The Persistent Path to Perfection, 1836–1902" (PhD diss., Drew University, 1989); Whidden, *The Judgment and Assurance: The Dynamics of Personal Salvation* (Hagerstown, MD: Review and Herald, 2012); Whidden, *Ellen White on Salvation* (Hagerstown, MD: Review and Herald, 1995), 131–142.

131. See, for example, Ellen G. White, *Desire of Ages* (Mountain View, CA: Pacific Press, 1911, 1940), 638.

132. See, for example, White, *Testimonies,* vol. 1, 133–134, 158, 163, 242–243.

133. White, *Selected Messages,* 1:373.

know whether I shall be saved or not." By living faith we must lay hold of his promise, for he has said, "Though your sins be as scarlet, they shall be as white as snow."[134]

Each one of you may know for yourself that you have a living Saviour, that he is your helper and your God. *You need not stand where you say, "I do not know whether I am saved."* Do you believe in Christ as your personal Saviour? If you do, then rejoice.[135]

The perishing sinner may say: "I am a lost sinner; but Christ came to seek and to save that which was lost. He says, 'I came not to call the righteous, but sinners to repentance' (Mark 2:17). *I am a sinner, and He died upon Calvary's cross to save me. I need not remain a moment longer unsaved.* He died and rose again for my justification, and *He will save me now.* I accept the forgiveness He has promised."[136]

Confronting some Adventist ministers who were "talking fears and doubts" as to whether they would be saved, she challenged, "Brethren, you have expressed many doubts; but have you followed your Guide? You must dispense with [H]im before you can lose your way; for the Lord has hedged you in on every side."[137] Climaxing a powerful appeal to trust in Christ, she declared, "Faith comes by the Word of God. Then grasp His promise, 'Him that cometh to Me I will in no wise cast out.' John 6:37. Cast yourself at His feet with the cry, 'Lord, I believe; help Thou mine unbelief.' You can never perish while you do this—never."[138]

The dilemma of present versus ultimate assurance, which the earlier reformers all wrestled with, was also addressed by Ellen White. Despite the possibility of backsliding, she believed in present assurance and security: "If you are right with God today, you are ready if Christ should come today."[139] Regarding her own hope of ultimate perseverance, she declared,

---

134. Ellen G. White, "The Christian a Guardian of Sacred Trusts," *Signs of the Times* (April 4, 1892), par. 3, emphasis added.

135. Ellen G. White, "The Need of Missionary Effort," *General Conference Bulletin* (April 10, 1901) par. 14, emphasis added.

136. Ellen G. White, *Selected Messages,* 1:392, emphasis added.

137. Ellen G. White, "The Christian's Refuge," *Review and Herald* (April 15, 1884), par. 13, emphasis added.

138. White, *Desire of Ages,* 429.

139. Ellen G. White, "One Day at a Time," *In Heavenly Places* (Washington, DC: Review and Herald, 1967), 227.

"I rejoice that Jesus has a firm hold of us. Our grasp [on Him] is feeble and easily broken, but our safety depends upon the firm hold Jesus has upon us," and that He "ever liveth to make intercession for us."[140] Trusting not in themselves, but in their immortal, divine Intercessor, Christians can and should have abundant evidence of present assurance; and the grace that gives present assurance will also sustain to the end all who continue in a trusting, obedient relationship with Jesus.

This might sound like a tautology: if believers persist in faith, they shall persevere. But the reality is that to one who remains faithful every day, one day in the succession of days will be the last, and present assurance will have persevered into ultimate salvation. Augustine spoke of a "gift of perseverance" as if it were something magical, something quite "other" than simply "keeping on keeping on" with Jesus.[141] But in the Wesleyan-Adventist view, perseverance is a gift of grace to be embraced by choice and received through faith moment by moment in the daily tests of life. Ultimate perseverance at the end of life is essentially the culmination of the minutes and hours of daily perseverance in faith, repentance, forgiveness, submission, and obedience, in order to keep the relationship with Christ unbroken. Faith is invisible, but genuine faith bears fruit, and the character of the fruit provides visible proof of the quality of the faith. Thus deeds are necessarily involved in the judgment simply because they provide visible evidence of the invisible faith.[142]

This is why Ellen White insists on distinguishing between salvation and assurance of salvation. *Salvation* means being on God's list for eternal life—or in biblical terms, *having* your name in the Book of Life. *Assurance of salvation* means *knowing* that your name is in the Book of Life.[143]

140. Ellen G. White to James White, July 27, 1878 (Letter 42, 1878), quoting Heb. 7:25, quoted in Ellen G. White, *The Upward Look* (Washington, DC: Review and Herald, 1982), 222.

141. Augustine, *On Rebuke and Grace* 26 (NPNF[1], 5:482); idem, *On Perseverance* 1 (NPNF[1], 5:526).

142. For detailed treatments of assurance in the final judgment, see Whidden, *The Judgment and Assurance: The Dynamics of Personal Salvation*; John T. Anderson, *Investigating the Judgment: Patterns of Divine Judgment* (Hagerstown, MD: Review and Herald, 2003); Hans K. LaRondelle, *Assurance of Salvation* (Nampa, ID: Pacific Press, 1999), 93–101; Whidden, *Ellen White on Salvation*, 131–142.

143. See Philippians 4:3; Revelation 3:5; 13:8; 17:8; 20:12–15.

CONCLUSION

Considering the fact that five centuries have elapsed since Luther began lecturing at Wittenberg,[144] there is a remarkable degree of unity among the Protestant expositors on the basic principles of assurance. Though there are minor differences of perspective on details, there is a Protestant consensus on several great scriptural foundations.

The five Protestants considered—Luther, Calvin, Arminius, Wesley, and White—all agree that *human merit plays no part in assurance.* Even though all agree that the testimony of a pure conscience constitutes evidence of salvation, nevertheless, they all deny that such evidence involves any human merit. Forgiveness and new birth are a gift of grace. Sanctification is a gift of grace. Sinners, who are by definition rebels, can never be the source of any saving merit. All merit for salvation originates with Christ and His atoning sacrifice on the cross.

All the Protestants considered here agree that *the promises of Scripture, certifying the character of God, form the objective foundation of assurance.* Scripture testifies that "God is love." He desires "all men to be saved and to come unto the knowledge of the truth." He is "not willing that any should perish, but that all should come to repentance."[145] Therefore, each believer may declare: "The promises of Scripture declare that God loves all; therefore God loves me; therefore I know that if I accept His gift of forgiving and regenerating grace, He will also give me the transforming grace and persisting grace to continue faithful in relationship to Him as long as life shall last."

All the above Protestants agree that, after the testimony of Scripture to the character of God, *there are two further evidences of assurance: the inward witness of the Holy Spirit, and the visible fruit of the Spirit in the life of the believer.* The inward witness of the Spirit (Rom. 8:16; 1 Cor. 2:12; Gal. 4:6; Eph. 1:17–18) is a *subjective* evidence of salvation; yet it is verifiable, because it is always accompanied by a third evidence of salvation, the fruit of the Spirit in a life conforming to the will of God revealed in Scripture. The fruit of the Spirit in a transformed life can be *objective* evidence,

---

144. Luther began lecturing at the University of Wittenberg on the Psalms in 1513. Grosse, *Salvation and Certitude,* 68; cf. Roland H. Bainton, *Here I Stand: A Life of Martin Luther* (Nashville, TN: Abingdon, 1950), 46–53.

145. 1 John 4:8; 1 Timothy 2:4; 2 Peter 3:9.

because it is tested by the *objective* Word of God and can be *objectively* discerned by other people. A life conforming to the will of God in Scripture is, from the internal perspective of the individual, a potentially *subjective* evidence, since one's reading of Scripture and one's evaluation of one's own motives and behavior can both be *subjective*. But to the extent that one's behavior is verifiable by multiple trustworthy external witnesses, the testimony of a faithful life can also provide *objective* evidence of assurance.

Because both the witness of the Holy Spirit and the transformation of the human life are rooted in a continually growing relationship with Christ and the Holy Spirit (John 15:1–8; 17:3), *ultimate assurance is found only in the context of an ongoing relationship with Christ.* As Hebrews 4:2 says, even the gospel will be of no benefit unless "mixed with faith" in the hearers. In other words, believers enter by faith into a life-changing relationship with Christ which leads to faith-based obedience (Rom. 1:5).

Regarding ultimate perseverance, Augustine was partly right: perseverance is a gift of grace (Phil. 1:6). But it is not an unconditional guarantee. To the contrary, Scripture warns: "Let him who thinks he stands take heed lest he fall" (1 Cor. 10:12; cf. 9:27; Heb. 6:4–9; 10:26, 36). Whereas Augustine seems to see perseverance as a one-time, miraculous, and irreversible gift, the Protestant consensus, especially in the Arminian-Wesleyan-Adventist line, is that the grace of perseverance is given daily, in the midst of the daily tests of life. Daily God's children receive grace to resist temptation and to bear patiently the annoyances and disappointments that are a normal part of human life. Daily they receive repentance (Rom. 2:4) and forgiveness for all the ways in which their characters still "fall short of the glory of God" (Rom. 3:23–24). Thus by grace, through faith, believers may "work out [their] own salvation with fear and trembling." In "fear and trembling," because they know they can fail and fall; but in faith and hope because they also know that "it is God who works in [them] both to will and to do for His good pleasure" (Phil. 2:12–13). Thus by daily abiding in Christ, they ultimately persevere, and one day they will see Him face to face, whom they have known and trusted through Scripture, faith, and prayer.

CHAPTER 18

WIND AND THE "HOLY WIND": DIVINE ASSURANCE OF SALVATION

Jo Ann Davidson

While the wind is itself invisible, it produces effects that are seen and felt. So the work of the Spirit upon the soul will reveal itself in every act of him who has felt its saving power.
—Ellen G. White, *Desire of Ages*, 173

About a quarter before nine, while he was describing the change which God works in the heart through faith in Christ, I felt my heart strangely warmed. I felt I did trust in Christ, Christ alone for salvation.
—John Wesley, *Journal 2*, May 24, 1738

The stone streets of Jerusalem carried the steps of a prominent member of the Jewish clergy to meet with Jesus one evening. This would be an advantageous time to have a private conversation because Jesus was always surrounded by clamoring crowds of people during the day. Introduced as a Pharisee in the Gospel of John narrative, Nicodemus is portrayed as a conscientious follower of Jewish tradition. Also called "a ruler of the Jews" (John 3:1), Nicodemus was likely a member of the Sanhedrin. His nocturnal audience with Jesus probably was to protect his professional reputation. After all, Jesus was not of the established clerical aristocracy, having never earned professional Jerusalem credentials. And His ministry was just getting started. But Nicodemus had heard of (and perhaps seen) Jesus performing miracles and could not doubt His impressive power.

He addresses Jesus: "Rabbi, we know that You are a teacher come from God; for no one can do these signs that You do unless God is with him" (John 3:2).[1] Using the esteemed title "Rabbi," Nicodemus shows respect and perhaps seeks to put himself in as good a light as possible. With the plural "we," Nicodemus perhaps includes himself within a group of those who were impressed with the young Galilean.

Jesus ignores Nicodemus's introductory niceties. Instead, He reveals His divine nature by addressing the heart of His guest.[2] "Verily, verily, I say unto thee, Except a man be born again,[3] he cannot see the kingdom of God" (John 3:3).[4] The "verily, verily" with which Jesus begins calls for serious attention.[5] The final destiny of Nicodemus will depend upon how he accepts these words: "I say to you, unless one is born again, he cannot see the kingdom of God." This is a categorical, uncompromising statement and some of the most solemn words Jesus will ever utter. The "new birth" is the absolute foundation of any hope for salvation and thus for eternal life. It constitutes the fundamental ABCs of true religion.

In all likelihood Nicodemus had not expected this turn in the conversation. He is a devout Pharisee, well versed in the Levitical code, and feels assured of God's favor. Surely all his years of study and zealous obedience of the law should count for something. Perhaps he is slightly irritated that such sentiments should be applied to him, wondering why Christ is not

---

1. Unless otherwise indicated, all Scripture quotations are taken from the New King James Version®. Copyright © 1982 by Thomas Nelson. Used by permission. All rights reserved. Italics in Scripture quotes reflect emphasis added by author.

2. Ellen White writes poignantly of this moment: "Instead of recognizing this salutation, Jesus bent His eyes upon the speaker, as if reading his very soul. In His infinite wisdom He saw before Him a seeker after truth. He knew the object of this visit, and with a desire to deepen the conviction already resting upon His listener's mind, He came directly to the point, saying solemnly, yet kindly, 'Verily, verily, I say unto thee, Except a man be born from above, he cannot see the kingdom of God,' John 3:3, margin," *Desire of Ages* (Boise, ID: Pacific Press, 2006), 168.

3. The Greek, *anōthen*, can mean either "again" or "from above."

4. The King James Version is used for this quotation to catch the phrase "Verily, verily," which is a translation of the formulaic Greek "*Amèn, amèn.*"

5. Three times in this conversation with Nicodemus Jesus uses the authoritative "verily, verily" (John 3:3, 5, 11), underscoring the supreme importance of this discussion. Nowhere else in the Gospels does Jesus speak of the new birth so comprehensively.

complimenting his elite position as a religious leader in the capital city of Jerusalem. By virtue of his birth as an Israelite, moreover, he is assured of a place in the kingdom of God. Yet to this prominent Jewish ruler Jesus insists, "You must be born again." If He had said this to some obvious sinner, Nicodemus would have agreed, "Yes, *that* person *needs* to be converted." However, Nicodemus was one of the revered people in the Jewish religion. He had come to discuss other matters. Instead, Jesus "laid bare the foundation principles of truth," speaking of the need for "spiritual regeneration."[6] Instead of more theological knowledge, a new heart is absolutely necessary. Unless this dramatic change takes place, entering the kingdom of God will not be possible.

Jesus keeps reiterating this vital point in different ways: "unless one is born again" or "born of the Spirit" (John 3:3, 6). Improvement in outward behavior, keeping the law more earnestly, is not what is necessary. Something more radical is called for. Jesus also expresses the "unless clause" other times: "Unless you repent, you will all likewise perish" (Luke 13:3, 5); "Unless you are converted, and become as little children, you will by no means enter the kingdom of heaven" (Matt. 18:3); "Unless your righteousness exceeds the righteousness of the scribes and pharisees, you will by no means enter the kingdom of heaven" (Matt. 5:20). All these "unless" clauses really mean the same thing.

What is "regeneration," the "new birth," that Jesus insists on? It may be easier to describe what it is *not*. It is not going to church or even serving the church in various offices. Christians may pride themselves on regular church attendance, and attending church is a good thing. But it is not necessarily proof of regeneration. Others say, "I am trying to do what is right. I am attempting to keep the Ten Commandments." But according to Christ's definition to Nicodemus in John 3, this is not the "new birth." Nor does baptism guarantee regeneration. Because, sadly, a person may be baptized into the visible Church and still not be reborn. Baptism is essential, but it cannot replace the need for the new birth: "Unless one is born again, he cannot see the kingdom of God" (John 3:3).

Other believers may urge that they always participate in the Lord's Supper. And this is commendable. Jesus affirms this practice: as often as believers do it, they commemorate His death till He comes (1 Cor. 11:26).

---

6. Ellen G. White, *Desire of Ages* (Mountain View: CA, Pacific Press, 1940), 171.

But even this does not ensure that the new birth has occurred. Jesus states it so plainly that there can be no mistake: "Unless one is born again, he cannot see the kingdom of God" (John 3:3).

Another person might think that regular prayer life indicates regeneration. Though it will surely be a part of a regenerate person's life, prayer does not ensure that the new birth has happened. The solemn nature of Christ's statement to Nicodemus, who had not even outwardly asked for clarification, allows for no misunderstanding. Nicodemus didn't look like the type of person who needed the new birth. He wasn't a drunkard, a gambler, or a thief. He was an honorable member of the Sanhedrin, which was a high religious position. He was satisfied with "salvation by works," but now he hears that salvation is a gift of God. It is not brought about by anything a person does—just as a person can do nothing about his or her natural birth. Jesus insists: "Unless one is born again, he cannot see the kingdom of God."

The human heart is evil by nature. Paul quotes numerous passages from the Psalms to back up this point in Romans 3:10–18:

> *"There is none righteous, no, not one;*
> *There is none who understands;*
> *There is none who seeks after God.*
> *They have all turned aside;*
> *They have together become unprofitable;*
> *There is none who does good, no, not one."*
> *"Their throat is an open tomb;*
> *With their tongues they have practiced deceit";*
> *"The poison of asps is under their lips";*
> *"Whose mouth is full of cursing and bitterness."*
> *"Their feet are swift to shed blood;*
> *Destruction and misery are in their ways;*
> *And the way of peace they have not known."*
> *"There is no fear of God before their eyes."*

Augustine of Hippo, commenting on the nature of the human in Romans 5, decries, "From the moment, then, when 'by one man sin entered into the world, and death by sin, and so death passed upon all men, in whom all sinned,' the entire mass of our nature was ruined beyond doubt."[7] Jacob Arminius expresses similar inabilities of fallen humans: "In his lapsed and

---

7. Augustine, *On Original Sin*, 34; *NPNF*, First Series, 5:248.

sinful state, man is not capable, of and by himself, either to think, to will, or to do that which is really good."[8] Arminius goes on to assert that only through renewal by the Holy Spirit can the human do good: "It is necessary for him to be regenerated and renewed in his intellect, affections or will, and in all his powers, by God in Christ through the Holy Spirit, that he may be qualified rightly to understand, esteem, consider, will, and perform whatever is truly good."[9] In a similar vein, Ellen White confirms that what Nicodemus needed was not an improvement of his abilities, but a complete transformation by the Holy Spirit: "The Christian's life is not a modification or improvement of the old, but a transformation of nature. There is a death to self and sin, and a new life altogether. This change can be brought about only by the effectual working of the Holy Spirit."[10]

So what *can* a person do? That was the question that Nicodemus asked. According to Jesus, it is absolutely impossible to bring about the new birth on one's own. There must be a new creation, new life—and this demands the work of the Creator. During the Creation (Gen. 1 and 2), human beings did not just suddenly appear. No human help was needed—or possible. The Creator brought human life into existence. It is the same with the creation of new life. It is just as impossible for people to create themselves out of nothing as it is to make themselves holy before God.

When Jesus cried out on the cross, "It is finished" (John 19:30), something extraordinary happened! Salvation was assured. The task of His children is to accept His finished work. There is no hope for any as long as they try to work out salvation by what they do. Well they might ask with Nicodemus, "How can these things be? You mean, all the good things that I work at so hard don't help? Aren't we supposed to work out our salvation 'with fear and trembling'?" (Phil. 2:12). However, the position Jesus takes never varies. He insists that His children must receive salvation first before they can work it out.

In attempting to explain this spiritual principle, Jesus uses the analogy of wind. Perhaps He and Nicodemus are feeling a strong breeze that night as Jesus speaks: "The wind blows where it wishes, and you hear the

---

8. (Jacob) James Arminius, *The Writings of Arminius*, 3 vols. (Grand Rapids, MI: Baker, 1956), 1:252.

9. Ibid.

10. White, *Desire of Ages*, 172.

sound of it, but cannot tell where it comes from and where it goes. So is every one who is born of the Spirit" (John 3:8). No one understands the wind. It may be blowing southward close by, and a hundred miles further south, blowing northward. No one can fully explain wind currents. No one can control the wind. It acts independently of human control. But just because a person cannot explain the wind doesn't mean he or she denies that it exists—claiming there is no such thing as the wind. It would be foolish to try to persuade anyone that wind doesn't exist, because everyone has seen its effects.

Some of the best known conversions in history include a dramatic point in time: Paul and the blinding light in Acts 9, Augustine and the call to "pick it up and read" in *Confessions* 8.29,[11] and John Wesley's Aldersgate experience where his "heart was strangley warmed." These famous conversions may well be the exceptions rather than the norm for Christian conversion. In the context of the story of Nicodemus and the Holy Spirit acting on the heart, Ellen White suggests that,

> A person may not be able to tell the exact time or place, or to trace all the circumstances in the process of conversion; but this does not prove him to be unconverted. By an agency as unseen as the wind, Christ is constantly working upon the heart. Little by little, perhaps unconsciously to the receiver, impressions are made that tend to draw the soul to Christ.[12]

There are many different ways impressions are made, even though a person may not realize it. Then, at a time the Holy Spirit knows is best for that individual, He comes with an appeal that brings the person to surrender to Jesus. Conversion then becomes apparent to the person and those around him or her.[13] This wooing by the Spirit of God and the results are as unexplainable as the wind. The wind cannot be seen, but its effects can be. The reality of the

11. Maria Boulding, trans., *Saint Augustine: The Confessions*, 2nd ed. (Hyde Park, NY: New City Press, 2012), 206.

12. White, *Desire of Ages*, 172.

13. Steven Guthrie writes eloquently about the Holy Spirit's power: "The Spirit moves in ways we do not expect and acts with a power we cannot easily describe. . . . When we remember that the Spirit is the *ruach*, we remember to be humble before a sovereign God, whose thoughts are higher than our thoughts and whose ways are higher than our ways," *Creator Spirit: The Holy Spirit and the Art of Becoming Human* (Grand Rapids, MI: Baker Academic, 2011), 10.

new birth will be revealed in the newborn person's life—apparent to the person and those around as the "Holy Wind," the Holy Spirit[14] blows His saving power through the soul. Ellen White's description is graphic:

> When the Spirit of God takes possession of the heart, it transforms the life. Sinful thoughts are put away, evil deeds are renounced; love, humility, and peace take the place of anger, envy, and strife. Joy takes the place of sadness, and the countenance reflects the light of heaven. No one sees the hand that lifts the burden, or beholds the light descend from the courts above. The blessing comes when by faith the soul surrenders itself to God. Then that power which no human eye can see creates a new being in the image of God.[15]

The Apostle Paul also encourages Titus:

> But when the kindness and the love of God our Savior toward man appeared, not by works of righteousness which we have done, but according to His mercy He saved us, through the washing of regeneration and renewing of the Holy Spirit, whom He poured out on us abundantly through Jesus Christ our Savior, that having been justified by His grace we should become heirs according to the hope of eternal life. (Titus 3:4–7)

The precise way it happens Jesus does not explain. Even so, He assures that the effects of the new birth will be experienced and seen. God does everything that He can to bring salvation to everyone who wants it. The prophet Isaiah quotes God's wistful words: "What more could have been done to My vineyard that I have not done in it?" (Isa. 5:4). He sent His prophets—many were rejected and some killed. God then sent His beloved Son, and He was murdered. Now the Holy Spirit has been given to convict humanity of its need for salvation and to bring about the new birth because the only way to get into the Kingdom of God is to be "born" into it. No one need worry that God has in reserve something else to make salvation possible.

> God's intent is a saving intent, and the scope of his salvation is worldwide. His love for the whole human race expresses itself in the giving of his only Son to die on the cross ([John 3:]16). This "giving" is more specific than "sending" (v. 17). God "sent" his Son into the world (the Incarnation), but he **gave** his Son in death (the Passion) so that the world might be saved and

---

14. The same Greek word *pneuma* can mean "wind" or "spirit."

15. White, *Desire of Ages,* 173.

not condemned (v. 17). The universality is qualified, however, by the phrases **everyone who believes** in verse 15 and **whoever believes** in verse 16. To gain eternal life, a person must believe, just as the Israelites had to look at the bronze snake in order to be healed (Num 21:8–9).[16]

Jesus also employs a striking Old Testament event to help Nicodemus understand this vital truth. This is something to which this learned man could better relate. When the people of Israel were dying from deadly snakes in the wilderness, "the LORD said to Moses, 'Make a fiery serpent, and set it on a pole; and it shall be that everyone who is bitten, when he looks at it, shall live'" (Num. 21:8). Concerning these fiery serpents, the lifted up image, and the method of the cure, John Wesley comments, "This method of cure was prescribed that it might appear to be God's own work and not the effect of nature or art." Wesley continues, quoting Paul in Romans 8:3, "The serpent signified Christ, who was 'in the likeness of sinful flesh,' though without sin."[17] Augustine shares a similar insight: "Now there is this difference between the figurative image and the real thing: the figure procured temporal life; the reality, of which that was the figure, procures eternal life."[18] Ellen White drives this message of the power of God through Christ home:

> Many Israelites had regarded the sacrifice in the temple service as being able in itself to set them free from sin. God desired to teach them that it had no more value than the brazen serpent. It was to lead their minds to the Savior. Whether needing healing of their deadly wounds or pardon of their deadly sins, they could do nothing for themselves except show faith in God's provision.[19]

---

16. J. Ramsey Michaels, *New International Biblical Commentary: John* (Peabody, MA: Hendrickson Publishers and Paternoster Press, 1989), 59, emphasis in original.

17. John Wesley, *Wesley's Notes on the Bible* (Grand Rapids: Francis Asbury Press, 1987), 127, comments on Numbers 21:8.

18. Augustine, "Lectures or Tractates on the Gospel According to St. John," *NPNF*, First Series, 7:85; comments on John 3:6–21.

19. William Hendriksen is sensitive to this point: "Now, in John 3:14 the words 'As Moses . . . so must the Son of man' clearly indicate that the event recorded in Numbers 21 is a type of the lifting up of the Son of man. . . . The following points of comparison are either specifically mentioned or clearly implied in 3:14, 15 (cf. also verse 16):

   a. In both cases (Numbers 21 and John 3) death threatens as a punishment for sin.

   b. In both cases it is God himself who, in his sovereign grace, provides a remedy.

Those who had been bitten by the serpents might have questioned how there could be any help in that brazen symbol. They might have demanded a scientific explanation. But no explanation was given. They must accept the Word of God to them through Moses or else perish without looking.[20]

The same happens with the new birth—humanity must look and live.

The light shining from the cross reveals the love of God. His love is drawing us to Himself. If we do not resist this drawing, we shall be led to the foot of the cross in repentance for the sins that have crucified the Saviour. Then the Spirit of God through faith produces a new life in the soul. The thoughts and desires are brought into obedience to the will of Christ. The heart, the mind, are created anew in the image of Him who works in us to subdue all things to Himself. Then the law of God is written in the mind and heart, and we can say with Christ, "I delight to do Thy will, O my God" (Psa 40:8).[21]

Does humanity today need to grasp the same truth of the uplifted serpent that Jesus used to teach Nicodemus? Paul tells us that we are justified by faith apart from observing the law (Rom. 3:21–8). It cannot be obedience to the law of God, but faith in the blood of Christ that brings each of us a just justification. Commenting on verse 27, Wesley says, "The law of faith is that divine constitution which makes faith, not works, the condition of

---

c. In both cases this remedy consists of something (or some One) which (who) must be lifted up, in public view. [Many commentators add something like this: as the uplifted serpent was not an actual serpent but one of brass, so also Christ is not really a partaker of sin but only "made in the likeness of sinful flesh."]

d. In both cases, those who, with a believing heart, look unto that which (or: look unto the One who) is lifted up, are healed.

Here, as always, the Antitype far transcends the type. In Numbers the people are face to face with *physical death*; in John, mankind is viewed as exposed to *eternal death* because of sin. In Numbers it is *the type* that is lifted up. This type—the brazen serpent—has no power to heal. It points forward to the *Antitype*, Christ, who does have this power. In Numbers the emphasis is on *physical healing*: when a man fixed his eye upon the serpent of brass, he was restored to health. In John it is *spiritual life*—everlasting life—that is granted to him who reposes his trust in the One who is lifted up.

The lifting up of the Son of man is presented as a '*must*.' . . . It is not *a* remedy; it is *the only possible* remedy for sin," *Exposition of the Gospel According to John*, New Testament Commentary (Grand Rapids, MI: Baker, 1953), 138, emphasis in original.

20. White, *Desire of Ages*, 173.

21. Ibid., 175.

acceptance."[22] Every sinner, like Nicodemus, must allow the gentle work of the Holy Spirit to bring us to a willingness to recognize our sinful need and be saved by our lifted up Saviour. In the words of Ellen White, "Through faith we receive the grace of God; but faith is not our Savior. It earns nothing. It is the hand by which we lay hold upon Christ, and appropriate His merits, the remedy for sin." The message of prevenient grace flows down the centuries: humans cannot even repent without Him.[23] The struggle of Augustine is a case in point: "I was groaning in spirit and shaken by violent anger because I could form no resolve to enter into a covenant with You, though in my bones I knew that this was what I ought to do, and everything in me lauded such a course to the skies."[24] Augustine's will held back, powerless, until, empowered by God, he allowed himself to trust God. "Repentance comes from Christ as truly as does pardon."[25]

Even though Adam's fall wrought us all natural sinners, if a person is lost, it will not be because Adam fell, but because the gift of salvation is refused. If a person is lost, it will not be because a person is a sinner but because the "remedy" was spurned: "How shall we escape if we neglect so great a salvation?" (Heb. 2:3). For one who had been bitten by the deadly serpents in the wilderness, it would have done no good to look at the wound. Likewise it does no good to focus on the wound of sin. It is only the Savior who has power to save. Looking at the pole which held up the brazen serpent was not enough. A person must look beyond the pole to the Crucified Savior—who "takes away the sin of the world" (John 1:29). Jesus has provided the only remedy for sin—and it is offered to the whole world. "He 'must' be lifted up. There is no other way for God or for human beings to alter the drastic sin situation of humankind except that Jesus be 'lifted up.' He *must* die. There were no other alternatives even for God. . . . And His giving of His Son demonstrates 'the reality, enormity, and salvific power of the love of God for a sinful world and this human race which lives in that world of sin.'"[26]

---

22. John Wesley, *Notes on the Bible*, 498, comments on Romans 3:27.

23. Ellen G. White, *Steps to Christ* (Battle Creek, MI: Review and Herald, 1908), 26: "We can no more repent without the Spirit of Christ to awaken the conscience than we can be pardoned without Christ."

24. Augustine, *Confessions* 8.19, quoted in Boulding, *Saint Augustine,* 200.

25. Ibid. Cf. Acts 5:31.

26. Beauford H. Bryant and Mark S. Krause, *The College Press NIV Commentary: John,*

The sacrifice of Jesus for our sins is clearly taught throughout the New Testament. In the Old Testament, the truth of salvation provided by the actions of God for a sinful humanity is also taught. Isaiah recognized the universality of human sinfulness: "But we are all like an unclean thing, and all our righteousnesses are like filthy rags" (Isa. 64:6). David illustrates the need for God's action to change us: "Create in me a clean heart, O God, and renew a steadfast spirit within me" (Ps. 51:10). Ezekiel describes the work of the Holy Spirit within a human long before Paul wrote Romans: "I will give you a new heart and put a new spirit within you; I will take the heart of stone out of your flesh and give you a heart of flesh. I will put My Spirit within you and cause you to walk in My statutes, and you will keep My judgments and do them" (Ezek. 36:26–27).

A person can be lost, but not because he or she is a sinner. That person will be lost because he or she doesn't accept salvation. Roger Fredrikson is right:

> Here is the great paradox, the two-edged meaning of Jesus' coming. He came in love to save, to heal, and to offer spiritual birth. He did not come to condemn or judge. But His coming sharpens the issue. Now we must decide! There is both wondrous possibility and great peril in Nicodemus's coming to Jesus. If he chooses to lay aside all his preconceived ideas and learning and accepts Jesus as the One who has come down from heaven, he will be born again! But if he chooses to turn aside, to leave, to work out his own salvation by his own stubborn efforts, however noble, he stands under condemnation and will perish.[27]

The new birth comes by accepting Christ, taking God at His Word. The astonishing promise of John 3:16[28] may have dimmed through familiarity,

---

NT Series, ed. Jack Cottrell and Tony Ash (Joplin, MO: College Press Publishing Company, 1998), 97.

27. Roger L. Fredrikson, *The Communicator's Commentary: John*, ed. Lloyd J. Ogilvie (Waco, TX: Word Books, 1985), 86. Fredrikson then brings the analogy home: "Here is the mystery of evil, that darkness which keeps each of us from accepting the great gift, that rebellious pride which will not allow us to go through the water of repentance and receive the empowering of the Spirit. There is an egocentricity in each of us that constantly insists I can work out my own salvation. It is the cross, the lifting up of the Son of Man, that finally unmasks this ego and thus becomes the agent of discrimination and judgment (1 Cor 1:18)," ibid.

28. "The verb 'loved' has the prominent position in the sentence. Jesus wanted all to know that it was God's love that was bringing eternal life to the world. The Son of Man who descended from heaven and is in heaven has brought to us the truth of this assertion ([John] 3:13; 1:18).

but all people can trust this precious promise of God more than they can rely upon their own hearts. If people still have confidence in each other, human beings who frequently are deceptive, why should they not believe God's amazing promise?

Faith simply believes God's testimony. It is not a leap in the dark. God has never asked anyone to believe without giving that person something to believe in. Just as the wind gives evidence of its presence, so does salvation. The evidence is revealed over and over again in the lives of those who experience the new birth. To be born again, or "born of the Spirit," is not an intensification or more determined resolution to be good. No, something brand-new commences: having "one's life radically transformed by the power of God. It is like beginning life over again, with new perceptions and new relationships."[29] Ellen White speaks eloquently of the power of the Cross to bring about the new birth:

> I marvel that professing Christians do not grasp the divine resources, that they do not see the cross more clearly as the medium of forgiveness and pardon, the means of bringing the proud, selfish heart of man into direct contact with the Holy Spirit, that the riches of Christ may be poured into the mind, and the human agent be adorned with the graces of the Spirit, that Christ may be commended to those who know Him not.[30]

How does one generate faith? The glorious assurance is that, while individuals cannot generate it, faith itself is a gift from God. So is the air itself, but a person has to breathe it. The food everyone eats is also God's gift, but each person has to eat it. "Faith comes by hearing, and hearing by the Word

---

"God's motive (love), action ('gave'), and gift (His Son) are one inseparable unit. Love could not be love without its expression and its gift. Love such as this is a high, holy love that is a noble expression of God's nature and will. . . . Both verb forms, 'loved' and 'gave,' are in the historical aorist tense to emphasize the act as a definite fact." Thoralf Gilbrant and Tor Inge Gilbrant, *The New Testament Study Bible: John,* ed. Stanley M. Horton (Chicago, IL: Donnelley and Sons, 1987), 71.

29. Michaels, *New International Biblical Commentary: John,* 55. Ellen White also refers to the new birth experience: "It is impossible for finite minds to comprehend the work of redemption. Its mystery exceeds human knowledge; yet he who passes from death to life realizes that it is a divine reality. The beginning of redemption we may know here through a personal experience," *Desire of Ages,* 173.

30. Ellen G. White, *Signs of the Times,* Sept. 24, 1902.

of God" (Rom. 10:17). This is not describing a person sitting down and waiting for faith to come with some kind of strange mystical sensation. Rather, this text speaks of taking God at His Word, that He is empowering both the individual's will and actions. A glass of water will refresh a thirsty person, but not just by looking at it. There may be a fresh loaf of bread on the table and a person may acknowledge that it is there. But unless the bread is eaten, that person will still be hungry. As the body needs and feeds on water and food, so must the soul feed on Christ. If a drowning person sees a rope thrown out for rescue, looking at the rope will do no good. It must be taken hold of. Looking at a medicine bottle will not help the healing process—the medicine must be taken. The dying Israelites might have believed that the brazen serpent was lifted up—but unless they looked at it, they could not live.

A person may say, "I have no strength. If thrown a rope, I could not hold on." But Romans 5:6 promises, "For when we were still without strength, in due time Christ died for the ungodly." Jesus has come to give strength to the weak. The Holy Spirit, as persistent as the wind, brings the conviction, the invitation, and the empowerment to accept.

Another may say, "I cannot see." Christ answers, "I am the light of the world" (John 8:12). He came not only to give light but to "open blind eyes" (Isa. 42:7). Others may be afraid they will fall and their conversion will not hold. Then it is good to remember that it is God that does the holding: "My help comes from the LORD, who made heaven and earth. He will not allow your foot to be moved; He who keeps you will not slumber ... The LORD is your keeper. ... The LORD shall preserve you from all evil; He shall preserve your soul" (Ps. 121:2–3, 5, 7).[31] It is the work of the shepherd to keep the sheep. And Jesus has promised that He is the "good shepherd" (John 10:11, 14).

And descriptions of new birth experiences found in Scripture can encourage everyone: Zacchaeus (Luke 19:1–10); the Ethiopian eunuch to whom Philip gave a Bible study in a chariot (Acts 8:26–39); Cornelius and

---

31. God must have been in earnest to be sure this point is understood! "Fear not, for I am with you; be not dismayed, for I am your God. I will strengthen you, yes, I will help you, I will uphold you with My righteous right hand" (Isa. 41:10). "Now to Him who is able to keep you from stumbling, and to present you faultless before the presence of His glory with exceeding joy" (Jude 24). Jesus even expressed wonderment that Nicodemus did not understand: "Are you the teacher of Israel, and do not know these things?" (John 3:10).

his household (Acts 10). Jesus obviously wants the experience of the new birth to be accepted, for He repeats it many times: "Most assuredly, I say to you, he who hears My word and believes in Him who sent Me has everlasting life, and shall not come into judgment, but has passed from death unto life" (John 5:24).

Hence, the encounter of Nicodemus with Jesus in the gospel of John serves as the prototype for all encounters of those who dare to seek the uplifted One who alone can save us from sin through the regeneration of the Holy Wind.

> In the interview with Nicodemus, Jesus unfolded the plan of salvation, and His mission to the world. In none of His subsequent discourses did He explain so fully, step by step, the work necessary to be done in the hearts of all who would inherit the kingdom of heaven. At the very beginning of His ministry He opened the truth to a member of the Sanhedrin, to the mind that was most receptive, and to an appointed teacher of the people. But the leaders of Israel did not welcome the light. Nicodemus hid the truth in his heart, and for three years there was little apparent fruit.
>
> But Jesus was acquainted with the soil into which He cast the seed. The words spoken at night to one listener in the lonely mountain were not lost. For a time Nicodemus did not publicly acknowledge Christ, but he watched His life, and pondered His teachings. In the Sanhedrin council he repeatedly thwarted the schemes of the priests to destroy Him. When at last Jesus was lifted up on the cross, Nicodemus remembered the teaching upon Olivet: "As Moses lifted up the serpent in the wilderness, even so must the Son of man be lifted up: that whosoever believeth in Him should not perish, but have eternal life." The light from that secret interview illumined the cross upon Calvary, and Nicodemus saw in Jesus the world's Redeemer.[32]

Like Nicodemus we may find ourselves walking in a spiritual night, seeking to know in darkness He who is the light of the world. The Jesus who visited with Nicodemus in the gospel narrative and was lifted up on the cross is today the same Savior and Lord who invites us to accept His salvation. With so great a gift also comes the gift of the Holy Spirit. Both divine gifts of love are really one gift bestowed on all who would dare to believe. For God so loved the world that He "gave."

---

32. White, *Desire of Ages*, 176–177.

CHAPTER 19

ASSURANCE OF SALVATION: THE DYNAMICS OF CHRISTIAN EXPERIENCE

Woodrow W. Whidden

These things I have written to you who believe in the name of the Son of God, that you may know that you have eternal life, and that you may continue to believe in the name of the Son of God.

—1 John 5:13

The Seventh-day Adventist reactions to the issue of the believer's personal assurance of salvation definitely unfold in the setting of the Wesleyan/Arminian, synergistic tradition. The gist of this includes what Wesleyan Scholar Randy Maddox refers to as the dynamics of "responsible grace."[1] This explanatory concept emerges out of a marked involvement with sanctifying and perfecting grace. Thus one who is living the privileged life of victory over temptation and sin, through the grace of Christ, will not only demonstrate moral "responsibility," but his or her character will also feature the spiritual goal of living "responsively" to the calling, convicting, converting, justifying, and perfecting graces of Christ. Whatever grace that God has to offer, the believer will manifest patterns of responsiveness to it.

---

1. This expression is taken from Randy L. Maddox's survey of Wesley's theology entitled *Responsible Grace: John Wesley's Practical Theology* (Nashville, TN: Kingswood Books, 1994).

Now for many "evangelical Arminians" (be they Wesleyans, Free Will Baptists, or Seventh-day Adventists) such a vision of Christian discipleship is challenging enough. But Seventh-day Adventists have felt called (from their Bible study) to pursue the issue with some very challenging, even sobering, eschatological factors. The foremost of these is the doctrine of the Pre-Advent Investigative Judgment, which is chronologically followed by an apocalyptic period featuring "times of trouble" and an irreversible "close of probation" when every human case will be finally settled, "once and for all" for either eternal salvation or damnation. Thus the final settlement of every person's eternal destiny will then be decidedly revealed at the second coming of Jesus. And thus the pressing, practical question is this: Can there be any genuine assurance of salvation when the eschatological stakes seem so imposing, even downright scary?

The answer given by Bible-believing, Arminian Seventh-day Adventists, formatively tutored by the writings of Ellen G. White, is that it is indeed possible to persevere through the above-mentioned closing events scenario. And this can be experienced by faith in Christ which can engender a balanced sense of saving assurance, preparatory to greeting Jesus in peace at His second coming. But before presenting the case for such an experience of genuinely assured salvation for the eschatologically conditioned believer, a bit of perspective from the larger Christian tradition on the very practical issues of Christian assurance will be helpful.

SECURITAS, DESPERATIO, AND *CERTITUDO*[2]

Over the last two thousand years of Christian reflection, there has emerged a clear pattern of teaching regarding the tensions which have normally played out in the collective Christian search for personal assurance. Such tensions normally emerge between the extreme challenges called *securitas* and *desperatio*. Both extremes have been seen as inimical to genuine assurance.

---

2. The discussion which follows regarding these key terms is significantly informed by Keith D. Stanglin's study of Arminius's views on the assurance of salvation, *Arminius on the Assurance of Salvation: The Context, Roots, and Shape of the Leiden Debate, 1603–1609* (Leiden and Boston: Brill, 2007).

Securitas describes those who think they are assuredly saved, but who are in fact self-deceived. These are the Christians who have tended to attitudes of presuming on the grace of Christ and have fallen for the self-deceptions associated with cheap grace, indulging in various excuses for sinful lifestyles. And the long tradition of pastoral admonition has warned such believers that they are playing fast and loose with grace as they tread dangerously close to the very brink of damnation. Arminians have deemed this deadly concoction to be a false elixir and have warned that the Calvinist/Reformed preoccupation with perseverance has *de facto* indulged in this attractive concoction for way too long.

But many of the Augustinian/Reformed partisans in this long history of admonition have tended to see the dangers of *desperatio* as the greater contributor to a lack of Christian assurance. *Desperatio* refers to the condition of either creeping or utter despair when Christians have approached the point where their personal salvation seems practically impossible. This often results because of perceived failures to live a life of victory over temptation and sin. And thus it comes as no surprise that the Augustinian/Reformed advocates have leveled the charge that Arminian teaching (that salvation can truly be lost) is the greatest contributor to the evils of *desperatio*! In other words, they have claimed that unless one accepts their version of salvation (as the fruit of an irresistible grace that cannot be lost), there is no real antidote for Christian despair. Thus they claim that their version of assurance is the only viable alternative which can lead to genuine *certitudo*.

So who has the better part of the argument when it comes to the attainment of the alleged golden mean of *certitude*, a balanced experience which effectively avoids both cheap grace and deadening despair? Contra the Reformed Calvinists, it seems clear that the Arminian/Wesleyan solution contains the best theological and practical path to the golden mean of the genuine article of Christian assurance—the *certitudo* of free grace. This latter alternative can also be identified with the longer Christian tradition of the freely chosen patterns of "responsible grace"! Thus what follows attempts to lay out the details of this dynamic path to the assurance of salvation, an assurance that can even surmount the rigorous terrors of a pre-Advent investigative judgment and the frightful scenarios of earthly history's last great apocalyptic crisis—Adventist style!

THE GRACIOUS RESOURCES FOR GENUINE *CERTITUDO*

The *A Priori* Category

The rich resources of God's redeeming power have been manifested in two important categories of grace. The first has to do with what has been called the *a priori* of God's provisions for salvation. Such factors include not only His irrepressible love for sinners, but such love's gracious provisions that inhere in the atoning work of Christ. In the Incarnate life, death, resurrection, ascension, and priestly intercessions of Christ, all that needed to be done to save the entire human race has been done.

Furthermore, this *a priori* of divine grace includes all that God has been doing and is still doing to effectively communicate the saving provisions of Christ's atoning work to all who will respond in faith to His gracious offers of redemption. And these communicating factors include the calling, awakening, or convincing power of the Spirit (prevenient grace), converting, regenerating (repentance and new birthing grace), justifying (forgiving grace), transforming (sanctifying and perfecting grace), equipping (spiritual gifting,) and glorifying grace (the gift of immortality at the second coming). And when any believer begins to reflectively ponder the wonders of these *a priori* privileges, one wonders how anyone could ever be lost!

Further reflection on the graces most relevant to genuine *certitudo* assurance indicates that all of these factors have inherently essential contributions to make to the genuine article of assurance. Yet what is pleasantly surprising is that there is a significant unanimity between the Reformed and Arminian versions of these assuring *a priori* factors of grace.

But the unanimity is not complete and where the real differences emerge, they relate to (1) the very nature of God's love and (2) the role that sanctification plays in the life of the assured Christian. One other factor which undergirds this whole saving sequence is the shared evangelical conviction that all are totally depraved by their experience with sin and nothing but God's grace can redeem and grant the assurance that salvation is real and possible. But again, it must be emphasized that the controversial factors center on how God's love is understood and how optimistic believers should view the ability of transforming grace to really and truly free believers from the power of sin before glorification.

With regard to God's love, the key contrasting perspectives revolve around whether love divine is persuasive and yet resistible (the Arminian position) or whether it is both limited to and only administered irresistibly to a select group called the "elect" or the "predestined" (the Augustinian/Reformed position). Regarding the effectiveness of sanctifying or transforming grace, the Reformed position has always been wary of most perfection emphases. In some marked contrast, Arminians have normally been more optimistic about what God's grace can do (this side of glorification) to make loving obedience a cardinal characteristic of the assuredly redeemed.

Later more will be said about these key, controverted components of saving grace when discussing the key factors which contribute to a genuine Christian *certitudo*. And such differences will make a significant contribution to the case that the Arminian way of salvation is inherently more efficacious than the Reformed version when it comes to any effectual experience of a balanced assurance of salvation. But returning to those factors, there is one other major set of graced components which factor into any legitimate experience of Christian assurance, namely, the *a posteriori* factors.

The *A Posteriori* Category

This category of grace includes such factors as the direct witness of the Spirit (Rom. 8:16) and that believers are God's adopted children of grace. This is a grace which emerges during and after conversion when believers sense that God is directly communicating to individual "spirits" (minds) that such believers are the children of God. This is a grace which is very closely akin to the believer's experience with the Spirit's illumination of the Word of God so that he or she can not only understand the great plan of salvation, but receive the studied conviction that this plan envisions the possible reality that every believer can be the beneficiary of the great redemption plan. Without such a deeply personalized conviction that the truths of the Bible are intended for each and every sinner, the plan of salvation will be merely a doctrinal wonder that one can only contemplate, but never truly experience.

Now this aspect of saving experience has been technically called by both the Reformed and Arminian advocates the *syllogismus mysticus*. This rather clumsy sounding Latin expression simply means that any individual believer can actually, in a deeply mystical way, perceive that the Spirit of God has spoken to him or her directly that he or she is personally a child of God. The language of syllogism has reference to the fact that each person can logically conclude from his or her experience that he or she has been and is being personally and redemptively communicated with through the deep convictions and comforts of the Holy Spirit.

Now very closely related to this is a second *a posteriori* experience called the *syllogismus practicus*. Once again, this technical language has reference to the more practical manifestations of the "fruit of the Spirit" in the life of the believer. This factor is probably the one that is more familiar to Seventh-day Adventist Arminians. Simply stated, if one has experienced a personal rooting of faith in Christ, the Bible assures that individual that these manifestations of the Holy Spirit will not be lagging far behind in the life of saving faith. Put another way, if any believer does not actually manifest the fruit of faith, it is pretty good evidence that the root of faith is rotten at its core and is not the genuine article.

In addition to the specific qualities listed in Galatians, such fruit is often understood to include a whole array of spiritual phenomena. These normally include ethical consistency, attitudes of gratefulness to God for His mercy, patience with the foibles of others, an attitude of penitence and Christian humility as the normal daily meat and drink of the converted disciple of Christ, a love for the study of the Scripture and the place of prayer, attendance at corporate worship, zeal for Christian service, and a desire to contemplate and converse on matters having to do with Christ and eternity (to name but a few of the most important practical fruits of life in the Spirit and grace of Christ).

Implications of the *A Priori* and the *A Posteriori* Factors

Now what is really interesting is that both the Arminians and the Reformed believers and writers have all agreed that these factors, both the *a priori* and the *a posteriori* factors, are absolutely necessary for anyone to experience genuine Christian conversion and receive the gift of the assurance of salvation (the coveted *certitudo*).

Both the Reformed and the Arminian partisans agree that all of the graces of Christ must be factored into any genuine experience of Christ. Without the *a priori* provisions of salvation being effectively communicated to the believer, there will be no real saving union with Christ by faith and no real chance to experience the blessing of genuine assurance.

Furthermore, there is general agreement that without the *a posteriori* experiential implications of the workings of God's grace in one's life, there will be no deep personal realization that any believer can know that he or she has actually become a converted child of the King! These *a posteriori* factors include both the "mystical" (*syllogismus mysticus*) and the "practical" (*syllogismus practicus*) experiences of grace. If these factors are not abundantly apparent, no believer can have any viable evidence that he or she is a believer (in the Arminian sense), or among the predestined "elect" (in the more Reformed or Calvinistic sense). So, what can be concluded about these factors in Christian experience?

The key issue at stake in this reflection is to simply make the point that all believers are dependent on not just the *a priori* factors, but also on the full panoply of the *a posteriori* factors in the experience of saving assurance. Thus it is safe to conclude that there are really no discernible advantages which are the unique privileges of the Reformed/Calvinistic believer. The only major differences between the Reformed and the Arminian experience of assurance do, in fact, orbit around the *a priori* of how any believer understands God's love (is it persistently persuasive or is it irresistible?). Therefore both camps are in the same evidential boat when it comes to the manner in which the possibilities of transforming grace can contribute to either the assurance of salvation or the lack thereof.

Now here is the interesting and informative bottom line regarding any supposed assurance advantages claimed by the Calvinists: If God's grace is irresistible, how can anyone know that he or she is inevitably going to be found among the elect, especially when it is patently apparent that no person has been specifically prophesied (in either the Bible or any other inspired documents) to be irresistibly placed among the elect! And why is this so? Simply because no such prophecy exists!

With these simple facts in hand, there is only one obvious conclusion—Reformed Calvinists do not have any real advantage(s) when it comes to their ability to detect whether they are among the chosen elect of God or not. Thus they are also practically obliged to search out the powerful factors inherent in the *a priori* factors of God's gracious provisions (and His ability to communicate them). Furthermore they also, along with their fellow Arminian pilgrims, must search the contours of their personal experience of grace for any evidence of the *a posteriori* blessings that they are evidently and assuredly saved.

Once more it needs to be asked: Do the Reformed Calvinists truly possess any inherent advantages when it comes to their claim of the assuring comforts of the irresistible election teaching and their proclaimed privileges of irremissible perseverance (their salvation cannot be lost—thus "once saved always saved")? Arminians are not convinced by the Reformed claims.

Other Complicating Factors of Christian Experience

Now that both Reformed and Arminian partisans have all been consigned to the task of searching out the contours of their respective personal experiences of salvation, there are a few other practical matters which all Christians need to keep in mind regarding the search for assurance. And such matters are usually associated with the common experience of what earlier Christians referred to as *lucta*. This phenomenon includes the wrestling that often transpires in the soul between the forces of the good and evil. These battles can become very intense, and in the heat of such tribulations it can be easily concluded that such exposed weaknesses mean that one is not really saved! This is especially troubling to those who naturally struggle with depression, especially when they are called upon to endure periods when the "witness of the Spirit" is not speaking all that emphatically or clearly.

One other relevant factor that must be mentioned is the teaching of John Calvin on "temporary faith," which can easily lead to despair.[3] As Keith Stanglin points out, "the reason that the category of temporary faith undermines assurance is the great correspondence between true and temporary faith."[4] Can a Calvinist really believe that such could be true? In fact, this is readily admitted by them, especially when persons who claim to be saved are not looking or acting all that Christlike. Once again, the common experience of both Calvinists and Arminians becomes quite apparent, leading to the obvious conclusion that both camps must come up with filtering factors by which they can discern between true and false faith (be it "temporary" or patently "false") in Christian salvation experience.

---

3. See Stanglin's discussion on page 183 of *Arminius on the Assurance of Salvation*.

4. Ibid., 184.

So, what can be practically concluded at this juncture? It seems that the key issues between Calvinists and Arminians regarding the assurance of salvation come down to the issue of who has the better theology of God's love. This is especially relevant when it comes to God's loving ways in election and predestination and His power to forgive and transform. Practically speaking, evangelical, Bible-believing Calvinists and Arminians are very similar in their views on forgiving and justifying grace for true believers. But as already mentioned, their respective views on election and sanctification do manifest significant variances. What should be concluded regarding these variances in teachings on assurance? First, the issues of election and perseverance will be examined.

ELECTION, "ONCE SAVED ALWAYS SAVED," AND ASSURANCE

Some Preliminary Observations on Irresistible Election

While the issue of perseverance (i.e., once saved, always saved versus the teaching that believers can lose their salvation) has been the most controversial issue, first some preliminary observations on the issue of "irresistible election" and how it informs the issue of the personal assurance of salvation must be addressed. Even though most contemporary Reformed/Calvinist Christians reject the idea of irresistible election, the issue remains pertinent to a significant number of Reformed Christians who still emphasize that election is irresistible. While they claim that such irresistible grace is a great boon to assurance, the facts are that the stakes for any ultimate realization of the assurance of salvation must be greatly reduced. And why does this seem to be the case?

The answer is very simple: If the vast majority of sinners are irresistibly predestined to damnation, this immediately and significantly reduces the "pool" of possible candidates for election to salvation, which is normally deemed to be but a small remnant anyway.[5] When this concept is contrasted with the Arminian view, the results are quite instructive.

---

5. It is very clear that Calvin claimed that the pool of candidates for divine election to salvation included only "that little number whom he [God] has reserved for himself," or "only a few people." These quotations from Calvin are quoted in François Wendel, *Calvin: The Origins and Development of His Religious Thought* (New York: Harper & Row, Publishers, 1963), 279–280.

Since the Arminian view claims that the benefits of the atonement of Christ have always been intended to potentially save all sinners, it then becomes abundantly clear as to which teaching is inherently more optimistic about the possibility of a greater number of sinners being assuredly saved. In fact, it is safe to say that the classic Calvinistic doctrine, which teaches a great restrictedness in the number of possible persons who will be irresistibly elected, is thereby simply more inherently negative about the possibility of salvation for the many.[6]

To put it as bluntly as it can be stated: If the pool of candidates for salvation is already quite small, then the chances of anyone being among the elect, with its alleged assurances of salvation, are also proportionally quite minimal—to say the least! Therefore, even though Arminians also admit to a small pool of souls who will ultimately receive salvation, they at least teach that every sinner has a chance of ending up in the "saving pool" of the redeemed elect. This is simply due to the fact that Arminians understand the Bible to teach that the choice of salvation is ultimately contingent on the decisions of every individual person, not some secret decision unilaterally made by God. Thus the question must be asked: Is there or is there not an obvious contrast between the Arminian and the Calvinist positions, especially when the latter teaches that the decision for salvation and damnation is totally and irresistibly determined by the inscrutable wisdom of God? If the answer is affirmative, then it seems obvious that the Arminian believer will be much less prone to worry about reduced statistical chances or even arbitrary rejection (the Calvinists call it "reprobation") since he or she is convinced that God lovingly and mercifully desires, even longs for, all persons to be saved.

Therefore, the Arminian believers should then simply be more optimistic about their chances to receive not only salvation, but also the assurance that such a great salvation (offered on such a universal scale) will prove so alluringly desirable that the saved will be loath to carelessly

---

6. Most certainly Arminians also need to admit that Christ's universal offer of salvation will be embraced, but only by a relative few (compare 1 Tim. 2:3–4, Tit. 2:11 and 2 Pet. 3:9). This admittance is based on the testimony of Jesus which clearly states that the vast majority of humanity will not positively embrace His gracious offer of redemption (Matt. 7:13–14). But this is a far cry from the Calvinist concept which claims that the small number is due to God's sovereign choice, not the choices of those who could have chosen to be in the Kingdom.

mishandle such a precious gift! Logically, then, Arminian believers should logically be the most assured Christians in the world!

While a significant majority of modern Reformed/Calvinists have given up on the classic doctrine of irresistible election and want to say, in good Arminian fashion, that all sinners can be saved, they continue on to offer the important qualification that the ones who do respond to God's universal offer will suddenly find themselves in His irresistible, saving clutches once they say yes to grace. In other words, once God lovingly hooks any responsive sinner, that person is in the Gospel boat to stay (whether he or she wants to stay or not).

The question then immediately presents itself: Why would God respect any believer's freely chosen decision to be initially saved, but then immediately deny that person the option of voluntarily choosing to leave His "loving" embrace? With this rather searching question, it only seems logical to make a further enquiry. What is it, then, that is truly at the heart of the "once saved, always saved" concept?

The Basic Rationale of the "Once Saved, Always Saved" Doctrine

At the risk of some repetition, all participants in the debates over Christian assurance need to be very clear as to the basic rationale which undergirds the thinking of the "once saved, always saved" position. What its partisans boldly and confidently assert is that God simply will not allow those who have responded to His call to salvation to slip from His grasp. Thus the Lord providentially makes it impossible for any of His initially responsive children, being defined as those who have accepted Him as their Savior, to fall away from their saving relationship with Him. This forceful retention of the saved has been represented by two basic versions that have received widespread, popular acclaim.

The first version teaches something to the effect that God will so forcefully hem in or surround the responsive believers with compelling, saving influences that they will find it impossible to backslide. Thus they simply will not, since they effectively cannot, renege on their salvation commitment to the Lord. Moreover, if any alleged believers should begin to stray from their saving relationship with God, the Holy Trinity will either irresistibly protect them from any temptation to apostasy, or chastise them with a chain of providential circumstances so as to discourage any ultimate slippage from their assured status among the redeemed.

But what about those alleged believers who give the appearance of losing their salvation or back sliding away from the Lord's irrevocable embrace? This question points to the most common explanation, which is effectively the second popular version of irresistible perseverance. What this version claims is that such believers were never really or truly saved in the first place. A good example of this conceptual claim has been articulated by influential, contemporary Reformed theologian Millard J. Erickson.

Erickson begins by clearly affirming "once saved, always saved:" "The practical implication of our understanding of the doctrine of perseverance is that believers can rest secure in the assurance that their salvation is permanent; nothing can separate them from the love of God. Thus they can rejoice in the prospect of eternal life. There need be no anxiety that something or someone will keep them from attaining the final blessedness that they have been promised and have come to expect."

But not surprisingly, Erickson then feels the need to face up to the nettlesome issue of the commonly manifested attitudes of sinful presumption which so often accompany the idea that such a salvation is so secure that it cannot be lost: "On the other hand, however, our understanding of the doctrine of perseverance allows no room for indolence or laxity. It is questionable whether anyone who reasons, 'Now that I am a Christian, I can live as I please,' *has really been converted and regenerated.*"[7] In other words, if someone manifests persistent evidence of apostasy, that person was simply never truly converted in the first place. And with these interesting conclusions, Erickson has summarily made the argument almost impossible to deal with at any truly coherent, practical level. What is to be made of such logic?

An Arminian Response

First, it must be admitted, even from the Arminian perspective (which says that salvation can be lost), that it could well be true that there are believers whose tendency toward apostasy suggests that they were never genuinely converted in the first place. Jesus's parable of the sower clearly suggests that there are "believers" who are "way-side," "rocky," or "thorny"

---

7. Millard J. Erickson, *Christian Theology*, 2nd ed. (Grand Rapids, MI: Baker Books, 1998), 1007, emphasis added.

ground types of professed Christians whose faith lacks lasting, deep roots. Furthermore, these wavering souls can ultimately give way to the cares of evil influences which normally plague their salvation pilgrimage (Luke 8:11–15).

But the line of argument mounted by the Calvinists attempts to deny the possibility of apostasy. Such a denial simply ignores the question as to whether any given believer can be genuinely converted, and then either heedlessly wander away by careless neglect or be led away by strong temptations and go on to openly renounce the saving power of God in his or her life. After all, Jesus did plainly say that the great Adversary works in such a way as to snatch the "word out of their hearts, lest they should believe and be saved" (v. 12).

Furthermore, many Reformed teachers conveniently ignore the fact that our Lord also made the highly suggestive point that a person can "believe and be saved" (Acts 16:31). And finally, the context explicitly says that the seed which fell "on the rocks" did "receive the word with joy" and "for a while" did "believe"—strongly implying that their belief did effectually save them, if only temporarily (Matt. 13:3–8, 20–21).

Now if Jesus's teaching about "believing" and being "saved" has any merit, the question then becomes: Does such an experience of belief, which ultimately fails or languishes, prove to be no belief at all? Or were Jesus's "rocky" variety of believers simply mentioned in order to put forward a sensible, cautionary warning to all Christians to be watchful lest they carelessly fall into such "rocky" circumstances? For the Calvinist teachers (such as Erickson), the answer is that they were never saved in the first place!

For the Arminian interpreters, however, it seems obvious that such struggling believers could have been truly saved but just proved not to be vigilant enough in their walk with Jesus. Thus such a lack of vigilance is not inevitably caused by some secret will of the electing God, but it is simply due to a lack of attentiveness on the part of the careless believers who have the distinct possibility of finding healing for their back-sliding ways.

So what about believers who are at the stage of personal experience where their faith enters the stormy waters of intense struggle (i.e., the previously mentioned *lucta*—literally wrestling with or battling the world, the flesh, and the devil) and have not yet achieved the fuller or richer, settled trust of persevering children of God? Should such persons be told that they were never saved in the first place? From an Arminian perspective, this approach is incomprehensible and such believers should be given the benefit of the doubt and then be strongly encouraged to look again to the Lord in faith for the healing of their propensity to backslide and ultimately fall away.

Thus the debate returns to the issue of who has the better response, the Arminians or the Calvinists? Put another way, it seems patently obvious that both the Calvinists and the Arminians need to be able to effectively discern the marks or evidences of their election to salvation if they are to be blessed with the gracious article of genuine assurance.

The avowedly Calvinistic Erickson immediately makes this point: Genuine faith manifests itself in the fruit of the Spirit. "Assurance of salvation, the subjective conviction that one is a Christian, results from the Holy Spirit's giving evidence that he is at work in the life of the individual. The Spirit's work results in conviction on biblical grounds that God will enable the Christian to persist in that relationship—that nothing can separate the true believer from God's love."[8]

Therefore, in the light of these considerations, the comments of Jerry Moon seem to be abundantly justified when he claims that the "doctrine of 'once saved, always saved,' is simply a theoretical guarantee of eternal security, not an actual guarantee, since in that theological system (Reformed/Calvinistic), *one cannot infallibly know that one was 'once saved.'*"[9] And once more, consider the common privileges and challenges of all (both Calvinist and Arminian) who would be united to Christ by a saving faith which justifies, sanctifies, and assures. Moreover, an important aspect of such privileges is that the Spirit of God will not leave any believer bereft of the illuminating power of the Spirit's direct "Witness" and its more indirect working which sparks the "witness of our own spirit."

---

8. Erickson, *Christian Theology,* 1007–1008.

9. These judicious comments by Moon are just one key point that he makes in his wonderful lecture regarding Ellen White's true teachings on the issue of assurance of salvation. Part of Moon's lecture has been adapted and included in my book *The Judgment and Assurance: The Dynamics of Personal Salvation.* See "Part IV: Special Adventist Challenges," in the chapter titled "Ellen G. White on the Assurance of Salvation: Are Her Writings a Help or a Stumbling Block?" (Hagerstown, MD: Review and Herald Publishing Association, 2012), 153–172.

SOME FINAL CONSIDERATIONS ON PERSEVERANCE

Probably the most important principles for experiencing the assurance of salvation relate to the issues that the believer's security in God is linked to (1) his or her faith-union with Christ and (2) the extreme importance of maintaining and not forsaking this relationship. Do not the Bible and personal faith testimonies of believers in Christ resonate with these important principles?

It seems that the Calvinistic brothers and sisters, in their longing for a secure relationship to Christ, have overemphasized the importance of the moment of redemption. And this imbalanced emphasis has inevitably led to the neglect of salvation's long-term relational dynamics. The long-haul relational dynamics, not so much the initial moment of the realization of redemption, are what truly generate the critical core of the issue of the Christian's salvation assurance. Most certainly the initial moment of conversion and justification and its deep commitments are absolutely foundational! This, however, does not immediately negate the personal choices of faith's ongoing responsibilities in the believer's saving walk with the Lord.

The initial moment of saving faith is the beginning of the Christian's pilgrimage, not an experience of being irresistibly hooked by Christ. To the contrary, it is the beginning of a lifetime of responsive and responsible give and take which steadily grows and deepens into the mutuality of a dynamic, loving relationship. Therefore, this more relational vision (version) of salvation seems closer to the biblical portrait that portrays a God who is lovingly self-giving in the interest of His children's reconciliation. This stands in clear contrast to the questionable vision of God as some sort of relentless "manipulator" deity who is intent on kicking in the doors of people's hearts and forcefully binding them to Himself. Thus it seems that the Arminius-inspired Carl Bangs was correct—"grace is not a force; it is a Person"![10]

Now there is some truth to the fact that God's pursuit of humanity does have some sovereign aspects to it. Most certainly, God must always take the sovereign initiative in the salvation of His people. And, in this sense, He does

---

10. Bangs, quoted in Roger E. Olson in *Arminian Theology: Myths and Realities* (Downers Grove, IL: IVP Academic, 2006), 164.

come knocking at the doors of His people's hearts—whether they want Him to or not. But the truth is that He simply does not knock down their doors! Instead of irresistible force, He offers winsome appeals and suggests motives that seek to elicit a positive, love-engendered response from His people.[11]

Furthermore, many Arminians will readily attest that God's persistent pursuit of them can, on occasion, feel downright compelling (though it never ultimately forces anyone's will). Contemporary Methodist theologian Geoffrey Wainwright has sagely recalled an old truism: "When push comes to shove in Christian experience and witness, Arminians preach the assurance of salvation in a manner worthy of a Calvinist and Calvinists seek salvation through prayers which sound very much like those of a free-will Methodist."[12]

Indeed, many can testify to the persistence with which God has sought them and nurtured them; and it can, on occasion, feel like the solicitations of a watchful "mother bear." Moreover, the persistent, prayerful intercessions of many Calvinists evoke the need for human cooperation with God's providences in seeking the salvation of the lost. But neither of these positions necessitates either a doctrine of irresistible, deterministic election and perseverance, or some bald doctrine of humanistic, natural free-will.[13]

With a proper emphasis on the central importance of salvation being understood or conceived of as a complete process of co-operant interaction between the Savior and the individual believer—all the way from initial belief until glorification, here are some cautionary caveats regarding the "once saved, always saved" version of Christian assurance.

A Cautious Critique of Irresistible Perseverance

First, the believer's hope is in Christ, not ultimately in a once-for-all decision made in response to an altar call during some local church revival, evangelistic series, summer camp, or camp meeting. What is most important is that

---

11. Ellen G. White, *Desire of Ages* (Mountain View, CA: Pacific Press Publishing Association, 1989), 22, 487, 759; idem, "The Compelling Message," *Review and Herald* (September 24, 1895), 609; "Serve the Lord with Gladness," *Review and Herald* (January 14, 1890), 18.

12. Geoffrey Wainwright, quoted in Woodrow W. Whidden, *The Judgment and Assurance: The Dynamics of Personal Salvation* (Hagerstown, MD: Review and Herald Publishing Association, 2010), 125.

13. Ibid.

the believer remains constantly attentive by keeping his or her focus on Jesus and His abundant graces and nurtures the spiritual discipline of responsive sensitivity to the leading of the Spirit through the ministry of the Word.

Second, the focus of the Reformed version of perseverance is on faith itself. But important as faith is, its primary focus is not to be on itself. Faith is a gift of God that has no real virtue in and of itself, except that its great efficacy is found in the One whom it lays hold of.

Furthermore, saving faith is not to be primarily defined as an exercise in giving mental assent to an abstract theoretical guarantee of irrevocable assurance. Rather, biblical faith is better defined as a heartfelt trust in Christ that embraces Him as the One and only Person capable of keeping believers effectively convinced that their salvation is steadily assured. Herbert Douglass has succinctly expressed it this way: the "secret" of Christian assurance is that "we are not to trust in our faith, but in God's faithfulness."[14]

Therefore any present blessings of the assurance of salvation have much more to do with the believer's current faith-focus on Christ than it does in what faith did in some supposed "once for all time" claiming of salvation during a particularly moving altar call. Any initial exercise of faith that claims salvation at the instigation of the Spirit during any altar call is of vital importance. But it is only a conscious beginning. Therefore, persevering assurance is much more the result of an ongoing focus on Christ rather than on faith itself and its past exercise.

Third, as has been acknowledged by Millard Erickson, the "once saved, always saved" version of assurance has been persistently vexed with a checkered history of presumption and antinomian attitudes on the part of many Calvinists. It was this troubling tendency that provoked John Wesley and the vast majority of later Arminian Christians to strongly and persistently oppose the Calvinistic version of Christian election, perseverance, and assurance.

Moreover, at a very elemental level of pastoral concern, many can personally attest to the wisdom of the long-standing Wesleyan/Arminian aversion to Calvinistic inspired versions of assurance. Such troubling cheap-grace attitudes are still all too evident among Reformed-oriented believers.

---

14. Herbert E. Douglass, *Should We Ever Say, "I Am Saved"?: What It Means to Be Assured of Salvation* (Nampa, ID: Pacific Press Publishing Association, 2003), 26.

The idea that believers can go on knowingly transgressing God's law and still be considered saved is currently very much alive and well at the popular level among many professed believers who seek to excuse themselves from the duty of confronting their lingering propensities to indulge the habit of their "darling" sins. Furthermore, the issue includes not just indulgence in known defects, but an all-too-common refusal to embrace strong convictions of the Spirit's call to incorporate new moral and practical duties into their personal Christian walk. The fruit of the irresistible grace teachings is simply not good.

In the face of these persistently common attitudes of "cheap-grace," antinomian excuses for sin[15] and the self-evident fact that the Calvinists have no real, built-in advantages (either theologically or practically) when it comes to the assurance of salvation, on balance, the Wesleyan/Arminian (and Adventist) version of the personal assurance of salvation is the preferred biblical, theological, and practical route for believers to take in their walk with the Lord.

DOES AN EMPHASIS ON SANCTIFICATION DESTROY ASSURANCE?

This question raises one more important query: What should be the resort for the struggling Christian who is led to doubt the assurance of his or her salvation? Should it be a preoccupation with how many victories she or he has had in overcoming his or her character defects? Probably not. But does that do away with sanctified progress as a factor in aiding the struggling Christian's attempt to regain assured spiritual equilibrium? Certainly not! But before briefly addressing these dynamics, it needs to be emphatically stated that the blessings of justifying and forgiving grace are the main default resorts for all believers, be they Calvinist/Reformed or Arminian.

The knowledge that Jesus is constantly standing as humanity's Advocate with the Father, moment by moment seeking to draw people to Himself and

---

15. We do want to make it clear that not all Calvinist/Reformed Christians manifest these attitudes; but it is all too evident in their corridors of influence, including the experiences of numerous Seventh-day Adventists who have been either implicitly or explicitly affected by the popular preaching and publishing venues of Calvinisitic/Reformed teaching. We just sense that the Arminian venue offers, on balance, a better way.

reminding them that He is constantly reckoning penitent, responsive believers as perfect for the sake of Christ, is a wonderful tonic for any struggling sinner. But such considerations must never be isolated from the twin blessing of character transformation which is the fruit of Christ's transforming grace (a grace that He also mediates to humanity as the Advocating High Priest in the heavenly sanctuary). So, what is the assuring relationship between the justifying and sanctifying merits of Christ?

While there are no justifying merits in the fruitful obedience and character growth of the true believer, the very practical truth is that one of the very reasons why Jesus grants the twin blessings of justifying and sanctifying grace is so that every believer will be granted clearer spiritual perception when it comes to the preciousness and expensiveness of the merits of justifying grace. Sin and character defects always have a blinding effect on any believer. This is the reason that attitudes of presumption and cheap grace are so deadly to any genuine assurance of salvation.

But when the believer is growing in God's love through the grace of character transformation, and as his or her ability to perceive the awfulness of sin and the infinitely expensive, precious privileges of forgiveness and justifying grace increases, the more assured the believer will become. God's love, therefore, is expressed not only in merciful forgiveness, but also in gracious character transformation. The stronger the character, the more perfect will be the believer's perceptions of God's assuring love for him or her.

These reflections on forgiveness and transforming grace lead to the final consideration of this reflection: the positive, though reserved manner with which James Arminius embraced the issues of sanctification and the experience of Christian perfection. If character perfection truly does enable believers to more clearly grasp the privileges of God's merciful, loving forgiveness, why then should their thoughts turn negative any time some earnest "holiness" person (Adventist, Wesleyan, or Free Will Baptist) reminds them of the blessings of perfection and character change? The truth is that believers should be open to the following, wisely balanced counsels of Arminius.

"But while I never asserted that a believer could perfectly keep the precepts of Christ in this life, I never denied it, but always left it as a matter which has still to be decided." Thus, while Arminius was not preoccupied with perfection, he went on to offer sage counsel about disputes over the issue: "I think the time may be far more happily and usefully employed in prayers to obtain what is lacking in each of us, and in serious admonitions that every one endeavor to proceed and press forward towards the mark of perfection, than when spent in such disputations."[16]

CONCLUSION

Most certainly the personal assurance of salvation should be the privilege of every responsive and responsible believer in Christ. But what is becoming most apparent is that the Reformed/Calvinists do not possess any substantive theological or practical advantages over the Arminian/Adventist believers. In fact, if what has been discussed in this chapter has any ring of truth to it, the Arminian theological and spiritual resources are eminently more prone to be practically efficacious in generating the genuine article of true Christian assurance of salvation.

Therefore, with a balanced soteriology (the blessed *a priori's*) and a judicious, perceptive invocation of the privileges of Christian experience inherent in the enlightening power of the various witnesses of the Holy Spirit to their "spirits," all sincere believers should be able to march forward to the kingdom of God with Christ's "blessed assurance" providing spiritual steadiness to each step along the way.

Such appropriations of faith, enlightened and complemented by the transforming power of the "Spirit" of God, will assuredly carry any sincere believer through the trying times, be they fear of the investigative judgment, the close of probation, the personal and apocalyptic "times of trouble," or even the latest challenging sermon on perfecting grace. Truly the resources are more than sufficient to carry each believer all the way to the eternal gates of glory. Amen and Amen!

---

16. Arminius, quoted in Carl Bangs, *Arminius: A Study in the Dutch Reformation* (Nashville, TN: Abingdon Press, 1971), 347.

CHAPTER 20

ASSURANCE IN THE JUDGMENT

Richard M. Davidson

The Bible is replete with references to divine judgment. In the Old Testament one can find over three hundred examples of divine legal proceedings (covenant lawsuits), followed by executive judgments.[1] A full-orbed biblical theology of God's judgment includes seven different phases of universal divine judgment in Scripture, centered in the cross of Christ.[2] Seventh-day Adventists believe that we are now living in the fourth phase of this sevenfold judgment, which is commonly termed the "Pre-Advent Judgment."[3] This judgment is seen as a fulfillment of the Day of Atonement (*Yom Kippur*) typology of Leviticus 16.[4] As in Jewish

---

1. See Richard M. Davidson, "The Divine Covenant Lawsuit Motif in Canonical Perspective," *Journal of the Adventist Theological Society [JATS]* 21 (2010): 45–84.

2. Jiří Moskala, "Toward a Biblical Theology of God's Judgment: A Celebration of the Cross in Seven Phases of Divine Universal Judgment (An Overview of a Theocentric-Christocentric Approach)," *JATS* 15 (2004): 138–165. These seven phases include: (1) Old Testament pre-Cross judgments (Gen. 3:9–19); (2) the Cross judgment (John 12:31–32); (3) personal judgments whenever the gospel is preached (John 5:22–24); (4) pre-Advent investigative (trial) judgment (Dan. 7–8); (5) judgment at the second coming of Christ (Rev. 19:17–21); (6) millennial review judgment (Rev. 20:4–6); and (7) the "Great White Throne" judgment after the millennium (Rev. 20:7–15).

3. The biblical basis for this understanding is conveniently summarized by Marvin Moore, *The Case for the Investigative Judgment: Its Biblical Foundation* (Nampa, ID: Pacific Press, 2010).

4. See the summary of biblical data in Richard M. Davidson, "The Good News of Yom Kippur in Seventh-day Adventist Theology," *Shabbat Shalom* 54, no. 2 (2007): 4–8.

theology, *Kippur* is interpreted by Adventists as a time for the completion of a divine investigative (legal trial) phase of judgment dealing with
human beings.[5] Daniel 7:9–10 records the prophet's vision of this heavenly eschatological judgment: "I watched till thrones were put in place,
and the Ancient of Days was seated. . . . The court was seated, and the
books were opened."[6] The three angels' messages of Revelation 14 present this judgment as an integral part of the gospel—*euangelion*
[εὐαγγέλιον], "good news": "Then I saw another angel flying in the
midst of heaven, having the everlasting gospel [*euangelion* (εὐαγγέλιον
= 'good news')] to preach to those who dwell on the earth . . . saying
with a loud voice, 'Fear God and give glory to Him, for the hour of His
judgment has come" (Rev. 14:6–7).

Is the message of divine judgment in Scripture really reassuring good
news? The answer to this existential question cannot be given simply as
an academic biblical study. Hence, with the encouragement of the editors
of this volume, in this study I combine biblical data with personal experience.[7] I have not always considered the judgment to be good news. While
growing up as a fourth-generation Seventh-day-Adventist Christian, I
used to tremble when the subject of divine judgment was mentioned. I
listened to numerous evangelistic sermons on the subject, and I heard the

---

5. For the Jewish understanding, see, e.g., *b. Roš Haš. 16a*: "For it has been taught: 'All
are judged' on New Year and their doom is sealed on the Day of Atonement." cf. Philip Birn-
baum, *High Holyday Prayer Book: Yom Kippur* (New York: Hebrew Publishing Co., 1960),
508, quoted in *Seventh-day Adventist Bible Students' Source Book*, ed. Don F. Neufeld and
Julia Neuffer (Washington, DC: Review and Herald Publishing Association, 1962), 9:62:
"On Rosh Hashanah their destiny is inscribed, and on Yom Kippur it is sealed."

6. Unless otherwise indicated, all Scripture quotations are taken from the New King
James Version®. Copyright © 1982 by Thomas Nelson. Used by permission. All rights
reserved. Italics in quotations from Scripture reflect emphasis added by the author.

7. I first published my personal experience with regard to the judgment in an article,
"Assurance in the Judgment," *Adventist Review*, January 7, 1988, pp. 18–20. Here I retell it in
an expanded form and further develop the theology of Christian assurance in a more scholarly format. See also my article, "Good News of Yom Kippur," *JATS* 2/2 (Autumn 1991):
4–27, from which some of the concepts of this chapter are adapted, sometimes using the
same or similar wording in order to retain the freshness and accuracy of first expression,
but here further developed and updated, as my thinking and research on the subject has
matured and expanded. In this chapter these concepts are now placed in a new framework
of seven reasons for assurance in the judgment.

evangelists read the solemn biblical pronouncements: "For God shall bring every work into judgment, with every secret thing, whether it be good, or whether it be evil" (Eccl. 12:14, KJV); "Therefore the ungodly shall not stand in the judgment" (Ps. 1:5); "For we must all appear before the judgment seat of Christ, that each one may receive the things done in the body, according to what he has done, whether good or bad" (2 Cor. 5:10). The prospect of my name coming up in the heavenly court, with all my sins brought before God and the on-looking universe, made me think, *I'll never make it! I surely hope my name doesn't come up today.*

Throughout teenage and young-adult years, the subject of the judgment had an unsettling effect on me. Even as a young pastor, I avoided preaching about the judgment. After several years of pastoral ministry, I conducted a prayer meeting series on the Psalms, following the outline of the classic work on the Psalter by C. S. Lewis[8]—except that I skipped his chapter dealing with the judgment. Then my conscience smote me, and I decided to see what the Psalms really taught about the judgment.

I was surprised to see that the Psalmist often welcomed and even rejoiced over the coming judgment (e.g., Pss. 82:8; 96:11–13). But I could hardly believe my eyes when I read that David longed for *his own case* to come up in judgment. Several times David prayed, "Judge me, O LORD!" (Pss. 7:8; 26:1; 35:24; 43:1).[9] He seemed to be saying, in effect, "Hurry up, Lord! Send the judgment. Bring it on! Let my name come up. I can hardly wait!"

How could David pray such a prayer? He had not only *thought* about committing adultery and murder and lying but had actually carried out

---

8. C. S. Lewis, *Reflections on the Psalms* (New York: Harcourt, Brace, 1958).

9. The Hebrew of these four psalms all have the same imperative verb plus first-person common singular object pronoun *shaphteni* "Judge me!" The first three of these psalms are explicitly identified as Davidic, according to their superscription. The fourth has the superscription "A Contemplation of the sons of Korah." This may refer to the melody and not to the lyrics, in light of Psalm 88:1 where the superscription identifies the psalm as "a psalm of the sons of Korah" but then adds that it is also "a contemplation of Heman the Ezrahite"; it seems that in this case the sons of Korah wrote the tune and Heman the lyrics. Ellen White attributes the words of Psalm 42 (and thereby also Ps. 43, which is integrally—structurally and thematically—linked with Ps. 42) to David. See Ellen White, *Education* (Boise, ID: Pacific Press, 1952), 164 (cf. idem, *Gospel Workers* [Hagerstown, MD: Review and Herald], 1915), 257; *Testimonies to the Church* (Boise, ID: Pacific Press, 1948), 4:534–535.

these actions. Did he not understand how serious his sin was or how certain the judgment? His prayer of deep repentance after the power rape[10] of Bathsheba and the murder of her husband indicates that he did understand: "For I acknowledge my transgressions, and my sin is always before me. Against You, You only, have I sinned, and done this evil in Your sight—that You may be found just when You speak, and blameless when You judge" (Ps. 51:3–4).

David grasped the seriousness of his sin and the solemnity of the judgment. But he also grasped the message of the gospel. He understood that even though he was a great sinner, his sins could be atoned for by the blood of the Substitute. He prayed: "Purge [Heb. *khata'* in *piel*, 'cleanse from sin'] me with hyssop [the plant used to apply the blood of the Passover sacrifice upon the doorposts of the house; Lev. 14:4–6; Num. 19:18; Exod. 12:22], and I shall be clean" (Ps. 51:7). In effect, he prayed, "Cleanse me with the blood of the Lamb of God, my Substitute, and I shall have assurance of acceptance with You in the judgment."

My personal study through the years has brought to light at least seven biblical reasons for joyous assurance in the judgment. The remainder of this chapter develops each of these reasons.

CHRIST IS OUR SUBSTITUTE

As just mentioned with the testimony of David, the Bible teaches that the antitypical Lamb of God has been accepted as our Substitute. When we receive Christ, we are covered with the robe of His righteousness (Isa. 61:10; Zech. 3:4; cf. Gen. 3:21).[11] The Lord says to Satan, the great Accuser of the brethren (Rev. 12:10), "The LORD rebuke you, Satan!" (Zech. 3:2). We are forgiven and exonerated, pronounced "not guilty." We need no longer have anxiety about our acceptance with God. "We may enjoy the favor of God. We are not to be anxious about what Christ and God think of us, but about what God thinks of Christ, our Substitute."[12] What does God

---

10. See Richard M. Davidson, "Did King David Rape Bathsheba? A Case Study in Narrative Theology," *JATS* 17, no. 2 (Autumn 2006): 81–95.

11. See also Ellen G. White, *Christ's Object Lessons* (Hagerstown, MD: Review and Herald, 1941), 170, 206, 311.

12. Ellen G. White, *Selected Messages* (Washington, DC: Review and Herald, 1958), 2:32–33.

think of Christ our Substitute? He is accepted. Thus when we are in Christ, we may know that we are "accepted in the Beloved" (Eph. 1:6).

Assurance in the judgment is good news—almost too good to be true. And I dared not believe it even as a seminary student. I was privileged to take the course called Righteousness by Faith, taught by one of the leading Christian expositors of righteousness by faith. I studied hard for the course, and for the only time in my academic career, I received an A+ on the final exam. Imagine—an A+ in Righteousness by Faith! I had "arrived." Yet I had never personally experienced righteousness by faith.

I had been taught by earnest and well-meaning but misguided teachers that we should never claim assurance of salvation. One statement in particular was given to us to memorize: "Those who accept the Saviour, however sincere their conversion, should never be taught to say or to feel that they are saved."[13] It is tragic that the context of this passage was not recognized. In this statement the author is warning against the erroneous belief of "once saved, always saved." It does not teach that one could never have present assurance of salvation. In the very same paragraph is found the assurance that we can "give ourselves to Christ and know that He accepts us."[14]

For several years after graduating from the Seminary, many of my sermons were focused on Christ but were lacking the assurance in Christ. One summer, after we had finished pitching tents for the upcoming camp meeting, a pastor friend of mine, recognizing my spiritual plight, asked me directly, "Do you have assurance of salvation?" I answered, "I hope so!" Then he began to share the powerful promises of Scripture. He asked me to read John 6:47: "Most assuredly, I say to you, he who believes in Me *has* eternal life." "Do you believe in Jesus?" he queried. I answered, "Of course! I'm a pastor." He proceeded to drive the question home with another, "Then do you have eternal life?" I could only reply: "I hope so!" So he told me to read another passage, 1 John 5:13: "These things I have written to you who believe in the name of the Son of God, that you may *know* that you *have* eternal life." Once again he probed, "Do you believe in the name of the Son of God?" My answer "Of

---

13. White, *Christ's Object Lessons*, 155.

14. Ibid.

course!" was followed by his question, "then do you know that you have eternal life?" And my response, "I hope so!" After many rounds of reading the promises, followed by questions by my pastor friend, and my answers of "I hope so!" I finally dared to say, "Yes! I have eternal life, not because I feel it, but because God has promised it." And my life has never been the same. I later discovered the same magnificent affirmation of Gospel assurance in the words of Ellen White: "If you give yourself to Him, and accept Him as your Saviour, then, sinful as your life may have been, for His sake you are accounted righteous. Christ's character stands in place of your character, and you are *accepted* before God just as if you had not sinned."[15] This has become my favorite passage in the entire Ellen White corpus.

The glorious good news that Christ is my Substitute brought to me that same peace and joy as described by those who accepted the gospel message after the Seventh-day Adventist General Conference session in 1888. Ellen White expressed my own experience in her description of the events at the Ottawa, Kansas, camp meeting in 1889: "Light flashed from the oracles of God in relation to the law and the gospel, in relation to the fact that Christ is our righteousness, which seemed to souls who were hungry for the truth, as light too precious to be received."[16] I identified with the young pastor at that camp meeting who "saw that it was his privilege to be justified by faith; he had peace with God, and with tears confessed what relief and blessing had come to his soul."[17]

How precious is the doctrine of Christian assurance, even during the time of the judgment. In ancient Israel on the Day of Atonement (the Hebrew day of judgment), the "daily" (*tamîd* "continual") sacrifice continued to burn on the altar of burnt offering (Num. 28:2–7; 29:7–11), and the incense continued to waft over the inner veil, fill the holy of holies, and cover the holy ark (Exod. 30:7–10). So during the anti-typical Day of Atonement, we are still accepted by God solely on the basis of the atoning blood and intercessory merits of Christ. Christ is my Substitute who has paid the penalty for my sins with His blood.

---

15. Ellen G. White, *Steps to Christ* (Nampa, ID: Pacific Press, 1956), 62. Italics added.

16. White, *Selected Messages*, 1:356.

17. Ibid.

CHRIST IS OUR LAWYER/ADVOCATE

In the judgment, Christ is also our Advocate, our Lawyer. "And if anyone sins, we have an Advocate [παράκλητος (*paraklētos*)] with the Father, Jesus Christ the righteous" (1 John 2:1). Our heavenly Advocate has never lost a case that has been committed to Him (John 18:9). A courtroom loses its fear for the one being tried if the lawyer can guarantee that he has never and will never lose a case that is committed to his hands. This is what Jesus promises, based upon His sacrifice in our behalf.

In the heavenly assize, Christ eloquently and persuasively pleads our case based upon His blood: "Jesus, the mediator of a new covenant, and . . . purifying blood which pleads more insistently than Abel's" (Heb. 12:24, NJB; cf. Mic. 7:9). In the judgment "Jesus pleads in their [His followers'] behalf His wounded hands, His bruised body; and He declares to all who would follow Him: 'My grace is sufficient for thee.' 2 Corinthians 12:9."[18] The word "plead" used to trip me up, as I visualized the Son begging the Father to change His mind and love and forgive me because of Christ's blood. But I came to realize that in the context of the investigative judgment, the word "plead" is a legal term for what a lawyer does: he "pleads the case" of his client. So Jesus presents the evidence in behalf of the ones He is representing. The Father does not need to be begged to love and forgive us—He also is on our side. "For God [the Father] so loved the world that He [the Father] gave His only begotten Son" (John 3:16).

I used to have some old doctrinal books in my basement, with various artists' depictions of the repentant sinner standing in the heavenly courtroom when his name came up for judgment. Invariably, the face of the true child of God appeared filled with terror, sweat was pouring down from his brow, and worst of all, God's child was standing all alone in the courtroom. Are these accurate portrayals? They do correctly emphasize that there is a real investigative judgment now transpiring in heaven, where cases of the living will one day be examined. In a manner of speaking, "we must all appear before the judgment seat of Christ" (2 Cor. 5:10). But the illustrators that picture the repentant sinner standing in terror all alone in the midst of the heavenly tribunal have missed the crucial biblical point: "He [our Advocate] always lives to make intercession for them" (Heb. 7:25). For those in

---

18. White, *Great Controversy* (Mountain View, CA: Pacific Press, 1950), 489; see also 482.

Christ, the heavenly courtroom is a friendly place. Our heavenly Lawyer stands beside them with His arm around them, as it were; He "does not excuse their sins, but shows their penitence and faith, and, claiming for them forgiveness, He lifts His wounded hands before the Father and the holy angels, saying: I know them by name. I have graven them on the palms of My hands."[19] I am thankful that in a recent fire at our house those old books with their distorted illustrations of the judgment were consumed, so that they will not mislead my children or grandchildren as they did me.

Christ is my Lawyer who has never lost a case that has been committed to Him. That is assuring good news.

CHRIST IS THE STAR WITNESS IN OUR BEHALF

To the church at Laodicea (the name means "people of the judgment"), representing the people who are living during the time of the pre-Advent judgment, Christ reveals Himself as the "Faithful and True Witness" (Rev. 3:14). Not only does He warn the Laodicean people of their true spiritual condition; but for those who repent of their sins and open the door of their hearts for Him to come in and dine with them, He also testifies in their behalf in the heavenly assize.[20] As their Star Witness as well as Advocate, He brings evidence to the heavenly jury in support of His people that silences the false accusations of the adversary. Christ is my Star Witness in the heavenly assize. Yet He is not only our Substitute, our Lawyer/Advocate, our Star Witness. . . .

CHRIST IS OUR JUDGE

While still on earth, Jesus announced, "For the Father judges no one, but has committed all judgment to the Son" (John 5:22).[21] Our Elder Brother,

---

19. White, *Great Controversy*, 484.

20. For evidence of the legal setting of this divine "Witness" (μάρτυς [*martys*]) and of the messages to the seven churches (Rev. 2–3) and even the book of Revelation as a whole, see William Shea, "The Covenantal Form of the Letters to the Seven Churches," *AUSS* 21 (1983): 71–84; and Alan S. Bandy, *The Prophetic Lawsuit in the Book of Revelation*, New Testament Monographs 29 (Sheffield, England: Sheffield Phoenix Press, 2010).

21. Cf. John 5:27, 30; Ellen G. White, *Seventh-day Adventist Bible Commentary*, vol. 7A (Hagerstown, MD: Review and Herald, 1985), 7:989; idem, *Desire of Ages* (Mountain View,

our Best Friend, is the Judge. This Judge has never made a mistake, and He is on our side. He is not a stern, harsh magistrate seeking to damn all He can, but a loving, gracious God seeking to save all He can. With tender pleading He urges us to accept the provisions of the court so He can exonerate us:

> "Therefore I will judge you, O house of Israel, every one according to his ways," says the LORD God. "Repent, and turn from all your transgressions, so that iniquity will not be your ruin. Cast away from you all the transgressions which you have committed, and get yourselves a new heart and a new spirit! For why should you die, O house of Israel? For I have no pleasure in the death of one who dies," says the LORD God. "Therefore turn, and live." (Ezek. 18:30–32)

The multiple function of a single individual in the judgment may seem strange to our modern Western legal system, but it is entirely in keeping with the biblical concept of administering justice.[22] At the city gates the same elder(s) could convene the judicial proceedings, argue as an advocate, give testimony, and render the verdict. At the Israelite sanctuary the priest not only did all of this (Deut. 17:8–13) but also bore the penalty of the sins (Lev. 10:17).

With Christ as our Substitute and Surety, our Advocate and Mediator, our Witness and Friend and Judge, what better assuring news can we ask for? The One who has paid the price for our sins is our Lawyer who has never lost a case committed to Him, our Faithful and True Witness testifying on our behalf, and also the Judge. How can we lose our assurance in such a courtroom scene? We can lose assurance only if we refuse to accept the provisions of salvation that Christ freely offers daily to us as a gift.

CA: Pacific Press, 1940), 210; idem, *Testimonies for the Church* (Boise, ID: Pacific Press, 1948), 9:185. It is true that according to Daniel 7 the Ancient of Days does preside in the investigative judgment (White, *Great Controversy*, 479), but it appears that when the investigative judgment is over, Christ then assumes the role of Supreme Judge in order to pronounce the sentence and execute the judgment. See the analysis of the pertinent Ellen White quotations in Robert W. Olson, comp., "The Investigative Judgment in the Writings of Ellen G. White," Ellen G. White Estate pamphlet, 25 February 1980.

22. See Hans J. Boecker, *Law and the Administration of Justice in the Old Testament and Ancient Near East* (Minneapolis, MN: Augsburg Press, 1980), 34–35.

What we have described thus far is the *basis* of our acceptance in the judgment—justification by faith.[23] The ground of our salvation in the judgment is totally what Christ has done for us by shedding His blood at Calvary, then applying His blood for the pardon of our sins and covering us with His robe of righteousness as we daily give ourselves to Him and take Him as our Savior. This is the ultimate and only *foundation* of our assurance, both now and in the judgment. Yet there are three more reasons for joyous assurance in the judgment.

CHRIST IS OUR PURIFIER

On the Day of Atonement in ancient Israel, while maintaining the continual (*tamîd*) intercessory ministry, the priest carried out an additional service, as summarized in Leviticus 16:30: "For on that day the priest shall make atonement for you, to *cleanse* you, that you may be clean from all your sins before the LORD." Throughout the year the people received forgiveness and cleansing for their sins by faith in the ministry of Christ who was to come, but at the end of the year there was a special work of cleansing the sanctuary (Lev. 16:15–20), which involved a special work of purification for the people (Lev. 23:27–32). In the antitype, according to the prophecy of Daniel 8:14, at the end of the 2,300-day prophecy, "then the sanctuary shall be cleansed."[24] Seventh-day Adventists interpret this prophecy as pointing primarily to the cleansing of the heavenly sanctuary (Heb. 9:23–28), but as the heavenly sanctuary is being cleansed, there is a corresponding special work of cleansing to be accomplished in the soul temple of each individual worshiper.

In his depiction of the end-time pre-Advent judgment, Malachi portrays the cleansing work the Messiah, the Messenger of the Covenant: "For He is

---

23. For a comprehensive biblical study of the meaning of justification by faith, see Richard M. Davidson, "How Shall a Person Stand before God? What Is the Meaning of Justification?" in *God's Character and the Last Generation*, ed. Jiří Moskala and John C. Peckham (Nampa, ID: Pacific Press, 2018), 58–102.

24. For evidence that the word נִצְדַּק (*nitsdaq*) in Daniel 8:14 has (among other meanings) the semantic connotation of "purify, cleanse" in a judgment setting, see especially Eric M. Livingston, "A Study of צדק (*tsdq*) in Daniel 8:14, Its Relation to the 'Cleanse' Semantic Field, and Its Importance for Seventh-day Adventism's Concept of the Investigative Judgment" (PhD diss., University of New England, Australia, 2007); cf. Richard M. Davidson, "The Meaning of *Nitsdaq* in Daniel 8:14," *JATS* 7, no. 1 (1996): 107–119.

like a refiner's fire and like launderer's soap. He will sit as a refiner and a puri-fier of silver; He will purify the sons of Levi, and purge them as gold and silver, that they may offer to the LORD an offering in righteousness" (Mal. 3:2–3).[25]

Also in the context of eschatological judgment, Ezekiel records God's promise of cleansing for His people:

> Then I will sprinkle clean water on you, and you shall be clean; I will cleanse you from all your filthiness and from all your idols. I will give you a new heart and put a new spirit within you; I will take the heart of stone out of your flesh and give you a heart of flesh. I will put My Spirit within you and cause you to walk in My statutes, and you will keep My judgments and do them. (Ezek. 36:25–27)

What is crucial to note in each of these passages is *who* takes responsi-bility for doing the cleansing. Mark what the texts say: "the priest shall make atonement for you, to cleanse you" (Lev. 16:30); "He [the Messenger of the Covenant] will purify the sons of Levi" (Mal. 3:3); "I [the LORD] will cleanse you . . . I will . . . cause you to walk in My statutes" (Ezek. 36:25, 27).[26] God Himself assumes ultimate responsibility for the cleansing and for the obedience of His people.

I formerly thought that during the time of the pre-Advent investigative judgment I needed to cleanse myself—to try harder, to lift myself up by own bootstraps, to use my willpower to subdue all my sins, in order to be good enough for Jesus to accept me. But I found by experience that there was no victory in that kind of exercise. Even if I could somehow manage to keep from sinning outwardly, I still wanted to sin. My thoughts and motives were still polluted. And then came the joyous message of righteousness by faith. I came to realize that I do not undergo a work of cleansing in order

---

25. See White's application of this passage to the end-time investigative judgment, in *Great Controversy*, 425.

26. For full discussion of the interpretation of this passage, see James Matua, "The Spirit of the Lord and Obedience to the Law: An Exegetical, Intertextual, and Theological Study of Ezekiel 36:27" (PhD diss., Andrews University, forthcoming). Matua shows how the original Hebrew of this verse reads "I [God] will do . . . and you [God's people] will do," implying that God supplies the motivation and power to obey, and the people freely co-operate in "working out" what God "works in." The equivalent passage in the New Testa-ment is Philippians 2:12–13: "Work out your own salvation with fear and trembling, for it is God who works in you both to will and to do for His good pleasure."

for God to accept me; rather, I receive cleansing because He has already accepted me. And it is God who promises to provide both the motivation and power for me to be cleansed and live the life of holiness.

The Day of Atonement brings a call to holiness, but the life of holiness is rooted in justification by faith in the atoning blood of Christ.[27] Ellen White forcefully summarizes this relationship between justification by faith and holy living in a way that resonates with my own personal experience:

> There are conscientious souls that trust partly to God, and partly to themselves. They do not look to God, to be kept by His power, but depend upon watchfulness against temptation, and the performance of certain duties for acceptance with Him. There are no victories in this kind of faith. Such persons toil to no purpose; their souls are in continual bondage, and they find no rest until their burdens are laid at the feet of Jesus.
>
> There is need of constant watchfulness, and of earnest, loving devotion; but these will come naturally when the soul is kept by the power of God through faith. We can do nothing, absolutely nothing, to commend ourselves to divine favor. We must not trust at all to ourselves nor to our good works; but when as erring, sinful beings we come to Christ, we may find rest in His love. God will accept every one that comes to Him trusting wholly in the merits of a crucified Saviour. Love springs up in the heart. There may be no ecstasy of feeling, but there is an abiding, peaceful trust. Every burden is light; for the yoke which Christ imposes is easy. Duty becomes a delight, and sacrifice a pleasure. The path that before seemed shrouded in darkness becomes bright with beams from the Sun of Righteousness. This is walking in the light as Christ is in the light.[28]

The cleansing of our soul temple is by virtue of Christ's blood alone, and Christ by His Spirit takes responsibility for this cleansing as we allow Him to do His purifying work in our lives. At the same time, it is true that when our name comes up in the heavenly courtroom, there is an examination of the heavenly records (Dan. 7:10; 12:1). According to

---

27. See Leviticus 16:30, where it states that "on this day [Yom Kippur] shall atonement be made for you, to cleanse you; from all your sins you shall be clean before the LORD" (RSV). Note that the focus of even the people's "cleansing" is upon the atonement made by the blood of the Substitute.

28. White, *Selected Messages*, 1:353–354.

Adventist understanding of the biblical data, the cleansing of the sanctuary involves an investigative judgment, in effect, a judgment according works.

In the years following the discussion of righteousness by faith in the General Conference of 1888, some advocates of Christian assurance within Adventism (e.g., Albion Ballenger) felt that a belief in assurance of salvation could not be reconciled with the Adventist teaching regarding concerning the pre-Advent investigative judgment of the saints, and they therefore chose to retain the belief in assurance of salvation and jettison the belief in the pre-Advent investigative judgment.[29] This view that Gospel assurance is incompatible with an investigative judgment has again been advocated by some Adventists in recent decades. However, the biblical evidence discussed in the Daniel and Revelation Committee (DARCOM) and other scholarly research has shown that a choice between Christian assurance and the investigative judgment is unnecessary. Both doctrines are biblically sound.[30] Furthermore, research has shown that the examination of the deeds or "works" of God's professed people[31] as part of the eschatological judgment is clearly found in Scripture, as Adventists have consistently asserted,[32] and as many Christian theologians of various denominations recognize.[33]

---

29. See the analysis and critique of Ballenger's view in Roy Adams, *The Sanctuary Doctrine: Three Approaches in the Seventh-day Adventist Church*, vol. 1, Andrews University Seminary Doctoral Dissertation Series (Berrien Springs, MI: Andrews University Press, 1981), 91–164.

30. See especially Ivan Blazen, "Justification and Judgment," in *Seventy Weeks, Leviticus, and the Nature of Prophecy*, vol. 3, ed. Frank Holbrook; Daniel and Revelation Committee Series (Washington, DC: Biblical Research Institute, 1986), 339–388; cf. Moore, *The Case for the Investigative Judgment, passim.*

31. Blazen, "Justification and Judgment," in *Seventy Weeks*, 353–368, examines the major passages supporting this position (Rom. 2:16; 8:5–13; 14:10, 12; 1 Cor. 3:13; 4:5; 6:9; 2 Cor. 5:9–10; Gal. 5:21; 6:7–8; Eph. 5:5–6; Col. 3:5–6; 1 Thess. 4:6; Heb. 2:1–3; 10:26–31). In my own study, I have found at least one hundred biblical passages which either explicitly or implicitly affirm judgment according to works. See Richard M. Davidson, "Final Justification According to Works: Is N. T. Wright Right?" (paper presented at the national convention of the Evangelical Theological Society, Atlanta, Georgia, November 19, 2010), 3–10.

32. Blazen, "Justification and Judgment," in *Seventy Weeks*, 353–368, reviews various attempts to resolve the tension between justification and judgment, and shows the biblical mandate to retain the tension and understand it in terms of the "dynamic, salvation-historical" perspective of the "already" and the "not yet."

33. See, e.g., N. T. Wright, *Justification: God's Plan and Paul's Vision* (Downers Grove,

The Christian church since shortly after the apostolic period has struggled to bring together what seemed like two disparate teachings of Scripture: the assurance of salvation by grace and the judgment according to works. My study on this subject has persuaded me that the biblical message of the antitypical Day of Atonement enables a more harmonious and clear understanding and proclamation of these two realities than ever before. The Day of Atonement contains the key to keeping in balance the relationship both between grace and works, and between assurance and judgment.

This balance can be seen in the literary placement of the primary Day of Atonement passage, Leviticus 16, within the framework of Leviticus and of the entire Pentateuch. Recent literary studies have shown how the entire Pentateuch is arranged in a chiastic structure, with Leviticus as the central book of the Pentateuch:[34]

C. Leviticus

B. Exodus   **B'. Numbers**

A. Genesis   **A'. Deuteronomy**

Within this central Pentateuchal book of Leviticus, other scholars have shown that the central chapter of Leviticus is chapter 16.[35] Thus Leviticus 16, focusing on Yom Kippur, is the very center of Torah.[36]

IL: IVP Academic, 2009), 184–185; other scholars are cited in Davidson, "Final Justification According to Works," 1–31. See Richard M. Davidson, "Final Justification According to Works: Is N. T. Wright Right?" (paper presented at the national convention of the Evangelical Theological Society, Atlanta, Georgia, November 19, 2010), 3–10; to be published in *JATS* (forthcoming).

34. See Yehuda Radday, "Chiasm in Tora," *Linguistica Biblica* 19 (1972): 21–23; idem, "Chiasmus in Hebrew Biblical Narrative," in *Chiasmus in Antiquity*, ed. John Welch (Hildesheim: Gerstenberg Verlag, 1981), 84–86.

35. William Shea, "Literary Form and Theological Function in Leviticus," in *The Seventy Weeks, Leviticus, and the Nature of Prophecy*, ed. Frank Holbrook, Daniel and Revelation Committee Series, vol. 3 (Washington, DC: Biblical Research Institute, 1986), 131–168; and Wilfried Warning, *Literary Artistry in Leviticus*, BibInt 35 (Leiden: Brill, 1999), 86–87, 178.

36. Rolf Rendtorff, "Leviticus 16 als Mitte der Tora," *BibInt* 11 (2003): 252–258.

Here is the chiastic structure of Leviticus, as analyzed by William Shea, reformatted in customary chiastic display style and including only the main (bold) items of the structure:

CHIASTIC STRUCTURE OF LEVITICUS[37]

"Justification" (blood)	"Sanctification" (holiness)
D. chap. 16: Day of Atonement	
C. chaps. 11–15:	**C'. chaps. 17–20:**
Personal Laws	Personal
of Uncleanness	Moral Laws
B. chaps. 8–10:	**B'. chaps. 21–22:**
Priestly History	Priestly Legislation
A. chaps. 1–7:	**A'. chaps. 23–25:**
Cultic Legislation	Cultic Legislation

Notice in Shea's diagram that the book of Leviticus is divided into two halves, each with a different emphasis: "the first half of the book covers the sacrificial system; the second outlines the way the people are to live."[38] In the first half the underlying theme is "blood," while the leading motif of the second half is "holiness." Or, as Shea summarizes in the headings of each half: "justification" and "sanctification." And right in the middle of the book stands chapter 16, the message of the Day of Atonement.

Literary form highlights theology. The literary-structural setting of Leviticus underscores the balanced Gospel message: we are saved by grace alone—by the blood of Christ's sacrifice. Yet we are judged according our works of holiness, which are the natural fruit of atoning grace. The efficacy of the blood for the believer becomes manifest by its holy fruit.[39]

---

37. Shea, "Literary Form and Theological Function," 149.

38. Ibid., 150.

39. Cf. White, *Christ's Object Lessons*, 312 (discussing the investigative judgment): "Righteousness is right doing, and it is by their deeds that all will be judged. Our characters are revealed by what we do. The works show whether the faith is genuine."

Ivan Blazen succinctly summarizes the relationship between justification by faith and judgment according to works:

> The investigative judgment, rightly understood, is in harmony with justification by faith and judgment according to works. It encompasses within itself the ingredients of these two fundamental teachings. . . . Plainly, the investigative judgment does not deal merely with the sins of mankind but with the forgiveness of Christ. Consequently, when the whole package is put together, and justification by faith and future judgment according to works are seen as the content of the investigative judgment, it can be stated that there are two questions this judgment answers. First, has the sinner sought and received Christ's forgiveness of his sins? Second, has this forgiveness brought forth good fruit in his life? . . . . Only when the answer to such questions is a fundamental Yes can the final revelation of God's forgiveness and mercy be extended to believers.[40]

The concept of fruits of righteousness at the final judgment is especially evident in the New Testament passage of Philippians 1:6, 9–11:

> And I am sure that he who began a good work in you will bring it to completion at the day of Jesus Christ. . . . And it is my prayer that your love may abound more and more, with knowledge and all discernment, so that you may approve what is excellent, and may be pure and blameless for the day of Christ, filled with the *fruits of righteousness* which come through Jesus Christ, to the glory and praise of God. (RSV)

This concept of fruits of righteousness at the last judgment does not destroy Christian assurance in the judgment. As Blazen puts it, "If justification *grants* assurance, judgment *guards* it. *It guards it from the illusion that assurance is possible without a fundamental relationship to Christ and a committed following of Christ.*"[41] In the final judgment, works of faith in the life of the Christian provide the evidence that his or her faith is genuine. But the ultimate ground of one's acceptance in the judgment is not the believer's Spirit-enabled works, but the imputed righteousness of Christ. "While the character of Christ can be imitated and approximated, the infinite character of His goodness can never be equaled." Hence, as Blazen points out, "two things must remain true for the [final] judgment:

---

40. Blazen, "Justification and Judgment," in *Seventy Weeks*, 379–381.
41. Ibid., 367.

(1) the sanctified fruit of justification must be present, but (2) justification itself must continue its function of pardon."[42]

In the Day of Atonement assurance and judgment meet and take on ultimate meaning. This is assuring good news indeed.

CHRIST IS OUR VINDICATOR

David prayed, "Judge me, O LORD my God, according to Your righteousness" (Ps. 35:24, NASB); it may better be translated as captured by many modern versions: "Vindicate Me!" (NKJV, ESV, NIV, RSV). The outcome of the eschatological judgment is certain. It is "in favor of the saints of the Most High" (Dan. 7:22). The judgment brings condemnation upon the little horn power, and Satan who is ultimately behind this power, and at the same time brings vindication for God's people who have been falsely accused by Satan. John the Revelator delivers the same basic message as Daniel regarding the vindication of God's people: "for the accuser of our brethren, who accused them before our God day and night, has been cast down" (Rev. 12:10).

I was delighted to learn, from examining the more than three hundred examples of covenant lawsuits (investigative judgments) in Scripture, that the preponderance of legal proceedings are for the purpose of vindicating God's people.[43] In fact, the concept of judgment in Scripture is generally a positive one, and the primary usage of judgment terminology refers to God's work of justification, salvation, deliverance, and vindication of His people.[44]

This assurance of vindication in the judgment will become more and more precious to us in the last days, as persecution begins, as God's people are falsely accused, and as guilty verdicts are rendered against them by the highest earthly courts.[45] In such bleak circumstances, God's people confidently trust that in the investigative judgment the truth will come out and justice will be served. Like Job, who in a setting of cosmic investigative judgment[46] faced false accusers, God's end-time people can confidently proclaim:

---

42. Ibid.

43. Davidson, "Divine Covenant Lawsuit Motif," 83.

44. See Jiří Moskala, "The Gospel According to God's Judgment: Judgment as Salvation," *JATS* 22 (2011): 28–49.

45. See Revelation 12:17; 13:11–17; and White, *Great Controversy,* 582–592.

46. For analyses of the book of Job as a רִיב (*rîb*) or covenant lawsuit, see especially

"For I know that my Vindicator [margin] lives, and at last he will stand upon the earth; and after my skin has been thus destroyed, then from my flesh I shall see God, whom I shall see on my side!" (Job 19:25–27, RSV).[47]

Ellen White powerfully captures the picture of our final vindication in the pre-Advent investigative judgment:

> John in holy vision beholds the faithful souls that come up out of great tribulation, surrounding the throne of God, clad in white robes, and crowned with immortal glory. What though they have been counted the offscouring of the earth? In the investigative judgment their lives and characters are brought in review before God, and that solemn tribunal reverses the decision of their enemies. Their faithfulness to God and to His Word stands revealed, and Heaven's high honors are awarded them as conquerors in the strife with sin and Satan.[48]

The investigative judgment reveals to the unfallen universe the standing of the saints before God. The salvation of God's people is not placed in jeopardy. While those who have neglected and rejected the provisions made for their salvation have good reason for anxiety, for those who belong to Christ the investigative judgment is a reason for exuberant singing. For thousands of years (since the death of Abel) the blood of the martyrs has been crying out, "How long, O Lord, holy and true, until You judge and avenge our blood on those who dwell on the earth?" (Rev. 6:9–10). At last Yom Kippur is here! The final judgment has begun—the process through which God reveals to the unfallen inhabitants of the universe the evidence in favor of His people, the reality of their repentance and faith as demonstrated by the faithful fruits of their actions, and His forgiveness of their sins. Satan's accusations against His people are shown to be false, and the full truth can finally come out vindicating God's people.

B. Gemser, "The *Rîb*- or Controversy-Pattern in Hebew Mentality," in *Wisdom in Israel and in the Ancient Near East*, ed. Martin Noth and D. Winton Thomas, *VTSup* 3 (Leiden: Brill, 1955), 120–37; Heinz Richter, *Studien zu Hiob* (Berlin: Evangelische Verlagsanstalt, 1959); Sylvia Scholnick, "Lawsuit Drama in the Book of Job" (PhD diss., Brandeis University, 1976); and Claus Westermann, *The Structure of the Book of Job* (Philadelphia, PA: Fortress, 1981).

47. See the analysis of this passage by Gordon E. Christo, "The Eschatological Judgment in Job 19:21–29: An Exegetical Study" (PhD diss., Andrews University, 1992). According to this literary analysis of the book of Job, this passage stands at the chiastic apex of the book.

48. Ellen G. White, *Our High Calling* (Washington, DC: Review and Herald, 1961), 361.

Truly the first angel's message—"The hour of His judgment has come"—is part of the "eternal good news" (Rev. 14:6–7).

Vindication of the saints in the judgment is assuring good news. But the best news of assurance is saved for last. And it is ultimately not about us, but about God Himself.

THE VINDICATION OF GOD

The assuring good news of Yom Kippur has implications far beyond our personal experience. The plan of redemption focuses not only (or even primarily) upon our personal salvation. The Bible presents a theocentric view of salvation history. For example, Ezekiel, in the larger context of the earthly type of the antitypical investigative judgment[49] underscores the "bigger picture"—the cosmic dimension. In Ezekiel 36:22–23 (and again in 39:27–28), God reveals to Judah the ultimate result of their judgment: "through you I vindicate my holiness before their eyes [the eyes of the onlooking nations]" (ESV). It is for their sakes, to vindicate His character before the onlooking intelligences, that God acts.

The investigative judgment is not conducted to reveal to God who are His and who are not. He who is omniscient knows who are His (Isa. 46:9–10; John 10:4, 14, 27; 2 Tim. 2:19; Heb. 4:13). It is for the sake of assuring the onlooking universe that serves as the jury in the cosmic investigative judgment (1 Cor. 4:9, NIV). God, who throughout biblical history consistently has set forth the evidence in open court through "mini-investigative-judgments" (i.e., covenant lawsuits) before executing judgment upon any individuals or nations,[50] does not depart from this procedure in the final judgment. Since the rise of evil in the universe, the cosmic conflict has been concerning the character of God, with Satan accusing God of being unjust and/or unmerciful.[51] At the end of the Great Controversy, in the final

---

49. See Richard M. Davidson, "In Confirmation of the Sanctuary Message," *JATS* 2/1 (Spring 1991): 97–100; idem, "The Chiastic Literary Structure of the Book of Ezekiel, "in *To Understand the Scriptures: Essays in Honor of William H. Shea*, ed. David Merling (Berrien Springs, MI: The Institute of Archaeology/Siegfried H. Horn Archaeological Museum, 1997), 71–93.

50. See Davidson, "Divine Covenant Lawsuit Motif," passim, for discussion of this consistent procedure of God throughout history.

51. See the biblical evidence for this conclusion in Richard M. Davidson, "Back to the

heavenly assize, all the universe will have opportunity to witness "one great and final reaffirmation of all that He [Christ] has accomplished through the plan of salvation";[52] and they will be able to attest to the justice and truthfulness of God's dealings with humankind. Satan's charges against God will be proven false.

The mind-boggling aspect about this cosmic trial is that we have a part in God's vindication. Note how in Ezekiel 36:23 (ESV) God says that "*through you* I vindicate my holiness before their eyes," and then in succeeding verses He describes the work of cleansing that He will perform for His people.

In the Old Testament type, Judah's sins and the resulting captivity caused surrounding nations to charge that God could not keep His promises to His people. In gathering them from captivity and cleansing them, He vindicated His holy character from the false accusations (Ezek. 36:17–32). So in the antitype, against Satan's false claim that God cannot fulfill His new covenant promises, God gathers His faithful people to Himself at the consummation of history and through the power of His Spirit demonstrates the ultimate effectiveness of the gospel. The new covenant promise—"I will put my Spirit within you, and cause you to walk in my statutes and be careful to observe my ordinances" (Ezek. 36:27)—will find ultimate fulfillment among God's remnant people. They will become fully settled into the truth as it is in Jesus. Sealed as the spiritual 144,000, they will have the name (character) of the Lamb and the Father written on their foreheads (Rev. 7:4; 14:1). Then the investigative judgment can close for the living (Rev. 22:11).[53] No glory will accrue to the people—"It is not for your sake that I will act, declares the Lord God; let that be known to you" (Ezek. 36:32, ESV). To God alone be the glory!

Not only does God vindicate His character by revealing the faithfulness of the *saints*. Ezekiel 38:16, 22–23 (RSV) uses the same language to

Beginning: Genesis 1–3 and the Theological Center of Scripture," in *Christ, Salvation, and the Eschaton*, ed. Daniel Heinz, Jiří Moskala, and Peter M. van Bemmelen (Berrien Springs, MI: Old Testament Publications, 2009), 5–29.

52. William Shea, "Theological Importance of the Preadvent Judgment," in *Seventy Weeks*, 327.

53. See Doug Bennett, "The Good News About the Judgment of the Living," *Adventist Review* 16 (June 1983): 14–15, for evidence that probation does not close upon the living until after the latter rain and the sealing; cf. White, *Selected Messages*, 1:66; idem, *Early Writings* (Hagerstown, MD: Review and Herald, 1945), 85–86.

describe the final judgment upon the *wicked*, and in particular their leader:

> In the latter days I will bring you [Gog, symbol of Satan leading his wicked hordes] against my land, that the nations may know me, when *through you, O Gog, I vindicate my holiness before their eyes.*... With pestilence and bloodshed I will enter into judgment with him [Gog]; and I will rain upon him and his hordes and the many peoples that are with him, torrential rains and hailstones, fire and brimstone. So I will show my greatness and my holiness and make myself known in the eyes of many nations. Then they will know that I am the Lord.[54]

The final judgment reveals not only the ultimate effectiveness of the gospel but also the full ripening of iniquity (Rev. 14:18). In Revelation 16 the seven last plagues serve the purpose of revealing that God's final judgments find no answering chord of repentance in the hearts of the wicked—they only curse God all the more (Rev. 16:9, 11). God reveals Himself to be just and yes, merciful, in bringing the Great Controversy to an end. Before the Cosmic Conflict is over, even the rebels, though still unrepentant, will admit that God is just (Isa. 45:20–23; Rom. 14:11; Phil. 2:10–11). The mouth of Satan himself, the ringleader in the conflict, will finally be silenced as his charges against God are shown to be false.

At the grand climax to the Great Controversy, there will be a time of great rejoicing—and the good news will be about the vindication of God in the judgment. The redeemed will sing the song of Moses and of the Lamb: "Great and marvelous are Your works, Lord God Almighty! Just and true are Your ways, O King of the saints!" (Rev. 15:3). The angel of the water will say, "Just are you, O Holy One, who is and who was, for you brought these judgments" (Rev. 16:5, ESV). Another from the altar will cry, "Even so, Lord God Almighty, true and righteous are Your judgments!" (Rev. 16:7). After this "the loud voice of a great multitude in heaven, crying out, 'Hallelujah! Salvation and glory and power belong to our God, for his judgments are true and just . . .'" (Rev. 19:1–2, ESV).

---

54. For discussion of the Gog and Magog passages in Ezekiel and Revelation, see Jiří Moskala, "The Historical-Eschatological/Apocalyptic Fulfillment of the Gog and Magog Prophecy in Ezekiel 38–39," in *Christ, Salvation, and the Eschaton*, 287–313; and idem, "Toward the Fulfillment of the Gog and Magog Prophecy of Ezekiel 38–39," *JATS* 18, no. 2 (Autumn 2007): 243–273.

The message of the antitypical Yom Kippur—of the whole final judg-ment including the pre-Advent investigative trial, the millennial review, and post-millennial execution of the sentence—swells to a grand climax of assurance. The entire universe will be sure that God is just and true in all His ways, including the saving of His people. Thus, God's saved people have assurance forever. By means of the entire process of end-time judg-ment, God fully vindicates His character of love, and thus the universe will be rendered eternally secure. Assurance in the judgment will give way to assurance for eternity!

EPILOGUE

And you, being dead in your trespasses and the uncircumcision of your flesh, He has made alive together with Him.[1] —Colossians 2:13

But God demonstrates His own love toward us, in that while we were still sinners, Christ died for us. —Romans 5:8

Christ was treated as we deserve, that we might be treated as He deserves. He was condemned for our sins, in which He had no share, that we might be justified by His righteousness, in which we had no share. He suffered the death which was ours, that we might receive the life which was His. "With His stripes we are healed."[2]

This volume has been an attempt to address the most tenacious of all human questions: "What must I do to be saved?" The conflict that began in heaven, and is known as the great controversy between Christ and Satan, spilled over to the earth shortly after its creation and resulted in the Fall of the first couple. It was at that time that God enacted the plan of salvation that was established before the foundations of the world (Rev. 13:8). At the center of God's plan of salvation is Jesus Christ—a pre-existent, co-eternal divine being, in whom "dwells all the fullness of the Godhead bodily" (Col. 2:9). He chose to become a human, live a human life, die a sacrificial death on the cross, be resurrected, and become the mediator of the eternal covenant in the heavenly sanctuary. The cross of Christ stands at the core of God's plan of salvation as the singular most important event in the history of the universe. Without it, the plan of salvation would not be possible. As Paul said: "I determined not to know anything among you except Jesus Christ and Him crucified" (1 Cor. 2:2). Ellen White expressed it this way: "The sacrifice of Christ as an atonement for sin is the great truth around which all other truths cluster. In order to be rightly understood and appreciated, every truth in the Word of God, from Genesis to Revelation, must be studied in the light that streams from the cross of Calvary. I present before you the great, grand monument of mercy and regeneration,

---

1. Unless otherwise indicated, all Scripture quotations are taken from the New King James Version®. Copyright © 1982 by Thomas Nelson. Used by permission. All rights reserved.

2. Ellen G. White, *Desire of Ages* (Mountain View, CA: Pacific Press, 1898), 25.

salvation and redemption,—the Son of God uplifted on the cross."[3] Thus, Jesus and His accomplishment on the cross form the central theme of this volume.

But God did more than die for humanity. Faced with the total obliteration of human ability to reach out to Him, through the agency of prevenient grace He allowed fallen humans to once again "have the privileges and the opportunities" of free human beings.[4] Humans were thus supernaturally enabled to respond to the offer of God's grace, given to them at the very beginning. What must we do, then, to have eternal life? The Apostle John answers: "Believe in the name of the Son of God, that you may know that you have eternal life" (1 John 5:13). This "believing" depends on God's continual enabling that empowers us to maintain a constant "connection with Christ by faith and the continual surrender of [our] will to [His]."[5] As long as this happens in our lives, Christ "will work in us to will and to do according to His good pleasure" (Phil. 2:13).[6] Elen White States:

> Jesus imparts all the powers, all the grace, all the penitence, all the inclination, all the pardon of sins, in presenting His righteousness for man to grasp by living faith—which is also the gift of God. If you would gather together everything that is good and holy and noble and lovely in man and then present the subject to the angels of God as acting a part in the salvation of the human soul or in merit, the proposition would be rejected as treason.[7]

Thus, together with the Reformers, we can exclaim *Soli Deo Gloria! Glory to God alone!* The entire plan of salvation, from first to last, belongs to God. There never has been and never will be the possibility of human contribution to salvation aside from simply responding to God's grace, given to us "while we were still sinners" (Rom. 5:8). It is this grace that enables us to accept the free gift of salvation and empowers us to lead lives pleasing to God. It is, thus, through Christ's life of humility and suffering, as well as His sacrificial death on the cross, that the true nature of God has been revealed to humanity. To this good and beautiful God, who made all of this possible, this volume is dedicated.

3. Ellen G. White, *Gospel Workers* (Washington, DC: Review and Herald, 1948), 315.

4. Ellen G. White, "Christ the Propitiation for Our Sins," *Atlantic Union Gleaner*, vol. 2, no. 33 (August 19, 1903): 1.

5. Ellen G. White, *Steps to Christ* (Mountain View, CA: Pacific Press), 62.

6. Ibid., 62–63.

7. Ellen G. White, *Faith and Works* (Hagerstown, MD: Review and Herald, 2003), 24.

CONTRIBUTORS

CONTRIBUTING EDITORS

Martin F. Hanna, PhD, associate professor of systematic theology, Seventh-day Adventist Theological Seminary, Andrews University, Michigan

Darius W. Jankiewicz, PhD, professor of historical theology, Seventh-day Adventist Theological Seminary, Andrews University, Michigan

John W. Reeve, PhD, associate professor of church history, Seventh-day Adventist Theological Seminary, Andrews University, Michigan

OTHER CONTRIBUTING AUTHORS

Roy Adams, PhD, retired associate editor of the *Adventist Review*, Maryland

Ivan T. Blazen, PhD, professor emeritus of religion-theological studies, School of Religion, Loma Linda University, California

Jo Ann Davidson, PhD, professor of systematic theology, Seventh-day Adventist Theological Seminary, Andrews University, Michigan

Richard M. Davidson, PhD, J. N. Andrews Professor of Old Testament Interpretation, Seventh-day Adventist Theological Seminary, Andrews University, Michigan

Denis Fortin, PhD, professor of historical theology, Seventh-day Adventist Theological Seminary, Andrews University, Michigan

Roy E. Gane, PhD, professor of Hebrew Bible and ancient near east languages, Seventh-day Adventist Theological Seminary, Andrews University, Michigan

Norman R. Gulley, PhD, research professor, school of religion, Southern Adventist University, Tennessee

Abner Hernandez-Fernandez, PhD, faculty member in theology, Universidad de Montemorelos, Mexico

George R. Knight, PhD, professor emeritus of church history, Seventh-day Adventist Theological Seminary, Andrews University, Michigan

Hans K. LaRondelle, ThD, professor emeritus of theology (deceased), Andrews University, Michigan

John K. McVay, PhD, president, Walla Walla University, Washington

Nicholas P. Miller, JD, PhD, professor of church history, Seventh-day Adventist Theological Seminary, Andrews University, Michigan

Jerry A. Moon, PhD, professor emeritus of church history, Seventh-day Adventist Theological Seminary, Andrews University, Michigan

Jiří Moskala, ThD, PhD, dean and professor of Old Testament exegesis and theology, Seventh-day Adventist Theological Seminary, Andrews University, Michigan

Jon Paulien, PhD, dean and professor of religion-theological studies, School of Religion, Loma Linda University, California

Woodrow W. Whidden, PhD, professor emeritus of religion, College of Arts and Sciences, Andrews University, Michigan

SCRIPTURE INDEX

JEREMIAH

EZEKIEL

DANIEL

HOSEA

JOEL

AMOS

JONAH

ACTS

ROMANS

HEBREWS

JAMES

1 PETER

2 PETER

1 JOHN

JUDE

SUBJECT INDEX

A

Abasciano, Brian, 55n56
Abelard, Peter, 181–182
Abraham
  blessing of, 48, 56, 64, 304
  covenant with, 64, 218
  descent from, 70, 80
  in God's presence, 306
  justified by faith, 303–304, 305–306
accountability, 18
Achtemeier, Paul, 81, 81n27
Adam, 22, 91, 249–250
  Eve and, innocence of, 120–121
  garments of light worn by, 131–132,
    131n29
  impact of sin of, 93–94, 95–97, 98–99,
    109
  Jesus as Second, 29, 102n49, 117n117,
    137, 139, 265, 268
  Seth born "in the image of," 129
Adams, Roy, 90
adikia (unrighteousness), 155
adoption as God's children, 74, 76, 317, 347,
  348, 379–380
Adventism. *See also* White, Ellen G.
  Arminianism and, xii–xiii, 169–170
  assurance in, 350–357, 375–394,
    395–416
  Calvinist influence on, 392n15
  depravity in, xii, 116–117, 160, 169–171,
    298–299, 352
  intercession of Christ in, 201n60,
    221–240, 357
  prevenient grace in, 116–117, 298–299
  as reformation, 351
  struggles within, 285
  theodicy at heart of, 17–18
  Wesleyanism and, 116

Advocate
  Christ as, 228, 235, 318, 321, 392–393,
    401–403
  God as, 223
Alexander, Desmond, 250
Amos
  on God's "knowing," 63
  remnant theology of, 66
Anabaptists, 4, 5–7, 110–111, 110n87
  successors to, 111n96
Andreasen, M. L., 155n23
animals, sacrificing, 136, 136n43, 138, 193,
    193n19, 193n21, 205n78, 244
anomia (lawlessness), 151
Anselm of Canterbury, 10, 176, 179
anthropology
  high, x, 93, 94–95, 99n38, 100, 104–106,
    272
  low, x, 93, 101–102, 103, 106, 107–110,
    112–113
  medieval, xi, 103–107
  post-Reformation, 110–117
  pre-fifth century, x, 93–99
antinomianism, 297, 391–392
apokatástasis (restoration), 242, 242n3
Apologists, 94–99, 94n10
apostasy, 343–345, 343n81, 386–387
apostles, Jesus choosing, 70
Apostles' Creed, 177
apostolic council, 66n6
Apostolic Fathers, x, 94, 94n5
"appoint," 40n20
Arianism, 184
Arminianism, xi–xii, 168–169, 170, 171,
  375–376
  advantages of, 394
  and Calvinism, similarities between,
    390
  five points of, xi, xii

Hunt, David P., 42n25
Hus, Jan, 278, 278n76
Hyatt, Darlene, 53n50

I

idolatry, 320
Ignatius of Antioch, 263
illumination, 295
imago Dei, 95, 97, 120–121, 249–250
  Christ as, 199
  dominion and, 249, 257
  intact, 162–163
  marriage and, 252
  marring of, by sin, 9, 109, 129, 133, 137,
    162–163
  reflecting, 344n86
  restoration of, x, 49, 140, 226, 298, 320,
    367
impurity, 247–248
incarnation, 175, 183n22
indulgences, 279
infants, sin and, 109, 110–111, 129, 129n27
  Aquinas on, 104–105
  in Augustine's thought, 101–102,
    102n49, 269
  in Pelagian thought, 101, 103–104, 268
Innocents, Massacre of, 101n44
intercessor, Jesus as, 221–240, 392–393
  vs. appeasing, 224–225
  biblical support for, 223–224
  the cross as basis for, 225–226
  dual nature and, 225, 226–228
  ministry of, ending, 238
  praise for, 240
  redemptive ministry of, 226, 227–240
  revealing God, 226–227
  saving, 234–236, 240
  terms for, 227, 228–230
  transforming believers, 236–237, 240, 393
  vindication through, 237–239, 240
Irenaeus, 95–96, 178, 265–266, 265n22, 330
Isaiah, 24n11, 26

remnant theology in, 66
Revelation and, 253, 253n25
Servant Songs in, 67, 69, 206, 223, 249n19
on sin, 371
vineyard parable in, 69, 367
Israel, 79–83. *See also* "remnant"
  choosing God, 64–65
  chosenness of, 51n46, 54n53, 55, 56n59,
    62–67, 72, 81–82
  as clay, 53n51, 78
  disobedience of, 54n54, 55, 56, 67, 71,
    78–79
  eschatological hope for, 79–80
  "fullness" of, 57
  Gentiles joining, 65
  as God's "firstborn," 63
  God's love for, 62
  messianic prophecies and, 71, 84
  salvation open to, 53–54
  unbelief of, 52n49, 53, 78–83

J

Jacob and Esau, 78, 80, 81, 82
James (apostle), 41
  on perfection, 319
  on sin, 92, 130
Jankiewicz, Darius W., 89
Jennings, Timothy R., 235, 237
Jeremiah, temple speech of, 66
Jerusalem. *See* New Jerusalem
Jerusalem *vs.* Babylon, 24
Jesus Christ. *See also* intercessor, Jesus as
  as advocate, 221–240, 318, 321, 392–393,
    401–402
  believers identified with, 234–236,
    310–313
  birth of, 129n27
  chosen, 69–71
  confessing, 79, 81–83
  the cross revealing, 215, 215n132
  death of, not punishment, 186
  deceit denounced by, 152

righteousness in, 251, 251n22
New Jerusalem, 25, 30
    gates of, always open, 251
    like Eden, 247, 249–250
    as temple city, 246–248
Nicodemus, 361–363, 365–370, 373n31,
    374
Norris, Frederick W., 264n19

O

obedience
    assurance and, 337, 392–393
    Eden narrative centered on, 135
    grace enabling, 315–316, 337
    as remedy to sin, 95, 97, 100, 265
    and sin as disobedience, 96, 100
Oden, Thomas, 162, 287, 291, 293, 294
olive tree
    branches broken off of, 80–81
    Gentiles grafted onto, 55, 55n56
Olson, Roger, 7, 107, 113, 114n111, 168,
    276, 278n76, 291–292, 294
omission, sinning by, 130, 154
"once saved, always saved" doctrine,
    385–386, 399. *See also* perseverance
    critiques of, 386–388, 390–392
"ontological righteousness," 106
open future, 39n18
opheiletai (obligation), 262
ordinatio, 275, 275n66
Origen, 261n3
    on grace and merit, 261–262, 262n4,
        266–267
    on Jesus's Sonship, 267n33
    original sin and, 97–98
    on ransom theory of atonement, 178
    on the Trinity, 98n32
original sin, x, 96–97, 96n25, 98–99, 101–
    102, 106–107. *See also* Pelagianism
    in Adventism, 298
    baptism and, 102, 104–105, 110–111,
        166–167

in biblical text, 119–143
definitions of, 120n2
as illness, 105–106
in Reformation thought, 107–110
in Wesley's thought, 114
orthodoxy *vs.* orthopraxy, 276

P

Packer, J. I., 198, 198n47, 202nn62–63,
    203n70, 211n109, 212n117
paganism, sacrifice in, 205n78, 209–210,
    225
Parable of the Sower, 386–387
Parable of the Wedding Feast, 70
paradox, 88n39
parakletos (advocate), 228, 230
Passover, 218
Paul, 41–42, 47–57, 72–83
    on assurance, 335–336, 337
    Athens sermon of, 41–42, 41n23
    cruciformity in, 216–217
    denial formula used by, 51n46
    on foreknowledge, 36, 36n11, 47–57
    on grace, 261, 262
    interpreting, 78n23
    Jewish "kinsmen" of, 79–83
    metaphor in, 203–204
    "mystery" in, 47–48, 48n39
    olive tree metaphor of, 55, 55n56
    on perfection, 317, 318–319, 320
    reconciliation in, 194, 196–200, 196n37
    on sin, 92, 129, 302–303
    slavery language in, 164
    sorites in, 48, 48n40, 51
    spiritual inability in, 163
Paulien, Jon, 173
peace, reconciliation leading to, 196n37
Peckham, John C., 51n45
Pelagianism, x, 93, 99–103, 166–168, 182,
    184, 268–269. *See also* Augustine of
    Hippo; semi-Pelagianism
Pelagius, 99–102, 99n41, 100n42, 166–167, 268

as irresistible, 292–293

Luther on, 279

response to God enabled by, 296, 389–390

vs. sanctifying grace, 266–267, 282–283

universality of, 292

Wesley on, 114–116, 282–283

will freed by, 293, 418

pride, 23–24, 26

priests

and breastplate of High Priest, 246–247

God's people as, 246

sins of, 147

promise

children of, 80, 81

of God, as trustworthy, 335–338, 339, 372, 399–400

prophets

foreknowledge and, 38n17, 39–41, 44, 47, 50–56, 58, 71

free will in, 86

killing of, 367

marriage metaphor in, 63

"remnant" theology in, 65–67

on sin, 150–151, 154

propitiation *vs.* expiation, 209, 209n102

Psalms, 149–157, 305–306, 397–398, 397n9

pseudos (lie, deceit), 152

purification of sin, 398, 404–411

Puritanism, 13–14

Q

Quell, Gottfried, 146, 146n2, 147, 149, 151–152

R

Racovian Catechism, 184n23

Ramm, Bernard, 163, 164

ransom, atonement as, 177–179, 185, 187, 207–208, 207n88

reason as Christ's gift, 267

rebellion, 150, 151–152, 156. *See also* sin

reconciliation

among humans, 251–252

atonement as, 189, 189n1, 190–191, 191n10, 194–220, 243–244

the cross in, 181, 189–220, 306

God's Fatherhood and, 197–198, 199–200

of humans to God, not vice-versa, 224–225, 225nn10–11

metaphors for, 202–204

"now" and "not yet" aspects of, 199, 201, 407n32

ongoing, 199, 201, 221–240

peace as outcome of, 196n37

"receiving," 197

terms for, 194–195, 197n40, 199, 199n51, 199n54, 200n56, 200n58

of the universe, 19–32, 199–200, 213n121, 220, 241–258

redemption, 29n19, 30, 208, 389

as ransom, 177–179, 192n17, 193, 207–208

sacrifice and, 136, 311, 348

Rees, Brinley Roderick, 270

Reeve, John W., 259

Reformation theology

assurance and, 334, 335–345

grace asserted by, xi, 278–285

post-Reformation developments of, xi–xii, 110–117

sin in, 107–110

regeneration. *See* new birth

relationships. *See also* reconciliation

atonement in, 190–191, 195, 196, 219–220, 243–252

justification in, 212

as "knowing," 215

sanctification and, 309–310

sin breaking, 131–134, 141, 153–154, 195–196, 199, 252

remiyyah (deceit), 150, 152–153, 156

Satan
accusing believers, 237–238, 411
accusing God, 3, 22, 187n26
Azazel and, 243n6
binding of, 276
Christ hated by, 28n17
Christ tempted by, 21
in Eden, 21, 23, 28, 121–126
Job and, 21–23, 28
Joshua accused by, 66
names of, 26–27
as prince of this world, 21–22, 28, 250
rebellion of, 22–26
slandering God, 27, 27n13, 31–32,
  122–123, 123n11
symbols for, 23–26
as tempter, 121–126
transaction between God and, 177–179
victory over, 213–214, 237–239, 411–416
war of, against love, 20, 24, 26–30
satisfaction, atonement as, 179–181
Saul (king), 38, 59
scapegoat, 243n6
Schreiner, Thomas R., 82n28, 88n39
Scripture
assurance in, 346, 348–349, 358
gezerah shawah and, 306
Holy Spirit's aid in interpreting, 266, 379
judgment in, 395–398
prevenient grace illuminating, 296–297
Second Advent, 25, 29, 140, 142n58,
  350–351, 376
Second Great Awakening, 13
securitas, 376–377
self, crucifying, 318–319
semi-Pelagianism, 103, 103n54, 103n57,
  104, 168, 170
in Adventism, 285
alternative model, 271, 273, 274–275
condemnation of, 271
cooperative model, 271–273, 275, 285
medieval, 276–277
serpent, 28, 29, 121–126, 121n7, 142. *See*

also Satan
death and, 133
touching tree of knowledge of good and
  evil, 124, 124n17
Servant, Messiah as God's, 67, 69, 84
servant leadership, 216
Servant Songs, 67, 69, 206, 223, 249n19
Seth, 129
Seventh-day Adventist Church Manual, 298,
  298n26
shame, 131–132
Shea, William H., 25n12, 409
Shedd, William, 103
Shellrude, Glen, 37n15, 45n32
sight, Christ giving, 373
Simon (sorcerer), 155
sin, 89–171. *See also* the Fall; infants, sin and
biblical lexicon of, 145–157
commission of, *vs.* inclination toward,
  111, 128, 154–157
complexity of, 153–157
confession of, 150, 284, 317
conviction of, 294, 295, 347–348, 373, 392
corruption of, in believer, 108, 154–157,
  159–171
covenant theology and, 134–140
and death, 29n19, 95
definitions of, 24, 126n21, 127–131,
  141–142, 155
as disobedience, 96, 100
dying to, 155n23, 310–311, 318–319
Eden narrative and, 119–143
eradication of, 222n2
excusing, in self, 316, 320–321, 323
the Flood resulting from, 141–142,
  142n58
God punishing, 179–181, 185–187
God's hatred of, 186, 210, 229
history of theology of, 91–117
law transgressed by, 128–129, 143, 151,
  155, 185–186
learning, 97, 101
lordship of, 307–308, 310

love of, 19, 24
subordinationism and, 98n32
trust, 283
vs. fear, 132–133, 335, 337–340
in God *vs.* in faith, 391
in perseverance, 333, 335, 337–340,
399–400
sin stemming from lack of, 127–128,
128n24, 142–143, 196
Tuckett, C. M., 214
Tyconius, 272–273
type *vs.* antitype, 368n19
Tyre, king of, 23–26

U

unbelief, 53, 57, 130–131
Unitarianism, 184, 184n24
universe
inhabited planets of, 21n7
love reconciling, 19–32, 199–200,
213n121, 220, 241–258
unrighteousness, 155. *See also* sin
Uriah, 151

V

"verily, verily," 362, 362n4, 362n5
"vessels" of wrath or glory, 53, 53n50
Vick, Edward, 170
victory, the cross as, 213–214
vindication
by Christ, 411–413
of God, 413–416
through believers, 414–415
violation of norms, sin as, 147
voluntarism, 7

W

Wainwright, Geoffrey, 390
Walker, Williston, 110n87

Watson, Richard, 12
Weber, Otto, 66
Wenham, Gordon, 132
Wesley, Charles, 154, 282
Wesley, John, 11, 12, 12n24, 77, 113–116
anthropology of, 114, 114n105
Arminianism and, 113, 113n102,
327–328
on assurance, 345–350, 358, 391
death feared by, 345–346
on faith, 369–370
"heart strangely warmed," 282, 346, 361
infant baptism and, 115n114
on perseverance, 349–350, 391
and sanctification without perfectionism,
281–283
Wesley, Samuel, 11
Wesley, Susanna, 11
Whidden, Woodrow W., 260, 325
White, Ellen G., 283–285, 351
Arminius and, 113n99
on assurance, 344n86, 352n120,
354–357, 358, 399, 400
conversion and, 353–354, 372n29, 374
on the cross, 201n60, 225n11, 351, 372,
417–418
on depravity and grace, 116, 116n117,
170–171, 299, 352–353
on election made sure, 45n32
on the fiery serpent, 368–369
on first sin, 128n24
on foreknowledge, 38n17, 40n19
on forgiveness, 306, 370n23
on God's goodness, 352, 355–356
on grace, 16–17, 116–117, 284–285, 290,
292, 299, 351, 406
on the great controversy, 186–187,
187n26, 353
on holiness of believers, 406, 409n39
on the Holy Spirit, 361, 367, 370n23, 372
on human nature, 160
on intercession of Christ, 221n1, 222n3,
231n20, 233, 235, 238–239